P9-CAU-839

Fourth Edition

CULTURE, PEOPLE, NATURE

An Introduction to General Anthropology

MARVIN HARRIS
UNIVERSITY OF FLORIDA

HARPER & ROW, PUBLISHERS, New York
Cambridge, Philadelphia, San Francisco,
London, Mexico City, São Paulo, Singapore, Sydney

Sponsoring Editor: Alan McClare
Project Editor: Susan Goldfarb
Cover and Text Design: Helen Iranyi
Design Coordination: Barbara Bert
Cover Photo: © Frerck, Woodfin Camp
Text Art: Vantage Art, Inc.
Photo Research: Mira Schachne
Production: Jeanie Berke
Compositor: The Clarinda Company
Printer and Binder: R. R. Donnelley & Sons Company

CULTURE, PEOPLE, NATURE: An Introduction to General Anthropology
Fourth Edition

Library of Congress Cataloging in Publication Data

Harris, Marvin, 1927–
Culture, people, nature.

Bibliography: p.
Includes index.
1. Anthropology. I. Title.
GN25.H37 1985 301 85-2580
ISBN 0-06-042656-X

Illustration credits begin on page 579.

85 86 87 88 9 8 7 6 5 4 3 2 1

BRIEF CONTENTS

PREFACE xv

1. WHAT DO ANTHROPOLOGISTS STUDY? 1
2. ORGANIC EVOLUTION 9
3. THE HUMAN PEDIGREE AND HUMAN NATURE 19
4. THE FIRST HOMINIDS 41
5. THE ORIGINS OF *HOMO SAPIENS* 71
6. RACE, HUMAN VARIATION, AND THE FORCES OF EVOLUTION 93
7. THE NATURE OF CULTURE 113
8. THE OLD WORLD PALEOLITHIC 129
9. THE NEOLITHIC AND THE RISE OF CITIES AND STATES 151
10. THE SECOND EARTH 173
11. ECOLOGY, ENERGY, AND POPULATION 203
12. ECONOMY, EXCHANGE, CONTROL 227
13. THE ORGANIZATION OF DOMESTIC LIFE 249
14. KINSHIP, LOCALITY, AND DESCENT 271
15. LAW, ORDER, AND WAR IN EGALITARIAN SOCIETIES 289

16. THE POLITICAL ECONOMY OF THE STATE 309

17. STRATIFIED GROUPS: CLASS, CASTE, MINORITY, ETHNICITY 329

18. UNDERDEVELOPMENT AND CULTURAL CHANGE 355

19. POVERTY AND CULTURE 377

20. LANGUAGE AND CULTURE 393

21. VARIETIES OF RELIGIOUS EXPERIENCE 415

22. RELIGION AS ADAPTATION 443

23. THE ARTISTIC ANIMAL 467

24. PERSONALITY AND SEX 485

25. HISTORY OF THEORIES OF CULTURE 513

GLOSSARY 533

BIBLIOGRAPHY 541

CREDITS 579

INDEX 583

DETAILED CONTENTS

PREFACE xv

1. WHAT DO ANTHROPOLOGISTS STUDY? 1

Why Anthropology? 6
The Diversity of Anthropological Theories 7
Summary 8

2. ORGANIC EVOLUTION 9

Reproduction 10
Chromosomes, Genes, and DNA 10
The Inheritance of Genes 11
Dominant and Recessive Genes 14
The Forces of Evolution 15
Natural Selection and the "Struggle for Survival" 17
Speciation: Fast or Slow? 17
Summary 18

3. THE HUMAN PEDIGREE AND HUMAN NATURE 19

From Animal to Primate 20
The Order Primates 22
The Anthropoidean Superfamilies 26
Characteristics of the Hominoidea 28
Family Hominidae Versus Family Pongidae and Family Hylobatidae 30
Hominid Sexuality 38
Language and Culture 38
Summary 39

4. THE FIRST HOMINIDS 41

An Evolutionary Clock 42
From Hominoid to Hominid 42
Homo habilis 54
Tools and the Plio-Pleistocene Hominids 56
Tool Use Among Contemporary Monkeys and Apes 58
Infrahuman Culture and the Evolution of the Hominids 61
Hunting and the Plio-Pleistocene Hominids 65
Summary 69

5. THE ORIGINS OF *HOMO SAPIENS* 71

Homo erectus 72
Archaic *Homo sapiens* 84
The Neandertals and *Homo sapien sapiens* in Europe 87
Summary 91

6. RACE, HUMAN VARIATION, AND THE FORCES OF EVOLUTION 93

Races as Populations 94
Frequencies versus Archetypes 94
Clines 96
The Explanation of Human Polymorphisms 101
Polymorphisms and Racial Antiquity 105
Summary 111

7. THE NATURE OF CULTURE 113

Definitions of Culture and Society 114
Enculturation and Cultural Relativism 115
Limitations of the Enculturation Concept 117
Diffusion 119
Mental and Behavioral Aspects of Culture 122
Emic and Etic Aspects of Culture 123
Emics, Etics, and Cattle Sex Ratios 124
The Universal Pattern 125
Alternative Research Strategies 125
Summary 127

8. THE OLD WORLD PALEOLITHIC 129

Gene-Culture Coevolution 130
Cultural Takeoff 130
Prehistoric Periods 131
Lower Paleolithic Developments 131
Middle Paleolithic Developments 133
The Upper Paleolithic 135
Upper Paleolithic Art 139
Homo sapiens sapiens and the Middle/Upper Transition 143
The End of the Paleolithic 143
The End of the Paleolithic in World Perspective 147
Summary 148

9. THE NEOLITHIC AND THE RISE OF CITIES AND STATES 151

The Neolithic 152
The Neolithic in the Middle East 152
The Origins of Agriculture 155
The Domestication of Animals 157
Early Neolithic in Northeastern Africa 158
The Causes of the Neolithic 160
The Neolithic "Revolution" 161
The Urban Revolution and the Rise of the State 164
The East Asian Neolithic 167
The Neolithic in Southeast Asia 169
The African Neolithic 171
Summary 171

10. THE SECOND EARTH 173

When Was America Discovered? 174
The New World Paleolithic 175
Archaic Traditions 177
The New World "Neolithic" 178
A Mesoamerican Sequence 180
The Development of New World States; the Mesoamerican Highlands 186
The Role of Animal Domesticates 190
Developments North of Mexico 191
The Development of States in South America 192
The Meaning of the "Second Earth" 194
Summary 199

11. ECOLOGY, ENERGY, AND POPULATION 203

Ecology and Ecosystems 204
Evolution of Energy Production 204
Modes of Food Production 205
The Influence of the Environment 206
Carrying Capacity and the Law of Diminishing Returns 208
Expansion, Intensification, and Technological Change 209
Hunter-Gatherer Ecology 210
A Slash-and-Burn Food Energy System 211
The High Cost of Pigs 213
Energy and Pastoral Nomadism 214
Industrial Food Energy Systems 216
The Myth of Increased Leisure 218
Cultural Checks on Population Growth 220
Contraception Techniques 221
Postconception Techniques 221
The Influence of Disease 223
Population Pressure and Cultural Evolution 224
Summary 225

12. ECONOMY, EXCHANGE, CONTROL 227

Definition of Economy 228
Exchange 228
Reciprocal Exchange 229
The Problem of the Freeloader 229
Reciprocity and Trade 231
The Kula 233
Redistributive Exchange 235
Reciprocity Versus Redistribution 235
The Cultural Ecology of Redistribution and Reciprocity 238
The Origin of Destructive Potlatches 239
Stratified Redistribution 240
Price-Market Exchange: Buying and Selling 241
Money 241
Capitalism 244
"Primitive Capitalism?" The Kapauku Case 245
Landownership 246
Summary 247

13. THE ORGANIZATION OF DOMESTIC LIFE 249

The Domestic Sphere of Culture 250
The Nuclear Family 250
Alternatives to the Nuclear Family 251
Polygamy and the Nuclear Family 252
The Extended Family 255
One-Parent Domestic Group 257
What Is Marriage? 258
Legitimacy 259
Functions of Marriage 261
Marriage in Extended Families 261
Domestic Groups and the Avoidance of Incest 263
Preferential Marriages 268
Summary 268

14. KINSHIP, LOCALITY, AND DESCENT 271

Kinship 272
Descent 272
Descent Rules 273
Cognatic Descent Groups: Bilateral Variety 276
Cognatic Descent Groups: Ambilineal Variety 277
Unilineal Descent Groups 277
Postmarital Locality Patterns 278
Causes of Bilateral Descent 279
Determinants of Cognatic Lineages and Clans 279
Determinants of Unilineal Lineages and Clans 280
Causes of Patrilocality 281
Causes of Matrilocality 281
Causes of Avunculocality 283
Kinship Terminology 284
Summary 286

15. LAW, ORDER, AND WAR IN EGALITARIAN SOCIETIES 289

Law and Order in Band and Village Societies 290
"Primitive Communism" 290
Mobilizing Public Opinion: Song Duels 292
Mobilizing Public Opinion: Witchcraft Accusations 294
Headmanship 296
Blood Feud 298
Nonkin Associations: Sodalities 299
Warfare Among Hunters and Gatherers 300
Warfare Among Village Agriculturalists 302
Warfare and the Regulation of Population Growth 302
Game Animals and Warfare: The Yanomamo 304
Summary 307

16. THE POLITICAL ECONOMY OF THE STATE 309

Bigmanship 310
Big Men and Warfare 311
Chiefs, War, and Redistribution: Trobrianders and Cherokee 312
Limitations of Chiefly Power 314
From Chiefdom to State 315
An African Kingdom: Bunyoro 316
Feudalism 317
A Native American Empire: The Inca 318
The State and the Control of Thought 320
Thought Control in Modern Contexts 321
The State and Physical Coercion 324
The Fate of Prestate Bands and Villages 325
Summary 327

17. STRATIFIED GROUPS: CLASS, CASTE, MINORITY, ETHNICITY 329

Class and Power 330
Sex, Age, and Class 331
Emics, Etics, and Class Consciousness 331
Economic Exploitation 333
Peasant Classes 333
Ruling Classes: The Soviet Union 337
Is There a Ruling Class in the United States? 338
The Concentration of Wealth in the United States 339
Class and Life-Style 341
Class Mobility 344

Minorities and Majorities 345
Assimilation Versus Pluralism 347
Castes in India 349
Caste from the Top Down and Bottom Up 350
Summary 353

18. UNDERDEVELOPMENT AND CULTURAL CHANGE 355

Colonialism and Underdevelopment 356
Indonesia and Japan 357
Japan 360
The Green Revolution 361
Mexican Wonder Wheat 362
The Green Revolution in Bangladesh 363
Limits to Technification and Industrial Growth 365
Bullock Versus Tractor 366
Population and Development 367
The Image of Limited Goods 370
Sisal in Brazil 372
San Pedro: A Success Story 372
Summary 375

19. POVERTY AND CULTURE 377

The Culture of Poverty 378
Deferred Gratification and the Futility of Work 380
Now Whose Fault is That? 382
Getting Drunk in Denver 383
Values and the Matrifocal Family: The Flats 385
The Welfare Connection 388
"The Broken Fountain" 389
Summary 392

20. LANGUAGE AND CULTURE 393

Semantic Universality 394
Arbitrariness 395
Duality of Patterning 396
Phonemic Systems 396
Morphemes 398
Grammar: Rules Governing the Construction of Morphemes 399
Grammar: Syntax 399
Deep Structure 399
Apes and Language 400
Language Acquisition 403
The Equivalence of All Grammars 404
Generality and Specificity 404
Language, Social Class, and Ethnicity 405
Language, Thought, and Causality 407
Obligatory Elitism and Sexism 409
Linguistic Change 410
Language and Consciousness 412
Summary 412

21. VARIETIES OF RELIGIOUS EXPERIENCE 415

Animism 416
The Three Souls of the Jivaro 417
Animatism and Mana 418
Natural and Supernatural 418
Sacred and Profane 419
Magic and Religion 421
The Organization of Religious Beliefs and Practices 422
individualistic Beliefs and Rituals: The Eskimo 423
The Patterning of Individualistic Beliefs and Rituals 425
Shamanistic Cults 426
Tapirapé Shamanism 427
Shamans, Witchcraft, and Witch-Hunts 429
Communal Cults 430
Communal Rites of Solidarity: Totemism 430
Communal Rituals: Rites of Passage 433
Circumcision 433
Ecclesiastical Cults 437
The Religion of the Aztecs 438
Summary 441

22. RELIGION AS ADAPTATION 443

Religion and Political Economy: High Gods 444
Imperial Religion 445
Human Sacrifice and Cannibalism Among the Aztec 446
Revitalization 448
Native American Revitalizations 449

Cargo Cults 453
Christianity and Revitalization 454
Revitalizations in Europe 456
Taboo, Religion, and Ecology 458
The Sacred Cow 459
The Secret of Voodoo 462
Summary 463

23. THE ARTISTIC ANIMAL 467

What Is Art? 468
Art as a Cultural Category 468
Art and Invention 470
Art and Cultural Patterning 472
Art and Religion 475
Art and Politics 477
The Evolution of Music and Dance 479
The Complexity of Primitive Art: Campa Rhetoric 480
Myth and Binary Contrasts 481
Summary 482

24. PERSONALITY AND SEX 485

Culture and Personality 486
Childhood Training and Personality 486
Male Initiation and Childhood Training 488
Patterns and Themes 489
Basic Personality and National Character 490
Oedipus and Personality 492
Culture and Mental Illness 494
Cultural Definitions of Male and Female 497
A Male-Supremacist Complex? 498
Sexual Politics 500
Religion and Sexual Politics 502
Sex Roles and Ethnography 503
Trobriands Revisited 503
Warfare and the Male-Supremacist Complex 505
Masculinity, War, and the Oedipus Complex 507
Varieties of Sexual Experience 507
Homosexuality 508
Sex Roles in Industrial Society 509
Sex Roles for the Future 510
Summary 511

25. HISTORY OF THEORIES OF CULTURE 513

The Enlightenment 514
Nineteenth-Century Evolutionism 514
Social Darwinism and Racism 515
Marxist Evolutionism 517
The Reaction to Nineteenth-Century Evolutionism 517
Diffusionism 518
British Functionalism and Structural Functionalism 518
Culture and Personality 519
The New Evolutionism 519
Dialectical Materialism 520
Cultural Materialism 521
Structuralism 521
Particularizing Approaches 522
Racial Determinism: IQ 522
Sociobiology 525
Determinism, Science, and the Individual 527
Probabilistic Causality 528
Summary 529

GLOSSARY 533

BIBLIOGRAPHY 541

CREDITS 579

INDEX 583

FIGURES

1.1 Anthropologists at Work 2–4
2.1 Double Helix Model of DNA 10
2.2 Human Chromosome Karyotype 12
2.3 Reduction Division 13
2.4 Crossing Over 14
3.1 Egg-Laying Mammals 21
3.2 A Wallaby Mother and Child 22
3.3 Gibbon Foot 22
3.4 Primate Grips 23
3.5 Visual Acuity 24
3.6 Rhesus Mother and Child 25
3.7 Prosimians 27
3.8 Old World Monkey Dentition; New World Monkey Dentition 28
3.9 Gibbons 29
3.10 Suspensory Feeding 30
3.11 Juvenile Orangutans 30
3.12 Adult Male Gorilla 31
3.13 Gorilla; *Homo sapiens* 31
3.14 Human Foot; Gorilla Foot 32
3.15 Human Pelvis; Chimpanzee Pelvis 33
3.16 Gorilla Vertebral Column; Human Vertebral Column 34
3.17 Base of Human Skull 35
3.18 Gorilla Skull; Human Skull 35
3.19 Gorilla Jaw; Human Jaw 36
3.20 Gelada Baboons 37
3.21 Yellow Baboon (*Papiocynocephalus*), Suborder Anthropoidea, Superfamily Cercopithecoidea 39
4.1 Evolutionary Clock 43
4.2 *Aegyptopithecus zeuxis* 44
4.3 Y Pattern 44
4.4 *Propliopithecus haeckeli* 45
4.5 *Aeolopithecus chirobates* 45
4.6 *Dryopithecus fontani* 46
4.7 *Ramapithecus* Mandible 46
4.8 *Gigantopithecus* 47
4.9 "Lucy" 47
4.10 Earliest Hominid Footprint 49
4.11 *A. afarensis* Toe Bones 51
4.12 The Taung Child's Mandible 52
4.13 Australopithecines 53
4.14 Laetoli 53
4.15 Hadar 54
4.16 Olduvai Gorge 55
4.17 OH 7 56
4.18 KNM 1470 56
4.19 Olduvai Chopper 57
4.20 Omo Tools 57
4.21 Jane Van Lawick-Goodall 59
4.22 Chimpanzee Termiting 60
4.23 Japanese Monkey Culture 65
4.24 Japanese Monkeys Washing Wheat 66
4.25 Chimpanzees Meat Eating 67
5.1 Cranial Cavities 72
5.2 *Pithecanthropus IV* 73
5.3 *Pithecanthropus V* 73
5.4 *Meganthropus* 74
5.5 *Homo erectus* 74
5.6 The Earliest *Homo erectus* (KNM-3733) 75
5.7 Olduvai Gorge 77
5.8 Oldowan Choppers 78
5.9 Acheulian Hand Ax from Olduvai Gorge 78
5.10 Implements from Sinanthropus Levels of Choukoutien Cave 79
5.11 Biface Manufacture 82
5.12 Ambrona (Spain) 83
5.13 Japanese Women Pearl Divers at Work 84
5.14 Swanscombe 85
5.15 Steinheim (I) 85
5.16 Steinheim (II) 86
5.17 "Rhodesian Man" 86
5.18 *Homo soloensis* 86
5.19 Classic Neandertal and *Homo sapiens sapiens* 87
5.20 Classic Neandertal 88
5.21 Early South Central European *Homo sapiens sapiens* 88
5.22 Shanidar Neandertal 89
5.23 Tabūn Mandible 90
5.24 Skhūl Neandertal 90
5.25 Air Passages of Chimp, Neandertal, and Human 90
6.1 Native Australians 96
6.2 Brazilian Portraits 97
6.3 Unity of Humankind 98–99
6.4 Normal Blood Cells and Sickling Blood Cells 103
6.5 Heat Dispersal and Body Shape 106
6.6 Mullen's Alley, 1888 108
6.7 Rickets 109
7.1 Techniques of Eating 115
7.2 Passing Culture On 116
7.3 Culture, People, and the Sun 118
7.4 Punk Rocker 119
7.5 Diffusion 120–121

7.6 Rules for Breaking Rules 122–123
8.1 Acheulian Hand Ax 132
8.2 Paleolithic Side Scraper 133
8.3 Improved Acheulian Hand Ax and Technique 134
8.4 Levalloisian Tortoise Core Technique 134
8.5 Mousterian Implements 135
8.6 Mousterian Tortoise Core 136
8.7 Mousterian Jewelry 137
8.8 Mousterian Ritual Object 137
8.9 Upper Paleolithic Blade 138
8.10 Upper Paleolithic Blade Technique 138
8.11 Upper Paleolithic Implements 139
8.12 Venus Statue 140
8.13 Spear Thrower 140
8.14 Paleolithic Masterpieces 141
8.15 Paleolithic Notations 142
8.16 Woolly Mammoths 147
9.1 Hilly Flanks, Northern Iraq 153
9.2 Site of Zawi Chemi Shanidar 155
9.3 Tell Mureybat 156
9.4 Emmer Spike 157
9.5 Excavation at Jarmo 159
9.6 Jericho 162
9.7 Çatal Hüyük 163
9.8 Çatal Hüyük Neolithic Wall Painting 163
9.9 Eridu 165
9.10 Stonehenge 167
9.11 Pan-p'o 168
9.12 Shang Bronze Metallurgy 170
9.13 Taro Plants 171
10.1 Meadowcroft Rock Shelter 174
10.2 New World Paleolithic Projectile Points 177
10.3 Folsom Point Embedded in Ribs of an Extinct Bison 178
10.4 La Venta Pyramid 182
10.5 Olmec Head, San Lorenzo, Mexico 183
10.6 Cuello Site 184
10.7 Mayan Temple, Palenque, Chiapas, Mexico 185
10.8 Tikal 187
10.9 Teotihuacán 188
10.10 Ruins of Tula, Hidalgo, Mexico 189
10.11 Chinampas of Xochimilco 190
10.12 Mississippian Mound 193
10.13 Tiahuanaco 194
10.14 Chan Chan 195
10.15 Machu Picchu, Peru 196
10.16 Pre-Columbian Metallurgy 197
10.17 Mayan Glyphs 198
11.1 Planting in a Swidden 206
11.2 Philippine Mountainside Terraces 207
11.3 Graph Showing Relationship Between Carrying Capacity and Point of Diminishing Returns 209
11.4 !Kung Women Returning to Camp 210
11.5 "Cooking" the Garden 212
11.6 Dispatching a Pig 214
11.7 Irrigation Dam 215
11.8 Pastoral Nomads 216
11.9 Industrial Agriculture 217
11.10 Labor-Saving Devices That Don't Save Work 218–219
11.11 Machiguenga at Work 220
11.12 Breast Feeding Older Children 222
12.1 San Reciprocity 230
12.2 New Guinea Market 232
12.3 Kapauku of Western New Guinea 233
12.4 Kula Canoe 234
12.5 Semai Hunter 236
12.6 Kwakiutl of the Northwest ca. 1900 237
12.7 Potlatch 238
12.8 Tokyo Stock Exchange 242
12.9 Shell and Dog Tooth Money 243
13.1 Japanese Nuclear Family 251
13.2 Polygyny 253
13.3 Polyandry 254
13.4 Extended Family, United States 255
13.5 Taiwan Marriage 256
13.6 Bride-Price 262
13.7 Dowry 263
13.8 Kibbutz Boys and Girls 265
13.9 Cleopatra 266
14.1 How to Read Kinship Diagrams 274
14.2 Bilateral Descent 274
14.3 Ambilineal Descent 275
14.4 Patrilineal Descent 275
14.5 Matrilineal Descent 275
14.6 Cross Cousins and Parallel Cousins 276
14.7 Kindreds 276
14.8 Cognatic Lineage 277
14.9 Patrilineages 278
14.10 Avunculocality 281
14.11 Eskimo Terminology 285
14.12 Hawaiian Terminology 286
14.13 Iroquois Terminology 287
16.1 Solomon Island Chiefs 311
16.2 Cherokee Chief 313
16.3 Tikopia Chief and His "Honor Guard" 314
16.4 Mukama of Bunyoro 316

16.5 Sacsahuaman 319
16.6 Stratification: The King of Morocco 320
16.7 The Great Pyramid of Khufu 321
16.8 Thought Control in Two Modern States 322
16.9 New York City, July 14, 1977 326
17.1 Poverty and Power 330
17.2 The Soviet Ruling Class 332
17.3 Albanian Peasants 335
17.4 Chinese Peasants 336
17.5 Peruvian Peasants 337
17.6 Ecuadorian Peasants 337
17.7 Members of the Ruling Class? 341
17.8 Class and Life-Style 341
17.9 Class and Life-Style 342
17.10 Caracas Shantytown 343
17.11 Squatters in Lima 344
17.12 Ethnic Identity 346
17.13 Apartheid 347
17.14 Untouchables 350
17.15 Bombay Laundry 351
18.1 Underdevelopment 357
18.2 Java Rice Terraces 359
18.3 Rice Harvest, Java 363
18.4 Planting Wheat in Bangladesh 364
18.5 Crowded Third World 368
18.6 Image of Limited Goods 371
18.7 Sisal Worker 373
18.8 San Pedro, Guatemala 374
19.1 Mother-Centered Family 379
19.2 Dead-End Job 380
19.3 Newfoundlanders 383
19.4 Navajo Youth 384
19.5 Pruitt-Igoe 386
19.6 Another Solution 387
19.7 Children of the Flats 387
19.8 Lower East Side 388
19.9 Naples 390
20.1 Parts of Oral Passage 397
20.2 Washoe 401
20.3 Lana Using Yerkish to Communicate with a Computer 401
20.4 Koko 402
20.5 Nim Chimpsky 403
20.6 Class and Speech 406
20.7 Indo-European Family of Languages 412
21.1 Gururumba Medicine 419
21.2 Sacred and Profane 420
21.3 San Curing 422
21.4 Level of Religious Organization 424
21.5 Sioux Vision 425
21.6 Tapirapé Shaman 427
21.7 Sabbat 429
21.8 Dakota Sun Dance 431
21.9 Totemic Solidarity 432
21.10 Religion and Life Crises 434–435
21.11 Ndembu Circumcision Camp 435
21.12 Bull Roarer 436
21.13 Ndembu Monster 436
21.14 Ecclesiastical Cult 438
21.15 Temple of Quetzalcoatl 439
21.16 Tenochtitlán 440
22.1 Religion and Stratification 445
22.2 Aztec Sacrificial Knife 447
22.3 Skull Rack 447
22.4 Wovoka 450
22.5 Wounded Knee 451
22.6 Peyote Ceremony 452
22.7 John Frumm 453
22.8 Temple of Jerusalem 455
22.9 Jonestown, Guyana 457
22.10 Revitalization in Iran 457
22.11 Plow Animals in Rajastan, India 460
22.12 Sacred Cows 461
22.13 Haitian Cemetery 463
23.1 Chimpanzee Artists 469
23.2 Art Has Many Media 471
23.3 Solutrean Laurel Leaf Blade 472
23.4 Masks 473
23.5 Maori Canoe Prow 474
23.6 Mochica Pot 474
23.7 What Does It Mean? 475
23.8 Ba Kota Funerary Figures 476
23.9 Asmat Gravepost 477
23.10 Art and Architecture 477
23.11 Gold Death Mask of Tut 478
23.12 Art and Religion 478
23.13 Soviet Realism 479
23.14 Tetum House 483
24.1 Care of Children 487
24.2 Javanese Girl and Brother 488
24.3 The Relationship of Basic Personality to Ecology, Child-Rearing Practices, and Secondary and Projective Institutions 489
24.4 Psychodynamic Model of Relationship Between Low-Protein Diet and Severe Male Initiation 490
24.5 Berdache 491
24.6 Personality in a Complex Society 492
24.7 Freud's Milieu 493
24.8 Arctic Hysteria 495
24.9 Aggressive Male Games 498–499

24.10 Female Shaman 502
24.11 Interior of Men's House, New Guinea 502
24.12 Can the Gap Be Closed? 506
24.13 Hindu Erotic Art 508

TABLES

3.1 Categories and Taxons Relevant to Human Ancestry 20
5.1 Cranial Volume and Body Weights of Hominoidea 73
11.1 Time Devoted to Various Activities per Day by Machiguenga Married Men and Women 220
11.2 Rate of Growth of the Human Population 221
14.1 Principal Varieties of Postmarital Residence 278
14.2 Relationship Between Residence and Descent in the Ethnographic Atlas 283
15.1 Sex Ratios and Warfare 304
18.1 Inequalities in Social and Economic Development 366
18.2 World Population Estimates 368
22.1 Religion, Class, and Morality 445
24.1 World Records (1982) 506
24.2 Mangaian Sexuality 509
24.3 American and Hindu Coital Frequency 509

MAPS AND CHARTS

Important Fossil Sites in East and South Africa 50
Human Evolution Sites 62–63
Chronological Relationship of Principal Pleistocene Hominid Fossils 80–81
Distribution of Alleles of the ABO Blood Group System 101–102
Distribution of Falciparum Malaria in the Old World 104
Distribution of the Sickle-Cell Trait in the Old World 104
Archaeological Sites 144–145
Fertile Crescent Region 159
Beringia Land Bridge 176
Chronology of Cultural Evolution 200–201

PREFACE

More than ever, the global and comparative perspective of anthropology provides an indispensable framework for students who wish to understand the modern world. No other discipline attempts to illuminate so many different aspects of the human experience.

Despite the conservative trends that are affecting campus interest and values, the fourth edition of *Culture, People, Nature* continues to highlight problems confronting the disadvantaged. It seems to me more vital than ever for anthropologists to help sensitize students to the realities of social life as experienced by the less fortunate members of our endangered species.

In this edition, about one-third of the old material has been dropped to make room for the new; however, the overall size of this edition is unchanged. Naturally, some difficult choices had to be made.

New to the fourth edition is Chapter 25, "History of Theories of Culture," added to accommodate numerous requests from instructors that such material be included. Much of the discussion of racial differences in relation to intelligence and culture has been moved to this chapter. This material remains essential to the anthropological enterprise, and I hope it will not get lost in the shuffle.

Changes from the third edition reflect continuing advances achieved in human paleontology, social and cultural anthropology, primatology, prehistory, archaeology, and linguistics. Among the improved themes and sections are the treatment of the evolution of skin color, primate omnivory, the East Asian paleolithic, Amazonia settlement patterns and warfare, language acquisition, and sex and gender roles. New ethnographic sections have been added to explain Haitian "voodoo," life in a Naples slum, and Windigo "psychosis." Extensive revision of Chapter 24, "Personality and Sex," should be noted, especially the expanded treatment of female viewpoints. The survey material and bibliography have been brought up to date to represent what I hope is the "state of the art" as of late 1984.

A special effort has been made to improve the continuity of the book. New terms and concepts are defined when they are introduced and are then used to build higher-level concepts. Cross-referencing by chapter and page number, both forward and backward, has also been expanded and improved. This feature is designed to permit students who have not been assigned the whole book to acquaint themselves with relevant key terms and concepts presented in unassigned chapters. It is also intended to remind students of the book's cumulative thrust toward a comprehensive view of anthropology.

Let me take this opportunity to express special thanks to Madeline Harris, to Karen Griffin for her help in the bibliographical updating of this edition, to Phyllis Durell for her help in typing and retyping manuscripts, and to colleagues, students, and friends at the University of Florida in Gainesville for providing me with a friendly, stimulating, and safe place to work and think.

MARVIN HARRIS

1 WHAT DO ANTHROPOLOGISTS STUDY?

Anthropology is the study of humankind, of ancient and modern people and their ways of living. Since this subject is very large and complex, different branches of anthropology focus on different aspects or dimensions of the human experience. Some anthropologists study how our species, known scientifically as *Homo sapiens*, evolved from earlier species. Others study how *H. sapiens* came to possess the uniquely human facility for language, how languages evolved and diversified, and how modern languages serve the needs of human communication. Still others concentrate on the learned traditions of human thought and behavior known as *cultures*. They study how ancient cultures evolved and diversified and how and why modern cultures change or stay the same.

Within departments of anthropology at major universities in the United States the different perspectives of anthropology are usually represented by four fields of study: cultural anthropology (sometimes called social anthropology), archaeology, anthropological linguistics, and physical anthropology (Fried 1972)*.

Cultural anthropology deals with the description and analysis of cultures—the socially learned traditions—of past and present ages. It has a subdiscipline, *ethnography*, that systematically describes contemporary cultures. Comparison of these descriptions provides the basis for hypotheses and theories about the causes of human life-styles.

Archaeology assists cultural anthropology in this endeavor. Archaeologists dig up the remains of the cultures of the past, making it possible to study peoples who had no written history. Without the findings of archaeology we would not be able to understand the past, and without understanding the past we cannot understand the present.

Anthropological linguistics is the study of the great variety of languages spoken by human beings. Anthropological linguists attempt to trace the history of all known families of languages. They are concerned with

(a)

Figure 1.1 *ANTHROPOLOGISTS AT WORK* (*a*) Ethnographer Margaret Mead among the Manus islanders. (*b*) Archaeologist Ralph Solecki at Nahr Ibrahim, Lebanon, where excavations have reached Middle Paleolithic Levalloiso-Mousterian levels (see Ch. 8).

(b)

(c)

Figure 1.1 *(continued)*
(c) Physical anthropologist Richard Leakey and assistant Kimayou inspecting a fossil jaw near Lake Turkana, Kenya (see Ch. 4).
(d) Linguist Francesca Merlin with the speakers of a previously unknown language near Mt. Hagen, New Guinea.

(d)

AN ANTHROPOLOGICAL SCORECARD

Anthropologists frequently identify themselves with one or more specialized branches of the four major fields. The following is only a partial listing.

CULTURAL ANTHROPOLOGY

Applied Anthropology

Study and make proposals to solve practical problems and evaluate results.

Medical Anthropology

Study biological and cultural factors in health and disease and the treatment of the sick.

Urban Anthropology

Study city life.

Development Anthropology

Study the causes of underdevelopment and development among the less developed nations.

ARCHAEOLOGY

Historic Archaeology

Study cultures of the recent past by means of a combination of written records and archaeological excavations.

Industrial Archaeology

Historic archaeology that focuses on industrial factories and facilities.

Contract Archaeology

Conduct archaeological surveys for environmental impact statements and protection of historic sites.

PHYSICAL (BIOLOGICAL) ANTHROPOLOGY

Primatology

Study social life and biology of monkeys, great apes, and other primates.

Human Paleontology

Search for and study fossil remains of early human species.

Forensic Anthropology

Identify victims of murders and accidents.

Population Genetics

Study hereditary differences in human populations.

LINGUISTICS

Historical Linguistics

Reconstruct the origins of specific languages and of families of languages.

Descriptive Linguistics

Study the grammar and syntax of languages.

Sociolinguistics

Study the actual use of language in the communication behavior of daily life.

the way language influences and is influenced by other aspects of human life, and with the relationship between the evolution of language and the evolution of *H. sapiens*. They are also concerned with the relationship between the evolution of languages and the evolution of different cultures.

Physical anthropology (also called *biological anthropology*) grounds the other anthropological fields in our animal origins and our biologically determined nature. Physical anthropologists seek to reconstruct the course of human evolution by studying the fossil remains of ancient species. Physical anthropologists also seek to describe the distribution of hereditary variations among contemporary populations and to sort out and measure the relative contributions made by heredity, environment, and culture to human life.

The combination of all four fields of anthropology is known as *general anthropology*. This book is an introduction to the major findings in all four fields. Hence, it is an introduction to general anthropology.

WHY ANTHROPOLOGY?

Many disciplines other than anthropology are concerned with the study of human beings. Our animal nature is the subject of intense research by biologists, geneticists and physiologists. In medicine alone, hundreds of additional specialists investigate the human body, and psychiatrists and psychologists, rank upon rank, seek the essence of the human mind and soul. Many other disciplines examine our cultural, intellectual, and aesthetic behavior. These disciplines include sociology, human geography, social psychology, history, political science, economics, linguistics, theology, philosophy, musicology, art, literature, and architecture. There are also many "area specialists" who study the languages and life-styles of particular peoples, nations, or regions: "Latin Americanists," "Indianists," "Sinologists," and so on. What then is distinctive about anthropology?

The distinction of anthropology is that it is global and comparative. Other disciplines are concerned with only a particular segment of human experience or a particular time or phase of our cultural or biological development. But the findings of anthropology are never based upon the study of a single population, race, tribe, class, nation, time, or place. Anthropologists insist first and foremost that conclusions based upon the study of one particular human group or civilization be checked against the evidence of other groups or civilizations. In this way the relevance of anthropology transcends the interests of any particular tribe, race, nation, religion, or culture. In anthropological perspective, all peoples and cultures are equally worthy of study. Thus, anthropology is incompatible with the view of those who would have themselves and no one else represent humanity, stand at the pinnacle of progress, or be chosen by God or history to fashion the world in their own image.

Anthropologists believe that a sound knowledge of humankind can be achieved only by studying distant as well as near lands and ancient as well as modern times. By adopting this broad view of the totality of human experience, perhaps we humans can tear off the blinders put on us by our local life-styles and see ourselves as we really are.

Because of its biological, archaeological, linguistic, cultural, comparative, and global perspective, anthropology holds the key to many fundamental questions. Anthropologists have made important contributions to

*See the first page of the Bibliography for an explanation of the system of citations used in this book.

understanding the significance of humankind's animal heritage and hence to the definition of what is distinctively human about human nature. Anthropology is strategically equipped to study the significance of race in the evolution of cultures and in the conduct of contemporary life. It also holds the key to the understanding of the origins of social inequality in the form of racism, sexism, exploitation, poverty, and international underdevelopment.

In the words of Frederica De Laguna,

> Anthropology is the only discipline that offers a conceptual schema for the whole context of human experience. . . . It is like the carrying frame onto which may be fitted all the several subjects of a liberal education, and by organizing the load, making it more wieldy and capable of being carried (1968:475).

THE DIVERSITY OF ANTHROPOLOGICAL THEORIES

Although all anthropologists stress the importance of the multidimensional, broad, comparative, and global approach, they often disagree about the best way to go about explaining and understanding the human condition. Anthropologists do not agree that the similarities and differences in human thought and behavior are caused in ways that science can understand. Some hold that culture cannot and should not be studied the way scientists study natural phenomena. But others hold that anthropology can discover causal processes to the same degree that biologists discover the causes of biological evolution or meteorologists discover the causes of the weather. Even among anthropologists who believe that there are definite causes of institutions and of life-styles, however, disagreement exists about what these causes are.

The kinds of research that anthropologists carry out and the kinds of conclusions they stress are greatly influenced by the basic assumptions they make about the causes of cultural evolution. Basic assumptions made by anthropologists of different theoretical persuasions are called *research strategies*.

No textbook can conceivably be written so as to represent all the current research strategies with bias toward none and equal coverage for all. In the chapters to come the author has made a conscious effort to include alternative viewpoints on controversial issues. Inevitably, however, the author's own research strategy dominates the presentation. The point of view followed throughout is known as *cultural materialism*. This is one of the research strategies which holds that the primary task of anthropology is to give causal explanations for the differences and similarities in thought and behavior found among human groups. Unlike other scientifically oriented research strategies, however, cultural materialism makes the assumption that this task can best be carried out by studying the material constraints to which human existence is subjected. These constraints arise from the need to produce food, shelter, tools and machines and to reproduce human populations within limits set by biology and the environment. They are called *material* constraints or conditions in order to distinguish them from constraints or conditions imposed by ideas and other mental or spiritual aspects of human life such as values, religion, and art. For cultural materialists, the most likely causes of variation in the mental or spiritual aspects of human life are the variations in the material constraints affecting the way people cope with the problems of satisfying basic needs in a particular habitat.

This strategic assumption accounts for the

organization of the subjects to be treated in the following chapters. It explains why a great deal of emphasis is given to demographic, technological, economic, and ecological factors. Only after these basic material factors have been set forth can we attempt to describe and explain the varieties of domestic and political institutions, and the moral values, religious beliefs, and aesthetic standards of particular peoples. This does not mean that the mental and spiritual aspects of cultures are regarded as being somehow less significant or less important than production, reproduction, and ecology. Moral values, religious beliefs, and aesthetic standards are in one sense the most significant and most distinctively human of all our attributes. Their importance is not an issue. What is an issue is how we can best explain—if we can explain at all—why particular human populations have one set of values, beliefs, and aesthetic standards while others have different sets of values, beliefs, and aesthetic standards.

SUMMARY

Anthropology is the study of humankind. Its four major branches are cultural or social anthropology, anthropological linguistics, physical (or biological) anthropology, and archaeology. Its distinctive approach lies in its global, comparative, and multidimensional perspective. The combined approach of all four fields is known as general anthropology. Within anthropology there are many alternative research strategies. The research strategy followed in this book is cultural materialism. The aim of this strategy is to discover the causes of the differences and similarities in thought and behavior characteristic of particular human populations by studying the influence of material conditions.

2 ORGANIC EVOLUTION

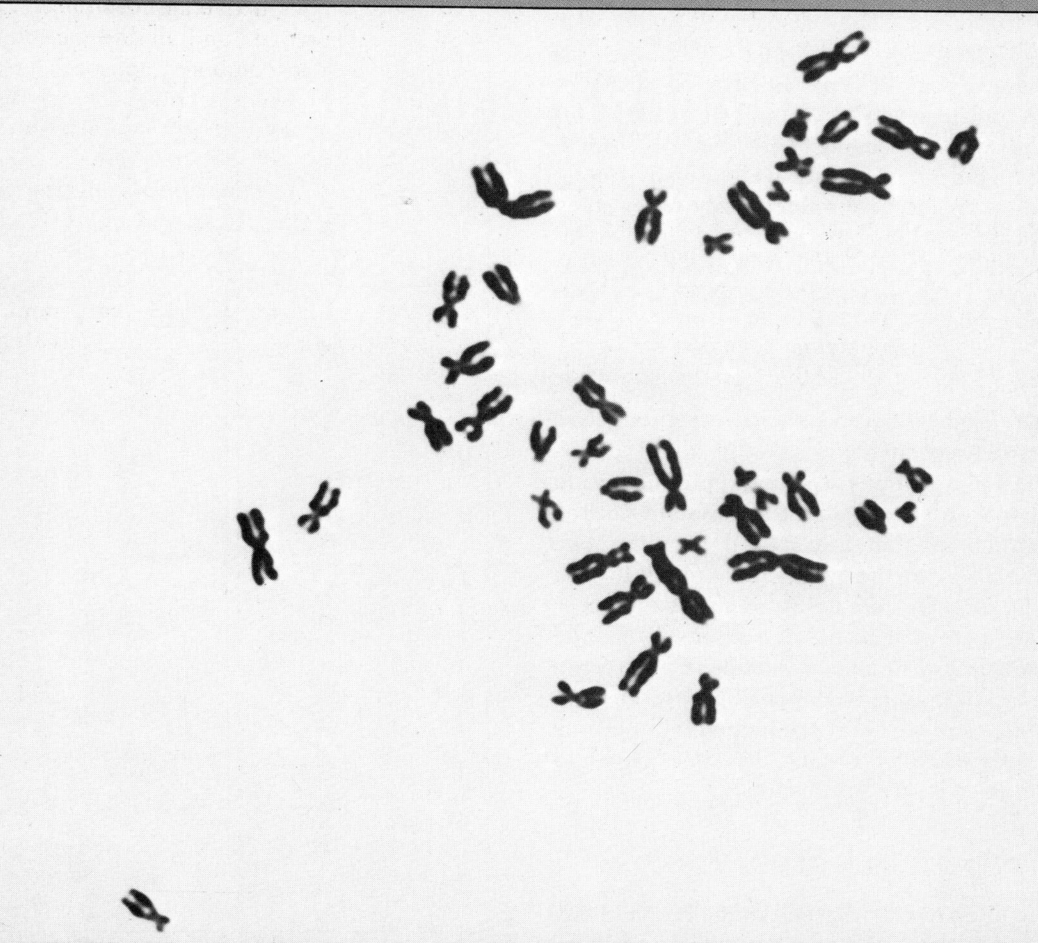

This chapter is concerned with the basic principles of biological heredity and biological evolution. These principles are essential for understanding how our species arose and how it acquired its distinctive human nature. Only the most basic aspects of the mechanisms of inheritance and the forces of evolution will be touched upon.

REPRODUCTION

Reproduction accomplishes two things: It makes a copy of a particular kind of organism and it makes a copy of the plans or instructions for making more such organisms. All higher organisms (as well as many simple forms of life) reproduce only after they transfer portions of their reproductive instructions to each other. When reproduction involves such transfers it is called sexual reproduction.

Why sex? Sexual reproduction is advantageous because it permits organisms to share slight differences in their reproductive instructions and to combine these differences in novel ways. Sexual reproduction, in other words, increases the variability of the instructions that are passed on from one generation to the next. Such variability, in turn, increases the ability of succeeding generations to withstand adverse environmental changes and to take advantage of new beneficial environmental opportunities. The advantages of sexual reproduction will become clearer when we discuss the forces of evolution later on in this chapter.

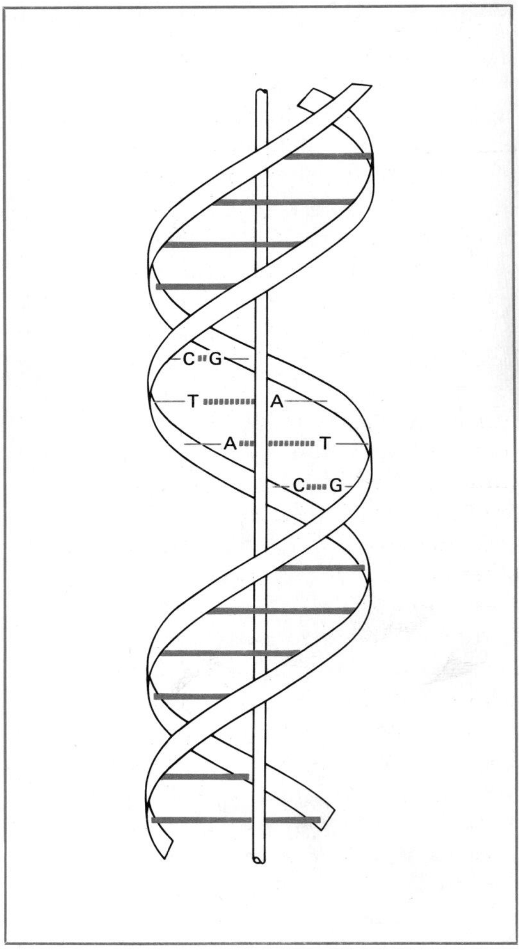

Figure 2.1 *DOUBLE HELIX MODEL OF DNA* C = cytosine; T = thymine; G = guanine; A = adenine. It is the sequence of these chemicals that determines the message carried by the DNA in the chromosomes.

CHROMOSOMES, GENES, AND DNA

The nucleus of every cell in the human body contains a set of structures known as *chromosomes*. Chromosomes are visible under a microscope shortly before and after cells reproduce by fissioning in half. At such times chromosomes have a thickened rodlike appearance; during the interval between fissionings, they become long, thin filaments and are difficult to see.

The fundamental units of heredity are called *genes*. These units are strung out along the chromosomes and occupy definite places, or *loci*. In recent years great strides have been made toward understanding the chemical nature of chromosomes and genes.

Chromosomes consist in large measure of molecules known as *DNA* (deoxyribonucleic acid). DNA has a spiral ladder–like shape. Its side pieces consist of sugar *(deoxyribose)* and phosphate, while its "rungs" consist of four chemicals (known as bases): adenine, thymine, cytosine, and guanine. The order in which these bases form the "rungs" constitutes the fundamental code governing the activites of each cell and the formation of new organisms. Each particular order of bases constitutes a "message" concerning the construction of one of 20 amino acids which are the building blocks of chains of proteins (which in turn are the essential constituents of all life processes). The messages are read off by molecules similar to DNA and transferred from the chromosomes to other parts of the cell, where the actual synthesis of various chains of amino acids is carried out. The portion of the DNA that contains the code for a particular chain of amino acids is called a *cistron*.

The correspondence between cistrons and genes remains somewhat in doubt, since the activity of a gene may be guided by more than one cistron. In general, however, it seems clear that genes are places *(loci)* on the DNA of the chromosome.

THE INHERITANCE OF GENES

To understand how species evolve, one must understand how the chromosomes and their genes are passed along from parent to offspring. Within ordinary body cells, chromosomes always occur in pairs. In sexually reproducing organisms one member of a pair represents the contribution of the male parent, and the other member the contribution of the female parent. Thus human beings have 46 chromosomes, of which 23 are inherited from the father and 23 from the mother. Our hereditary nature is determined when a sperm bearing 23 chromosomes unites with an ovum containing 23 chromosomes. Soon after this union, the chromosomes of similar structure from the sperm and ovum pair off and jointly communicate their hereditary instructions to the first cells of the new individual, which is called a *zygote*. The zygote proceeds to divide and differentiate until a whole embryo is constructed and a new human being is ready to be born.

Since it takes 23 + 23 = 46 chromosomes to create a new human being, it is clear that only one-half of a father's or mother's 46 chromosomes can be passed on to a particular child. The halving of the parental sets of 46 chromosomes takes place during the manufacture of the sex cells in the testes and ovaries. The chromosomes line up at the center of the sex cells and form pairs. It is entirely a matter of chance whether the member of the pair that has been contributed by the individual's father or the individual's mother lines up on the right or left. The chromosomes are then pulled to opposite sides of the cell (23, one member of each pair, to a side), and the cell then divides in two. Each new sex cell thus contains a new assortment of hereditary material created by the shuffling of the *homologous* chromosomes—the chromosomes that have similar genes on them—some coming from the mother and the rest from the father in a proportion governed by chance.

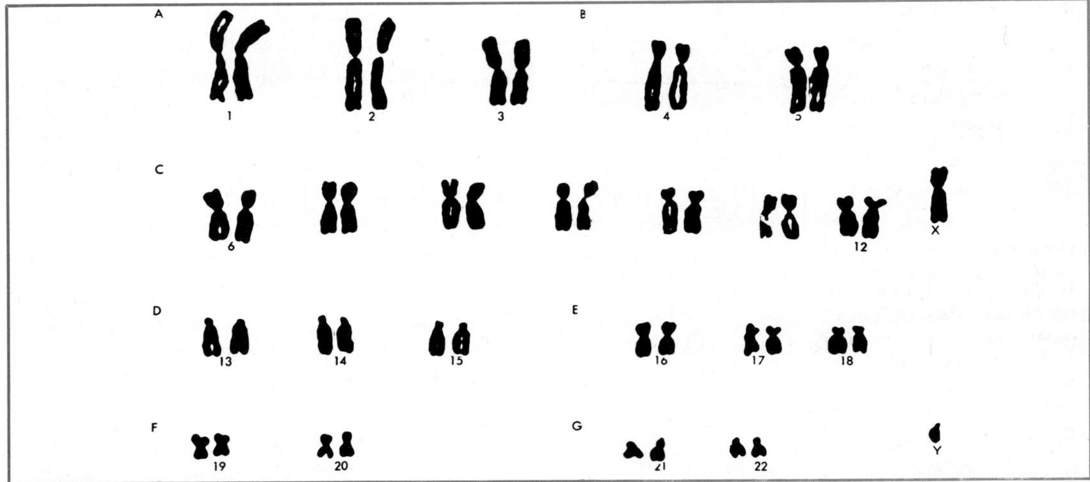

Figure 2.2 *HUMAN CHROMOSOME KARYOTYPE*
The set of chromosomes of a species is called its *karyotype*. Shown are the 23 pairs of human chromosomes. The X and Y, or sex chromosomes, are the 23d pair.

The fact that the chromosomes are independently assorted during the *reduction division* (Fig. 2.3) of the sex cells (reduction from 46 to 23 chromosomes) is a basic principle of genetics. *Independent assortment* means that hereditary information on one chromosome is passed along independently of the information on all the other chromosomes. It also means that although one-half of our chromosomes come from our father and one-half from our mother, there is no guarantee that one-quarter of our chromosomes come from each of our grandparents, and it is unlikely that precisely one-eighth of our chromosomes come from each of our great-grandparents. On the fifth ascending generation, where we have 64 grandparents, it is possible that some of these "ancestors" may not have contributed any genes at all to our heredity. This should have a sobering effect on people who delight in tracing their "roots" more than four generations back to royalty, first settlers, or other dignitaries.

The situation would be even more bleak for genealogists were it not for the fact that homologous chromosomes exchange segments (genes) with each other. This phenomenon is known as *crossing over* (Fig. 2.4), and it occurs just before reduction division, when the 23 pairs of chromosomes are lined up at the center of the cell. Because of crossing over, the chromosomes contributed by any particular ancestor do not remain intact throughout the generations. Thus several different ancestors may contribute genes to each of the 46 chromosomes possessed by one of their descendants, making it likely that each of as many as 64 ancestors could have contributed some genes to their great-great-great-great-grandchild. That their contribution would be exactly 1/64, however, is highly unlikely.

Genotype and Phenotype

When the genes at the same locus on a pair of homologous chromosomes contain precisely the same information, the individual

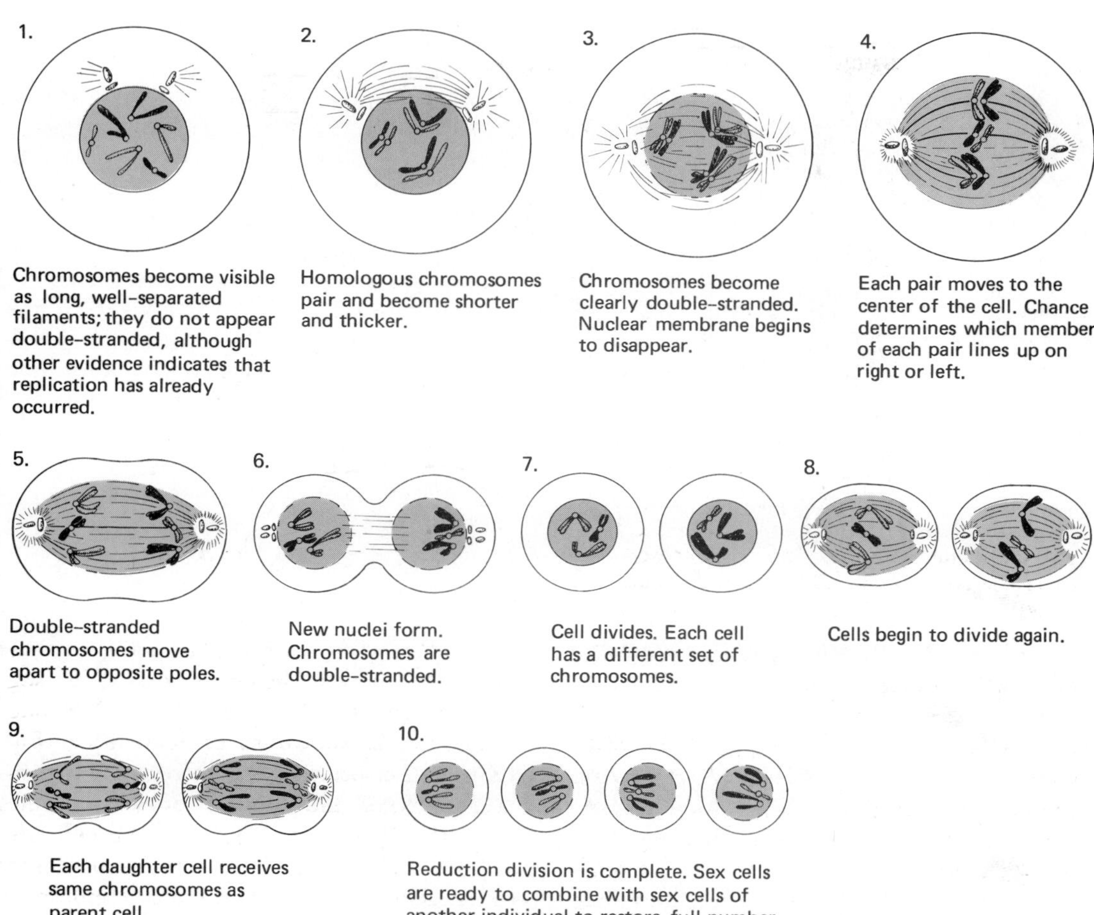

Figure 2.3 *REDUCTION DIVISION*
Schematic representation of steps responsible for the independent assortment of parental chromosomes in an individual's sex cells.

is said to be *homozygous* for the trait controlled by that gene. Often, however, the two genes will differ slightly and the individual is said to be *heterozygous*. The variant genes found at a given locus are called *alleles*.

Because the assortment of chromosomes in the sex cells is governed by chance, it is possible to predict the probable proportions in which two or more alleles will occur in the children of fathers and mothers whose genetic types are known. For example, suppose that at one locus there are two alleles: A and a. Because of the processes responsible for independent assortment, this means that three kinds of individuals may occur:

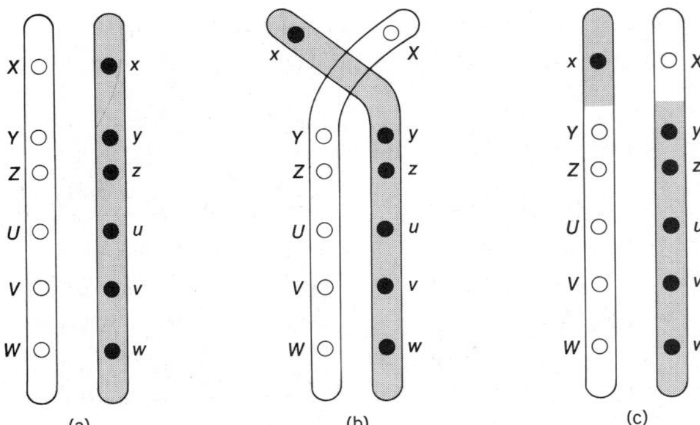

Figure 2.4 *CROSSING OVER*
Schematic representation of a pair of homologous chromosomes exchanging some of their genes during reduction division.

AA, Aa, and aa. Each of these combinations is called a *genotype*. The proportion in which genotypes will occur can be calculated from a simple device known as a *Punnett square*. If ovum and sperm have an equal chance of possessing either allele, the zygote has a one-half chance of being heterozygous Aa or aA, a one-quarter chance of being homozygous AA, and a one-quarter chance of being homozygous aa. The following Punnett square shows that the three genotypes can be expected to occur in the ratio 1AA:2Aa:1aa.

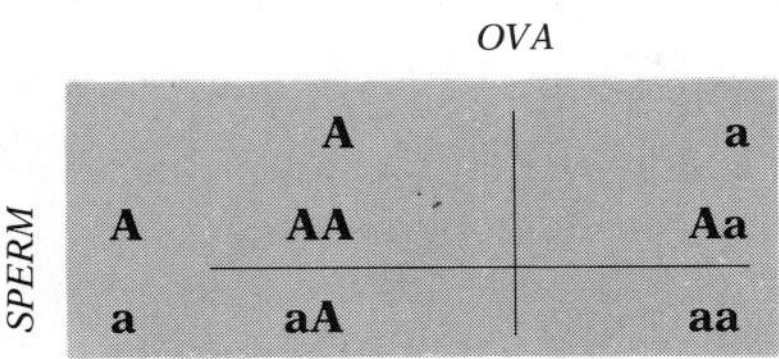

OVA

SPERM	A	a
A	AA	Aa
a	aA	aa

As the zygote matures, and as the organism is born, grows, and dies, its genetic traits interact with the environment of its particular life experiences. The interaction of genes with environment produces the organism's *phenotype*—its appearance. Organisms having similar genotypes may have dissimilar phenotypes, and vice versa. For example, people who are disposed by heredity to accumulate fat may keep themselves thin by strict dieting, while others predisposed by heredity toward thinness may make themselves fat by overeating. The important lesson here is that no organism is a product of its purely hereditary nature; nor is any organism purely the product of its environmental life experience. Rather, all individuals are the products of the interaction of their genes and their environment.

DOMINANT AND RECESSIVE GENES

Individuals who are heterozygous for a trait cannot always be identified as such by their appearance. Some alleles seem to have no effect on the appearance of a trait if they are in a heterozygous condition. Such alleles are said to be *recessive*. The alleles paired with recessives are said to be *dominant*.

In the above example, suppose that A is dominant and that a is recessive. The ratio of the genotypes will not change, but individuals AA, Aa, and aA will all have the same phenotype (under similar environmental conditions).

This discovery was first made by Gregor Mendel, the founder of modern genetics. Crossing red-flowered peas with white-flowered peas, Mendel obtained a generation of peas all of which had red flowers:

	w	w
R	Rw	Rw
R	Rw	Rw

The reason for this is that all the white-flowered peas were homozygous for the recessive gene w, and all the red-flowered peas were homozygous for the dominant gene R. None of the phenotypes shows the presence of the recessive gene. Then, by crossing the red-flowered heterozygotic peas with each other, Mendel showed that the recessive gene was still present in the genotype:

	R	w
R	RR	Rw
w	wR	ww

Approximately one out of every four pea plants—those homozygous for the recessive w—now bore white flowers.

Although the above Punnett square indicates three genotypes, which occur in the ratio 1:2:1, there are only two phenotypes, which occur in the ratio 3:1. Many human traits—such as eye color and color blindness, as well as hemophilia, sickle-cell anemia, and other hereditary diseases—are governed by systems of dominant and recessive genes in which heterozygous individuals are phenotypically indistinguishable from those who are homozygous for a dominant allele. This often makes the heterozygotes carriers of harmful traits. In some instances, however, the heterozygotes have an advantage over the homozygote dominants even though the homozygote recessives may be the victims of fatal diseases. The resistance against malaria enjoyed by persons heterozygous for sickle-cell anemia is a classic instance of *heterozygous superiority*. It should be emphasized that not all recessive genes are harmful.

Contrary to popular misconception, dominant alleles do not tend to become more frequent in a population as time goes by. The frequencies of dominant and recessive alleles as well as the frequencies of all other genes are determined by the forces of evolution, and it is to these that we now turn.

THE FORCES OF EVOLUTION

In large populations the frequency of occurrence of genes would remain stable were it not for certain forces. Any process which changes the frequency of genes in a population is an evolutionary force. Biologists generally identify four major evolutionary forces.

1. Drift The proportions of genes in each generation may differ purely as a result of the chance factors in the way genes and chromosomes are inherited. In extreme cases, involving very small populations and low gene frequencies, alleles present in one generation may disappear entirely from the next. Suppose that in an isolated population only one individual out of a total population of 100 is carrying an allele for curly hair. By chance, it might happen that none of that person's children would inherit that allele and, as a result, there would no longer be any people with curly hair in that population. Another form of drift may occur when part of one population migrates and takes with it to its new homeland a pool of genes that is not representative of the original group. All the curly-headed individuals, for example, might by accident emigrate at once from one island to another. This kind of genetic drift is called the *founder effect*.

All changes in gene frequencies that arise simply from the statistically unrepresentative nature of successive generations or of migrant groups are examples of evolution by drift (Birdsell 1981:64–65).

2. Gene Flow Since populations that make up a species are never completely isolated from each other, there is usually some interbreeding between them. When interbreeding between populations takes place on a large scale, many alleles may occur in new proportions in the new gene pool. For example, as a result of gene flow, the population of modern Brazil has gene frequencies which were not characteristic of the Africans, Europeans, and native Americans who contributed to the formation of the population of Brazil (ibid.: 66–67).

Gene flow often results from migration and subsequent hybridization, but not all migrations result in gene flow (e.g., when there is migration to a previously unpopulated habitat).

3. Mutations Mutations are alterations or "errors" in the DNA code, or changes in the structure or number of chromosomes, that result in new alleles or chromosomes. Many physical and chemical factors may play a role in the failure of a gene or of a whole chromosome to duplicate itself. Radiation, for example, is a well-known cause of mutations in many species. Under natural conditions, human mutations may occur anywhere from once every 20,000 duplications to once every 10 million duplications. High rates of mutation will tend to alter the makeup of the gene pool. Regardless of their rate of occurrence, however, mutations may constitute the raw material for extensive evolutionary change if they are advantageous.

4. Natural Selection The most powerful force for evolutionary change arises from the variable *fitness* of genes and alleles. Fitness refers purely to the number of progeny, the reproductive success, associated with the alleles at a particular locus. The more progeny, the higher the fitness. Alleles associated with higher fitness will increase in frequency, at the expense of alleles having lower fitness. The process by which high-fitness genes replace low-fitness genes is called *natural selection.* Natural selection denotes any change in gene frequency brought about by differential fitness. Natural selection may act upon mutations or upon the existing repertory of genes. When acting upon mutations, natural selection can rapidly increase the frequency of a new allele even if the mutation recurs only once in a million duplications. If environmental conditions change to favor alleles already present in the gene pool, natural selection can rapidly raise their frequency also. An example of the power of natural selection to raise the frequency of a rare gene is the evolution of penicillin-resistant strains of bacteria. The alleles conferring resistance are present in normal populations of bacteria but in only a small percentage of individuals. As a result of the differential reproductive success of such individuals, however, the resistant genotype soon becomes the most common genotype.

As a result of natural selection, organisms may be said to become *adapted* to the needs and opportunities present in their environments. An adaptive trait is one that confers relatively high levels of fitness. It is important to remember that there is no absolute fixed level of fitness that guarantees the perpetuation of a species. The essence of organic evolution is its opportunism. A vast range of natural experiments is always being carried out, leading inevitably to the modification and replacement of hitherto highly adapted species (Alland 1970). As a result of changes in the physical and organic environments, traits which were once adaptive may become maladaptive. The evolutionary record shows that as conditions change, better-adapted species replace those that are less well adapted or maladapted. In most instances these new species cannot be regarded as either more or less complex, "advanced," or "efficient" than their predecessors. They are simply better adapted under the circumstances.

NATURAL SELECTION AND THE "STRUGGLE FOR SURVIVAL"

The information contained in the genetic code is not sufficient to produce a new organism. For that, the genes need space, energy, and chemical substances. These vital ingredients must be obtained from the environment according to directions contained in the genes.

Unless a parent organism dies immediately after producing a single copy of itself, reproduction tends to increase the size of a population. As a population increases, a point is reached sooner or later at which the space, energy, and chemical substances needed for constructing new organisms become more difficult to obtain. If each organism produces several copies of itself, population expansion occurs very rapidly. In a short time there is not sufficient space, energy, or chemical nutrients to permit all the members of the population to reproduce at the same rate. Some genotypes, enjoying greater fitness, will come to constitute an increasing proportion of the population. That is, they will be selected by natural selection.

Fitness is associated with many different kinds of factors. It may be related to the organism's ability to resist disease, to gain or hold space more securely, or to obtain energy in larger or more dependable amounts, as well as to the increased efficiency and dependability of some aspect of the reproductive process itself.

It was Charles Darwin and Alfred Wallace who formulated the basic principles of how organic evolution could result from natural selection. Under the influence of the prevailing philosophy of economic competition, however, both Darwin and Wallace accepted Thomas Malthus's concept of a "struggle for survival" as the main source of selection for reproductive success. Thus, in the nineteenth century natural selection was pictured incorrectly as the direct struggle between individuals for scarce resources and sexual partners, and even more erroneously as the preying upon and destruction of one another by organisms of the same species. Although within-species killing and competition sometimes do play a role in organic evolution, the factors promoting differential reproductive success are in the main not related to an organism's ability to destroy other members of its own population or to prevent them from obtaining nutrients, space, and mates.

Today, biologists recognize that natural selection favors cooperation within species as often as it favors competition. In social species the perpetuation of an individual's genes often depends as much on the reproductive success of its close relatives as on its own survival and reproduction. Many social insects even have "altruistic" sterile "castes" which assure their own genetic success by rearing the progeny of their fertile siblings (see p. 525).

SPECIATION: FAST OR SLOW?

Darwin pictured evolution taking place as a result of the slow accumulation of slight adaptive changes. Eventually enough differences would accumulate in a population so that it gradually became unable to interbreed with other populations. As a result of this increasing *reproductive isolation*, a new species would emerge. This view of speciation is called *phyletic gradualism*. It has recently been criticized for its failure to account for certain aspects of the fossil record (see the following chapter), namely, the long periods during which many species do not seem to change at all and the suddenness with which new species often appear. An alternative view of speciation is called *punctuated equilibrium.* According to this view, species are not always accumulating new adaptive changes; they are already very well adapted and hence are in "equilibrium" with their habitats. Only after millions of years, and sometimes tens of millions of years, will this equilibrium be "punctuated" by a species-forming "event." Such an event might be triggered by a change in environment or an opening up of the possibility of utilizing a new habitat, and might at one extreme take only a few hundred years to complete (Eldredge and Tattersall 1982:59; Eldredge and Gould 1972). Although punctuated equilibrium has been represented by the popular media as a fundamental challenge to Darwin's view of evolution, it is in reality no such thing. Most biologists find no difficulty in accepting the possibility of both gradual and sudden speciation events, with most new species originating over intermediate time spans (hundreds of thousands of years). The most important point about speciation is not the rate at which it occurs but that it occurs as a result of the four major natural forces of evolution—drift, gene flow, mutation, and natural selection—and not as a result of divine intervention, as scientists believed before Darwin's time.

The next three chapters are concerned with the particular sequence of adaptations and evolutionary transformations that led to the emergence of our species, *Homo sapiens.*

SUMMARY

H. sapiens is an evolutionary product. Organic evolution is a consequence of the interaction of reproductive and evolutionary processes. Reproductive processes depend on the replication of genetic information encoded by the DNA molecules found at active loci on the chromosomes. In human and other sexually reproducing organisms, genes are randomly shuffled during reduction division. This results in the independent assortment of hereditary traits. The actual assemblage of genes on an organism's chromosomes is its genotype; its phenotype is the actual appearance of an organism as a result of the suppression of recessive alleles and the interaction of the genotype with the environment. Biological evolution begins with changes in the frequency of genes found in a given population. Four major forces account for gene frequency changes: drift, migration, mutation, and natural selection. Of these, natural selection is the most powerful, since it accounts for the adaptedness of species. Phyletic gradualism and punctuated equilibrium are alternative views of the rates of speciation. Both conform to Darwin's view that speciation results from natural processes.

3 THE HUMAN PEDIGREE AND HUMAN NATURE

This chapter is concerned with the problem of defining human nature. It describes the anatomical and behavioral traits that we share in common with our distant relatives in the animal kingdom. Then it focuses upon the anatomical and behavioral traits that we share with our closest relatives in the animal kingdom. Finally, it identifies those traits that only human beings possess.

FROM ANIMAL TO PRIMATE

Biologists use Latin terms to classify organisms by means of a standard set of increasingly inclusive categories ranging upward from species to kingdom. They call the various types of organisms within each category *taxons*. The objective of such categorization is to group all organisms having a common ancestor in the same taxon. So if one is interested in the question "What is human nature?" part of the answer surely lies in learning about the taxons to which our ancestors belong. All of these taxons have contributed something to human nature.

As Table 3.1 shows, our species has a pedigree defined by 14 taxonomic categories within the animal kingdom.

Human beings are Animalia: mobile multicelled organisms that derive energy from ingestion ("eating"). Animalia are radically different from members of the plant kingdom, from the bacteria, from one-celled creatures (Protista), and from fungi.

We are also Chordata, the animal phylum, all of whose members possess (1) a *no-*

Table 3.1 CATEGORIES AND TAXONS RELEVANT TO HUMAN ANCESTRY

Category	Taxon	Common Description
Kingdom	Animalia	Animals
Phylum	Chordata	Animals with notochords
Subphylum	Vertebrata	Animals with backbones
Superclass	Tetrapoda	Four-footed vertebrates
Class	Mammalia	Vertebrates with body hair and mammary glands
Subclass	Theria	Mammals bearing fetal young
Infraclass	Eutheria	Mammals that nourish young in womb
Order	Primates*	Primates
Suborder	Anthropoidea*	All monkeys, apes, and humans
Superfamily	Hominoidea*	Apes and humans
Family	Hominidae*	Humans and their immediate ancestors
Genus	*Homo*	Human species living and extinct
Species	*Homo sapiens*	Modern human species
Subspecies	*Homo sapiens sapiens*	All contemporary human beings

*The English words primate, anthropoid, hominoid, and hominid are often used as informal substitutes for Primates, Anthropoidea, Hominoidea, and Hominidae, respectively. Some categories used by biologists (e.g., "cohort" and "tribe") are not needed to define our ancestry. Disagreement exists about mammalian subclasses and infraclasses.

tochord, a rodlike structure that provides internal support for the body; (2) *gill pouches,* lateral slits on the throat; and (3) a hollow nerve chord ending in a brain. (We display the first two of these features only when we are embryos.) The Chordata contrast radically with some 24 different animal phyla such as the sponges, the stinging jellyfish, the flatworms, the roundworms, the mollusks, and the arthropods (insects, crustaceans, millipedes, spiders).

Human beings are also Vertebrata, uniquely distinguished from other subphyla of the Chordata by two features: (1) In all adult Vertebrata the notochord is surrounded or replaced by a column of cartilaginous or bony discs (the vertebrae); and (2) The brain is encased within a bony covering (the skull, or *cranium*).

Among the Vertebrata we belong in the superclass Tetrapoda, which means literally "four-footed," as distinguished from Pisces, the superclass of the fish. The Tetrapoda are divided into four classes: Amphibia, Reptilia, Aves (birds), and Mammalia. Our class, Mammalia, is distinguished from the others by: (1) milk-secreting mammary glands; (2) hair; and (3) incisor, canine, and molar teeth for cutting, tearing, and grinding, respectively. In addition, mammals share with birds the capacity to maintain their bodies at a constant temperature.

The Mammalia are usually divided into two subclasses: Theria, mammals like us that do not lay eggs, and Prototheria, egg-laying mammals, of which the spiny anteater (*Echidna*) and the duckbill (*Ornithorhynchus*) are the best-known and the only surviving representative genera (Fig. 3.1). Both the spiny anteater and the duckbill are found only in Australia, Tasmania, and New Guinea. They have mammary glands but no teats, hair (formed into spines in the case of the Echidna), and a rudimentary body thermostat. The duckbill copulates in the water and incubates its eggs inside a burrow for about 10 days. The spiny anteater is more land-dwelling and has a pouch into which it places its young after they hatch.

(a)

(b)

Figure 3.1 *EGG-LAYING MAMMALS*
The *Echidna,* or spiny anteater *(a),* and the *Ornithorhyncus,* or duckbill platypus *(b),* are representatives of the mammalian subclass Prototheria.

The subclass Theria, which does not lay eggs, is divided into two living infraclasses: Metatheria, or *marsupials,* and our own infraclass, Eutheria. The principal characteristic of Eutheria is the presence of the *placenta,* a unique nutrient and waste-exchanging structure that enhances fetal de-

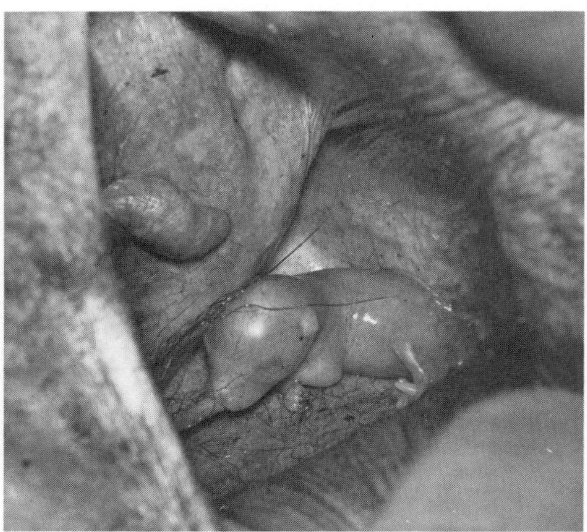

Figure 3.2 *A WALLABY MOTHER AND CHILD*
Among the metatherian, the tiny newborn young complete their fetal development inside the mother's pouch.

velopment within the mother's body. Metatheria lack part or all of the placental structure. Instead, many, though not all, have an external pouch in which the tiny newborn young complete their fetal development (Fig. 3.2). Besides familiar marsupials, such as the kangaroo and the opossum, the metatherians occur in a dazzling variety of forms. Many live an arboreal life feeding on insects and fruits; others are predators; others dig tunnels; others are aquatic; still others are jumpers and gliders. There are marsupials that resemble mice and others that evoke comparisons with foxes, minks, wolves, and squirrels. These resemblances are of great theoretical interest because they are not caused by descent from a common ancestor but by adaptations to similar ecological conditions.

Our infraclass, Eutheria, contains 16 orders, including, for example, insectivores, carnivores, and rodents. The order we belong to is called *Primates*, (pronounced "pri-mahtees"), a taxon that includes monkeys, apes, tarsiers, lemurs, and other close relatives.

THE ORDER PRIMATES

As compared with the earliest mammals, Primates have distinctive hands, feet, toes, toenails, fingernails, and eyes. Primates also tend to have few offspring per birth, prolonged infancies, and complex social behavior. They also are brainier and more intelligent than most mammals (Schwartz et al. 1978).

1. Prehensile Hands and Feet Primates have prehensile hands and feet, meaning that they have flexible fingers and toes that

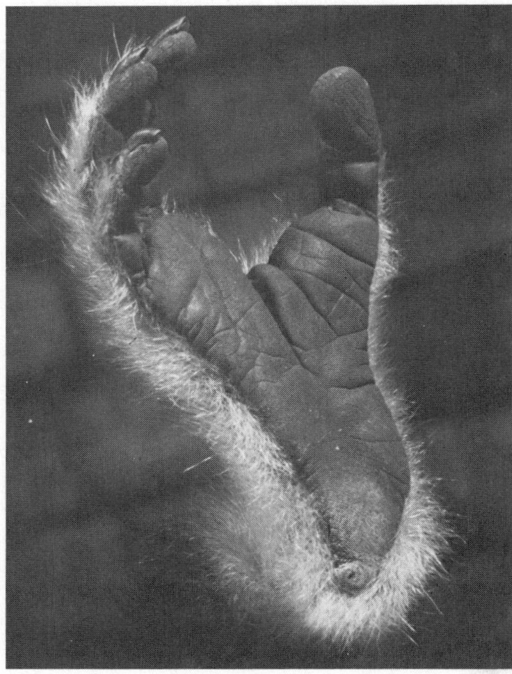

Figure 3.3 *GIBBON FOOT*
The big toe is prehensile and opposable.

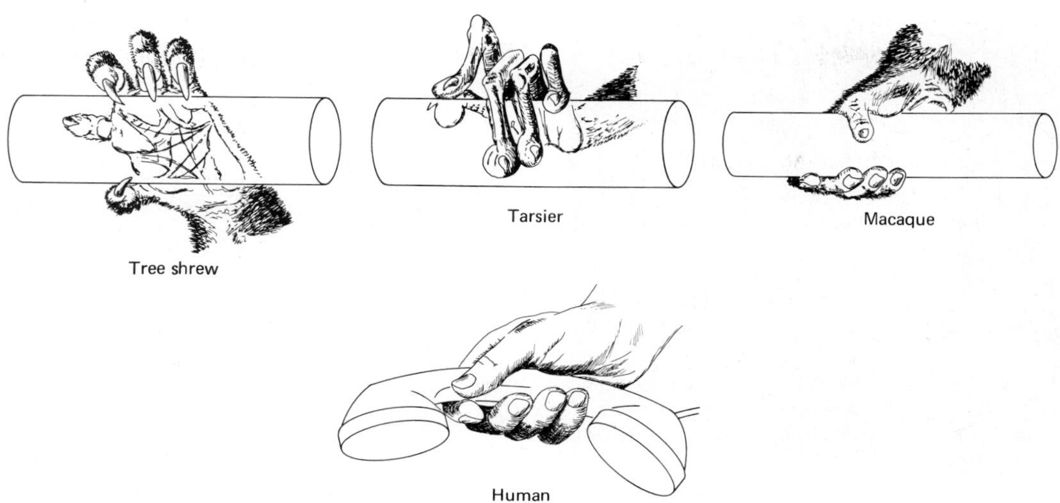

Figure 3.4 *PRIMATE GRIPS.*

are adept at grasping and clutching. In many primate species, the big toe and the thumb are *opposable*—the tips can be made to lie against the tips of the other digits (Fig. 3.3). Closely associated with prehensility is the absence or reduction of the claws used by several other mammalian orders for climbing, predation, and defense. Instead, most Primates have flat nails, which protect and reinforce the tips of their fingers and toes without interfering with prehensility (Fig. 3.4).

2. Specialized Functions of the Forelimb Primates have a highly developed ability to rotate, flex, and extend their forelimbs. This capability accounts for the distinction between arms and legs. Arms in conjunction with a prehensile hand are well suited for exploring the space under leaves and between branches and twigs and for clutching and drawing in fruits and berries, as well as for catching small animals and insects.

3. Visual Acuity Primate eyes are large proportionate to facial surface and are typically located toward the front of the head instead of at the sides (Fig. 3.5). This arrangement helps to produce the stereoscopic vision and the ability to gauge distances. Most Primates also have color vision. But in contrast to their well-developed sense of sight, Primates have a relatively poor sense of smell. Many other mammals get most of their information by sniffing the environment, and their eyes are located behind their snouts. Dogs, for example, lack stereoscopic vision and see only in black and white tones. They are literally led by their noses. The positioning of primate eyes is related to prehensility and to the mobility of the forelimbs. Typical primate feeding involves a grasping action that brings objects close to the mouth, where they are examined by the eyes before being swallowed. Snouted mammals, on the other hand, examine what they eat primarily by the sense of smell.

(a)

(b)

Figure 3.5 *VISUAL ACUITY*
A prosimian, the tarsier *(a)* is a nocturnal arboreal insect- and fruit-eating primate. It has binocular stereoscopic vision; disklike adhesive pads on its digits; elongated hind legs; and a long tail. These characteristics are all suited to hopping along tree limbs. Like the tarsier, the chimpanzee *(b)* has stereoscopic vision and depends greatly on the sense of sight.

4. Small Number of Offspring per Birth Primates tend to give birth to no more than two or three infants at a time, and a single offspring per birth is the rule among many primate species. In keeping with this characteristic, Primates have only two mammary glands (unlike dogs and cats and other mammals which have to nurse seven or eight infants at a time).

5. Prolongation of Pregnancy and Infancy Most mammalian orders that rely upon large numbers of offspring per birth for reproductive success have short pregnancies followed by rapid onset of sexual maturity and adulthood. Mammals that have large litters depend on numbers to compensate for defective births. A high proportion of the individuals in the litter are either stillborn or weeded out shortly after birth as a result of the competition among the littermates for the mother's milk and for her protection and care. In contrast, primates concentrate on one infant at a time and provide high quality care for that one infant until it is large enough to fend for itself. Compared with the rest of the animal kingdom, primate mothers pamper their babies (Fig. 3.6). This does not mean, however, that infanticide and child abuse are absent or rare in primate social life (Reite and Cains 1983).

6. Complexity of Social Behavior A further consequence of not having large litters is that primate patterns of behavior are highly social. This arises from the prolonged mother-child relationship and the intense care given to each offspring. Manual dexterity also adds to social interdependence, since it permits primates to groom each other's hair. Most primates spend their lives as members of groups

Figure 3.6 *RHESUS MOTHER AND CHILD*
A typical agile, alert, dexterous, and highly sociable monkey.

(although not necessarily the group they are born into), and these groups cooperate in finding food and in defending themselves against predators. Group life is facilitated among primates by relatively complex communication systems consisting of signals which indicate the presence of food, danger, sexual interest, and other vital matters. Primates need social companionship not only to survive physically but to mature emotionally. Many studies have shown that monkeys brought up in isolation display severe neurotic symptoms such as excessive timidity or aggressiveness (Harlow et al. 1966).

7. Enlargement of the Brain Most primates have a high ratio of brain weight to body weight. It is no accident that the Primates are among the brainiest as well as the most social of the mammals. The prolonged dependency of the primate infant, the large amount of auditory, visual, and tactile information passed between mother and offspring, the intense play among juveniles, and the mutual grooming among adults all presuppose a heightened ability to acquire, store, and recall information. It is also no coincidence that human beings, the brainiest of the Primates, are also the most social of the Primates. Our intelligence is above all an evolutionary consequence of our extremely intense social life. (Why ants and other social insects are not equally intelligent will become clear in Ch. 7.)

Primates and Life in the Trees

Most living and fossil Primates are found in tropical forest habitats. Several of the traits which distinguish the Primates from other mammals probably were selected for their advantages in an *arboreal*—tree-dwelling—way of life in these forests: prehensile hands and feet for moving up and down trunks and branches; forelimbs for exploring between leaves, plucking fruits and berries, and capturing and picking up small insects and reptiles; keen vision as a compensation for not being able to follow scents from branch to branch or tree to tree; and small numbers of offspring per birth as an adaption to the difficulty and dangers to both mother and offspring of having a litter cling to her as she runs and jumps high above the ground.

But life in the trees by itself is not sufficient to account for the earliest phases of primate evolution. Squirrels, for example, have claws and non-prehensile forelimbs, and lack stereoscopic vision, yet they are accomplished aerial acrobats. It seems likely that the grasping functions of primate hands and feet evolved primarily to facilitate cautious, well-controlled movements in pursuit of small animals and insects amid the lower branches and leaves. The stereoscopic vision of the Primates resembles that of predator cats and birds, which also evolved in relation to predation practiced against small animals and insects (Cartmill 1974).

There is little doubt that some of our remote ancestors lived in the trees. But as in the case of many other Primates species (e.g., baboons) our ancestors went on to adopt a *terrestrial*—ground-dwelling—way of life at some point in the past. When this took place will be discussed below.

Suborder Anthropoidea versus Suborder Prosimii

The order Primates contains two suborders: Anthropoidea and Prosimii. All monkeys, great apes, and human beings are Anthropoidea. The Prosimii consist of lemurs, lorises, tarsiers, and galagos (Fig. 3.7). These less familiar cousins of ours are found in Africa, Madagascar, India, and Southeast Asia.

The Anthropoidea are sometimes called the "higher primates." They have relatively larger and rounder skull cases, flatter faces, and mobile upper lips detached from the gums. This last feature is important for making facial expressions, which in turn figure in the development of more advanced forms of primate social life (since facial expressions assist in communicating feelings and intentions). Lorises and lemurs (but not tarsiers) have their upper lips attached externally to their nose by a moist strip of skin called a *rhinarium*, which can also be seen on the snouts of cats and dogs. We humans boast a dry nose and a dry, hairy upper lip. But the two vertical ridges under our nose suggest that someone in our family tree once had a rhinarium.

THE ANTHROPOIDEAN SUPERFAMILIES

The suborder Anthropoidea is made up of three superfamilies: (1) the Ceboidea, or New World monkeys; (2) the Cercopithecoidea, or Old World monkeys; and (3) the Hominoidea, which include all fossil and contemporary species of both apes and human beings.* Old and New World monkeys have different dental patterns that indicate an ancient divergence from a common primate or prosimian ancestor. Old World monkeys (but not Prosimii) have what is known as the cercopithecoid *dental formula:* $\frac{2.1.2.3}{2.1.2.3}$ (see Fig. 3.8). The numbers above the line denote from left to right the number of incisors, canines, premolars, and molars in an upper quadrant (quarter) of the jaw; the figures below the line, the numbers in a lower quadrant. (The total number of teeth equals the number in the upper quadrant times 2 plus the number in the lower quadrant times 2.) All New World anthropoids on the other hand have either $\frac{2.1.3.3}{2.1.3.3}$ or $\frac{2.1.3.2}{2.1.3.2}$ patterns. If your wisdom teeth have erupted, you may discover for yourself that we share a $\frac{2.1.2.3}{2.1.2.3}$ pattern with the Old World monkeys and apes.

*Some taxonomists distinguish two infraorders within the Anthropoidea, Catarrhini and Platyrrhini, with the superfamilies Cercopithecoidea and Ceboidea respectively placed within the former and the latter.

(a)

(b)

(c)

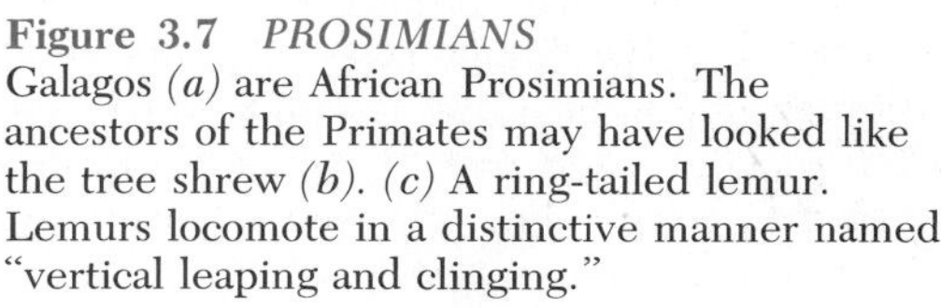

Figure 3.7 *PROSIMIANS*
Galagos *(a)* are African Prosimians. The ancestors of the Primates may have looked like the tree shrew *(b)*. *(c)* A ring-tailed lemur. Lemurs locomote in a distinctive manner named "vertical leaping and clinging."

CHARACTERISTICS OF THE HOMINOIDEA

The hominoids consist of apes and humans. There are two families of living apes: the Hylobatidae, which consist of siamangs and gibbons (the *lesser apes*); and the Pongidae, which consist of chimpanzees, gorillas, and orangutans (the *great apes*).

In general, the Hominoidea are larger than other Anthropoidea and have developed distinctive postures and modes of locomotion. Unlike most monkeys, three of the living Hominoidea—*Homo sapiens,* the gibbon, and siamang—seldom move on all fours. The gibbon and siamang are primarily *brachiators*—they swing from branch to branch with legs tucked up close to their bodies, propelled through graceful trajectories by extraordinarily long and powerful arms (Fig. 3.9).

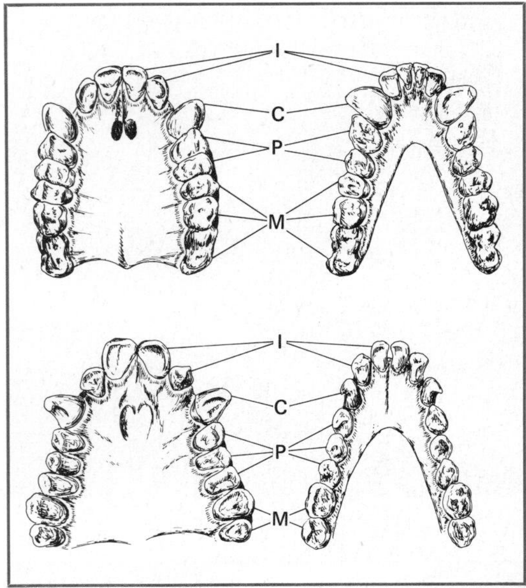

Figure 3.8 *OLD WORLD MONKEY DENTITION (top); NEW WORLD MONKEY DENTITION (bottom)*

Although the chimpanzee, gorilla, and orangutan also have long arms, they are too big and heavy as adults to brachiate energetically. Their long arms, however, are put to good use while they practice *suspensory feeding*—hanging by a combination of arms and prehensile feet and reaching out to pluck off fruity morsels from slender branches that cannot bear their weight (Figs. 3.10 and 3.11). In addition, the great apes have developed special forms of walking on the ground. This is especially true of the chimpanzee and gorilla, who spend the majority of their lives during the day on the ground. In this they are similar to ground-dwelling monkeys such as the baboons. But whereas baboons maintain the basic four-footed gait by walking on the palms of their hands, gorillas and chimpanzees practice *knuckle walking:* their long arms lock at the elbow into a rigid straight line, and their forward weight rests on their knuckles (Fig. 3.12). Orangutans usually walk on the sides of their fists during their fairly frequent visits to the ground (Tuttle 1969; Napier 1970; Galdikas-Brindamour 1975). The long, mobile arms of all the living pongids suggest that they all had ancestors who were vigorous brachiators and suspensory feeders.

H. sapiens also probably had ancestors who were brachiators and suspensory feeders since we too have mobile arms that are quite long in comparison with the length of our trunks. In our case, however, the capacity for brachiation was almost entirely given up in favor of *bipedalism* (two-leggedness). This resulted in the lengthening of our legs to a degree that is unique among the hominoids (Fig. 3.13).

Perhaps I should also add that the Hominoidea are probably more intelligent than the other primates, as our recent experiences with teaching chimps and gorillas to communicate suggests (see Ch. 20).

(a)

Figure 3.9 *GIBBONS*
These Hominoidea are assigned to the family Hylobatidea. Their entire anatomy reflects the influence of brachiation. Note especially the huge arms, long fingers, short legs, and short thumbs.

(b)

Figure 3.10 *SUSPENSORY FEEDING*
A young orang can eat with its feet as well as its hands.

Figure 3.11 *JUVENILE ORANGUTANS*
Note the long forelimbs suitable for brachiation and the prehensile feet with opposable big toes.

Common Ancestry of Apes and Humans

During the 1970s a new method for measuring the degree of relatedness between living species was developed by the biochemist Vincent Sarich (1974). Sarich's method is based on the analysis of blood proteins. When two species split off from a common ancestor, the components of amino acid chains in the blood begin to change, creating an increasing amount of immunological reaction between the two proteins. The greater the degree of change, the greater the "*immunological distance.*" Moreover, the rate of change seems to be quite constant across a broad range of species.

According to this immunological "clock," two of the great apes—gorillas and chimpanzees—and *H. sapiens* must have had a common ancestor no more than 5 or 6 million years ago. Their blood proteins are 99 percent similar, which makes them as closely related as such species as the horse and zebra or grizzly bears and polar bears (Poirier 1982:206).

Orangutans show a much greater amount of immunological distance; gibbons and siamangs show a still greater amount (see p. 46).

FAMILY HOMINIDAE VERSUS FAMILY PONGIDAE AND FAMILY HYLOBATIDAE

As we have just seen, the superfamily Hominoidea contains three families: (1) the Hominidae—all varieties of hominids, of which *H. sapiens* is the sole surviving representative; (2) the Pongidae—all contemporary and extinct varieties of great apes; and (3) the Hylobatidae—the gibbon and siamang and their fossil ancestors.

Figure 3.12 *ADULT MALE GORILLA*
Knuckle-walking involves anatomical modifications in the elbows as well as in the wrists and fingers.

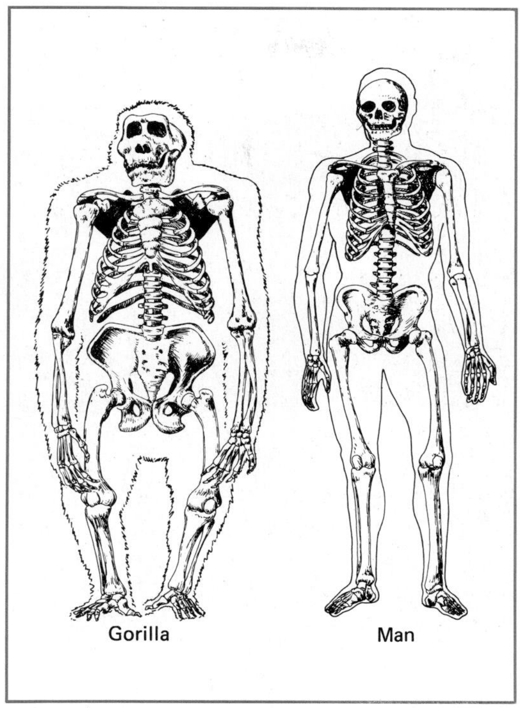

Figure 3.13 *GORILLA (left);* HOMO SAPIENS *(right)*

What distinguishes humans from apes? Setting aside behavioral traits associated with the evolution of culture for the moment, the most conspicuous anatomical differences all relate to the development of bipedalism in hominids. As we shall see in greater detail in the next chapter, the hominids gave up suspensory feeding and brachiation in favor of life spent mostly on the ground in a habitat that was relatively open or savannahlike. From this basic change of habitat and gait there arose a series of anatomical and behavioral adaptations which set the hominids off from the great apes. To understand who we are, we must begin from the ground up. In the beginning there was the foot.

1. The Foot The human bipedal gait was made possible by a rearward extension of the heel bone and a realignment of the big toe. Lifting power from our calf muscles raises the heel bone. Then a forward and upward spring is imparted by leverage against the big toe. Arches extending from front to rear and side to side keep the action springy. The big toe of the human foot, unlike the pongid toe, is lined up with the rest of the toes and has lost practically all its opposability. Whereas the pongid foot can be used to touch and grasp objects, the human foot is specialized for standing, walking, and running (Fig. 3.14).

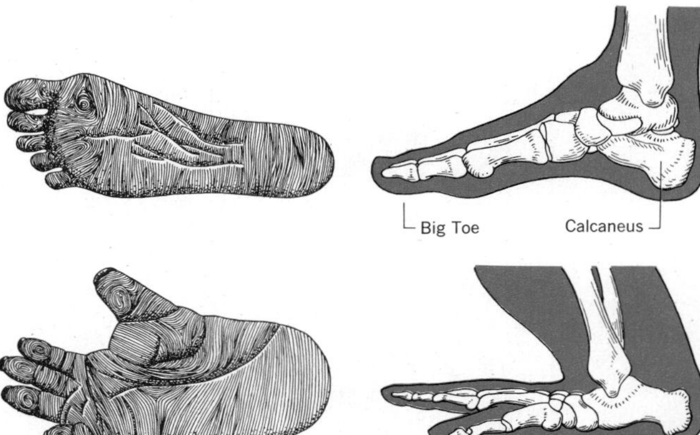

Figure 3.14 *HUMAN FOOT (top); GORILLA FOOT (bottom)*

2. **Arms and Hands** The great advantage of hominid bipedalism is that it frees the hands and arms to do things other than locomoting while moving about. The gorilla, the chimpanzee, and the orangutan depend upon their arms either for brachiation or for semierect walking. Hominids are the only animals that can comfortably travel long distances on the ground while carrying heavy objects in their hands. Moreover, the dexterity of the hominid hand is unsurpassed; in the gibbon and the orangutan the requirements of climbing and of brachiation interfere with the size and dexterity of their thumb. The chimpanzee and the gorilla are quite dexterous, but our thumb is larger, more heavily muscled, and more supple. The length and strength of the human thumb give us a uniquely precise grip, powerful yet delicate. This grip, almost as much a hallmark of humanity as bipedalism and braininess, has helped to make us the supreme artisans of the animal kingdom.

3. **The Lower Limbs** Human legs relative to trunk length are the longest among the Hominoidea (Fig. 3.13). The large calf of our lower leg is distinctive; the great apes lack prominent calf muscles. Even more dramatically human is the massive gluteal musculature, which, when we are not sitting on it, provides much of the force for walking up hill, straightening up after bending, and running and jumping.

4. **The Pelvic Girdle** In four-footed mammals the pelvis has the contour of a narrow tube to which the rear legs are attached at nearly a right angle. About one-half of the weight of an animal that moves on all fours is transmitted through the pelvis to the rear legs. Among the Pongidae the rear legs bear a higher percentage of the total body weight. The chimpanzee pelvis, for example, shows some flattening and strengthening as a result of its increased weight-bearing function. But in hominids the pelvis is basinlike, and the body's center of gravity passes directly through it (Fig. 3.15). The basinlike character of the human pelvis is completed by inward-turning vertebrae and their ligaments at the base of the spine, which close off the bottom portion of the pelvic cavity. A main function of the pelvis is to provide attachments for the powerful muscles that control the legs. The basin or

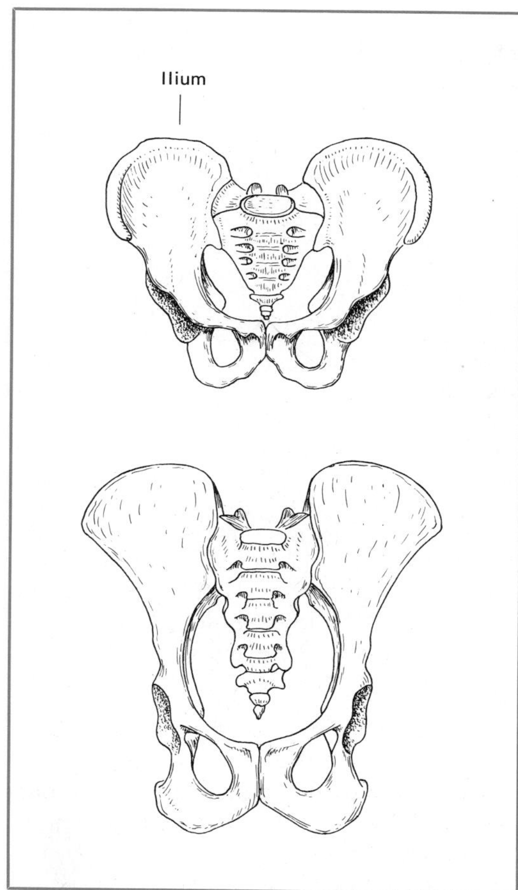

Figure 3.15 *HUMAN PELVIS (top); CHIMPANZEE PELVIS (bottom)*

ring shape of the human pelvis with its two broad-bladed hip bones increases the effective force of all the musculature involved in standing erect. Muscles attached to the hip bones and to other portions of the pelvis provide much of the power for moving the lower limbs.

5. The Vertebral Column To allow for upright posture, the human vertebral column has developed extra vertebrae which form a unique curve in the lumbar region (Fig. 3.16). Here the column bends forward over the center of the pelvis, and on meeting the pelvis reverses itself to form a "sickle" with the handle above. Without this curve, people would have a tendency to topple over backward. Although capable of supporting 700 pounds or more, our vertebral column is subject to malfunction. The intense pressures upon the cartilaginous discs between the vertebrae lead to their rupture and misalignment and to characteristically human "pains in the back." At its upper end (the cervical region), the human spinal column curves forward, then upward and slightly to the rear, meeting our skull at a point close to its center of gravity. The human neck vertebrae lack the long spiny rearward extensions that anchor the gorilla's large neck muscles (Harrison and Montagna 1969; Birdsell 1981:223 ff.).

6. The Neck The head pivots atop the vertebral column on a pair of bony knobs found at the base of our skulls. These knobs are called *occipital condyles* (Fig. 3.17). In pongids the main weight of the head is well forward of the pivot points. The powerful neck muscles needed for stability completely obscure the skeletal contour of the gorilla's cervical region. Modern hominids are different; our occipital condyles are very close to the head's center of gravity. Our head almost balances by itself at the top of the cervical curve, so we need only relatively small neck muscles and have a distinctively long, thin neck.

7. The Cranium The rear portion of the skull to which the neck muscles are attached is called the *nuchal plane* (Fig. 3.18). Among the pongids this area is very large and rises to form an abrupt angle with the rest of the head at the *nuchal crest*. In

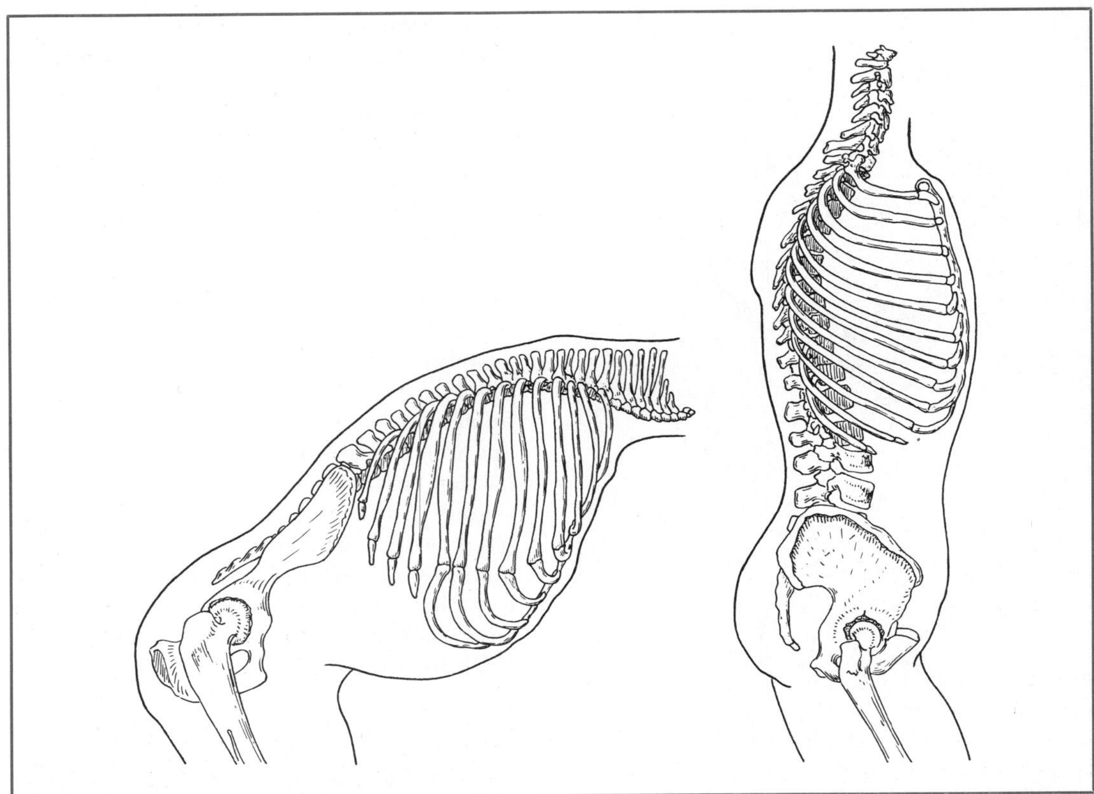

Figure 3.16 *GORILLA VERTEBRAL COLUMN (left); HUMAN VERTEBRAL COLUMN (right)*

H. sapiens the nuchal crest is absent, the area of the nuchal plane is smaller, and its position is underneath rather than at the rear of the skull. This gives a smooth, spherical contour to the rear of the human skull. The roundedness continues into the forehead region and is clearly related to the fact that our brain is the largest and heaviest of primate brains. Viewed from the rear, our skull is distinguished by its steeply rising side walls. Its maximum width is above rather than below the ears. A gorilla's head is more massive than ours, but a much smaller space is available inside. Much of its skull is taken up by the thick bones and prominent crests, which serve as attachments for muscles and as structural reinforcements. Such crests, as we shall see in the next chapter, are also found in certain extinct hominids.

8. The Face and Upper Jaw Among pongids the face extends well beyond the plane of the forehead. The forward thrust is continued by the upper jaw resulting in a shape known as *prognathism* (see Fig. 3.19). In contrast, the modern human

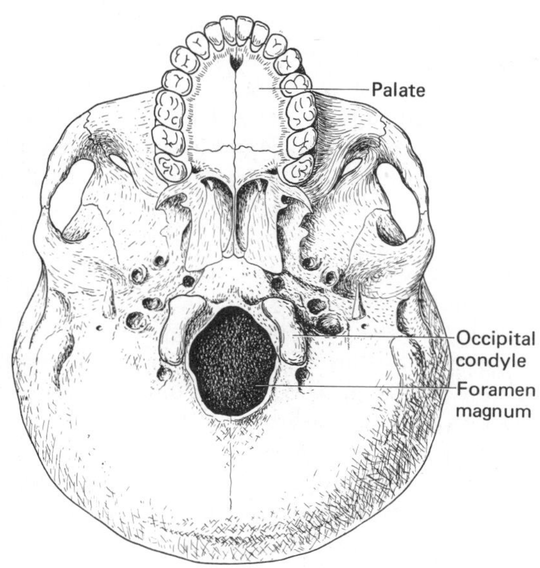

Figure 3.17 *BASE OF HUMAN SKULL*

upper jaw is *orthognathic;* it is aligned vertically with the forehead, directly under the eye sockets. Among gorillas there is a large bar over the eyes known as the *supraorbital torus.* This structure protects the upper face from the enormous pressure generated by the gorilla's massive jaws and powerful chewing muscles. With the exception of certain extinct species, hominids, in contrast, have smaller jaws, less powerful chewing muscles, and a smaller supraorbital torus. The introduction of cooked foods, which do not have to be chewed as vigorously as raw foods, may be responsible for the reduced size of the *H. sapiens* jaw.

9. Jaws and Teeth Our chewing equipment is one of our most important and distinctive features. Fossilized fragments of jaws and even of single teeth are relied on for tracing hominid ancestry and for distinguishing between hominid and pongid taxons. Modern pongids have a *dental arcade* in which long parallel rows of molars and premolars are joined by a U-shaped curve of canines and incisors. In contrast, the hominid arcade is parabolic and greatly compressed to conform to the orthognathism of the hominid face. A pongid's incisors and canines are large in comparision with its molars and massive in comparison with a hominid's incisors and canines; a hominid's incisors and canines are small in comparison with its molars (Fig. 3.19).

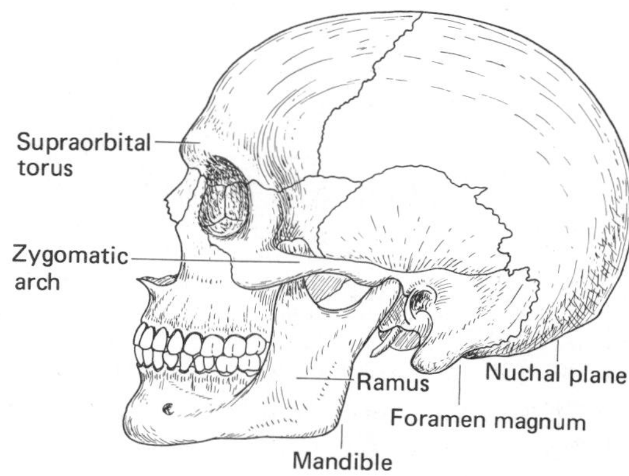

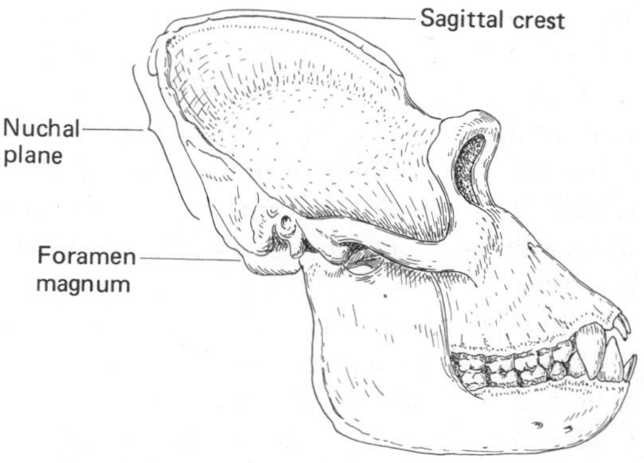

Figure 3.18 *HUMAN SKULL (top); GORILLA SKULL (bottom)*

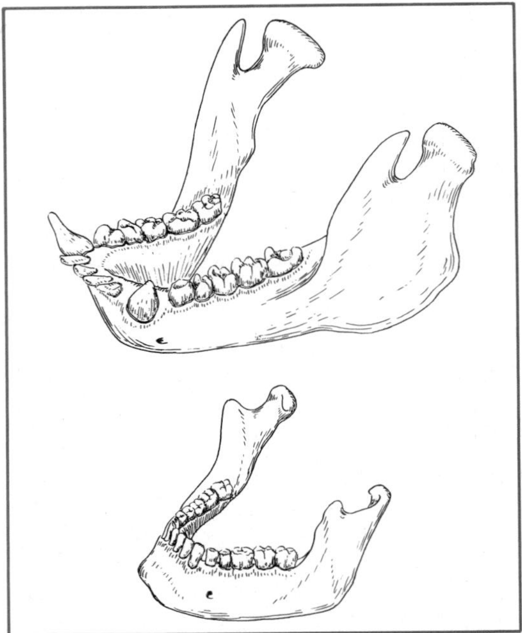

Figure 3.19 *GORILLA JAW (top); HUMAN JAW (bottom)*

These differences imply fundamentally different feeding adaptations. The massive size of the pongid's front teeth probably relate to the use of incisors and canines to cut and rip the outer covering of woody shoots, such as bamboo, and celery and the tough skin of forest fruits. The dental pattern characteristic of hominids—small incisors and canines relative to large molars—suggests a different diet, one based on substances that are easily processed into bite-size portions by the front teeth but that thereafter must be subjected to a considerable amount of grinding and milling before they can be swallowed. From his studies of seed-eating and grass-eating baboons, Clifford Jolly (1970) developed the theory that the distinctive features of hominid dentition were adaptations to small, tough morsels such as grass seeds, stems, and gritty roots. Such a diet requires the processing of large quantities of small and/or gritty items. To subsist the animal must feed very often, and the molars must stay in virtually continuous use, milling and grinding the seeds and stems. The importance of teeth for milling and grinding in the adaptation of our ancestors is suggested by the flexible way in which our lower jaw is hinged, which enables both back-to-front and side-to-side rotary motions as we chew. Recent criticisms of Jolly's theory have de-emphasized the adaptation to seeds and small morsels. The hominid dental pattern could also represent an adaption to bamboo-, nut-, or leaf-eating habits (Wolpoff 1982:503).

Another feature suggestive of grinding and milling is the delayed eruption of the hominid molars, so that as the front molars are worn down they are replaced by fresh molars to the rear. A final aspect of this pattern is that hominid molars are higher than they are either broad or long. This is another feature that would provide a selective advantage in resisting the attrition produced by prolonged milling action (Simons 1968; Simons and Ettel 1970).

Another definitive feature of hominid dentition is that our canines project only slightly or not at all above the level of the adjacent teeth. In contrast, pongid canines, especially the upper canines, are so large that they need spaces in the opposite arcade in order for the jaws to shut tightly. Canines are especially conspicuous among the male pongids. In addition to ripping stalks and opening hard-covered fruits, they are used to threaten predators, females, and junior males. Since we have neither large canines nor other large teeth, our jaws have lost the defensive or offensive capacity which jaws serve in so many other animals (Sheets and Gavan 1977).

The basic pattern of hominid dentition weighs heavily against the popular stereotype that our ancestors were bloodthirsty "killer apes." In fact, just the opposite seems to be true (see p. 68). Deprived of canines, and equipped with fingernails and toenails instead of claws, we humans are anatomically curiously harmless creatures. Naked, without weapons or a knowledge of judo or karate, we would find it virtually impossible to kill any large animal, including our own adult fellow humans. (Fists, so prominent in fictional American fighting, are too fragile to do lethal damage, and bare-

Figure 3.20 *GELADA BABOONS*
Female on right is in estrus, as indicated by brightly colored "necklace."

footed kickers break their toes.) This does not mean that our ancestors were vegetarians; on the contrary, as we shall see, they were undoubtedly both meat and plant eaters, or *omnivores*.

HOMINID SEXUALITY

Among all living Primates, except human beings, the female is sexually receptive during only a few days before and after the mature ovum passes from the ovary to the uterus. This is the period during which fertilization must take place if the ovum is to become implanted in the uterus wall. With the maturation of the ovum, the primate female displays sexual receptivity in accordance with monthly or seasonal rhythms. By means of smell and visual signals she invites the males to copulate (Fig. 3.20). Among some Primates, females in heat have multicolored swellings in the region of the anus and vagina. Sexual receptivity in chimpanzees, for example, is signaled by a bright pink swelling in the anal-genital skin, and during this period as many as 20 male chimpanzees have been observed copulating with a single female (van Lawick-Goodall 1965). (However, some chimps form consort pairs at such times.)

Although the menstrual cycle of the human female is similar in many respects to that of the pongids and other Primates, there are no external signs indicating the period of maximum fertility. Indeed, women usually cannot tell when they are ovulating. Since there are no clear signs of the fertile period, the reproductive success of human females depends on their being sexually receptive during the entire estral cycle. (This characteristic is often misstated. Human females are not "continuously sexually receptive," as some anthropologists would have it.) Human sexual relationships, therefore, need not be sporadic and discontinuous as in animals that have rutting seasons or periods of heat, but can serve as the basis for long-term male-female bonding. At the same time the weakness of biological rhythms governing sexuality means that male-female relationships can be more readily shaped by cultural conventions. These features of human sexuality help to account for the intensely cooperative nature of human male-female bonding. Human males and females not only cooperate in the care and feeding of their offspring but they take care of and feed each other more regularly and over longer stretches of time than any other vertebrate species.

LANGUAGE AND CULTURE

Many animals possess learned traditions that are passed on from one generation to the next and that constitute a rudimentary form of culture. As we shall see in the next chapter, chimpanzees and other Primates make and use tools as a result of such learning. However, it is only among the hominids that culture has become a primary source of adaptive behavior, more important than biological evolution involving changes in gene frequencies. Able to stand and walk erect, their forelimbs freed entirely from locomotor and support functions, the earliest hominids probably manufactured, transported, and made effective use of tools as a primary means of subsistence. Apes, on the other hand, survive nicely with only the barest in-

Figure 3.21 *YELLOW BABOON* (PAPIOCYNOCEPHALUS), *SUBORDER ANTHROPOIDEA, SUPERFAMILY CERCOPITHECOIDEA*
Hominids lack prominent canines characteristic of many monkeys and great apes. [*Mark Boulton/National Audubon Society*]

ventory of such tools. Hominids, ancient or modern, have probably always depended on some form of culture for their very existence.

Closely linked with the capacity for cultural adaptations is the uniquely human capacity for language and for language-assisted systems of thought. While other Primates use complex signal systems to facilitate social life, human languages are qualitatively different from all other animal communication systems. The unique features of human languages—to be discussed in Chapter 20—undoubtedly arise from genetic adaptations related to the increasing dependence of the earliest hominids on social cooperation and on culturally acquired modes of subsistence. Human infants are born with the kind of neural circuitry that makes learning to talk as natural for them as learning to walk. This circuitry in turn represents the kind of mental "wiring" useful for a creature that needs to store and transmit large amounts of information not in the genes but in the brain.

SUMMARY

H. sapiens shares some traits with all animals. The animals with which we share the most traits are the Chordata, Vertebrata, Tetrapoda, Mammalia, Theria, Eutheria, Primates, Anthropoidea, and Hominoidea. The ancestors of each of these taxons were also our ancestors. Our closest evolutionary relatives are the other members of the Primates order, especially the members of the anthropoidean suborder. We share the following traits with other Primates: (1) prehensile hands; (2) legs and extremely mobile arms specialized for different functions; (3) stereoscopic color vision; (4) one or two babies per birth episode; (5) long pregnancies and a long period of infant dependency; (6) intense social life; and (7) large brains relative to body size. Most of these traits reflect an actual or ancestral adaptation to an arboreal way of life in tropical forest habitats.

With Old World monkeys we also share the cercopithecoid dental formula, and with the great apes we share large body size and a high degree of intelligence.

The anthropoidean suborder includes monkeys, apes, and human beings, all of whom are descended from a common primate ancestor. Among apes, the pongids—gorillas, chimpanzees, and orangutans—bear the closest resemblance to hominids. Like the pongids, the hominids probably had an ancestor who brachiated and practiced suspensory feeding but who subsequently developed additional specialized modes of walking on the ground.

Living hominids are distinguished from pongids by (1) feet specialized for walking; (2) extremely dexterous hands; (3) long legs relative to trunk length; (4) basinlike pelvis; (5) lumbar curve; (6) head balanced on top of spine; (7) smooth, spherical, enlarged cranium; (8) small jaws; (9) reduced canines, parabolic dental arcade, and orthognathic face (Fig. 3.21). Behaviorally, hominids have highly developed languages and cultures. Among living representatives at least, hominid females do not have seasonal and monthly periods of sexual receptivity.

Many of the traits that distinguish hominids from pongids are functionally related to the peculiar bipedal gait adopted by the hominids when they abandoned the forest habitat and ventured forth into more open country.

4 THE FIRST HOMINIDS

This chapter focuses on the fossil evidence for the evolution of the earliest hominids. *Fossils* are rocklike relics formed by the substitution of minerals for bone and tissue and which therefore preserve the shape of a long-dead organism. The fossils of our earliest ancestors are usually found only in fragments. Here popular curiosity runs high. Who were the first human beings? Are we descended from fierce, carnivorous "killer apes" or from mild-mannered vegeterians? The pace of discovery of new evidence bearing on these questions quickens from year to year. At the present moment only tentative conclusions can be drawn and the student must be prepared to cope with conflicting interpretations offered by different experts.

AN EVOLUTIONARY CLOCK

Geologists divide the history of the earth into eras which are subdivided into periods and epochs. Life probably began about 3 or 4 billion years ago, but the first microorganisms were not fossilized and disappeared without leaving traces that can be found today. It was not until about 600 million years ago that the first animals appeared that were large enough and hard enough to leave abundant fossil remains. As shown in Figure 4.1, the phylum Chordata, subphylum Vertebrata, and superclass Tetrapoda were present about 400 to 350 million years ago. Mammals appeared between 225 and 180 million years ago during the Mesozoic era. There were primates toward the end of the Mesozoic or the beginning of the Cenozoic era 70 to 60 million years ago. Between 40 and 25 million years ago, during the Oligocene epoch, the Anthropoidea became abundant. In the next epoch, the Miocene, the Hominoidea became widespread. The earliest unmistakable hominids did not appear until the Pliocene, which began about 5 million years ago. There may have been ground-dwelling, bipedal, tool-using hominids throughout the entire Pliocene epoch. The genus *Homo* appeared close to the Pliocene–Pleistocene transition, and our own species, *Homo sapiens,* close to the end of the Pleistocene. If the evolutionary clock from the origin of life to the present is reduced to the scale of 1 year, human beings make their appearance at about 8 P.M. on New Year's Eve.

FROM HOMINOID TO HOMINID

The earliest of the Primates lived during the Paleocene and Eocene. They resembled the Prosimii and were probably the ancestors of today's lemurs and tarsiers.

From the Paleocene to the Oligocene, the Primates underwent several *adaptive radiations*, that is, rapid filling out of new ecological niches with new genera and species. These adaptive radiations were followed by widespread extinctions of the new genera and species, possibly as a result of competition with arboreal rodents and with the ancestors of the modern anthropoids. Another adaptive radiation took place during the Oligocene, when the ancestors of today's apes and monkeys actually appear in the fossil record for the first time.

The two top contenders for the earliest anthropoids are a late Eocene fossil from the

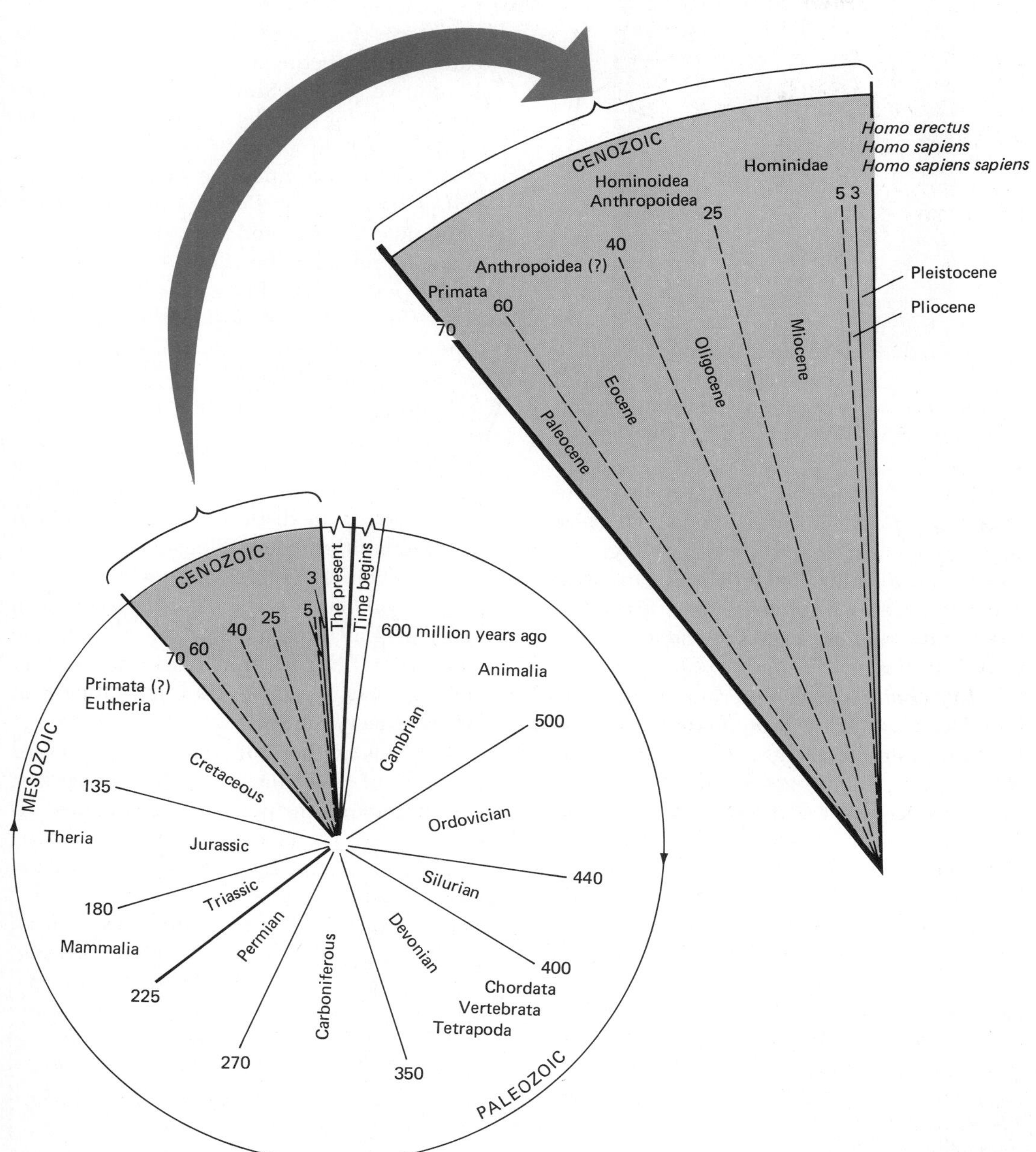

Figure 4.1 *EVOLUTIONARY CLOCK*

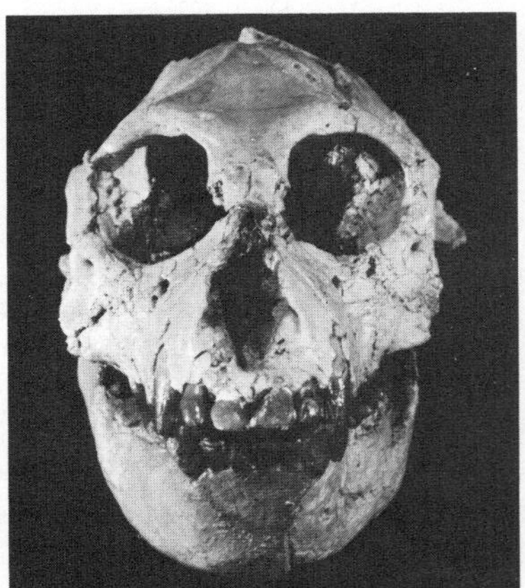

Figure 4.2 AEGYPTOPITHECUS ZEUXIS
An early common ancestor of the hominoids and hominids; from Egypt.

Pondaung Hills in Burma (Maw, Ciochon, and Savage 1979) and an early Oligocene fossil from Fayum, Egypt. The Burma specimen is called *Paundaungia* and the Egyptian specimen is called *Aegyptopithecus* (Fig. 4.2).

Aegyptopithecus has certain dental features which make it a candidate for the earliest ape as well as the earliest anthropoid. The molars of apes and hominids have five cusps arranged in a Y pattern, whereas monkeys have four cusps arranged in parallel rows. *Aegyptopithecus* has a pronounced Y-5 pattern (Fig. 4.3). With its 4-inch-long skull and projecting canines it resembles a diminutive gorilla. Similar to *Aegyptopithecus* except for smaller canines is another apelike fossil, *Propliopithecus* (Fig 4.4). Another Oligocene ape, *Aeolopithecus* (Fig. 4.5), also found at Fayum, displays many gibbonlike features and has been discounted as a contender for the ancestry of either the great apes or the Hominidae by some experts (Simons 1968). Altogether some six genera of Oligocene Primates species have been identified at Fayum.

During the next epoch, the Miocene, various kinds of apes appear in widely separated parts of the Old World (but none in the New World). Two major groups have been distinguished: the Dryopithecinae and the Ramapithecinae (Pilbeam 1978). The Dryopithecinae (Fig. 4.7), whose name means "woodland ape," have been found in areas of East Africa, Europe, the Middle East, the U.S.S.R., India, and China that were heavily forested. They first appear in late Oligocene times.

The Ramapithecinae appear only toward the end of the Miocene, and having first been identified in India, they are named af-

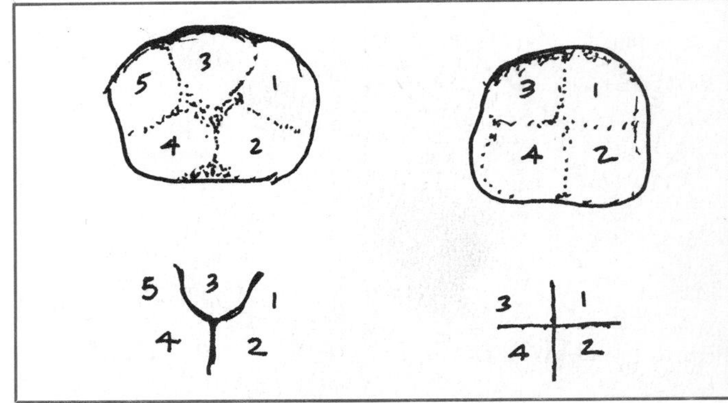

Figure 4.3 *Y PATTERN*
Ape and hominid molars display Y pattern of cusps, as illustrated on left. Monkey molars display + pattern, right.

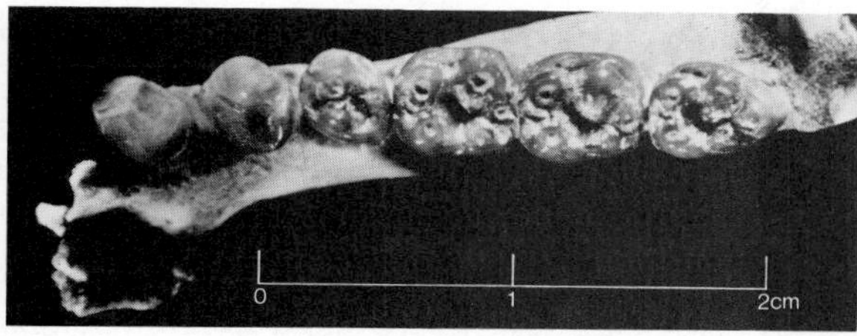

Figure 4.4 PROPLIOPITHECUS HAECKELI

ter the Indian god Rama. There is some evidence that one or more of the Dryopithecinae were the ancestors of the Ramapithecinae (Pickford 1982). The earliest of the group is *Ramapithecus* of Kenya, which lived about 14 million years ago (Fig. 4.7). But like the Dryopithecinae, the Ramapithecinae were a diverse group that survived over a time span of several million years. They ranged in size from the small (less than 3 feet tall)*Ramapithecus* to *Gigantopithecus*, an Asian variety whose jaws and teeth and body were almost twice as massive as a modern gorilla's (Fig. 4.8). What the Ramapithecinae have in common is that they were all probably partially adapted to living outside of the forests and to eating tough and less nutritious plant food that requried much milling and grinding before it could be swallowed. This can be deduced from the heavy coating of enamel on their teeth, the worn-down condition of the molars, and the greater size of the molars as compared with the front teeth. Since these traits are also distinctive of the hominids (see below), it seems likely that one of the Ramapithecinae was the ancestor of the Hominidae. At one time the top candidate for this "honor" was little *Ramapithecus* itself along with several nearly identical specimens found in Pakistan and India, all of which were known only from teeth and jaws. Sad to say, when the faces that go with these jaws and teeth began to be discovered, *Ramapithecus* lost its hominid pretensions. It is now regarded as the ancestor of the orangutan (Pilbeam 1982; Wolpoff 1982).

These recent finds have vindicated the immunological method for assessing the degree of relatedness of living species. These finds place the separation of orangutan ancestors from gorilla, chimpanzee, and hu-

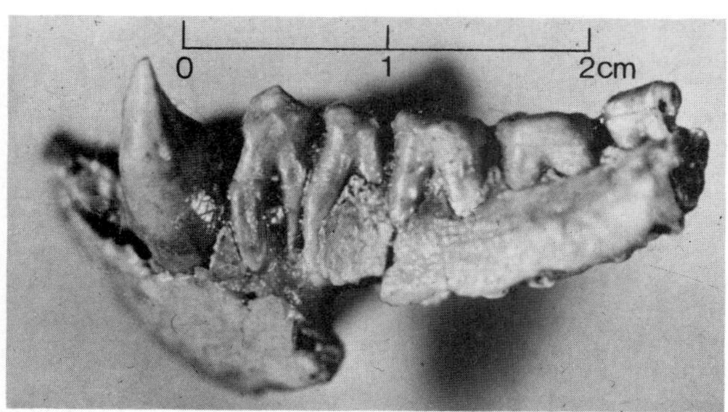

Figure 4.5 AEOLOPITHECUS CHIROBATES

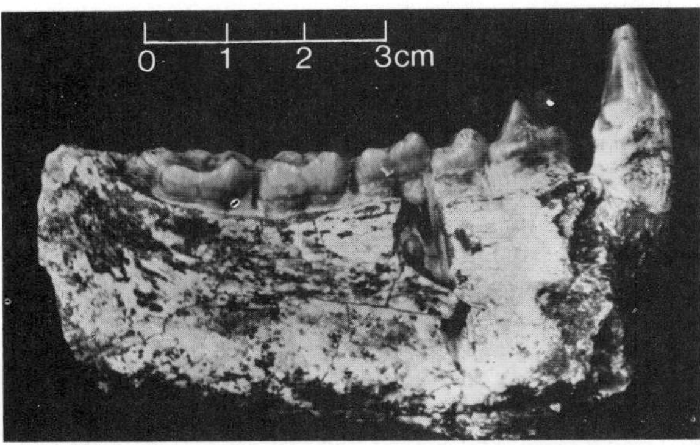

Figure 4.6 DRYOPITHECUS FONTANI

man ancestors in the mid-Miocene, as predicted by Vincent Sarich (1974) and his collaborators. As we saw in the last chapter (p. 30) according to the immunological clock, gorillas, chimpanzees, and *H. sapiens* had a common ancestor no more than 6 or 5 million years ago. With *Ramapithecus* no longer eligible for the title "earliest hominid," the way has now been cleared to reconcile the immunological clock with the fossil record. The common ancestor of humans and the two great apes of Africa is now generally presumed to have lived toward the end and not the middle of the Miocene. As discussed below, the earliest definite hominids appear as far back as 5 to 4 million years ago; therefore, the time span for the development of these hominids may have to be compressed into a million years or less. From the perspective of punctuated equilibrium theory (see p. 13), this does not present any great difficulty. None of this speculation, however, is an adequate substitute for finding the actual fossil evidence for the common ancestor in question. The search goes on.

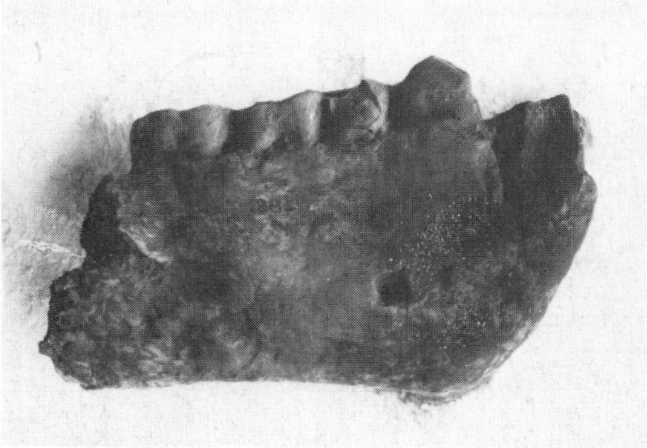

Figure 4.7 RAMAPITHECUS *MANDIBLE*
Compare the size of the canines with the size of the canines in Figs. 4.2 and 4.6.

The Plio-Pleistocene Hominids

The front-running candidates for the earliest definite hominids are a small group of fossils found at Laetoli in Tanzania and dated to about 3.6 million years B.P. (years before the present) (M. Leakey et al. 1976) and a larger group found at Hadar, Ethiopia, and dated to between 3.2 and 2.9 million years B.P. or between 3.6 and 3.0 million years B.P., depending on which expert you believe (Boaz 1983 or Walter and Aronson 1982).

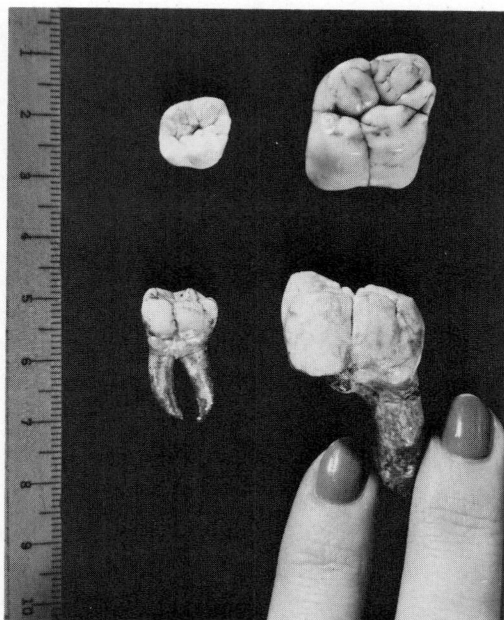

Figure 4.8 GIGANTOPITHECUS
Molar teeth on right compared to modern human teeth on left.

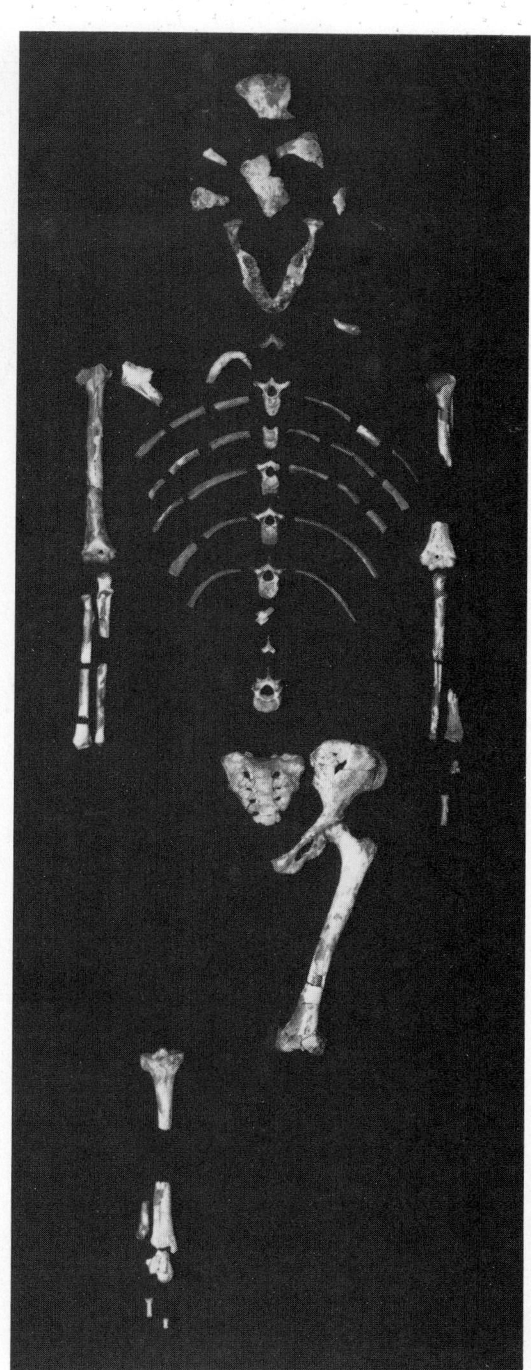

In the opinion of Donald Johanson and Tim White (1979), all these fossils represent a single hominid species for which they have proposed the name *Australopithecus afarensis* (after the Afar region in Ethiopia in which the Hadar sites are located). One of their most famous finds is "Lucy," a small female *A. afarensis*. Approximately 40 percent of her skeleton is preserved, including pelvic, arm, and leg bones (Fig. 4.9). As seen by Johanson and White, *A. afarensis*

Figure 4.9 *"LUCY"*
Found by Don Johanson and Tim White at Hadar; proposed as the ancestor of the genus Homo.

HOW FOSSILS ARE DATED

Carbon Fourteen (^{14} C)

A certain percentage of the carbon in every organism's body consists of the isotope ^{14}C. This isotope decays at a constant rate into an isotope of nitrogen. But the ratio of ^{14}C to ^{12}C is kept constant as long as the organism takes in fresh supplies of ^{14}C through eating and breathing. When it dies, however, the ratio of ^{14}C to ^{12}C begins to fall at a constant rate, namely, by one-half every 5730 years. Knowing the ratio of ^{14}C to ^{12}C, one can calculate the year that the organism died. This method is unreliable beyond 70,000 years and thus is used mainly in archaeology, not in paleontology.

Potassium–Argon (^{10}K–^{40}Ar)

During volcanic eruptions a bed of ash containing the isotope of potassium , ^{40}K, is laid down. This isotope decays into the isotope of argon, ^{40}Ar, at the rate of one-half every 1.31 billion years. Fossils found below or above dated beds of volcanic ash can thus be assigned upper or lower dates. This method is reliable up to several million years, but fossils are not always conveniently sandwiched between layers of volcanic ash (Fleming 1977).

Fission Track Dating

The most abundant isotope of uranium, ^{238}U, makes microscopic tracks as it spontaneously fissions in glassy substances associated with volcanic activity. The older the specimen, the larger the number of tracks. Since the rate of fissioning is constant, all one need know is the amount of ^{238}U that was originally present in the specimen. This is determined by laboratory techniques involving neutron bombardment. Depending on the richness of the specimen in ^{238}U, this method can supply accurate dates ranging from a few hundred years to 3 billion years (Macdougall 1976).

Geomagnetic Dating

During the history of the earth, the magnetic poles have altered their position from time to time. The dates of these "magnetic events" have been calculated by various isotope decay methods. The minerals in sedementary strata respond to magnetic fields and point toward the position of the magnetic poles when they were deposited and solidified. They thus contain a record of the dated magnetic events which took place during their formation.

Several other dating methods are also available and new ones are being added virtually every year.

Figure 4.10 *EARLIEST HOMINID FOOTPRINT*
Discovered at Laetoli, Tanzania, by Mary Leakey, a series of these footprints demonstrate the existence of bipedal hominids over 3 million years ago.

was the ancestor of two different lines of hominids (Johanson and Edey 1981). One of these lines led to the first member of the genus *Homo*, namely, *Homo habilis* (see below). The other line led to the extinct creatures known as *A. africanus* and *A. robustus*. In the line that led to *H. habilis* (and ultimately to *H. sapiens*), brain capacity increased, teeth and jaws remained small and adapted to an omnivorous diet, and physique remained slender. On the other hand, in the line that led to *A. africanus* and *A. robustus*, brain capacity remained stationary, teeth and jaws got larger and progressively more adapted for chewing coarse vegetable matter, the cranium developed gorillalike crests and buttresses, and physique grew massive. The separation of the extinct side line, *Australopithecus*, occurred between 3.0 and 2.5 million years ago and the transition from the *A. africanus* to *A. robustus* about 2 million years ago. The extinction of this line was complete about 1 million years ago.

Johanson and White's evolutionary scenario, however, is not beyond dispute. The principal alternative interpretation of the fossil evidence for the period between 4 and 1 million years ago is that which is advocated by Richard Leakey. According to Leakey, the remains classified by Johanson and White as *A. afarensis* do not all belong to the same taxon. The Hadar remains are in fact quite variable: some individuals (such as Lucy, appear to have been a little more than 3½ feet tall and to have weighed about 60 pounds, while others were 5 feet tall and weighed up to 150 pounds. Some, like Lucy, had a more simian V-shaped jaw than others. Johanson and White attribute this variability to *sexual dimorphism* (differences between the sexes), with larger specimens representing males and smaller representing females. Such a degree of *dimorphism* is characteristic of contemporary apes, and hence it is not unreasonable to suppose that the closer we get to a common ancestor with the apes, the greater the differences between male and female hominids.

This explanation is rejected by Richard Leakey. According to Leakey, the Hadar remains testify to the existence of two and pos-

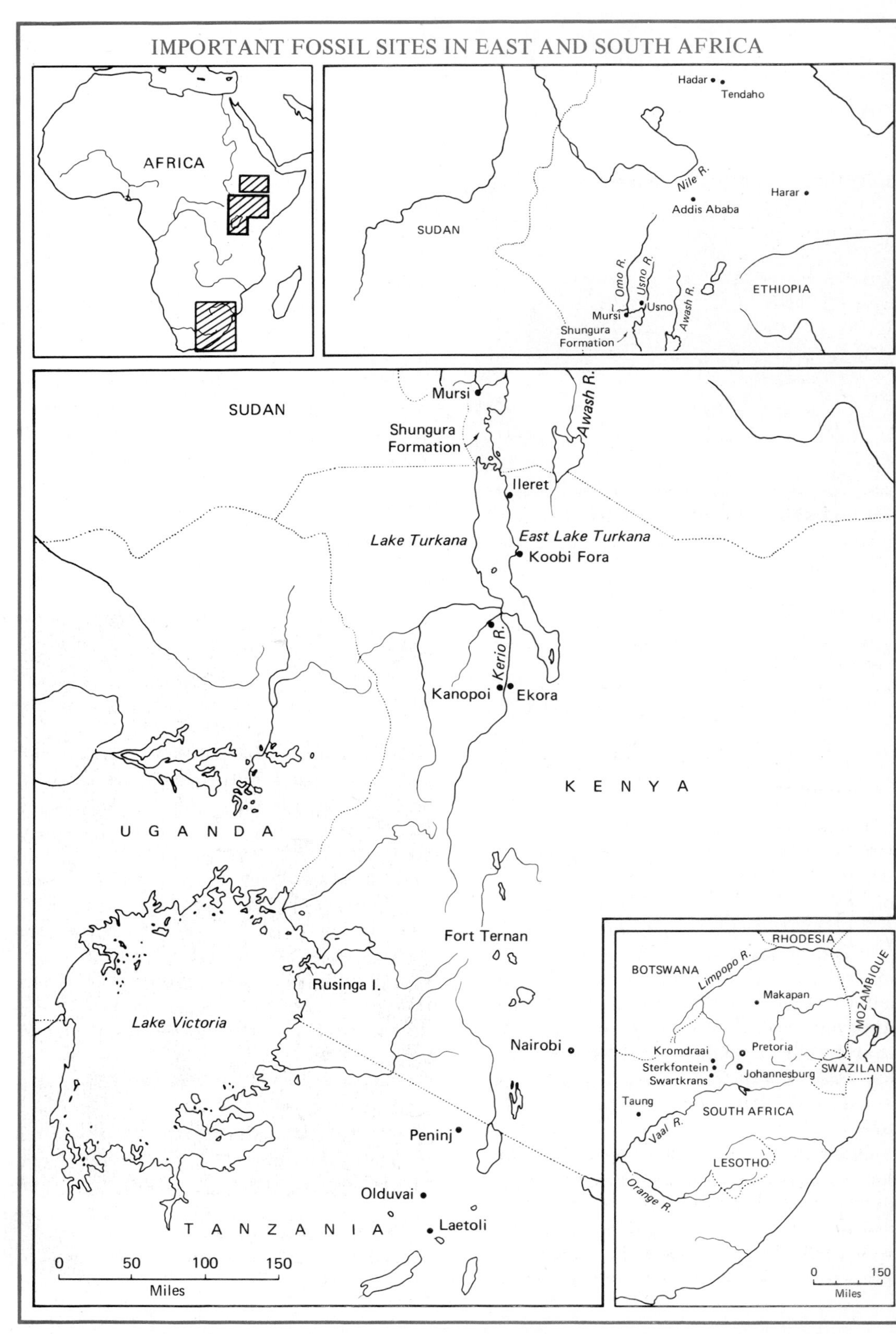

IMPORTANT FOSSIL SITES IN EAST AND SOUTH AFRICA
AFRICA
Hadar
Tendaho
Nile R.
Harar
Addis Ababa
SUDAN
Omo R.
Usno R.
Awash R.
ETHIOPIA
Mursi
Usno
Shungura Formation
SUDAN
Mursi
Shungura Formation
Awash R.
Ileret
East Lake Turkana
Lake Turkana
Koobi Fora
Kerio R.
Kanopoi
Ekora
K E N Y A
U G A N D A
Fort Ternan
Rusinga I.
Lake Victoria
Nairobi
Peninj
Olduvai
Laetoli
T A N Z A N I A
0 50 100 150
Miles
RHODESIA
BOTSWANA
Limpopo R.
MOZAMBIQUE
Makapan
Kromdraai
Pretoria
Sterkfontein
Swartkrans
Johannesburg
SWAZILAND
Taung
SOUTH AFRICA
Vaal R.
LESOTHO
Orange R.
0 150
Miles

sibly three different hominid species: the *Homo* line, represented by the species (1) *H. habilis* ("handyman"), and the *Australopithecus* line possibly already divided into two species, (2) *A. robustus* and (3) *A. africanus.* Leakey sees all three lines existing side by side for several million years (Walker and R. Leakey 1978; R. Leakey and Walker 1980).

Bipedalism and *Australopithecus*

Johanson and White claim that *A. afarensis* was an efficient, fully bipedal terrestrial hominid. They base their claim on an analysis of the pelvis, leg bones, and foot bones found at Hadar and on a remarkable 75-foot-long trail of footprints found at Laetoli, Tanzania (M. Leakey 1979; Charteris, Wall, and Nottrodt 1982). These footprints (Fig. 4.10), preserved in volcanic ash, date to 3.5 million years ago. They were laid down by two or three hominids who ranged from 4 to 5 feet in height, as determined by the ratio of foot length to stride length.

> "Make no mistake about it . . . they are like modern human footprints. . . . There is a well-shaped modern heel with a strong arch and a good ball of the foot it front of it. The big toe is straight in line. It doesn't stick out on the side like an ape toe. . ." (T. White quoted in Johanson and Edey 1981:250).

Richard and Mary Leakey dispute this interpretation. They are not ready to concede that the Laetoli jaw and footprints belong to *Australopithecus,* preferring instead to interpret them as evidence for the existence of *Homo.*

Other authorities also dispute the claim that the Hadar foot and leg bones were completely adapted to bipedalism and reject the idea that the Laetoli footprints could have been made by a creature like Lucy. The principal evidence against the Johanson-White interpretation is that the toe bones found at Hadar are curved in a manner that is similar to a great ape's toe bones (Fig. 4.11). From this is can be inferred that *A. afarensis* and possibly other australopithecines of more recent times were still more adept at tree climbing than *Homo,* although this does not necessarily preclude them from having had an efficient bipedal gait. It is interesting to note that the larger of the Hadar australopithecines seem to have had a more fully bipedal adaptation than the smaller ones. If size differences reflect sex differences (and not species differences), then it seems plausible that the male Hadar australopithecines, like male great apes, spent more time than females on the

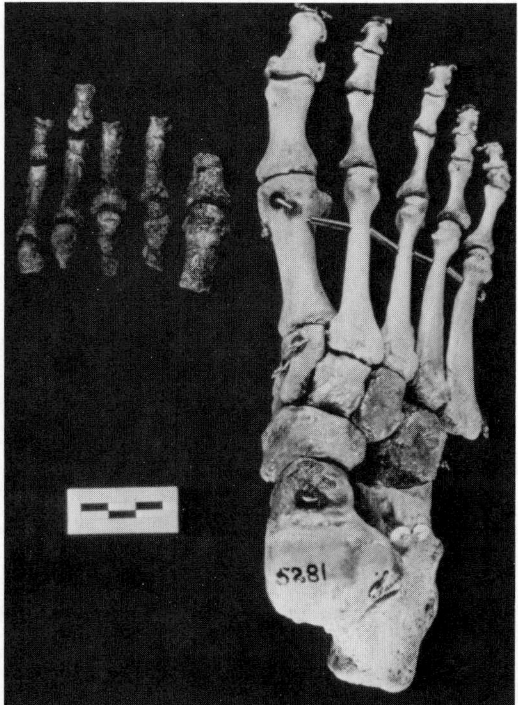

Figure 4.11 A. AFARENSIS *TOE BONES* Curvature suggests that *A. afarensis* was still adept at tree climbing. Compare with human toe bones *(right).*

ground, while females stayed in the trees more often for protection from predators (Lewin 1983; Stern and Susman 1983). Tree climbing may also have figured in the adaptations of *A. africanus* and *A. robustus,* but if so, it was to a lesser extent than among the Hadar group (Stern and Susman 1983:313). Therefore, in the matter of locomotion, *A. afarensis* may be a "missing link":

"In our opinion *A. afarensis* is very close to what can be called a "missing link." It possesses a combination of traits that had travelled well down the road toward full-time bipedality, but which retained structural features that enabled it to use the trees efficiently for feeding, resting, sleeping or escape (ibid.:314).

Johanson has recently agreed that examination of the Hadar group's vertebrae tends to confirm this picture of a semiarboreal adaptation in which "climbing and acrobatic activities may have been proportionately more important than they are in modern humans" (Cook et al. 1983:100).

The Later Australopithecines

Raymond Dart discovered the first *Australopithecus* specimen at Taung, South Africa, in 1924 (Fig. 4.12). It was he who gave it the generic name *Australopithecus,* meaning "southern ape." Since then hundreds of teeth and over a thousand fragments of skulls, jaws, leg bones, foot bones, pelvises, and other body parts attributed to the australopithecines have been found. Despite their name, the australopithecines were not apes. They were primitive bipedal hominids, neither ape nor human. All australopithecines possessed characteristically hominid jaws and teeth. Their dental arcade was rounded; their small canines projected

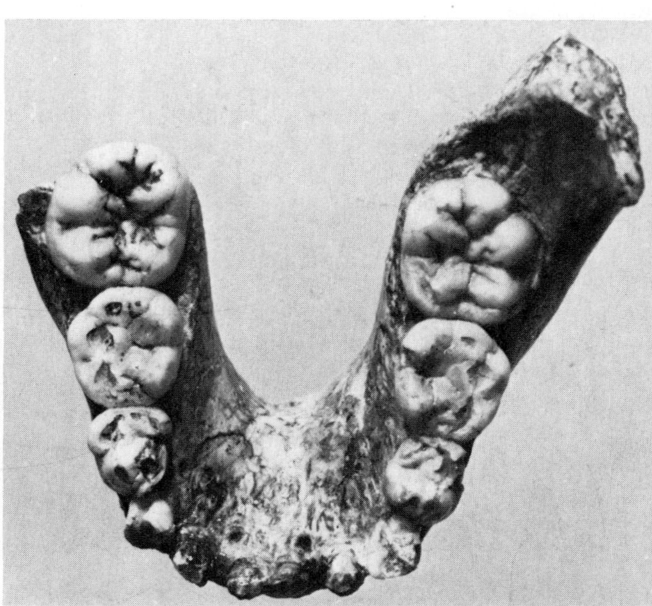

Figure 4.12 *THE TAUNG CHILD'S MANDIBLE*
The first *Australopithecus* to be discovered.

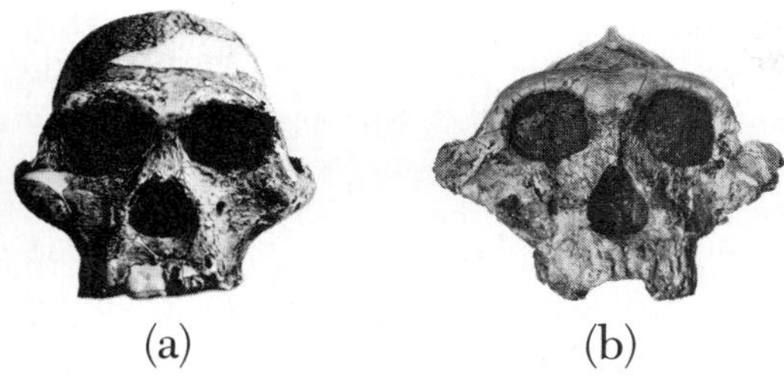

Figure 4.13 *AUSTRALOPITHECINES*
Graciles *(a)* had smaller jaws and teeth and smaller crests than the robusts *(b)*.

slightly or not at all; and their incisors were relatively small as compared with their premolars and molars. On the other hand, all australopithecines had braincases whose volume falls below the human range.

It has long been agreed that some of the australopithecines were more "robust"—larger, heavier—whereas others were more "gracile"—smaller, lighter. The robusts had massive jaws and huge molar teeth, heavy brow ridges, and remarkable bony crests and flanges along the top and side of their skulls to which massive chewing muscles were attached; the graciles had smaller jaws and teeth and smaller crests or none at all (Fig 4.13). Average cranial volume of the graciles was 442 cubic centimeters, whereas the average of the robusts was 517 cubic centimeters (Holloway 1973). (The modern gorilla's cranial volume ranges from 420 to 752 cubic centimeters, and the modern human's ranges from about 1000 to 2000 cubic centimeters.) Some of the graciles may have weighed as little as 45 pounds, while some of the robust specimens may have weighed

Figure 4.14 *LAETOLI*
Tanzanian site at which some of the oldest hominid remains have been found.

over 150 pounds (Robinson 1973). According to Henry McHenry (1974), the average height of the South African graciles was 4 feet 9 inches, of the South African robusts 5 feet and of the East African robusts 5 feet 4 inches.

It seems likely that these differences represent the overlapping presence of two species, which have been named *A. africanus* (the graciles) and *A. robustus*. (Some authorities distinguish further between robust types and use the designation *A. boisei* for the East African robusts, reserving *robustus* for the southern forms.)

There are indications that the robusts and the graciles may have lived in close proximity between 3 and 2 million years ago in at least one site, namely, East Lake Turkana, Kenya (formerly Lake Rudolph), and that they were present together in other regions as well (Howell and Coppens 1976). However, with the discovery of the fossils from Laetoli and Hadar (Figs. 4.14 and 4.15), there is growing recognition that the gracile form was ancestral to the robust form. Lucy closely resembles *A. africanus*. As we have seen, according to one view, *A. africanus* was in turn ancestral to *A. robustus* and these two species did not overlap each other for any considerable period. The apparent overlap between them in the period 3 to 2 million years ago at Lake Turkana is explained away as an indication of the kind of variability that one would expect in a rapidly evolving lineage.

HOMO HABILIS

Several decades after Dart's original discovery at Taung, most experts had formed the opinion that the australopithecines, especially the gracile variety, were the ancestors of *H. sapiens*. With its bipedal gait, virtually human dentition, and ape-sized brains, *A.*

Figure 4.15 *HADAR*
Ethiopian site at which the remains of the putative ancestor of the australopithecines and of the earliest human beings have been found.

Figure 4.16 *OLDUVAI GORGE*
One of the principal sites in Tanzania. (Mary Leakey in the foreground).

africanus admirably met the requirements for a missing link between apes and human beings. But the veteran fossil hunter Louis Leakey took strong exception to this view, arguing that not enough time had elapsed between the latest australopithecines and the then earliest known *Homo* species (i.e., *H. erectus*—see the next chapter) for one to be the ancestor of the other. In 1961 Leakey discovered several cranial fragments in Bed I at the bottom of Olduvai Gorge (Fig. 4.16) in northern Tanzania, which he claimed had a cranial volume greater than any australopithecine and which represented a more advanced hominid. He eventually gave this individual (specimen OH 7—Olduvai hominid 7) the name *H. habilis* ("handyman") (Fig. 4.17). Olduvai Bed I has been dated by the potassium-argon decay method (see box on p. 48) to 1.75 million years. This claim for a third line was strengthened when Richard Leakey (Mary and Louis's son) discovered the remains of a remarkably advanced skull at East Turkana in Kenya, known for the time being by its catalog number—KNM 1470 (Kenya National Museum 1470) (Fig. 4.18). With a cranial volume of 755 cubic centimeters, KNM 1470 was at first dated to 2.5 million years, which made its descent from an australopithecine highly unlikely. Revision of this date to 1.8 million years (the same as Louis Leakey's *H. habilis*), and the Hadar and Laetoli finds, has subsequently weakened the Leakeys' case for an early *Homo*. A simpler scenario is to regard *H. habilis* as a descendant of the australopithecines present at Hadar (and Laetoli) 1 million years earlier. But no firm conclusion as to which view is correct can be drawn. Richard Leakey still expects to find evidence for a separate hominid line leading to *H. habilis* as far back as 5 million years ago. Given the amazing success of the Leakey family as fossil hunters, Richard Leakey's views may yet win out.

The extinction of the australopithecine line about 1 million years ago was undoubtedly related in some fashion to competition with the genus *Homo*. *A. robustus* was probably not much more intelligent than modern chimpanzees or gorillas. Its habitat in the savannahs and plains overlapped with that of the early members of the genus *Homo*, whose intelligence and cultural mode of adaptation compensated for their less massive physique. As the population and

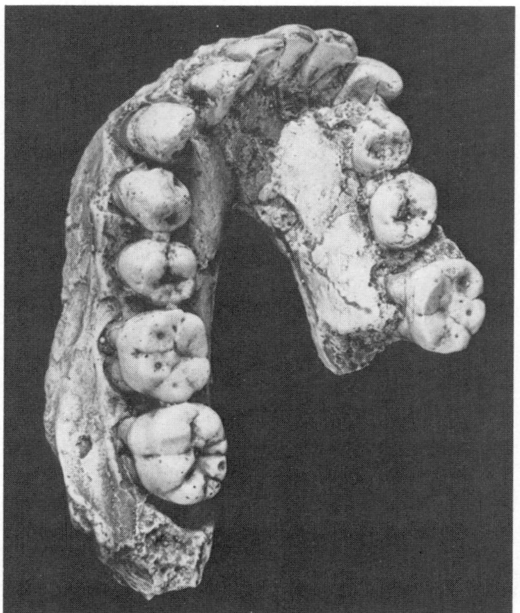

Figure 4.17 *OH 7*
The original *Homo habilis* (handyman) of Olduvai Gorge.

Figure 4.18 *KNM 1470*
This skull may be 2.5 million years old, and its volume is greater than that of the australopithecines that were living at the same time. Front view (top); side view (bottom).

range of activities of the descendants of *H. habilis* increased, the small-brained line of hominids came to an end.

TOOLS AND THE PLIO-PLEISTOCENE HOMINIDS

The evidence for two or three separate lines of hominids living in the same general region for upward of 2 million years has upset traditional views of the forces responsible for the evolution of human beings. For a while, after the discovery of the first australopithecines, these forces seemed self-evident. The earliest hominids were thought to be small-brained bipedal animals who had left the safety of the forest to forage (i.e. search for food) in the grasslands and savannahs. These relatively small animals with their conspicuously small canines had adapted to their habitat by means of manufactured tools and weapons. Dart, the first to discover the australopithecines, thought that they manufactured many different kinds of bone, horn, and tooth implements. With the discovery of very ancient and very simple stone tools—over 1 million years old—at Olduvai and at other sites in North, East, and South Africa, the probability that the australopithecines were toolmakers increased. Yet the fossil remains of the australopithecines and the stone artifacts were never closely united at a given site. Dart's bone-horn-tooth tools were soon dismissed by many authorities as the remains left after meat eating by carnivores rather than toolmaking by hominids (Brain 1978; 1981).

At last, in 1959, Louis Leakey discovered a robust australopithecine skull in Bed II at Olduvai, which was surrounded by a variety of choppers (Figs. 4.19 and 4.20), scrapers, hammerstones, and other stone tools. This might have proved once and for all that the australopithecines were the makers of the most ancient tools were it not for the fact that Leakey also simultaneously discovered the remains of the first *H. habilis* 6 inches below (and therefore older than) the *robustus* specimen. From this he deduced that *H. habilis* had made the tools and had used them to catch and eat the australopithecines. However, stone tools dating to more

Figure 4.19 *OLDUVAI CHOPPER*
One of the basic tools presumably manufactured by *Homo habilis*.

Figure 4.20 *OMO TOOLS*
These tools, found at Omo in Ethiopia, may have been manufactured as long ago as 3 million years.

than 2 million years B.P. (before the present), much older than those found at Olduvai, were soon found at East Turkana and Omo in Ethiopia (Fig. 4.20). At Hadar, stone tools dating to 2.5 million years have been found. If these dates hold up, there must be serious consideration of the likelihood that stone tools were made by australopithecines or by hominids closely resembling australopithecines.

It is Richard Leakey's opinion that toolmaking and tool using were relatively unimportant for the australopithecines but important for *H. habilis*. In addition, Richard Leakey has suggested that *H. Habilis* practiced a "mixed economy," whereby females gathered plant foods and males scavenged and hunted for meat and both sexes pooled their daily spoils at a home base. In such an economy, digging sticks and containers would have been even more important than stone tools. (Unfortunately, only the stone tools have survived the ravages of time.) This theory gives *H. habilis* a whole way of life which is quite different from that of the australopithecines. However, it deepens the mystery surrounding the development of hominid bepedalism. If the bipedal gait was not selected because of its adaptive advantages with respect to tool use and hand-carrying capabilities, why did it evolve?

TOOL USE AMONG CONTEMPORARY MONKEYS AND APES

Paleontological and archaeological data do not prove definitely that all the earliest hominids used tools. But studies of modern-day animals favor the conclusion that the australopithecines as well as *H. habilis* made and used tools.

A *tool* is an object, not part of the user's body, which the user holds or carries during or just prior to use and which is used to alter the form or location of a second object with which it was previously unconnected (cf. Beck 1975). By this definition, when a sea gull opens a clam shell by dropping it on a rock, the rock is not a tool. But when a vulture drops a rock on an egg, the rock, having been carried, is a tool. Similarly, a chimpanzee banging a fruit against a rock is not using a tool; but one that bangs a rock against the fruit is using a tool. Many animals will haul up or pull in objects attached to vines or strings. For this to constitute tool use, the animal itself must create the connection between the vine or string and the object (by tying, wrapping, or hooking it).

Experimental approaches to behavior show that most mammals and birds are "intelligent" enough to learn to make and use simple tools under laboratory conditions. Under natural free-ranging conditions the capacity to make and use tools is expressed less frequently, because most animals can get along quite effectively without having to resort to artificial aids. Natural selection has adapted them to their particular habitat by providing body parts such as snouts, claws, teeth, hooves, and fangs. But natural selection has occasionally favored tool use as a normal mode of existence even among insects. The wasp *Ammophilia urnaria*, for example, hammers the walls of its burrow with a pebble held in its mandibles. Several species of birds apparently have a predisposition to use tools as a supplement to their beaks. Galapagos finches, for example, break off small twigs and use them to push insects out of inaccessible holes and crannies. Jane van Lawick-Goodall (1968) has observed Egyptian vultures breaking ostrich eggs by hurling stones at them with their beaks. The Satis bowerbird paints the inside of its nest with the aid of a bark wad held between the tips of its beak. Occasional tool use is also reported among mammals: elephants scratching their backs with branches held in their trunks, and sea otters swimming on their backs and breaking shellfish against stones placed on their chest. It is highly probable that all tool-using performances among birds and mammals are dependent upon learning and socialization. Finches reared in isolation, for example, do not acquire the technique of using twigs (Pronko 1969; Fellers and Fellers 1976).

Although Primates are intelligent enough to make and use tools, their anatomy and normal mode of existence disincline them to develop extensive tool-using repertories. Among monkeys and apes the use of the hand for tool use is inhibited by the importance of the forelimbs in walking and climbing. That is probably why the most common tool-using behavior among many different species of monkeys and apes is the repelling of intruders with a barrage of nuts, pine cones, branches, fruits, feces, or stones. Throwing such objects requires only a momentary loss of the ability to run or climb away if danger threatens.

Among free-ranging Primates the most accomplished tool user is the chimpanzee. Over a period of many years, Jane van Lawick-Goodall and her associates have studied the behavior of a single population of free-ranging chimpanzees in the Gombe National Park in Tanzania (Fig. 4.21). One of their

Figure 4.21 *JANE VAN LAWICK-GOODALL*
Making friends with a young chimpanzee in Gombe National Park, Tanzania.

Figure 4.22 *CHIMPANZEE TERMITING*
A stick carefully stripped of leaves is inserted into the nest. The chimpanzee licks off the termites that cling to the stick when it is withdrawn.

most remarkable discoveries is that the chimpanzees "fish" for ants and termites. (Fig. 4.22). "Termiting" involves first breaking off a twig or a vine, stripping it of leaves and side branches, and then locating a suitable termite nest. Such a nest is as hard as concrete and impenetrable except for certain thinly covered tunnel entrances. The chimpanzee scratches away the thin covering and inserts the twig. The termites inside bite the end of the twig, and the chimpanzee pulls it out and licks off the termites clinging to it. Especially impressive is the fact that the chimpanzees will prepare the twig first and then carry it in their mouths from nest to nest while looking for a suitable tunnel entrance (van Lawick-Goodall 1968). Anting provides an interesting variation on this theme. The Gombe chimps "fish" for a species of aggressive nomadic driver ant which can inflict a painful bite. Upon finding the temporary subterranean nest of these ants, the chimps make a tool out of a green twig and insert it into the nest entrance. Hundreds of fierce ants swarm up the twig to repel the invader:

> The chimpanzee watches their progress and when the ants have almost reached its hand, the tool is quickly withdrawn. In a split second the opposite hand rapidly sweeps the length of the tool . . . catching the ants in a jumbled mass between thumb and forefinger. These are then popped into the open, waiting mouth in one bite and chewed furiously (McGrew 1977:278).

Chimpanzees also manufacture "sponges" for sopping up water from an inaccessible hollow in a tree. They strip a handful of leaves from a twig, put the leaves in their mouth, chew briefly, put the mass of leaves in the water, let them soak, put the leaves to their mouths, and suck the water off. A similar sponge is employed to dry their fur, to wipe off sticky substances, and to clean the bottoms of chimpanzee babies. Gombe chimpanzees also use sticks as levers and digging tools to pry ant nests off trees and to widen the entrance of subterranean beehives.

Elsewhere other observers have watched chimpanzees in their native habitats pound or hammer tough-skinned fruits, seeds, and nuts with sticks and stones. One chimp in the Budongo Forest, Uganda, used a leaf on a twig to fan away flies (Sugiyama 1969).

Chimpanzees appear to go further than other Primates in using weapons and projectiles. They hurl stones, feces, and sticks with considerable accuracy. One Gombe chimp threw a large stone at an adult bush pig, hitting it and driving it off long enough for another chimp to rush in and capture the piglet that it was guarding (Teleki 1981:336).

Under semicontrolled conditions, chimpanzees have been observed to wield long clubs with deadly aim. One investigator (Kortlant 1967) built a stuffed leopard whose head and tail could be moved mechanically. He set the leopard down in open country inhabited by chimpanzees, and when the chimpanzees came into view he animated the leopard's parts. The chimpanzees attacked the leopard with heavy sticks, tore it apart, and dragged the remnants off into the bush.

It has long been known that chimpanzees in zoos and laboratories readily develop complex patterns of behavior involving tool use. Provided with a box on which to stand, sticks that fit together, and bananas out of reach, they quickly learn to push the box under the bananas, put the sticks together, stand on the box, and knock down the bananas. Captive chimpanzees will also spontaneously employ sticks to pry open boxes and doors and to break the mesh on their cages. Belle, a female chimpanzee at the Delta Regional Primate Station, cleaned her companion's teeth with a pencillike object manufactured from a twig (McGrew and Tutin 1973).

The kinds of tool-using behavior that captive primates exhibit outside their native habitat are perhaps even more significant than what they normally do in their natural setting. In order for tool use to become an integral part of an animal's behavioral repertory, it must contribute to the solution of everyday problems that the animal cannot solve as efficiently by relying on its own body parts. The ease with which chimpanzees and other Primates expand their tool-using repertory outside their normal habitat is thus extremely significant for assessing the potential for tool use among the Plio-Pleistocene hominids. It seems likely that no radical reorganization of the brain or sharp increase in intelligence was needed for the hominids to expand their tool-using behavior. The australopithecines need not have been "smarter" than the average chimpanzee in order to make regular use of clubs and projectiles to repel predators, stones to smash bones and cut hides, and sticks to dig for roots and tubers (Kitahara-Frisch 1980).

INFRAHUMAN CULTURE AND THE EVOLUTION OF THE HOMINIDS

The great evolutionary novelty represented by culture is that the "capabilities and habits" of culture-bearing animals are acquired through social heredity rather than through the more ancient process of biological heredity (see p. 11). By *social heredity* is meant the shaping of a social animal's behavior in conformity with information stored in the brains of other members of its society. Such information is not stored in the organism's genes. (Yet it must be stressed that actual cultural responses always depend in part upon genetically predetermined capacities and predispositions.)

There appears to be no specific genetic information that is responsible for chimpanzee termiting and anting. True, in order for this behavior to occur, genetically determined capacities for learning, for manipulating objects, and for omnivorous eating must be present in the young chimpanzee. But these general biological capacities and predispositions cannot explain termiting and anting. Given nothing but groups of young chimpanzees, twigs, and termite nests, termiting and anting are unlikely to occur. The miss-

HUMAN EVOLUTION SITES

CHINA
1. Zhoukoudien, Hopei province
2. Yuanmou, Yunnan province
3. Maba, Guandong province
4. Lantian, Shaanxi province

BORNEO, Island of
5. Niah Cave, Sarawak

JAVA, Island of
6. Trinil and Djetis

INDIA
7. Siwalik Hills

IRAQ
8. Shanidar Cave

ISRAEL
9. Amud (Sea of Galilee)
10. Mount Carmel (Tabūn and Skhūl)
11. Hazorea

ISRAEL-OCCUPIED WEST BANK OF JORDAN
12. Nazareth

EGYPT
13. Fayum

SUDAN
14. Singa

ETHIOPIA
15. Omo
16. Hadar

KENYA
17. Lake Turkana
18. Fort Ternan
19. Olorgesailie
20. Lothagam Hill

TANZANIA
21. Olduvai Gorge
22. Gombe Stream Reserve
23. Laetoli

SOUTH AFRICA
24. Makapan
25. Kromdraai
26. Sterkfontein
27. Taung
28. Florisbad
29. Swartkrans
30. Nelson's Bay
31. Saldanha Bay

LIBYA
32. Hava Fte

ALGERIA
33. Ternfine
34. Ain Hen

MOROCCO
35. Jebel Igh

20°
0°
160°
140°
20°
40°
80°
60°
60°
60°
Areal Scale 1: 100,000,000²
1
2
3
4
5
6
7
8
9
12
15
16
17
18
19
20
21
22
23
25
26
29
8
PAIN
6. Bañolas
7. Torralba and Ambrona
REECE
8. Petralona
UGOSLAVIA
9. Krapina
UNGARY
0. Vértesszöllös
ITALY
41. Monte Circeo
42. Quinzano
43. Saccapastore
CZECHOSLOVAKIA
44. Stranska
45. Gánovce
GERMANY
46. Ehringsdorf
47. Steinheim
48. Heidelberg
49. Neander Valley
50. Lehringen
51. Bilzingsleben
FRANCE
52. Tautevel
53. Le Lazaret
54. Montmaurin
55. Orgnac-l'Aven
56. Fontéchevade
57. Monsempron
58. La Chapelle-aux-Saints
59. Le Moustier
60. Vallonet
61. La Chaise
62. Saint-Acheul
63. Arago
BELGIUM
64. Spy
ENGLAND
65. Clacton-on-Sea
66. Swanscombe

ing ingredient is the information about terminting and anting that is stored in the brains of the adult chimpanzees. This information is displayed to the young chimpanzees by their mothers. Among the Gombe chimpanzees, the young do not begin termiting until they are 18 to 22 months old. At first their behavior is clumsy and inefficient, and they do not become proficient until they are about 3 years old. Van Lawick-Goodall witnessed many instances of infants watching intently as the adults termited. Novices often retrieved discarded termiting sticks and attempted to use them on their own. Anting, with its risk of being bitten, takes longer to learn. The youngest chimp to achieve proficiency was about 4 years old (McGrew 1977:282). The conclusion that anting is a cultural trait is strengthened by the fact that chimps at other sites do not exploit driver ants even though the species is widely distributed throughout Africa. At the same time, other groups of chimps do exploit other species of ants and in ways which differ from the Gombe tradition. For example, chimps in the Mahali mountains 170 km south of Gombe insert twigs and bark into the nests of tree-dwelling ants, which are ignored by the Gombe chimps (Nishida 1973).

The most extensive studies of infrahuman culture have been carried out with Japanese macaques. Primatologists of the Primate Research Institute of Kyoto University have found among local monkey troops a wide variety of customs and institutions based on social learning. The males of certain troops, for example, take turns looking after the infants while the infants' mothers are feeding. Such baby-sitting is characteristic only of the troops at Takasaki-yama and Takahashi. Other cultural differences have been noted too. When the monkeys of Takasaki-yama eat the fruit of the *muku* tree, they either throw away the hard stone inside or swallow it and excrete it in their feces. But the monkeys of Arashi-yama break the stone with their teeth and eat the pulpy interior. Some troops eat shellfish; others do not. Cultural differences have also been noted with respect to the characteristic distance that the animals maintain among themselves during feeding and with respect to the order of males, females, and juveniles in line of march when certain troops move through the forest.

The scientists at the Primate Research Institute have been able to observe the actual process by which behavioral innovations spread from individual to individual and become part of a troop's culture independently of genetic transmission. To attract monkeys near the shore for easier observation, sweet potatoes were set on the beach. One day in 1953 a young female began to wash the sand from the sweet potatoes by plunging them in a small brook that ran through the beach. This washing behavior spread throughout the group and gradually replaced the former rubbing habit. Nine years later, 80 to 90 percent of the animals were washing their sweet potatoes, some in the brook, others in the sea (Fig. 4.23). When wheat was spread on the beach, the monkeys of Koshima at first had a hard time separating the kernels from the sand. Soon, however, one of them invented a process for removing sand from the wheat, and this behavior was taken over by others. The solution was to plunge the wheat into the water (Fig. 4.24): The wheat floats and the sand drops to the bottom (Itani 1961; Miyadi 1967; Itani and Nishimura 1973).

Given the presence of rudimentary cultures among contemporary monkeys and apes, there seems little reason to deny that the bipedal australopithecines possessed

Figure 4.23 *JAPANESE MONKEY CULTURE* A female monkey of Koshima troop washing a sweet potato.

fairly large repertoires of socially conditioned responses including the making and using of tools.

HUNTING AND THE PLIO-PLEISTOCENE HOMINIDS

Playwright Robert Ardrey wrote a best-seller entitled *African Genesis* on the theme that the australopithecines, unlike all previous "apes," were killers armed with lethal weapons. According to Ardrey, we are a "predator whose natural instinct is to kill with a weapon" (1961:316). It should be noted, however, that an emphasis upon hunting among the australopithecines or *H. habilis* need not have produced a nature any more fierce or bloodthirsty than that of contemporary apes and monkeys, most of whom readily take to diets that include meat (Fig. 4.25). Chimpanzees, as well as baboons and other Primates, frequently attack and eat small terrestrial animals (Hamilton and

(a)

(b)

Figure 4.24 *JAPANESE MONKEYS WASHING WHEAT*
(a) Members of Koshima troop separating wheat from sand by placing mixture in water. *(b)* Central figure carrying the mixture in its left hand. Two monkeys in foreground are floating the wheat and picking it up.

Busse 1978; McGrew et al. 1979). During a year of observation near Gelgil, Kenya, Robert Harding (1975) observed 47 small vertebrates being killed and eaten by baboons. Their most common prey were infant gazelles and antelopes. Over the course of a decade, chimpanzees of the Gombe National Park are known to have eaten 95 small animals—mostly infant baboons, monkeys, and bush pigs (Teleki 1973). Chimpanzee meat eating and terrestrial hunting have been observed in both forested and semiforested habitats (Suzuki 1975). About 10 percent of a chimpanzee's total time devoted to feeding is taken up by predation on mammals (Teleki 1981:327). Chimpanzees are also known to scavenge dead animals (Hasegawa et al. 1983). It is virtually certain, therefore, that the Plio-Pleistocene hominids were to some degree hunters and scavengers. But the extent and nature of this hunting and scavenging remains very much in doubt, as does its significance for the evolution of culture.

Much of the hunting carried out by chimpanzees is done cooperatively, and the eating of the prey animals involves an unusual amount of sharing and intense social interaction. Gombe chimpanzees pursue various prey species "in a coordinated manner, with 2 to 9 adults (almost always males) positioning and repositioning themselves to maintain an enclosure, sometimes for an hour or more, to effectively anticipate and cut off all potential escape routes of the prey" (Teleki 1981:332). By "begging," by removing pieces without permission, or by recovering dropped fragments of meat, 15 chimpanzees (again mostly males) obtained shares of one 3-kilogram carcass over a 9-hour period. Occasionally voluntary offers are made (ibid.: 333). "Begging" for other kinds of food is also quite common.

(a)

(b)

Figure 4.25 *CHIMPANZEES MEAT EATING* *(a)* Two males devouring a bushbuck. Male on right is threatening female, whose arm appears in upper right *(b)*, begging for a morsel.

A begging individual may reach out to touch the food or the lips of the possessor of the food, or he may hold out his hand toward him (palm up), sometimes uttering small whimpers. . . . The response to such gestures varied according to the individuals involved and the amount of food. Often the possessor pulled the food away from the begging individual or threatened him. . . . Almost always when chimpanzees held their hands to the mouth of the possessor, the latter eventually responded by pushing out a half-chewed lump of food (van Lawick-Goodall 1972:79).

These observations make it clear that food sharing among adults can no longer be said to occur exclusively among hominids, although it is clear that sharing among chimpanzees is rudimentary by comparison with human food-sharing patterns.

Early Hominid Meat Eating

While meat eating seems to occupy an important place in the diet of many anthropoids, none of the anthropoids, including the australopithecines, exhibit the kind of dental patterns which would identify them as specialized *carnivores* (i.e., exclusively or mainly meat eaters). Mammals that consume large quantities of meat (from large animals as opposed to insects) have an unmistakable dental pattern: large canine teeth for puncturing and ripping; enlarged premolars shaped like long, narrow blades for shearing and cutting; and small, narrow molars. Inspection of a convenient domestic cat will reveal only one small molar in each quadrant. Nothing could be more ill-suited to the needs of a "killer ape" than the set of 12 massive, high-crowned, flat "grinders" possessed by both *H. habilis* and australopithecines and, to a lesser extent, by *H. sapiens* (Isaac and Crader 1981:40).

It is generally agreed that the australopithecines, like most primates, were *omnivores* (i.e., they ate both plant and animal foods). Exactly what portion of their diet consisted of meat is unknown (Stahl 1984). Attempts to prove that they actually consumed significant quantities of meat by microscopic examination of the pattern of wear on teeth have been inconclusive (Walker 1981).

The best evidence for meat eating as an important but not primary means of subsistence among the early hominids comes from patches of discarded stone tools and broken animal bones that have been found at Olduvai and other early Pleistocene sites. Comparison of the distribution of bones and tools at these sites with the distribution of bones and tools left behind at the camps of modern hunter-gatherers suggests that the bone accumulations were probably the result of hominid activity. It is impossible to state whether the animals represented by the bones were hunted or simply scavenged (Binford 1983:56–70).

It should be stressed that with the exception of the Eskimo and other Arctic peoples, contemporary "hunters" are hunter-gatherers (one should really say gatherer-hunters). By far the major share of food calories and most of the protein of these populations come from the gathering and collecting of roots, fibers, seeds, fruits, nuts, grubs, frogs, lizards, and insects (see Ch. 11). From analogies with what is actually known about the way contemporary hunter-gatherers live, it seems likely "that foods such as tubers, roots, fruits, nuts, eggs, insects,and other small animals were quantitatively the main items of early hominid diet" (Isaac and Crader 1981:94).

An important new line of evidence bearing on early hominid diet involves the comparison of the human gut with the guts of other primates. According to Katherine Milton (1984), the human gut has a reduced large intestine as compared to the intestines of gorillas, orangutans, and other primates that consume large quantities of low-grade fibrous plant foods. These "bulk feeders" do not travel far in search of their food, which is readily obtainable in the form of stalks, leaves, and unripe fruit. Primates whose gut proportions resemble those of humans tend to be "quality" feeders through whose intestines food moves very rapidly and who therefore must follow a strategy of going after ripe fruit, insects, and small game found in widely dispersed patches. According to this view, the earliest hominids would have been selected for their ability to find patches of high-quality resources, including insects, fruit, nuts, small game, and an occasional big game animal carcass they could scavenge.

Bipedalism is a more efficient mode of locomotion in the less heavily forested savannah habitats where the earliest hominids seem to have lived. It would then have been a small step for them to have intensified their efforts to capture more and larger game with increased social cooperation and tool use, leading in turn to selection for bigger brains and greater intelligence.

While almost all anthropologists reject the killer-ape scenario for hominid evolution, the provisioning of meat, even in small quantities, seems to offer an important clue to the origins of human social life. Regardless of whether meat was obtained through hunting, collecting, or scavenging, it would have encouraged the development of a division of labor, especially between males and females. Sharing of meat between males and females would have made long-term bonding between the sexes and joint provisioning of offspring advantageous.

This further implies that individuals carried tools and containers over long distances and returned with diverse products of their daily foraging expeditions to a home base. A final implication of this scenario is that there was selection for improved communication and symbolizing abilities to facilitate the production and exchange of food and the manufacture of tools and other artifacts.

> It seems very likely that the portability and high food value of meat helped establish an adaptive complex that involves the transport and sharing of food obtained by the complementary endeavor of different members of the same society (Isaac and Crader 1981:95).

But a word of caution: Although in all modern-day hunting and gathering societies men specialize in hunting and women specialize in gathering, we cannot conclude that this was the case among the Plio-Pleistocene hominids. To the extent that limited hunting was practiced by *H. habilis*, both males and females could have engaged in it. And there is no reason to suppose that female *H. habilis* could not have scavenged for meat as effectively as the males. The fundamental requirement for achieving advanced hominid status need not have been the sexual division of labor into male hunters and female gatherers, but the pooling of food at mealtimes (N. Tanner 1983).

SUMMARY

This chapter deals with the evolution of the hominoids and hominids from the Oligocene epoch (about 35 to 22 million years ago) to Plio-Pleistocene times (about 5 to 1.5 million years ago). Although the first "apes" and Old World monkeys appeared during the Oligocene and perhaps as early as the Eocene, it is not possible to identify a hominid lineage until much later. By late Miocene and early Pliocene times (about 12 to 8 million years ago), there were two main groups of hominoids: the Dryopithecinae, adapted to woodland habitats, and the Ramapithecinae, adapted to open country habitats. The Ramapithecinae display several hominid traits, and they lasted well into the Pliocene (12 to 3 million years ago). However, the relationship between the Miocene Hominoidea and the first pongids and first hominids is not known as yet.

The earliest definite hominids have been found at Laetoli in Tanzania and Hadar in Ethiopia. The name *Australopithecus afarensis* has been proposed for this group, which is seen by some experts to be the ancestor of all the later hominids including *H. habilis* and the australopithecines. Other experts contend that *A. afarensis* fossils do not comprise a single taxon and that the ancestors of *H. habilis* and of the australopithecines had already diverged prior to 4 million years ago.

All of these hominids were fully bipedal, lived in savannah habitats, were equipped with large molar teeth and small canines, and consumed both plant and animal foods. On the basis of analogies with tool use by contemporary monkeys and apes, it is probable that both the australopithecines and *H. habilis* made and used some kinds of tools, although not necessarily the stone tools that have been found at the earliest sites. Also on the basis of analogies with modern Primates, it is probable that the australopithecines as well as *H. habilis* had acquired social traditions or cultures. However, *H. habilis,* with its enlarged cranial capacity, probably had advanced further than the other hominids toward culturally patterned means of subsistence and social life with a consequent decrease in dependence on genetically programmed or instinctual patterns of behavior.

Again on the basis of analogies with modern human and primate groups, it seems likely that the increased reliance on culture arose primarily from the advantages to be gained from sharing food, especially meat, between males and females and the joint provisioning of children by adults of both sexes. There is nothing in the fossil record to indicate that it is human nature to be a "killer ape." Rather, it is human nature to be the animal that is most dependent on social traditions for its survival and well-being.

This inference is strengthened by the fact that the canine teeth in the earliest hominids are considerably smaller than in the great apes and other anthropoids. Canines, which are especially prominent in males, are natural stabbing and ripping weapons useful not only for defense against predators but for intimidating females and juveniles (Fig. 3.8). Their failure to project beyond the level of the adjacent teeth in *A. afarensis* suggests that the hominids were already adapted to a greater reliance on artificial weapons and cultural practice than other hominoids.

As the earliest hominids came to rely more on tool use and other cultural patterns of behavior, they were selected for larger brains and improved learning skills. This adaptive trend eventually resulted in the emergence of *H. habilis,* with its bigger brain and a tool kit of stone implements.

5 THE ORIGINS OF *HOMO SAPIENS*

This chapter focuses on the evolution of the hominids from Plio-Pleistocene times to the recent past. It sets forth the evidence concerning the extinction of the australopithecines and the further evolution of *Homo habilis* into the single remaining hominid species and subspecies, *H. sapiens sapiens*.

HOMO ERECTUS

By 1.5 million years ago *H. habilis* had evolved into a bigger-brained species call *H. erectus*. The most obvious difference between *H. erectus* and the earlier hominids is the increased cranial volume—an average of 1050 cubic centimeters as compared with 636 cubic centimeters for *H. habilis* and considerably less for the australopithecines (see Table 5.1). Some *H. erectus* skulls have volumes that overlap with that of *H. habilis*, while others have volumes that overlap with that of *H. sapiens* (Fig. 5.1).

Homo erectus in Java

The first *H. erectus* was found in 1891 by Eugene Dubois, a Dutch physican, near Trinil on the Island of Java in Indonesia. It consisted of a skull cap with heavy brow ridges and a low cranial vault, and a leg bone which resembled that of modern *H. sapiens*. Dubois gave his find the name *Pithecanthropus erectus*, or "upright ape-man" (Figs. 5.2 and 5.3). Recently, the leg bone has been found to be much less old than the skull cap and is no longer regarded as part of a *H. erectus*.

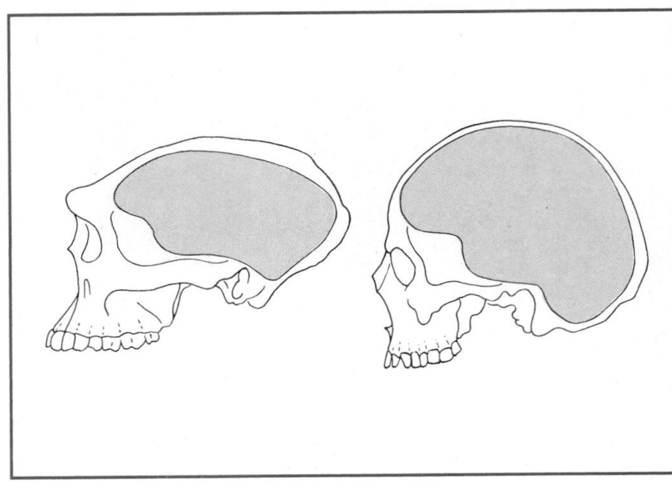

Figure 5.1 *CRANIAL CAVITIES* *Homo erectus* (left) and *Homo sapiens* (right).

Table 5.1 CRANIAL VOLUME AND BODY WEIGHTS OF HOMINOIDEA

Taxon	Volume (cc)	Weight (kg)
Chimpanzee	395	45
Australopithecus afarensis	415	37
A. africanus	442	35
A. robustus	530	44
Homo habilis	636	48
H. erectus	1050	53
H. sapiens	1230	57

SOURCE: McHenry 1982:161.

Altogether there are about a dozen skulls, several leg bones, and many teeth and other bones of *H. erectus* known from various sites in Java. The cranial volume of the skulls ranges from about 700 to 1100 cubic centimeters, with the larger volumes generally associated with the more recent specimens. The earliest Javanese *H. erectus* is about 1.5 million years old—about the same as the oldest *H. erectus* of Africa; the latest in the Javanese series is about 0.5 million years old. One early specimen, formerly called

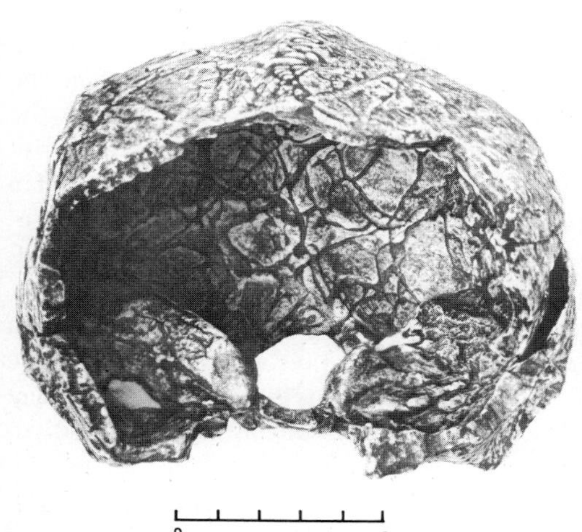

Figure 5.2 PITHECANTHROPUS IV

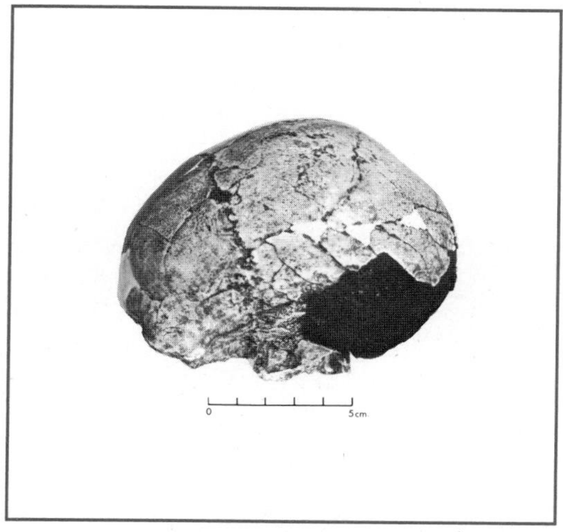

Figure 5.3 PITHECANTHROPUS V
Also known as *Homo modjokertensis*.

Meganthropus, has a lower jaw that closely resembles *H. habilis* from Olduvai and Lake Turkana (Fig. 5.4).

All of the skulls of the Java *H. erectus* have thick bones, large brow ridges, a low receding forehead (which is "pinched" behind the eye sockets), and a "weak" or absent chin. These features are generally more marked in the older specimens (Sartono 1975; Jacob 1975).

Fossils very similar to *Pithecanthropus* have been found in China, Europe, and Africa. In recognition of the fact that all of these specimens are undoubtedly members of the genus *Homo*, they have been assigned the name *H. erectus* (a misleading name since, as we have seen, *A. afarensis* was fully bipedal at least a million years before *H. erectus* appeared on the scene).

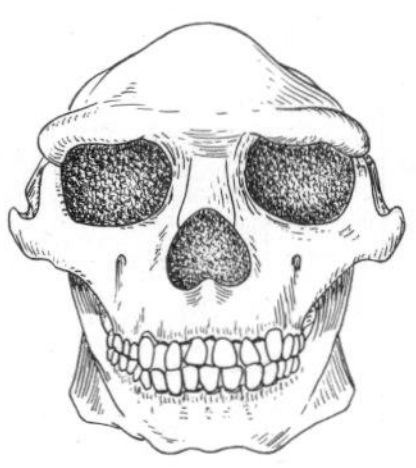
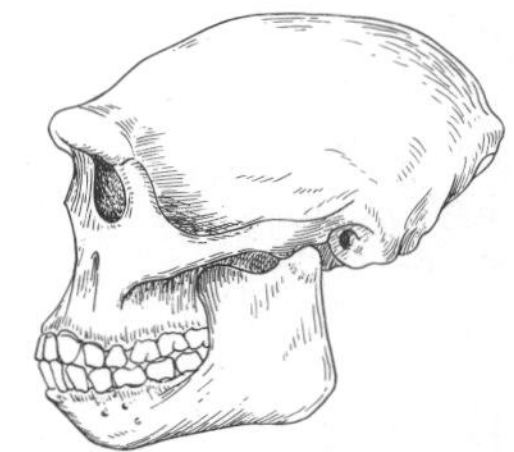

Java *Homo erectus* (male)

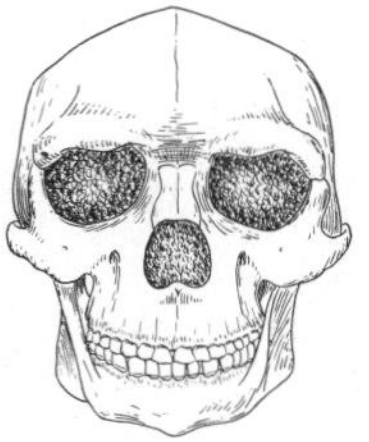
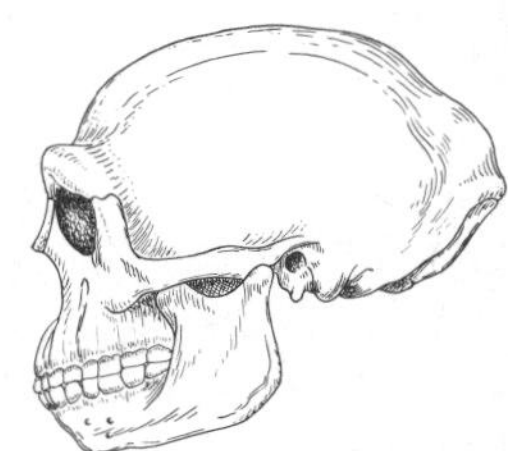

China *Homo erectus* (female)

Figure 5.5 HOMO ERECTUS
Male from Java (top) and female from Peking (bottom).

Homo erectus in China

H. erectus in China was originally named *Sinanthropus pekinensis*. A rich assortment of *H. erectus* crania and teeth have been found at Zhoukoudian (formerly spelled Choukoutien) near Peking; hence the name "China Peking man." Cranial volume starts toward the upper end of the Java *H. erectus* range. It averages about 1050 cubic centimeters with an upper limit of 1300 cubic centimeters which is above the present-day human average. The cranial vault bones are thinner than those of Java *H. erectus*; the brow ridges somewhat reduced; and the area behind the temple less pinched. But other features clearly align the Zhoukoudian fossils with *H. erectus* of Java and elsewhere: the low, elongated cranial vault; prominent brow ridges; heavy chinless jaw; and forward-jutting face (Fig. 5.5). Although accurate dating has not been achieved, there is general agreement that the Zhoukoudian *H. erectus* is not as old as the Javanese remains and that the Zhoukoudian remains derive from the period between 300,000 and 700,000 years ago (Aigner 1976).

However, isolated *H. erectus* teeth found at Yuanmou, Yunnan, and a jaw found at

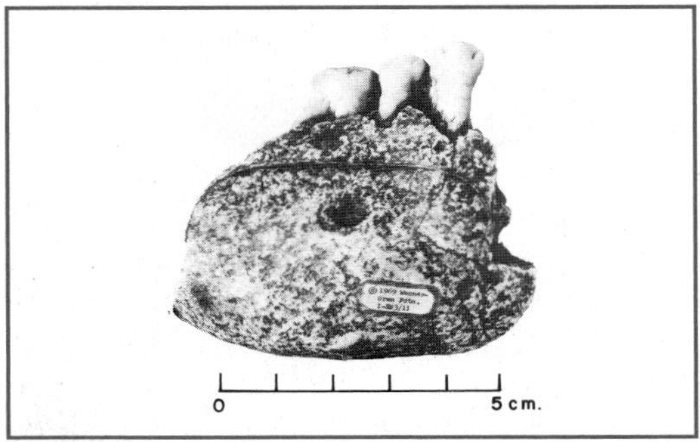

Figure 5.4 MEGANTHROPUS

Lantian, Shaanxi, may be considerably older and more closely resemble the more rugged *H. erectus* of Java and Africa (Rukang 1982:474).

Homo erectus in Africa

H. erectus has also been found in three different parts of Africa. In the north, large chinless jaws formerly assigned to the genus *Atlanthropus* were found at Ternifine, Algeria, with dates estimated to be between 700,000 to 500,000 B.P. In Morocco, near Rabat, Casablanca, and Sale, *H. erectus* remains that seem to be transitional to *H. sapiens* have been dated to about 200,000 years B.P.

In East Africa, *H. erectus* has been found in the Afar region of Ethiopia (the "Bodo skull"), in Bed II at Olduvai, Tanzania, and at Lake Turkana, Kenya. The latter, called KNM 3733 (Fig. 5.6), is one of the earliest and best-preserved specimens. At Olduvai and Lake Turkana, *H. erectus* lived at a time when *A. robustus* had not yet become extinct, about 1.6 million years ago.

Finally, in South Africa, there is evidence for another extremely early *H. erectus* among the remains found at Swartkrans.

It should be stressed that the earlier of the *H. erectus* finds resemble *H. habilis* and even in some instances *A. africanus*. Not unexpectedly, there is considerable disagreement concerning where to draw the line among them. Some experts insist that *H. habilis* is nowhere distinct enough from *H. erectus* to warrant a separate taxon. Some insist that the Swartkrans fossils belong to *A. africanus*. A complicating factor is the possibility that the more rugged and hence presumably more "primitive" specimens may actually be males of the same species (Wolpoff et al. 1976).

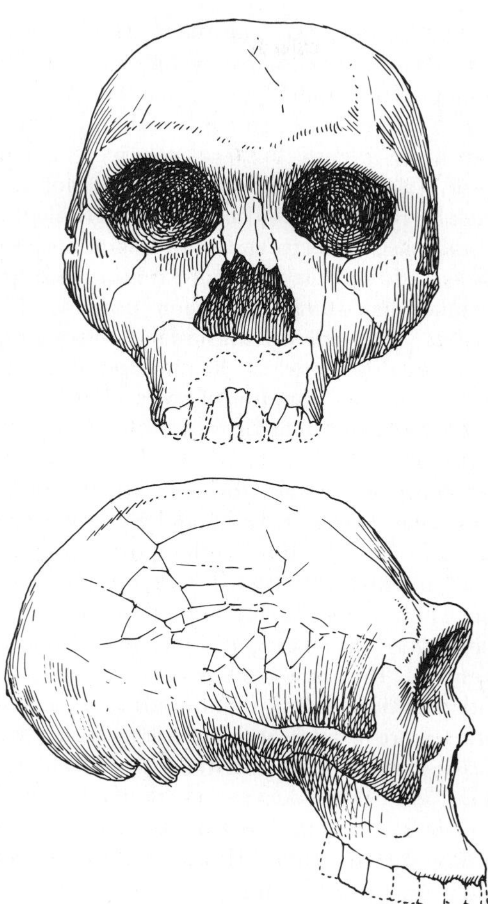

Figure 5.6 *THE EARLIEST* HOMO ERECTUS *(KNM-3733)*
Found east of Lake Turkana and provisionally dated to 1.6 million years, this member of the genus *Homo* was alive at the same time as the australopithecines.

Homo erectus in Europe

Remains of *H. erectus* in Europe are much less abundant than in Asia or Africa and are the subject of continuing controversies. Although tools dating back as much as 1 million B.P. have been found in Europe, pointing to the existence of some kind of early hominid, no *H. erectus* bones definitely older than 500,000 years have been identified. Possibly the oldest of the finds is the Mauer jaw (formerly known as "Heidelberg man"), which is extremely broad and robust and lacks a chin but has relatively small teeth. Claims have been advanced for *H. erectus* remains at Verteszöllös, Hungary, on the basis of teeth and skull fragments and associated with stone tools reminiscent of Zhoukoudian tools. Another possible *H. erectus* site is Bilzingsleben, Germany, where a thick-headed, heavy-browed hominid left a large number of stone, bone, and antler tools and hearths indicative of the use of fire.

Other contenders for *H. erectus* status have been found at Arago and Montmaurin, France. The trouble with these and yet other possible *H. erectus* finds in Europe is that their ages remain uncertain. Many of them were discovered prior to the development of the new radiometric, magnetic, and chemical dating techniques. Previously dates were established by reference to the classic scheme of Pleistocene continental glaciations. This scheme, with its four advances and retreats, is now known to have grossly oversimplified the succession of cold and warm periods during the past 1.5 million years (see pp. 80–81). Attempts to apply the new techniques have resulted in widely discrepant dates in the 300,000 to 100,000 B.P. range (Cook et al., 1982). If these new dates are correct, most of the European fossils previously regarded as *H. erectus* probably should be regarded as forms transitional between *H. erectus* and the early or "archaic" *H. sapiens* (Sigmon and Cybulski 1981). Part of the uncertainty about dates arises from the fact that fossils from the period in question are too recent to be dated by the potassium-argon method and too old to be dated by the carbon 14 method.

Homo erectus Cultures

It seems clear that *H. erectus* possessed a higher capacity for cultural behavior than *H. habilis* or the australopithecines. The extinction of the australopithecines suggests that hominids were subject to intense selection for more complex and efficient tool use and socially acquired patterns of subsistence on the basis of cooperation, division of labor, and food sharing.

At Olduvai Gorge (Fig. 5.7), the oldest deposits (1.75 million years B.P.) contain a stone tool industry called *Oldowan*. Several hundred stone tools have thus far been removed from Beds I and II, most of which fall into the category called *choppers* (Fig. 5.8). Oldowan choppers were made by knocking flakes off of one end of a tennis-ball-sized piece of lava rock. They may have served as cutting tools for meat processing or woodworking. There are also crude scrapers and possibly hammer stones. About a million years passed with only minor refinements, resulting in the industry called *Developed Oldowan*. Presumably *H. habilis* was the manufacturer of some of these tools, yet for reasons previously discussed, the possibility that the australopithecines also made them should not be dismissed.

Coincident with *H. erectus* there appeared a second tool tradition known as the *Acheulian*. Its characteristic implements are *bifaces*—pebbles and/or large flakes that are worked on both sides to produce a variety of well-formed cutting, scraping, and piercing edges and points. Of these, the most typical is the *hand ax* (Fig. 5.9), a multipurpose instrument probably evolved out of the Oldo-

Figure 5.7 *OLDUVAI GORGE*
Excavation exposing various "beds" on the side of the gorge.

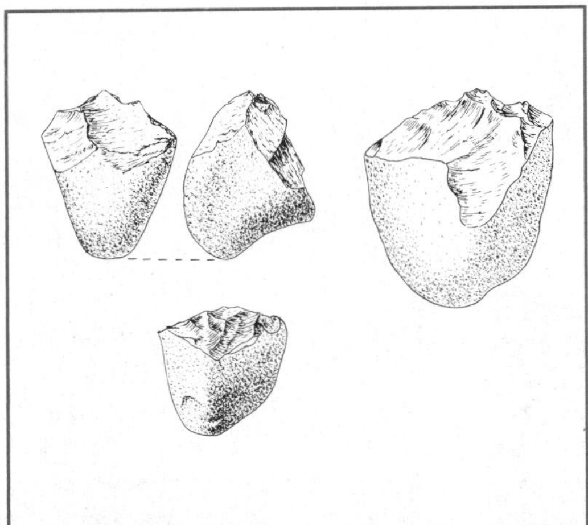

Figure 5.8 *OLDOWAN CHOPPERS*

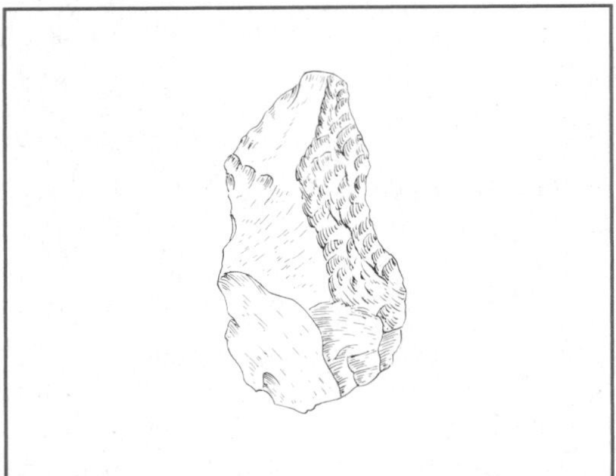

Figure 5.9 *ACHEULIAN HAND AX FROM OLDUVAI GORGE*

wan chopper—although not necessarily at Olduvai itself (M. Leakey 1975).

> While Oldowan toolmakers simply modified the circumference of pebbles in their effort to produce a tool, Acheulian craftsmen usually completely transformed pebbles, chunks, or large flakes so that it is now often impossible to determine on what kind or shape of object a finished hand-axe was made (Butzer 1971:437).

For some 500,000 years, from about 1.5 to 1 million B.P., the Oldowan and Acheulian traditions seem to have existed side by side at Oldowan. There is no good explanation for their coexistence. Some possibilities: Oldowan and Acheulian were tool industries associated with different kinds of camps at which the same *H. erectus* groups did different things. Or they represent two different "tribal" cultures of *H. erectus;* or they represent the more developed cultures of *H. erectus* and the less developed cultures of *H. habilis* or the australopithecines. Finally, they may simply result from the use of different raw materials (Jones 1979; Stiles 1979).

Acheulian implements similar to those found at Olduvai Gorge form part of a widespread stone tool tradition (Feifar 1976). They are named after the site in France where such tools were first identified. Acheulian hand axes have been found virtually everywhere in Africa and Eurasia wherever *H. erectus* or other early fossil humans lived.

Up until recently it was believed that a separate tool tradition known as the *chopper-chopping tool tradition* was characteristic of *H. erectus* in China and other parts of East Asia. The chopper-chopping tradition was allegedly marked by the absence of hand axes and the presence of choppers and cleavers (Fig. 5.10). It is now clear that tools of the chopper-chopping tradition occur in Europe as well as in East Asia, and that numerous hand axes were made in East Asia as well as in Europe during early and mid-Pleistocene times (Yi and Clark 1983). For example, at Verteszöllös in Hungary there are thousands of chopper cores and flakes but no hand axes, while at Chon-Gok-Ni in Korea, 50 hand axes and Acheulian-type cleavers have been found (Yi and Clark 1983:183).

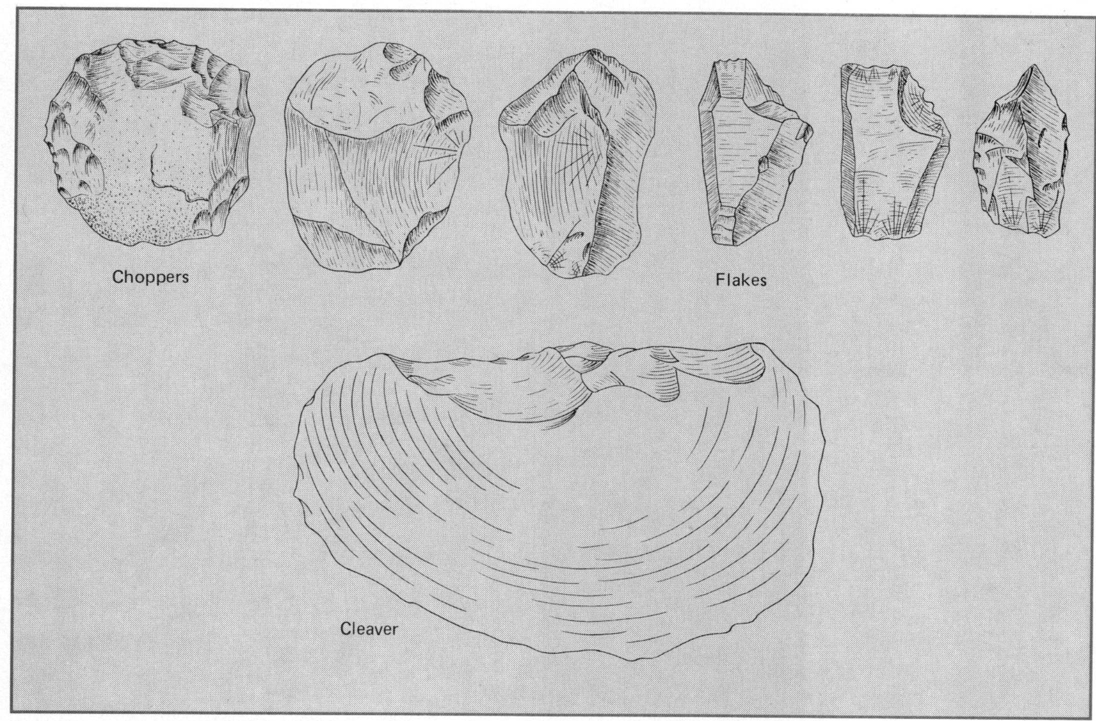

Figure 5.10 *IMPLEMENTS FROM SINANTHROPUS LEVELS OF CHOUKOUTIEN CAVE*

Hand axes were probably multipurpose instruments that served to break soil and roots, to hack off branches, and to dismember game (see p. 131). The *H. erectus* tool kit usually also included smaller flake instruments for trimming wood, cutting meat and sinew, and scraping hides. Such flakes are the natural by-products of the manufacture of biface tools (Fig. 5.11).

The advancing cultural achievements of *H. erectus* are also indicated by the food refuse found at Acheulian sites; the bones of elephants, horses, wild cattle, and other large mammals are common. Some of these animals may have been killed with wooden spears fashioned by flake tools. At Clacton in Essex, England, the 300,000-year-old forepart of a yew-wood lance whose tip may have been hardened by fire is the earliest evidence of such spears. This fragment resembles a complete 8-foot yew-wood fire-hardened lance found at Lehringen embedded between the ribs of an extinct type of elephant that lived in Saxony, West Germany, at 125,000 B.P. (Butzer 1971).

At Zhoukoudian, *H. erectus* also seems to have hunted large mammals. Here the debris includes bones of deer, bison, horse, rhinoceros, elephant, bear, hyena, and tiger. *H. erectus* in China as in Europe seems to have learned how to use fire. Deep layers of charcoal fragments and pieces of carbonized bone have been discovered at the Zhoukoudian site.

CHRONOLOGICAL RELATIONSHIP OF PRINCIPAL PLEISTOCENE HOMINID FOSSILS

Million years B.P.		European glaciations	EUROPE: Fossil beds	EUROPE: Fossils	SOUTHEAST ASIA: Fossil beds and caves	SOUTHEAST ASIA: Fossils	EAST ASIA: Caves	EAST ASIA: Fossils
.010	Upper Pleistocene	Warm						
.035	Upper Pleistocene	Cold		Cro-Magnon	Niah Cave	*H. sapiens sapiens*	Upper cave	*H. sapiens sapiens*
.050	Upper Pleistocene	Warm						
.075	Upper Pleistocene	Cold		Classic Neandertals		Solo (Archaic *H. sapiens*)		
.125	Upper Pleistocene	Warm		Archaic *H. sapiens*				Maba Dali (Archaic *H. sapiens*)
.145	Middle Pleistocene	Cold		Arago Montmaurin (*H. erectus*)				
.300	Middle Pleistocene	Warm		Steinheim Swanscombe				
	Middle Pleistocene						Lower Cave	
.400	Middle Pleistocene	Cold		Vértesszöllös (*Homo erectus*)			Zhoukoudien	*Sinanthropus* (*H. erectus*)
	Middle Pleistocene			Bilzingsleben (*Homo erectus*)	Trinil			
.700	Middle Pleistocene	Warm		Mauer (*Homo erectus*)		*Pithecanthropus* I, II, III, VI, VII, VIII (*H. erectus*)		
	Middle Pleistocene			Prezletice (*Homo erectus*)				
1.	Middle Pleistocene	Cold						
1.3	Middle Pleistocene	Warm	Calabrian			?		Lantian (*H. erectus?*)
1.75	Lower Pleistocene	Cold						Yuanmou (*H. erectus*)
2.	Lower Pleistocene	Warm			Djetis	*Pithecanthropus* V (modjokertensis)		
	Lower Pleistocene		Villafranchian					
2.5	Lower Pleistocene	Cold				*Pithecanthropus* IV *Meganthropus*		
3.	Lower Pleistocene							
4.	Pliocene							
5.	Pliocene							

EAST AFRICA AND ETHIOPIA		SOUTH AFRICA		NORTH AFRICA	MIDDLE EAST		
Fossil beds	Fossils	Caves	Fossils	Fossils	Fossils	European glaciations	Million years B.P.
							.010
	Sinja (*H. sapiens sapiens*)		Florisbad (Archaic *H. sapiens*)	Hava Fteh Jebel Ighoud	Jebel Qafzeh Skhūl Amud Tabūn Shanidar Archaic *H. sepiens* and *H. neanderthalensis*)		.035
							.050
	LH 18 (Archaic *H. sapiens*)					Wurm	.075
							.125
	Afar-Omo-Kibish and Rhodesian (Archaic *H. sapiens*)		Saldanha (Archaic *H. sapiens*)	Rabat, Casablanca (*H. erectus?*)		Riss	.145
							.300
						Mindel*	.400
Olduvai IV	OH 12 (*H. erectus*)			*Atlanthropus* (*H. erectus*)	Hazorea (*H. erectus*)		.700
Olduvai III	OH 9 (*H. erectus*)					Gunz*	1.
Olduvai II	(*A. robustus*)						1.3
Olduvai I	OH 7 (*H. habilis*)	Kromdraai Swartkrans	Telanthropus (*H. erectus*)			Donau*	1.75
ast Turkana	KMN 1470 (*H. habilis?*) KMN 3733 (*H. erectus*)		*Australopithecus robustus*				2.
							2.5
Omo Laetoli Hadar	? *Australopithecus afarensis* ?	Sterkfontein Makapansgat	*Australopiethcus africanus*				3.
							4.
							5.

*"These terms are so highly controversial that usage . . . should be discontinued." (Butzer 1971:23)

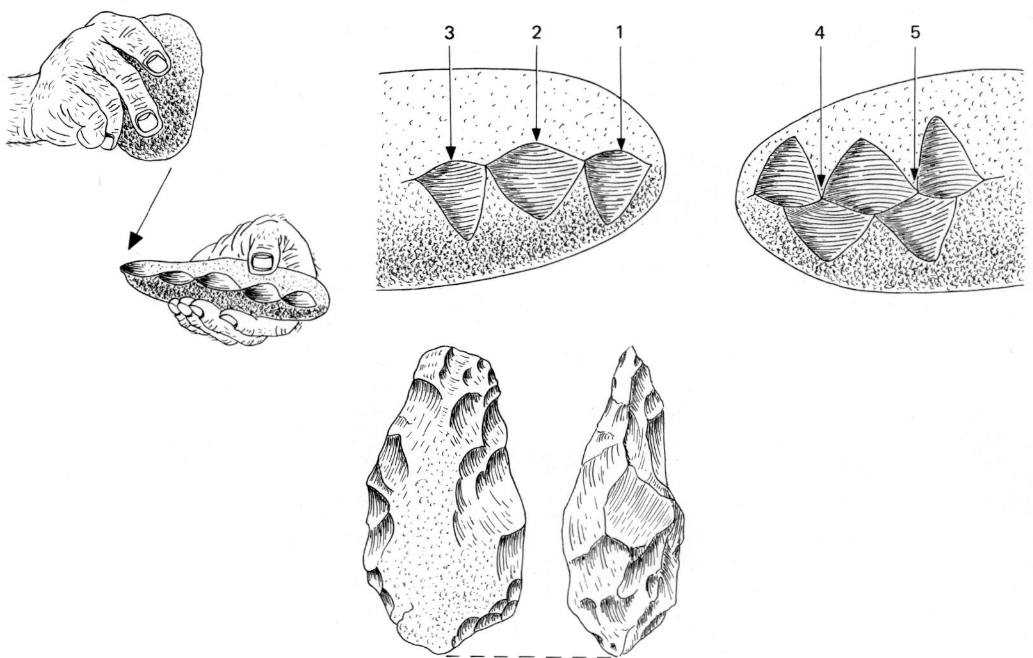

Figure 5.11 *BIFACE MANUFACTURE*
Core is held in one hand and blows 1, 2, 3, are delivered with hammer stone held in other. Core is turned over and blows 4 and 5 are delivered creating cutting edge. Acheulian hand ax (bottom) was made in this manner. Flakes (not shown) may also have been used as tools.

The Cultural Consequences of Big-Game Hunting

A number of lines of evidence converge toward the inference that *H. erectus* was a more regular and more proficient hunter of large animals than *H. habilis* or the australopithecines. At sites such as Olorgesailie in Kenya, Terra Amata in France, and Torralba and Ambrona in Spain, large accumulations of bones of single species suggest that surrounds and drives were utilized (Fig. 5.12). Furthermore, control over fire would make drives and surrounds more effective and would have permitted the manufacture of fire-hardened wooden spears. Finally, the high level of craft embodied in Acheulian stone implements suggests that effective hunting equipment, such as bolas, wooden clubs, nets, lines, deadfalls, and hidden pits, were not beyond the technological competence of *H. erectus*.

Among modern hunting-and-gathering peoples, the hunters of large game are usually men. The kill usually occurs far from a "home base" or camp. The quarry is usually dismembered where it has fallen, and if it is very large, women and children are summoned to help carry the parts back to the campsite. Instead of accompanying the men on the hunt, women and children look for vegetable foods, grubs, insects, and small animals. Most contemporary hunting groups exhibit this division of labor (but female gathering activities are more intensive in tropical and temperate regions than in the Arctic). Hence, it is assumed that *H. erectus* hunting-and-gathering groups must have been organized in a similar fashion.

The projection of the sex roles of contemporary hunting peoples back upon the *H. erectus* of a million years ago merits extreme skepticism. There is no direct evidence that big-game hunting was carried out exclusively or primarily by *H. erectus* males; nor is there any direct evidence that women alone did the baby-sitting. On physiological grounds one expects females who are in advanced pregnancy or who are nursing newborn infants to confine their economic contribution to relatively sedentary activities close to camp or home base. At other times, however, mothers can readily participate in far-reaching expeditions. Precisely this sort of shift has been observed among chimpanzees, among whom the extent to which females participate in heterosexual foraging groups depends on whether or not the individual is pregnant or nursing. (J. K. Brown 1970; Williams 1971; van den Berghe 1972; Williams 1973). In some contemporary hunting-and-gathering groups the role of woman as hunter is not insignificant (Morren 1973; Leacock 1973). A home base populated exclusively by females and children is not theoretically more adaptive than a home base populated by nursing females, children, and males awaiting the return of hunting parties composed of both males and females (Fig. 5.13). The fact that males control the weaponry of hunting and warfare in all known contemporary human groups is not sufficient evidence for the belief that this was true of *H. erectus* populations. Consid-

Figure 5.12 *AMBRONA (SPAIN)*
Early Acheulian human occupation site, with tusks and other parts of several carcasses of elephants.

eration must be given to the possibility that the beliefs and practices associated with male control of the technology of hunting and warfare originated in relatively recent times.

ARCHAIC *HOMO SAPIENS*

Between 300,000 and 50,000 B.P., *H. erectus* evolved into and was replaced by larger-brained but still low-browed and big-boned forms of hominids who are known as *archaic H. sapiens*, the earliest members of our own species.

Archaic *Homo sapiens* in Europe

As discussed above (p. 76), there is a problematical group of fossils in Europe which seem to be intermediate between *H. erectus* and *H. sapiens* and which probably date to between 300,000 and 200,000 B.P. These include the fossils found at Arago and Montmaurin, France, and perhaps even those at Verteszöllös and Bilzingsleben (Cook et al. 1982). Prior to the redating of these finds it was believed that the earliest archaic *H. sapiens* in Europe were Swanscombe (Fig. 5.14) and Steinheim (Fig. 5.15), from England and Germany, respectively. These finds have cranial capacities within the *sapiens* range, but their cranial vaulting and the thickness of their bones suggest a status intermediate between *H. erectus* and *H. sapiens*.

Abundant remains of additional archaic *H. sapiens* have been found in Spain, Germany, Italy, France, Greece, and Yugoslavia

Figure 5.13 *JAPANESE WOMEN PEARL DIVERS AT WORK*
This female specialty suggests that the exclusion of women from the role of hunters cannot be attributed to the need for women to remain at home and take care of children. Children can readily be left at home and cared for by older siblings or men.

Figure 5.14 *SWANSCOMBE*

for the time period of 250,000 to 75,000 B.P. Fontechevade (Fig. 5.16) and Krapina are two of the better-known examples.

African Archaic *Homo sapiens*

During the initial period of anthropological inquiry into the origins of *H. sapiens*, research was conducted mostly by European scientists, who found it more convenient to work in Europe than elsewhere. As a result, the number of European archaic *H. sapiens* fossil specimens is much larger than the number of such specimens from any other region.

In Africa, from the Sahara to the Cape of Good Hope, *H. erectus* populations were probably replaced or were being replaced by archaic *sapiens* populations at least as early as in Europe. Several of the *H. erectus* fossils from North Africa seem to be transitional to archaic *H. sapiens* and have dates comparable to those of Arago, Montmaurin, Swanscombe, and Steinheim in Europe.

Previous estimates of the dates of such African archaic *H. sapiens* as "Rhodesian man," a rugged low-crowned skull with a capacity of 1300 cubic centimeters (Fig. 5.17) and "Saldanha man," a somewhat less rugged contemporary found 90 miles from the Cape of Good Hope, had suggested that populations little different from *H. erectus* were still alive in Africa as recently as 30,000 B.P. (Coon 1962). This view is almost certainly incorrect. Although the precise dates remain unknown, a reevaluation of the archaeological and faunal evidence suggests that the Rhodesian and Saldanha populations lived more than 125,000 years ago (Klein 1973). Moreover, other archaic *sapiens* are now known to have lived in the Omo and Afar regions of Ethiopia earlier than 125,000 B.P. (Butzer 1971:444; Conroy et al.; Rightmire 1983). In 1980 the discovery of Laetoli hominid 18 with an estimated age of 120,000 years provided additional evidence for an early appearance of *H. sapiens* in Africa (Day, M. Leakey, and Magori 1980).

As in Europe and the Middle East, archaic *H. sapiens* populations probably lived on in Africa to 40,000 B.P. Large-brained but low-browed fossils have been found at Jebel Ighoud in Morocco, dating from 43,000 B.P.; Hava Fteh in Cyranaica, Libya, from, 40,000 B.P.; and Florisbad, Orange

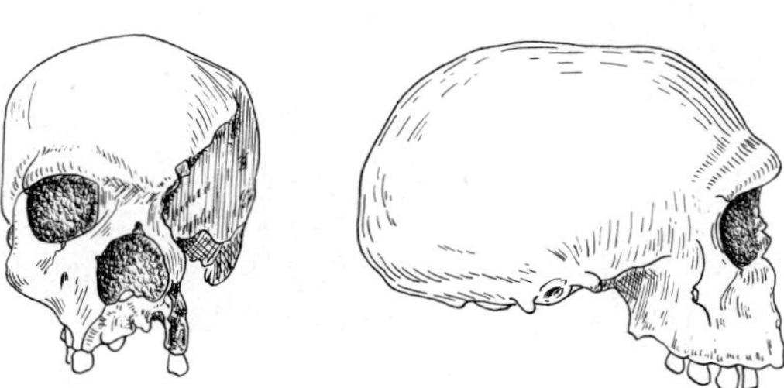

Figure 5.15 *STEINHEIM*
Intermediate between *Homo erectus* and Neandertal.

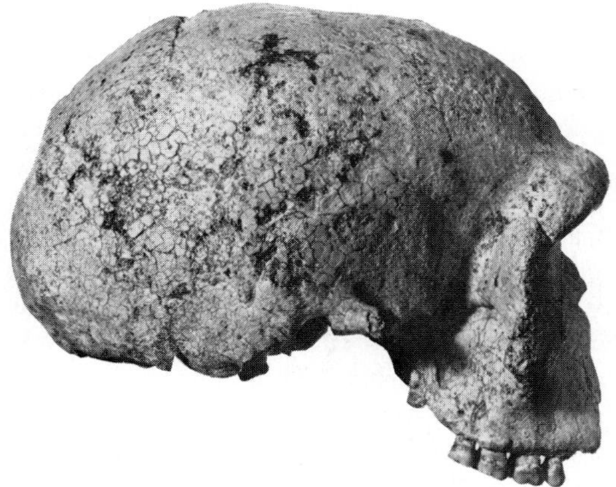

Figure 5.16 *STEINHEIM*
Archaic *H. sapiens* from West Germany.

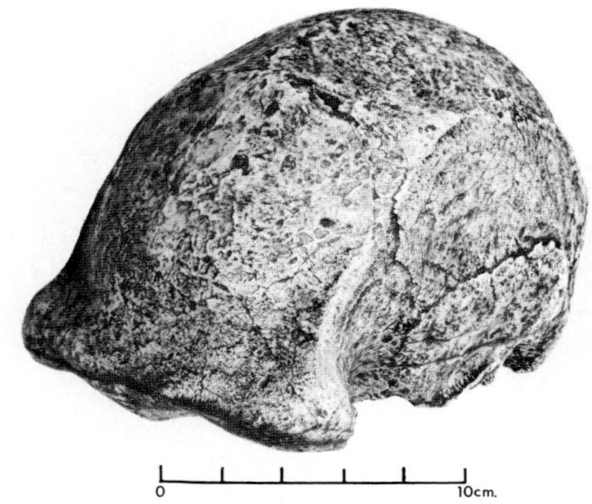

Figure 5.18 HOMO SOLOENSIS
Archaic *Homo sapiens* from Ngandong, Java.

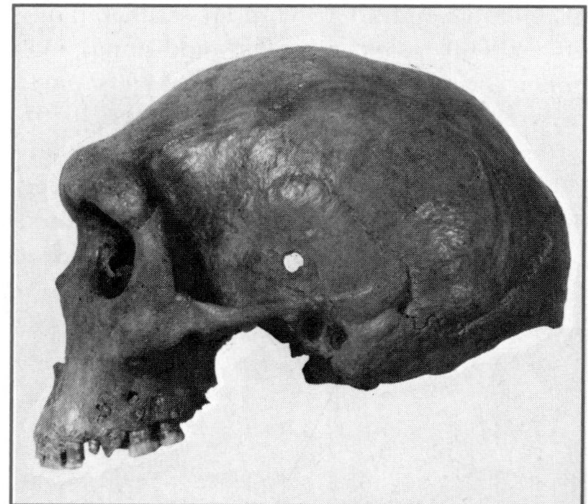

Figure 5.17 *"RHODESIAN MAN"*

Free State, more than 44,000 B.P. (Rightmire 1978). There is no evidence for the view that the development of African archaic *sapiens* was retarded or for the view that the archaic *sapiens* lingered on longer in Africa than elsewhere.

Archaic *Homo sapiens* in Asia

In Asia, archaic *H. sapiens* (similar in many respects to those of Europe and Africa) contemporaneously begin to appear in the fossil record. One of the best known finds is the Maba, Guangdong, skull (formerly spelled Mapa, Kwantung). It represents a big-brained, low-browed individual who lived about 125,000 years ago. Recently, there has been a renewal of interest in paleoanthropology in China and several additional archaic *H. sapiens* have come to light. So far, the Dali skull discovered in 1978 in Shaanxi "is the most complete fossil found in China between *H. erectus* and modern *H. sapiens*" (Rukang 1982). It has a cranial volume of 1200 cubic centimeters, a long, low cranial vault, and moderately thick bones.

In Java, so-called Solo man is another archaic *H. sapiens*. It has heavy brow ridges, a sloping forehead, and a cranial capacity of 1200 cubic centimeters and dates to about 75,000 B.P. (Fig. 5.18).

THE NEANDERTALS AND *HOMO SAPIENS SAPIENS* IN EUROPE

Between 75,000 and 40,000 B.P., Europe and the Middle East were inhabited by a group of archaic *H. sapiens* known as *Neandertals*. The first Neandertal was found in 1856 in the Neander-Tal (Neander Valley), Germany.* Neandertals tend to be markedly prognathic, with heavy brow ridges, robust, chinless jaws, and low brows reminiscent of *H. erectus*. Yet their average cranial capacity (1500 cc) was greater than that of most *H. sapiens sapiens!* (Fig. 5.19) Finds have been made at many localities which bordered the glaciers that covered northern Europe during the Upper Pleistocene; for example, at Spy in Belgium, Le Moustier and La Ferassie in France, and Monte Circeo in Italy (Fig. 5.20).

One of the most important diagnostics of the Neandertals is the extreme forward position of their teeth as compared both with earlier European archaic *H. sapiens* populations and with modern *H. sapiens sapiens*. In Neandertals the tooth row begins 2 or 3 centimeters farther forward of the ascending portion (*ramus*) of the mandible than in *H. erectus* or *H. sapiens sapiens* (Howells 1975). It has been suggested that this feature may reflect selection for jaws useful in chewing of animal hides and in other cold-climate industrial activities. All authorities

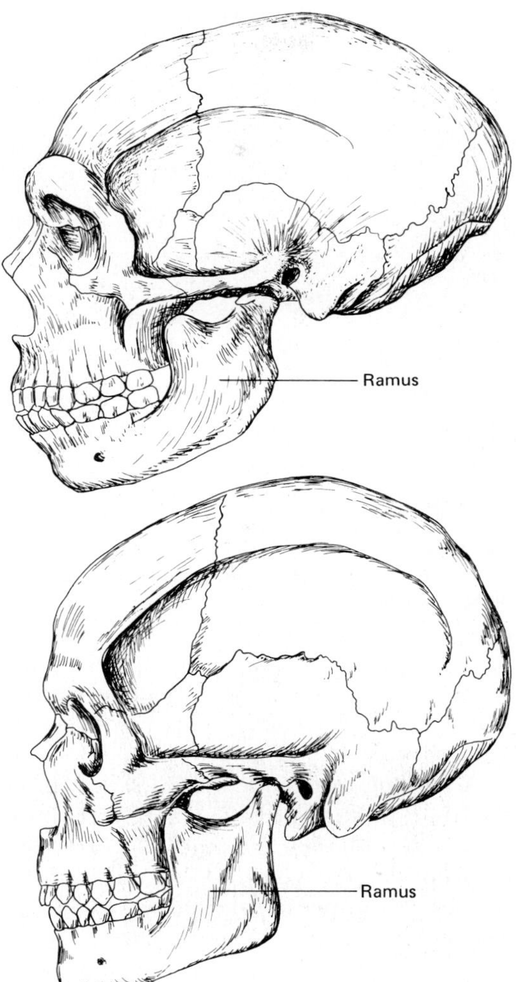

Figure 5.19 *CLASSIC NEANDERTAL (top) AND* HOMO SAPIENS SAPIENS *(bottom)* Note that the Neandertal third molar is forward of the ramus. This feature may reflect emphasis on chewing of animal hides.

agree that the Neandertals of Europe were members of the genus *Homo*, but a few continue to assign them to a separate species: *H. neanderthalensis*. The emerging consen-

*"In 1864, when King introduced the taxon *Homo neanderthalensis*, the spelling of the trivial name followed accepted German orthography. 'Thal,' meaning valley, was spelled with an 'h,' although it was silent in pronunciation. Later, established German usage changed, and the silent 'h' in words like 'tal,' 'tor,' etc., was dropped. Thus, Neandertal man should be written without the 'h,' although, according to the International Code, the taxon *Homo neanderthalensis* must continue to be written as first proposed. Since English speakers tend to pronounce the 'h,' it is hoped that future discussions of the Neandertals will . . . write the term without an 'h' " (Mann and Trinkaus 1974:188).

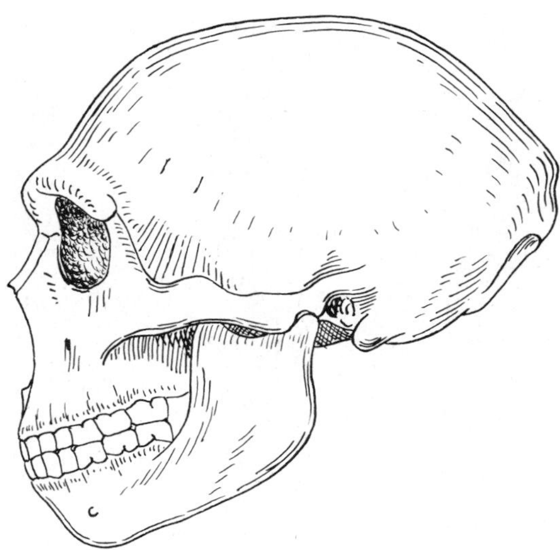

Figure 5.20 *CLASSIC NEANDERTAL* Found at La Ferassie, France, and dated to about 50,000 B.P.

sus is that all of the "classic" Neandertals belong to an archaic subspecies known as *H. sapiens neanderthalensis*.

According to some authorities, the Neandertals, despite their large cranial capacities, were not in the lineage that led to *H. sapiens sapiens* but were a locally specialized species or subspecies adapted to severe glacial climates that became extinct about 50,000 to 40,000 B.P. According to still other accounts, the classic Neandertals were exterminated by *H. sapiens sapiens* who swept into Europe from the Middle East during a warm interval in the last continental glaciation. Even if this catastrophe (for the Neandertals) did take place, it seems unlikely that the Neandertals would not have contributed some of their genes to their more modern replacements (Saben 1977).

Considerable evidence exists, however, for regarding the south central European Neandertals as the direct ancestors of *H. sapiens sapiens*. In the region that includes parts of Hungary, Austria, Rumania, and Czechoslovakia, there is a definite shift toward more *sapiens*-like features from earlier to later specimens. This shift is not evident in the western and northern parts of Europe, where the classic Neandertals did die our very rapidly, presumably as a result of competition from *H. sapiens sapiens* (Smith 1982:685). The earlier south central Neandertals closely resemble the "classic" western Europe Neandertals. But the later specimens exhibit intermediate features such as reduced brow ridges, narrow noses, higher foreheads, and less massive bone structure. At the same time, the earliest *H. sapiens sapiens* from south central Europe have brow ridges, bone thickness, nose structure, and tooth dimensions that are reminiscent of the late Neandertals. These earliest *H. sapiens sapiens* have been found at numerous sites in the region dating from 35,000 to 25,000 B.P. (Fig. 5.21).

The gradualness of the transition from Neandertals to modern *H. sapiens sapiens* in

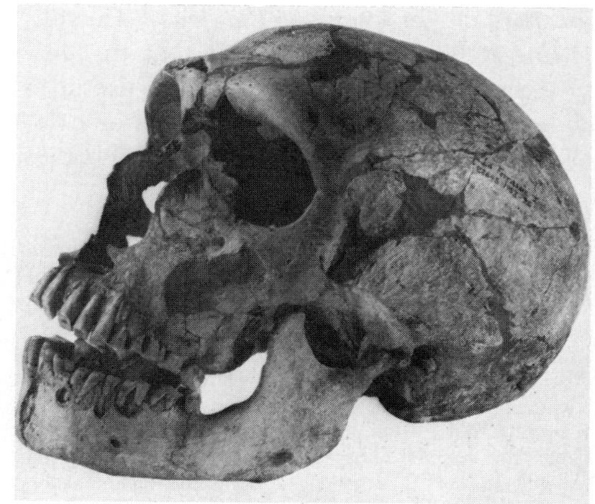

Figure 5.21 *EARLY SOUTH CENTRAL EUROPEAN* HOMO SAPIENS SAPIENS

south central Europe seems to weigh against the theory that all Neandertals were killed off by a sudden invasion of physically and culturally advanced populations. Two other possibilities remain: the observed intermediate forms represent (1) the hybridization of Neandertals with *H. sapiens sapiens* who originated outside of the region or (2) the local evolution of *H. sapiens sapiens* from the later Neandertals.

In order for the first interpretation to be valid there must be evidence for the emergence of *H. sapiens sapiens* in some other nearby region considerably earlier than 35,000 B.P. Does such evidence exist?

Neandertals and *Homo sapiens sapiens* in the Middle East

The logical place to look for the source of European *H. sapiens sapiens* genes is in the Middle East. Neandertals lived in the Levant (today's Lebanon, Syria, Israel, and Jordan) and Iraq about the same time as they did in Europe, and they were replaced by *H. sapiens sapiens* at about the same time as in Europe. The earliest Middle Eastern Neandertals are from Shanidar cave in Iraq and date to between 60,000 and 45,000 B.P. These specimens closely resemble classic western European Neandertals (Fig. 5.22). Forms intermediate between Neandertals and *H. sapiens sapiens* have been found at a cave called Tabūn on Mt. Carmel, Israel, dating to 50,000 B.P. (Fig. 5.23). And finally, the first *H. sapiens sapiens* appear at Skhūl, another cave on Mt. Carmel, and Jebel Qafzeh near Nazareth between 40,000 to 30,000 B.P. (Fig. 5.24). Unless these dates are changed, it would appear that the Middle East has its own Neandertal–*H. sapiens sapiens* transition and that this transition did not occur substantially earlier than in south central Europe (Smith 1982:689).

Figure 5.22 *SHANIDAR NEANDERTAL* It rests on cave floor still embedded in the matrix.

The Emergence of *Homo sapiens* in Africa and East Asia

For historical reasons, more is known about the transition to *H. sapiens sapiens* in Europe than in Africa or East Asia. Ongoing research will eventually redress the balance. But enough is known to suggest that the transition occurred at about the same time throughout much of the Old World. One of the earliest *H. sapiens sapiens* is from Southeast Asia. A fully modern skull with a ^{14}C date of 35,000 B.P. (Harrison 1976) has been found in Niah Cave on the island of Borneo. In the Upper Cave at Zhoukoudian local varieties of *H. sapiens sapiens* appeared about 25,000 B.P. In Africa, *H. sapiens sapiens* with a date of about 23,000 B.P. have been identified at Sinja, in the Sudan.

The Significance of "Sapienization"

The replacement of archaic *H. sapiens* by *H. sapiens sapiens* suggests that there is some adaptive advantage associated with a more globular shape and less rugged construction of the human cranium. This adaptive advan-

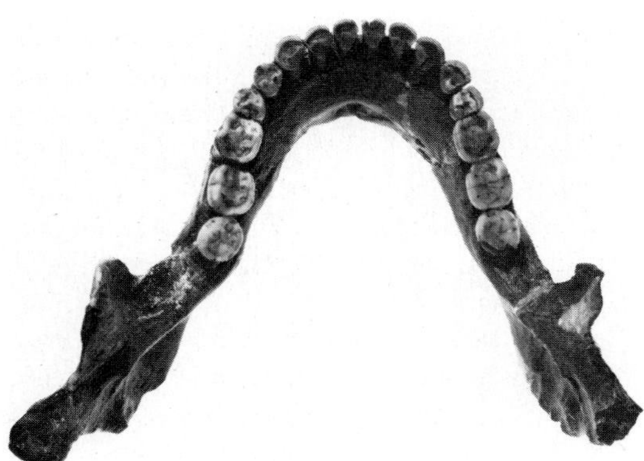

Figure 5.23 *TABŪN MANDIBLE*
A transitional Neandertal found on Mt. Carmel.

tage cannot consist simply in a greater volume of brain matter, since many archaic *H. sapiens* actually have greater cranial capacities than modern-day human beings. One suggestion is that the less rugged features represent a diminution of the muscularity of the neck and face as more efficient hunting-and-gathering technologies were developed with the evolution of culture in the late Pleistocene. Another related suggestion is that sapienization is really a kind of "feminization" brought about by a decrease in sexual dimorphism, again related to increased reliance on tools and weapons rather than on brute strength. Neither of these suggestions, however, really gets at the reason for the globular shape of the modern human cranium.

One of the most provocative and controversial ideas for explaining this globular shape is that it is related to the development of speech. Philip Lieberman and his associates have shown that the human vocal tract has a unique ability to produce certain vowel and consonant sounds as a function of the enlarged size of our pharynx—the sound-resonating portion of our throats between the vocal cords and the back of the mouth (Lieberman, Crelin, and Klatt 1972). The comparatively small size of the chimpanzee's pharynx, for example, seems to explain why we have been able to teach them to communicate with us in the medium of sign language but not in the medium of spoken words (see p. 400). The Neandertal vocal tract resembles the chimpanzee vocal tract (Fig. 5.25). This resemblance is related to the Neandertal's short neck and prognathic face. Lieberman concludes that it was only with the appearance of the fully rounded cranium and reduced prognathism of modern *H. sapiens sapiens* that the hominid vocal tract achieved the shape needed to make sounds such as [i], [u], or [a], which are essential components in all human languages. Further studies of the base of the skull of Neandertals and archaic *H. sapiens* have tended to confirm Lieberman's unfavorable picture of the location and size of the larynx and pharynx in pre–*sapiens sapi-*

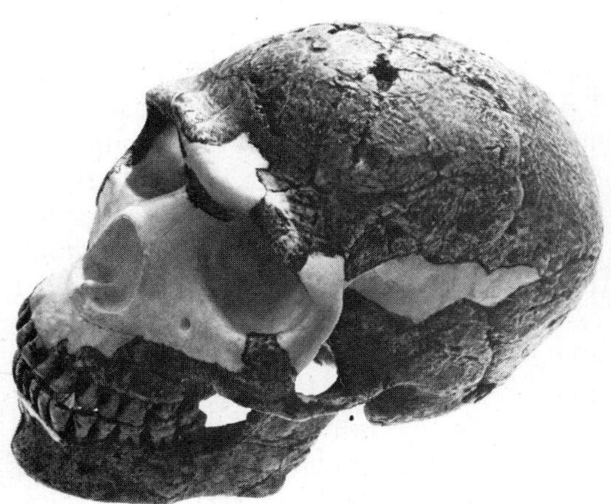

Figure 5.24 *SKHŪL NEANDERTAL*

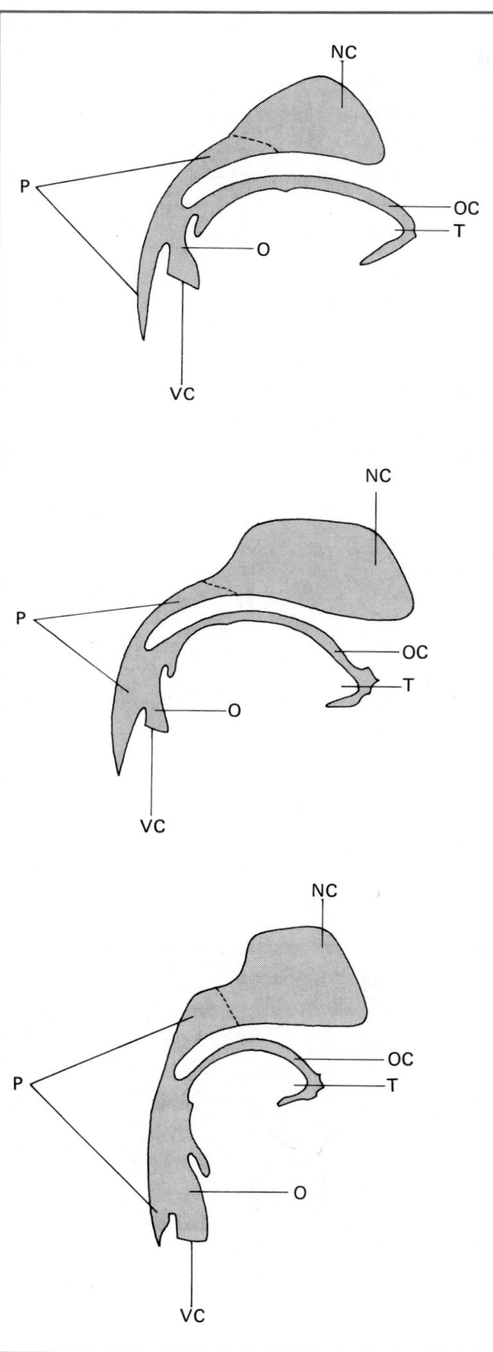

ens fossils (Laitman, Heimbuch, and Crelin 1979; Laitman and Heimbuch 1982; Krantz 1980). Other experts, however, challenge the validity of Lieberman's techniques for reconstructing the Neandertal vocal tract (Carlisle and Siegel 1974; Lieberman and Crelin 1974; Mann and Trinkaus 1974; Lieberman 1978).

Regardless of why sapienization took place, its results have immense significance for human destiny. For the past 35,000 years, there has been only one hominid genus, species, and subspecies in the world. In no part of the world, however remote, are there people whose nature is less human than the rest.

SUMMARY

The Plio-Pleistocene hominids were succeeded by progressively bigger-brained and culturally more proficient hominids. *H. erectus*, the earliest of these, inhabited a vast region including Africa and most of southern Eurasia and Indonesia. *H. erectus* originated the stone tool technology characterized by biface traditions and the Acheulian hand ax, learned to control fire, and learned to hunt big animals. The experts do not agree on where *H. erectus* first developed, and it is possible that there was a parallel development throughout Africa and southern Eurasia. After 500,000 B.P. *H. erectus* evolved into archaic forms of *H. sapiens*. It is impossible to say exactly when and where the first *H. sapiens* emerged, since the earliest archaic forms strongly resemble *H. erectus*.

Figure 5.25 *AIR PASSAGES OF CHIMP (top), NEANDERTAL (middle), AND HUMAN (bottom)*
P = pharynx; NC = Nasal cavity; T = tongue; O = opening of larynx into pharynx; VC = vocal chords.

Moreover, there appear to have been parallel developments throughout the Old World in Europe, Asia, Africa, and Indonesia. Hence, one can speak of a general process resulting in the appearance of big-brained hominids. The main evolutionary force operating throughout this period was selection for increased cultural capacity in the form of increased intelligence and language facility. It is not known when the first languages were spoken, but there is some anatomical evidence suggesting that the human speech apparatus was not perfected until after the appearance of archaic *H. sapiens* or even not until *H. sapiens sapiens*.

The date at which *H. sapiens sapiens* appears does not vary by more than a few thousand years in all the regions of the Old World. In the view of some experts the archaic *H. sapiens* such as *H. sapiens neanderthalensis* evolved directly into *H. sapiens sapiens*. Others see species or subspecies like the Neandertals or the Rhodesian, Omo, or Solo types as comprising divergent specialized and isolated populations which became extinct without contributing to the *H. sapiens sapiens* gene pool. All agree, however, that by 35,000 B.P. there was only one species of hominid left in the world and that no contemporary human population can be regarded as biologically more or less human than any other.

6 RACE, HUMAN VARIATION, AND THE FORCES OF EVOLUTION

This chapter concludes the discussion of the evolution of the hominids by focusing on the hereditary biological variations, or *polymorphisms*, that characterize different *Homo sapiens sapiens* populations around the globe. These variations are the source of obsolete scientific and popular concepts of race. How did these variations originate and what is their biological significance? They are best understood as the consequence of processes governed by the forces of evolution rather than as aspects of racial inheritance.

RACES AS POPULATIONS

In biological taxonomies, a *race* denotes a large, geographically isolated population within a species which has had little or no *gene flow* with other populations for a long time. Such a population may be considered an incipient species. If its isolation as a breeding unit were to continue, and if it were subject to selection pressures not found elsewhere, it could evolve into a divergent species.

There is no doubt that the species *H. sapiens sapiens* consists of different populations which can justifiably be labeled races. However, as we shall see in a moment, the races which most people distinguish, such as "black," "yellow," and "white" races (or "Negroids," "Mongoloids," and "Caucasoids"; or "African," "Asian," and "European"), are not taxonomically valid categories. The discrepancy between popular ideas about race and scientific principles of taxonomy is so great that an increasing number of anthropologists advocate that the concept of race ought to be dropped from anthropology textbooks (Montagu 1974; Fried 1968; Littlefield, Lieberman, Reynolds 1982). It would indeed be preferable to substitute the concept of *population* for the concept of race.

A population is simply any group of people whose members interbreed with more than random frequency and who exhibit different gene frequencies when compared with neighboring groups of people. The position adopted in this book is that expressed by Wenda Trevathan (1982:652):

> To sidestep race, treat it as though it did not exist as a valid or invalid concept in physical anthropology, is to take the ostrich approach at best, unethical at worst.

FREQUENCIES VERSUS ARCHETYPES

The definition of race as a population in which one or more genes occur with a particular frequency contradicts popular and once scientifically accepted notions about the racial divisions of *H. sapiens*. In the traditional view, *H. sapiens* was thought to consist of a fixed number of races. The same races that exist today were supposed to have existed in the past, perhaps from the very beginning of hominid evolution. Moreover, every true member of a race was thought to possess a particular assemblage of hereditary traits that always made it possible to identify everyone's racial origin.

These traditional race-defining traits consisted of external characteristics that are readily noticeable, such as coloration of the skin, hair, and eyes; hair form; amount of hair on body, face, and head; thickness of nose and lips; shape of the face and head; body mass and stature, and so forth.

The existence of several races of continental scope was inferred from "bundles" of these traits. Thus Europeans have pale skin, straight or wavy hair, large amounts of body hair, noses of narrow to medium width, and medium to tall stature. Native central Africans have dark brown or black skin; their hair form is wiry, the amount of body hair is medium, lips and noses are relatively thick, and stature is medium to tall. East Asians have pale to light brown skin, straight black hair, dark brown eyes with *epicanthic folds* (flaps over the eyes, giving them a slanted look), short to medium stature, and relatively hairless faces and bodies.

But several misconceptions about the nature of these "bundles" result from a failure to think of them in terms of gene frequencies and the principle of genetics. Many people imagine that there must be a racial archetype, that is, that somewhere there is a perfect representative of blacks or of whites who possesses all the attributes of his or her race. But it follows from the principle of genetics that the traits in the bundle will not stay together but will assort independently (see p. 13). Moreover, from the standpoint of the population being called a race, the frequencies of the various genes responsible for the traits in the bundle will change through time as a result of the forces of evolution (see p. 16). Therefore there is no fixed racial archetype.

The independently assortable nature of the traits used in popular racial taxonomies can also be seen in the complex patternings of skin color, hair form, and so forth found among populations who cannot be said to be black, white, or yellow (or Caucasoid, Negroid, or Mongoloid). At least one-half of the population of the world today displays bundles of racial traits not anticipated in popular sterotypes. For example, millions of people with thin lips and thin noses, wavy hair, but dark brown to black skin live in northern Africa. The native inhabitants of southern Africa have epicanthic eye folds, light brown to dark brown skin, and tightly spiraled hair. India has millions of people with straight or wavy hair, dark brown to black skin, and thin lips and thin noses. On the steppes of central Asia, epicanthic eye folds combine with wavy hair, light eyes, considerable body and facial hair, and pale skins. In Indonesia there is a high frequency of epicanthic folds, light to dark brown skin, wavy hair, thick noses, and thick lips. Varied combinations of brown to black skin, with contrastive forms and quantities of hair and facial features are found among the inhabitants of the Islands of Oceania. One of the most interesting bundles of traits occurs among the Ainu of northern Japan, who have light skins, thick brow ridges, and are among the hairiest people in the world. Finally, in Australia pale to dark brown skin color and wavy blond to brown hair are found. (Fig. 6.1).

The absurdity of trying to cram all populations into the mold of three or four racial categories is well illustrated by the system of racial identity currently employed in the United States. In the American folk taxonomy, if one parent is "black" and the other is "white," the child is "black" despite the fact that by the laws of genetics, half of the child's genes are from the black parent and half from the white. The practice of cramming people into racial pigeonholes becomes even more absurd when black ancestry is reduced to a single grandparent or great-grandparent. This produces the phenomenon of the "white" who is socially classified as "black." The arbitrary nature of this practice extends to many ostensibly scientific studies of "blacks" and "whites." Most American blacks have received a significant portion of their genes from recent European ancestors. When samples of American blacks are studied (as in intelligence testing, see

Figure 6.1 *NATIVE AUSTRALIANS*
The native Australians exhibit an unusual combination of light, wavy hair and dark skin.

Ch. 25), the assumption that they genetically represent Africans is incorrect. Both scientists and laymen would do well to emulate the Brazilians (Fig. 6.2), who identify racial types not by 3 or 4 terms but by 300 or 400 (Harris 1970; Meintel 1978).

Frequencies

A similar misconception about race is that some "pure-blooded" individuals are more representative than others of the racial type or "essence." Curly-haired, thick-lipped, dark-skinned Europeans are regarded as somehow less authentically European than light-skinned, light-eyed Europeans. But every individual whose genes enter a population's gene pool is an authentic member of that population. When speaking of Europeans as having straight to wavy hair, one must not forget that many Europeans have curly hair. Similarly, a small percentage of Europeans have epicanthic folds. Europeans who are less than 5 feet tall are no less European than those who are 7 feet tall. Similarly, both the 4½-foot Ituri Mbuti and the 7-foot Watusi are Africans. If one ignores individuals who do not conform to what a "typical" African is supposed to look like, one violates the concept of race as a population. The genes of everyone in the population's gene pool count equally in determining the population's gene frequencies.

Physical anthropologists sometimes divide Europeans into Baltics, Nordics, Alpines, Dinarics, and Mediterraneans. Adding similar subgroups around the world yields classifications that have tens or even hundreds of groupings. But within all such subgroups, traits like hair form, skin color, and stature continue to vary widely. Even if one takes each of the 2000 or so "tribes" known to ethnographers and declares each a "race," no individuals could be found who would represent the true or pure type of their groups (Hiernaux 1969).

CLINES

The genes responsible for differences in skin color, hair form, and the other traits used to define racial categories are not distributed randomly over the globe. They usually occur with gradually increasing or decreasing frequency from one population to another. Such distributions are called *clines*. For example, the frequency of the genes responsible for dark skin color gradually increases as one moves from Mediterranean Europe south along the Nile or across the Sahara

Figure 6.2 *BRAZILIAN PORTRAITS*
The great variety of facial types in Brazil suggests that it is futile to think about human beings in terms of a small number of fixed and sharply distinct races.

		4	10								
		5	11	17	21	25	29	34			
		6	12	18	22	26	30	35		39	
1	2	7	13	19	23	27	31	36	37	40	
		8	14				32		38	41	42
	3	9	15				33				43
			16	20	24	28					

1 Mauritania
2 Tunisia
3 Eq. Guinea
4 Sweden
5 Denmark
6 Italy
7 Libya
8 Niger
9 Burundi
10 Finland
11 Hungary
12 Greece
13 Egypt
14 Sudan
15 Ethiopia
16 Zanzibar
17 Ukraine
18 Iraq
19 Yemen
20 Madagascar
21 USSR
22 Iran
23 Pakistan
24 Mauritius
25 USSR
26 Afghanistan
27 Pakistan
28 Maldive Is.
29 Tuva (USSR)
30 Nepal
31 India
32 India
33 India
34 Mongolia
35 China
36 Burma
37 Laos
38 Malaysia
39 Japan
40 Philippines
41 Indonesia
42 Ponape
43 Fiji

Figure 6.3 *UNITY OF HUMANKIND*
There are no sharp breaks in the distribution of racial types across Africa and Eurasia. (Only men are shown because of the difficulty of obtaining a comparable set of photos of women in which the women would all be dressed alike and have similar hairdos. This difficulty results from the domination by men of U.N. missions and consular posts.)

and into central Africa. There are no sharp breaks anywhere along the way. Similarly, the incidence of epicanthic folds gradually increases from west to east across Asia, whereas the frequency of wavy hair gradually increases in the reverse direction, toward Europe (Fig. 6.3).

Clines result from two evolutionary processes: gene flow and selection. One can expect a gradual change in gene frequencies with distance as a result of the gradual spread of genes through adjacent populations. A similar pattern will result if there is an adaptive advantage for a gene and if that advantage varies with latitude, longitude, or altitude. Skin color, for example, has a clinal pattern from lower to higher latitudes related to the gradually changing intensity of the sun's rays from equatorial to Arctic regions (see below).

In either case, clines contradict the popular notion that there are archetypes and purebloods and sharp differences between the members of different races. And when the clines are a result of gene flow, they contradict the scientific definition of race as population that breeds in isolation from other populations.

Blood Groups and Race

The more genetic traits that one uses to define races, the less likely it is that the traits will form a bundle that vary in a coherent fashion from one population to another. This can be seen in the case of the alleles which determine the immunological properties of blood. These alleles at one time were thought to be the best possible source of a genetic classification of the races. Unlike traits such as skin color or hair form, the precise genetic mechanism for the inheritance of the blood groups is well understood, and thousands of controlled blood-group studies have been made throughout the world. The best-known series is the *ABO system*, which is based on three alleles, A, B, and O at a single locus. All human beings have a genotype that puts them in either blood group phenotype A, B, AB, or O. (We shall ignore the complexities of the subtypes which, in any event, make the distribution even more erratic.) The relationship between the alleles and phenotypes is as follows:

Genotype	*Blood Group Phenotype*
OO	O
AO	A
AA	A
BO	B
BB	B
AB	AB

The O allele has the widest distribution, occurring on all continents and crosscutting all racial divisions (see maps on pp. 101–102). Type O occurs with a frequency of 70–80 percent in Scotland, central Africa, Siberia, and Australia. Type A is equally unmindful of traditional racial boundaries. Africa, India, and southern and northern China all have 10–20 percent frequencies, while Japan, Scotland, and much of aboriginal Australia are in the 20–29 percent bracket. Asians have frequencies of type B ranging from 10–30 percent, yet the native American, whose ancestors were Asians are in the 0–5 percent range, a frequency shared by the Australian aborigines. West Africa and eastern Europe both show type B frequencies of about 15–20 percent. Similar racially nonconforming distributions are characteristic of other blood systems, such as MNS and Rh (cf. Hulse 1973; Kelso 1974), although some degree of match-up can be achieved by using the statistical technique known as multivariate analysis (Cavalli-Sforza and Edwards 1965; Stern 1973:319).

THE EXPLANATION OF HUMAN POLYMORPHISMS

As many as 30 percent of all human gene loci are estimated to have one or more alleles. The resultant variations in genotypes and phenotypes are called *polymorphisms*. Traditional ideas about race make very small contributions toward understanding why these polymorphisms occur and why they are distributed unevenly from one population to the next.

The failure of the idea of racial archetypes to explain the distribution of polymorphisms accounts in large measure for the declining interest which physical anthropologists have shown in using the concept of race (Livingstone 1982).

Physical anthropologists have found it much more productive to approach the problem of genetic polymorphisms from a dynamic evolutionary viewpoint and to study the role of natural selection and the other evolutionary forces in bringing about variations in gene frequencies.

For example, there is considerable evidence linking the ABO series with different resistances to diseases which may affect reproductive success such as smallpox, bubonic plague, and food poisoning by toxic

DISTRIBUTION OF ALLELES OF THE ABO BLOOD GROUP SYSTEM

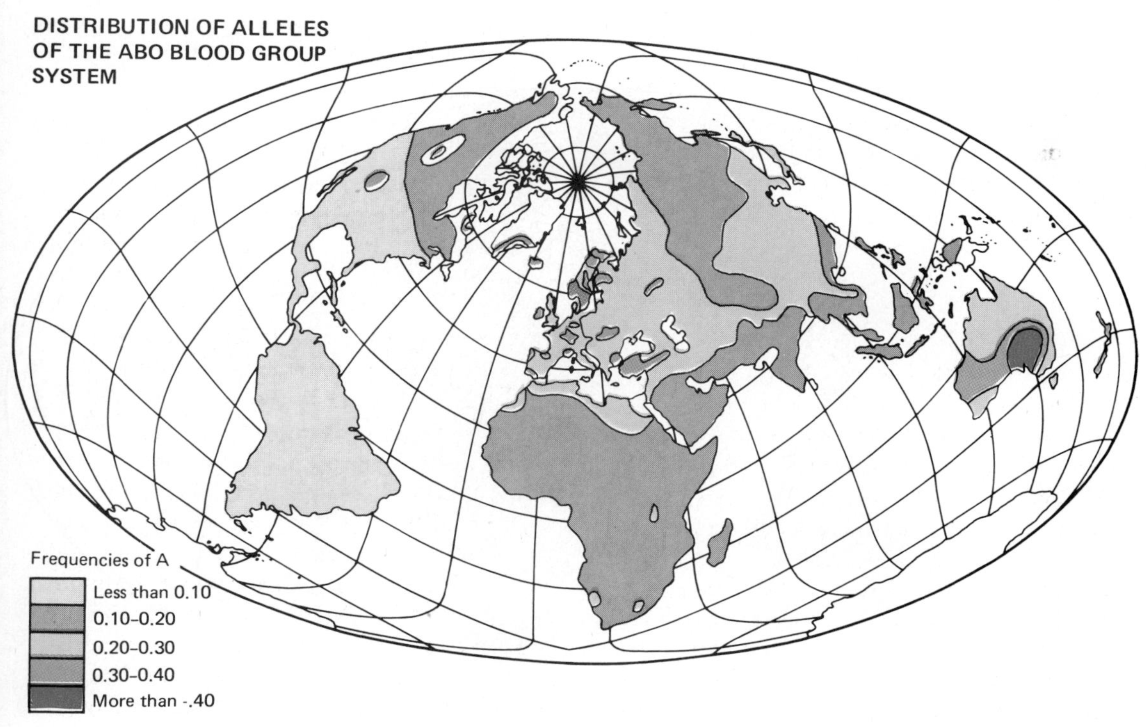

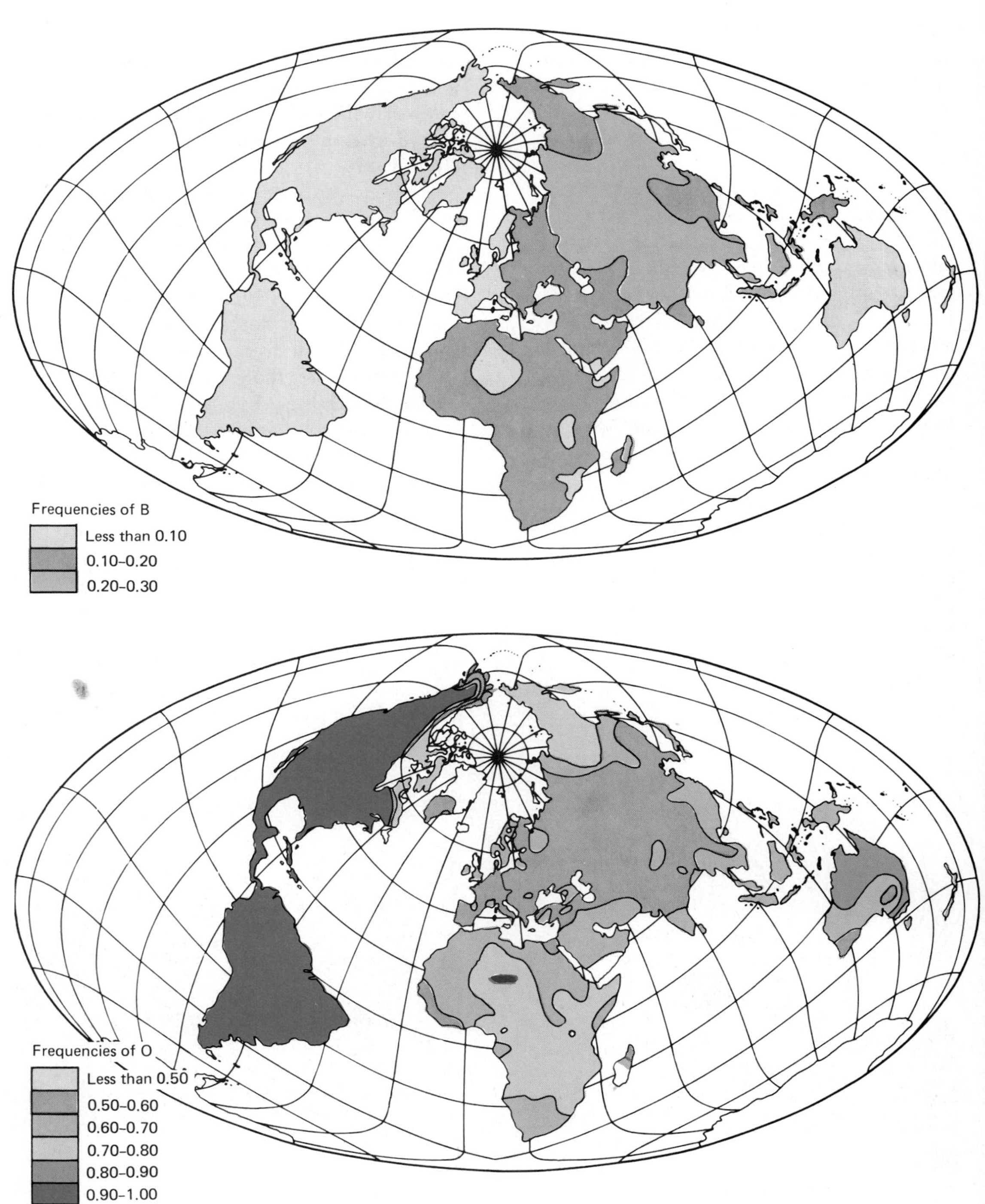
Frequencies of B
Less than 0.10
0.10–0.20
0.20–0.30
Frequencies of O
Less than 0.50
0.50–0.60
0.60–0.70
0.70–0.80
0.80–0.90
0.90–1.00

bacteria. (There are also linkages with duodenal ulcers and stomach cancer, but these may occur too late in life to affect reproductive success.) Hence the explanations for blood type polymorphism may have to be sought primarily in the history of transient exposures of different populations to different diseases rather than in racial ancestry.

One of the most interesting cases of polymorphism is the allele responsible for the disease known as *sickle-cell anemia.* The red blood cells of persons afflicted with this congenital defect are sickle shaped instead of round and are incapable of transporting normal amounts of oxygen (Fig. 6.4). An individual falls victim to this potentially lethal defect only when both parents carry the allele for sickling. Individuals who have inherited the allele from one parent show only mild symptoms. The sickling allele was first noted among Africans and among Americans of African descent. Its highest frequencies, about 20 percent, occur in central Africa; but it was discovered that the same allele also occurs in Greece, Turkey, Yemen, India, and Burma. In each of these countries, the sickling allele occurs most frequently in zones of endemic malaria (see maps on p. 104). It was found that individuals who have the deleterious allele in a heterozygous form have a high degree of resistance to this disease. In areas of endemic malaria, the allele in a heterozygous form protects more individuals from death due to malaria than it kills in its homozygous form as a result of anemia. Thus it seems likely that natural selection is responsible for the distribution of the trait.

Another interesting polymorphism is the ability to taste the bitter substance *phenylthiocarbamide,* or PTC. Tasters have the dominant allele T whereas nontasters are homozygous for the recessive allele t. The frequency of t ranges from 60 percent among Asian Indians to 10 percent among native Americans. A possible explanation may lie in the fact that goiter, produced by a malfunction of the thyroid gland, is more common among nontasters than among tasters. PTC chemically resembles certain substances which inhibit thyroid function. Hence the ability to taste PTC as a bitter substance may be related to the ability to detect any foods that adversely affect

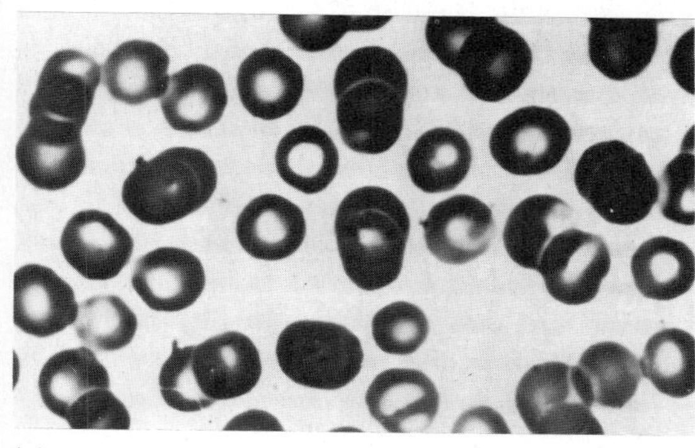
(a)

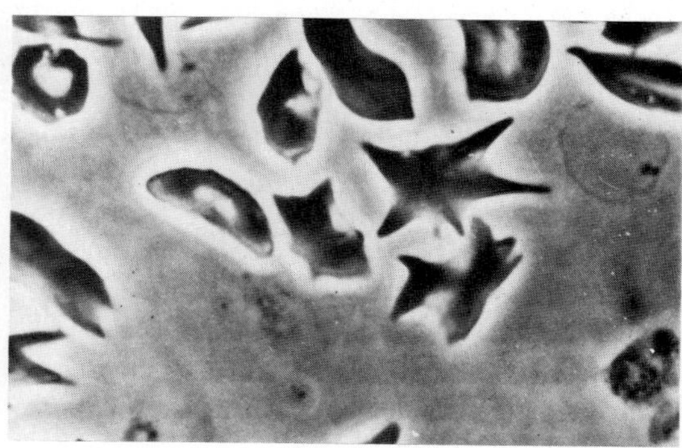
(b)

Figure 6.4 *NORMAL BLOOD CELLS (a) AND SICKLING BLOOD CELLS (b).*

DISTRIBUTION OF
FALCIPARUM MALARIA
THE OLD WORLD
Modified Briesemeister Projection
Areal Scale 1:150,000,000²

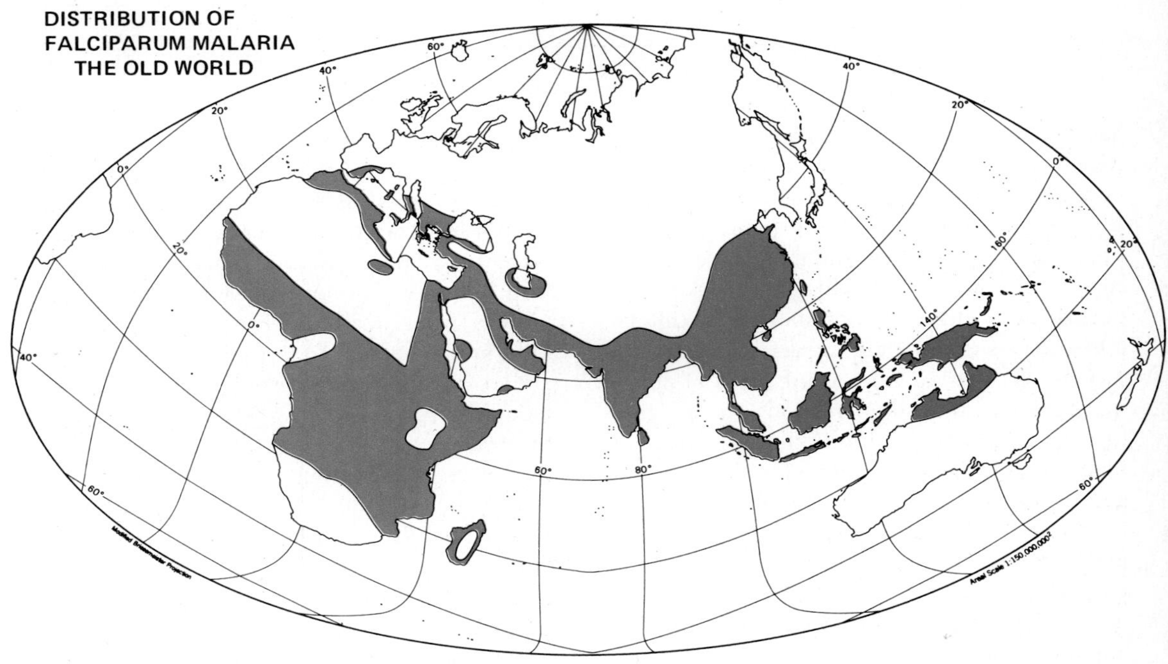

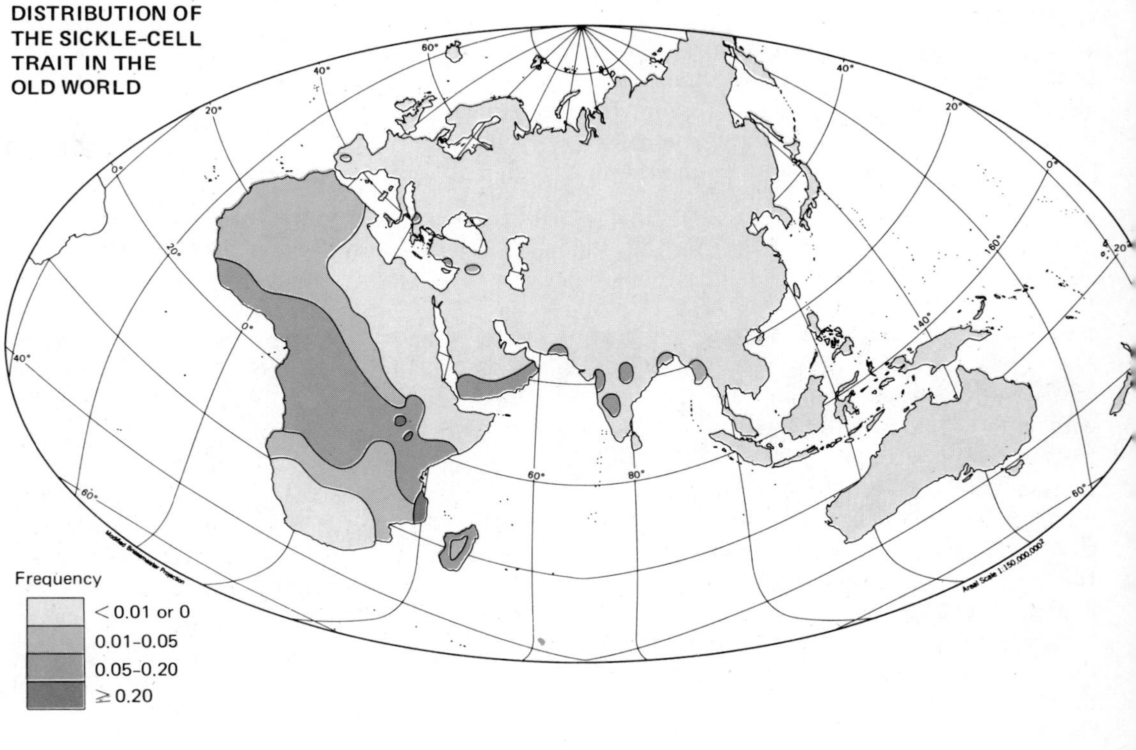

DISTRIBUTION OF
THE SICKLE-CELL
TRAIT IN THE
OLD WORLD
Modified Briesemeister Projection
Areal Scale 1:150,000,000²
Frequency
< 0.01 or 0
0.01–0.05
0.05–0.20
≥ 0.20

thyroid function (Cavalli-Sforza and Bodmer 1971:215).

Lactase deficiency is still another polymorphism. The ability to digest milk is dependent on the ability to produce the enzyme lactase, which breaks down the complex milk sugar lactose into simpler sugars. Most adult mammals, including most *H. sapiens*, lose the ability to produce lactase as juveniles or adults and suffer severe forms of indigestion when they consume large quantities of unfermented milk. This presumably has an adaptive value since it prevents competition between mature individuals and infants for mother's milk. However, in populations whose subsistence depends on drinking large quantities of milk from dairy animals, there is a higher incidence of the allele which makes it possible for adults to produce lactase. Where, as in the case of northern Europeans, fluid milk was the principal source of calcium, selection for lactase-sufficient adults was especially intense (Harrison 1975; Paige and Bayless 1978; Simoons 1982, Harris 1983).

POLYMORPHISMS AND RACIAL ANTIQUITY

Scientists formerly believed that the races that we see today always existed in the past. This idea can be traced back to pre-Darwinian biologists, who believed that species were unrelated to each other and that each species had its immutable nature fixed by God. Although no anthropologists propose that racial taxons are absolutely immutable, some, nonetheless, continue to argue that today's major races were already in existence hundreds of thousands of years ago (Coon 1962:658).

The principal difficulty with this view is that the classification of races is based primarily on external and superficial traits such as skin color, hair form, eye color, and so forth. These leave no traces of themselves in the fossil skulls and bones that constitute the only source of our knowledge about archaic *H. sapiens*. Therefore, no one knows what the total range of human variation was like 50,000 years ago. Modern-day images of what the races look like ought not to be projected back upon our remote ancestors. Most of our ancestors were probably neither blacks nor whites nor Asians nor anything else that would be familiar to us.

The concept of a race as an ancient breeding isolate is further contradicted by consideration of the causes of genetic polymorphisms. As we have just seen, human polymorphisms may result from selection of advantageous alleles. If traits used for racial classification are strongly adaptive, they cannot be used as evidence of common biological descent.

For example, suppose a group with a low-sickling frequency moves into an area of endemic malaria inhabited by an unrelated people who have a high frequency of sickling alleles. After a number of generations (predictable by genetic equations) the frequency of sickling will increase among the immigrants, and after a relatively short time the natives and the immigrants will become indistinguishable with respect to the sickling trait. Yet their ancestors were quite unrelated.

An even more rapid distortion of phylogenetic relationships will take place if there is cultural as well as natural selection in favor of one genotype at the expense of another. Cultural selection may come into play in the form of differential treatment of infants or potential mates on the basis of some trait that may be directly or indirectly linked to adaptive biological consequences.

To take a hypothetical example, suppose that epicanthic folds confer an adaptive advantage upon peoples who live and hunt amid the glare of arctic snows. The greater success of the heavy-lidded hunter might gradually receive recognition in the form of an aesthetic bias in favor of individuals with the epicanthic trait. Since infanticide was probably one of the most important means of population control during prehistoric times (see p. 223), this aesthetic bias might influence the decision not to rear a particular child. If cultural selection of this sort were added to the higher death rate among hunters who lacked the epicanthic fold, very rapid change in gene frequencies would follow, especially since archaic human populations were very small.

Distributions of several of the traditional racial traits have been studied for clues concerning their possible adaptive significance. Results thus far have been inconclusive. A number of interesting suggestions have related racial differences to temperature, humidity, and other climatological factors. For example, the long narrow noses of Europeans may have resulted from the need to raise extremely cold, damp air to body temperature before it reached the lungs. The generally rounded squat form of the Eskimos can be viewed as another type of adaptation to cold. A spherical shape presents a maximum of body mass to a minimum of body surface. This links maximum heat production to maximum heat conservation (i.e., the greater the biomass, the more heat generated; the smaller the surface area, the less heat that is lost). A tall, thin body form, on the other hand, combines a minimum of body mass with a maximum of body surface leading to maximum heat loss (Fig. 6.5). This may explain the characteristics of the tall, thin Nilotic Africans who inhabit regions of intense arid heat. Finally, some physical anthropologists explain the tightly wound hair spirals known as peppercorns, found among the native peoples of southern Africa, as heat-dispersing adaptations. By leaving empty spaces on the head, the peppercorn "facilitates heat loss at high temperature" (Coon 1965:112).

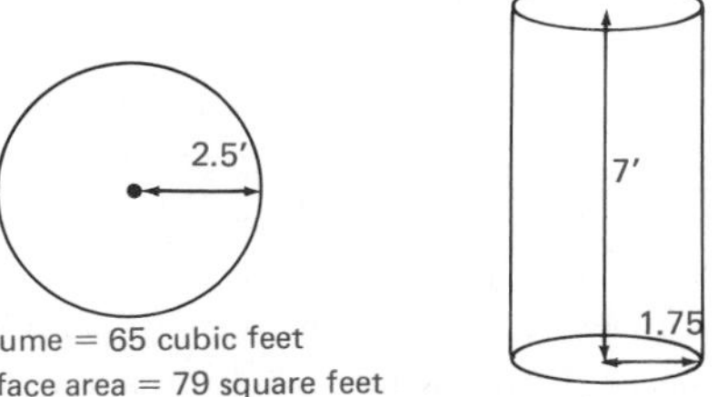

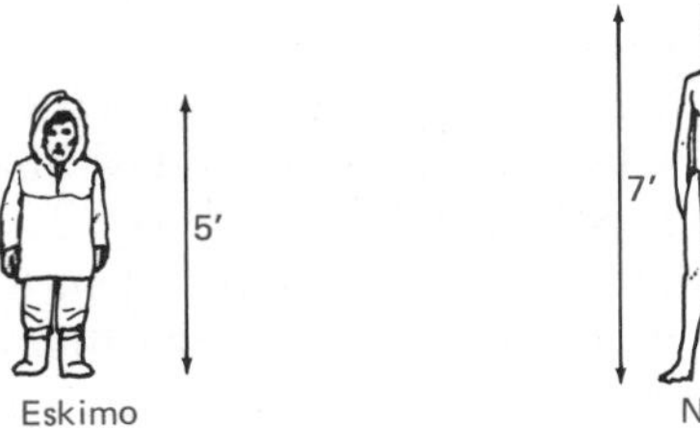

Sphere and cylinder have equal volumes. But cylinder has larger surface area. Therefore, it radiates heat more efficiently than sphere. Eskimo body-build is adapted to conserving heat, and Nilotic body-build to radiating it.

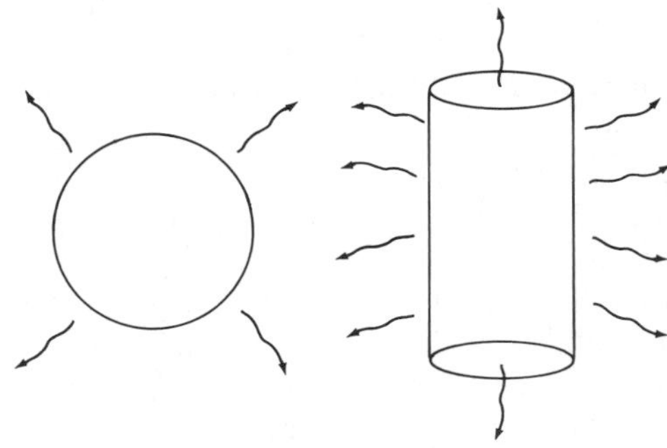

Figure 6.5 *HEAT DISPERSAL AND BODY SHAPE*

More Polymorphism: The Case of Skin Color

Most human beings are neither very fair nor very dark, but brown. The extremely fair skin of northern Europeans and their descendants, and the very black skins of central Africans and their descendants, are special adaptations. They probably represent the divergent outcome of natural and cultural processes acting on earlier brown-skinned ancestors shared by modern-day blacks and whites—ancestors who lived possibly as recently as 15,000 to 10,000 B.P.

Human skin owes its color to the presence of particles known as *melanin*, the same substance which allows lizards to change their color and which makes octopus ink black. In humans the primary function of melanin is to protect the upper levels of the skin from being damaged by the ultraviolet wavelength of sunlight that penetrates the atmosphere. This radiation poses a critical problem for our species because we lack the dense coat of hair that acts as a sunscreen for most mammals. Hairlessness has its advantages: it allows abundant sweat glands to cool our bodies through evaporation, thereby bestowing on our species the unique ability to pursue and run down swift game animals over long distances during the midday heat (besides providing the spectacle of 15,000 runners trying to win the Boston marathon). But hairlessness has its price. It exposes us to two kinds of radiation hazards: ordinary sunburn with its blisters, rashes, and risk of infection; and skin cancers, including malignant melanoma, one of the deadliest diseases known. Melanin is the body's first line of defense against these afflictions. The more melanin particles, the darker the skin, the less risk of sunburn and all forms of skin cancer (Malkenson and Keane 1983).

Malignant melanoma is primarily a disease of light-skinned individuals of northern European parentage with a history of exposure to intense solar radiation. One of the highest rates of all forms of skin cancer is found in Australia where the white population is primarily of northern European descent. Solar radiation is implicated for two reasons: the rate quadrupled coincident with an increase in outdoor sports and the wearing of scanty attire; and the rate varies with the amount and intensity of solar radiation from north to south (Ariel 1981).

In the United States, where one-third of all new cancers per year are skin cancers, the rate of malignant melanoma increased sixfold from 1935 to 1975, again in tandem with the rise in popularity of outdoor sports and the relaxation of dress codes. Predictably, malignant melanoma occurs most frequently among urban whites who live in cities like Dallas and Fort Worth and least frequently among those who live in Detroit or Minneapolis. Men, more likely to go shirtless than women, get it on the upper torso. Women get it on their legs, less frequently on their backs, and practically never on their seldom-exposed breasts (ibid.).

In Europe the evidence seems contradictory: Norwegians get it 20 times more frequently than sun-drenched Spaniards. But there is an obvious explanation. Not only are Norwegians and Swedes generally fairer than Spaniards, they have taken to nude and seminude sunbathing with fanatic zeal, at home during their short summer and abroad during their winter vacations.

In contrast, malignant melanoma rarely occurs among heavily pigmented central Africans and their New World descendants. An added twist is that when very dark-

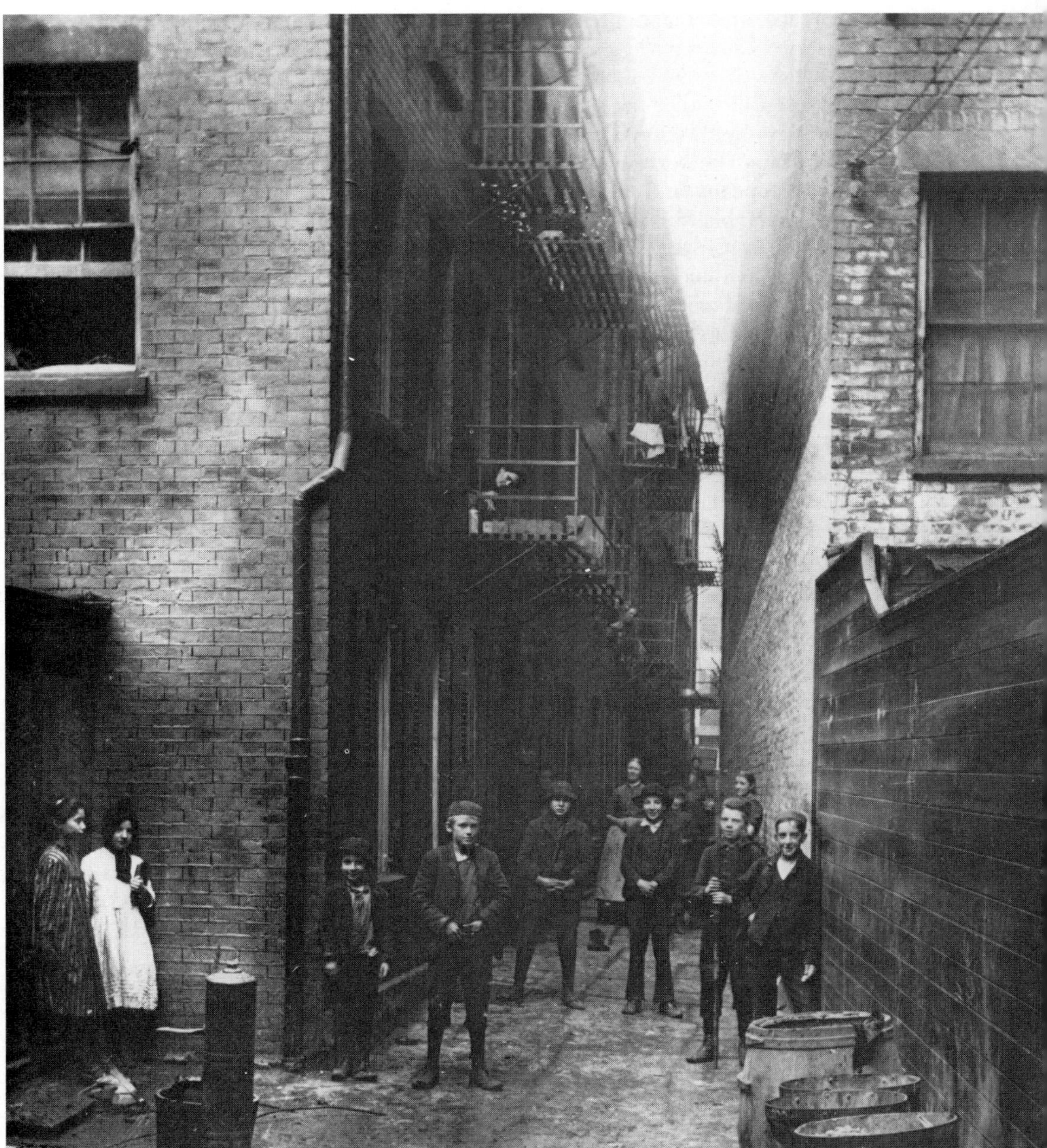

Figure 6.6 *MULLEN'S ALLEY, 1888*
Lacking both sunlight and dietary sources of vitamin D, the children of the urban industrial slums fell victim to rickets, despite their light skin color.

skinned individuals get malignant melanoma, they get it on the most depigmented parts of their bodies—the soles of their feet, palms of their hands, and their lips. To paraphrase Irving Ariel, a leading authority on skin cancer, black is certainly beautiful when it comes to malignant melanoma (ibid.).

If exposure to solar radiation had nothing but harmful effects, natural selection would have favored inky black as the color for all human populations. But the sun's rays do not present an unmitigated threat. As it falls on the skin, sunshine converts a fatty substance in the epidermis into vitamin D. (The substance is 7-dehydrocholesterol, and the conversion process is known as photolysis.) The blood carries vitamin D from the skin to the intestines (technically making it a hormone rather than a vitamin), where it plays a vital role in the absorption of calcium. In turn, calcium is vital for the growth and strength of every bone in the body. Without it, bones become soft and grotesquely deformed, and people fall victim to the crippling diseases—rickets and osteomalacia (Figs. 6.6 and 6.7). In women, calcium deficiencies can manifest themselves in deformed birth canals which make childbirth lethal for both mother and fetus (Malkenson and Keane 1983; Molnar 1983:162 ff).

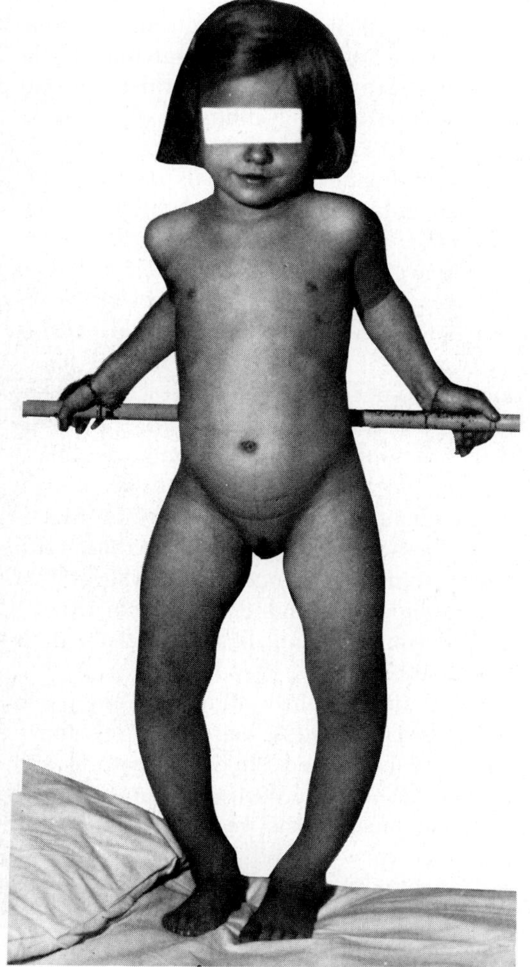
Figure 6.7 *RICKETS*
A young victim.

While vitamin D can be obtained from a few foods—primarily the oils and livers of marine fish—inland populations must rely on the sun's rays and their own skins for the supply of this crucial substance. The particular color of a human population's skin therefore represents in large degree a trade-off between the hazards of too much versus too little solar radiation: acute sunburn and skin cancer on one hand, and rickets and osteomalacia on the other. It is this trade-off that largely accounts for the preponderance of brown people in the world and for the general tendency for skin color to be darkest among equatorial populations and lightest among populations dwelling at higher latitudes.

At middle latitudes the skin follows a strategy of changing colors with the seasons. Around the Mediterranean basin, for example, exposure to the summer sun is high risk for cancer but low risk for rickets; more melanin is produced and people grow darker (i.e., they get suntans). Winter reduces the risk of sunburn and cancer; less melanin is produced and the tan wears off.

The correlation between skin color and latitude is not perfect because other factors such as the availability of foods containing vitamin D and calcium, regional cloud cover during the winter, amount of clothing worn, and cultural preferences may work for or against the predicted relationship. Arctic-dwelling Eskimos, for example, are not as light-skinned as expected, but their habitat affords them a diet that is exceptionally rich in both vitamin D and calcium.

The Mediterranean farming and dairying people who settled northern Europe about 6000 years ago (see p. 166) must have been acutely endangered by rickets. As they migrated northward they had to cover themselves with heavy garments for protection against the long, cold, cloudy winters. But unlike the Eskimo, their farming and dairying economy did not provide them with marine fish rich in vitamin D. Fair-skinned, nontanning individuals who could utilize the weakest and briefest doses of sunlight to synthesize vitamin D would have been strongly favored by natural selection. During the frigid winters, only a small circle of a child's face could be left to peek out at the sun through the heavy clothing, thereby favoring the survival of individuals with translucent patches of pink on their cheeks characteristic of many northern Europeans.

Depigmentation went a long way toward solving the problem of producing vitamin D in the skins of these displaced Mediterraneans. But vitamin D by itself will not prevent rickets. There also has to be an adequate intake of calcium. The dairy animals which the migrants had with them were a splendid resource in this regard. Not only is milk rich in calcium but it has recently been discovered that the sugar in milk—lactose—also facilitates the absorption of calcium (Simoons 1982). But in order to take advantage of the antiricketic properties of milk, another genetic obstacle had to be overcome. The migrants had to acquire the ability to digest lactose in adulthood as well as childhood. As discussed above, malabsorption of large quantities of lactose leads to debilitating cramps and diarrhea, conditions that are adverse for calcium absorption (or digestion in general). So it is no accident that northern Europeans have both distinctively fair skins and an unusual ability to digest copious quantities of fresh fluid milk.

If light-skinned individuals on the average had only 2 percent more children per generation, the changeover in their skin-color-gene frequencies could have begun 5000 years ago and reached present levels well before the beginning of the Christian era (Cavalli-Sforza 1972). But natural selection need not have acted alone. Cultural selection may also have played a role. It seems likely that whenever the migrants consciously or unconsciously had to decide which infants to nourish and which to neglect, the advantage would go to those with lighter skin, experience having shown that such individuals tended to grow up to be taller, stronger, and healthier than their darker siblings.

To account for the evolution of black skin in equatorial latitudes, one has merely to reverse the combined effects of natural and cultural selection. With the sun directly overhead most of the year, and clothing a hindrance to work and survival, vitamin D was never in short supply. Skin cancer was the main problem, and what nature started, culture amplified. Darker infants were favored by parents because experience showed that they grew up to be freer of disfiguring and lethal malignancies.

It is interesting to note that the darkest-skinned Africans inhabit the most heavily forested parts of Africa. One of the negative aspects of heavy pigmentation is that the skin absorbs heat in direct proportion to its darkness. Thus it is known that blacks are about 15 percent more susceptible to heat stroke than whites (Baker 1958). Increased susceptibility to heat stroke might be a serious disadvantage in hunting and running down animals in open or savannah habitats. If hunting took place primarily in tropical forest settings, the negative effect of very dark skin might not be significant.

SUMMARY

Modern *H. sapiens* is a polymorphic species consisting of many partially isolated breeding populations some of which have traditionally been assigned to the taxonomic category, race. With its implications of a subspecies on the verge of branching off to form a new species, the term race is strictly speaking a taxonomically inappropriate designation for any contemporary human population.

Modern concepts of populations and genetic processes cannot be reconciled with the traditional division of the species into three or four major races. In the traditional view these races were like archetypes whose essence was expressed by "pure-blooded" individuals and whose distinctiveness was as old as the species. As populations, however, groups such as Europeans, East Asians, and Africans possess no such attributes. First of all, there is no individual who can be considered a "pureblood" who is more representative of a population than others of "mixed blood." To have any scientific validity, the characterization of a population must refer to frequencies of genes, and individuals do not have frequencies of genes. Second, the traditional racial taxons cannot be reconciled with the existence of genetic clines associated with intermediate or transitional gene frequencies. There is no justification for regarding these clines as the product of hybridization between hypothetical pure races which once existed in the past. Instead, the clines point to the existence of constantly shifting gene frequencies resulting from natural selection, drift, and gene flow. Finally, the traditional racial divisions are based on a bundle of traits which do not vary coordinately with the gene frequencies of other genes such as those involved in the ABO blood groups. Such nonconforming distributions are predictable from Mendel's law of independent assortment.

By setting aside the traditional concept of race, physical anthropologists can place the study of human polymorphisms on a sound genetic and evolutionary basis. The ABO blood groupings, sickle-cell anemia, and PTC tasting are examples of polymorphisms whose genetic mechanisms are well understood. With additional research it may eventually be possible to explain the distribution of the alleles responsible for these traits in terms of natural selection in relation to medical and nutritional factors. The implication of such factors in the explanation of many polymorphisms casts additional doubt on the antiquity of present-day races. Selection can rapidly alter the frequency of an allele in a convergent direction among populations that have been genetically isolated or in divergent directions in populations that have high rates of gene flow. The extent to which features such as stature, hair form, nose shape, and epicanthic folding can be explained by adaptive processes remains to be seen. Heat and cold stress have been viewed as possible sources of selection pressure for these traits. A complex set of adaptive processes involving melanin, solar radiation, skin cancer, lactose malabsorption, and vitamin D deficiency have been implicated in the correlation between pale skin and northern habitats and dark skin and tropical habitats.

7 THE NATURE OF CULTURE

In this chapter we lay the basis for the study of cultural evolution and of cultural differences and similarities. Certain general features of human cultures will be discussed and a strategy for studying cultural differences and similarities will be described.

DEFINITIONS OF CULTURE AND SOCIETY

As we have seen, *culture* refers to the socially acquired traditions which appear in rudimentary form among mammals, especially Primates. When anthropologists speak of a human culture, they usually mean the total socially acquired life-style of a group of people including patterned, repetitive ways of thinking, feeling, and acting (Fig. 7.1).

The definition of culture as consisting of patterns of acting (behavior), as well as patterns of thought and feeling, follows the precedent set by Sir Edward Burnett Tylor who was the founder of academic anthropology in the English-speaking world and the author of the first general anthropology textbook:

> Culture . . . taken in its wide ethnographic sense is that complex whole which includes knowledge, belief, art, morals, law, custom, and any other capabilities and habits acquired by man as a member of society. The condition of culture among the various societies of mankind, in so far as it is capable of being investigated on general principles, is a subject apt for the study of laws of human thought and action (1871:1).

Some anthropologists, however, restrict the meaning of culture exclusively to the mental *rules* for acting and speaking shared by the members of a given society. These rules are seen as constituting a kind of "grammar" for behavior. Actions are then regarded as "social" rather than "cultural" phenomena. It is this distinction that some anthropologists seek to make when they write about social anthropology as distinguished from cultural anthropology (Goodenough 1970). No confusion can result from the more inclusive definition if care is taken to indicate whether the culturally determined ideas inside people's heads or the culturally determined activities of their bodies, or both, are being discussed.

There is one other kind of distinction between social and cultural that is also quite common. Some sociologists and anthropologists employ the term *social* to refer to the relationship between the groups within a society. In this book, social groups and the relation of one social group to another will be regarded as aspects of culture (mental and behavioral). The family, for example, is a social group that conforms to and exhibits a particular society's culture of domestic life.

What then is the definition of society? The term *society* signifies a group of people who share a common habitat and who are dependent on each other for their survival and well-being. Some societies, where marrying within the group prevails, are coincident with populations as defined in the previous chapter. But where ethnic, racial, and other kinds of in-marrying groups exist *within* the society, the society as a whole cannot be considered a biological population. Nonetheless, the boundaries between societies are usually characterized by breeding discontinuities and lowered rates of gene flow.

In referring to patterns of culture characteristic of certain kinds of groups within a society, anthropologists often use the term *subculture*. This term indicates that the culture of a society is not uniform for all its members. Thus, even small societies may

Figure 7.1 *TECHNIQUES OF EATING*
Power of enculturation is vividly apparent in diverse eating practices. Chinese girls eating rice.

have male and female subcultures, while in larger and more complex societies one encounters subcultures associated with ethnic, religious, and class distinctions.

Finally, the term *sociocultural* should be noted. This term is short for "social and cultural" and is useful as a reminder that society and culture form a unit or a system.

ENCULTURATION AND CULTURAL RELATIVISM

The culture of a society tends to be similar in many respects from one generation to the next. In part this continuity in life-ways is maintained by the process known as *enculturation*. Enculturation is a partially conscious and partially unconscious learning experience whereby the older generation invites, induces, and compels the younger generation to adopt traditional ways of thinking and behaving. Thus, Chinese children use chopsticks instead of forks, speak a tonal language, and dislike milk because they have been enculturated into Chinese culture rather than into the culture of the United States. Enculturation is primarily based upon the control that the older generation exercises over the means of rewarding and punishing children. Each generation is programmed not only to replicate the behavior of the previous generation but to reward behavior that conforms to the patterns of its own enculturation experience and to punish, or at least not reward, behavior that does not so conform (Fig. 7.2).

The concept of enculturation (despite its limitations as discussed below) occupies a central position in the distinctive outlook of modern anthropology. Failure to comprehend the role of enculturation in the maintenance of each group's patterns of behavior and thought lies at the heart of the phenomenon known as *ethnocentrism*. Ethnocentrism is the belief that one's own patterns of behavior are always natural, good, beautiful, or important, and that strangers, to the extent that they live differently, live by savage, inhuman, disgusting, or irrational standards. People who are intolerant of cultural differences usually ignore the following fact: Had they been enculturated within another group, all those supposedly savage, inhuman, disgusting, and irrational life-styles

(a)

(b)

(c)

(d)

Figure 7.2 *PASSING CULTURE ON*
In Bali *(a)* a man reads to his grandchildren from a script on narrow bamboo strips. In Afghanistan *(b)*, father with son reading from Koran. In Moscow *(c)*, a ballet class. In Taos, New Mexico *(d)*, father teaching child to dance.

would now be their own. Exposure of the fallacy of ethnocentrism leads to tolerance for and curiosity about cultural differences.

Anthropologists are tolerant of and curious about cultural differences. Some, however, have gone further and adopted the viewpoint known as *cultural relativism*, according to which each cultural pattern is regarded as being intrinsically as worthy of respect as all the rest. Although cultural relativism is a scientifically acceptable way of relating to cultural differences, it is not the only scientifically admissible attitude. Like everybody else, anthropologists make ethical judgments about the value of different kinds of cultural patterns. One need not regard cannibalism, warfare, human sacrifice, and poverty as worthy cultural achievements in order to carry out an objective study of these phenomena. Nor is there anything wrong with setting out to study certain cultural patterns because one wants to change them. Scientific objectivity does not arise from having no biases—everyone is biased—but from taking care not to let one's biases influence the result of the research process (Jorgensen 1971).

LIMITATIONS OF THE ENCULTURATION CONCEPT

Under present world conditions no special wisdom is required to realize that enculturation cannot account for a considerable portion of the life-styles of existing social groups. It is clear that replication of cultural patterns from one generation to the next is never complete (Fig. 7.3). Old patterns are not always faithfully repeated in successive generations, and new patterns are continually being added (Fig. 7.4). Recently the rate of innovation and nonreplication in the industrial societies has reached proportions alarming to adults who were programmed to expect that their children's behavior would duplicate their own. This lack of cross-generational continuity has been called the *generation gap*. As explained by Margaret Mead:

> Today, nowhere in the world are there elders who know what the children know; no matter how remote and simple the societies are in which the children live. In the past there were always some elders who knew more than any children in terms of their experience of having grown up within a cultural system. Today there are none. It is not only that parents are no longer guides, but that there are no guides, whether one seeks them in one's own country or abroad. There are no elders who know what those who have been reared within the last twenty years know about the world into which they were born (1970:77–78).

Clearly enculturation cannot account for the generation gap and for other consequences of rapid cultural change such as the shift from manufacturing jobs to service and information jobs in the United States (Harris 1980). Enculturation, in other words, can account for the continuity of culture; but it cannot account for the evolution of culture.

Even with respect to the continuity of culture, enculturation has important limitations. Every replicated pattern is not the result of the programming that one generation experiences at the hands of another. Many patterns are replicated because successive generations adjust to similar conditions in social life in similar ways. Sometimes the programming received may even be at variance with actual patterns; people may be enculturated to behave in one way but be obliged by conditions beyond their control to behave in another way. For example, enculturation is responsible for replicating the patterns of behavior associated with driving a car. Another replicated pattern consists of stalled traffic. Are automobile drivers pro-

(a)

(b)

grammed to make traffic jams? On the contrary, they are programmed to keep moving and to go around obstacles. Yet traffic jams are a highly patterned cultural phenomenon.

Poverty requires a similar analysis, as we will see in a later chapter. Many poor people find themselves living in houses, eating food, working, and raising families according to patterns that replicate their parents' subculture not because their parents wanted them to follow these patterns, but because

Figure 7.3 *CULTURE, PEOPLE, AND THE SUN*
Relationship between people and the sun is mediated by culture. Sunbathing *(a)* is a modern invention. On the beach at Villerville in 1908 *(b)*, only "mad dogs and Englishmen went out in the midday sun" . . . without their parasols.

they confront political and economic conditions which perpetuate their poverty (see Ch. 19).

DIFFUSION

Whereas enculturation refers to the passing of cultural traits from one generation to the next, *diffusion* refers to the passing of cultural traits from one culture and society to another (Fig. 7.5). This process is so common that the majority of traits found in any society can be said to have originated in some other society. One can say, for example, that much of the government, religion, law, diet, and language of the United States was "borrowed" or diffused from other cultures. Thus the Judeo-Christian religions come from the Middle East; parliamentary democracy comes from Western Europe; the food grains in our diet—rice, wheat, corn—come from ancient and distant civilizations; and the English language comes

Figure 7.4 *ENCULTURATION CAN'T EXPLAIN THIS*
A "punker."

from the amalgam of several different European tongues.

Early in this century (see p. 518), diffusion was regarded by many anthropologists as the most powerful explanation for sociocultural differences and similarities. The lingering effects of this approach can still be seen in popular attempts to explain the similarities among major civilizations as the result of the derivation of one from another—Polynesia from Peru, or vice versa; lowland Mesoamerica* from highland Mesoamerica, or vice versa; China from Europe, or vice versa; the New World (the Americas) from the Old, and so forth. In recent years, however, diffusion has lost ground as an explanatory principle. It is true that, in general, the closer two societies are to each other, the greater will be the cultural resemblance between them. But these resemblances cannot simply be attributed to some automatic tendency for traits to diffuse. It must be kept in mind that societies close together in

*Mesoamerica is Mexico plus Central America.

Figure 7.5 *DIFFUSION*
Can you reconstruct the diffusionary history of the objects and activities shown in these scenes? Headman in Arnhem, Australia, summoning his clanspeople to a meeting with a solar-powered portable radio (a); Mongolian metropolis (*b*); Brazilian woodsman (*c*).

(a)

(b)

space are likely to occupy similar environments; hence the similarities between them may be caused by the effects of similar environmental conditions (Harner 1970). Moreover, there are numerous cases of societies in close contact for hundreds of years that maintain radically different ways of life. For example, the Incas of Peru had an imperial government while the nearby forest societies lacked centralized leadership of any kind. Other well-known cases are the African Ituri forest hunters and their Bantu agriculturalist neighbors; the "apartment house" Pueblos and their marauding, nomadic Apache neighbors in the southwest United States. Resistance to diffusion, in other words, is as common as acceptance. If this were not the case, there would be no struggle between Catholics and Protestants in Northern Ireland; Mexicans would speak English (or U.S. citizens Spanish), and Jews would accept the divinity of Jesus Christ. Furthermore, even if one accepts diffusion as an explanation, there still remains the question of why the diffused item originated in the first place. Finally, diffusion cannot account for many remarkable instances in

(c)

which people who are known never to have had any means of contact invented similar tools and techniques and developed remarkably similar forms of marriage and religious beliefs.

In sum, diffusion is no more satisfactory as a mode of explanation of similar cultural traits than is enculturation. If nothing but diffusion and enculturation were involved in determining human social life, then we should expect all cultures to be the same and to stay the same; this is clearly not the case.

It must not be concluded, however, that diffusion plays no role in sociocultural evolution. The nearness of one culture to another often does influence the rate and direction of change as well as shape the specific details of sociocultural life, even if it does not shape the general features of the two cultures. For example, the custom of smoking tobacco originated among the native peoples of the Western Hemisphere and after 1492 spread to the remotest regions of the globe. This could not have happened if the Americas had remained cut off from the other continents. Yet contact alone obviously does not tell the whole story, since hundreds of other native American traits, like living in wigwams or hunting with bow and arrow, were not taken up even by the colonists who lived next door to native Americans.

MENTAL AND BEHAVIORAL ASPECTS OF CULTURE

By talking with people, anthropologists learn about a vast inner mental world of thought and feeling. This inner world exists on different levels of consciousness. First, there are patterns that exist far below consciousness. The rules of grammar are an example of such "deep structures." Second, there are patterns that exist closer to consciousness and that are readily formulated when the proper questions are asked. People can usually formulate values and norms and proper codes of conduct for activities such as weaning babies, courting a mate, choosing a leader, treating a disease, entertaining a guest, categorizing kin, worshiping God, and thousands of additional commonplace activities. But such rules, plans, and

(a)

(b)

Figure 7.6 *RULES FOR BREAKING RULES*
Cultural behavior cannot be predicted from the knowledge of a simple set of rules.

(c)

values may not ordinarily be formalized or completely conscious. Finally, there are equally numerous, fully conscious, explicit, and formal rules of conduct and statements of values, plans, goals, and aspirations that may be discussed during the course of ordinary conversations, written in law codes, or announced at public gatherings (e.g., rules about littering, making bank deposits, playing football, trespassing, and so on).

But conversations are not the only source of anthropological knowledge about culture. In addition, anthropologists observe, measure, photograph, and take notes about what people do during their daily, weekly, or annual rounds of activities. They watch how births take place, attend funerals, go along on hunting expeditions, watch marriage ceremonies, and attend thousands of other events and activities as they actually unfold. These actual events and activities constitute the behavioral aspect of culture.

The relationship between the mental and behavioral aspects of culture is highly complex and the subject of considerable disagreement. Cultures not only have rules for behavior, but rules for breaking the rules for behavior—as when one parks in front of a sign that says "No Parking" and gambles on not getting a ticket (Fig 7.6). To make matters worse, there is the problem of distinguishing between the culture's own version of its mental rules and behavioral events and the mental rules and behavioral events as they appear to the scientific observer.

EMIC AND ETIC ASPECTS OF CULTURE

The distinction between mental and behavioral events does not resolve the question of what constitutes an adequate description of a culture as a whole. The problem is that both the thoughts and behavior of the participants can be viewed from two different perspectives: from the perspective of the participants themselves and from the perspective of the observers. In both instances scientific, objective accounts of the mental and behavioral fields are possible. In the first instance the observers employ concepts and distinctions that are meaningful and appropriate to the participants; in the second instance they employ concepts and distinctions that are meaningful and appropriate to the observers. The first way of studying culture is called *emics* and the second way is called *etics* (see Ch. 20 for the derivation of these terms from *phonemics* and *phonetics*). The test of the adequacy of emic descriptions and analyses is whether they correspond with a view of the world natives accept as real, meaningful, or appropriate. In carrying out emic research, anthropologists attempt to acquire a knowledge of the categories and rules one must know in order to think and act as a native. They attempt to learn, for example, what rule lies behind the use of the same kin term for mother and mother's sister among the Bathonga; or when it is appropriate to shame house guests among the Kwakiutl; or when to ask a boy or a girl out for a date among U.S. teenagers.

The test of the adequacy of etic accounts, however, is simply their ability to generate scientific theories about the causes of sociocultural differences and similarities. Rather than employ concepts that are necessarily real, meaningful, and appropriate from the native point of view, the anthropologist now uses categories and rules derived from the data language of science, which are often unfamiliar to the native. Etic studies often involve the measurement and juxtaposition of activities and events that native informants find inappropriate or meaningless.

EMICS, ETICS, AND CATTLE SEX RATIOS

The following example demonstrates the importance of the difference between emics and etics in nonlinguistic aspects of culture. In the Trivandrum district of the state of Kerala in southern India, farmers insist that they would never deliberately shorten the life of one of their animals—that they would never kill it or starve it to death—thereby affirming the standard Hindu prohibition against the slaughter of cattle. Yet among Kerala farmers the mortality rate of male calves is almost twice as high as the mortality rate of female calves. In fact, male cattle 0–1 year of age are outnumbered by female cattle of the same group in a ratio of 67:100. The farmers themselves are aware that male calves are more likely to die than female calves, but they attribute the difference to the relative "weakness" of the males. "The males get sick more often," they say. When asked to explain why male calves get sick more often, some farmers suggest that the males eat less than the females. Finally, some farmers even admit that the male calves eat less because they are not allowed to stay at the mother's teats for more than a few seconds. But none could say that since there is little demand for traction animals in Kerala, male cattle are culled and female cattle are reared. The emics of the situation are that no one knowingly or willingly would shorten the life of a calf. Again and again farmers affirm that every calf has the "right to live" regardless of its sex. But the etics of the situation are that cattle sex ratios are systematically adjusted to the needs of the local ecology and economy through preferential male "bovicide." Although the unwanted calves are not slaughtered, many are more or less starved to death. In other parts of India, where different ecological and economic conditions prevail, etic "bovicide" is practiced more against female rather than male cattle, resulting in some states in an adult cattle sex ratio of over 200 oxen for every 100 cows (see Ch. 22 for more discussion on the emics and etics of cattle in India).

The comparison of etic and emic versions of culture gives rise to some of the most important and intriguing problems in anthropology.

THE UNIVERSAL PATTERN

In order to compare one culture with another, the anthropologist has to collect and organize cultural data in relation to cross-culturally recurrent aspects or parts of the social and cultural whole. The structure of these recurrent aspects or parts is called the *universal pattern.*

Anthropologists agree that every human society has provisions for behavior and thoughts related to making a living from the environment, having children, organizing the exchange of goods and labor, living in domestic groups and larger communities, and for the creative, expressive, playful, aesthetic, moral, and intellectual aspects of human life. However, there is no agreement on how many subdivisions of these categories should be recognized nor on what priority they should be given when it comes to the conduct of research. In subsequent chapters, the following universal pattern will be used:

1. **Infrastructure** Consists of the etic and behavioral activities by which each society satisfies minimal requirements for subsistence—the *mode of production*—and by which each society regulates population growth—the *mode of reproduction.*

2. **Structure** Consists of the economic and political etic and behavioral activities by which every society organizes itself into groups that allocate, regulate, and exchange goods and labor. Depending on whether the focus of organization is on domestic groups or on the internal and external relationships of the whole society, one may speak of *domestic economies* or *political economies* as universal components on the structural level.

3. **Superstructure** Consists of behavior and thought devoted to artistic, playful, religious, and intellectual endeavors plus all the mental and emic aspects of a culture's infrastructure and structure.

ALTERNATIVE RESEARCH STRATEGIES

Anthropologists do not agree on what is the best way to go about explaining the evolution of cultures and the great variety of cultural differences as well as similarities. As in any discipline, anthropologists follow a number of alternative *research strategies,* that is, basic models (or paradigms) consisting of principles which organize and guide the collection of data and the formulation of hypotheses and theories (Kuhn 1970; Lakatos 1970; Clarke 1972; Lauden 1977). The main alternatives can be grouped into *idiographic* and *nomothetic* strategies. Idiographic strategies are those which assume that chance and human spontaneity dominate all human phenomena and that it is, therefore, futile to look for any grand design in history or to seek for recurrent cause-and-effect relationships as the explanation of sociocultural differences and similarities (see Ch. 25).

THE ETIC AND BEHAVIORAL COMPONENTS OF THE UNIVERSAL PATTERN

INFRASTRUCTURE

Mode of Production The technology and the practices employed for expanding or limiting basic subsistence production, especially the production of food and other forms of energy, given the restrictions and opportunities provided by a specific technology interacting with a specific habitat.

Technology of subsistence
Techno-environmental relationships
Ecosystems
Work patterns

Mode of Reproduction The technology and the practices employed for expanding, limiting, and maintaining population size.

Demography
Mating patterns
Fertility, natality, mortality
Nurturance of infants
Medical control of demographic patterns
Contraception, abortion, infanticide

STRUCTURE

Domestic Economy The organization of reproduction and basic production, exchange, and consumption within camps, houses, apartments, or other domestic settings.

Family structure
Domestic division of labor
Domestic socialization, enculturation, education
Age and sex roles
Domestic discipline hierarchies, sanctions

Political Economy The organization of reproduction, production, exchange, and consumption within and between bands, villages, chiefdoms, states, and empires.

Political organization, factions, clubs, associations, corporations
Division of labor, taxation, tribute
Political socialization, enculturation, education
Class, caste, urban, rural hierarchies
Discipline, police/military control
War

SUPERSTRUCTURE

Behavioral Superstructure

Art, music, dance, literature, advertising
Rituals
Sports, games, hobbies
Science

Nomothetic strategies, on the other hand, make the assumption that there is a considerable degree of uniformity and lawfulness in cultural phenomena. They emphasize the recurrent rather than the unique aspects of the human social and cultural experiences. However, they differ widely in the amount of orderliness they expect to find and in the causal importance they assign to the levels and categories of the universal pattern.

The existence of alternative research strategies and the necessity of choosing among them is to be expected in any discipline. Indeed, it has been suggested by philosophers of science that science progresses only as a result of the competition between alternative research strategies. Commitment to a particular strategy, however, does not mean that the others have nothing to contribute and can safely be ignored. No strategy can pretend to have an exclusive monopoly on the truth. Students interested in a brief description of some of the major alternative research strategies should turn to Chapter 25.

SUMMARY

A culture consists of the socially acquired ways of thinking, feeling, and acting of the members of a particular society. Cultures maintain their continuity by means of the process of enculturation. In studying cultural differences, it is important to guard against the habit of mind called ethnocentrism, which arises from a failure to appreciate the far-reaching effects of enculturation on human life. Enculturation, however, cannot explain how and why cultures change. Moreover, not all cultural recurrences in different generations are the result of enculturation. Some are the result of reactions to similar conditions or situations.

Whereas enculturation denotes the process by which culture is transmitted from one generation to the next, diffusion denotes the process by which culture is transmitted from one society to another. Diffusion, like enculturation, is not automatic and cannot stand alone as an explanatory principle. Neighboring societies can have both highly similar as well as highly dissimilar cultures.

Culture, as defined in this book, consists of thoughts that take place inside of people's heads plus the human behavior that takes place all around them. Unlike other social animals which possess only rudimentary cultures, human beings can describe their thoughts and behavior from their own point of view. In studying human cultures, therefore, one must make explicit whether it is the native participant's point of view or the observer's point of view that is being expressed. These are the emic and etic points of view, respectively. Both mental and behavioral aspects of culture can be approached from either the emic or etic points of view. Emic and etic versions of reality often differ markedly. However, there is usually some degree of correspondence between them. In addition to emic, etic, mental and behavioral aspects, all cultures share a universal pattern. The universal pattern as defined in this book consists of three main components: infrastructure, structure, and superstructure. These in turn consist respectively of the modes of production and reproduction; domestic and political economy; and the creative, expressive, aesthetic, and intellectual aspects of human life. The definition of these categories is essential for the organization of research and differs according to the research strategy one adopts.

Research strategies are basic models, or paradigms, which organize the collection of data and the formulation of hypotheses. In anthropology there are two basic kinds of research strategies: the idiographic and nomothetic. Idiographic strategies reject the possibility of discovering general causal processes in human cultures; they emphasize the unique and/or emic aspects of social life. The nomothetic strategies share in common the assumption that cultures can be analyzed as causally determined systems, but they differ widely in the scope of their interests, the priorities they give to the components of the universal pattern, their ability to explain both differences and similarities, and the breadth and coherence of their theories.

8 THE OLD WORLD PALEOLITHIC

The anthropological study of cultural evolution begins with the facts and inferences of prehistoric archaeology. Archaeology is to anthropology as paleontology is to biology. Without archaeology anthropologists could neither describe nor explain the course of cultural evolution. Because of the great sweep of time and space studied by archaeologists, anthropology enjoys a unique position among the social sciences. Anthropologists can observe the operation of long-range trends and formulate and test causal theories of cultural evolution.

This chapter traces the evolution of Old World cultures from the earliest known artifacts indicative of gathering, hunting, and scavenging modes of production up to the threshold of the domestication of plants and animals.

GENE-CULTURE COEVOLUTION

As we have seen (Ch. 4), hominids were not initially selected for their braininess, but for their upright gait. Why bipedalism was selected for is still a matter of debate; but it is clear that once hands were no longer needed for walking or running, tool use could become far more important than it is among modern-day monkeys and apes. Tools such as clubs, digging sticks, and stone hammers and knives could be carried in the hands without endangering the ability to explore, move about, and flee from danger. The making and using of these tools could then benefit from the shared experiences of many individuals.

As tool using became more important, natural selection favored brainier individuals who were better able to encode and transmit behavioral tradition. This in turn led to more and better tools and an ever-greater reliance on enculturation as a source of appropriate behavior; this in turn led to still brainier varieties of hominids.

Thus, for several million years the evolution of culture and the evolution of the human brain and body into an increasingly efficient learning machine were part of a single evolutionary process. The simple stone tools associated with the ape-sized brains of the earliest hominids became more complex, more skillfully made, and more specialized for particular cutting, digging, and throwing tasks as *Homo habilis* was succeeded by *Homo erectus* and later by *Homo sapiens*. This feedback between culture and genetic change is known as *gene-culture coevolution* (Lumsden and Wilson 1983). It is characteristic of the earliest phases of cultural evolution. With the emergence of *H. sapiens*, however, cultural evolution has been proceeding at a far more rapid rate than genetic evolution. Gene-culture coevolution is no longer a fundamental aspect of cultural evolution.

CULTURAL TAKEOFF

With the appearance of *H. sapiens*, the relationship between cultural and biological evolution underwent a profound change. For the last 100,000 years the average size of the human brain has not increased—in fact, it has decreased as we saw in Chapter 5. Yet the complexity and rate of change of human sociocultural systems have increased by many orders of magnitude. This fact makes it clear that to understand the last 100,000 years of the evolution of culture, primary emphasis must be given to processes that are distinctive to culture. Natural selection and organic evolution lie at the base of culture; but once the capacity for culture became fully developed, a vast number of cultural differences and similarities could arise and disappear entirely independent of changes in genotypes. This topic is discussed in Chapter 25 in connection with the research strategy known as *sociobiology* (p. 525).

PREHISTORIC PERIODS

Stone implements provide most of the evidence about the earliest phases of cultural evolution. Hence archaeologists divide the entire period of early prehistory into *lithic* (meaning "stone") ages. Three such ages are recognized in the cultural evolution of Europe: *Paleolithic* (old stone age), *Mesolithic* (middle stone age), and *Neolithic* (new stone age). These ages were of drastically different lengths: the Paleolithic lasted over 2 million years (longer in Africa and Asia) while the Mesolithic and Neolithic combined did not last more than 10,000 years. Paleolithic cultures were based on hunting, fishing, and gathering rather than on farming or stock raising. Groups were small, the total population of the world was only a few million, and the groups were widely dispersed. To make efficient use of available plant and animal resources, the Paleolithic hunter-gatherers ranged over a wide territory and probably did not settle at any one campsite, cave, or shelter for more than a few weeks or months at a time.

Three subdivisions are generally recognized: (1) the long *Lower Paleolithic*, dominated by simple Oldowan tools, core biface tools, and simple flake tools; (2) the brief *Middle Paleolithic*, characterized by an enlarged and refined repertory of core tools, flake points, and other flake tools; (3) the still briefer *Upper Paleolithic*, characterized by an enlarged and refined repertory of *blade tools* (see p. 135) and by many specialized ivory, bone, and antler implements and artifacts.

In the same highly general perspective, one may characterize the Neolithic as the age of cultural systems based on domesticated plants and animals. Group size and total population were larger and settlement was more nucleated. To make efficient use of the domesticated plants, permanent settlements or villages replaced the temporary camps of the Paleolithic hunters and gatherers. The transition to Neolithic farming communities took place under a variety of conditions in various parts of the Old and New Worlds. The Mesolithic denotes this transitional age in Europe. Ages transitional between hunting and gathering infrastructures and farming infrastructures in other parts of the world have local or regional names.

LOWER PALEOLITHIC DEVELOPMENTS

The earliest tools known (Hadar, about 2.5 million years) and the earliest tool tradition, the Oldowan, have already been described (p. 76). The Oldowan choppers can be seen as the logical antecedents of the first Acheulian bifaces, or "hand axes" (Fig. 8.1). The Acheulian tool kit included many different kinds of hand axes, often made from flakes rather than from cores—*polyhedrals* (multifaceted, rounded stones) of unknown function, knives, and scrapers made from cores, as well as significant numbers of large-flake cleavers and scrapers and other small-flake tools (Fig. 8.2). As previously discussed, so-called Developed Oldowan and Acheulian tools seem to have coexisted at Olduvai and other African sites for 500,000 years (p. 78).

The hand ax is the most intriguing of the Lower Paleolithic tools. Hand axes are

Figure 8.1 *ACHEULIAN HAND AX*

found all over the Old World in association with *H. erectus*, archaic *H. sapiens*, and even *H. sapiens sapiens*. Hand axes are almond to triangular in shape and are flaked bifacially to produce two converging edges all around. (Fig. 8.3). Despite the fact that our ancestors used them for about 2 million years, today no one is certain what they were used for or how. Some archaeologists think they were hafted and used for chopping; others see them as hand-held and used for butchering bones, cutting meat, scraping hides. It has recently been suggested that they were hurled upward as a projectile to land point down on the head of small game animals (O'Brien 1981). A more plausible solution is that they were hand-held and used to skin and butcher animals. In experiments carried out with flakes and hand axes that were replicas of Acheulian tools found at Olduvai, Peter Jones discovered that the hand ax was more efficient and less tiring in skin cutting, skin removal, and meat cutting than flake tools. Surprisingly, when held in the proper manner, the hand ax did not cut Jones's hand even though it had sharp edges all around the perimeter (Jones 1980:160).

The greatest enigma of the lower Paleolithic, however, is why it lasted so long and why so little change took place over such a vast stretch of time involving so many tens of thousands of generations of hominid beings. In Olduvai Gorge the "monotony" of the Acheulian tradition is not relieved for a million years. In the words of Arthur Jelinek, this evidence suggests

> a qualitatively different kind of cultural activity from that familiar to us in the activities of *Homo sapiens sapiens*. There is thus good reason to refer to this lower Paleolithic pattern as representing a paleocultural behavior which differed significantly from the cultural behavior of modern man (1977:28).

Presumably the critical difference revolves around the capacity to communicate by means of language. Yet it must be kept in mind that it was during this long paleocultural epoch that the genus *Homo* learned to use and control fire, to hunt large animals, and to make open-air shelters out of skins or out of leaves and brush.

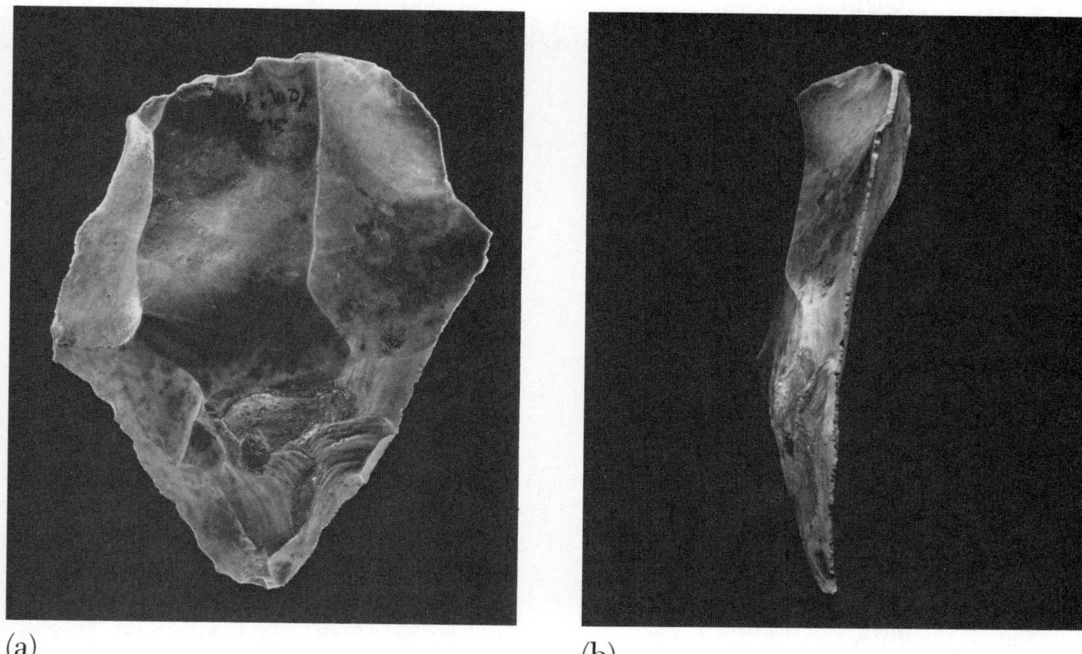

(a) (b)

Figure 8.2 *PALEOLITHIC SIDE SCRAPER*
The long, almost straight right-hand edge of this 200,000-year-old tool is the working edge. Front view (*a*) and side view (*b*).

MIDDLE PALEOLITHIC DEVELOPMENTS

At the end of the Lower Paleolithic, Acheulian assemblages were enriched by flake tools produced by an ingenious method known as the *Levallois* technique (Fig. 8.4). A tortoise-shaped core of flint was prepared as if one were about to produce a thick hand ax, except that shaping proceeded on only one side of the tortoise core. Next a transverse blow was struck at one end of the core, creating a ledge, or *striking platform.* Then, a longitudinal blow was administered to the striking platform, detaching a thin elongated flake with sharp, straight edges. Levalloisian cores and flakes have been found throughout Africa and Europe and usually mark the transition to Middle Paleolithic industries. Euro-African Middle Paleolithic tool kits also contain varying percentages of hand axes and other Acheulian-type implements. Points that might have been attached to spears make their appearance. They were fashioned from Levallois and other kinds of flakes and were light enough and sharp enough to have functioned as effective projectiles.

In many regions, Middle Paleolithic flake-tool assemblages conform to the type of industry known as *Mousterian.* These assemblages consist of small flakes removed from Levallois and other disc-shaped cores which were subjected to secondary flaking based on soft-hammer and pressure tech-

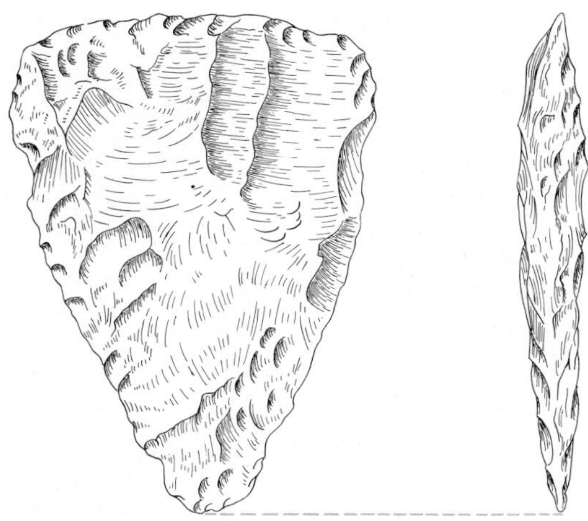

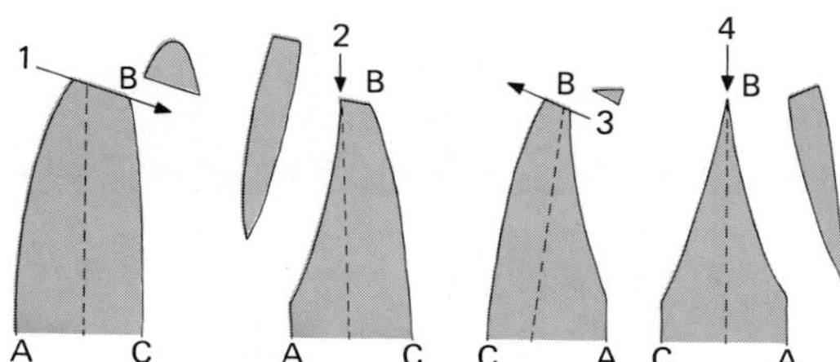

Figure 8.3 *IMPROVED ACHEULIAN HAND AX AND TECHNIQUE*
Blows may have been delivered by bone or wood hammers. Flakes could have been used as tools also.

niques (Figs. 8.5 and 8.6). (Some prehistorians use the term "Mousterian" to cover all Middle Paleolithic industries.) Middle Paleolithic tool kits thus usually included a few hand axes and numerous flake tools such as several varieties of points, scrapers, notched flakes for shaving wood, burins, and borers. A high degree of control had been achieved over the secondary flaking or retouching of working edges, and special bone instruments presumed to have been employed for this purpose are found at many Middle Paleolithic sites. It has been shown that excellent retouching and trimming can also be achieved by biting the edge of a flake with one's teeth (Gould, Koster, and Sontz 1971).

The transition from Acheulian industries to Middle Paleolithic industries occurred quite abruptly in Europe, the Middle East, and Africa and at approximately the same time—about 100,000 B.P. (Beaumont and Vogel 1972; Deacon 1975; J. D. Clark 1975). This makes the Middle Paleolithic roughly equivalent to the period during which archaic varieties of *H. sapiens,* including *H. sapiens neanderthalensis,* appeared throughout the Old World. There is considerable evidence that cultural "take-off" occurred at this time. Special importance has been attached by Alexander Marshack (1976) to the discovery of what appear to be personal adornments in the form of pendants made out of reindeer bone and the canine tooth of a fox and of bones engraved with fine lines and zigzags at sites in France and Bulgaria

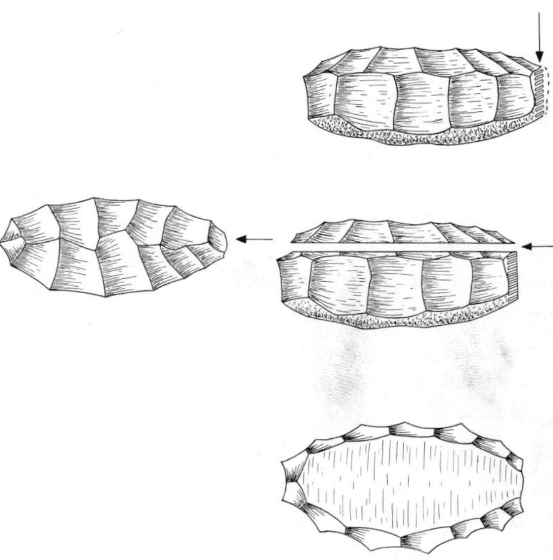

Figure 8.4 *LEVALLOISIAN TORTOISE CORE TECHNIQUE*
Left view shows Levalloisian flake. Right view shows (top to bottom) making platform, striking flake from nucleus, looking down on core after flake detached.

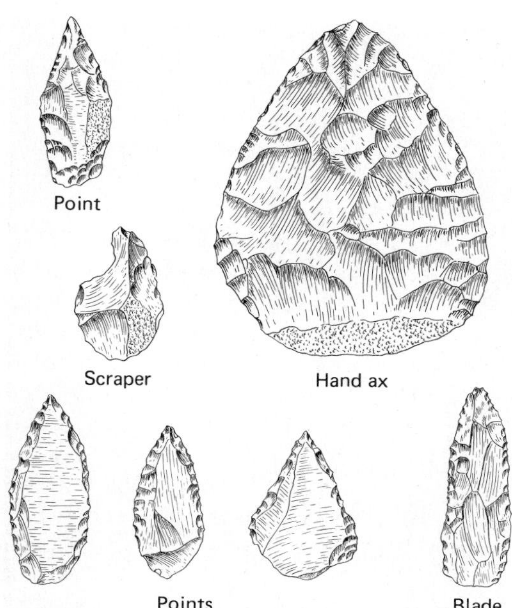

Figure 8.5 *MOUSTERIAN IMPLEMENTS*

(Fig. 8.7). An incised and polished section of a mammoth's tooth from the Mousterian at Tata, Hungary, may have functioned as some sort of ritual object (Fig. 8.8). These items seem to imply the existence of social meanings that could only be comprehended and communicated within a community which not only possessed a social tradition of toolmaking, but also an advanced form of language. Similar conclusions are suggested by the occurrence of funerallike ceremonies at many Neandertal burial sites. For example, the 55,000-year-old skeletons from Skhūl cave had their knees drawn up toward the chest. One of the Skhūl males had apparently been interred with the jaws of a wild boar resting on top of him, indicative of some concept of care of the dead. At Shanidar masses of bachelor buttons, hollyhocks, hyacinths, and other flowers were interred with a Neandertal man who died 60,000 years ago (Solecki 1971). Other Middle Paleolithic sites indicate that red ochre—a dye associated with blood and magical powers among many modern aboriginal populations—was also used in some kind of funerary ritual (Constable 1973).

At other Middle Paleolithic burials, hunting tools and the bones of meat offerings are also found, suggesting that death may already have been interpreted as a journey to a distant land. During this journey perhaps the meat would be needed to nourish the hunter, but upon arrival there would be plenty of game to hunt. All such interpretations, however, remain highly speculative.

THE UPPER PALEOLITHIC

The Upper Paleolithic is characterized by a marked increase in blade tools and by a great florescence of ivory, bone, and antler implements. Flakes that have parallel edges and that are twice as long as they are broad are known technically as *blades* (Fig. 8.9). Blade tools have been found at numerous Mousterian Middle Paleolithic sites and with Levallois tools at Lower Paleolithic sites in East Africa. A few blades have even been found in Oldowan assemblages. But the blade tools of these earlier ages occur with less frequency and do not display the high level of craft and virtuosity of the Upper Paleolithic blade tools (Fig. 8.10).

Bone, ivory, and antler tools also occur earlier than the Upper Paleolithic, but the variety, abundance, and craft of the Upper Paleolithic bone, ivory, and antler artifacts "is clearly on a scale and of a nature quite different from the possible instances of Mousterian bone working" (Straus 1982:185). Another distinctive feature of Upper Paleolithic technology is the development of *composite tools* (i.e. tools that have several

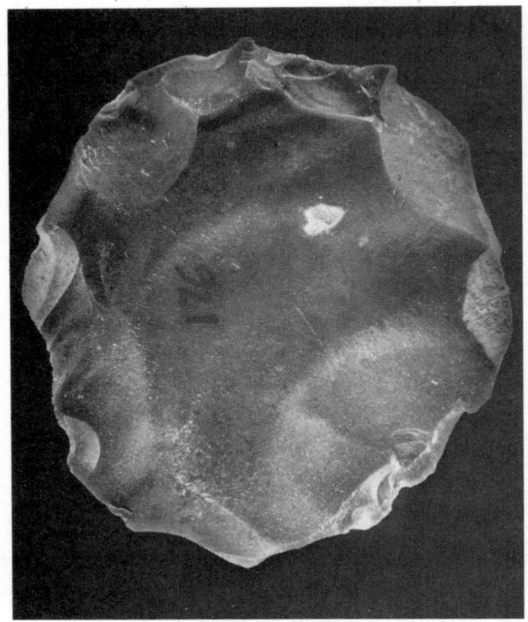

(a)

(b)

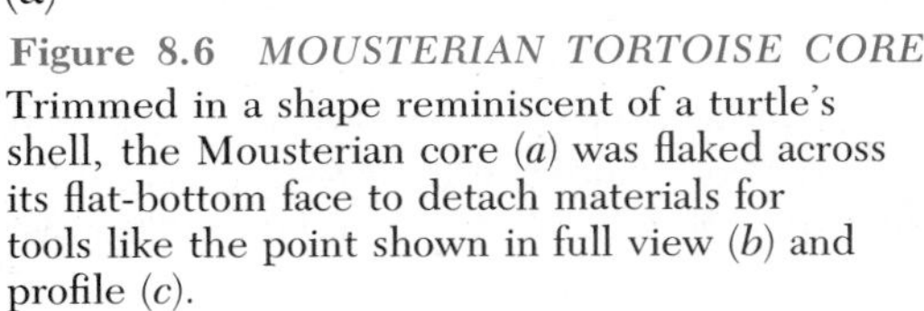

Figure 8.6 *MOUSTERIAN TORTOISE CORE* Trimmed in a shape reminiscent of a turtle's shell, the Mousterian core (*a*) was flaked across its flat-bottom face to detach materials for tools like the point shown in full view (*b*) and profile (*c*).

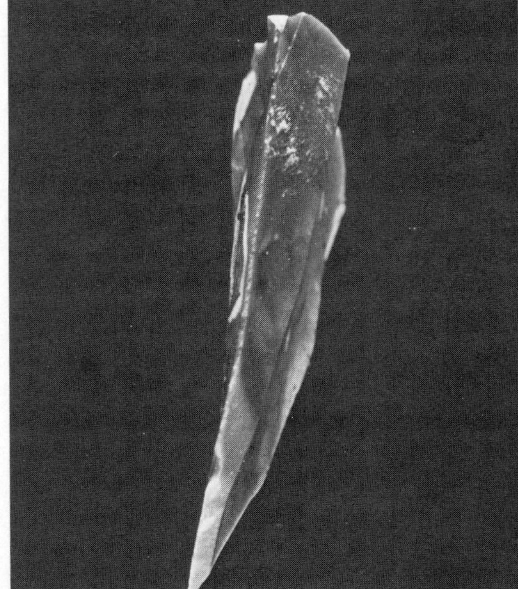

(c)

parts)—such as harpoons and hafted weapons and projectiles. Projectile points which have special shoulders or tongs for attachment to spears, plus evidence for the use of traps, nets, and weirs, "suggest the development of technologies far more complex and specialized than those of the middle Paleolithic" (ibid.).

In Europe, industries transitional between the Middle Paleolithic and the Upper Paleolithic are known as the *Châtelperronian* (about 37,000 to 34,000 B.P.) and the *Perigordian* (about 32,000 B.P.); both are notable for a mixture of Middle Paleolithic tools together with pointed blade knives, blade burins (for work in wood and bone), bone awls, and bone points suitable for spears and arrows (Fig. 8.11). Almost as early as the Perigordian is the *Aurignacian*, characterized by fine blades, knives, scrapers, and burins. Bone awls, pierced antlers thought to have been used as arrow straighteners, and bone spearheads with a cleft base for hafting are also common (Fig. 8.12). The earliest examples of representational art known in the world have been recovered from a middle Aurignacian site in Vogelherd, West Germany, dating to 30,000 B.P. The finds consist of superb statuettes of animals and of crude human figurines (Marshack 1976:274). Somewhat later and centered in southern Russia and central Europe is the industry known as the *Gravettian*, distinguished by small blade knives whose backs have been blunted, perhaps to protect the user's fingers, bone awls, and various objects of personal adornment such as bone beads, bracelets, and pins (Fig. 8.12). Many of the bone and ivory objects are decorated with incised geometric designs. The most notable of the Gravettian artifacts are numerous small figurines depicting pregnant women with enlarged breasts and buttocks. The figurines, known as *Venus statues* (Fig. 8.12), are carved in stone, bone, and ivory, and they may have possessed some ritual significance associated with the fertility of women and animals or with women suffering from hormone imbalances that were given religious significance (Kopper and Grishman 1979). Some 60 examples have been recovered from sites all the way from France to Siberia. As indicated by skeletal remains, the Gravettians hunted mammoth, horse, reindeer, bison, and other large herd animals. They made their camps both in the open and at the mouths of caves and rock shelters. In southern Russia archaeologists have identified the remains of a Gravettian mammoth hunter's animal-skin dwelling set in a shallow pit 40 feet long and 12 feet wide. In Czechoslovakia round floor plans, reminiscent of American Indian tepees or wigwams, have also been found.

At about 23,000 B.P. another Upper Paleolithic industry known as the *Solutrean* is found throughout much of France and

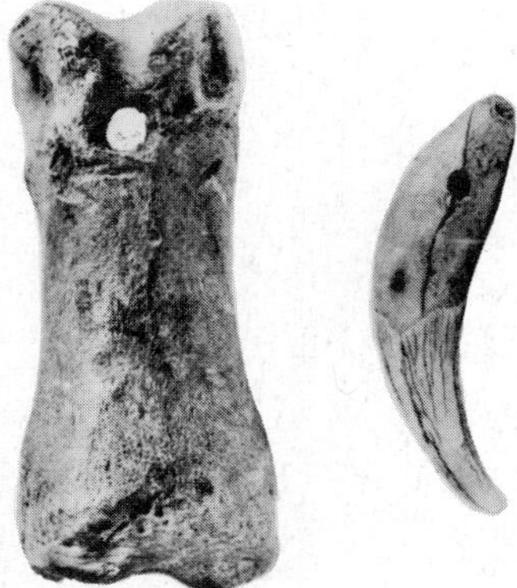

Figure 8.7 *MOUSTERIAN JEWELRY* Mousterian pendants from the site of La Quina, France, made from a reindeer phalange and the canine of a young fox (natural size).

Figure 8.8 *MOUSTERIAN RITUAL OBJECT* Carved from the section of a mammoth molar, it resembles the Australian "churinga."

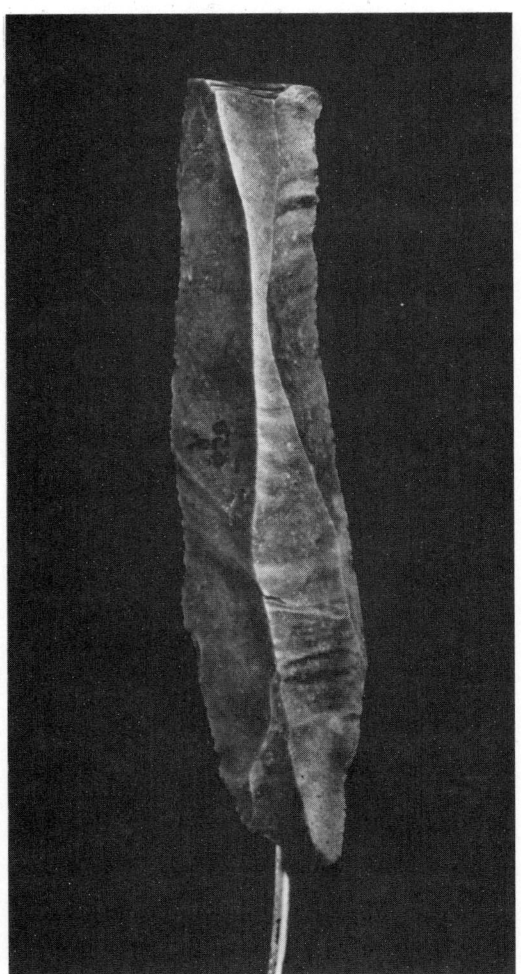

Figure 8.9 *UPPER PALEOLITHIC BLADE* Basic form of many Upper Paleolithic instruments. Specialized tools were made by retouching edges and ends. This blade is 4 inches long and only one-quarter inch thick.

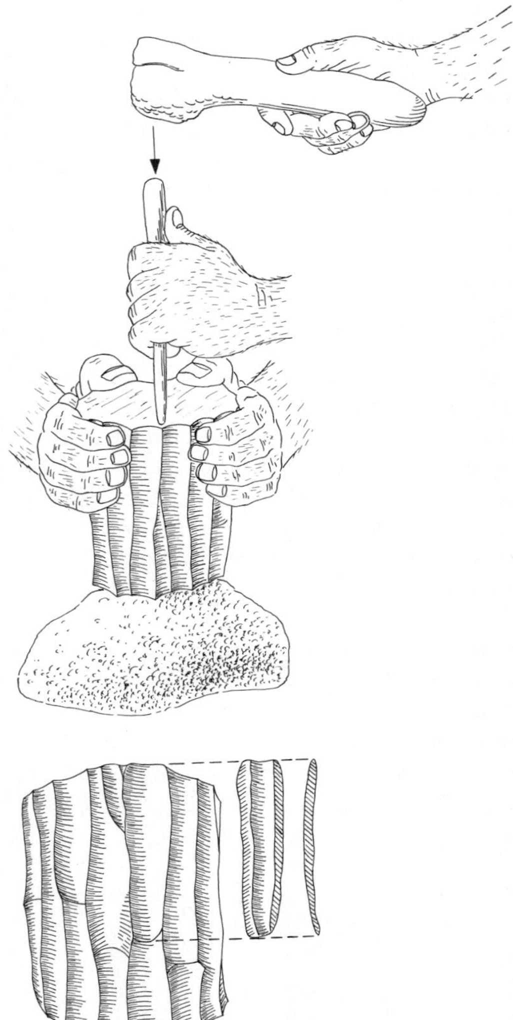

Figure 8.10 *UPPER PALEOLITHIC BLADE TECHNIQUE*

Spain. The most famous Solutrean artifacts are magnificently flaked symmetrical daggers and spear points made in the shape of long, thin laurel leaves. The Solutreans also made finely worked stemmed and barbed points. Needles found at Solutrean sites indicate that skin clothing must have been sewn to form-fitting shapes.

The richest of the European Upper Paleolithic industries is known as the *Magdalenian* and ranges in time from about 16,000 to 10,000 B.P. (Bordes 1968). The Magdalenians added harpoons to the inventory of hunting weapons. The barbed points of these harpoons were made of bones and antler. Fine bone needles attest to the probable importance of tailored clothing. For hunting, the early Magdalenians used the spear-thrower, a short rod or slat with a notch or hook at one end (Fig. 8.13). The hook fits into the butt end of the spear. The spear-thrower increases the force with which a spear can be hurled. Toward the end of the Magdalenian, the bow and arrow were probably in use as depicted in some of the cave paintings of France and Spain. Magdalenian lance heads, harpoon points, and spear-throwers were often decorated with carvings of horses, ibex, birds, fish, and geometrical designs, some of which may be notations representing lunar cycles and seasonal changes (below).

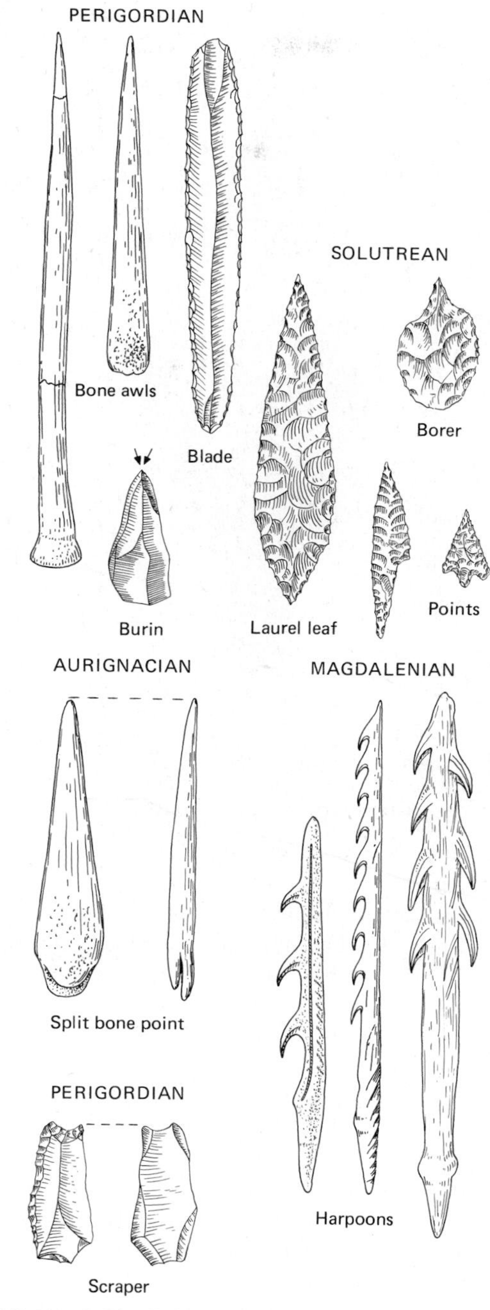

Figure 8.11 *UPPER PALEOLITHIC IMPLEMENTS*

UPPER PALEOLITHIC ART

The control achieved by Upper Paleolithic peoples over the techniques of tool manufacture in stone, bone, ivory, antler, and wood was reflected in their mastery of several ritualized art forms. On the walls and ceilings of deep caves in Spain and France, in hidden galleries far from the light of day, Upper Paleolithic peoples painted and engraved pictures of the animals they hunted. To a lesser extent, similar paintings are found in caves across Europe as far Russia. An occasional human figure—sometimes wearing a mask—outlines of hands, pictographs, and geometric symbols also occur, but the vast majority of the paintings and engravings depict horses, bison, mammoths, reindeer, ibex, wild boars, wild cattle, woolly rhinoceros, and other big-game animals. In spite of the magnificent economy of line and color, so much admired today, Upper Paleolithic cave art must be considered

Figure 8.12 *VENUS STATUE*
Reconstructed from fragments, showing typical enlargement of buttocks and breasts.

at least as much an expression of culturally established ritual as of individual or cultural aesthetic impulses. The animals were often painted one on top of another even though unused surfaces were available, indicating that they were done first and foremost as ritual rather than as art (Fig 8.14). It is generally assumed that the paintings were some form of hunting magic, but their precise function cannot be reconstructed reliably. All that can safely be asserted is that the hunters were impressed by the power and beauty of the animals whose death made their own lives possible (Ucko and Rosenfeld 1967; Leroi-Gourhan 1968; Conkey 1981).

A number of attempts have been made to interpret various painted and incised geometric designs—dots, grids, scratches, lines—on Upper Paleolithic cave walls and on antler and bone implements. The theory has recently been advanced that the holes and lines found on certain antler and bone plaques and "batons" (Fig. 8.15) were records of the passage of days and phases of the moon (Marshack 1972a and b). Although these marks can be interpreted in other ways, there is no reason to doubt that the artists responsible for the amazingly realistic scenes on the cave walls would also have had the capacity to observe and record the phases of the moon and other celestial events, thereby preparing the way for the development of the first calendars.

Figure 8.13 *SPEAR THROWER*
This Arunta hunter is using an implement first found in the Magdalenian phase of the Upper Paleolithic.

(a)

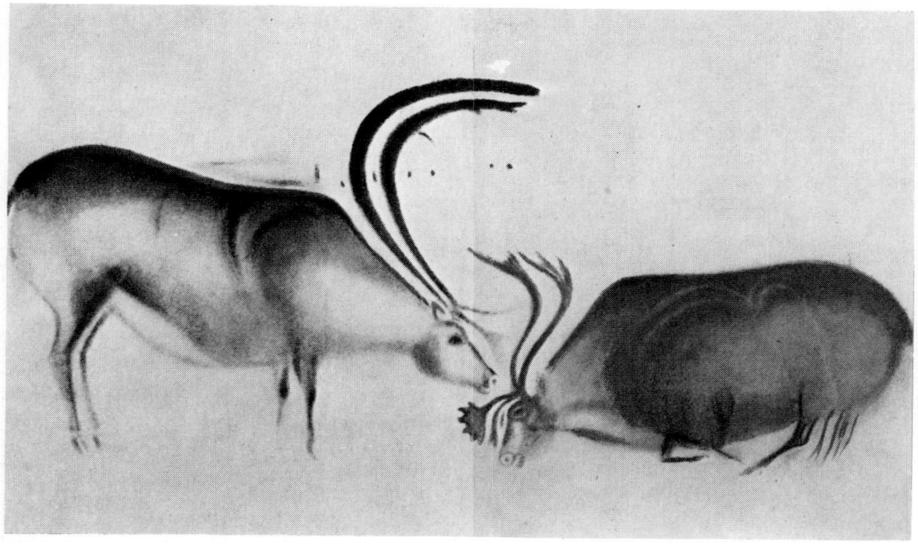

(b)

Figure 8.14 *PALEOLITHIC MASTERPIECES*
It is as if Picasso were to paint on a canvas already used by Rembrandt. (*a*) Altamira, Spain; (*b*) La Caverne de Font de Gaume, France.

The sudden appearance of personal adornments and representational and decorative art in the late Middle and early Upper Paleolithic provides additional evidence that cultural take-off was associated with the transition from archaic *H. sapiens* to *H. sapiens sapiens*. As Alexander Marshack (ibid.) has suggested, the kind of shared symbols implicit in nonutilitarian engraved lines or figurines is different from the symbolism implicit in the manufacture of a hand ax. A Paleolithic youth could learn what the meaning of a hand ax was by watching one being made and used. But he or she would have

(a)

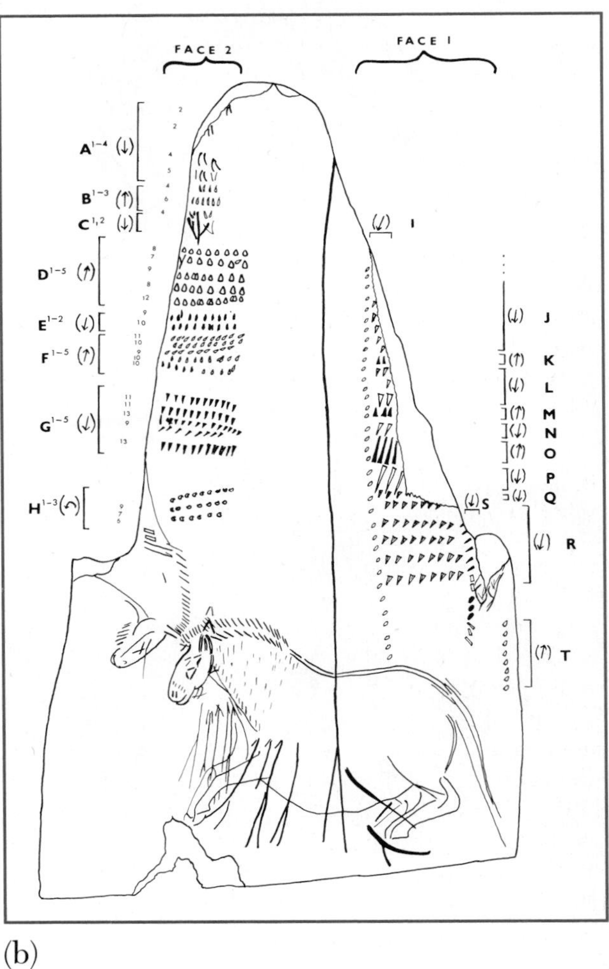

(b)

Figure 8.15 *PALEOLITHIC NOTATIONS*
(*a*) Antler found at La Marche, France. (*b*) Drawing of same antler, flattened out to show two sets of notations and horses that have been repeatedly engraved. It is thought that the notations were a record of the passage of 7½ lunar months.

to be told what the meaning of a zigzag line or a Venus statue was.

According to some authorities, the Upper Paleolithic marks the end of scavenging of large animals as an important source of meat and the development of regular communal hunts resulting in surpluses, which were stored during winter months.

In exploiting migratory game herds and the annual return of spawning fish such as salmon, Upper Paleolithic peoples displayed a developed sense of time and an ability to anticipate future events. By comparison with Middle Paleolithic sites, Upper Paleolithic sites seem to indicate larger and more permanent settlements and higher regional population densities (Binford 1982). Other characterizations of the Upper Paleolithic stress the increasing complexity of symbolic and artistic endeavors and the use of ornaments and insignia as a means of identifying individuals and corporate groups (White 1982).

HOMO SAPIENS SAPIENS AND THE MIDDLE/UPPER TRANSITION

Sequences of Paleolithic industries similar to those in Europe also occur in Africa and Asia. For example, Levallois techniques and Mousterian industries succeed Acheulian traditions at Fauresmith in South Africa and at many other African sites. There is even a Mousterianlike flake industry in North China. By 40,000 to 30,000 B.P., bone, flake, and blade tools were being made on every continent (except Antarctica). For the period 20,000 to 10,000 B.P. it is impossible to say that any particular region had achieved decisive technological advantages over the others. To be sure, there was a great deal of variation in the specific content of the tool kits of the Eurasian mammoth hunters, the Southeast Asian forest-dwellers, and the Australian hunters of marsupials, but this variation probably reflected local adaptation more than different levels of technological progress (Bricker 1976).

It is clear that in general there is a correlation between the appearance of *H. sapiens sapiens* and the transition to Upper Paleolithic cultures. The extent to which this correlation can be attributed to gene-culture coevolution is unknown. The problem is that essentially Mousterian tool kits remain in use at some Upper Paleolithic sites after the Neandertals and other archaic *H. sapiens* had become extinct (Wenke 1980:193). And as we have seen, ritual symbolism and blade and bone tools were used to some extent before the appearance of *H. sapiens sapiens*. An intriguing discovery was made in 1978 at Saint-Cesaire Nance consisting of a classic Western Neandertal skeleton in association with Châtelperronian artifacts (Smith 1982:685). The implication of this discovery is that the Western Neandertals were in the midst of a transition to Upper Paleolithic cultures. This strengthens the view presented in Chapter 5 that *H. sapiens neanderthalensis* evolved into *H. sapiens sapiens* and suggets that culture-gene coevolution may have been responsible for the distinctive components of Upper Paleolithic cultures and Upper Paleolithic human types.

THE END OF THE PALEOLITHIC

Despite the many technological triumphs of the Paleolithic, the basic mode of subsistence remained essentially what it had been since Acheulian times. All human groups continued to have some variety of a hunting, gathering, fishing mode of production. To be sure, neither the environmental opportunities for hunting and gathering nor the technological inventory available for exploit-

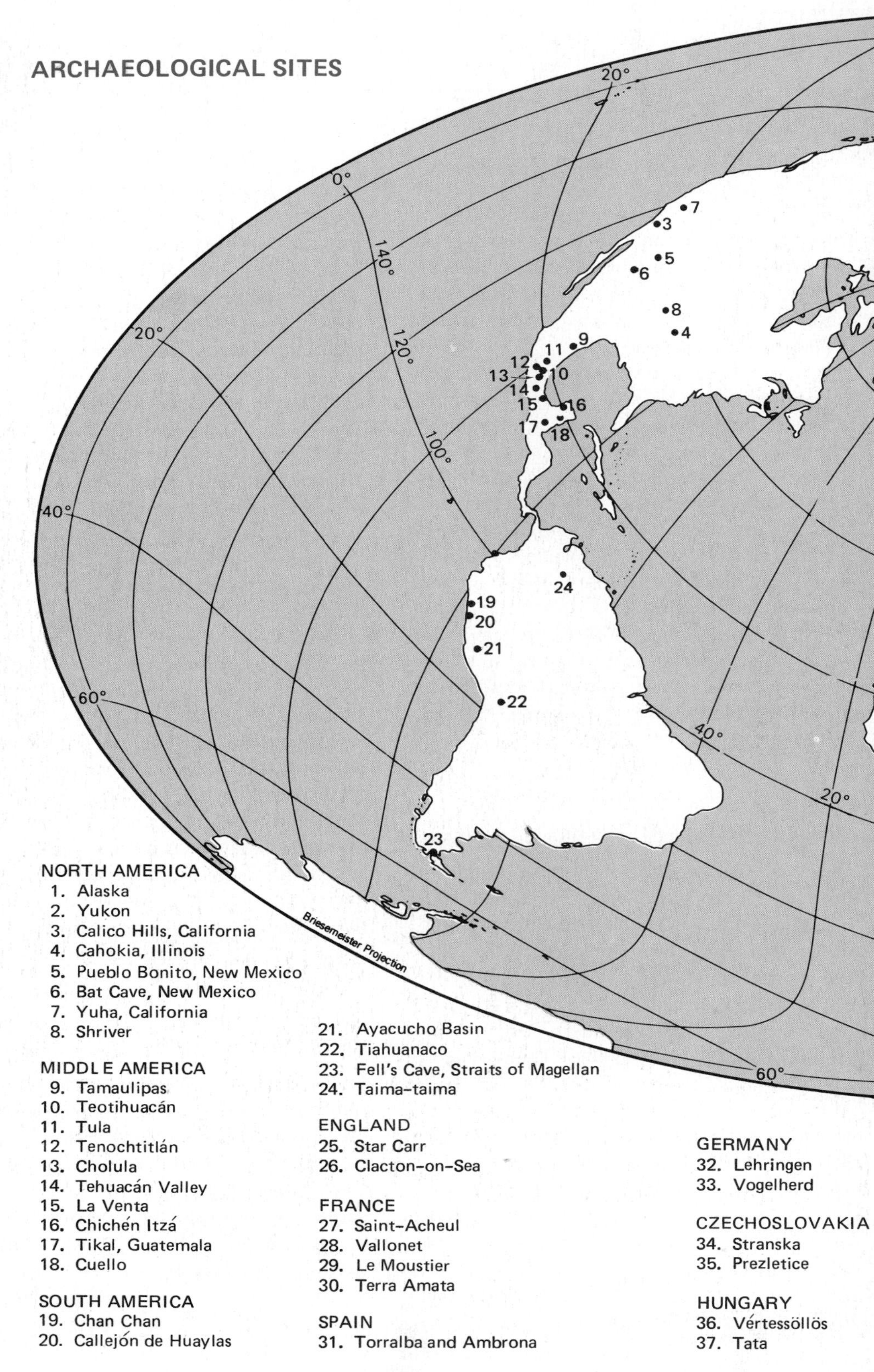
ARCHAEOLOGICAL SITES
Briesemeister Projection
NORTH AMERICA
1. Alaska
2. Yukon
3. Calico Hills, California
4. Cahokia, Illinois
5. Pueblo Bonito, New Mexico
6. Bat Cave, New Mexico
7. Yuha, California
8. Shriver
MIDDLE AMERICA
9. Tamaulipas
10. Teotihuacán
11. Tula
12. Tenochtitlán
13. Cholula
14. Tehuacán Valley
15. La Venta
16. Chichén Itzá
17. Tikal, Guatemala
18. Cuello
SOUTH AMERICA
19. Chan Chan
20. Callejón de Huaylas
21. Ayacucho Basin
22. Tiahuanaco
23. Fell's Cave, Straits of Magellan
24. Taima-taima
ENGLAND
25. Star Carr
26. Clacton-on-Sea
FRANCE
27. Saint-Acheul
28. Vallonet
29. Le Moustier
30. Terra Amata
SPAIN
31. Torralba and Ambrona
GERMANY
32. Lehringen
33. Vogelherd
CZECHOSLOVAKIA
34. Stranska
35. Prezletice
HUNGARY
36. Vértessöllös
37. Tata

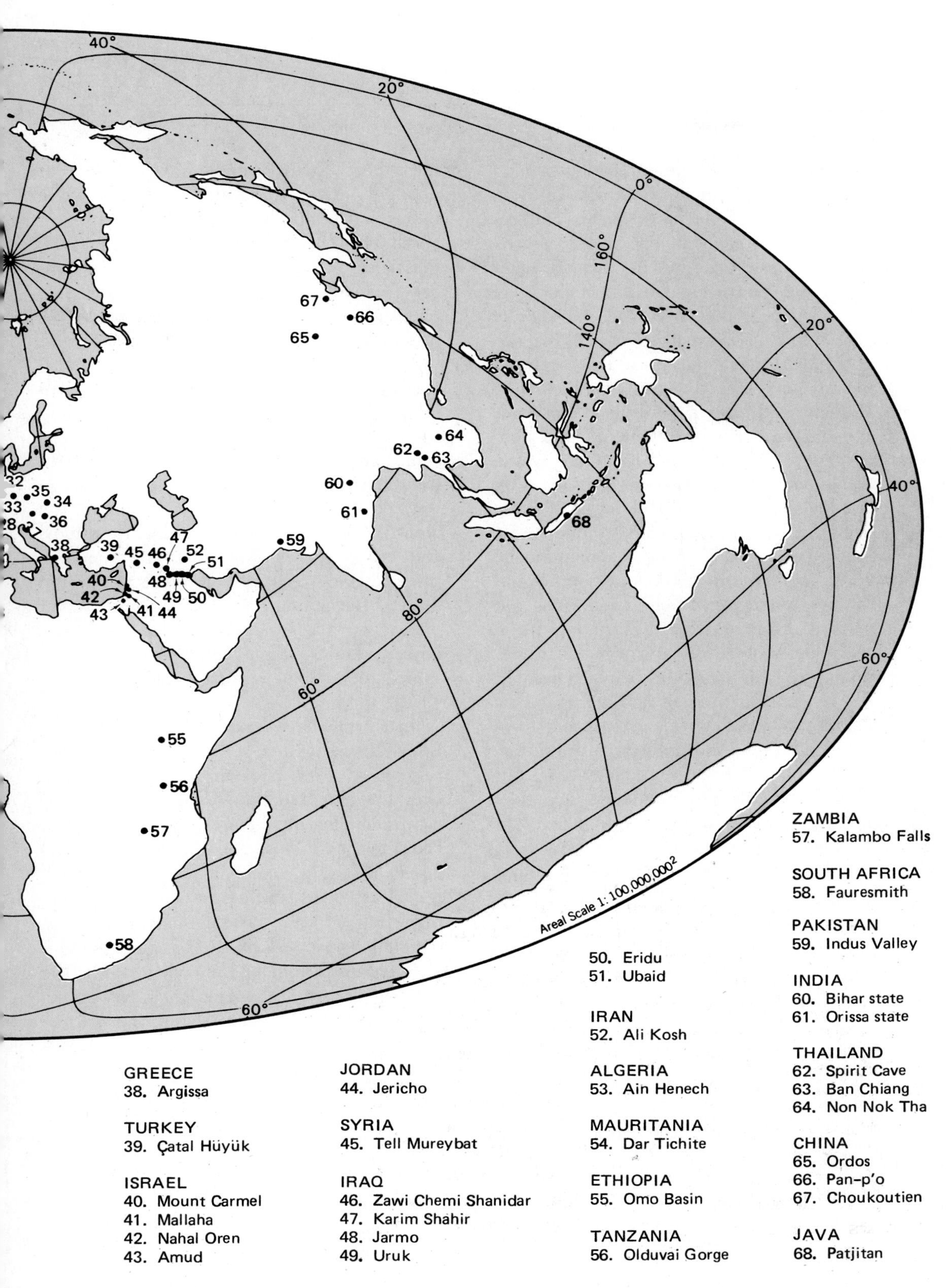
40°
20°
0°
160°
140°
20°
40°
60°
80°
60°
60°
Areal Scale 1: 100,000,000²
GREECE
38. Argissa
TURKEY
39. Çatal Hüyük
ISRAEL
40. Mount Carmel
41. Mallaha
42. Nahal Oren
43. Amud
JORDAN
44. Jericho
SYRIA
45. Tell Mureybat
IRAQ
46. Zawi Chemi Shanidar
47. Karim Shahir
48. Jarmo
49. Uruk
50. Eridu
51. Ubaid
IRAN
52. Ali Kosh
ALGERIA
53. Ain Henech
MAURITANIA
54. Dar Tichite
ETHIOPIA
55. Omo Basin
TANZANIA
56. Olduvai Gorge
ZAMBIA
57. Kalambo Falls
SOUTH AFRICA
58. Fauresmith
PAKISTAN
59. Indus Valley
INDIA
60. Bihar state
61. Orissa state
THAILAND
62. Spirit Cave
63. Ban Chiang
64. Non Nok Tha
CHINA
65. Ordos
66. Pan-p'o
67. Choukoutien
JAVA
68. Patjitan

ing the natural environment had remained constant. Throughout the hundreds of thousands of years of glacial advances and retreats, climatic zones underwent drastic changes. These changes in turn brought about a constantly changing succession of plant and animal life. With each advance of the glaciers, warm-weather species of animals were driven south, tundras replaced plains, plains replaced forests, forests turned to deserts, and elsewhere deserts bloomed. The quality and nutritive value of the Paleolithic diet was determined as much by the local abundance of plants and animals as by technology. Inefficient technology yielded a high standard of living when there was a great abundance of plants and animals, whereas even the most efficient hunting and collecting technologies and techniques did not stave off hunger and extinction when game and plant resources became scarce. Human well-being was thus directly related to the response of animals and plants to natural conditions. Paleolithic groups may have influenced these conditions by burning forests to increase grassland grazing areas. But for the most part the only influence they could exert was negative, through overkill and uncontrolled gathering.

The vulnerability of the hunting and gathering mode of production is well illustrated in the transition from the Upper Paleolithic to the terminal Pleistocene cultures of northern and western Europe. Toward the end of the last glaciation, the region south of the glaciers received a flow of meltwater favoring the growth of grassy plains on which herds of horses, bison, mammoths, and reindeer grazed. As the glaciers retreated, lush virgin grasslands formed into which these animals spread followed by their human predators. Both animal and human populations prospered, but unbeknown to either, their mutual way of life was doomed. The Eurasian grasslands were merely a temporary ecological phase. At about 12,000 B.P. trees began to invade the grasslands. Underneath the leafy forest canopy, no grass could grow. By 10,000 B.P. much of the so-called *Pleistocene megafauna* had become extinct in Europe. Gone were the woolly mammoth and rhino, steppe bison, giant elk, and wild ass (Fig. 8.16). No doubt the marvelously skilled Upper Paleolithic hunters themselves contributed to this ecological catastrophe, just as New World hunters probably played a role in the extinction of the Pleistocene megafauna in the New World (see p. 178). Elephants, rhinos, and other genera had survived numerous prior advances and retreats of grasslands and forests throughout the Pleistocene. What was new in the situation may have been the unprecedented efficiency of Upper Paleolithic technology (Butzer 1971; Kurtén 1972).

In Europe this period is called the *Mesolithic.* It was a time of intense local ecological change. Forests of birch and pine spread over the land, and the hunters made their camps in clearings along riverbanks and at lakesides, estuaries, and the seashore. The forests sheltered game such as elk, red deer, roe deer, wild cattle (aurochs), and wild pigs. But to locate these animals, new tracking skills were needed. Forest-dwelling animals would disappear from view unless the kill was prompt and silent. Thus, it is no accident that at a Mesolithic site, Star Carr in England, archaeologists have found the earliest European evidence—about 9500 B.P.—of the long and successful symbiosis between people and dogs (Clutton-Brock 1969). In the forest the dog's sense of smell directed the hunter to within bowshot of evasive prey. But hunting under forested conditions, even with improved bows and hound dogs, could not yield the quantities of meat that were formerly obtained by following the herds of reindeer and bison. Thus, the Mesolithic people turned increasingly to a *broad spectrum* of plant foods and fish, mollusks, and other riverine and maritime sources of food. Along the seacoast the heaped-up debris of centuries of Mesolithic shellfish eating formed mounds called *kitchen middens*. Although clams, oysters, and mussels are good sources of protein, it took a lot of eating for a hungry person to fill up on such food.

THE END OF THE PALEOLITHIC IN WORLD PERSPECTIVE

There is considerable evidence that the European Mesolithic was a regional manifesta-

Figure 8.16 *WOOLLY MAMMOTHS*
Artist's rendering of one of the species of big-game animals that became extinct in Europe at the end of the last glaciation.

tion of a worldwide cultural-ecological trend leading to broad-spectrum modes of production which took place at somewhat different times but within a range of about 6000 years (about 15,000 to 7,000 B.P.). This trend is marked by the exploitation of mollusks, marine mammals, fish, birds, seeds, nuts, and other dispersed and energetically costly food sources. In the Near East, for example, the people called the *Natufians* who lived about 10,500 B.P. supplemented their hunting of animals like gazelle and deer with harvesting of wild grain while fishing with nets, harpoons, and fishhooks (for more on the Natufians, see the next chapter). A similar complex can be found in Nubia and Upper Egypt between 15,000 and 9,000 B.P. along the margins of the Nile Valley where the broad spectrum included wild grains and seeds, birds, fish, and some larger animals (Krzyzaniak 1981). A broad-spectrum mode of production provided the basis for what Jerome Jacobson (1979:481) has called a "full-fledged Mesolithic village" located on a lakeshore in the state of Uttar Pradesh in India and dating to about 10,300 B.P. Comparable developments can be discerned in China in the lake region of Yunnan Province and in Japan where shellfish middens (refuse heaps) resembling European Mesolithic middens date to 9000 B.P. Finally, as will be seen in our discussion of New World prehistory (Ch. 10), broad-spectrum modes of production also occur at the end of the Pleistocene at sites in Mexico, the Peruvian coast, and the Mississippi Valley.

As we shall see (p. 178), this recurrent trend appears to be indicative of an imbalance between population and Upper Paleolithic big-game hunting-and-gathering modes of production. Environmental change, an increase in population density, intensification of traditional hunting patterns leading to depletion of traditional food resources, and some form of population pressure appear to be critical factors leading to Mesolithic-like broad-spectrum adaptations (G. Clark 1981; Yessner 1981; Harris 1977; M. Cohen 1977).

SUMMARY

Cultures evolved slowly and for long periods not at all during most of the Pleistocene. There appears to have been a close relationship between the emergence of *H. sapiens* and the point of culture "take-off."

The longest and most ancient age of hominid prehistory is called the Paleolithic. This age began at least 2.5 million years ago as indicated by the simple stone tools found at Hadar. It lasted until about 10,000 years ago. The mode of production practiced throughout that entire period was the scavenging, hunting, gathering, or fishing of the natural life-forms. There were no domesticated plants or animals.

During the Lower Paleolithic, a transition occurred from the earliest Oldowan chopper and flake industries to the core-biface industries of the Acheulian tradition. It is assumed that one evolved into the other although the two overlapped for 500,000 years at Olduvai. The principal diagnostic of the Acheulian is the hand ax, probably a multipurpose instrument, but its precise functions are unknown. The Acheulian industry is closely associated wth European and African *H. erectus*, although in west Europe it may have displaced earlier local industries. During the Lower Paleolithic, big-game hunting techniques were improved, simple shelters constructed, and controlled use of fire introduced.

It was only at the transition between the

Lower and Middle Paleolithic, about 125,000 to 100,000 B.P., that fundamental changes in tool technology occurred. The best-known innovation is the Levallois tortoise-core method for the preparation of flake tools. The European Middle Paleolithic is often called the Mousterian period, and it is closely associated with the Neandertals. Elsewhere, the Middle Paleolithic is associated with other archaic *H. sapiens*. Much of the tool manufacture during the Middle Paleolithic involved soft-hammer techniques and secondary flaking, retouching, and trimming. Points suitable for spears appear. Toward the end of the Middle Paleolithic a few personal adornments, incised decorations, and a considerable amount of burial ritual suggest that fundamental changes in symbolizing faculties were taking place.

The Upper Paleolithic begins about 30,000 years ago and is closely associated with the emergence of *H. sapiens sapiens*. There is a great production of ivory, bone, and antler implements. Blades and other stone tools become highly specialized and beautifully crafted. Needles suggest the use of skin clothing in northern latitudes. Many other basic inventions were made. Personal adornments, representational paintings and figurines, and incised symbols proliferate, all suggesting a quantum leap in the quality of the symbolizing process.

In Europe the Upper Paleolithic peoples were hunters of the big game that inhabited the grasslands which developed after the retreat of the last continental glaciers. After 10,000 years ago, reforestation, aided to an unknown degree by human hunting, destroyed this megafauna. Hence, the European Mesolithic is characterized by coastal, riverine, and forest-adapted cultures. The dog was domesticated to aid in forest hunting. Many other basic technological inventions suitable for exploiting a broad spectrum of coastal, riverine, and forest habitats were introduced. Similar patterns of broad-spectrum adaptations occur widely at the end of the Pleistocene in both the Old World and the New World in the time period of 15,000 to 7,000 B.P.

It seems likely that the end of the Paleolithic represented relatively hard times for many of the descendants of the Upper Paleolithic big-game hunters. In Europe the new technoenvironmental relationship also had rather drastic consequences upon the cave art. Both the herd animals and the ritual art depicting them disappeared at about the same time. The aesthetic component in Mesolithic rituals expressed itself in geometric designs and symbols incised on tools and weapons and painted on pebbles. In a very general sense the end of the cave art may reflect the failure of ritual paintings to prevent the destruction of Upper Paleolithic ecosystems (G. Clark 1967).

Because of the disappearance of the cave art, some prehistorians view the Mesolithic as a time of cultural decline or even degeneration. However, this view fails to give proper weight to the uninterrupted vitality of cultural innovation during the period. The domestication of the dog surely is an achievement no less significant than the cave paintings. To meet the challenge and the opportunity provided by the great abundance of trees, new techniques were developed for making and hafting woodworking tools. For the first time, axes were produced by grinding rather than by flaking processes. Fishhooks, fish spears, and harpoons were perfected; fish nets and bark floats, boats and paddles, sleds and skis were also either invented or improved upon. One of the most important experiments involved an increase in the amount of settlement, as local groups camped for longer periods of time near renewable resources such as shellfish beds or fishing streams. Thus, far from being degenerate, it was a time of great technological diversification and technological experimentation, as new ways to make the best of the altered natural circumstances were tried out. The stage was being set for momentous changes.

9 THE NEOLITHIC AND THE RISE OF CITIES AND STATES

This chapter describes the further evolution of cultures from the end of the Mesolithic to the rise of cities and states in the Old World. We shall see that between 10,000 and 2,000 B.P., as a result of the domestication of plants and animals, more changes of a fundamental nature were introduced into Old World cultural beliefs and practices than in all the previous millions of years of cultural evolution.

THE NEOLITHIC

Neolithic literally means "new stone age." When the term was first introduced in the nineteenth century, it gave recognition to the appearance of stone implements which had been prepared by the techniques of grinding and polishing. Today the term *Neolithic* is used not to designate new stone-working methods but new methods of food production. During the Neolithic greater control over the reproduction of plants and animals was achieved by the development of farming and stock raising. This in turn provided the material basis for high-density, sedentary settlements and for rapid population increase. During the Neolithic, *H. sapiens*, changed from a rare to an abundant species. Farming and stock raising also set the stage for profound alterations in domestic and political economy centering on access to land, water, and other basic resources, and for the emergence of differences in wealth and power. Without agriculture the development of cities, states, and empires could not have occurred. All that is regarded today under the rubric of industrial society arose ultimately in response to that same great transformation.

What is domestication? Domestication involves a complex symbiotic relationship between human populations, the *domesticators,* and certain favored plants and animals, the *domesticates.* The domesticators destroy or clear away undesirable flora and fauna from the domesticates' habitats. They adjust the supply of space, water, sunlight, and nutrients, and they interfere in the reproductive activity of the domesticates to ensure maximum favorable use of available resources. Domestication usually involves genetic changes. For example, a key difference between wild and domesticated varieties of wheat, barley, and other cereals is that wild grains break off upon ripening and fall to the ground on their own, whereas ripe domesticated grains remain intact even when roughly handled. Indeed, the ripe domesticated grains must be pulled or beaten off if they are to be made available for human consumption. In the case of American Indian maize, the ripe kernels do not fall off at all, and the plant is incapable of reproducing itself without human assistance. Other instances of this phenomenon are found in the banana plant and date palm. The final step in domestication occurs when the domesticate is removed from its natural habitat to an area that is markedly different, or when, as a result of cultivation, its original habitat is markedly transformed (cf. Barrau 1967).

THE NEOLITHIC IN THE MIDDLE EAST

One of the earliest archaeologically known transitions from hunting and gathering to a Neolithic mode of production took place in the Middle East*. This region extends from

*Archaeologists refer to this region as the *Near East.* Almost everyone else, including the news media, refers to it as the *Middle East.*

the Jordan Valley, northward to southern Turkey, eastward to the headwaters of the Tigris and Euphrates rivers in Syria and Iraq, and southward along both flanks of the Zagros Mountains (Fig. 9.1), which form the border between Iraq and Iran. Domesticated barley, wheat, goats, sheep, and pigs, dating between 11,000 and 9,000 B.P., have been identified at a number of sites in this region. There is some evidence that the area of earliest domestication, especially of cattle, pigs, and goats, extended as far west as Greece (Protsch and Berger 1973; cf. Bökönyi, Braidwood, and Reed 1973). Also, it seems likely that leguminous plants including peas, lentils, broad beans, and chickpeas were domesticated almost at the same time as the basic grain crops (Zohary and Hopf 1973).

The region in which the Middle Eastern Neolithic transformation occurred corresponds roughly to the regions in which wheat, barley, peas, lentils, goats, and sheep occur naturally in a wild state (Harlan 1978; Zohary and Hopf 1973). At the end of the Pleistocene, Middle Eastern peoples incorporated these plants and animals into their food supply through hunting and gathering techniques. The culture of these preagricultural peoples was a local form of the terminal Paleolithic (or a Middle Eastern version of the Mesolithic). Much of the big game had become extinct as early as 20,000 B.P. (M.N. Cohen 1977:132). Like the European Mesolithic peoples, the terminal Pleistocene Middle Easteners had tool kits containing barbed harpoons, bone needles, and fishhooks. They exploited a broad spec-

Figure 9.1 *HILLY FLANKS, NORTHERN IRAQ*
The Zagros Mountains are in the background.

trum of food resources: small game, fish, turtles, seasonal waterfowl, terrestrial and marine snails, mussels, and crabs, as well as legumes, nuts, fruits, and other plant foods. One critical difference, however, was that the Middle Easterners made increasing use of grass seeds, including the wild ancestors of wheat and barley. The absence of these wild grains from the broad spectrum of resources that could be exploited in western Europe explains perhaps why the Neolithic transformation did not originate directly from the western European Mesolithic base.

The contribution grains made to the food supply was at first relatively minor. Their use was limited by a number of technical problems. First, the ripening of wild wheat and barley occurs during a 3-week period in the late spring. Hence if the wild grains were to form part of the diet during any extended portion of the year, a rather large amount had to be harvested. Moreover, to make use of such a harvest, a considerable amount of additional labor was needed to process the seeds. The processing technology was in itself quite complex since the seeds had to be cleaned, roasted (in order to crack the husks), husked, winnowed, ground, and cooked. Carrying around the heavy stones needed for grinding would be especially troublesome for groups with a nomadic hunting-and-gathering mode of production. The obvious solution to these difficulties was to settle in relatively permanent dwellings where the grain could be stored and the heavy grinding and roasting equipment left in place. Middle Eastern groups had begun to settle down in permanent villages a thousand or more years before domesticated varieties of wheat and barley were in use (D. Harris 1975; Flannery 1973).

At Mt. Carmel in Israel, for example, prehistoric people known as the Natufians carved out basin-shaped depressions at the front of their rock shelters, laid courses of stone pavement, and built rings of stone around what appear to be permanent hearths. In the Jordan River Valley, at the 10,000 B.P. site of Mallaha, stone foundations of round houses with plastered storage pits have been excavated. Flint "sickles" also found at these sites indicate that the Natufians harvested wild grains. Such instruments reveal their function by a special sheen that is acquired by flint blades used to cut grass stems. Evidence of preagricultural grain-cutting, grain-roasting, or grain-storing village life has been found at Zawi Chemi Shanidar in Iraq (Fig. 9.2) at the upper drainage of the Tigris River and at Karim Shahir on the flanks of the Zagros Mountains, both dating from 12,000 to 10,000 B.P. (Solecki 1964). Evidence of preagricultural village life dating to 10,000 B.P. has also been discovered at Tell Mureybat on the headwaters of the Euphrates River in Syria (Fig. 9.3). Here clay-walled houses, grinding stones, and roasting pits have been found, together with 18 different types of wild seeds including wild wheat and barley. The discovery of preagricultural sedentary villages has revolutionized previous theories concerning the origin of agriculture. Prior to 1960 it was generally believed that settled village life must have come after, not before, the development of domesticates. It is now recognized, however, that hunters and gatherers can live in relatively dense and sedentary settlements if the resources they exploit are concentrated in restricted areas as, for example, mollusk beds, fish that migrate upstream to spawn, and fields of wild grasses.

J.D. Harlan has shown that stands of wild

Figure 9.2 *SITE OF ZAWI CHEMI SHANIDAR*
One of the earliest villages in Iraq. Mortars in foreground attest to the importance of cereals in diet.

wheat still grow thick enough in Turkey and other parts of the Middle East for an individual using a flint-bladed sickle to harvest a kilogram of grain per hour—enough for a family of experienced plant collectors working over a 3-week period to gather more grain than they could possibly consume in a whole year. As Kent Flannery has remarked, "After all, where can you go with a metric ton of cleaned wheat? It requires storage facilities, and it requires that they be sufficiently waterproof so the grain does not sprout during the moist winter season"(1973:280).

THE ORIGINS OF AGRICULTURE

Thus the preagricultural villages in the Middle East were adaptations to the need to store the wild grain, process it into flour, and convert it into flat cakes or porridge. The construction of houses, walls, roasters, grinders, and storage pits may be viewed as capital investment in grain futures. The people who made such an investment would be very reluctant to give it up in order to move to another site.

In order for their system of wild grain collection to remain viable for any length of

Figure 9.3 *TELL MUREYBAT*
Site of preagricultural sedentary village.

time, the collectors had to refrain from harvesting all the stalks in a particular field. Selective harvesting of this sort is still practiced by many contemporary hunting-and-gathering peoples precisely to ensure future harvests from the same wild stands. Thus, with selective grain harvests supplemented by hunting and other collecting activities, villages were able to feed themselves without having to move.

But selective grain harvesting is not as efficient as agriculture proper and cannot support dense regional populations. The trouble is that in their wild state, wheat and barley have heads that consist of a brittle axis to which the seed husks are affixed. When it is ripe, the axis (called a *rachis)* shatters easily (Fig. 9.4). Harvesters may move through a field of wild grains, cutting off the entire ear or stripping the husk-encased seeds with their fingers. Either way, their activity shatters the most brittle heads (if the wind has not already done so), and these are the ones that reseed themselves. What the harvesters need are plants whose ripened seeds will not be dislodged by next year's winds before the harvesters can get to them. Yet these are the ones they take home to eat. And so the harvesters would seem to be unconsciously selecting against the very feature that is most essential for the breeding of domesticated grains. How was this selection reversed? One theory is that when sheaths of tough rachis grain were brought to the village to be threshed and winnowed, tough rachis seeds would accidentally be scattered in the area around the houses where human waste and garbage provided ideal growing conditions. The next step would be deliberate planting of these tough rachis seeds in the favored area around the village. Finally, it would be recognized that sowing seeds from a few plants with good harvesting qualities produced whole fields of tough rachis plants. Another change involved selection for husks that did not adhere firmly to the seeds and that could easily be detached during threshing. In the wild varieties the husks had to be heated and then pounded and winnowed in order to get at the grain. This may explain the presence of roasting pits and subterranean earth ovens in the earliest villages (see above). Other desirable genetic changes—leading to larger ears with multiple rows of seeds—were easily achieved by following one simple rule: Don't eat the seeds from plants that have the most desirable features; plant them. This rule implies that the actual planting and cultivation of cereal grains began *before* the genetic changes characteristic of domesticates had occurred. This seems to be confirmed at Tell Abu Hureya in Syria where the remains of weeds that are known to be associated with modern cultivated fields appear in association with the remains of wheat grains that are indistinguishable from wild types (Fagan 1983:193).

THE DOMESTICATION OF ANIMALS

Which came first—the domestication of sheep and goats or the domestication of wheat and barley? No definite answer can or should be given. The Old World animal and plant domesticates and the people who depended on them were interrelated parts of a unitary process. As humans began to obtain their food energy in a new way, plants and animals were forced into new relationships with each other. The wild grasses—including the ancestors of wheat and barley—had been a major food source for wild sheep and goats. As permanent villages more and more often came to be located in the middle of dense fields of grain, herds of wild sheep

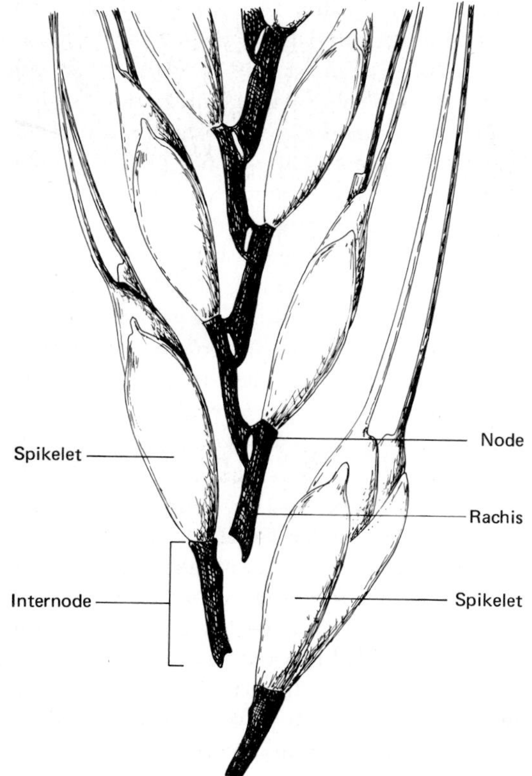

Figure 9.4 *EMMER SPIKE*

and goats would be forced into closer and closer contact with people. With the aid of dogs, the people could begin to control the movements of these herds, keeping the sheep and goats permanently on the margins of the grainfields, allowing them to eat the stubble but keeping them away from the ripe grain. Hunting, in other words, may have become greatly simplified. The hunters no longer had to go to the animals; instead, the animals, finding the lush fields of concentrated vegetation irresistible, came to the hunters. This would have resulted in a temporary increase in meat production. In the long run, however, the spread of agriculture inevitably leads to the depletion and eventual extinction of regional game resources. Unless measures are taken to control the rate of production, wild species find their natural range lands greatly diminished, and the hunters find it easier to locate their quarry. The domestication of sheep and goats, therefore, can be looked upon as the first great conservation movement. By deliberately feeding the endangered animals and by slaughtering only males and protecting the females, sheep and goats were kept off the growing list of valuable species that had become extinct since the end of the Pleistocene.

Many modern-day hunter-gatherers and village horticulturalists keep animals as pets. It was not lack of knowledge about animals that prevented Mesolithic peoples from raising large numbers of such pets and making use of them for food and other functions. Rather, the principal problem was that humans would soon run out of food for themselves if they had to share it with animals. But the cultivation of grains opened new possibilities: sheep and goats thrive on stubble and other inedible portions of domesticated plants. On a small scale they could be penned, fed on stubble, and milked and slaughtered selectively. Breeding for desirable genetic features, unlike the initial phases of plant domestication, would have been quite straightforward. Animals that were too aggressive or that grew too slowly or that were too delicate would have been eaten before they reached reproductive age. On theoretical grounds, therefore, it is likely that the domestication of plants and animals in the Middle East occurred synchronously as part of a general regionwide process of cultural and ecological change. This seems to be confirmed by the early dates at which both plant and animal domesticates begin to appear.

At Zawi Chemi Shanidar, one of the earliest villages in Iraq, domesticated sheep appeared shortly after 11,000 B.P., and the earliest domesticated goats have been found at Ali Kosh in Iran, dating to 9500 B.P., along with domesticated wheat and barley. At Jericho in Jordan there were domesticated varieties of wheat, barley, and goats by 9000 B.P., and the same complex is found at Jarmo (Fig. 9.5) in Iraq by 8800 B.P. (Higgs and Jarman 1972; Herre and Röhrs 1978; Harlan 1978; Protsch and Berger 1973).

Many other Neolithic sites of similar antiquity have been excavated, and new ones are being brought to light every year.

EARLY NEOLITHIC IN NORTHEASTERN AFRICA

Investigations carried out in Egypt and the Sudan during the last two decades indicate that the Neolithic transition occurred at about the same time in this region as in the rest of the Middle East (i.e., southwestern Asia). There was an early phase of intensive collecting of wild barley and wild wheat associated with milling stones and mortars.

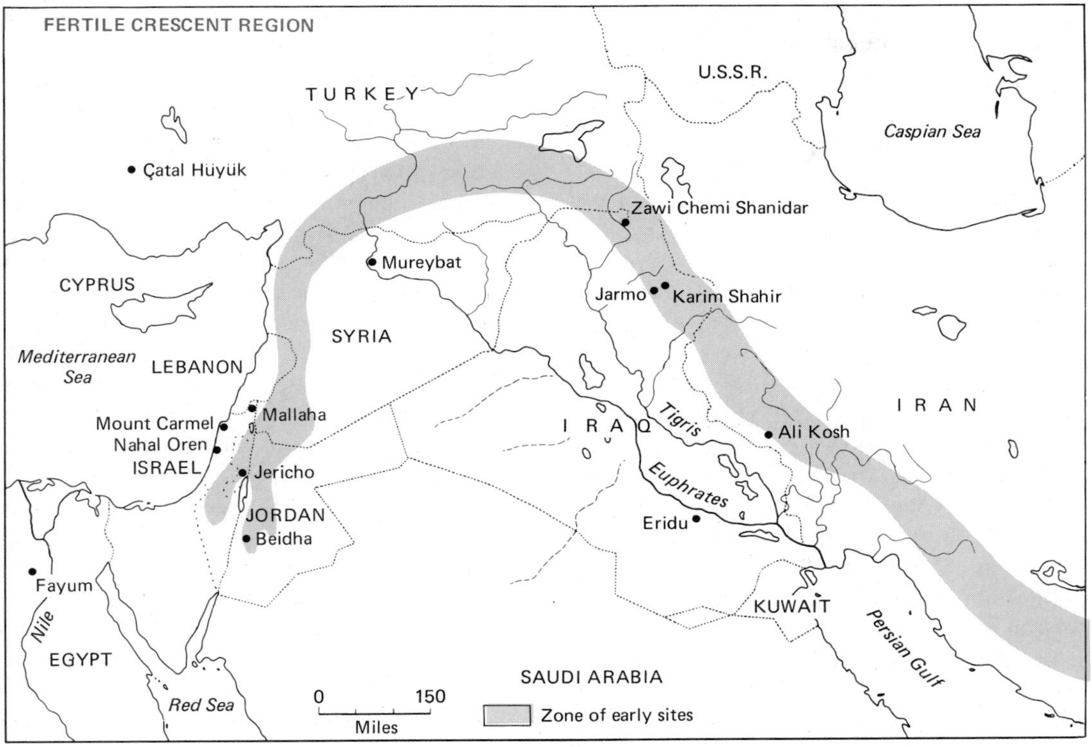

FERTILE CRESCENT REGION

TURKEY
U.S.S.R.
Caspian Sea
Çatal Hüyük
Zawi Chemi Shanidar
CYPRUS
Mureybat
Jarmo
Karim Shahir
SYRIA
Mediterranean Sea
LEBANON
Mount Carmel
Mallaha
Nahal Oren
ISRAEL
Jericho
JORDAN
Beidha
IRAQ
Tigris
Euphrates
Ali Kosh
IRAN
Eridu
Fayum
Nile
EGYPT
Red Sea
SAUDI ARABIA
KUWAIT
Persian Gulf
0 150
Miles
Zone of early sites

Figure 9.5 *EXCAVATION AT JARMO*
One of the earliest Neolithic villages in Northeast Iraq where barley, wheat, goats, sheep, and dogs were all in use by 8500 B.P.

But the extremely early radiocarbon dates (18,000 to 14,000 B.P.) previously assigned to these complexes have been shown to be erroneous (Wendorf et al. 1984). Evidence for domesticated cattle in oases of the Egyptian western desert with dates of 9700 to 8250 B.P. has also been found. And full Neolithic complexes with domesticated cattle, sheep, goat, wheat, barley, and date palms had appeared by 7800 B.P. (Krzyzaniak 1981; Wendorf and Schild 1981).

THE CAUSES OF THE NEOLITHIC

Early attempts to understand the transition to the Neolithic were distorted by a belief that all hunters and gatherers led "nasty, mean, brutish" lives and that they engaged in a grim, never-ending search for game and edible morsels. More recently, as we shall see in Chapter 11, anthropologists have shown that hunters and gatherers enjoy higher standards of health and nutrition and considerably more leisure than most peasant farming peoples (Sahlins 1972). However, this "affluence" can be maintained only by strict limitation of the size of the hunter-gatherer population and only as long as climatic and ecological conditions remain favorable to the survival and reproduction of the edible plants and animals. There is considerable evidence that the earlier post-Pleistocene Middle Easterners confronted a deteriorating ecological situation and were experiencing increasing population pressure. The broad-spectrum mode of hunting and collecting itself can be interpreted as a response to a decline in the availability of larger protein-rich game animals and calorie-rich plants. The fact that seed collecting—with its elaborate requirements for processing into flour—assumed such prominence among the Natufians and other pre-Neolithic hunter-gatherers suggests that they could maintain their standard of living only by working longer and harder than the peoples of the Upper Paleolithic. Indeed, there is some justification for interpreting the time of the broad-spectrum modes of production in Europe, the Middle East, and in other regions just before the development of agriculture as a prehistoric "crisis" in food production (M. N. Cohen 1977; Binford 1983:210–212).

In the absence of modern contraceptive and abortion techniques, limitation of population growth cannot be achieved without paying heavy psychological and physical penalties. The principal means that are available to preindustrial peoples are abstention from heterosexual intercourse, prolongation of breast feeding to 3 or 4 years (see p. 221), dangerous abortions, and infant and child deaths through neglect or abuse. Adoption of the farming mode of production would have lessened the need to use these psychologically and physically costly remedies for relieving the population pressure brought on by the food crisis. By controlling the rate at which plants capture the energy of the sun, agriculture makes it possible for denser human populations to exist in a habitat previously exploited only by hunting and gathering. Moreover, agriculture lessens the cost of rearing children. Among hunters and gatherers, additional children are costly because infants must be carried over long distances, and male children do not become effective hunters until they are adolescents. But with agriculture, the more children, the more plants and animals that can be taken care of. Children can be put to work at an early age in a number of simple tasks connected with planting, weeding, and herding and can easily "pay" for themselves—at least as long as there is plenty of land available (or game, where there are no domesticated animals; see p. 370). Moreover, with agriculture, women are freed from much of the burden of having to carry infants over long distances each day. In permanent village situations there is less need for long-distance travel and hence less of a penalty associated with shortening the span of years between the rearing of one infant and another. Perhaps it was this reduction in "cost" per child per woman more than any other factor that was responsible for the initial concentration on seed gathering even before plants and animals were domesticated (Sussman 1972; Sengel 1973; Dumond 1975; Lee 1979:312ff).

Early Neolithic villages such as Çatal Hüyük (see next section) attest to a high standard of living enjoyed by all villagers on an equal basis without class distinctions. Animal fats and proteins (meat and dairy products) were probably as abundant per capita as during the times of the Upper Paleolithic big-game hunters. However, population increased rapidly, surpassing earlier rates of growth. The rate during the Paleolithic is estimated to have been only 0.0015 percent per year (see Table 11.2), yielding a population in the Middle East of about 100,000 in the year 10,000 B.P. (Carneiro and Hilse 1966). It is estimated that the rate increased to 0.1 percent between 10,000 and 6,000 B.P. This amounts to a doubling of population every 700 years. Thus, starting with 100,000 people in 10,000 B.P., the population of the Middle East probably reached 3.2 million shortly before 6000 B.P.—a thirtyfold increase in 4000 years. By this time, however, the original domesticates and Neolithic techniques could no longer maintain the same high per capita return for labor input that had been characteristic of the years when land was abundant and population was small. Animal fats and protein in particular probably became scarcer on a per capita basis because of the utilization of grazing lands for food crops and because of the high costs of feeding livestock on grains. This situation was worsened by inequalities in access to goods and services related to the emergence of the state.

THE NEOLITHIC "REVOLUTION"

Once the threshold to full Neolithic status was crossed, new domesticates, tools, productive techniques, and forms of social life appeared with explosive rapidity. True, this "explosion" went on from 10,000 to 5,000 B.P., but during those 5000 years technology, social organization, and ideology changed more drastically than during the preceding 2 or 3 million years.

For reasons probably related to an increase in warfare, walled towns were built shortly after the appearance of domesticated plants and animals. The most astonishing of these towns was Jericho (Fig. 9.6), whose earliest walls and towers date to 10,000 B.P. Situated in an oasis, Jericho probably controlled the Dead Sea salt trade; it covered 10 acres and had a population estimated at 2000 (Hamblin 1973). By 8750 B.P. some Middle Eastern adobe-brick towns covered 30 or more acres.

One such site in southern Turkey, Çatal Hüyük (Mellart 1975), contains a dazzling array of art objects, woven cloth, murals, and wall sculpture (Fig. 9.7). The people of Çatal Hüyük grew barley and three varieties of wheat. They kept sheep, cattle, goats, and dogs. The people lived in adjoining rectangular one-story, sun-dried brick houses opening on courtyards. There were no doors; entrance was gained through holes in the flat roofs. Initially there was considerable hunting of wild species, especially of aurochs (wild cattle). By about 8000 B.P. the wild cattle were replaced by smaller domesticated cattle (Todd 1978). As at Jericho, the prosperity of Çatal Hüyük may have been based on its control of trade. It seems likely that the village was a center for the domestication, breeding, and export of cattle for which it received a variety of imported arti-

Figure 9.6 *JERICHO*
The ruins lie near permanent springs, 700 feet below sea level.

(a)

(b)

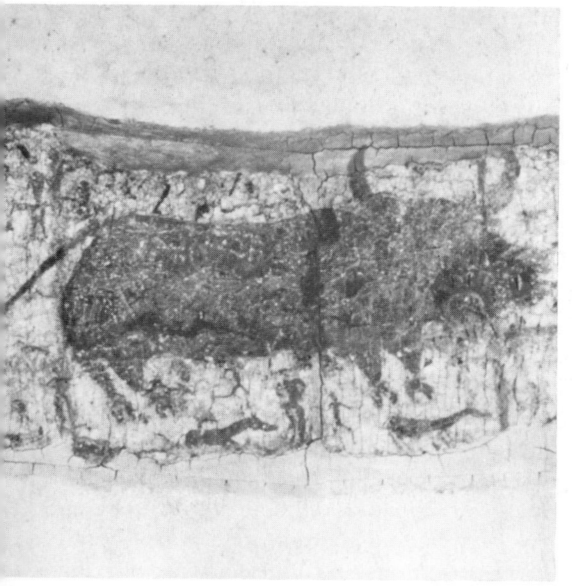

Figure 9.7 *CATAL HÜYÜK*
View of rooms and walls (*a*) and bull's head wall sculpture (*b*).

Figure 9.8 *ÇATAL HÜYÜK NEOLITHIC WALL PAINTING*
Cattle played a prominent role in the economy and in religious and artistic life.

facts and raw materials including 35 different kinds of minerals (Sherratt 1982:14). Çatal Hüyük's wall paintings—the earliest known paintings on a house wall—depict a large bull, 6 feet long, other animals being hunted, dancing men, and vultures attacking human bodies. Colors include red, pink, mauve, black, and yellow (Fig. 9.8).

EARLIEST EVIDENCE OF ANIMAL DOMESTICATION

Dog	14,000 B.P.	Palegawara, Iran
Sheep	11,000 B.P.	Zawi Chemi Shanidar, Iraq
Cattle	9,700 B.P.	Western Desert, Egypt
Goat	9,500 B.P.	Ali Kosh, Iran
Pig	9,000 B.P.	Cayonu, Turkey
Guinea pig	8,000 B.P.	Ayacucho Basin, Peru
Silk moth	5,500 B.P.	Hsi-Yin-t'sun, China
Llama	5,500 B.P.	Andean Highlands, Peru
Ass	5,000 B.P.	Nile Valley, Egypt
Bactracian Camel	5,000 B.P.	Southern U.S.S.R.
Dromedary	5,000 B.P.	Saudi Arabia
Horse	5,000 B.P.	Ukraine, U.S.S.R.
Honeybee	5,000 B.P.	Nile Valley, Egypt
Water buffalo	4,500 B.P.	Indus Valley, Pakistan
Duck	4,500 B.P.	Middle East
Yak	4,500 B.P.	Tibet
Chickens	4,000 B.P.	Indian Valley, Pakistan
Cat	3,600 B.P.	Egypt
Goose	3,500 B.P.	Germany
Reindeer	3,000 B.P.	Pazyryk Valley, Siberia

THE URBAN REVOLUTION AND THE RISE OF THE STATE

Once cattle were domesticated a whole series of additional technological and environmental innovations and interactions followed. Harnessed to plows, which were invented by 5500 B.P. or earlier, cattle made it possible to farm a variety of new zones. As population increased, village settlements spread out over the fertile but rainless southern portion of the Tigris-Euphrates Valley. Confined at first to the margins of the natural watercourses, dense clusters of villages and towns came increasingly to rely on artificial irrigation to water their fields of wheat and barley. By 6350 B.P. monumental mud-brick temples reared up from the center of major towns such as Eridu (Fig. 9.9) and Al Ubaid. Finally, as at Uruk between 5800 and 5200 B.P., there appeared the first cities whose streets, houses, temples, palaces, and fortifications covered hundreds of acres and were surrounded by thousands of acres of irrigated fields.

The catalog of technological achievements now included spinning and weaving (earlier Neolithic inventions), as well as ceramics, smelting and casting of bronze, baked brick, arched masonry, the potter's wheel, sailing ships, the first wheeled vehicles, writing, calendrical time-reckoning, weights and measures, and the beginnings of mathematics. Here, for the first time, human communities became divided into rulers and ruled, rich and poor, literate and illiterate, townspeople and peasants, artists, warriors, priests, and kings.

Briefly considered, the process of state formation in Mesopotamia (the area between the Tigris and Euphrates rivers) seems to have involved a number of factors which recurred in other regions where cities and states developed after the appearance of simple farming villages. Mesopotamian soils were extremely fertile, but because of the deficiency in rainfall, irrigation was needed to expand and intensify agricultural production. As population density increased, competition within and between local settlements for access to and control over the water needed for irrigation also increased. Mesopotamia was also deficient in stone, metal ores, wood, and many other raw materials. These deficits were made up by extensive trade with other regions, and the need to organize and control trading activities blended with the need to organize and control the waterworks and to regulate the distribution of the grain harvests. The task of organizing production, distribution, trade, and defense was gradually taken over by a political-religious-military hierarchy, which formed the nucleus of the first state bureaucracies.

Figure 9.9 *ERIDU*
Remains of large tower at center and of temple below.

These elite groups provided services in the form of calendrical calculations, provision of emergency rations, support of artisan specialists, and religious ceremonials. They eventually developed into exploitative classes whose despotic power rested on control over police-military force. By imposing various forms of taxation, the first dynastic ruling classes succeeded in diverting a substantial portion of the farming population's harvests into state enterprises, thereby preventing the peasant food producers from slackening their productive efforts or from enjoying the leisure or security that are intuitively but erroneously associated with the adoption of advanced technologies. More and more intensive irrigation merely provided additional means of consolidating and intensifying the ruling elite's power over people and nature. We shall take a closer look at the processes responsible for the rise of class-stratified state societies and some alternative theories of state formation in Chapter 16 (cf. Childe 1952; Wittlogel 1957; Braidwood and Willey 1962; R. McC. Adams 1966, 1972; Mitchell 1973; Carneiro 1970; Cohen and Service 1978; Haas 1982).

The Spread of the Neolithic

The Neolithic spread by a combination of diffusion and independent reinventions, constantly being adapted and readapted to different ecological and cultural contexts. In some instances, all of the basic crops and animals were taken over wholesale by neighboring peoples; in others, the complex was spread by invading immigrants who displaced earlier hunter-gatherer populations. The spread of the Neolithic was still not complete 12,000 years after it began. A handful of societies continued to live by hunting and gathering, either because their habitat was too cold or dry to practice farming or because they could make a better living by exploiting the natural flora and fauna.

The spread of the Neolithic into Europe was slowed by the fact that the ecosystem of the Mesolithic European hunters was basically different from the one that gave rise to the Middle Eastern Neolithic complex of domesticated animals. The latter, with the exception of the pig (see below), could not be transferred directly into forested regions. Hence the spread of agriculture into Europe involved substantial modifications in the original Neolithic system. For this reason, Europe followed a course toward urbanization and state formation that was fundamentally different from that of the Middle East (see p. 334). Even the grains, as in the case of rye, oats, and millet, had to undergo considerable modification in order to survive in the generally colder and damper European climate. By 8500 B.P. farming communities were well established in Greece. In the next millennium they had advanced into the Hungarian plains and up the Danube River. To make these regions suitable for agriculture and stock raising, the Neolithic invaders burned the forests, practicing a form of agriculture known as *slash-and-burn* (see p. 205). No doubt the native hunter-gatherers sometimes adopted the new mode of production on their own and interbred with the invaders.

By 8000 B.P. farming infrastructures including wheat, barley, cattle, and pigs had become established at Argissa-Maghula in Greek Thessaly. The same complex reached Bulgaria at about 7500 B.P., southern Italy about 7000 B.P., and Britain and Scandanavia between 6000 and 5000 B.P. (Renfrew 1973). As noted previously (p. 107), the spread of the Neolithic complex into northern Europe involved some degree of gene-culture coevolution with respect to light skin color and lactose tolerance in adults.

Figure 9.10 *STONEHENGE*
Neolithic ceremonial center on Salisbury Plain, Wiltshire, England. Megalithic structure implies existence of large, coordinated labor supply, a considerable degree of centralized planning, and an agricultural mode of production.

With the clearing of the forests, the Neolithic colonists settled down to more intensive forms of agriculture and stock raising. Their settlements grew larger and more permanent, trade increased, and their society became more hierarchical and bellicose, reaching the level of political organization known as chiefdoms (see p. 312) by about 5500 B.P. in central Europe and by 5000 B.P. in northern Europe and England. It is these chiefdoms which carried out the construction of Europe's megalithic (large stone) monuments, the most famous of which is Stonehenge (Fig. 9.10), begun about 4800 B.P. and completed about 3100 B.P. (Daniel 1980:87).

THE EAST ASIAN NEOLITHIC

The Neolithic reached Afghanistan and Pakistan by about 5000 B.P. and the Indus Valley in India by 4500 B.P. (Vishnu-Mittre 1975). Beyond this point, however, the role of diffusion becomes obscure. There is mounting evidence that China and Southeast Asia were the centers of one or more Neolithic food-producing "revolutions" based on a complex of domesticates different from

Figure 9.11 *PAN-P'O*
The Chinese have built a museum to protect the site of their earliest village.

those of the Middle East and largely or entirely independent of Middle Eastern influences.

Recent radiometric datings have pushed the beginnings of sedentary village life in China back before 6000 B.P. One of the earliest sites is at Pan-p'o (Fig. 9.11) in the semiarid loess highlands bordering the upper reaches of the Yellow River. Here there were village settlements employing a form of field agriculture involving domesticated millet and domesticated pigs and dogs. The well-patterned graveyards, painted pottery, and prototypes of the characters used in the Chinese form of writing indicate that still earlier Neolithic and protoagricultural sites remain to be discovered. Like the earliest Middle Eastern agricultural sites, Pan-p'o and the other early villages of China are found away from the principal watercourses and the most fertile river valleys. These circumstances make it difficult to interpret the millet at Pan-p'o as anything other than the product of an independent development. For if the millet had been obtained through diffusion, one would expect to find it applied first in regions of more abundant rainfall or in the river valleys. Although the virgin loess soils of China are highly fertile, they have the drawback of requiring a year of exposure to the air before they become productive. Moreover, the major varieties of millet found at Pan-p'o have wild ancestors that grew both in China and Europe.

The earliest domesticated millet in Europe has been found at Argissa, Greece, with a date of 7500 B.P. Considering the length of time it took wheat and barley to reach India, it seems highly unlikely that there was any connection between the onsets of European and Chinese millet farming. It is even more improbable that the domestication of the pig in the West had anything to do with its domestication in the East. The pig was a marginal component in the agricultural complex of the Middle East, but in China the pig has always played a central role.

Millet apparently provided the energy basis for the first Chinese cities, which were located along the central floodplains of the great bend of the Yellow River, dating to about 4000 B.P. Eventually, in the period 3300 to 3000 B.P., wheat and barley reached China and were incorporated into the agricultural system. But by that time two additional important crops, rice and soybeans—unknown in Europe and the Middle East—were also being used. The Middle Eastern plow and oxen arrived even later—2200 B.P.

All this indicates that the early North China system of field agriculture and stock raising had developed independently of the Middle Eastern Neolithic (Ho 1975, 1978; Harlan 1978; Chang 1973). Moreover, there is increasing evidence that there may have been a second independent transition to the Neolithic in central China in the Lower Yangtze and Huai river plains and a third independent transition in the southeastern coastal regions (Chang 1977a and b). The details of these sequences are still obscure, however.

The earliest archaeologically known dynastic state in China is Shang, dated to about 3700 B.P. (Chinese legend refers to a still earlier civilization called Hsia). Shang was centered in the lower Huangho Basin in Honan province and was based on irrigated rice, wheat, and millet farming. The Shang possessed wheeled vehicles, horses, cattle, a system of writing, and an advanced knowledge of bronze metallurgy (Fig. 9.12). Their capital near Anyang was enclosed by a huge earthen wall, had residential districts inhabited by craft specialists, and royal tombs displaying evidence of human sacrifice. Life in this early dynasty, despite the basically independent origins of Chinese civilization, bore remarkable similarities to early dynastic life in the Middle East (Chang 1980; Young 1982).

THE NEOLITHIC IN SOUTHEAST ASIA

The Neolithic in North China and the Middle East was based upon the domestication of grains whose wild ancestors were adapted to semiarid temperate upland habitats. The possibility must be kept open that the transition to settled Neolithic village life was also independently achieved in humid semitropical habitats of Southeast Asia through the domestication of root crops, especially yams and taro (Harlan 1978; D. Harris 1975; Hutterer 1976; Meacham 1977). Remains of such crops decompose more readily than grains and are difficult to recover archaeologically. There is no doubt that a concern with broad-spectrum plant gathering extends about as far back in time in Southeast Asia as in the Near East. At Spirit Cave in northwest Thailand, 11,500-year-old remains of almonds, candle nuts, betel nuts, peppers, gourds, phaseolus beans, peas, cucumbers, and other edible plants have

(a)

(b)

Figure 9.12 *SHANG BRONZE METALLURGY*
(*a*) Rhinoceros container, Eastern Zhou, 475–221 B.C.; (*b*) Bird-shaped wine vessel, Shang dynasty, 13th–11th century B.C..

been identified. Some of these plants may have been domesticated, but expert opinion is divided (Gorman 1969, 1978; Solheim 1970; Vishnu-Mittre 1975; Yen 1977).

The role of rice in the development of a distinctive Southeast Asian Neolithic is still poorly understood. Species of wild rice occurred in almost all the riverine deltas and estuaries of southern and southeastern Asia, but it is possible that the first cultivated varieties were grown in interior savannah habitats and other dry-land settings (Chesnov 1973). One theory is that the first Southeast Asian cultivated plants were taro (Fig. 9.13) and yams. Taro grows wild in swampy areas, and yams grow wild in forest areas. Transfer of yams into swampy areas would have required mounding and drainage. Rice could have grown initially as a weed in the irrigated upland taro fields (Condominas 1972). Thus far, however, the earliest archaeological evidence for rice cultivation in Asia is found at two sites on the low-lying northeastern plateau, or piedmont, of Thailand. At Non Nok Tha elaborately incised cord-marked pottery, domesticated cattle, and dry-rice agriculture seem to have been present at about 6500 B.P. (Bayard 1968). At the second site, Ban Chiang, wet-rice farming seems to date from 5500 B.P. (Gorman 1978). This evidence suggests that if taro and/or yams were actually the first crops grown in the region, then the beginnings of agriculture in Southeast Asia may have taken place at about 9000 B.P.—or roughly at the same time as in the Middle East. Chester Gorman (1978) has proposed that rice itself may have been the earliest Southeast Asian domesticate and that the beginning of the Neolithic in that region was related to the rise in sea level at the end of the last glaciation. This rise in sea level reduced the land area of Southeast Asia by one-half, subjecting the Upper Paleolithic hunters and gatherers to population pressure analogous to that experienced at the end of the Pleistocene by the big-game hunters of Europe and the Middle East (M.N. Cohen 1977).

Figure 9.13 *TARO PLANTS*
Possibly one of the first plants to be domesticated in Southeast Asia. These are growing in Hawaii.

THE AFRICAN NEOLITHIC

The transition to agriculture began in the Upper Nile Valley at a date that was about the same as and with a mix of plants and animals similar to those found in southwestern Asia. It was not until 3150 B.P. that this complex reached Dar Tichitt in Mauritania. But agriculture based on a set of forest-adapted crops independently domesticated in West Africa south of the Sahara may have been practiced as early as 4500 B.P. (Munson 1976; Ellis 1979). The principal staple in this region would have been the African yam (McIntosh and McIntosh 1981, 1983). It seems likely that the failure of the Neolithic to spread as rapidly into Africa south of the Sahara as it did elsewhere is related to the continued viability of big-game hunting throughout most of this region long after the Pleistocene megafauna became extinct elsewhere.

SUMMARY

The domestication of plants and animals and the development of the first Old World agricultural modes of production took place during the archaeological period known as the Neolithic. The transition to the Neolithic from Mesolithic or Upper Paleolithic cultures probably occurred independently in China and in Southeast Asia. The evidence is not yet complete enough to rule out the possibility that these or other regions crossed the threshhold to the Neolithic as early as the Middle East and northeast Africa did.

The transition in the Middle East and northeast Africa was preceded by a change from specialized big-game hunting to broad-spectrum hunting and gathering bearing a resemblance to the western European Mesolithic, except for the increasing importance of wild grains. These wild grains made sedentary village life possible some 2000 years before plants and animals were domesticated. A presumed advantage of sedentary village life with a diet based on wild grains was that it reduced the burden of carrying infants. Domestication of both the wild grains and the wild animals attracted to the grains gradually emerged from the commitment to sedentary settlements. The tough rachis varieties of barley and wheat received favored treatment and gradually replaced the brittle varieties, while sheep and goats were fed on stubble and selected for useful behavioral and physical traits.

The completion of the transition to farming and stock raising brought additional benefits in the form of greater production per capita of proteins and carbohydrates, thus relieving temporarily the population pressure associated with the period of broad-spectrum hunting and gathering. However, additional population growth rapidly raised the density of human settlements, forcing the spread of agriculture into regions deficient in rainfall as well as in other natural resources. These deficits were overcome by irrigation agriculture and by trade. With population density on the rise, competition for access to irrigable lands and vital trade goods increased the incidence of warfare. The need to organize the irrigation works, control trade, and coordinate military and police activities was met by the emergence of incipient bureaucracies and the division of society into rulers and ruled.

The Neolithic complex spread from southeastern to northwestern Europe during the period 9000 to 5000 B.P., slowed by the necessity of readapting the domesticates to the cool and forested European habitats.

In China, the fact that the earliest domesticates were millets and pigs suggests an independent origin for the transition from the East Asian Upper Paleolithic to the Neolithic and the subsequent development of cities and states. There may even have been three independent centers of domestication in China alone: the Middle Yellow River valley, the Lower Yangtse, and the South China coast.

In Southeast Asia there may have been an independent Neolithic transition involving root crops, legumes, and rice. The archaeological evidence for this area remains extremely tentative, however. The most suggestive data is from northwest Thailand where a broad spectrum of plants, some of which may have been domesticated have been found with dates ranging up to 11,500 B.P.

West Africa and Africa south of the Sahara adopted a Neolithic way of life very late. A possible independently developed Neolithic transition based on yams took place in West Africa by about 4500 B.P. Conservation of Pleistocene big-game animals may have made the Neolithic adaptation less necessary and less appealing to the hunter-gatherers of Africa south of the Sahara.

10 THE SECOND EARTH

This chapter outlines the main archaeological evidence for the evolution of cultures in North and South America. We shall see that there are both significant differences as well as remarkable similarities in the evolution of cultures in the "New" and "Old" Worlds. Moreover, we shall see that in the main, cultural evolution in North and South America was not dependent on the Old World developmental sequences and that the comparison of the archaeology of the two hemispheres, therefore, provides us with a "second earth"—a testing ground for theories about sociocultural processes.

WHEN WAS AMERICA DISCOVERED?

The ancestors of the American "Indians" reached *Homo sapiens* status in the Old World. No fossil hominoids have been found in the Americas, nor does anyone expect them to be found. The dental formula of the New World ceboidean monkeys indicates they diverged from the Old World hominoid line 30 to 40 million years ago. Nonetheless, controversy surrounds the question of how long humans have been living in the New World.

Persistent efforts to prove that the Americas were penetrated by Asian hunter-gatherers as early as 50,000 to 25,000 B.P. have not been substantiated. Evidence of early occupations, such as a skeleton found at Yuha, California (Childers and Minshall 1980) and bone artifacts found at Old Crow Flats in Alaska (Morlan 1978), can only be regarded as inconclusive. Several claims for great antiquity such as for 70,000-year-old flints and 50,000-year-old skeletal remains from southern California have been discredited (Taylor et al. 1983). The status of the claim for tools and hearths from highland Mexico and Peru said to be over 20,000 years old also remain to be verified (MacNeish 1978). But given the fact that reliable radiometric evidence from the Meadowcroft rock shelter (Fig. 10.1) near Pittsburgh definitely places hunter-gatherers in Eastern North America by 19,000 years ago, dates of 25,000 to 20,000 B.P. do not seem unreasonable for other North American sites. The

Figure 10.1 *MEADOWCROFT ROCK SHELTER*
East face of the excavation.

earliest remains at Meadowcroft consist of sophisticated blade knives and small bifaces, but no projectile points (Adovasio and Carlisle 1984).

The most likely origin of the first Americans was Asia. This seems probable, first of all, because native Americans of today phenotypically resemble Asians. Like East Asians, they have straight black hair, epicanthic folds, and very little body hair. It seems unlikely that these features could be derived from either European or African ancestries. Asia is also indicated as their place of origin if we consider how the first Americans could have gotten to the New World.

The migrations probably began during the late Pleistocene-Upper Paleolithic. This was long before the invention of oceangoing craft. Hence it is extremely improbable that the first Americans crossed either the Atlantic or the Pacific oceans. On the other hand, they could easily have entered the New World over the Bering Straits, across which on a clear day, one can see Alaska from Sieria. Actually, at the maximum of the last continental glaciation, there was no water at all between Siberia and Alaska. At maximum glacial advance an amount of moisture sufficient to reduce the level of the oceans by at least 300 feet was held on land in the form of ice. Since the Bering Straits are less than 300 feet deep, the earliest migrants had neither to swim nor hop from one iceberg to another in order to enter the Western Hemisphere. The first unsung "discoverers of America" could easily have walked across on dry land. When the sea was down only 150 feet, they could have walked across on a "bridge" between 100 to 200 miles wide. At its maximum, Beringia, as this now submerged land is called, was 1000 miles wide.

Even without the land bridge, the Bering Straits would not have been much of a barrier. From time to time the straits still freeze over solid enough for people and animals to walk across on the ice. Moreover, there was no lack of motive for such crossings. Like other Upper Paleolithic peoples, the first Americans were hunters of migratory herbivores, especially of mammoths, horses, caribou, bison, and musk oxen. These and other large mammals abounded in great unexploited herds from Alaska to Tierra del Fuego.

The Beringia Bridge was above water between 50,000 and 37,000 B.P. and again from 25,000 to 15,000 B.P. But the hunters who used the bridge confronted an additional obstacle: mile-high walls of ice covered most of Alaska, blocking the way south. The blockage was not total, however. At various intervals there existed an ice-free corridor that connected the north coast of Alaska with the great plains east of the Rockies. This corridor was open from 36,000 to 32,000 B.P., from 28,000 to 20,000 B.P., and from 13,000 B.P. on. Migrations southward of people and animals must have taken place during at least one of these intervals, and it is not unlikely that all three opportunities were utilized.

THE NEW WORLD PALEOLITHIC

Considerable uncertainty surrounds the question of the kinds of equipment and modes of production the first Americans brought with them on their journey from Asia. Evidence is accumulating year by year, however, which points to a close correspondence between the earliest known American tool kits and the discoidal-core and edge-retouched flake tools that were used in northeast Asia during Upper Paleolithic times (Fig. 10.2). Traces of this earliest lithic complex have been found both in northwest Alaska and near Ayacucho, Peru, with dates centering on 16,000 B.P. and at

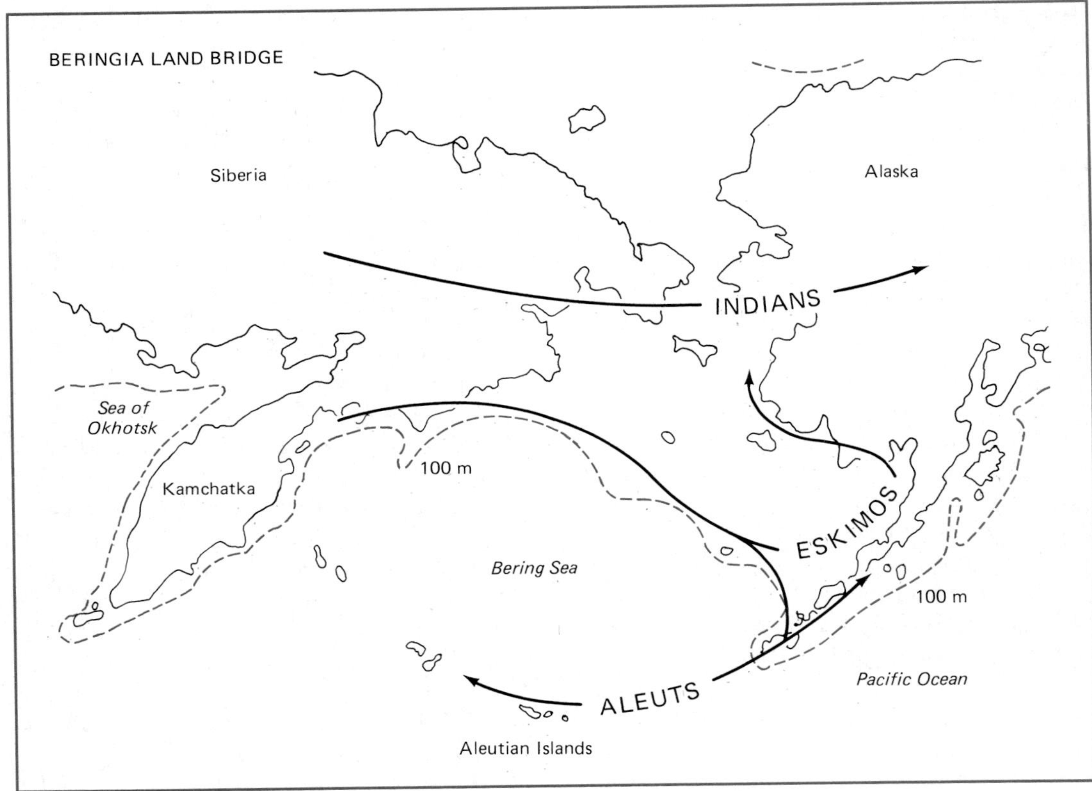

Taima-taima, Venezuela, where a quartzite projectile point, was recovered inside the pelvic bone of a juvenile mastodon killed at least 13,000 and possibly more than 14,000 years ago. Other tools found at Taima-taima include a knife, scrapers, and rough stones used as choppers or pounders (Bryan et al. 1978).

Tools manufactured from flakes struck from discoidal-prepared cores by a technique reminiscent of Old World Levalloisian tortoise cores have been found at the Shriver site in northwest Missouri with estimated dates even earlier than those of Taima-taima (Reagan et al. 1978). These tools establish the existence of an early phase of American hunter-gatherer technology, which preserved many features of Old World Upper Paleolithic origin and which preceded the development of distinctive New World tool types. They were discovered in strata underlying more advanced native American tools, which previously had been thought by many archaeologists to be the earliest types. It now seems likely, however, that the distinctive and more advanced American traditions developed several thousand years after the penetration of both

North and South America by the first bands of Upper Paleolithic hunter-gatherers.

Paleo-Indian Traditions

These more advanced traditions have as their mainstay pressure-flaked blade projectile points with fluted surfaces on thinned basal edges. They are grouped together and called the Paleo-Indian traditions and have dates ranging from 11,000 to about 9,000 B.P. or later, depending on the region. In North America two *assemblages* (i.e., patterned sets of artifacts) of the Paleo-Indian tradition are recognized: Clovis and Folsom.

Clovis is characterized by large fluted points found at sites where mammoths were killed and butchered on the high plains of Oklahoma, Colorado, New Mexico, and southern Arizona (although Clovis points are also found in the prairie and eastern woodlands as well). *Folsom* assemblages are characterized by Folsom and Sandia points, which were used to kill now extinct species of bison on the Central Plains from Montana to Texas (Fig. 10.3). At the Shriver site the discoidal-core tools lay underneath a Folsom-type assemblage. Separate but possibly related regional big-game traditions of comparable age have also been found in the Valley of Mexico, in the Andes from Argentina to Chile, and in Venezuela. One of the most interesting assemblages is that of Fell's Cave near the Strait of Magellan. Here stone tools, including fluted points, were found with the remains of extinct ground sloths and American horses, revealing that the ancestors of the American "Indians" had already spread out from Alaska to the tip of South America 11,000 years ago.

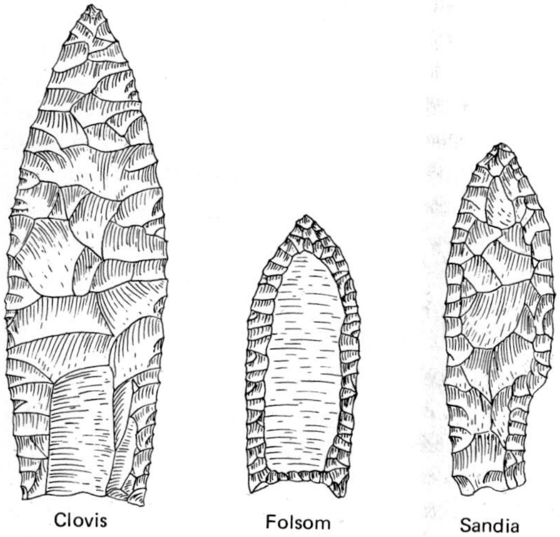

Clovis and Folsom assemblages dominate almost all of the archaeological sites in North America from 11,500 to 9,000 B.P. From the tools and the associated remains of slaughtered animals, it seems clear that the predominant mode of production was the specialized hunting of large game, closely paralleling the terminal Upper Paleolithic in the Old World. "Only occasional, and often questionable, pieces of grinding equipment occur with these sites; actual plant remains are almost never found; and fish, shellfish, and fishing equipment are scarce or absent" (M.N. Cohen 1977:130).

Clovis Folsom Sandia

Figure 10.2 *NEW WORLD PALEOLITHIC PROJECTILE POINTS*

ARCHAIC TRADITIONS

Only after 10,000 to 9,000 B.P. do sites with numerous milling stones, suggesting a significant concentration on seeds and other plant foods, begin to be common. As in the European Mesolithic, many forest, coastal, and riverine habitats now became populated and increased attention was paid to fish, shellfish, and other aquatic resources. Although not all archaeologists agree, there is much to be said in favor of viewing North

Figure 10.3 *FOLSOM POINT EMBEDDED IN RIBS OF AN EXTINCT BISON*
An historic discovery, altering the conception of the antiquity of the American Indian presence in the New World.

and South American modes of production from 10,000 B.P. on as various native American versions of the broad-spectrum hunting and gathering systems which characterized European and Middle Eastern Mesolithic and incipient agricultural times in China and Southeast Asia (Lynch 1983:125).

As in the Old World, a basic cause of the shift to broad-spectrum food production may have been the extinction of many species of large animals which had flourished during Pleistocene times. In the New World these extinctions involved considerably more species than in the Old World. Thirty-one genera died out, including mastodons, mammoths, big-horn bison, camels, tapirs, horses, pigs, several kinds of goats and sheep, musk ox, varieties of antelopes, oxen, yaks, giant beavers, giant armadillos, giant ground sloths, giant rodents, saber-toothed tigers, and species of bears, wolves, and coyotes. The relative importance of human overkill and of natural factors associated with the retreat of the last glaciation in these extinctions is the subject of considerable debate. The people who were equipped with Clovis and Folsom weaponry were undoubtedly extremely efficient hunters. Indeed, one could reasonably interpret their advanced stone-working skills as both a response to and a cause of the increasing scarcity of big game brought about initially by environmental changes. It seems likely that they heightened the stress experienced by the Pleistocene fauna. At the very least, one can say that they did not prevent the extinction of many valuable species and, as we shall see, this was to have dire consequences in later times.

THE NEW WORLD "NEOLITHIC"

The explanation of the origins of New World agriculture constitutes an outstanding scientific achievement. Many details remain unknown, but there is one basic fact: The domestication of plants and animals by Americans did not depend on the diffusion of farming or stock raising from any of the Old World centers of domestication. This means that diffusion is also unlikely to account for the other remarkable similarities between the Old and the New World, such as the development of sedentary village life, cities, states, empires, monumental architecture, writing, and metallurgy. The independent origins of New World agriculture lends weight to the view that there is a tendency for human cultures to evolve with considerably higher probabilities in some directions rather than in others. It further suggests that explanations for both differences and similarities in prehistory and history must be sought in the study of processes that tend to produce similar sociocultural consequences under similar conditions.

There had always been strong circumstantial evidence for postulating an independent native American development of agriculture. The inventory of New World crops consists almost entirely of domesticates whose wild prototypes grew only in North and South America. At the time of contact with the first Europeans, this inventory was as diverse and nutritionally satisfactory as that of the combined Middle Eastern and Southeast Asian plant complex. It included grains such as maize, amaranth, and quinoa. It also included legumes like black beans, string beans, and lima beans and other important vegetables like squash, melons, and tomatoes. Among the root crops were manioc, potatoes, and sweet potatoes. There were also peanuts and condiments such as chili peppers, cacao, and vanilla; narcotics and stimulants such as coca and tobacco; and useful fiber-yielding plants such as henequen, maguey, cotton, and sisal. (Cotton was independently domesticated in the Old World and the New World.) A variety of agricultural systems ranging from slash-and-burn to irrigation were used to raise these crops (Matheny and Gurr 1983).

The joining of native American domesticates with those of the Old World after 1492 had massive consequences all over the world. For example, sugar combined with cacao yielded chocolate. Sugar cane, which had been domesticated first in Southeast Asia, was then planted in Brazil and the Caribbean islands to make sugar for chocolate and to sweeten coffee and tea. It was the attempt to find cheap labor for the sugar plantations that led to the development of the slave trade and that forced migrations of tens of millions of African blacks to the New World. Maize was taken to China where it provided extra calories for a population explosion in the sixteenth century. Manioc became a staple food crop of tropical populations throughout Africa. The potato was taken to Ireland, where it sustained a population explosion followed by crop failures, a famine, and a mass exodus to America. Tobacco was taken to Europe, then sent back to Virginia, where it provided the impetus for the development of plantation slavery in the United States (Wolf 1982).

Until the 1960s many anthropologists were unwilling to concede that the native Americans had been able to domesticate these important plants without help from the Old World. This view persisted because of the apparent chronological priority of plant domestication in the Middle East, China, and Southeast Asia. Thus it was suggested that a boatload of post-Neolithic migrants from across the Atlantic or Pacific had washed up in Mexico, Brazil, or Peru, bringing with them the *idea* of plant domestication. Some archaeologists even argued that the voyagers must have brought maize with them since the wild ancestors of maize had not yet been identified (Godfrey and Cole 1979; cf. Schneider 1977).

Diffusionist theories of New World agricultural origins have been decisively refuted by the identification of the ancestral forms of maize and of the sequence of modification that these forms underwent as they were domesticated. The most important discoveries were made by Richard S. MacNeish in the highlands of the Mexican State of Tamaulipas and in Tehuacán Valley in the State of Puebla in 1958 and 1964, respectively. MacNeish showed that in both of these rather arid upland areas the domestication of maize and other native American plants was the product of a series of cultural and ecological interactions that were determined by specific local conditions.

Controversy surrounds the identity of the actual wild predecessor of maize. One possibility is that maize was domesticated from the grass called *teosinte* (Fig. 10.5), which still grows wild in the area. Teosinte has been crossed with modern maize, and the results are extremely similar to the earliest corn cobs. Like modern popcorn teosinte can be popped by being heated, or cracked or ground, or softened up for eating by soaking in water (Flannery 1973; Beadle 1981). Between 5000 and 3000 B.P. the primitive varieties of maize were improved by selection and cross breeding, lost their ability to seed themselves, and acquired the large numbers of rows of kernels found in modern varieties. These modern varieties of maize, like many other domesticated plants, are dependent on humans for continued survival.

At any rate, the domestication of maize must antedate 7000 B.P. because the people who lived in the Tehuacán Valley at that time were already growing a primitive form of maize that had a small cob with two or three rows of soft-husked seeds and toughened rachis (see p. 157).

Over the next 3000 years further selection and hybridization produced varieties more closely resembling the ones now in use. So the native Americans on their own not only domesticated maize, but they also subjected it to a great amount of selection and morphological change and adapted it to as wide a geographical range as any major food plant (Flannery 1973). In this process Euro-Asian or African "ideas" about other crops could not have played a significant role (Pickersgill and Heiser 1975).

A MESOAMERICAN SEQUENCE

As described by Richard MacNeish, 12,000 years ago the Mexican highlands were occupied by hunting and gathering peoples whose way of life was probably similar to that found elsewhere in North America at approximately the same time level. But the animals hunted in Tamaulipas and Tehuacán seem not to have been as large or as abundant as those that the Clovis and Folsom big-game hunters depended on. After the extinction of the Pleistocene fauna in highland Mesoamerica, grinding stones appear along with a broad-spectrum pattern of dependence on small animals, such as deer, rabbits, gophers, rats, turtles, and birds, plus a wide variety of plants, including the ancestors of domesticated squash, avocados, maize, and beans.

During the Ajuereado phase (12,000–9,000 B.P.), the horse, antelope, giant turtle, large jackrabbit, large rodents, and probably the mammoth became extinct. Early in the phase the emphasis was on hunting; later, grinding tools became prominent. Initially, meat constituted between 76 to 89 percent of calorie intake depending on the season. People lived in small seminomadic groups called *bands* (see p. 205). Their movements were irregular.

During the next phase (El Riego, 9000–7000 B.P.) meat fell to about 31 to 69 percent of calorie intake. Seed collecting became as important as hunting. Seed and fruit pit planting gradually emerged as part of a careful scheduling of movements from one ecological zone to another as the seasons changed. The earliest plant domesticates were squash, amaranth, chili peppers and avocados, but these contributed only 1 percent of calorie intake. Bands were larger and population density higher.

During the Coxcatlan phase (7000 – 5400 B.P.) maize and beans were domesticated. Eight percent of calories now came from the domesticates. Meat declined further to 23 to 62 percent depending on the season.

Next came the Abejas phase (5400 – 4300 B.P.) during which meat provided only 15 percent of the calorie intake for part of the year while the plant domesticates furnished 21 percent.

It was not until 3500 B.P., during the Ajalpan phrase, that hamlets and permanent houses were built. Meat had by then been reduced to below 25 percent of calorie intake, but wild plants still bulked large in the diet.

Large permanent villages did not appear in Tehuacán until after 2850 B.P. (MacNeish 1978). But in other highland valleys, villages containing over 300 persons who lived in wattle and daub huts began to appear shortly after 3500 B.P. (Flannery 1973). In the transition to still larger aggregates of villages and states in the highlands, the studies at Tehuacán "strongly indicate that a major causal factor was the development of water control and various kinds of irrigation agriculture" (MacNeish 1972:93).

Lowland Mesoamerican Sequences

At some point between 5000 and 4000 B.P., maize was brought down from its native highland habitat and adopted by lowland tropical forest peoples in Vera Cruz and Guatemala. Unlike the highland peoples, the lowlanders had already settled down to a form of village life based on the exploitation of a broad spectrum of riverine and coastal flora and fauna by 4900 B.P. and perhaps as early as 7300 B.P., *prior* to the arrival of maize. Along the Gulf Coast of Vera Cruz and Tabasco, these early maritime, sedentary, and preagricultural villages formed the basis for the development of the *Olmec,* the first chiefdom and incipient state of North America. (As discussed below, lowland preagricultural maritime villages along the coast of Peru were the basis for the growth of the earliest chiefdoms and incipient states in South America.) Being sedentary, these villages were "preadapted" to agriculture. They easily added the exploitation of crops such as squash and peppers to their broad-spectrum mode of production. With the diffusion of maize from the highlands, they began to concentrate on agriculture, their population grew more dense, and their political organization more complex.

Early Olmec sites are marked by carved stone monuments and earthen platforms. At the best-known Olmec site, La Venta, there is an earth-fill pyramid shaped like a volcano with gullied slopes. It is 105 feet in height and 420 feet in diameter (Fig. 10.4). Construction was underway by 3000 B.P. As at several other Olmec localities, 9-foot-high round-faced stone heads (Fig. 10.5), stone altars, tombs, and stelae (monolithic carved columns) also occur. Basalt for these constructions had to be transported from quarries over 50 miles away (Coe 1968). The Olmec sites appear to be associated with natural levees produced by meandering rivers on which intensive forms of maize agriculture were practiced. This was combined with fishing, shellfishing, turtling, and some terrestrial hunting. The levee land was the best suited for growing maize, but its area was limited. It appears likely that the building of the monuments and the development of the chiefdoms was related to the control of these productive lands by a ruling elite to

Figure 10.4 *LA VENTA PYRAMID*
Landing strip and oil refinery were not built by the Olmec.

meet the needs of an increasing population. Olmec rulers also probably controlled extensive trade networks. The Olmec subsistence base, however, was not ample enough to support the kinds of dense populations which are associated with fully developed states; by 2400 B.P., the Olmec heartland was no longer a flourishing part of Mesoamerica.

The Rise and Fall of the Maya

Developments somewhat similar to those characteristic of the Olmec took place in the Yucatán peninsula among the Maya. The earliest known Maya ceremonial structure—a low masonry platform—was begun about 4600 B.P. (Fig. 10.6) at the Cuello site in Belize (Hammond 1982). At this time the area was heavily forested and agriculture was based on the slash-and-burn method (see p. 205). During the next 2000 years, the forest cover in the Cuello area was greatly reduced, possibly as the result of repeated burning at shorter and shorter intervals. By about 2500 B.P. the Maya were practicing a more intensive form of maize agriculture—the raised-field method—involving the drainage and mounding of low-lying swampy areas, plus the cultivation of fruit trees mulched with household wastes. By A.D. 300 this new mode of production had given rise to a rapid increase in population, the development of ruling elites, the construction of hundreds of ceremonial centers, and the emergence of numerous chiefdoms and states (Hammond and Miksicek 1981; Turner and Harrison 1981).

Although the precise nature of the Maya states remains a matter of controversy, it is clear that the Maya achieved a high degree of political centralization and urbanization, as well as great sophistication in learning, architecture, and sculpture. The Maya maintained far-flung trade networks into the highlands, and it is likely that their development was stimulated by trade and warfare with the more powerful states that arose in the highlands at roughly the same time as the Maya states began to flourish.

Between A.D. 300 and 900, Maya ceremonial centers were at their maximum. Elaborately ornamented multiroom buildings were constructed on top of supporting platforms and grouped symmetrically around plazas. Ball courts for ceremonial games, stelae and altars incised with calendrical and historical hieroglyphics, and massive statuary were also part of the plaza complexes. Towering over all were great, truncated pyramids (Fig. 10.7) with stone facing and flights of steps leading to temples at their crests (Coe 1977; Henderson 1981). In addition there were scores of medium-sized but still imposing centers, plus several

Figure 10.5 *OLMEC HEAD, SAN LORENZO, MEXICO*
The massiveness and abundance of Olmec monuments suggests the existence of state-level institutions.

hundred smaller ones. Tens of thousands of hamlets housed a population of several million people.

Most of the ceremonial centers are located within 1 kilometer of seasonally wet swampy lands on high grounds near permanent sources of water, and the largest ones are remarkably evenly spaced at about a day's walk (26 kilometers) apart (Harrison 1982).

It has been estimated that at Tikal (Fig. 10.8), the largest of the Maya centers, there was a population of 45,000 people in an area of 123 square kilometers (Haviland 1970). Most of these people lived on small farms an hour's walk away from the main civic centers. The size of the central residential group of rulers, priests, bureaucrats, and artisans was much smaller. Based on analogies with modern-day descendants of the Maya, some of the civic and ceremonial centers may have been relatively empty most of the year, filling up with people only on ceremonial occasions when they also probably served as market centers for the dispersed populations (Vogt 1969).

Although the lowland Maya area is heavily forested, it is subject to an annual dry season. Moreover, because the bedrock forming the Yucatán Peninsula is limestone, almost all surface water sinks into the ground and disappears during the dry spell. All the lowland Maya civic centers are, therefore, located in the vicinity of natural waterholes or are associated with artificial reservoirs. Thus it is possible that the Maya rulers con-

Figure 10.6 *CUELLO SITE*
The earliest known ceremonial structure in the New World.

trolled access to sources of drinking water, which were critical for survival during years of drought. But it is unlikely that Maya social life was characterized by extreme differences in power, since the dispersed farmers could not easily be taxed or rounded up for *corvée* (forced labor). This suggests that much of the labor involved in lowland monumental construction was voluntarily donated or at least compensated for in food or trade goods rather than coerced (Vogt and Cancian 1970).

There is increasing evidence that the Maya intensified agriculture as population density increased. The need for locating settlements adjacent to artificial or natural sources of drinking water and areas suitable for raised-field cultivation restricted the mobility of Maya farmers and obliged them to utilize more concentrated and labor-intensive methods of production. Permanent or short-fallow fields were created by mounding wet soil dug from networks of drainage canals, which were probably also exploited for their aquatic flora and fauna (Turner 1974; Matheny 1976; Hammond 1978; Harrison and Turner 1978; Dickson 1981).

The relative lack of potential for expansion of the lowland rainfall agricultural modes of production is probably related to the sudden collapse of Maya civilization about A.D. 800. Not only were the major ceremonial centers abandoned, but the Peten region, which contained the largest sites became virtually uninhabited and to this day has yet to recover its former glory. (There was a postclassic form of Maya state at

Figure 10.7 *MAYAN TEMPLE, PALENQUE, CHIAPAS, MEXICO*
This structure covers a tomb which was reached by an interior stairway.

Chichen Itza and Mayapan in northern Yucatán but these are generally recognized as being colonial dominions of a highland-based empire known as the Toltecs.) A theory that accounts for most of the relevant facts is that as the population increased, the rulers attempted to intensify agricultural production by stepping up tax and labor demands on the commoner farmers. The farmers responded by intensifying their agricultural efforts, progressively shortening fallow periods until infestations of weeds and grass and soil erosion and soil exhaustion made it impossible to sustain high yields. At Tikal there is evidence that the hillsides lost their topsoil, which collected in basins, drainageways, and alluvial flats, creating conditions adverse for raised-field agriculture. Alteration in patterns of rainfall caused by excessive forest clearing may also be implicated. Additional crises may have been produced by the silting up of drinking water reservoirs. The deleterious effects of Maya activities on the soils of the Peten are still visible after 1000 years of abandonment (Cowgill 1964; Willey and Shimkin 1971; Sanders 1972; Cook 1972; Culbert 1973; Willey 1977; Olson 1978; Hamblin and Pitcher 1980; Adams, Brown, and Culbert 1981; Flannery 1982; Marcus 1983). These ecological changes would have increased competition between the various centers and increased popular discontent. Wars, peasant revolts, and the disruption of trade routes would then have brought the final ruination of the classical Maya world.

THE DEVELOPMENT OF NEW WORLD STATES; THE MESOAMERICAN HIGHLANDS

In the highlands a fundamentally different kind of potential for growth existed. Here the developmental sequence of cultures displays certain remarkable parallels to what transpired during the urbanization of the Middle East.

The first agricultural settlers of the highland region known as the basin of Mexico entered the southern and southwestern parts of the basin at the comparatively late date of 3400 to 3200 B.P., apparently only after adjacent regions more favorable to agriculture had already been utilized for several centuries. The first settlers practiced a form of slash-and-burn rainfall agriculture on the hillsides at middle altitudes above the basin floor where they could obtain a balance between maximum amounts of rainfall and minimum amounts of crop-limiting frosts. Between 2900 and 2200 B.P. the less favored central part of the basin filled with settlements and population growth gradually moved on to the still less favorable northern fringe where rainfall was lowest (500 – 600 mm annually). It was here, in the valley of Teotihuacán some 25 miles northeast of modern-day Mexico City, that the first great imperial city of the New World was founded.

Because of the scarcity and irregularity of rainfall in this part of the valley, the villages near Teotihuacán made increasing use of the set of permanent springs from which water flowed at a rate of about 60,000 liters (15,840 gallons) a minute. By using this water for irrigation, they overcame the limitations imposed by frost and rainfall. But to make use of it, they had to invest much more labor to build and maintain the dams, canals, and drainage works than was needed under the rainfall systems. By 2200 B.P. there were three large villages and about 25 hamlets in the Teotihuacán Valley, most of which still probably depended on rainfall agriculture. Between then and A.D. 100 the dispersed population of the valley rather suddenly coalesced into a single large center

Figure 10.8 *TIKAL*
The largest of the Maya centers.

close to the springs. Teotihuacán thereafter grew at an explosive rate and by A.D. 500 it covered an area of 20 square kilometers (7.7 square miles) and had a population of over 100,000 people. Control over strategic trade routes also undoubtedly played a role in this expansion (Charlton 1978). There was formal planning of the city's residential and civic precincts as indicated by the grid pattern of the avenues and alleys, markets in various districts, and exclusive quarters allotted to craft specialists (Millon 1970). In the middle of Teotihuacán there is a complex of public buildings and monuments that, by comparison, dwarf even those of Tikal and render the Olmec sites puny. The central monument is the so-called Pyramid of the Sun (Fig. 10.9), still among the world's largest artificial structures. Measuring 670 meters (200 ft) in height and over 2,133 meters (700 ft) on a side, this edifice contains 840,000 cubic meters of fill. A second, smaller pyramid contains 210,000 cubic meters, which makes it about twice as big as the Olmec

(a)

Figure 10.9 *TEOTIHUACÁN*
(*a*) Panoramic view with Pyramid of the Sun in the center. (*b*) Closeup of the Pyramid of the Sun. Compare this to Figure 10.8.

pyramid at La Venta. The civic buildings of Tikal cover only a small fraction of the area of Teotihuacán's ceremonial complex (Sanders and Price 1968; Millon 1973). With the emergence of Teotihuacán the Mesoamerican highlands entered a period of imperial rivalry and extensive warfare.

At about A.D. 700 Teotihuacán was abandoned. Once again there is reason to suspect that overintensive use and depletion of natural resources played a role in combination with internal and external unrest and wars. Deforestation in the hillsides surrounding

(b)

Teotihuacán may have changed the pattern of rainfall runoff and diminished the flow of irrigation water for the network of spring-fed canals (Sanders, Santley, and Parsons 1979; Nichols 1982).

The basin of Mexico, however, unlike the Maya's Peten, never became depopulated. A succession of neighboring highland imperial centers took Teotihuacán's place. The first of these was located at Cholula, where there is an unexcavated pyramid even bigger than the Pyramid of the Sun. Then from A.D. 968 to 1156 the reigning empire was that of a people called the *Toltecs*, whose capital was at Tula (Fig. 10.10). Their influence extended as far as the Yucatán.

The final and greatest of the empires in the native imperial lineage of Mesoamerica was that of the Aztecs, whose capital, Tenochtitlán, contained well over 100,000 inhabitants when Cortez's disbelieving eyes first glimpsed its gardens, causeways, markets, pyramids, and temples (Wolf 1959; Coe 1977; Vaillant 1966). Aztec agriculture involved an even more intensive mode of production than Teotihuacán. It was based on massive flood control, desalinization, and drainage works, which made it possible to raise crops year round on misnomered "floating gardens," or *Chinampas* (Fig. 10.11). These were actually raised mounds built up out of the mud and debris of lakeside lands and interconnected for drainage and transportation by a complex network of canals (Carasco 1978). As Jeffry Parsons writes,

> The continued operation and maintenance of the entire Chinampa system was possible only through a massive system of dams, sluice gates, gates and canals that regulated the water level within narrow limits. . . . This critical water control system was so large, complex, and interconnected that it almost certainly was managed directly by the Aztec state (1976:253).

Figure 10.10 *RUINS OF TULA, HIDALGO, MEXICO*
This was the capital city of the pre-Aztec people known as the Toltecs. It was destroyed by invaders in 1160 A.D.

Figure 10.11 *CHINAMPAS OF XOCHIMILCO*
The gardens obviously do not float, as can be seen from the trees growing on them. Note corn growing in fields.

Despite the enormous productivity of *Chinampas* agriculture, there is evidence that the swift growth of population and the continuing depletion of natural resources during Aztec times had created a politically and ecologically unbalanced situation. The problem of procuring an adequate supply of animal fat and protein was especially acute, and the practice of cannibalism on a large scale under the auspices of the Aztec state religion may have been a compensation for the shortage of meat (see p. 448), (Harner 1976, 1978; Harris 1979a). The Aztecs, however, met a fate different from all previous New World civilizations. In A.D. 1519 they were conquered by invaders who arrived from another world, equipped with steel weapons and mounted on horses, animals that had not been seen in Mexico for 10,000 years.

THE ROLE OF ANIMAL DOMESTICATES

A major difference between the period of early agriculture in the Middle East and highland Mesoamerica was that the Americans retained their seminomadic way of life for a long time after they had begun to domesticate their basic food crops. Sizable highland Mesoamerican villages that predate 5000 B.P. have not yet been found. The ecological basis for this difference seems clear.

In the Middle East sedentary villages could have their plants and their animal protein too, since both plants and animals were domesticated at the same time. However, because of the more extensive range of extinctions affecting the New World Pleistocene fauna, opportunities for animal domestication were limited by a lack of suitable wild species. The only domesticated New World animal at all comparable to sheep, goats, or cattle is the llama. But the ancestors of this marginally useful beast did not survive in Mesoamerica. Although the ancient Peruvians domesticated the llama, there was no chance for the Mesoamericans to do so. The same is true of the guinea pig, which became an important source of animal protein in the Andes but never in Mexico.

The Mexicans ultimately did domesticate the turkey, the muscovy duck, the honeybee, and hairless dogs bred for meat, but these species were of no significance in the incipient agricultural phase and never did amount to much in later periods. One can only speculate why the Mesoamericans did not domesticate species such as tapirs, peccaries, and antelopes (Hunn 1982). Suffice to say they did not, nor has anyone else.

In the Middle East, sedentary village life was based upon the domestication of both plants and animals. Sedentism increased the productivity of the plant domesticates, which increased the productivity of animal domesticates, which increased the productivity of sedentary village life, and so on. In highland Mexico, however, the need to retain animal food in the diet worked against the abandonment of hunting. Hence, compared with the Middle East, the development of village sedentism in highland Mesoamerica did not precede the first phases of cultivation but followed it after a lapse of several thousand years. This difference in animal domestication probably accounts for the lag in the development of New World empires as compared with those of Europe and Asia and explains why it was the Old World that conquered the New and not vice versa.

DEVELOPMENTS NORTH OF MEXICO

Just as the Neolithic spread from the earliest centers of domestication into Europe, India, and parts of Africa, so too, in the New World, the basic Mesoamerican farming complex gradually affected the life-styles of people living in remote parts of North America. And again, as in the Old World, as the farming complex spread, it encountered diverse environments and was adapted and readapted by hundreds of different local cultures. Primitive varieties of corn were being planted in the vicinity of Bat Cave in southwest New Mexico as early as 5000 B.P. But, as at Tehuacán, agriculture did not lead immediately or inexorably to sedentary village life. Almost 3000 years elapsed before the first permanent villages appeared in the southwest. These consisted of small clusters of pit houses found in the valleys of the Mogollon Mountain Range in New Mexico at about 2300 B.P. Larger villages associated with a culture called Hohokam soon appeared in the valleys of the Salt and Gila rivers in southern Arizona. The Hohokam peoples built extensive irrigation systems fed by canals 30 miles long, reared pyramid mounds, and constructed Mexican-style ball courts (Jennings 1974).

The third great southwestern culture based on agriculture is called the Anasazi. These were the "pueblo" peoples of Arizona, New Mexico, Utah, and Colorado. At Pueblo Bonito, long before the coming of the first Europeans, people lived in an apartment house five stories tall containing 800 rooms. The Anasazi were forced to abandon many of their pueblos as a result of a prolonged drought that gripped the southwest during the thirteenth century (Jennings 1974).

Maize cultivation moved up the Mississippi and Ohio river valleys beginning about 3000 B.P., creating profound transformations in the life-styles of the seminomadic inhabitants. Although the spread of maize ushered in the first intensive forms of agriculture, many seminomadic North Americans in the eastern United States had already included such crops as gourds, sunflower seeds, sumpweed, and pumpkins in their broad-spectrum modes of production (Watson 1977). The three main phases of maize cultivation—known as Adena, Hopewell, and Mississippian—were marked by the construction of thousands of earth mounds, some containing burials and others that served as platforms for temples or residences (Fig. 10.12). Dense populations appeared during the Mississippian phase, giving rise to urban nucleations and elaborate temple-priest-idol cults that exhibited strong Mesoamerican influences. The greatest expression of this trend toward monumentality, urbanism, and state formation occurred at Cahokia near East St. Louis between A.D. 900 and 1100. Here, with energy derived from the Mexican plant food "trinity"—maize, squash, and beans—the Mississippians built a mound that was 100 feet high and covered 15 acres. Numerous additional large and small mounds, supporting houses and temples, surrounded the main structure. It is clear that the Mississippians had reached the incipient stages of state formation although there are theoretical reasons to suppose that their potential for growth was very restricted. These reasons will be discussed in Chapter 16 (Stoltman 1978).

The effects of the introduction of maize agriculture were less spectacular in the eastern woodlands where people, like the Iroquois and Delaware, continued to live in small villages and to rely on hunting and gathering as the major source of their food supply. Elsewhere in North America there were vast regions into which agriculture never penetrated. The peoples of the entire Pacific Coast from California to Alaska, for example, never abandoned their reliance on broad-spectrum hunting, wild-seed gathering, fishing, and shellfish collecting. One can only conclude that intensive farming offered no conspicuous advantages over the existing subsistence practices in these regions. This is especially true of the northwest Pacific Coast where people were able to live in large plankhouse permanent villages by exploiting annual upstream migrations of fish (see Ch. 12).

THE DEVELOPMENT OF STATES IN SOUTH AMERICA

The Andean region of South America was the center of an independently developed complex of domesticated animals and plants. This complex provided the basis for the rise of additional native American states and the largest of the New World empires.

The phase of big-game hunting in South America was followed as in the rest of the hemisphere by expansion of broad-spectrum modes of production into variegated habitats but especially into high-altitude and riverine and coastal regions. Although maize eventually became the principal crop of the Inca Empire and although the Andean region shared many other domesticates in common with Mesoamerica, several important New World plants and animals were specialties of the Andes. Chief among these are high-altitude tubers like the potato and high-altitude grains like quinoa. The discovery of two kinds of domesticated beans at Callejón de Huaylas, Peru, dating between 10,500 and

Figure 10.12 *MISSISSIPPIAN MOUND*
Winterville, Mound A.

7,500 B.P. suggests that plant domestication was under way at least as early in the Andes as in Mesoamerica (Kaplan, Lynch, and Smith 1973). The earliest maize in South America, dating between 6300 and 4800 B.P., has been found at Ayacucho in Peru, again indicating an antiquity almost as great as for the maize that MacNeish discovered in the Tehuacán Valley. (MacNeish also found the Ayacucho maize.) As for animals, it was only in the Andes that large herbivores—the llama and alpaca—were domesticated, possibly by 6000 B.P. (Browman 1976:469).

As in Mesoamerica, the earliest sedentary villages appear in coastal locales and precede the introduction of the first animal and plant food domesticates, which presumably originated elsewhere (Mosely 1983).

Along the coast of Peru the earliest chiefdoms may have been based on a infrastructure of maritime resources with virtually no contribution from domesticated food plants. According to Michael Moseley (ibid.), the people who built the first large coastal platform mounds and masonry monuments at about 4000 B.P. were nourished primarily by catches of a small fish, the *anchovetta*, which schools in vast numbers off the coast of Peru. Supplementary marine resources also included larger fish, mollusks, and water birds.

> Viewed as a complex, these marine resources are concentrated along the shoreline and in the nearshore waters. They are extremely abundant . . . and available throughout the year. The maritime interpretation holds that this resource complex underwrote the rise of large sedentary populations and supplied the foundation for the coastal civilization (ibid.:205).

This view has been challenged by J.S. Raymond (1981), whose calculations of the calorie yield of the maritime resources exploitable with a simple technology indicate that only a band-sized population could have subsisted on such resources. In Raymond's view, the builders of the first towns and temple complexes relied on root crops for their basic calorie needs and on maritime resources for their protein and fat. The use of root crops is difficult to confirm archaeologically because they decompose rapidly and leave no trace of their presence, unlike maize and other seed crops (cf. Quilter and Stocker 1983).

As additional domesticated plants were added to the agricultural repertory, settlements grew up in the floodplains of the Peruvian coastal rivers and were inhabited by as many as 3000 to 4000 people in the period 3900 to 3750 B.P. (M.N. Cohen 1975). Before and after the introduction of irrigation and maize, the coastal population underwent rapid growth. Canal systems extending across whole valleys were constructed, and the first small states made their appearance by 2350 B.P. to A.D. 1. Thereafter a series of wars and conquests led to the emergence of larger states, which united coastal valleys and highland valleys into single political units, such as the Tiahuanaco (Fig. 10.13) and Huari states (A.D. 550–800), followed by the Chimu Empire with its huge mud-walled city of Chan Chan (Fig. 10.14) and finally by the Inca Empire (Fig. 10.15), A.D. 1438–1525 (Lanning 1974; Isbell and Schreiber 1978; Jennings 1983; Collier, Tenato, and Wirth 1982). We shall discuss the organization of the Inca Empire in Chapter 16.

THE MEANING OF THE "SECOND EARTH"

Until the Spanish conquest, technology in the New World had been evolving along lines remarkably parallel to the Middle

Figure 10.13 *TIAHUANACO*
Ruins of the pre-Inca civilization near Lake Titicaca, Bolivia.

Figure 10.14 *CHAN CHAN*
Capitol of the Chimu Empire.

Eastern sequence. Nonetheless, native American technological change was definitely proceeding at a slower rate. Much of the "lag" can be attributed to the differential natural endowments of the Middle Eastern and nuclear American regions. As discussed above, the extinction of potential animal domesticates among the Pleistocene megafauna rendered the American Indians vulnerable to military conquest by Europeans mounted on horseback. The same megafauna extinction also deprived the American Indians of potential animal domesticates that might have served to provide traction for plows and for wheeled vehicles. (The Inca actually did have a form of plow that people pushed and

Figure 10.15 *MACHU PICCHU, PERU*
Ruins of an Inca fortress-city.

pulled). The preconquest Mesoamericans understood the principle of the wheel at least to the extent of putting wheels on children's toys. Presumably, given more time, these inventions and their applications would have been improved upon and extended.

Lack of steel tools also placed the native Americans at a great disadvantage during the European invasions. But the development of American metallurgical techniques had already passed beyond the hammering of sheet copper to the smelting and casting of copper, gold, silver, and several alloys (Fig. 10.16). Just before the Conquest, bronze mace heads and bronze knives were being made. Had the Americans not been conquered, would they have eventually discovered the superior qualities of iron and steel? It seems likely that they would have done so since they had already independently accomplished so many other technological achievements. For example, like their Old World counterparts, native American priests and rulers were concerned with the regulation of agricultural production. Under state and temple auspices, astronomical observations were carried out, which led to the development of calendars. Indeed, the Maya calendar was more accurate than its Egyptian counterpart. To keep calendrical records, as well as records of agricultural production, taxes, and other state affairs, hieroglyphic writing systems were invented by several Mesoamerican peoples (Fig. 10.17). Of special interest is the Maya system of vigesimal numeration (numbers with the base set at 20), which incorporated the principle of the zero. The zero was absent in the Middle Eastern, Greek, and Roman number systems. Without the concept of a zero quantity to mark the absence of the base number or its exponents, it is extremely difficult to perform arithmetical operations involving large numbers. In this respect, at least, the native Americans appear to have been ahead of their Old World counterparts.

Given the fact that the ecosystems of the Old World and the Americas were initially quite different, precise parallels leading toward urban and imperial societies in the two hemispheres should not be expected. Again and again, however, the peoples of the two hemispheres independently achieved convergent solutions to similar problems when

Figure 10.16 *PRE-COLUMBIAN METALLURGY*
Silver alpaca, llama, and figurine.

(a)

Figure 10.17 *MAYAN GLYPHS*
Symbols in form of stylized human faces and mythical animals, from Palenque (*a*); On Stela from Monte Alban (*b*).

(b)

the underlying technological, environmental, and demographic conditions were approximately similar.

After landing in Vera Cruz in 1519, Cortez marched to the Aztec capital, Tenochtitlán (today Mexico City), thereby ending the biological and cultural isolation of the earth's two worlds. Despite the fact that they had gone their separate ways for 20,000 years, Spain and Mexico were remarkably similar in some respects.

He passed through cities, towns, villages, markets and irrigated fields; he saw slavery, poverty, potentates, farmers, judges, churches, massive pyramids, roads, boats, pottery and textiles; in short he encountered a world whose almost every aspect he could understand in terms of his own experience as an urban Spaniard of the sixteenth century (Wenke 1980:555–556).

The meaning of the "second earth," therefore, is that sociocultural systems are subject to determining forces that select innovations and shape the course of cultural evolution. This does not mean that all cultures must travel through the same stages of evolution any more than that the principle of natural selection means all organisms must travel through the same stages of evolution. The determinism that governs cultural systems produces both similar and dissimilar trajectories of evolutionary transformation. It does this because the conditions under which the interaction between culture and nature takes place are enormously diverse. What the geological time perspective of archaeology teaches is that even when cultures diverge, their differences can usually be understood in terms of orderly, scientifically intelligible processes.

SUMMARY

Homo sapiens was the first hominid in the New World. The precise date of the "discovery of America" is not known. It definitely occurred before 14,000 B.P. and probably before 25,000 B.P. The discoverers were undoubtedly groups of Siberian big-game hunters who walked across the Bering Straits when it was frozen or above water. The earliest American tool types known were produced from discoidal cores and resemble Upper Paleolithic Asian tool types. By about 11,500 B.P. distinctive Paleo-Indian American traditions appeared. In North America these were characterized by the finely crafted fluted points and thin-based points of the Clovis and Folsom assemblages, which are associated with large animal kills. Lack of stone grinders suggests that Clovis and Folsom assemblages were used by highly advanced specialist big-game hunters for whom plant gathering was of secondary significance. There were similar Paleo-Indian adaptations in South America.

Traditions known as the Archaic appear about 10,000 B.P. They are characterized by broad-spectrum hunting, gathering, and fishing economies adapted to forested, riverine, and coastal habitats. This shift to broad-spectrum modes of production coincided as in the Old World Mesolithic with extinctions of megafauna. It is likely that post-Pleistocene climate changes and intensive predation by efficient hunters both contributed to the loss of numerous genera and species. As in the Old World, the broad-spectrum modes of production were practiced in diverse habitats, some of which contained plant and animal species suitable for domestication. New World domesticates covered a broad range of grains, root crops, legumes, and vegetables. Only a rather narrow range of animals was domesticated, however, as a result of the extent of the megafauna extinctions. The spread of New World crops, such as maize, cacao, manioc, and potatoes, has had an enormous impact on the history of the entire world since 1492. The fact that the major New World plant domesticates were unknown in the Old World strongly suggests an independent origin for New World agriculture. Recent discoveries of the gradual steps in the improvement of maize make this a virtual certainty.

A New World transition from broad-spectrum modes of production to agriculture is known from the valley of Tehuacán in the Mexican highlands. After the megafauna extinctions, small animals, birds, and a wide variety of plants—including many of the later domesticates—were the main source of

CHRONOLOGY OF CULTURAL EVOLUTION

Thousand years B.P.	EUROPE		MIDDLE EAST		EAST AND SOUTHEAST ASIA		AFRICA
	Site	Findings	Site	Findings	Site	Findings	Site
(A.D. 1500)							West Africa
1							
(A.D. 500)					Vietnam	First SE Asian city	
2							Southwestern Sahara
	Athens	First Olympic games					
3							Dar Tichitt
4	Argissa	Farming infrastructure			Huangho Basin Yellow River	Shang Dynasty Domestication of millet	
	England	Stonehenge begun					
5			Uruk	First cities	Ban Chiang	Wet rice farming	Egypt
6			Çatal Hüyük Al Ubaid Eridu	Town, murals Mud brick temples	China Pan-p'o	Writing Sedentary village life	Egypt
7					Non Nok Tha	Cord-marked pottery, domesticated cattle, dry rice agriculture	
	Argissa	Earliest domesticated millet					
8			Jarmo Jericho	Domesticated wheat, barley, goats			↑ Egyptian western desert ↓
9	Star Carr	Domesticated dogs	Ali Kosh Mallaha Jericho Zawi Chemi	Domesticated goats Round houses Walls and towers Domesticated sheep	Japan	Earliest known pottery	
10			Nahal Oren	Domesticated cereal	Spirit Cave	Edible plants (domesticated?)	
15							Wade Kublaniya North Africa
25	Vogelherd	Aurignacian art					
	Saint-Cesaire Nance	Neandertal in association with artifacts					
50			Skhūl Shanidar	Funeral rites?			
75							
100	Tata	Polished mammoth's tooth (Mousterian)					Faversmith
500							
1000							

AFRICA	SOUTH AMERICA		MESOAMERICA		NORTH AMERICA		Thousand years B.P.
Findings	Site	Findings	Site	Findings	Site	Findings	
First cities	Peru	Inca Empire	Tenochtitlán	Aztecs conquered			(A.D. 1500)
					Cahokia Southwest N. America	First city Pueblos appear	1
	Peruvian coastal rivers	First small states	Yucatán	Mayan chiefdoms			(A.D. 500)
Village clusters, paramount chiefs?			Teotihuacán Yucatán	Formation Mayan maize agriculture	Mogollan mtn. range	Pit houses	2
Transition to agriculture	Peruvian coastal rivers Coastal Peru	Large settlements Coastal platform mounds, masonry	Tehuacán La Venta Basin of Mexico	Large villages Earthfill pyramid Agricultural settlers	Mississippi, Ohio River valleys	Maize cultivation	3
							4
			Yucatán	Mayan masonry			
Writing	Ayacucho	↑ Maize domestication	Gulf Coast of Vera Cruz and Tabasco	Development of Olmec civilization	Bat Cave	Primitive corn domestication	5
First farming villages	Andes	Domesticated llamas ↓					6
			Tamualipas Tehuacán Valley	Domestication of maize			7
	Callejón de Huaylas	Domesticated beans					
							8
Domesticated cattle							9
	Callejón de Huaylas Taima Taima	Domesticated beans Projectile point, scrapers	Tehuacán	Hunter-gatherer band	Shriver	Discoidal core flakes	10
Milling stones Domesticated sheep	Ayacucho	Discoidal core, edge-retouched flakes			Meadowcroft Rock Shelter	Blade knives	15
					Old Crow Flats	Bone artifacts	25
							50
							75
Levallois flake tools							100
							500
							1000

subsistence for the small hunter-gatherer bands of Tehuacán. After 9000 B.P. grinding tools were prominent and meat began to lose its importance as a source of calories. In order to take advantage of the seasonal availability of wild plant foods in different ecozones, careful scheduling of band movements was necessary. The periodic return to fields of wild grains, squash, and other plants led to seed and fruit pit planting as a means of guaranteeing a regular harvest. Squash, amaranth, chili peppers, and avocados were the earliest domesticates. As more plant domesticates were added, regular planting and harvesting became a major focus of activity, but 3500 years elapsed before permanent houses and hamlets were built. In fact, sedentary villages were first built not by the incipient agriculturalists but by broad-spectrum hunter-gatherers living in lush coastal and riverine habitats. It seems likely that the delay in reaching sedentism in the highlands was related to the absence of animal domesticates and the reliance on wild species as a source of animal fats and proteins.

As in the Old World, agricultural modes of production laid the basis for the emergence of native American cities, states, and empires. Different regions, however, had different limits of growth. In the Mesoamerican lowlands, the Olmec and, to a greater degree, the Maya, supplemented slash-and-burn techniques with raised-field and other intensive forms of agriculture. Soil depletion and other effects of overintensification probably caused the collapse of the great Maya ceremonial centers and the depopulation of the Peten area. In the highlands the use of spring-fed canal irrigation at Teotihuacán and Chinampas near the Aztec capital of Tenochtitlán, together with extensive trade networks, encouraged the growth of larger and more powerful state systems. North of Mexico, on the other hand, there were many regions in which agriculture was never adopted. In general, the natural and cultural conditions north of Mexico were not suitable for the rise of native American states or empires.

The largest New World states and empires developed in the Andes region of South America including the adjacent Pacific Coast. Again, the distinctiveness of many Andean animal and plant domesticates points to a largely independent transition from small broad-spectrum villages along the coast to large agricultural communities in the irrigated river valleys. With a full range of grains, tubers, and vegetables, plus llamas and guinea pigs, the potential for growth of the Andean states was greater than that of Mesoamerica and was epitomized by the Inca Empire, which developed shortly before the Spanish conquest.

The independent origin of cities, states, and empires in the New World lends support to nomothetic research strategies and especially to those that are concerned with cultural evolutionary processes.

11 ECOLOGY, ENERGY, AND POPULATION

As the people of the Western world have recently come to realize, the amounts and kinds of energy used in daily life affect every aspect of human existence. In this chapter we will examine the interrelationships among energy production, the natural environment, and technology, and their joint effect on everyday patterns of work and leisure in different societies. We will also consider how the problem of controlling human population growth generates pressure to intensify and change modes of production.

ECOLOGY AND ECOSYSTEMS

Ecology is essentially the study of how the energy in sunlight is captured and stored by plants in different natural environments and how various "communities" of plants and animals make use of that energy, aided and abetted by one another and by inorganic factors such as soils, rainfall, and other environmental conditions. Systems by which communities of organisms capture, exchange, and use energy are known as *ecosystems*.

Because of the enormous versatility of culture, human beings are an important although not necessarily dominant feature in most ecosystems. The study of ecosystems that concentrates on the ecological relationships among human beings and their cultures and the rest of the organic and inorganic environment is known as *human ecology* (or cultural ecology). The production and exchange of energy provides the key to understanding the relations between human populations and the other living and nonliving components of ecosystems. This in turn furnishes the key to understanding many basic features of the infrastructural, structural, and superstructural aspects of sociocultural life.

EVOLUTION OF ENERGY PRODUCTION

During the time of the earliest hominids, all the energy utilized for the conduct of social life stemmed from food. *Homo erectus* does not appear to have mastered the use of fire until sometime between 1 million and 500,000 years ago, judging from charcoal fragments discovered at fossil sites in Hungary and China (Stahl 1984:151). Fire was used at first for cooking, for warmth, for hardening the tips of spears, and for driving game animals over cliffs or into ambushes, and possibly to favor the growth of desired plant species. During the Neolithic, animals began to provide energy in the form of muscle power harnessed to plows, sleds, and wheeled vehicles. At about the same time, considerable wood and charcoal fuel energy was expended to produce pottery. With the rise of incipient states (see p. 165), there was the beginning of the use of wind energy for sailing ships and wood energy for melting and casting metals. The energy in falling water was not tapped extensively until the medieval period in Europe. It is only in the last 200 or 300 years that the fossil fuels—coal, oil, and gas—began to dominate human ecosystems.

New sources of energy have followed each other in a logical progression, with mastery of later forms dependent on the mastery of the earlier ones. For example, in both the Old World and the New World the sequence of inventions that led to metallurgy depended upon the prior achievement of high-temperature wood-fire ovens and furnaces for baking ceramics, and this depended on learning how to make and control wood fires in cooking. Low-temperature metallurgical experience with copper and tin almost of necessity had to precede the use of iron and steel. Mastery of iron and steel in turn had to precede the development of the mining machines that made the use of coal, oil, and gas possible. Finally, the use of these fossil fuels spawned the Industrial Revolution, from which the technology for today's nuclear energy derives.

These technological achievements have steadily increased the average amount of energy available per human being from Paleolithic times to the present. This increase in energy does not necessarily mean that humankind's ability to control nature has steadily increased. The lesson of today's energy and ecology crisis is that the increased use of energy per capita does not necessarily bring a higher standard of living or less work per capita. Also, a distinction must be made between total amount of energy available and the efficiency with which that energy is produced and put to use.

MODES OF FOOD PRODUCTION

As we have seen, throughout most of humankind's presence on earth, food production was universally based on hunting and fishing and the collection or gathering of wild plants.

Hunter-gatherers are typically organized into small groups called *bands*, numbering from about 20 to 50 people (Barnard 1983). Bands consist of individual families who make camp together for periods ranging from a few days to several years before moving on to other campsites. Band life is opposed to village life, which is typically associated with agricultural modes of production. Band life is essentially migratory; shelters are temporary and possessions are few. One must be careful, however, not to overgeneralize, since hunter-gatherers inhabit a wide range of environments. The Eskimo—hunter-gatherers of the Arctic—necessarily have ecologies and cultures somewhat different from those of desert-dwelling groups. Moreover, as discussed above (p. 178), the earliest villages in both hemispheres are based on broad-spectrum modes of production, especially in habitats rich in maritime and riverine fauna.

Typically, agricultural peoples live in more permanent settlements than hunter-gatherers. But again, not all agricultural societies are alike. There are many varieties of agriculture, each with its ecological and cultural implications. *Rainfall agriculture* utilizes naturally occurring showers as a source of moisture; *irrigation agriculture* depends on artificially constructed dams and ditches to bring water to the fields. Several varieties of rainfall and irrigation agriculture, each with its own ecological and cultural implications, must also be distinguished. *Raised-field* systems (p. 185), combine aspects of rainfall and irrigation techniques.

To practice rainfall agriculture, the problem of replenishing the nutrients taken from the soil by successive crops must be solved. One of the most ancient methods for solving this problem, still widely practiced to this day, is known as *slash-and-burn* (see p. 211). A patch of forest is cut down and left to dry. Then the slash is set on fire and later the ashes, which contain a rich supply of nutrients, are spread over the area to be planted (Fig. 11.1). In regions of heavy rainfall, a slash-and-burn garden cannot be replanted for more than two or three seasons before the nutrients in the ashes become depleted. A new patch of forest is then cleared and burned. Slash-and-burn thus requires large amounts of land in fallow awaiting the regrowth of vegetation suitable for burning.

A totally different solution to the problem of maintaining soil fertility is to raise animals as well as crops and to use animal manure as fertilizer. This is known as *mixed farming*, and was once characteristic of the European and American small family farm. With the advent of the industrial era, soil fertility has come to depend primarily on chemical fertilizers, eliminating the need for raising animals and crops on the same farm.

In irrigation agriculture, soil fertility is less of a problem since the irrigation water often contains silt and nutrients that are automatically deposited on the fields. But irrigation agriculture varies greatly in type and in scale (Carlstein 1981:257ff.). Some irrigation systems are confined to terraces on the walls of mountain valleys, as in the Philippines (Fig. 11.2). Others embrace the flood plains of great rivers such as the Nile and the Yellow River. One form of irrigation involves mounding: mud is scooped from shallow lakes and piled up to form ridges in which crops are planted, as in the famous *Chinampas* of Mexico (see Fig. 10.11). In the Middle East, huge underground aqueducts called *qats* (or *qanats*) conduct water from mountain streams to distant desert farmlands (Wilkinson 1977). Throughout much of India, irrigation water is pulled up by ox-power from deep brick-lined wells or more recently pumped up electrically through drilled pipes. Irrigation, however, is not without its own problems. Heavily irrigated fields, for example, turn salty if the water table rises too close to the surface, rendering vast areas unsuitable for planting. It has also recently been found that the damming of rivers for hydroelectric power and irrigation in tropical habitats poses a health hazard by providing ideal breeding conditions for disease-carrying snails (Rhodes 1978).

Figure 11.1 *PLANTING IN A SWIDDEN*
This Amahuaca woman is using a digging stick to plant corn in a recently burned garden.

THE INFLUENCE OF THE ENVIRONMENT

Items of a food production technology interact with factors present in a particular environment. Similar kinds of technologies in different environments may lead to different energy outputs. For example, the productivity of irrigation farming varies according to the size and dependability of the water supply, the availability of flat terrain, and the amount of minerals in the water. Similarly, the productivity of slash-and-burn agriculture varies in relation to how much forest is available for burning and how quickly the forest can regenerate itself. It is thus really not possible to speak of technology in the abstract; rather, we must always refer to the interaction between technology and the conditions characteristic of a specific natural environment.

In industrial societies the influence of environment often appears to be subordinate to the influence exerted by technology. But it is incorrect to believe that industrial societies have liberated themselves from the in-

Figure 11.2 *PHILIPPINE MOUNTAINSIDE TERRACES*
These terraces, built by the Ifugao people, are among the engineering wonders of the preindustrial world.

fluence of the environment or that our species now dominates or controls the environment. It is true that replicas of American suburbs have been built in the deserts of Saudi Arabia and the snowfields of Alaska and that they can also be constructed on the moon. But the energy and material involved in such achievements derive from the interactions between technology and environment carried out in mines, factories, and farms in various parts of the world which are depleting irreplaceable reserves of oil, water, soil, forests, and metallic ores. Similarly, at all sites where modern technology extracts or processes natural resources or where any form of industrial construction or production takes place, the problem of disposing of industrial wastes, pollutants, and other biologically significant by-products arises. Efforts are now underway in many industrial nations to reduce air and water pollution and to prevent the depletion and poisoning of the environment. The costs of these efforts testify to the continuing importance of the interaction between technology and environment. These costs will continue to mount, for this is only the very beginning of the industrial era. In the centuries to come, the inhabitants of specific regions may pay for industrialization in ways as yet uncalculated.

CARRYING CAPACITY AND THE LAW OF DIMINISHING RETURNS

Factors such as abundance of game, quality of soils, amounts of rainfall, and extent of forests available for energy production set an upper limit on the amount of energy that can be extracted from a given environment by means of a given technology of energy production. The upper limit on energy production in turn sets an upper limit on the number of human beings who can live in that environment. This upper limit on population is called the environment's *carrying capacity*.

Extreme caution must be exercised before concluding that a particular culture can "easily" raise production by increasing the size of its labor force or by increasing the amount of time devoted to work. Carrying capacity is difficult to measure (Glassow 1978; Street 1969). Allegations of untapped environmental potential are often not based upon long enough periods of observation. Many puzzling features of human ecosystems result from adjustments that are made to recurrent but infrequent ecological crises, such as droughts, floods, frosts, hurricanes, and recurrent epidemics of animal and plant diseases that require long periods of observation. Moreover, a basic principle of ecological analysis states that communities of organisms adjust to the minimum life-sustaining conditions in their habitats rather than to the average conditions. One formulation of this principle is known as *Liebig's law of the minimum*. This law states that growth is limited by the minimum availability of any one necessary factor rather than by the abundance of all necessary factors. The short-time observer of human ecosystems is likely to see the average condition, not the extremes, and is likely to overlook the limiting factor (Jochim 1981:181).

Nonetheless, there is now much evidence that food production among preindustrial peoples is often only about one-third of what it might be if full advantage were taken of the environment's carrying capacity by means of the existing technology (Sahlins 1972). In order to understand why this "underproduction" occurs, we must distinguish between the effect of exceeding carrying capacity and the effect of exceeding the *point of diminishing returns* (Fig. 11.3). When carrying capacity is exceeded, production will begin to decline as a result of irreversible damage to the ecosystem. The depletion of soils is an example of the consequence of exceeding carrying capacity. Species extinctions, as in the case of the Upper Paleolithic hunters, is another example (see p. 178).

When the point of diminishing returns is exceeded, however, production may hold steady or may even continue to increase, even though there is less produced per unit of effort as a result of the growing scarcity or impoverishment of one or more environmental factors. The present condition of the ocean fisheries of the world is an example of exceeding the point of diminishing returns. Since 1970 the rate of return per unit of effort has declined by almost one-half, yet the total catch of fish has held steady (L. Brown 1978). A similar situation exists with respect to world agriculture and in the production of oil and gas (see below).

Except when thay are under certain kinds of political pressures, people will attempt to keep the ratio of output to input from falling below the point of diminishing returns by limiting the expansion of their production efforts; no one willingly wants to work more for less. Thus people may feel the need to change their routines and to institute cultural innovations long before carrying capacity is reached.

EXPANSION, INTENSIFICATION, AND TECHNOLOGICAL CHANGE

To understand the way human ecosystems operate, one must distinguish between expansion and intensification. If technology is held constant, production can be increased by putting more people to work or by having them work longer and faster. If this increase in input occurs without increasing the area in which food production is taking place, intensification has occurred. If, however, there is a proportionate increase in the area throughout which food production takes place so that the input per hectare or square kilometer remains the same, then the system is *expanding* or growing but not being intensified (Morren 1977:311).

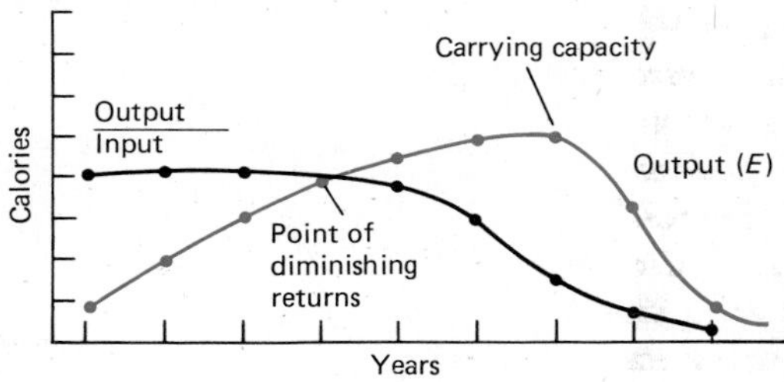

Figure 11.3 *GRAPH SHOWING RELATIONSHIP BETWEEN CARRYING CAPACITY AND POINT OF DIMINISHING RETURNS*
Production continues to increase even after point of diminishing returns is passed. But production cannot increase after carrying capacity is reached.

Since all modes of production (indeed, all modes of activity of any sort) depend on finite resources, expansion cannot continue forever. Sooner or later any further increase in production will have to depend on intensification. And intensification, more or less rapidly, must lead to the point of diminishing returns caused by the depletion of nonrenewable resources, and a drop in efficiency. If the intensification is sustained, sooner or later production will collapse and fall to zero.

The all-important condition in this scenario, however, is that the technology is held constant. In human ecosystems, a common response to diminishing returns is to change the technology. Thus, as suggested in the work of Ester Boserup (1965, 1981), when hunters and gatherers deplete their environments and pass the point of diminishing returns, they are likely to begin to adopt an agricultural mode of production; when slash-and-burn peoples pass the point of diminishing returns, they may shift to the cultivation of permanent fields using animal fertilizer; and when rainfall agriculturalists using permanent fields deplete their soils, they may shift to irrigation agriculture. The shift from preindustrial to industrial and petrochemical forms of agriculture can also be seen as a response to depletion and declining yield per unit of effort (Harris 1977).

HUNTER-GATHERER ECOLOGY

The !Kung San* are a hunting-and-gathering people who live in the Kalahari Desert on both sides of the border between Botswana and Namibia in southern Africa (Lee 1979). Like most hunter-gatherers, the !Kung San move about a great deal from one camp to another in search of water, game, and wild plant foods (Hayden 1981; Barnard 1983). They build only temporary shelters and have a minimum of possessions, yet they are well-nourished and moderately long-lived. As among most hunter-gatherers, the !Kung San men specialize in hunting while !Kung San women specialize in gathering, although on occasion women will bring a small animal back to camp and men will help in carrying loads of nuts (Fig. 11.4).

*The ! designates a sound which is not used in English, called a click. See p. 398.

The number of people in a !Kung camp varies from 23 to 40, with an average camp size of 31 (20 adults and 11 children). During a 4-week study period, Richard Lee calculated that 20 adults put in an average of 2.4 days per week on hunting and gathering. On any particular day, the number of people hunting or gathering varied from zero to 16.

About 60 percent of the calories consumed by a !Kung camp are provided by women's gathering activities. Women range widely throughout the countryside, walking about 2 to 12 miles a day round trip for a total of about 1500 miles a year each. On an average trip each woman brings back a load of from 15 to 33 pounds of nuts, berries, fruits, leafy greens, and roots whose proportions vary from season to season.

Men hunt on the average only every 3 or 4 days and are successful only about 23 percent of the time they hunt. Hunting is

Figure 11.4 *!KUNG WOMEN RETURNING TO CAMP*
They have been out gathering wild vegetables and are carrying digging sticks.

therefore not an efficient source of energy for the !Kung. For every calorie (above basal metabolism) expended on hunting, only about 3 calories worth of meat were produced. Of the average total of about 2355 calories consumed per person per day, meat provides about 19 percent, nuts and vegetables the rest. One nut, in particular, the mongongo, alone accounts for about 70 percent of the !Kung caloric intake and a large share of their protein as well.

Studies of the !Kung and other hunter-gatherers who have survived into modern times have dispelled the notion that the hunting-and-gathering way of life necessarily condemns people to a miserable hand-to-mouth existence, with starvation avoided only by dint of unremitting daily effort. About 10 percent of the !Kung are over 60 years of age (as compared with 5 percent in agricultural countries such as Brazil and India) and medical examination shows them to be in good health.

Judged by the large quantity of meat and other sources of protein in their diet, their sound physical condition, and their abundant leisure, the !Kung San have a high standard of living. The key to this situation is that their population is low in relation to the resources they exploit. There is less than one person per square mile in their land and their production effort remains far below carrying capacity, with no appreciable intensification (except in recent years due to the appearance of neighboring peoples who possess livestock). If the !Kung San were to double their effort at hunting from 2 days a week to 4, they would not only find it progressively more difficult to capture their prey, but they would run the risk of depleting the animal population below the point of recovery. In a sense, the !Kung San benefit from being at the mercy of the natural rates of increase of the plants and animals in their habitat; their mode of production obliges them to work less than agriculturalists or modern factory workers.

A SLASH-AND-BURN FOOD ENERGY SYSTEM

Roy Rappaport (1968, 1984) has made a careful study of the food energy system of the Tsembaga Maring, a clan living in semi-permanent villages on the northern slopes of the central highlands of New Guinea. The Tsembaga, who number about 204, plant taro, yams, sweet potatoes, manioc, sugarcane, and several other crops in small gardens cleared and fertilized by the slash-and-burn method (Fig. 11.5). Slash-and-burn is a more efficient method of meeting calorie needs than hunting, yielding 18 calories output for every 1 calorie of input. Thus, the Tsembaga are able to satisfy their caloric needs with a remarkably small investment of working time—only 380 hours per year per food-producer spent on raising crops, or about 7.2 hours per week. And at the same time the Tsembaga manage to feed almost ten times as many people as the !Kung and to live in permanent houses (except for routs caused by warfare).

Two environmental limits are especially pertinent to the Tsembaga and to other tropical slash-and-burn ecosystems. First, there is the problem of forest regeneration. Because of leaching by heavy rains and because of the invasion of insects and weeds, the productivity of slash-and-burn gardens drops rapidly after 2 or 3 years of use, and additional land must be cleared to avoid a sharp reduction in labor efficiency and output (Clarke 1976; Janzen 1973). Optimum productivity is achieved when gardens are cleared from a substantial secondary growth of large trees. If gardens are cleared when the secondary growth is very immature,

Figure 11.5 *"COOKING" THE GARDEN* Tsembaga Maring woman during the burning phase of swidden cycle.

only a small amount of wood-ash fertilizer will be produced by burning. On the other hand, if the trees revert to climax-forest size, they will be very difficult to cut down. Optimum regeneration may take anywhere from 10 to 20 years or more, depending on local soils and climates.

Thus in the long run, slash-and-burn ecosystems use up a considerable amount of forest per capita, but in any particular year only 5 percent of the total territory may actually be in production (Boserup 1965:31). The Tsembaga, for example, plant only 42 acres in a given year. Nonetheless, about 864 acres in their territory have been gardened. This is about the amount of forest that the Tsembaga would need if their population remains at about 200 people and if they burned secondary-growth garden sites every 20 years. Rappaport estimates that the Tsembaga had at their disposal an amount of forest land sufficient to support another 84 people without permanently damaging the regenerative capacities of the forest. However, the bulk of this land lies above or below the optimum altitude levels for their major crops and thus would probably somewhat diminish efficiency if put into use. All slash-and-burn peoples confront the ultimate specter of "eating up their forest" (Condominas 1978) by shortening the fallow period to a point where grasses and weeds replace trees. At least this is what has happened to other New Guinea peoples not too far from the Tsembaga (Sorenson 1972; Sorenson and Kenmore 1974). Nonetheless, there are situations, such as in the Amazon jungle, where vast untapped reserves of trees remain and where population densities are so low that the supply of burnable trees cannot be the factor limiting carrying capacity or determining the point of diminishing returns.

Many tropical slash-and-burn peoples, however, confront another problem that sets limits to the expansion of their population and the intensification of work effort. This problem is especially acute where the main staples are protein-deficient crops such as sweet potatoes, plantains, yams, manioc, and taro. Natural tropical forest ecosystems sustain a vast amount of *plant* biomass per acre, but they are very poor producers of *animal* biomass as compared, for example, with grasslands and marine ecosystems (Richards 1973). The animals that inhabit tropical forests tend to be small, furtive, and arboreal. As human population density rises, these animals quickly become very scarce and hard to find. The total animal biomass—the weight of all the spiders, insects, worms, snakes, mammals, and so on—in a hectare of central Amazon rain forest is 45 kilograms. This compares with 304 kilograms in a dry East African thorn forest. In East African savannah grasslands, 627 kilograms of large herbivores are found per hectare, far outweighing all the large and small animals found per hectare in the Amazon (Fittkau and Klinge 1973:8). Although plant foods can provide nutritionally adequate amounts of proteins if eaten in variety and abundance, meat is the most effective source of all the amino acids necessary for nutrition: fat, minerals, and vitamins. Hence, one of the most important limiting factors in the growth of slash-and-burn energy systems is thought to be the availability of meat (Gross 1975, 1982; Harris 1984). This issue, however, is the center of considerable controversy, and a discussion of the ecological and nutritional importance of meat and other forms of animal food appears in Chapter 15 (p. 306).

THE HIGH COST OF PIGS

Whatever etic ecological and nutritional reason there may be for it, there is no doubt that the Tsembaga, like virtually every other human group (Abrams 1983), highly prize fatty meat (vegetarians who abstain from meat usually prize animal protein and fat in the form of milk and yogurt). The Tsembaga, whose population density is 67 persons per square mile, compared with less than 1 per square mile among the !Kung San, have depleted the wild animals in their territory. But they have compensated for this by stocking their land with a domestic animal—the pig (Fig. 11.6). The Tsembaga's pigs root for themselves during the day but come home to a meal of sweet potatoes and food scraps in the evening. An average Tsembaga pig weighs as much as an average Tsembaga human, and Rappaport estimates that each pig consumes almost as much garden produce as each person.

IRRIGATION AGRICULTURE

Under favorable conditions, irrigation agriculture yields more calories per calorie of effort than any other preindustrial mode of food production. And among irrigation farmers, the Chinese have excelled for thousands of years (Fig. 11.7). A detailed study of the labor inputs and weight yield of agricultural production in precommunist times was carried out by the anthropologists Fei Hsiao-t'ung and Chang Chih-I (1947) in the village of Luts'un, Yunnan Province. Over 50 calories were obtained for each calorie of effort in the fields. The principal crops were rice, which accounted for 75 percent of the total, soybeans, corn, manioc, and potatoes. Because of the high productivity of their agriculture, the 700 people of Luts'un produced five times more food than they consumed. What happened to this *surplus*? It was diverted from the village to towns and cities; it was exchanged via markets and money for nonfarm goods and services; it was taxed away by the local, provincial, and central governments; it went into rent as payment for use of land; and it was used to raise large numbers of children and to sustain a high rate of population increase.

One of the most interesting features of Luts'un's energy system is that despite the high ratio of output to input, the average Luts'un farmer put in 1129 hours of work per year, far more than the average !Kung San hunter-gatherer.

The high population density of parts of China and of other societies that practice irrigation agriculture results from the fact that by expanding the amount of water fed to the

Figure 11.6 *DISPATCHING A PIG*
Pigs have great ritual significance throughout New Guinea and Melanesia. The people in this scene are Fungai Maring, neighbors of the Tsembaga Maring.

fields, increasing amounts of labor can be invested in production without substantial losses in the output-input ratio. Thus, instead of using the labor-saving potential of their technology to work less, irrigation agriculturalists opt for intensifying their effort and increasing their output.

ENERGY AND PASTORAL NOMADISM

Grains convert about 0.4 percent of photosynthetically active sunlight into human edible matter. If one feeds this grain to animals rather than to people and then eats the meat, 90 percent, on the average, of the energy available in the grains will be lost (National Research Council 1974). The loss in efficiency associated with the processing of plant food through domesticated animals accounts for the relatively infrequent occurrence of cultures whose mode of food production is that called *pastoral nomadism* (Fig. 11.8). Full pastoral nomads are peoples who raise domesticated animals and who do not depend upon hunting, gathering, or the planting of their own crops for a significant portion of their diet. Pastoral nomads typically occupy arid grasslands and steppes in which precipitation is too sparse or irregular to support rainfall agriculture and which cannot be irrigated because they are too high or too far from major river valleys. By specializing in animal husbandry, pastoral nomads can move their herds about over long distances and take advantage of the best pasture.

However, pastoral peoples must obtain grain supplements to their diet of milk, cheese, blood, and meat—the last always being a relatively small part of the daily fare. (As discussed in Ch. 9, pastoral and agricultural technologies evolved in interaction with each other.) The productivity of herding alone is not adequate to support dense populations. Grains are usually obtained through trade with agricultural neighbors who are eager to obtain hides, cheese, milk, and other animal products that are in short supply wherever preindustrial agricultural systems support dense populations. Pastoralists frequently attempt to improve their "bargaining" position by raiding the sedentary villagers and carrying off the grain harvest without paying for it. They can often do this with impunity, since their possession of animals such as camels and horses makes them highly mobile and militarily effective. Continued success in raiding may force the farming population to acknowledge the pastoralists as their overloads. Repeatedly in the history of the Old World, relatively

Figure 11.7 *IRRIGATION DAM*
Built on the Yuxi River to irrigate over 33,330 hectares in Qionglai County, China.

small groups of pastoral nomads—the Mongols and the Arabs being the two most famous examples—have succeeded in gaining control of huge civilizations based on irrigation agriculture. The inevitable outcome of these conquests, however, was that the conquerors were absorbed by the agricultural system as they attempted to feed the populations that had fallen under their control (Lattimore 1962; Lees and Bates 1974; Salzman 1971; Carlstein 1981:103).

However, because of their restricted energy base, most pastoral societies are dominated by the more powerful states in whose territories they live. Since pastoral societies tend to be decentralized and to lack their own state institutions, they cannot exert political pressure upon the governments to which they are subject and they lack modern weaponry and means of transport (Dahl 1979:262).

Figure 11.8 *PASTORAL NOMADS* Tuareg family and their most valuable possession.

INDUSTRIAL FOOD ENERGY SYSTEMS

It is difficult to estimate the output-input ratio of industrial agriculture because the amount of indirect labor put into food production exceeds the amount of direct labor (Fig. 11.9). An Iowa corn farmer, for example, puts in 9 hours of work per acre, which yield 81 bushels of corn with an energy equivalent of 8,164,800 calories (Pimentel et al. 1973). This gives a nominal ratio of 5000 calories output for every calorie of input! But this is a misleading figure. First of all, three-quarters of all the croplands in the United States are devoted to the production of animal feeds, with a consequent 90 to 95 percent reduction in human consumable calories. Indeed, the livestock population of the United States consumes enough food calories to feed 1.3 billion people (Cloud 1973). Second, enormous amounts of human labor are embodied in the tractors, trucks, combines, oil and gas, pesticides, herbicides, and fertilizers used by the Iowa corn farmer.

A misunderstood aspect of industrial food energy systems is the difference between higher yields per acre and the ratio of energy input to output. As a result of more and more intensive modes of production involving genetically improved crops, and higher dosages of chemical fertilizers and pesticides, yields per acre have steadily improved (N. Jensen 1978). But this improvement has been made possible only as a result of a steady increase in the amount of fuel energy invested for each calorie of food energy produced. In the United States 15 tons of machinery, 22 gallons of gasoline, 203 pounds of fertilizer, and 2 pounds of chemical insecticides and pesticides are invested per year. This represents a cost of 2,890,000 calories of nonfood energy per acre per year (Pimentel et al. 1975). This cost has increased steadily since the beginning of the century. Before 1910 more calories were obtained from agriculture than were invested in it. By 1970 it took 8 calories in the form of fossil fuels to produce 1 calorie of food. If the people of India were to emulate the U.S. system of food production, their entire energy budget would have to be devoted to nothing but agriculture (Steinhart and Steinhart 1974). In the words of Howard Odum (1971:15):

> A whole generation of citizens thought that the carrying capacity of the earth was proportional to the amount of land under cultivation and higher efficiencies in using the energy of the sun had arrived. This is a sad hoax, for industrial man no longer eats potatoes made from solar energy; now he eats potatoes made of oil.

Figure 11.9 *INDUSTRIAL AGRICULTURE*
Pea bean combines harvesting baby lima beans in the state of Washington. Are the men in the picture farmers?

(a)

Figure 11.10 *LABOR-SAVING DEVICES THAT DON'T SAVE WORK*
(*a*) The first assembly line. Ford's Highland Park, Michigan, magneto assembly line saved 15 minutes per unit and initiated the era of mass production in 1913. But the workers worked harder than ever. (*b*) All work and no play in a Russian television factory.

THE MYTH OF INCREASED LEISURE

Another common misconception concerning industrial and preindustrial modes of production is that industrial workers have more leisure than their preindustrial ancestors. The reverse seems to be true, however. With a 40-hour week and a 3-week vacation, the typical modern factory worker puts in close to 2000 hours per year under conditions hunters and gatherers would probably regard as "inhuman" (Fig. 11.10). When labor leaders boast about how much progress has been made in obtaining leisure for the working class, they have in mind the standard established in "civilized" nineteenth-century Europe, when factory workers put in 12 hours a day or more, rather than the standards observed by the !Kung.

Of course, these data fail to take into consideration other activities which might etically be classified as work. Preindustrial peoples are not merely idle when they are not sleeping or processing or producing food. In every culture much time and energy are devoted to additional tasks and activities, some of which are essential to subsistence. Unfortunately, anthropologists have seldom collected the appropriate data, and hence it is very difficult to generalize about how time is allocated to various tasks and activities in different cultures. A broader definition of "work," however, does not give the middle-class industrial wage earner or office worker an advantage over those peoples whose activity patterns have been studied with more care.

One of the best attempts to quantify daily activity patterns for a whole population has been carried out by Allen Johnson (1974) among the Machiguenga (Fig. 11.11), a slash-and-burn village people who live on the Upper Urubamba River on the eastern slopes of the Andes in Peru. Johnson randomly sampled what the members of 13 households were doing between the hours of 6 A.M. and 7 P.M. throughout an entire year. His results, given in Table 11.1, show that food production plus food preparation plus the manufacture of essential items such as clothing, tools, and shelter consume only 6.0 hours per day for married men and 6.3 hours per day for married women.

(b)

Figure 11.11 *MACHIGUENGA AT WORK* As in most slash-and-burn economies, Machiguenga men do the heavy work of felling trees and clearing the forest for new plantings.

If we add hours of commuting time and hours devoted to shopping, cleaning, cooking, and household maintenance to the 8 hours spent by U.S. urban wage workers at their places of work, the Machiguenga clearly come out ahead.

This leads to the question of why the great labor-saving potential of technology has been devoted to the ever-greater expansion of energy systems rather than to the achievement of an ever-greater amount of leisure based on a constant population and a constant level of production and consumption.

CULTURAL CHECKS ON POPULATION GROWTH

Most contemporary hunter-gatherer peoples have populations whose densities are considerably less than one person per square mile. If these groups are at all representative of prehistoric times, *Homo sapiens* must have been a very rare creature during the Paleolithic. Perhaps there were only 6 million people in the entire world in those times (Hassan 1981:199; Dumond 1975), certainly no more than 15 million (M. N. Cohen 1977:54), compared with almost 4 billion today. Whether one takes the upper or lower estimate, there is no doubt that for tens of thousands of years, the rate of growth of the human population was very slow (see Table 11.2). Potentially, human populations can easily double every 28 years, which is equivalent to an annual growth rate of about 2.5 percent. This was actually the observed rate of growth of the !Kung during the period 1963 to 1969 (Howell 1976a:141), and rates of 3.0 percent or more are common today among less developed countries. Yet for most of prehistory, population grew at only a fraction of this potential rate.

Another way to pose this problem is to consider the childbearing capacity of the human female. Among the Hutterites, a religious agrarian sect who live in Canada, each woman averages 10.7 live births during her

Table 11.1 TIME DEVOTED TO VARIOUS ACTIVITIES PER DAY BY MACHIGUENGA MARRIED MEN AND WOMEN

	Married men	Married women
Food production	4.4 hours	1.8 hours
Food preparation	0.2	2.4
Manufacture	1.4	2.1
Child care	0.0	1.1
Hygiene	0.3	0.6
Visiting	1.0	0.8
Idle	2.3	2.5
	9.6	11.3

SOURCE: Johnson 1975, 1978.

reproductive career. Yet in order to maintain the 0.0015 rate of increase of the Paleolithic, women would have had to average less than 2.1 children born and surviving to reproductive age. How and why did world population increase so slowly for so long?

CONTRACEPTION TECHNIQUES

Population-regulating mechanisms may operate prior to conception or after conception. Contrary to romantic beliefs about folk contraceptives, preindustrial people cannot prevent conception by anything resembling the "pill." Their chief means of preventing women from getting pregnant is abstention from heterosexual genital intercourse. A common form of abstention involves a taboo on such intercourse after a woman has given birth. Encouragement of homosexual relations also occurs, but its effect on birth rates is problematical (see p. 509). The practice of the operation known as clitoridectomy—the removal of part or all of the clitoris—occurs among a number of high-density agriculturalists in Africa and may influence pregnancy rates by diminishing a woman's desire. Some groups also practice *infibulation*, in which the lips of the vagina are sewed together. Like male castration, however, these operations are seldom reported among hunter-gatherers.

An effective means of lowering the number of conceptions per woman is to prolong breast feeding of children (Fig. 11.12). There are currently two theories that account for the contraceptive effects of prolonged breast feeding. One stresses the release of certain hormones that suppress ovulation. The other attributes the failure to resume ovulation to the difficulty in gaining weight while breast feeding. It is possible that a critical minimum percentage of body weight must be fat before a woman's body is prepared to embark upon another pregnancy (or the first one). The calorie drain imposed by breast feeding makes it difficult to pass this limit (Frisch and MacArthur 1974; Frisch 1978; see Huffman et al. 1978, 1979; Tyson and Perez 1978). Regardless of how breast feeding produces its contraceptive effect, there is growing accord that it does work and that it can lengthen the interval between birth and conception by as much as 3 or 4 years beyond the 3 months typical of healthy, sexually active nonnursing mothers (Howell 1976b; Lee 1979; Short 1984).

POSTCONCEPTION TECHNIQUES

The most effective barriers against rapid population growth are events that influence the life span of the newborn after conception

Table 11.2 RATE OF GROWTH OF THE HUMAN POPULATION

Period	World population at end of period	Percentage annual rate of growth during period
Paleolithic	5,000,000	0.0015
Mesolithic	8,500,000	0.0330
Neolithic	75,000,000	0.1000
Ancient empires	225,000,000	0.5000

SOURCE: Hassan 1978, 1971; Spengler 1974.

or birth has taken place. Most of these events are to some degree subject to human control. For example, almost all known cultures have a variety of methods for terminating unwanted pregnancies. The most common are those that traumatize or poison both mother and fetus. Tying tight bands, delivering blows to the abdomen, and jumping on boards laid across the abdomen are some of the physical traumas that produce abortion. Drinking of poisonous concoctions such as violent purgatives is a common form of chemical trauma. All these methods place the mother at as much risk as the fetus. For this reason, induced abortions are probably not a principal factor in population control among hunter-gatherers and other prestate and preindustrial peoples (Devereux 1967; Nurge 1975).

Many preindustrial peoples shorten the life of unwanted children after birth (Helm 1980; Miller 1981; Scrimshaw 1983). Shortening the lives of unwanted infants and children takes many forms. Fully conscious and deliberate acts of infanticide are reported from many cultures. Still others deny that they practice infanticide, yet have very high rates of infant mortality. When the rate of infant and child mortality is consistently higher for one sex than for the other, there is reason to believe that unwanted children are being fed more poorly or are being less well cared for, even if there is no conscious attempt to shorten their lives. The etic effect of neglect is probably more powerful than outright infanticide in slowing down the rate of population growth. Among measures affecting infant mortality, Susan Scrimshaw (1978) lists premature withdrawal of breast feeding without proper weaning foods; withdrawal of food from children who are sick; withholding of protein-rich foods from weak children; and careless treatment of the umbilical cord.

Considerable controversy surrounds the demographic importance assigned to infanticide and neglect. Some anthropologists hold that during the Paleolithic, between 25 to 50 percent of all infants who did not die from natural diseases had their lives shortened through some form of infanticide or neglect (Birdsell 1968, 1972; Hassan 1981). Others hold that prolonged breast feeding did away with the need for relying on infanticide and neglect. Among the !Kung San there appears to be very little overt or covert infanticide (although infant mortality is high). As emphasized by Richard Lee (1979) and Nancy Howell (1976b), prolonged breast feeding is the main method for slowing down population growth. However, the long-term growth rate of the !Kung population is 0.5 percent (Howell 1976a:150). This amounts to a doubling every 139 years. Had this rate been sustained for only the last 10,000 years of the Upper Paleolithic, the population of the earth would have reached 604,463,000,000,000,000,000,000 at the beginning of the Neolithic instead of the estimated 6 million mentioned above. Moreover, there is some evidence that prolonged dependence on mother's milk might lead to poor health in children whose diets do not contain mineral supplements. There is no iron or copper in mother's milk, for example. Too much breast feeding may be as dangerous to the child as too little, and as a matter of fact, the !Kung do have a high rate of infant mortality (Wilmsen 1979).

Figure 11.12 *BREAST FEEDING OLDER CHILDREN*
San women breast-feed their children for 4 or 5 years per child.

THE INFLUENCE OF DISEASE

Anthropologists who assign an important role to infanticide and neglect tend to minimize the effect of disease on Paleolithic rates of growth. Most of the great lethal epidemic diseases—smallpox, typhoid fever, flu, bubonic plague, and cholera—are primarily associated with dense urbanized populations rather than with dispersed hunter-gatherers or small village cultures. Even diseases like malaria and yellow fever were probably less important among low-density populations who could avoid swampy mosquito breeding grounds. (Knowledge of the association between swamps and disease is very ancient, even though mosquitoes were not recognized as disease carriers.) Other diseases such as dysentery, measles, tuberculosis, whooping cough, scarlet fever, and the common cold were also probably less significant among hunter-gatherers and early farmers (Armelagos and McArdle 1975; Black 1975; Cockburn 1971; Wood 1975). The ability to recuperate from these infections is closely related to the general level of bodily health, which in turn is heavily influenced by diet, especially by balanced protein levels (N. Scrimshaw 1977). The role of disease as a long-term regulator of human population is thus to some extent a consequence of the success or failure of other population-regulating mechanisms. Only if these alternatives are ineffective and population density rises, productive efficiency drops, and diet deteriorates will disease figure as an important check on population growth.

There is some evidence to indicate that Paleolithic hunter-gatherers were healthier than late Neolithic agriculturalists and the peasant farmers of preindustrial state societies. Exactly when and where a deterioration occured is the focus of much continuing research (Cohen and Armelagos 1984). It seems likely that for much of the Upper Paleolithic at least, "artificial" population controls rather than sickness were the principal factors governing rates of population growth (Handwerker 1983:20).

POPULATION PRESSURE AND CULTURAL EVOLUTION

All these natural and cultural mechanisms for regulating population have something in common. They all involve psychological, physiological, and behavioral "costs" that most people would prefer to avoid. Even the practice of prolonged breast feeding imposes restrictions or demands on the nursing mother. Abstinence from heterosexual genital intercourse constitutes a severe penalty for most adults, and traumatic abortion, infanticide, and premature deaths brought on by neglect, malnutrition, or disease are also clearly burdensome and unwanted. Hence to some degree, all preindustrial societies experience some form of *population pressure*—that is, physiological and psychological costs incurred on behalf of restraining population growth below the level that would result if there were no restraints on the birth rate and resources were infinite. Population pressure in this sense exists even if a preindustrial population is not growing or even if it is getting smaller. In general, population pressure increases at the point of diminishing returns (see p. 209) and is still greater when carrying capacity is reached.

Many anthropologists regard population pressure (in the sense of the high cost of artificially lowering population growth rates under preindustrial conditions) as an important "engine" of sociocultural evolution. Population pressure predisposes individuals, families, and whole societies to *intensify* the productive effort in order to lessen the need to use physically and psychologically costly means of limiting births and in order to provide better living conditions for infants and children suffering from malnutrition and neglect. Intensification, as we have seen, often leads to depletions that destroy ecosystems and compel people to adopt new modes of production.

Population pressure thus introduces an element of instability into all human ecosystems. This instability often interacts with purely natural sources of instability (sometimes called "perturbations"), such as changes in ocean currents and advances and retreats of continental glaciers, to bring about large-scale shifts in modes of production. As discussed below (see p. 302), population pressure probably played an important role in the development of warfare, the evolution of the state (p. 315), and the emergence of industrial society.

SUMMARY

The comparative study of infrastructures involves consideration of ecology and ecosystem variables, and these in turn require examination of the quantitative and qualitative aspects of energy production and consumption. Most of the energy flowing through preindustrial energy systems consists of food energy. The technology of energy production cannot be altered at whim. It has evolved through successive stages of technical competence in which the mastery of one set of tools and machines has been built on the mastery of an earlier set. Through technological advance, the energy available per capita has steadily increased. However, technology never exists in the abstract, but only in the particular instances where it interacts with a particular environment; there is no such thing as technology dominating or controlling the natural environment. Even in advanced industrial ecosystems, depletion and pollution of habitats add unavoidable costs to energy production and consumption. Technology interacting with environment determines carrying capacity, which is the upper limit of production, and hence of the human population density possible without depletion and permanent damage.

When carrying capacity is exceeded, production will decline precipitously. However, the fact that a food energy system is operating as much as two-thirds below carrying capacity does not mean that ecological restraints are absent. Culture energy systems tend to stop growing before reaching the point of diminishing returns, which is defined as the point at which the ratio of output to input begins to fall, holding technology constant. A distinction must also be made between the effects of growth and the effects of intensification. Growth may continue for a long time without leading to a decline in the ratio of output to input. Intensification, however, which is defined as increased input in a fixed area, may lead to critical depletions, diminishing returns, and irreversible damage to the habitat's carrying capacity. All the factors in ecosystems must be approached from the perspective of Liebig's law, which states that extremes, not averages, set the limits for carrying capacity.

A common human cultural response to declining efficiency brought about by intensification is to alter technology and thereby adopt new modes of production.

As in the example of the !Kung San, while hunter-gatherers output/input efficiency is low, especially for the male-dominated activity of hunting, by maintaining low population densities and avoiding intensification, hunter-gatherers can enjoy high standards of living. Slash-and-burn agriculturalists such as the Tsembaga Maring produce their caloric needs with greater efficiency than the !Kung San, but they have depleted the game animals in their habitat and must rely on costly domesticated pigs for their animal proteins and fats. By using irrigation agriculture, the people of Luts'un produce a large surplus. Despite their high output/input ratio, they work longer at food production than either the !Kung San or the Tsembaga.

Pastoralism is another but rare preindustrial mode of food production, which is practiced only in areas unsuitable for agriculture. The reason for this is that feeding plant food to domesticated animals rather than consuming crops directly results in a 90 percent reduction in the efficiency of conversion of sunlight to human food.

Industrial agriculture has achieved very high outputs at the cost of very high chemical and energy inputs. When input/output ratios include fuel costs, the efficiency of industrial agricultural systems has been falling, not rising. Finally, it is clear that many industrial peoples work harder for their basic subsistence than hunters and gatherers.

The reproductive capacity of human beings was held in check by cultural mechanisms for most of human history and prehistory. It was kept well below the potential rate of growth, which may be equal to a doubling every 28 years. The chief means of contraception involved prolonged breast feeding and abstention from genital heterosexual intercourse. Prolonged breast feeding may retard the onset of ovulation through the effect of nipple sucking on the hormonal system, or through the effect of the calorie cost of mother's milk on the ability of nursing mothers to increase the percentage of body fat above a critical threshold.

Postconception controls among band and village peoples include abortions, infanticide, and neglect of unwanted children. Nonmedical abortions depend on whole-body traumas produced by mechanical or chemical abuse and threaten the life of the mother. Infanticide, especially femal infanticide, is widespread, but it is often not given conscious recognition. Infanticide grades imperceptibly into various forms of neglect in which unwanted infants and children are underprotected from disease and malnutrition.

By using these techniques, band and village peoples can readily keep their populations well below carrying capacity and the point of diminishing returns. By doing so, they can maintain relatively high standards of health among those individuals who survive to adulthood. It seems unlikely that disease per se exercised a significant restraint on population growth as long as population density among band and village peoples remained low, settlements were dispersed over considerable distances, and calorie and protein consumption per capita remained high.

However, the most effective preindustrial modes of controlling reproduction involved considerable waste of human life and severe psychological or physical penalties. One can speak, therefore, of some degree of population pressure being present even when a population is steady or declining, in the sense that a price must always be paid to keep reproduction in balance with production.

Population pressure predisposes human groups to intensify production. In combination with natural perturbations, population pressure is therefore an important factor in shifts from one mode of production to another.

12 ECONOMY, EXCHANGE, CONTROL

This chapter initiates the comparative study of the structural or organizational aspects of the economic sectors of sociocultural systems. We focus on the distribution of goods and services by means of different modes of exchange and on alternative modes of controlling who gets what. Our focus of inquiry will thus be moving from the infrastructural to the structural components of sociocultural systems. This chapter is intended to form a link between the discussion of modes of production and later chapters devoted to the origin of the state and the maintenance of law and order in egalitarian and stratified societies.

DEFINITION OF ECONOMY

In a narrow sense, *economy* refers to the allocation of scarce means to competing ends. Most professional economists hold that human beings in general tend to "economize," that is, to allocate scarce means in such a way as to maximize the achievement of ends while minimizing the expenditure of means. Many anthropologists, however, see economy as the activities responsible for provisioning a society with its goods and services.

> An economy is a set of institutionalized activities which combine natural resources, human labor, and technology to acquire, produce, and distribute material goods and specialist services in a structured, repetitive fashion (Dalton 1969:97).

The two definitions of economy are not necessarily incompatible. Anthropologists stress the fact that motivations for producing, exchanging, and consuming goods and services are shaped by cultural traditions. Different cultures value different goods and services and tolerate or prohibit different kinds of relationships among the people who produce, exchange, and consume. For example, as we will see in a moment, some cultures emphasize cooperative acquisition and sharing of wealth, whereas others emphasize competitive acquisition and retention of wealth. Some cultures emphasize communal property; others emphasize private property. It is obvious, therefore, that "economizing" has different premises and different consequences in different cultural contexts. Yet it may be possible that underlying apparently diverse cultural specifications of means and ends, there is a common human calculus of minimizing costs and maximizing benefits that accounts for the origin and perpetuation of different economic systems. The viewpoint adopted in this book is that the existence of minimum cost–maximum benefit relationships is an empirical question that can be solved by empirical research (cf. Christenson 1982).

EXCHANGE

Most of what is produced by human labor is distributed by means of exchange. (The exceptions consist of instances of direct consumption by the producers themselves.) *Exchange* refers to the panhuman pattern of giving and receiving valuable objects and services. Except for meat sharing (p. 68), the joint provisioning of children by adult men and women is a form of giving and receiving confined to the hominids and important for the definition of what it means to be human. Human beings can not live without exchanging their labor or the products of their labor with one another (Robinson Crusoe was a taker if not a giver even before Friday arrived; hermits and religious recluses also inevitably depend on goods they take with them into the wilderness, and they usually render some kind of service in return.) However, the patterns of exchange differ markedly from one culture to another. Following the work of the economist Karl Polanyi, anthropologists have come to distinguish three main types of exchange: *reciprocal*, *redistributive*, and *market*. As discussed below, these different types of exchange are related to other differences on the infrastructural and structural levels of the universal pattern.

RECIPROCAL EXCHANGE

One of the most striking features of the economic life of band and prestate village societies is the prominence of exchanges that are conducted according to the principle known as *reciprocity*. In reciprocal exchanges the flow of labor products and services is not contingent upon any definite counterflow. The partners in the exchange take according to need and give back according to no set rules of time or quantity.

Richard Lee has written a succinct description of reciprocity as it occurs among the !Kung. In the morning, anywhere from 1 to 16 of the 20 adults in the !Kung band leave camp to spend the day collecting or hunting. They return in the evening with whatever food they have managed to find. Everything brought back to camp is shared equally, regardless of whether the recipients have spent the day sleeping or hunting (Fig. 12.1).

> Not only do families pool the day's production, but the entire camp—residents and visitors alike—share equally in the total quantity of food available. The evening meal of any one family is made up of portions of food from each of the other families resident. Foodstuffs are distributed raw or are prepared by the collectors and then distributed. There is a constant flow of nuts, berries, roots and melons from one family fireplace to another until each person resident has received an equitable portion. The following morning a different combination of foragers moves out of camp and when they return late in the day, the distribution of foodstuffs is repeated (Lee 1969:58).

Eventually all the adults will have gathered or hunted and given as well as received food. But wide discrepancies in the balance of giving and receiving may exist between individuals over a long period without becoming the subject of any special talk or action.

Some form of reciprocal exchange occurs in all cultures, especially among relatives and friends. In the United States or Canada, for example, husbands and wives, friends, and brothers, sisters, and other kin regulate and adjust their economic lives to a minor degree according to informal, uncalculated, give-and-take transactions. Teenagers do not pay cash for their meals at home or rent for their parents' car. Wives do not bill their husbands for cooking a meal. Friends give each other birthday gifts and Christmas presents. These exchanges, however, constitute only a small portion of the total acts of exchange among modern day North Americans. The great majority of exchanges in modern cultures involve rigidly defined counterflows that must take place by a certain time.

THE PROBLEM OF THE FREELOADER

As we know from our own experience with taking from parents and with birthday and Christmas gifts, failure to reciprocate in some degree will eventually lead to bad feelings even between close relatives and friends and husbands and wives. No one likes a "freeloader." Among band and village cultures, a grossly asymmetrical exchange also does not go unnoticed. Some individuals will come to enjoy reputations as diligent gatherers or outstanding hunters, whereas others acquire reputations as shirkers or malingerers. No specific mechanisms exist for obliging the debtors to even up the score. Yet there are subtle sanctions against becoming a complete freeloader. Such behavior generates a steady undercurrent of disapproval. Freeloaders are eventually subject to collective punishment. They may meet with violence because they are suspected of being bewitched or of bewitching others through the practice of sorcery.

What is distinctive about reciprocal exchange, therefore, is not that products and services are simply given away without any thought or expectation of return, but rather that there is (1) no immediate return, (2) no systematic calculations of the value of the services and products exchanged, and (3) an overt denial that a balance is being calculated or that the balance must come out even.

Is there no exchange, then, corresponding to what Bronislaw Malinowski called "pure gift"? Are we always to look for hidden, self-seeking, material motives whenever labor products are moved from one individual or group to another? Nothing of the sort is implied. The bestowal of gifts without any tangible reciprocity in services or products is a universal phenomenon. Indeed, this relationship is becoming increasingly

Figure 12.1 *SAN RECIPROCITY*
Men awaiting the distribution of meat from a small warthog.

common throughout the industrial world. In preindustrial contexts, parents generally expect and receive material reciprocity for their child-rearing efforts. Children begin to reciprocate by working at agricultural and household tasks at an early age, and this relationship continues into the old age of parents, who frequently end their lives with a net favorable balance of labor and products (Caldwell 1981). But all contemporary industrial states display a trend toward a lifetime exchange balance between parents and children that is favorable to the younger generation. Parents must rely increasingly on their own savings and state aid in the form of insurance, pensions, old-age social security, and other public welfare schemes to maintain themselves during periods of sickness and senility (Minge-Kalman 1978b).

There is, then, no question that some human beings will voluntarily give away their most valued possessions and expect nothing in return. But there is also no question that some human beings in every population will tend to become freeloaders if they get the chance. While every mode of production can tolerate a certain number of freeloaders, the line must be drawn somewhere. Hence, no culture can rely exclusively on purely altruistic sentiments to get its goods and services produced and distributed. What does occur, especially on the level of small band and prestate village societies, is that goods and services are produced and reciprocally exchanged in such a way as to keep the notion of material balance, debt, or obligation in an emically subordinate position. As in the case of modern Euramerican intrahousehold exchanges, this is accomplished by expressing the necessity for reciprocal exchanges as *kinship* obligations (see Ch. 13). These kinship obligations establish reciprocal expectations with respect to food, clothing, shelter, and other economic goods.

Kinship-embedded transactions constitute only a meager portion of modern exchange systems, whereas among band and village peoples almost all exchanges take place between kin, or at least intimate associates, for whom the giving, taking, and using of goods has sentimental and personal meaning.

RECIPROCITY AND TRADE

Reciprocity is thus the dominant form of exchange within band and prestate village societies. Even hunters and gatherers, however, want valuables such as salt, flint, obsidian, red ochre, reeds, and honey that are produced or controlled by groups with whom they have no kinship ties. Among band and village peoples, economic dealings between nonkin are based on the assumption that every individual will try to get the best of an exchange through chicanery and theft. As a result, trading expeditions are likely to be hazardous in the extreme and to bear a resemblance to war parties.

One interesting mechanism for facilitating trade between distant groups is known as *silent trade*. The objects to be exchanged are set out in a clearing, and the first group retreats out of sight. The other group comes out of hiding, inspects the wares, and lays down what it regards as a fair exchange of its own products. The first group returns and, if satisfied, removes the traded objects. If not satisfied, it leaves the wares untouched as a signal that the balance is not yet even. In this fashion the Mbuti of the Ituri Forest trade meat for bananas with the Bantu agriculturalists, and the Vedda of Sri Lanka trade honey for iron tools with the Sinhalese.

More developed trade relations are found among prestate agricultural villages. Condi-

Figure 12.2 *NEW GUINEA MARKET*
Man at left is giving yams in exchange for fish at right.

tions for the occurrence of trade markets seem to have been especially favorable in Melanesia. In Malaita in the Solomon Islands, women regularly trade fish for pigs and vegetables under the armed guard of their menfolk (Fig. 12.2). Among the Kapauku of western New Guinea (Fig. 12.3), full-fledged price markets involving shell and bead money (see below) may have existed before the advent of European control. Generally speaking, however, marketing and money as regular modes of trade are associated with the evolution of the state and with the enforcement of order by means of police and soldiers.

Perhaps the most common solution to the problem of trading without kinship ties or state-supervised markets is the establishment of special *trade partnerships.* In this arrangement, members of different bands or villages regard one another as metaphorical kin. The members of trading expeditions deal exclusively with their trade partners, who greet them as "brothers" and give them food and shelter. Trade partners attempt to deal with one another in conformity with the principle of reciprocity, deny an interest in getting the best of the bargain, and offer their wares as if they were gifts (Heider 1969).

THE KULA

The classic example of trade partnerships is described in Bronislaw Malinowski's *Argonauts of the Western Pacific*. The argonauts in question are the Trobriand Islanders who trade with the neighboring island of Dobu by means of daring canoe voyages across the open sea (Fig. 12.4). The entire complex associated with this trade is known as the *Kula*. According to the men who take these risky voyages, the purpose of the Kula trade is to exchange shell ornaments with their trade partners. The ornaments, known to the Trobrianders as *vaygu'a*, consist of armbands and necklaces. In trading with the Dobuans, who live to the southeast, the Trobrianders give armbands and receive necklaces. In trading with the people who live to the southwest, the Trobrianders give necklaces and receive armbands. The armbands and necklaces are traded in opposite directions from island to island and finally pass through their points of origin from the direction opposite to the one in which they were first traded.

Figure 12.3 *KAPAUKU OF WESTERN NEW GUINEA*
The men (wearing penis sheaths) are counting shell money.

Participation in the Kula trade is a major ambition of youth and a consuming passion of senior men. The *vaygu'a* have been compared with heirlooms or crown jewels. The older they are and the more complex their history, the more valuable they become in the eyes of the Trobrianders. Nothing is done with them except that on ceremonial occasions they are worn as ornaments; otherwise they remain in the house, where they are occasionally inspected and admired in private. Although regarded as a man's most valuable possessions, they can be used only to obtain other armbands or necklaces.

Each Kula expedition requires extensive social and ritual preparation. Minor gifts as well as *vaygu'a* are brought along to please the trade partners. These partnerships are usually handed down from one kinsman to another, and young men are given a start in the Kula trade by inheriting or receiving an armband or a necklace from a relative. When the expedition reaches shore, the trade partners greet one another and exchange preliminary gifts. Later the Trobrianders deliver the precious armbands, accompanied by ritual speeches and formal acts concerned with establishing the honorable, giftlike character of the exchange. As in the case of reciprocal transactions within the family, the trade partner may not be immediately able to provide a necklace whose value is equivalent to the armband just received. Although the voyager may have to return home empty-handed except for some preliminary gifts, he does not complain. He knows that his trade partner will work hard to make up for the delay by presenting him with an even more valuable necklace at their next meeting.

Why all this effort in order to obtain a few baubles of sentimental or aesthetic value? As is often the case, the etic aspects of the Kula are different from the emic aspects. The boats that take part in the Kula expedition carry trade items of great practical value in the life of the various island peoples who participate in the Kula ring. While the trade partners fondle and admire their priceless heirlooms, other members of the expedition trade for practical items. As long as everyone agrees that the expedition is not really concerned with such mundane necessities as coconuts, sago palm flour, fish, yams, baskets, mats, wooden swords and clubs, green stone for tools, mussel shells for knives, creepers and lianas for lashings, these items can be bargained over with impunity. Although no Trobriander would admit it, or even conceive how it could be true, the *vaygu'a* are valuable not for their qualities as heirlooms, but for their truly priceless gift of trade (cf. Uberoi 1962).

Figure 12.4 *KULA CANOE*
These large canoes are used by the Trobrianders for long-distance voyages.

REDISTRIBUTIVE EXCHANGE

The evolution of economic and political systems from bands and villages to states is in large degree a consequence of the development of coercive forms of exchange that supplement or almost entirely replace reciprocal exchange. Coercive forms of exchange did not appear in sudden full-blown opposition to reciprocal forms. Rather, they probably first arose through what seemed to be merely an extension of familiar reciprocal forms.

The exchange system known as *redistribution* can best be understood as such an extension. In redistributive exchange, the labor products of several different individuals are brought to a central place, sorted by type, counted, and then given away to producers and nonproducers alike. Considerable organizational effort is required if large quantities of goods are to be brought to the same place at the same time and given away in definite shares. This coordination is usually achieved by individuals who act as *redistributors*. Typically, the redistributor consciously attempts to increase and intensify production, for which he gains prestige in the eyes of his fellows. As we will see (Ch. 15), this attempt is closely related to increased population density, depletions, increased warfare, and the emergence of classes and the state.

Egalitarian and stratified forms of redistribution must be distinguished. As an *egalitarian* system of exchange, redistribution is carried out by a redistributor who has worked harder than anyone else producing the items to be given away, who takes the smallest portion or none at all, and who, after it is all over, is left with fewer material possessions than anyone else. In its egalitarian form, therefore, redistribution appears to be merely an extreme example of reciprocity; the generous provider gives everything away and for the moment gets nothing in return, except the admiration of those who benefit from his efforts.

In the *stratified* form, however, the redistributor withholds his or her own labor from the production process, retains the largest share, and ends up with more material possessions than anyone else.

Redistributive exchange, like reciprocal exchange, is usually embedded in a complex set of kinship relations and rituals that may obscure the etic significance of the exchange behavior. Redistribution often takes the form of a feast held to celebrate some important event such as a harvest, the end of a ritual taboo, the construction of a house, a death, a birth, or a marriage. A common feature of Melanesian redistributive feasts is that the guests gorge themselves with food, stagger off into the bush, stick their fingers down their throats, vomit, and then return to eating with renewed zest. Another common feature of redistributive feasting is the boastful and competitive attitude of the redistributors and their kin with respect to other individuals or groups who have given feasts. This contrasts markedly with reciprocal exchange. Let us take a closer look at this contrast.

RECIPROCITY VERSUS REDISTRIBUTION

Boastfulness and acknowledgment of generosity is incompatible with the basic etiquette of reciprocal exchanges. Among the Semai of Central Malaya, no one even says "thank you" for the meat received from another hunter (Fig. 12.5). Having struggled all day to lug the carcass of a pig home through the jungle heat, the hunter allows his prize to be cut up into exactly equal portions, which are then given away to the entire group. As Robert Dentan explains, to express gratitude for the portion received indicates that you are the kind of person who calculates how much you are giving and taking.

> In this context saying thank you is very rude, for it suggests first that one has calculated the amount of a gift and second, that one did not expect the donor to be so generous (1968:49).

To call attention to one's generosity is to indicate that others are in debt to you and that you expect them to repay you. It is repugnant to egalitarian peoples even to suggest that they have been treated generously. Richard Lee tells how he learned about this aspect of reciprocity through a revealing incident. To please the !Kung with whom he was staying, he decided to buy a large ox and have it slaughtered as a Christmas present. He spent days searching the neighboring Bantu agricultural villages looking for the largest and fattest ox in the region. Finally, he bought what appeared to be a perfect specimen. But one !Kung after another took him aside and assured him that he had been duped into buying an absolutely worthless animal. "Of course, we will eat it," they said, "but it won't fill us up—we will eat and go home to bed with stomachs rumbling." Yet when Lee's ox was slaughtered, it turned out to be covered with a thick layer of fat. Lee eventually succeeded in getting his informants to explain why they had claimed that his gift was valueless, even though they certainly knew better then he what lay under the animals skin:

> Yes, when a young man kills much meat he comes to think of himself as a chief or a big man, and he thinks of the rest of us as his servants or inferiors. We can't accept this, we refuse one who boasts, for someday his pride will make him kill somebody. So we always speak of his meat as worthless. This way we cool his heart and make him gentle (1968:62).

In fragrant violation of these prescriptions for modesty in reciprocal exchanges, redistributive exchange systems involve public proclamations that the host is a generous person and a great provider. This boasting is one of the most conspicuous features of the *potlatches* engaged in by the native Americans who inhabit the Northwest coast of the United States and Canada (Fig. 12.6). In descriptions made famous by Ruth Benedict in *Patterns of Culture*, the Kwakiutl redistributor emerges as a virtual megalomaniac.

Figure 12.5 *SEMAI HUNTER*
Among the Semai, reciprocity prevails.

Figure 12.6 *KWAKIUTL OF THE NORTHWEST CA. 1900*
The signs over the doors read: "Boston. He is the Head chief of Arweete. He is true Indian. Honest. He don't owe no trouble to white man" and "Cheap. He is one of the head chief of all tribes in this country. White man can get information."

Here is what the Kwakiutl chiefs had to say about themselves (1934:190):

I am the great chief who makes people ashamed.
I am the great chief who makes people ashamed.
Our chief brings shame to the faces.
Our chief brings jealousy to the faces.
Our chief makes people cover their faces by what he is continually doing in this world;
Giving again and again oil feasts to all the tribes.*

I am the only great tree, I the chief!
I am the only great tree, I the chief!

You are my subordinates, tribes.
You sit in the middle of the rear of the house, tribes.
I am the first to give you property, tribes.
I am your Eagle, tribes!

Bring your counter of property, tribes, that he may try in vain to count the property that is to be given away by the great copper maker, the chief.

In the potlatch the guests continue to behave somewhat like Lee's !Kung. They grumble and complain and are careful never to appear satisfied or impressed. Nonetheless, there has been a careful public count-

*Fish oil, not petroleum.

ing of all the gifts displayed and distributed (Fig. 12.7). Both hosts and guests believe that the only way to throw off the obligations incurred in accepting these gifts is to hold a counter potlatch in which the tables are reversed.

THE CULTURAL ECOLOGY OF REDISTRIBUTION AND RECIPROCITY

Why do the !Kung esteem a hunter who never draws attention to his generosity, whereas the Kwakiutl and other redistributor peoples esteem a man who can boast about how much he has given away? One theory compatible with min-max principles is that reciprocity reflects an adjustment to technological and environmental conditions in which an increase in production would rapidly lead to diminishing returns and environmental depletions. Hunters and gatherers seldom have an opportunity to intensify production without rapidly reaching the point of diminishing returns. Intensification poses a grave threat to such peoples in the form of faunal overkills. To encourage the !Kung hunter to be boastful is to endanger the group's survival. On the other hand, agricultural villages generally have greater leeway for increasing production by investing

Figure 12.7 *POTLATCH*
Spokesman for Kwakiutl chief making speech next to blankets about to be given away.

more labor. They can raise their standards of consumption if they work harder, and yet not immediately jeopardize their energy efficiency by depleting their habitats. The Kwakiutl are not agriculturalists, but they depended on the annual upriver runs of salmon and candlefish. Using aboriginal dip nets, it was impossible for the Kwakiutl and their neighbors to affect the overall rate of reproduction of these species. Hence, they depended on a highly intensifiable mode of production. Moreover, there were periodic fluctuations in the size of the annual migrations of these fish from one year to the next (Langdon 1979). Hence, it was ecologically feasible for the Kwakiutl to try to maximize production and to reward those who played a role in getting everybody to work harder with prestige and the privilege of boasting.

THE ORIGIN OF DESTRUCTIVE POTLATCHES

Potlatching came under scientific scrutiny long after the people of the Pacific Northwest had entered into trade and wage-labor relations with Russian, English, Canadian, and American nationals. Declining populations and a sudden influx of wealth had combined to make the potlatches increasingly competitive and destructive by the time Franz Boas began to study them in the 1880s (Rohner 1969). At this period the entire tribe was in residence at the Fort Rupert trading station of the Hudson's Bay Company, and the attempt on the part of one potlatch-giver to outdo another had become an all-consuming passion. Blankets, boxes of fish oil, and other valuables were deliberately being destroyed by burning or by throwing them into the sea. On one occasion, made famous by Ruth Benedict in *Patterns of Culture*, an entire house burned to the ground when too much fish oil was poured on the fire. Potlatches that ended in this fashion were regarded as great victories for the potlatch-givers.

It seems likely that before the coming of the Europeans, Kwakiutl potlatch feasts were less destructive and more like Melanesian feasts. Although rivalrous feasts are wasteful, the net increment in total production may exceed the loss due to gorging and spoilage. Moreover, after the visitors have eaten to their satisfaction, there still remains much food, which they carry back home with them.

The fact that guests come from distant villages leads to additional important ecological and economic advantages. It has been suggested that feasting rivalry between groups raises productivity throughout a region more than if each village feasts only its own producers. Second, as has been suggested for the Northwest Coast region by Wayne Suttles (1960) and Stuart Piddocke (1965), rivalrous intervillage redistributions may overcome the effects of localized, naturally induced production failures. Failure of the salmon runs at a particular stream could threaten the survival of certain villages while neighbors on other streams continue to catch their usual quotas. Under such circumstances, the impoverished villagers would want to attend as many potlatches as they could and carry back as many vital supplies as they could get their hosts to part with by reminding them of how big their own potlatches had been in previous years. Intervillage potlatches thus may have been a form of savings in which the prestige acquired at one's own feast served as a tally. The tally was redeemed when the guests turned hosts. If a village was unable year after year to give potlatches of its own, its prestige credit would disappear.

A third ecological function of potlatching is the shifting of population from less productive to more productive villages. When an impoverished and unprestigious group could no longer hold its own potlatches, the people abandoned their defeated redistributor-chief and took up residence among relatives in more productive villages. In this interpretation the boasting and the giving away and displaying of wealth were advertisements that helped to recruit additional labor power into the work force gathered about a particularly effective redistributor. Incidentally, if this hypothesis is correct, it is easier to understand why the Northwest Coast peoples lavished so much effort on the production of their world-famous totem poles. These poles bore the redistributor-chief's "crests" in the guise of carved mythic figures; title to the crests was claimed on the basis of outstanding potlatch achievements. The larger the pole, the greater the potlatch power, the more the members of poor villages would be tempted to change their residence and gather around another chief.

With the coming of the Europeans, however, there was a shift toward more destructive forms of redistribution. The impact of European diseases had reduced the population of the Kwakiutl from about 10,000 in 1836 to about 2000 by the end of the century. At the same time the trading companies, canneries, lumber mills, and gold-mining camps pumped an unprecedented amount of wealth into the aboriginal economy. The percentage of people prepared to claim the crests of achievement rose, while the number of people available to celebrate the glory of the potlatcher dropped. Many villages were abandoned; hence rivalry intensified for the allegiance of the survivors.

A final and perhaps the most important factor in the development of destructive potlatches was the change in the technology and intensity of warfare. As suggested by Brian Ferguson (1979), the earliest contacts in the late eighteenth century between the Europeans and the native Americans of the Northwest Pacific Coast centered on the fur trade. In return for sea otter skins, the Europeans gave guns to the Kwakiutl and their traditional enemies. This had a double effect. On the one hand, warfare became more deadly; and on the other, it forced local groups to fight one another for control of trade in order to get the ammunition on which success in warfare now depended. Small wonder, therefore, that as population declined, the potlatch chiefs were willing to throw away or destroy wealth that was militarily unimportant in order to attract manpower for warfare and the fur trade.

STRATIFIED REDISTRIBUTION

A subtle line separates egalitarian from stratified forms of redistribution. In the egalitarian form, contributions to the central pool are voluntary and the workers get back all or most of what they put into it or items of comparable value. In the stratified form, the workers must contribute to the central pool or suffer penalties, and they may not get back anything. Again, in the egalitarian form, the redistributor lacks the power to coerce followers into intensifying production and must depend on their goodwill; in the stratified form, the redistributor has that power and the workers must depend on his or her goodwill. The processes responsible for the evolution of one form of redistribution into another will be discussed in Chapter 15. Here we will only note that fully developed forms of stratified redistribution imply the existence of a class of rulers who have the power to compel others to do their bidding. The expression of this power in the realm of production and exchange results in the economic subordination of the labor force and its partial or total loss of control over production and exchange. Specifically, the labor force loses control over:

1. Access to land and raw materials
2. The technology of production
3. Work time and work schedules
4. Place and mode of production activity
5. Disposition of the products of labor

Forms of production and exchange that depend upon the coercive effects of power can be understood only within the framework of a combined political and economic analysis. All the concepts appropriate to the analysis of contemporary economic systems, such as wages, rent, interest, property, and capital, have a political dimension. Just as production and exchange in egalitarian societies are embedded in kinship institutions, the processes of production and exchange in state-level societies are embedded in institutions of political control (Haas 1982:173ff.).

PRICE-MARKET EXCHANGE: BUYING AND SELLING

Marketplaces occur in rudimentary form wherever groups of nonkin and strangers assemble and trade one item for another. Among band and village peoples, marketplace trading usually involves the barter of one valuable consumable item for another: fish for yams, coconuts for axes, and so forth. In this type of market, before the development of *all-purpose money* (see next section) only a limited range of goods or services is exchanged. The great bulk of exchange transactions takes place outside the marketplace and continues to involve various forms of reciprocity and redistribution. With the development of all-purpose money, however, *price-market exchanges* come to dominate all other forms of exchange. In a price market, the price of the goods and services exchanged is determined by buyers competing with buyers and sellers competing with sellers. Virtually everything that is produced or consumed comes to have a price, and buying and selling becomes a major cultural preoccupation or even obsession (Fig. 12.8).

It is possible to engage in reciprocal exchange using money, as when a friend gives a loan and does not specify when it must be repaid. Redistributive exchange can be carried out via money, as in the collection of taxes and the disbursement of welfare payments. Buying and selling on a price market, however, is a distinctive mode of exchange since it involves the specification of the precise time, quantity, and type of payment. Furthermore, unlike either reciprocity or redistribution, once the money payment is concluded, no further obligation or responsibility exists between buyer and seller. They can walk away from each other and never see each other again. Price-market exchanges, therefore, are noteworthy for the anonymity and impersonality of the exchange process and stand in contrast to the personal and kin-based exchanges of band and village economies. Now let us take a closer look at the nature of that strange entity we call money.

MONEY

The idea and practice of endowing a material object with the capacity of measuring the social value of other material objects, animals, people, and labor occurs almost universally. Such standard-of-value "stuffs" are widely exchanged for goods and services. Throughout much of Africa, for example, a young man gives cattle to his father-in-law and gets a wife in return (see p. 262). In many parts of Melanesia, shells are exchanged for stone implements, pottery, and

other valuable artifacts. Elsewhere beads, feathers, shark teeth, dog teeth, or pig tusks are exchanged for other valuable items and are given as compensation for death or injury and for personal services rendered by magicians, canoe-builders, and other specialists (Fig. 12.9). With rare and still controversial exceptions, however, these "money stuffs" lack some of the major characteristics of the money stuffs found in price-market economies. In price-market economies money is commercial or market money, an all-purpose medium of exchange. It has the following features:

1. **Portability.** It comes in sizes and shapes convenient for being carried about from one transaction to the next.
2. **Divisibility.** Its various forms and values are explicit multiples of each other.
3. **Convertibility.** A transaction completed by a higher-valued unit can be made just as well by its lower-valued multiples.
4. **Generality.** Virtually all goods and services have a money value.
5. **Anonymity.** For most purchases, anyone with the market price can conclude a transaction.
6. **Legality.** The nature and quantity of money in circulation is controlled by a government.

Although some of these traits may be associated with money in band and village economies, collectively the traits depend

Figure 12.9 *SHELL AND DOG TOOTH MONEY*
Manus dance and display their ceremonial money prior to exchange with trade partner. [American Museum of Natural History]

upon an economy in which selling and buying in a price market is a daily, lifelong occurrence. Where reciprocity, egalitarian redistribution, and trade-partner relations are the dominant modes of exchange, money in the modern dollar sense does not and cannot exist.

For example, cattle that are exchanged for wives are not the kind of currency you would want to take to the supermarket checkout counter, being neither very portable nor readily divisible. As employed in *bride-price* (see p. 262), cattle are frequently not convertible; that is, a large, beautiful, fat bull with a local reputation cannot readily be substituted for by two small and undistinguished animals. Furthermore, cattle lack generality since only wives can be "purchased" with them, and they lack anonymity because any stranger who shows up with the right amount of cattle will find that he cannot simply take the woman and leave the cattle. Cattle are exchanged

Figure 12.8 *TOKYO STOCK EXCHANGE*
The public sale and purchase of shares in companies and corporations is a fundamental feature of capitalist economies.

for women only between kinship groups who have an interest in establishing or reinforcing preexisting social relationships. Finally, cattle are put into circulation by each individual household as a result of productive effort that is unregulated by any central authority.

In other instances, noncommercial money stuff bears a greater resemblance to commercial money. For example, among the inhabitants of Rossel Island, which lies off the east coast of New Guinea, a type of shell money stuff occurs that has sometimes been confused with commercial money. The shells have portability, and they occur in 22 named units of value, that is, 1 to 22. These units, however, fall into three classes: numbers 1 to 10, numbers 11 to 17, and numbers 18 to 22. A person who borrows a number 1 shell must return a number 2. A person who borrows a number 2 must repay with a number 3. This continues through to a number 9. But a person who borrows a number 10 cannot be obliged to return a number 11. Thus the series 1 to 10 is divisible. Moreover, the series 1 to 10 has a considerable amount of generality, being used to buy such items as baskets and pots. But the two series 1 to 10 and 11 to 17 are neither divisible nor convertible with respect to each other. Similarly, the series 18 to 22 stands apart. There are only 60 shells in this series in circulation, and they are nonconvertible with respect to each other and to the other series. For example, a number 18 is the only shell that can be used for wife-purchase or for sponsorship of a pig feast. A number 20 is the only shell that can be used as indemnity for ritual murder. As George Dalton (1965) observes: "It is about as useful to describe a pig feast on Rossel as buying a pig with a no. 18 *ndap* as it is to describe marriage in America as buying a wife with a wedding ring."

CAPITALISM

Price-market exchange reaches its highest development when it is embedded in the form of political economy known as capitalism. In capitalist societies, buying and selling by means of all-purpose money extends to land, resources, and housing. Labor has a price called wages; and money itself has a price called interest. Of course, there is no such thing as a completely free market in which price is set wholly by supply and demand and in which everything can be sold. By comparison with other forms of political economy, however, capitalism is aptly described as a political economy in which money can buy anything. This being so, everyone tries to acquire as much money as possible, and the object of production itself is not merely to provide valuable goods and services, but to increase one's possession of money—that is, to make a profit and accumulate capital. *Capital* is any form of marketable wealth used or available for making a profit. The rate of capitalist production depends upon the rate at which profits can be made, and this in turn depends upon the rate at which people purchase, use, wear out, and destroy goods and services. Hence an enormous effort is expended on extolling the virtues and benefits of products in order to convince consumers that they should make additional purchases. Prestige is awarded not to the person who works hardest or gives away the greatest amount of wealth, but rather to the person who has the most possessions and who consumes at the highest rate. For example, the most prestigious profession in the United States—medical doctor—is also the one whose members make the most money.

In theory, Socialist and Communist political economies are supposed to replace price-market consumerism and the capitalist money obsession with egalitarian forms of redistribution and reciprocal exchanges. All contemporary Socialist societies, however, operate with price-market money economies, and many of them are as possession-oriented as capitalist societies. It is also questionable whether any of them has achieved the classlessness that is the prerequisite for truly egalitarian forms of redistribution (see Ch. 17).

Capitalism inevitably leads to marked inequalities in wealth based on differential ownership or access to resources and to the infrastructure of production. As in all stratified economies, political control is necessary to keep the poor from confiscating the wealth and privileges of the rich (Haas 1982:34ff). Some anthropologists, however, see many of the features of capitalism present in societies that lack state-administered laws and police-military means of control. Let us turn, therefore, to the question of the extent to which capitalism is foreshadowed in band and village societies.

"PRIMITIVE CAPITALISM"? THE KAPAUKU CASE

There is no doubt that, in general, band and village societies lack the essential features of capitalism because, as we have seen, their exchange systems are based on reciprocal and redistributive exchanges. In some cases, however, egalitarian reciprocal and redistributive systems may have certain features strongly reminiscent of contemporary capitalist arrangements. Upon closer inspection, as in the case of the Rossel Island "money," such resemblances usually can be shown to be superficial. Nonetheless, these cases are of special interest precisely because they reveal the abiding limitations imposed upon production, exchange, and consumption when there is no central political authority and hence where differential access to resources and technology cannot be sustained.

The Kapauku Papuans of West New Guinea (today, West Irian, Indonesia) are a case in point (see Fig. 12.3). According to Leopold Pospisil (1963), the Kapauku have an economy that is best described as "primitive capitalism." All Kapauku agricultural land is said to be owned individually; money sales are the regular means of exchange; money, in the form of shells and glass beads, can be used to buy food, domesticated animals, crops, and land; money can also be used as payment for labor. Rent for leased land and interest on loans are also said to occur.

A closer look at the land tenure situation, however, reveals fundamental differences between the political economy of Kapauku and capitalist peasant societies (see below). To begin with, there is no landowning class. Instead, access to land is controlled by kinship groups known as *sublineages* (see p. 278). No individual is without membership in such a group. These sublineages control communal tracts of land, which Pospisil calls "territories."

It is only within sublineage territories that one may speak of private titles, and the economic significance of these titles is minimal on several counts. (1) The price of land is so cheap that all the gardens under production have a market value in shell money less than the value of ten female pigs. (2) Prohibition against trespass does not apply to sublineage kin. (3) Although even brothers will ask each other for land payments, credit is freely extended among all sublineage members. The most common form of credit with respect to land consists merely of giving land on a loan, and in expectation that the favor will shortly be returned. (4) Each sublineage is under the leadership of a *headman* (see Ch. 15) whose authority depends on his generosity, especially toward the members of his own sublineage. A rich headman does not refuse to lend his kinsmen whatever they need to gain access to the environment, since "a selfish individual who hoards money and fails to be generous, never sees the time when his word is taken seriously and his advice and decisions followed, no matter how rich he may become" (Pospisil 1963:49).

Obviously, therefore, the wealth of the headman does not bestow the power associated with capitalist ownership. In Brazil, India, or other capitalist countries, tenants or sharecroppers can be barred from access to land and water regardless of their landlord's "reputation." Under the rules of capitalist landownership, it is of no significance to the sheriff and the police officers when they evict tenants that the landlord is being "selfish."

Pospisil states that differences in wealth are correlated with striking differences in consumption of food and that Kapauku children from poor homes are undernourished while neighbors are well fed. However, the neighbors are not members of the same sublineage. As Pospisil notes, sublineage kinsmen "exhibit mutual affection and a strong sense of belonging and unity" and "any kind of friction within the group is regarded as deplorable" (1963:39). It is true that certain sublineages are poorer than others. Sickness and misfortune of various sorts frequently lead to inequalities in physical well-being among the kinship units that are the building blocks of band and village societies. But such misfortunes do not lead to the formation of a poverty class as they do under true capitalism. Without central political controls, marked economic inequalities cannot be perpetuated for long, because the rich cannot defend themselves against the demand of the poor that they be given credit, money, land, or whatever is necessary to end their poverty. Under aboriginal conditions some Kapauku villagers might have starved while neighbors ate well; but it is extremely unlikely that those who starved did so because they lacked access to land, money, or credit.

A stingy redistributor in a band or village society is a contradiction in terms, for the simple reason that there are no police to protect such people from the murderous intentions of those whom they refuse to help. As Pospisil tells it:

> Selfish and greedy individuals, who have amassed huge personal properties, but who have failed to comply with the Kapauka requirement of "generosity" toward their less fortunate tribesmen may be, and actually frequently are, put to death. . . . Even in regions such as the Kamu Valley, where such an execution is not a penalty for greediness, a nongenerous wealthy man is ostracized, reprimanded; and thereby finally induced to change his ways (1963:49).

LANDOWNERSHIP

Ownership of land and resources is one of the most important aspects of political control. It is as much political as economic because unequal access to the environment implies some form of coercion applied by political superiors against political inferiors.

As we have just seen, certain forms of land and resource ownership do occur in band and village societies. Ownership of garden lands, for example, is often claimed by kin groups in village communities, but everybody belongs to such kin groups, and hence adults cannot be prevented from using the resources they need to make a living. Landownership by landlords, rulers, or the government, however, means that individuals who lack title or tenure may be barred from using land even if it leads to death through starvation.

As discussed in Chapter 16, ownership of land and resources results from systemic processes that select for more dense and more productive populations. Landownership is a great stimulus to production because it forces food producers to work longer and harder than they would if they had free access to resources. Landownership raises production mainly through the extraction of rent from the food producers. *Rent* is a payment in kind or in money for the opportunity to live or work on the owner's land. This payment automatically compels tenants to increase their work input. By raising or lowering rents, the landlord exercises a fairly direct measure of control over work input and production.

Because the extraction of rent is evolutionarily associated with an increase in food production, some anthropologists regard the payment of rent as indictive of the existence of *surplus* food—an amount greater than what is needed for immediate consumption by the producers. But it is important to note that the "surplus" food the landowner takes away as rent need not be a *superfluous* quantity from the producers' standpoint. The producers usually can very well use the full amount of their output to ease the costs of rearing children or to raise their own standard of living. If they surrender their produce, it is usually because they lack the power to withhold it. In this sense all rent is an aspect of politics, because without the power to enforce property titles, rent would seldom be paid. Thus there is a close resemblance between rent and taxation. Both depend on the existence of coercive power in the form of police and weapons that can be called into action if the taxpayer or tenant refuses to pay.

In certain highly centralized societies, such as in the ancient Inca Empire (see p. 318), there is no distinction between rent and taxes since there is no landlord class. Instead, the government bureaucracy has a monopoly over the means of extracting wealth from commoner food producers. States and empires also exercise direct control over production by setting regional or community quotas for particular crops and by conscripting armies of commoners to work on construction projects. Compulsory labor conscription, known as *corvée,* is merely another form of taxation. As discussed in Chapter 16, all of these coercive forms of extracting wealth from commoner food producers probably have their roots in the intensification of production, population pressure, warfare and the development of trade and stratified forms of redistribution.

SUMMARY

All cultures have an economy, a set of institutions that combine technology, labor, and natural resources to produce and distribute goods and services. To the extent that economizing takes place—that is, minimizing costs and maximizing benefits—it always takes place in a definite cultural context, and it is always embedded in institutional relationships such as kinship or politics. The question whether economies always function to increase benefits and diminish costs must be investigated empirically, but the possibility that apparently wasteful and "uneconomic" behavior such as gluttonous feasts represents economizing at a broader level of analysis should be kept in mind.

Modern-day price markets represent only one of several alternative modes of exchange. Buying and selling is not a universal trait. The idea that money can buy everything (or almost everything) has been alien to most of the human beings who have ever lived. Two other modes of exchange, reciprocity and redistribution, have played a more important economic role than price markets.

In reciprocal exchange the time and quantity of the counterflow is not specified. This kind of exchange can be effective only when it is embedded in kinship or close personal relationships. Daily food distribution among the !Kung San is an example of reciprocal exchange. Control over the counterflow in reciprocal exchange is achieved by communal pressure against freeloaders and shirkers. Reciprocity lingers on in price-market societies within kinship groups and is familiar to many of us as gift-giving to relatives and friends.

In the absence of price markets and police-military supervision, trade poses a special problem to people accustomed to reciprocal exchange. Silent barter is one solution. Another is to create trading partners who treat each other as kin. The Kula is a classic example of how barter for practical necessities is carried out under the cloak of reciprocal exchanges.

Redistributive exchange involves the collection of goods in a central place and its disbursement by a redistributor to the producers. In the transition from egalitarian to stratified forms of redistribution, production and exchange cross the line separating voluntary from coerced forms of economic behavior. In its egalitarian form, the redistributor depends on the goodwill of the producers; in the stratified form, the producers depend on the goodwill of the redistributor.

Redistribution is characterized by the counting of shares contributed and shares disbursed. Unlike reciprocity, redistribution leads to boasting and overt competition for the prestigeful status of great provider. The Kwakiutl potlatch is a classic example of the relationship between redistribution and bragging behavior. The predominance of redistribution over reciprocity may be related to the intensifiability of various modes of production. Where production can be intensified without depletions, rivalrous redistributions may serve adaptive ecological functions, such as providing an extra margin of safety in lean years and equalizing regional production. The development of destructive potlatches among Kwakiutl may have been caused by factors involved in the European contact situation, such as the intensification of warfare, trade for guns and ammunition, and depopulation.

Price-market exchange depends on the development of all-purpose money as defined by the criteria of portability, divisibility, convertibility, generality, anonymity, and legality. Although some of these features are possessed by limited-purpose standards of value in pre-state societies, price markets imply the existence of state forms of control.

The highest development of the price-market mode of exchange is associated with the political economy of capitalism, in which virtually all goods and services can be bought and sold. Since capitalist production depends on consumerism, prestige is awarded to those who own or consume the greatest amount of goods and services. Price-market exchanges are embedded in a political economy of control made necessary by the inequalities in access to resources and the conflict between the poor and the wealthy. The Kapauku illustrate the reasons why price-market institutions and capitalism cannot exist in the absence of such controls.

The relationship between political forms of control and modes of production and exchange focuses in many societies on the question of landownership. Rent, corvée labor, and taxation all reflect differential access to nature and technology. Thus, we see why the comparative study of economics must involve the study of the institutions in which economizing is embedded.

13 THE ORGANIZATION OF DOMESTIC LIFE

In this chapter we continue the comparative study of the structural level of sociocultural systems and examine the major varieties of domestic organizations. We will inquire whether all domestic groups are built up from a single form of family and whether there is a genetic basis for the exchanges of personnel that link domestic groups together. This chapter is primarily descriptive, but some theoretical explanations that are more fully elaborated in later chapters are discussed in a preliminary way.

THE DOMESTIC SPHERE OF CULTURE

All cultures have activities and thoughts that can usefully be lumped under the category of the domestic sphere of life. The basic ingredient in the etic notion of domestic life is a dwelling space, shelter, residence, or domicile, which serves as the place in which certain universally recurrent activities take place. But it is not possible to give a rigid checklist of what these activities are. In many cultures, domestic activities include preparation and consumption of food, cleaning, grooming, and disciplining of the young; sleeping; and adult sexual intercourse. However, there is no culture in which these activities are carried out exclusively within domestic settings. For example, sexual intercourse among band and village peoples more often takes place in the bush or forest than in the house where sleeping occurs. In other instances, sleeping itself takes place primarily away from the setting in which eating occurs and in still other instances domiciles may lack resident children, as when childless adults live alone or when children are sent off to school. The variety of combinations of activities characteristic of human domestic life is so great that it is difficult to find any single underlying common denominator for all of them. (One might insist that there must be at least mothers and very young children, but what about childless households?) This in itself, however, is an important fact, since no other species exhibits such an enormous range of different behaviors associated with patterns of eating, shelter, sleep, sex, and rearing of infants and children.

THE NUCLEAR FAMILY

Can a particular kind of group be found in all domestic settings? Many anthropologists believe there is such a group and refer to it as the *nuclear family*: husband, wife, and children (Fig. 13.1). According to Ralph Linton, father, mother, child is the "bedrock underlying all other family structures," and he predicted that "the last man will spend his last hours searching for his wife and child" (1959:52). George Peter Murdock found the nuclear family in each of 250 societies. He concluded that it was universal. According to Murdock (1949), the nuclear family fulfills vital functions that cannot be carried out as efficiently by other groups. The functions identified by Murdock are these: (1) sex, (2) reproduction, (3) education, and (4) subsistence.

1. The nuclear family satisfies sexual needs and diminishes the disruptive force of sexual competition.
2. The nuclear family guarantees the protection of the female during her long pregnancy and during the months and years of lactation.

Figure 13.1 *JAPANESE NUCLEAR FAMILY*
Industrialization in Japan has produced convergence toward a pattern of nuclear family life as in the United States.

3. The nuclear family is essential for enculturation. Only the coresident adult man and woman possess knowledge adequate for the enculturation of children of both sexes.
4. Given the behavioral specialties imposed upon the human female by her reproductive role, and given the anatomical and physiological differences between men and women, the sexual division of labor makes subsistence more efficient.

The nuclear family thus provides for heterosexual sex, reproduction, enculturation, and economic support more effectively than any other institution, according to this view.

It is important to investigate the validity of these claims at some length. The idea that the nuclear family is universal or nearly universal lends support to the view that non-nuclear family domestic units are contrary to human nature. In actuality, however, no one knows the limits within which human domestic arrangements must be confined in order to satisfy human nature and effectively carry out some or all of the four functions listed above.

ALTERNATIVES TO THE NUCLEAR FAMILY

Even though nuclear families can be found in the overwhelming majority of human cultures, it has long been obvious that every culture has alternative forms of domestic organization and that these frequently are more important—involve a higher proportion of the population—than the nuclear family. Furthermore, the four functions listed above can readily by carried out in the context of alternative institutions that may lie entirely outside the domestic sphere.

In the case of the nuclear family in modern industrial cultures this is evident with respect to enculturation and education. Enculturation and education in contemporary life are increasingly a nondomestic affair carried out in special buildings—schools—under the auspices of specialist nonkinspeople—teachers.

Many village and band societies also separate their children and adolescents from the nuclear family and the entire domestic scene in order to teach them the lore and ritual of the ancestors, sexual competence, or the military arts. Among the Nyakyusa of southern Tanzania, for example, 6- or 7-year-old boys begin to put up reed shelter playhouses on the outskirts of their village. These playhouses are gradually improved upon and enlarged, eventually leading to the construction of a whole new village. Between the ages of 5 and 11, Nyakyusa boys sleep in their parents' house; but during adolescence they are permitted to visit only during daylight hours. Sleeping now takes place in the new village, although the mother still does the cooking. The founding of a new village is complete when the young men take wives who cook for them and begin to give birth to the next generation (Wilson 1963).

Another famous variation on this pattern is found among the Masai of East Africa, where unmarried men of the same *age-set*, or ritually defined generation, establish special villages or camps from which they launch war parties and cattle-stealing raids. It is the mothers and sisters of these men who cook and keep house for them.

The common English upper-class practice of sending sons 6 years of age or older to boarding schools should also be noted. Like the Masai, the English aristocracy refused to let the burden of maintaining the continuity of their society rest upon the educational resources of the nuclear household.

In many societies, married men spend a good deal of time in special *men's houses*. Food is handed in to them by wives and children who are themselves forbidden to enter. Men also sleep and work in these "clubhouses," although they may on occasion bed down with their wives and children.

Among the Fur of the Sudan, husbands usually sleep apart from their wives in houses of their own and take their meals at an exclusive men's mess. One of the most interesting cases of the separation of cooking and eating occurs among the Ashanti of West Africa. Ashanti men eat their meals with their sisters, mothers, and maternal nephews and nieces, not with their wives and children. But it is the wives who do the cooking. Every evening in Ashanti land there is a steady traffic of children taking their mother's cooking to their father's sister's house (cf. Barnes 1960; Bender 1967).

Finally, there is at least one famous case—the Nayar of Kerala—in which "husband" and "wife" did not live together at all. Many Nayar women "married" ritual husbands and then stayed with their brothers and sisters. Their mates were men who visited overnight. Children born of these matings were brought up in households dominated by their mother's brother and never knew their father. We will return for a closer look at the Nayar in a moment.

POLYGAMY AND THE NUCLEAR FAMILY

Next we must consider whether the combination father-mother-child has the same

Figure 13.2 *POLYGYNY*
(a) Polygynous household, Senegal. Islamic law permits this man to take one more wife to fill his quota of four, providing he can take good care of her. *(b)* Sitting Bull. This famous Sioux chief is shown with two of his wives and three of his children. Polygyny was widespread among native American peoples. The photo was taken in 1882 at Fort Randall, South Dakota.

(b)

functional significance where either father or mother is married to and is living with more than one spouse at a time. This is an important question because plural marriage—*polygamy*—occurs to some extent in a least 90 percent of all cultures.

In one form, called *polygyny* (Fig. 13.2), a husband is shared by several wives; in another much less common form called *polyandry* (Fig. 13.3), a wife is shared by several husbands (we discuss the reason for the occurrence of polygyny and polyandry in Ch. 14). Is there a nuclear family when there are plural husbands or wives? G. P. Murdock suggested that nuclear families do exist in such situations. The man or woman simply belongs to more than one nuclear family at a time. But this overlooks the fact that plural marriages create domestic situations behaviorally and mentally very different from those created by *monogamous* (one husband, one wife) marriages.

Polygamous sexual arrangements, for example, are obviously quite different from those characteristic of monogamous marriages. The mode of reproduction is also different, especially with polygyny, because the spacing of births is easier to control when husbands have several wives. Also, distinctive patterns of nursing and infant care arise when the mother sleeps alone with her children while the father sleeps with a different wife each night (see p. 488). From the point of view of childrearing, there are special psychological effects associated with a father who divides his time among several mothers and who relates to his children through a hierarchy of wives. The monogamous U.S. or Canadian nuclear family places the focus of adult attention on a small group of full siblings. In a polygynous household, a dozen or more half-siblings must share the affection of the same man. Furthermore, the presence of co-wives or co-husbands changes the burden of childcare a particular parent must bear. For example, U.S. and Canadian parents are troubled by the question of what to do with children when both parents are preoccupied with adult-centered activities. But polygynous families have a built-in solution to the babysitting problem in the form of co-wives.

Turning finally to economic functions, the minimal polygamous economic unit often consists of the entire coresident production team and not each separate husband-wife pair. Under polygyny, for example, domestic tasks—nursing, grooming, cleaning, fetching water, cooking, and so on—frequently cannot be satisfactorily performed by a single wife. In polygynous societies, one of the main motivations for marrying a

Figure 13.3 *POLYANDRY*
This Tibetan woman (wearing the veil) is being married to the two men on the left, who are brothers.

second wife is to spread the workload and increase domestic output. It seems inappropriate, therefore, to equate nuclear families in monogamous domestic groups with husband-wife-child units embedded in polygamous domestic groups.

THE EXTENDED FAMILY

In many of the societies studied by anthropologists, domestic life is dominated by groupings larger than simple nuclear or polygamous families. The majority of existing cultures still carry on their domestic routines in the context of some form of *extended family*—that is, a domestic group consisting of siblings, their spouses and their children, and/or parents and married children (Fig. 13.4). Extended families may also be polygynous. A common form of extended family in Africa, for example, consists of two or more brothers, each with two or three wives, living with their adult sons, each of whom has one or two wives. Among the Bathonga of southern Mozambique, domestic life fell under the control of the senior males of the polygynous extended family's senior generation. These prestigious and powerful men in effect formed a board of directors of a family-style corporation. They were responsible for making decisions about the domestic group's holdings in land, cattle, and buildings; they organized the subsistence effort of the coresident labor force, especially of the women and children, by assigning fields, crops, and seasonal work tasks. They tried to increase the size of their cattle herds and supplies of food and beer, obtain more wives, and increase the size and strength of the entire unit. The younger brothers, sons, and grandsons in Bathonga extended families could reach adulthood,

Figure 13.4 *EXTENDED FAMILY, UNITED STATES*
The demand for labor was high on this Minnesota farm in 1895.

Figure 13.5 *TAIWAN MARRIAGE*
Groom's extended family assembled for wedding ceremony.

marry, build a hut, carry out subsistence tasks, and have children only as members of the larger group, subject to the policies and priorities established by the senior males. Within the Bathonga extended family households there really was no unit equivalent to a nuclear family, and this is true of extended families in many other cultures, whether they are monogamous or polygamous.

In traditional Chinese extended families, for example, marriage is usually monogamous (Fig. 13.5). A senior couple manages the domestic labor force and arranges marriages. Women brought into the household as wives for the senior couple's sons are placed under the direct control of their mother-in-law. She supervises their cleaning, cooking, and raising of children. Where there are several daughters-in-law, work tasks are rotated. One daughter-in-law cooks while the others work in the fields (Cohen 1976). The degree to which the nuclear family is submerged and effaced by these arrangements is brought out by a custom formerly found in certain Taiwanese households: "adopt a daughter-in-law; marry a sister." In order to obtain control over their son's wife, the senior couple adopts a daughter. They bring this girl into the household at a very early age and train her to be hardworking and obedient. Later they oblige their son to marry this stepsister, thereby preventing the formation of an economically independent nuclear family within their midst, while at the same time conforming to the rule against a brother marrying a sister (Wolf 1968).

Among the Rajputs of northern India, extended families take similar stern measures to maintain the subordination of each married pair. A young man and his wife are even forbidden to talk to each other in the presence of senior persons, meaning in effect that they "may converse only surreptitiously at night" (Minturn and Hitchcock 1963:241). Here the husband is not supposed to show an open concern for his wife's welfare; if she is ill, that is a matter for her mother-in-law or father-in-law to take care of: "The mother feeds her son even after he is married . . . she runs the family as long as she wishes to assume the responsibility."

As a final brief example of how extended families modify the nuclear constellation, there is Max Gluckman's (1955:60) wry comment on the Barotse of Zambia: "If a man becomes too devoted to his wife he is assumed to be the victim of witchcraft."

Why do so many societies have extended families? Probably because nuclear families frequently lack sufficient manpower and womanpower to carry out both domestic and subsistence tasks effectively. Extended families provide a larger labor pool and can carry out a greater variety of simultaneous activities (Pasternak, Ember, and Ember 1976).

ONE-PARENT DOMESTIC GROUP

Millions of children throughout the world are reared in domestic groups in which only one parent is present. This may result from divorce or death of one of the parents. But it also may result from inability or unwillingness to marry. The most common form of nonnuclear one-parent domestic arrangements is for the mother to be present and father to be absent. These are called *matrifocal* households. Mother more or less rapidly accepts a series of men as mates, usually one at a time, but sometimes polyandrously. The man and woman are usually coresident for brief periods, but over the years there may be long intervals during which mother does not have a resident mate.

At one extreme, associated with very rich or very poor women, mother and children may live alone. At the other extreme, mother and her children may live together with her sisters and her mother and constitute a large extended family in which adult males play only temporary roles as visitors or lovers.

Matrifocal households are best known from studies carried out in the West Indies (Blake 1961; M. G. Smith 1966; R. T. Smith 1973) and Latin America (Adams 1968; Lewis 1961, 1964), and among U.S. inner-city blacks (Furstenberg et al. 1975; Stack 1974; González 1970; Tanner 1974). However, the worldwide incidence of matrifocality has been obscured by the tendency to regard such domestic units as aberrant or pathological (Moynihan 1965). In describing domestic groups, social scientists frequently concentrate on the emically preferred or ideal form and neglect the etic and behavioral actualities. Mother-child domestic groups are often the result of poverty and hence are associated with many social ills and regarded as undesirable. But there is no evidence that such domestic arrangements are inherently any more pathological, unstable, or contrary to "human nature" than the nuclear family.

Matrifocal extended family households shade imperceptibly into *matrilocal* (see Table 14.1) extended family households. Among the matrilocal Nayar, for example, mother's mates never resided with mother and children. Moreover, unlike matrifocal households, Nayar households contained several generations of males related through females. It was one of the senior males—that is, a mother's brother—who was the head of the household, not a grandmother, as in the case of the extended matrifocal family.

WHAT IS MARRIAGE?

The diversity of human mating behavior and the differences between the emic and etic views of such behavior make it extremely difficult to give a simple definition of marriage. Among the many ingenious attempts to define marriage as a universally occurring relationship, the definition proposed by Kathleen Gough, who has studied among the Nayar, merits special attention. But it must be read more than once!

> Marriage is a relationship established between a woman and one or more persons, which provides that a child born to the woman under circumstances not prohibited by the rules of the relationship is accorded full birth-status rights common to normal members of his [or her] society or social stratum. (1968:68)

According to Gough, for most if not all societies, this definition identifies a relationship "distinguished by the people themselves from all other kinds of relationships." Yet Gough's definition seems oddly at variance with English dictionary and native Western notions of marriage. First of all, there is no reference to rights and duties of sexual access, nor even to simple sexual performance. Moreover, if Gough's definition is accepted, marriage need not involve a relationship between men and women. Gough merely specifies that there must be a woman and "one or more other persons" of undefined sex!

The main reason Gough does not mention sexual rights and duties is the case of the Nayar. In order to bear children in a socially acceptable manner, pubescent Nayar girls had to go through a 4-day ceremony that linked them with a "ritual husband." Completion of this ceremony was a necessary prerequisite for the beginning of a Nayar woman's sexual and reproductive career. Ideally, the Nayar strove to find a ritual husband among the men of the higher-ranking Nambodri Brahman caste. The members of this caste were interested in having sex with Nayar women, but they refused to regard the children of Nayar women as their heirs. So after the ritual marriage, Nayar women stayed home with their sisters and brothers and were visited by both Nambodri Brahman and Nayar men. Gough regards the existence of the ritual husbands as proof of the universality of marriage (although not of the nuclear family), since only children born to ritually married Nayar women were "legitimate," even though the identity of their fathers was uncertain.

But what can be Gough's reason for defining marriage as a relationship between a woman and "persons" rather than between "women and men"? There are several instances among African peoples—the Dahomey case is best known—in which women "marry" female "husbands." This is accomplished by having a woman, who herself is already usually married to a man, pay *bride-price* for a bride. [Bride-price is the transfer of valuables from husband's family to wife's family (see p. 262).] The female bride-price payer becomes a "female husband." She founds a family of her own by letting her "wives" become pregnant through relationships with designated males. The offspring of these unions fall under the control of the "female father" rather than of the biological *genitor* (see p. 260), that is, the biological father.

Wide as it is, Gough's definition ignores mating relationships that have no women at all. Some anthropologists also include such man-man relationships in their definition of marriage. For example, among the Kwakiutl, a man who desires to acquire the privileges associated with a particular chief can "marry" the chief's right or left side, or a leg or an arm.

In Euramerican culture, enduring mating relationships between coresident homosexual men or homosexual women are also often spoken of as marriage. It has thus been suggested that all reference to the sex of the people involved in the relationship should be omitted in the definition of marriage in order to accommodate such cases (Dillingham and Isaac 1975). Yet the task of understanding varieties of domestic organization is made more difficult when all these different forms of mating are crammed into the single concept of marriage. Part of the problem is that when matings in Western culture are refused the designation "marriage," there is an unjust tendency to regard them as less honorable or less authentic relationships. And so anthropologists are reluctant to stigmatize woman-woman or man-man matings or Nayar or matrifocal visiting mate arrangements by saying they are not marriages. But whatever we call them, it is clear that they cover an enormous behavioral and mental range. There is no scientific evidence that any one of them is less desirable or less human, provided that they do not involve the coercion, abuse, and exploitation of one of the partners (a provision that applies, of course, to Western man-woman monogamy as well).

Since the term *marriage* is too useful to drop altogether, a more narrow definition seems appropriate: *Marriage* denotes the behavior, sentiments, and rules concerned with coresident heterosexual mating and reproduction in domestic contexts.

To accommodate sensitivities that may be injured by using marriage exclusively for coresident heterosexual domestic mates, a simple expedient is available. Let such other relationships be designated as "noncoresident marriages," "man-man marriages," "woman-woman marriages," or by any other appropriate specific nomenclature. It is clear that these matings have different ecological, demographic, economic, and ideological implications, so nothing is to be gained by arguing about whether they are "real" marriages.

LEGITIMACY

The essence of the marital relationship, according to some anthropologists, is embodied in that portion of Gough's definition dealing with the assignment of "birth-status rights" to children. Children born to a married woman "under circumstances not prohibited by the rules of the relationship" (e.g., adultery) are legal or legitimate children. Children born to unmarried women are illegitimate. As Bronislaw Malinowski put it: "Marriage is the licensing of parenthood."

The case for the universality of marriage rests on the claim that every society draws an emic distinction between legitimate or legal child rearing and illegitimate or illegal child rearing. It is true that in all societies women are discouraged from attempting to rear children or dispose of their newborn infants according to their own whim and capacities. But the concept of legal or legitimate childbirth is not universal. Behind this concept lies the assumption that every society has a single, well-defined set of rules that identify legitimate and illegitimate births. There is the further assumption that those who violate these rules will be subject to punishment or disapproval. Both assumptions lack firm empirical support. Many societies have several different sets of rules defining permissible modes of conception and child rearing. Frequently enough, some of these alternatives may be esteemed more highly than others, but the less esteemed modes do not necessarily place children in a status analogous to that of Western illegitimacy (Scheffler 1973:754–755). For example, among Brazilians living in small towns there are four kinds of relationships between a man and a woman, all of which provide children with full birth rights: church marriage, civil marriage, simultaneous church and civil marriage, and consensual marriage. For a Brazilian woman the most esteemed way to have children is through simultaneous church and civil marriage. This mode legally entitles her to a portion of her husband's property upon his death. It also provides the added security of knowing that her husband cannot desert her and enter into a civil or religious marriage elsewhere. The least desirable mode is the consensual marriage, because the woman can make no property claims against her consort, nor can she readily prevent him from deserting her. Yet the children of a consensual arrangement can make property claims against both father and mother while suffering no deprivation of birthrights in the form of legal disadvantages or social disapproval as long as the father acknowledges paternity.

Among the Dahomey, Herskovits (1938) reported 13 different kinds of marriage determined largely by bride-price arrangements. Children enjoyed different birthrights depending on the type of marriage. In some marriages the child was placed under the control of the father's domestic group and in others under the control of a domestic group headed by a female "father" (see above). The point is not that the child is legitimate or illegitimate, but rather that there are specific types of rights, obligations, and groupings associated with different modes of sexual and reproductive relations. Most of the world's peoples are not concerned with the question of whether a child is legitimate, but with the question of who will have the right of controlling the child's destiny.

Various degrees of punishment and disapproval are administered to the woman who fails to fulfill the preferred conditions for motherhood. Even in this respect, however, it is false to assume that women are everywhere subject to some form of disapproval if they depart from the preferred course of child rearing. Everything depends on the larger domestic and social context in which the woman has become pregnant. No society grants women complete "freedom of conception," but the restrictions placed on motherhood and the occasions for punishment and disapproval vary enormously.

Where the domestic scene is dominated by large extended families and where there are no strong restrictions on premarital sex, the pregnancy of a young married woman is rarely the occasion for much concern. Under certain circumstances, an "unwed mother" may even be congratulated rather than condemned. Among the Kadar of northern Nigeria, as reported by M. G. Smith (1968), most marriages result from infant betrothals. These matches are arranged by the fathers of the bride and groom when the girl is 3 to 6 years old. Ten years or more may elapse before the bride goes to live with her betrothed. During this time, a Kadar girl is not unlikely to become pregnant. This will disturb no one, even if the biological father is a man other than her future husband:

> Kadar set no value on premarital chastity. It is fairly common for unmarried girls to be impregnated or to give birth to children by youths other than their betrothed. Offspring of such premarital pregnancies are members of the patrilineage . . .

of the girls's betrothed and are welcomed as proof of the bride's fertility (ibid.:113).

FUNCTIONS OF MARRIAGE

Every society regulates the reproductive activities of its sexually mature adults. One way of achieving this regulation is to set forth rules that define the conditions under which sexual relations, pregnancy, birth, and child rearing may take place and that allocate privileges and duties in connection with these conditions. Each society has its own sometimes unique combination of rules and rules for breaking rules in this domain. It would be a rather futile exercise to attempt to define marriage by any one ingredient in these rules—such as legitimation of children—even if such an ingredient could be shown to be universal. This point can be illustrated by enumerating some of the variable regulatory functions associated with institutions commonly identified as "marriage." The following list incorporates suggestions made by Edmund Leach (1968). Marriage *sometimes*

1. Establishes the legal father of a woman's children
2. Establishes the legal mother of a man's children
3. Gives the husband or his extended family control over the wife's sexual services
4. Gives the wife or her extended family control over the husband's sexual services
5. Gives the husband or his extended family control over the wife's labor power
6. Gives the wife or her extended family control over the husband's labor power
7. Gives the husband or his extended family control over the wife's property
8. Gives the wife or her extended family control over the husband's property
9. Establishes a joint fund of property for the benefit of children
10. Establishes a socially significant relationship between the husband's and the wife's domestic groups

As Leach remarks, this list could be greatly extended, but the point is "that in no single society can marriage serve to establish all these types of rights simultaneously, nor is there any one of these rights which is invariably established by marriage in every known society" (1968:76).

MARRIAGE IN EXTENDED FAMILIES

In extended families, marriage must be seen primarily in the context of group interests. Individuals serve the interests of the extended family: The larger domestic group never loses interest in or totally surrenders its rights to the productive, the reproductive, and the sexual functions of spouses and children. Marriage under these circumstances is aptly described as an "alliance" between corporate groups. This alliance influences present and future matings involving other members of these groups.

Among many societies, the corporate nature of marriage is revealed by the exchange of personnel or of valuable goods between the respective domestic groups in which bride and groom were born. The simplest form of such transactions is called *sister exchange* and involves the reciprocal "giving away" of the groom's sisters in compensation for the loss of a woman from each group.

Among many peoples around the world, corporate interests are expressed in the institution known as *bride-price* (Fig. 13.6). The wife-receivers give valuable items to

Figure 13.6 *BRIDE-PRICE*
Among the Kapauku, the bride-price consists of shell money.

the wife-givers. Of course, bride-price is not equivalent to the selling and buying of automobiles or refrigerators in modern industrial price-market societies. The wife-receivers do not "own" their woman in any total sense; they must take good care of her or her brothers and "fathers" (i.e., her father and father's brothers) will demand that she be returned to them. The amount of bride-price is not fixed; it fluctuates from one marriage to another. (In Africa the traditional measure of "bride wealth" was cattle, although other valuables such as iron tools were also used. Nowadays, cash payments are the rule.) Among the Bathonga, a family that had many daughter-sisters was in a favorable position. By exchanging women for cattle, they could exchange cattle back for women. The more cattle, the more mother-wives; the more mother-wives, the larger the reproductive and productive labor force and the greater the corporate material welfare and influence of the extended family.

Sometimes the transfer of wealth from one group to another is carried out in installments: so much on initial agreement, more when the woman goes to live with her husband, and another, usually final, payment when she has her first child. Failure to have a child often voids the marriage; the woman goes home to her brothers and fathers, and the husband gets his bride-price back.

A common alternative to bride-price is known as *bride-service* (sometimes called *suitor-service*). The groom or husband compensates his in-laws by working for them for several months or years before taking his bride away to live and work with him and his extended family. Bride-service may be involved in the conditions under which matrilocal residence tends to occur, as we will see in Chapter 14. If the suitor lingers on and never takes his bride home, he may be participating in an etic shift from patrilocal to matrilocal residence.

Bride-price and suitor-service tend to occur where production is being increased, land is plentiful, and the labor of additional women and children is seen as scarce and as being in the best interests of the corporate group (Goody 1976). Where the corporate group is not interested in or not capable of expanding production or in increasing its numbers, wives may be regarded as a burden. Instead of paying bride-price to the family of the bride, the groom's family may demand a reverse payment, called *dowry* (Fig. 13.7). When this payment consists of money or movable property instead of land, it is usually associated with a low or oppressed status for women.

The opposite of bride-price is not dowry but *groom-price,* in which the groom goes to work for the bride's family and the bride's family compensates the groom's family for the loss of his productive powers. This form of marriage compensation is extremely rare—only one well-documented case is known (Nash 1974)—probably for reasons having to do with the prevalence of male-supermacist institutions (see p. 499).

Figure 13.7 *DOWRY*
This Arab bride is exhibiting her wealth.

DOMESTIC GROUPS AND THE AVOIDANCE OF INCEST

All these exchanges point to the existence of a profound paradox in the way human beings find mates. Marriage between members of the same domestic group is widely prohibited. Husband and wife must come from separate domestic groups. The members of the domestic group must "marry out"—that is, marry *exogamously;* they cannot "marry in"—that is, marry *endogamously.*

Certain forms of endogamy are universally prohibited. No culture tolerates father-daughter and mother-son marriages. Sister-brother marriage is also widely prohibited, but it occurred, especially between half siblings, among the ruling classes of highly stratified societies such as those of the Inca and ancient Egypt (Bixler 1982). In the emics of Western civilization, sister-brother, father-daughter, and mother-son sex relations and marriages are called *incest.* Why are these sex relations and marriages so widely prohibited?

Explanations of nuclear family incest prohibition fall into two major types: (1) those that stress an instinctual component and (2) those that emphasize the social and cultural advantages of exogamy.

1. There is some evidence that children of opposite sex who live together during early childhood lose interest in each other as sexual partners. Boys and girls brought up together in "children's houses" on Israeli kibbutz (communal farms) seldom have sexual affairs and rarely marry each other (Shepher 1971; Spiro 1954). It has also been found that Taiwanese marriages of the adopt-a-daughter–marry-a-sister variety (see p. 256) in which husband and wife grow up together lead to fewer children, greater adultery, and higher divorce rates than

marriages in which husband and wife remain in different households until the marriage night (Wolf and Huang 1980).

These cases have been interpreted as proof of the existence of genetically based mechanisms which produce sexual aversions among people who grow up together. The existence of this aversion has been attributed to natural selection. It is held that individuals who lacked such an aversion and who mated incestuously tended to have fewer offspring. The reason they had fewer offspring was that incestuous matings increase the probability that harmful recessive alleles will occur in the homozygous state (see p. 13). Hence a genetically determined aversion against sex and marriage with one's earliest domestic companions—usually the members of one's nuclear family—was selected for (Wilson 1978:37–39; Bixler 1981; 1983).

Against this line of theories there are the following arguments: Marriage of the members of the same kibbutz is rendered unlikely by the small number of potential mates in the appropriate age cohort. Kibbutz members usually postpone marriage until after they have completed military service and come in contact with a broader selection of potential mates. Lack of sexual affairs between kibbutz boys and girls may reflect the traditional puritanical code of kibbutz life (Fig. 13.8). This code has been changing in recent years, and there is evidence that sexual affairs are becoming more common (Y. Cohen 1978; Kaffman 1977; Livingstone 1981). As for Wolf's data, the Taiwanese explicitly recognize that the adopt-a-daughter–marry-a-sister marriage is an inferior form of union. The preferred form of marriage, which involves the largest dowries and bride-price exchanges, and hence the greatest degree of support from both the bride and groom's extended family, is the one in which bride and groom remain separated until the marriage night. It is to be expected, therefore, quite apart from instinctual aversions, that live-together-as-children marriages will not be as successful as the more typical live-apart-as-children marriages.

Further difficulties with this theory arise when one considers the evidence for the harmful effects of homozygosity in small populations. It is true that in large modern populations incest leads to a high proportion of stillbirths and congenitally diseased and impaired children. But there is considerable doubt whether the same applies to small populations in band and village societies. As Frank Livingstone (1969) has pointed out, inbreeding leads to the gradual elimination of harmful recessive genes. If a small inbreeding group is able to overcome the higher rate at which impaired homozygotes initially occur, it will eventually reach a genetic equilibrium involving a lowered percentage of harmful alleles. The effect of close inbreeding depends upon the original frequency of harmful alleles. Theoretically, a succession of nuclear families could practice inbreeding for several generations without adverse effects. The parents of Cleopatra (Fig. 13.9), queen of Egypt, were the product of generations of close inbreeding between half brothers and half sisters within the Ptolemaic dynasty (van den Berghe and Mesker 1980; Bixler 1982). Apparently, brother-sister marriage was so much the vogue in ancient Egypt that commoners did it too (Hopkins 1980).

Modern populations carry a much greater "load" of harmful recessives than small demographically stable bands and villages. According to Livingstone, the chances of genetic catastrophes arising among groups that are already highly inbred is much less than in a modern outbred population. Small inbred village groups, such as the Kaingang of central Brazil, have remarkably low frequencies of harmful recessives. Most band and village peoples show little tolerance for infants and children who are congenitally handicapped and impaired. Such children are likely to become the victims of infanticide or systematic neglect and are unlikely to pass on their harmful alleles.

The proposal that intimacy triggers a genetically determined sexual aversion within the nuclear family is also contradicted by evidence of strong sexual

Figure 13.8 *KIBBUTZ BOYS AND GIRLS*
Does childhood familiarity lead to sexual avoidance?

Figure 13.9 *CLEOPATRA*
Product of 11 generations of brother-sister marriage.

attraction between father and daughter and mother and son. Freudian psychoanalysis indicates that children and parents of the opposite sex have a strong desire to have sexual encounters with each other. Indeed, in the case of the father-daughter and brother-sister relationship, at least, these wishes are acted upon more frequently than is popularly believed. Social workers, for example, estimate that tens of thousands of cases of these two varieties of incest occur in the United States annually (Armstrong 1978; Finkelhor 1979, 1980). Finally, the instinct theory of incest avoidance is hard to reconcile with the widespread occurrence of endogamous practices that are carried out simultaneously and in support of exogamic arrangements. Members of exogamous extended families, for example, frequently are involved in marriage systems that encourage them to mate with one kind of first cousin (*cross cousin*) but not another (*parallel cousin*, see p. 275). The difference between these two forms of inbreeding has not yet been explained satisfactorily by selection for heterozygosity (cf. Alexander 1977). Furthermore, the widespread preference for some form of cousin marriage itself weighs against the conclusion that exogamy expresses an aversion established by the harmful effects of inbreeding.

2. Nuclear family incest avoidance and other forms of exogamy among domestic groups can be explained in terms of demographic, economic, and ecological advantages. These advantages are not necessarily the same for all societies. It is known, for example, that band societies rely on marriage exchanges to establish long-distance networks of kinspeople. Bands that formed a completely closed breeding unit would be denied the mobility and territorial flexibility that are essential to their subsistence strategy. Territorially restricted, endogamous bands of 20 to 30 people would also run a high risk of extinction as a result of sexual imbalances caused by an unlucky run of male births and adult female deaths, which would place the burden for the group's reproduction on one or two aging females. Exogamy is thus

essential for the effective utilization of a small population's productive and reproductive potential. Once a band begins to obtain mates from other bands, the prevalence of reciprocal economic relations leads to the expectation that the receivers will reciprocate. The taboos on mother-son, father-daughter, and brother-sister marriages can, therefore, be interpreted as a defense of these reciprocal exchange relationships against the ever-present temptation for parents to keep their children for themselves, or for brothers and sisters to keep each other for themselves.

In this connection it is frequently overlooked that once marriage is prohibited between father-daughter and mother-son, sexual encounters between these pairs constitute a form of adultery. Mother-son incest is an especially threatening variety of adultery in societies which have strong male-supremacist institutions. Not only is the wife "double-dealing" against her husband, but the son is "double-dealing" against his father. This may explain why the least common and emically most feared and abhorred form of incest is that between mother and son. It follows that father-daughter incest will be somewhat more common since husbands enjoy double standards of sexual behavior more often than wives and are less vulnerable to punishment for adultery. Finally, the same consideration suggests an explanation for the relatively high frequency of brother-sister matings and their legitimizations as marriages in elite classes—they do not conflict with father-mother adultery rules.

After the evolution of the state, exogamic alliances between domestic groups continued to have important infrastructural consequences. Among peasants, exogamy also increases the total productive and reproductive strength of the intermarried groups. It permits the exploitation of resources over a larger area than the nuclear or extended families could manage on an individual basis; it facilitates trade; and it raises the upper limit of the size of groups that can be formed to carry out seasonal activities (e.g., communal game drives, harvests, and so on) that require large labor inputs. Furthermore, where intergroup warfare poses a threat to group survival, the ability to mobilize large numbers of warriors is decisive. Hence, in militaristic, highly male-centered village cultures, sisters and daughters are frequently used as pawns in the establishment of alliances. These alliances do not necessarily eliminate warfare between intermarrying groups, but they make it less common (Tefft 1975; Kang 1979; Podolefsky 1983), as might be expected from the presence of sisters and daughters in the enemy's ranks.

Among elite classes and castes, endogamy often combines with extended family exogamy to maintain wealth and power within the ruling stratum (see p. 344). But as already noted, even the nuclear family may become endogamous when there is an extreme concentration of political, economic, and military power. With the evolution of price-market forms of exchange, the extended family tends to be replaced by nuclear family domestic units. Domestic group alliances lose some of their previous adaptive importance and the traditional functions of the incest avoidance must be reinterpreted. Incest has been decriminalized in Sweden and there is an effort to do likewise in the United States (Y. Cohen 1978; DeMott 1980). Yet given the scientific knowledge that nuclear family incest is genetically risky in populations carrying a heavy load of harmful recessives, the repeal of antiincest legislation seems unlikely and unwise.

The possibility that incest avoidance is genetically programmed in *Homo sapiens* has received some support from field studies of monkey and ape mating behavior. As among humans, father-daughter, mother-son, and brother-sister matings are uncommon among our nearest animal relatives. However, to some extent, the avoidance of sex by these pairs can be explained in terms of male dominance of sexual rivalry. There is no experimental evidence suggesting that there is an aversion to incest per se among monkeys and apes. Moreover, even if such an instinctual aversion did exist, its significance for human nature would remain in doubt (cf. Demarest 1977).

PREFERENTIAL MARRIAGES

The widespread occurrence of exogamy implies that the corporate interests of domestic groups must be protected by rules that stipulate who is to marry whom. Having given a woman away in marriage, most groups expect either material wealth or women in exchange. Consider two domestic groups, A and B, each with a core of resident brothers. If A gives a woman to B, B may immediately reciprocate by giving a woman to A. This reciprocity is often achieved by a direct exchange of the groom's sister. But the reciprocity may take a more indirect form. B may return a daughter of the union between the B man and the A woman. The bride in such a marriage will be her husband's father's sister's daughter, and the groom will be his wife's mother's brother's son. (The same result would be achieved by a marriage between a man and his mother's brother's daughter.) Bride and groom are each other's cross cousins (see p.275). If A and B have a rule that such marriages are to occur whenever possible, then they are said to have *preferential cross-cousin marriage*.

Reciprocity in marriage is sometimes achieved by several intermarrying domestic groups that exchange women in cycles. For example, A→B→C→A; or A⟷B and C⟷D in one generation and A⟷D and B⟷C in the next, and then back to A⟷B and C⟷D. These exchanges establish domestic alliances that are known as *circulating connubia*. They are enforced by preferential marriage with appropriate kinds of cousins, nephews, nieces, and other kin types.

Another common manifestation of corporate domestic interest in marriage is the practice of supplying replacements for in-marrying women who die prematurely. To maintain reciprocity or to fulfill a marriage contract for which bride-price has been paid, the deceased woman's brother may permit the widower to marry one or more of his wife's sisters. This custom is known as the *sororate*. Closely related to this practice is the preferential marriage known as the *levirate*, in which the services of a man's widows are retained within the domestic unit by having them marry one of his brothers. If the widows are old, these services may be minimal, and the levirate then functions to provide security for women who would otherwise not be able to remarry.

Thus the organization of domestic life everywhere reflects the fact that husbands and wives usually originate in different domestic groups that continue to maintain a sentimental and practical interest in the marriage partners and their children.

SUMMARY

The structural level of sociocultural systems is made up in part by interrelated domestic groups. Such groups can usually be identified by their attachment to a living space or domicile in which activities such as eating, sleeping, marital sex, and nurturance and discipline of the very young take place. However, there is no single or minimal pattern of domestic activities. Similarly, the nuclear family cannot be regarded as the minimal building block of all domestic groups. While nuclear families occur in almost every society, they are not always the dominant domestic group, and their sexual, reproductive, and productive functions can readily be satisfied by alternative domestic and nondomestic institutions. In polygamous and extended families, the father-mother-child subset may not enjoy any practical existence apart from the set of other relatives and their multiple spouses. And there are many instances of domestic groups which lack a coresident husband-father. Although children need to be nurtured and protected, no one knows the limits within which human domestic arrangements must be confined in order to satisfy human nature. One of the most important facts about human domestic arrangements is that there is no single pattern which can be shown to be more "natural" than any other.

Human mating patterns also exhibit an enormous degree of variation. While something similar to what is called marriage occurs all over the world, it is difficult to specify the mental and behavioral essence of the marital relationship. Man-man, woman-woman, female father, and childless marriages make it difficult to give a minimal definition of marriage without hurting someone's feelings. Even coresidence may not be essential, as the Nayar and other single-parent households demonstrate. Even when we restrict the definition of marriage to coresident heterosexual matings that result in reproduction, there is a staggering variety of rights and duties associated with the productive sexual and reproductive functions of the marriage partners and their offspring.

In order to understand coresident heterosexual reproductive marriage in extended families, marriage must be seen as a relationship between corporate groups as much as between cohabiting mates. The divergent interests of these corporate groups are reconciled by means of reciprocal exchanges which take the form of sister exchange, bride-price, suitor-service, dowry, and groom-price. The common principle underlying these exchanges, except for dowry, is that in giving a man or woman away to another extended family, the domestic corporation does not renounce its interests in the offspring of the mated pair and expects compensation for the loss of a valuable worker.

Most domestic groups are exogamous. This can be seen as the result of genetic programming or social and cultural adaptation. The discussion of exogamy necessarily centers on the incest prohibitions within the nuclear family. Father-daughter, sister-brother, and mother-son matings and marriages are almost universally forbidden. The chief exception is brother-sister marriages which occur in several highly stratified state societies among the ruling elites. The genetic theory of incest avoidance stresses evidence from Taiwan and Israel, which suggests that children reared together develop a sexual aversion to each other. This aversion is seen as genetically adaptive since it would reduce inbreeding and thereby reduce the risk of harmful homozygosity. Other interpretations of the Taiwan and Israel studies can be made. A purely cultural theory of incest avoidance can be built out of the need for bands and domestic groups to defend their capacity to engage in reciprocal marriage exchanges by preventing parents from keeping their children for themselves. The precise nature of the infrastructural and structural advantages derived from incest avoidance varies from the band, to village, to the state level. In the future the perpetuation of the incest taboos may be related exclusively to the increasing genetic dangers associated with close inbreeding in populations carrying a large load of harmful recessive alleles.

Exogamy and incest avoidance form only a small part of the spectrum of preferred and prohibited marriages which reflect the pervasive corporate interests of domestic groups. Preferences for certain kinds of marriage exchanges create circulating connubia in which reciprocity between domestic groups may be direct or indirect. Such preferences may be expressed as a rule requiring marriage with a particular kind of cousin. Preferential marriage rules such as the levirate and sororate also exemplify the corporate nature of the marriage bond.

14 KINSHIP, LOCALITY, AND DESCENT

This chapter continues the discussion of domestic organization. It examines the principal mental and emic components of domestic groups and relates them to the etic and behavioral aspects of those groups. It also sets forth some of the theories that relate the mental and behavioral variations in domestic organization to infrastructural conditions.

KINSHIP

The study of domestic life in hundreds of cultures all over the world has led anthropologists to conclude that two ideas or mental principles are involved in the organization of domestic life everywhere. The first of these is the idea of *affinity*, or of relationships through marriage. The second is the idea of *descent*, or parentage. People who are related to each other through descent or a combination of affinity and descent are relatives, or *kin*. The domain of ideas constituted by the beliefs and expectations kin share about one another is called *kinship*. The study of kinship, therefore, must begin with the mental and emic components of domestic life.

DESCENT

Kinship relations are often confused with biological relations. But the emic meaning of descent is not the biological meaning of descent.* As discussed previously (p. 261), marriage may explicitly establish "parentage" with respect to children who are biologically unrelated to their culturally defined "father." Even where a culture insists that descent must be based on actual biological fatherhood, domestic arrangements may make it difficult to identify the biological father. For these reasons, anthropologists distinguish between the culturally defined "father" and the *genitor*, the actual biological father. A similar distinction is necessary in the case of "mother." Although the culturally defined mother is usually the *genetrix*, the widespread practice of adoption also creates many discrepancies between emic and etic motherhood.

Theories of reproduction and heredity vary from culture to culture, "but so far as we know, no human society is without such a theory" (Scheffler 1973:749). Descent, then, is the belief that certain persons play an important role in the creation, birth, and nurturance of certain children. As Daniel Craig (1979) has suggested, descent implies the preservation of some aspect of the substance or spirit of people in future generations and thus is a symbolic form of immortality. Perhaps that is why parentage and descent are universally believed in.

In Western folk traditions, married pairs are linked to children on the basis of the belief that male and female make equally important contributions to the child's being. The male's semen is regarded as analogous to seed, and the woman's womb is analogous to the field in which the seed is planted. Blood, the most important life-sustaining and life-defining fluid, supposedly varies according to parentage. Each child's body is thought of as being filled with blood ob-

*British social anthropologists restrict the term "descent" to relationships extending over more than two generations and use "filiation" to denote descent relationships within the nuclear family (Fortes 1969).

tained from mother and father. As a result of this imagery, "blood relatives" are distinguished from relatives who are linked only through marriage. This led nineteenth-century anthropologists to use the ethnocentric term *consanguine* (of the same blood) to denote relations of descent.

Descent need not depend upon the idea of blood inheritance, nor need it involve equal contributions from both father and mother. The Ashanti, for example, believe that blood is contributed only by the mother and that it determines only a child's physical characteristics. The Ashanti believe that a child's spiritual disposition and temperament is the product of the father's semen. The Alorese of Indonesia believe that the child is formed by a mixture of seminal and menstrual fluids, which accumulate for 2 months before beginning to solidify. Many other cultures share this idea of a slow growth of fetus as a result of repeated additions of semen during pregnancy. For the polyandrous Tamil of the Malabar Coast of India, the semen of several different males is believed to contribute to the growth of the same fetus. The Eskimo believe that pregnancy results when a spirit child climbs up a woman's bootstraps and is nourished by semen. The Trobrianders profess a famous dogma denying any procreative role to the semen. Here also, a woman becomes pregnant when a spirit child climbs into her vagina. The only physical function of the Trobriand male is to widen the passageway into the womb. The Trobriand "father," nonetheless, has an essential social role, since no self-respecting spirit child would climb into a Trobriand girl who was not married.

A similar denial of the male's procreative role occurs throughout Australia; among the Murngin, for example, there was the belief that the spirit children live deep below the surface of certain sacred waterholes. For conception to take place, one of these spirits appears in the future father's dreams. In the dream the spirit child introduces itself and asks its father to point out the woman who is to become its mother. Later, when this woman passes near the sacred waterhole, the spirit child swims out in the form of a fish and enters her womb.

Despite the many different kinds of theories about the nature of procreative roles, there is worldwide acknowledgment of some special contributory action linking both husband and wife to the reproductive process, although they may be linked quite unevenly and with vastly different expectations concerning rights and obligations.

DESCENT RULES

By reckoning descent relationships, individuals are apportioned different duties, rights, and privileges with respect to other people and with regard to many different aspects of social life. A person's name, family, residence, rank, property, and basic ethnic and national status may all depend on such *ascriptions* through descent independent of any *achievements* other than getting born and staying alive. (Ascribed statuses and achieved statuses are found in all cultures.)

Anthropologists distinguish two great classes of descent rules: the *cognatic* and the *unilineal*. *Cognatic descent rules* are those in which both male and female parentage are used to establish any of the above-mentioned duties, rights, and privileges. Unilineal descent rules restrict parental links exclusively to males or exclusively to females (Fig. 14.1). The most common form of cognatic rule is *bilateral descent*, the reckoning of kinship evenly and symmetrically along maternal and paternal lines in ascending and descending generations through individuals of both sexes (Fig. 14.2).

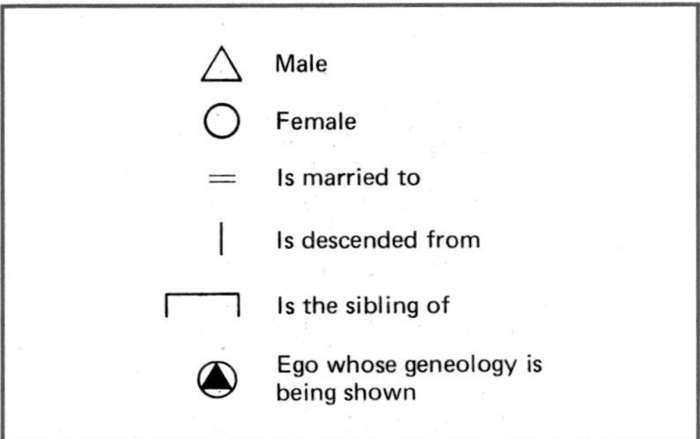

Figure 14.1 *HOW TO READ KINSHIP DIAGRAMS*

The second main variety of cognatic rule is called *ambilineal* descent (Fig. 14.3). Here the descent lines traced by *ego** ignore the sex of the parental links, but the lines do not lead in all directions evenly. As in bilateral descent, ego traces descent through males and females, but the line twists back and forth, including some female ancestors or descendants but excluding others and including some male ancestors and descendants and excluding others. In other words, ego does not reckon descent simultaneously and equally through mothers, fathers, and grandparents.

There are also two main varieties of unilineal descent: *patrilineality* and *matrilineality*. When descent is reckoned patrilineally, ego follows the ascending and descending genealogical lines through males only (Fig. 14.4). Note that this does not mean that the descent-related individuals are only males; in each generation there are relatives of both sexes. However, in the passage from one generation to another only the male links are relevant; children of females are dropped from the descent reckoning.

When descent is reckoned matrilineally, ego follows the ascending and descending lines through females only (Fig. 14.5). Once again, it should be noted that males as well as females can be related matrilineally; it is only in the passage from one generation to another that the children of males are dropped from the descent reckoning.

One of the most important logical consequences of unilineal descent is that it segregates the children of siblings of the opposite sex into distinct categories. This effect is especially important in the case of cousins. Note that with patrilineal descent, ego's father's sister's son and daughter do not share common descent with ego, whereas ego's father's brother's son and daughter do share

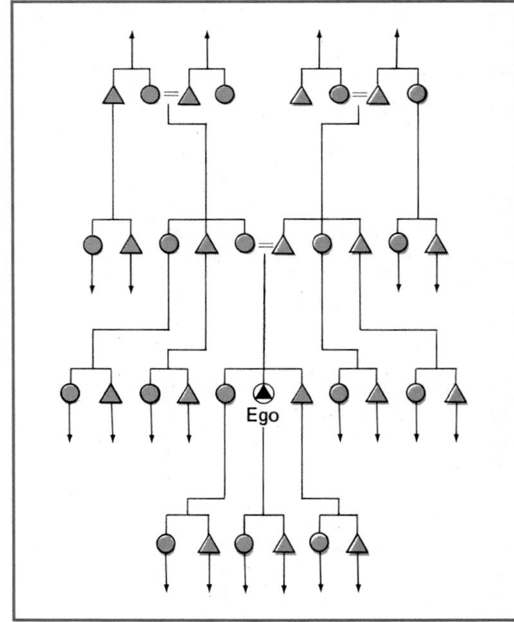

Figure 14.2 *BILATERAL DESCENT* Everyone on the diagram has a descent relationship with ego.

*Anthropologists employ the word *ego* to denote the individual from whose point of view kinship relations are being reckoned. It is sometimes necessary to state whether the reference person is a male ego or a female ego.

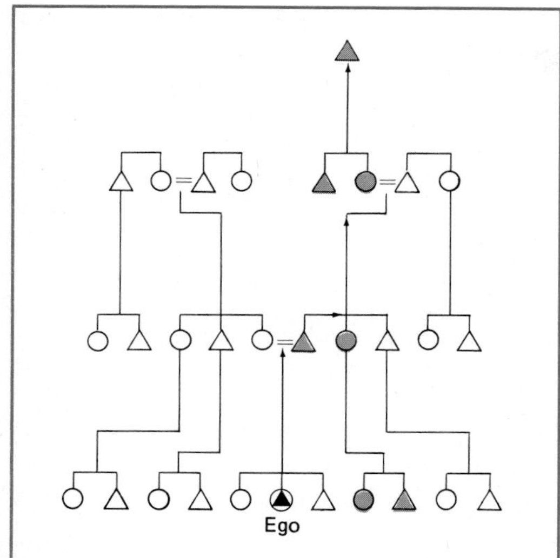

Figure 14.3 *AMBILINEAL DESCENT*
Ego traces descent through both males and females, but not equally and not simultaneously.

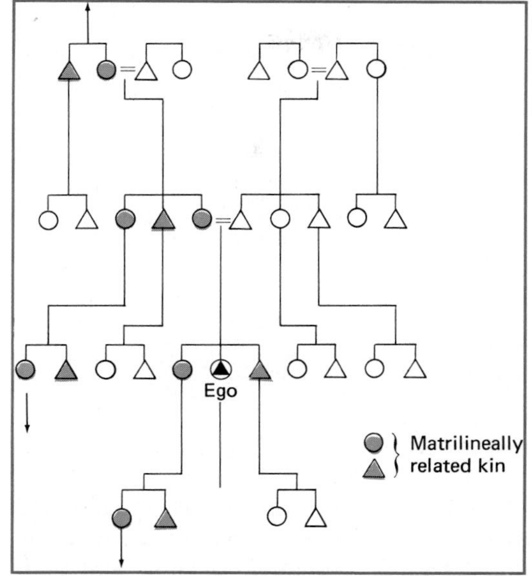

Figure 14.5 *MATRILINEAL DESCENT*
Descent is traced exclusively through females.

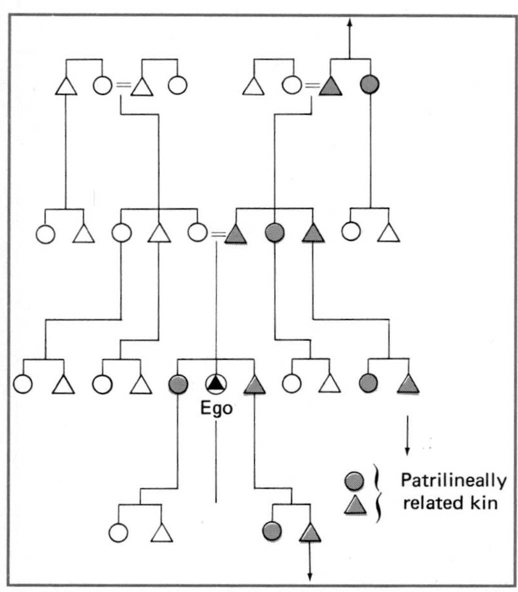

Figure 14.4 *PATRILINEAL DESCENT*
Descent is traced exclusively through males.

common descent with ego. In the case of matrilineal descent, the same kind of distinction results with respect to ego's "cousins" on the mother's side. Children whose parents are related to each other as brother and sister are known as *cross cousins;* children whose parents are related to each other as brother and brother, or sister and sister, are known as *parallel cousins* (Fig. 14.6).

Anthropologists distinguish an additional variety of descent rule, called *double descent,* in which ego simultaneously reckons descent matrilineally through mother and patrilineally through father. This differs from unilineal descent, in which descent is reckoned only through males or only through females but not both together.

Many other combinations of these descent rules may also occur. In all cultures, for example, there is some degree of bilat-

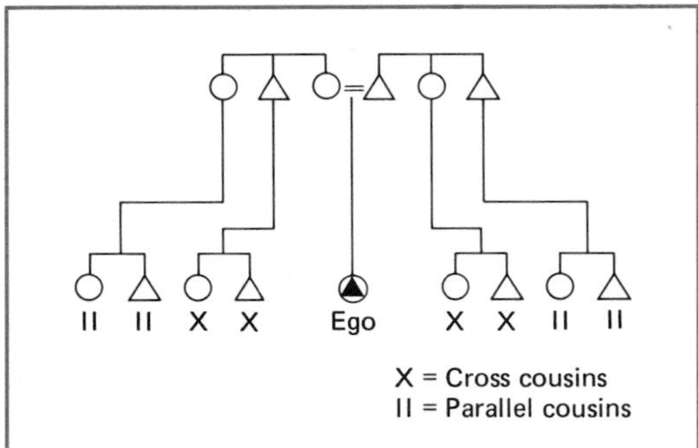

Figure 14.6 *CROSS COUSINS AND PARALLEL COUSINS*

eral descent in the reckoning of rights and obligations. If a society observes patrilineal descent in the grouping of people into land-owning domestic groups, this does not mean that ego and mother's brother's daughter do not regard each other as having special rights and obligations. Modern Euramerican culture is strongly bilateral in kin group composition and inheritance of wealth and property; yet family names are *patronymic*—that is, they follow patrilineal descent lines. The point is that several varieties of descent may occur simultaneously within a given society if the descent rules are pertinent to different spheres of thought and behavior.

Each of the above descent rules provides the logical basis for mentally aligning people into emic kinship groups. These groups exert great influence on the way people think and behave in both domestic and extra-domestic situations. An important point to bear in mind about kinship groups is that they need not consist of coresident relatives; that is, they need not be domestic groups. We proceed now to a description of the principal varieties of such groups.

COGNATIC DESCENT GROUPS: BILATERAL VARIETY

Bilateral descent applied to an indefinitely wide span of kin and to an indefinite number of generations leads to the concept of groups known as *kindreds* (Fig. 14.7). When modern-day Americans and Europeans use the word "family"and have in mind more than just their nuclear families, they are referring to their kindreds. The main characteristic of the kindred is that the span and depth of bilateral reckoning is open-ended. Relatives within ego's kindred can be judged as "near" or "far" depending on the number of genealogical links that separate them, but there is no definite or uniform principle for making such judgments or for terminating

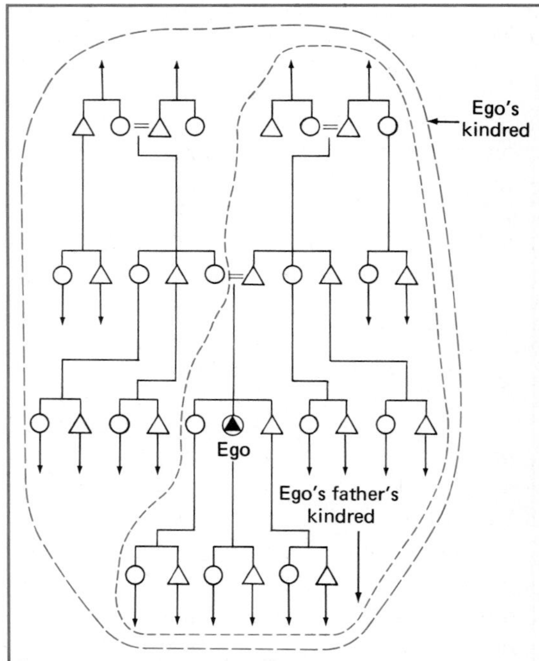

Figure 14.7 *KINDREDS*
Children have kindreds that are different from either parent's kindred.

the extension of the kinship circle. An important consequence of this feature, as shown in Figure 14.7, is that egos and their siblings are identified with a kindred whose membership cannot be the same for any other persons (except for ego's *double cousins*—cousins whose parents are two brothers who have exchanged sisters). This means that it is impossible for coresident domestic groups to consist of kindreds and very difficult for kindreds to maintain corporate interests in land and people.

COGNATIC DESCENT GROUPS: AMBILINEAL VARIETY

The open-ended, ego-centered characteristics of the bilateral kindred can be overcome by specifying one or more ancestors from whom descent is traced either through males and/or females. The resultant group logically has a membership that is the same regardless of which ego carries out the reckoning. This is the *cognatic lineage* (the terms *ramage* and *sept* are also used) (Fig. 14.8).

The cognatic lineage is based on the assumption that all members of the descent group are capable of specifying the precise genealogical links relating them to the lineage founder. A common alternative, as in the ambilineal "clans" of Scotland, is for the descent from the lineage founder to be *stipulated* rather than *demonstrated*. This can be done easily enough if the name of the founder gets passed on ambilineally over many generations. After a while many of the persons who carry the name will belong to the group simply by virtue of the name rather than because they can trace their genealogical relationship all the way back to the founding ancestor. An appropriate designation for such groups is *cognatic clan*. [In recent times, some members of Scots clans have different surnames as a result of patronymy and must demonstrate descent (Neville 1979).]

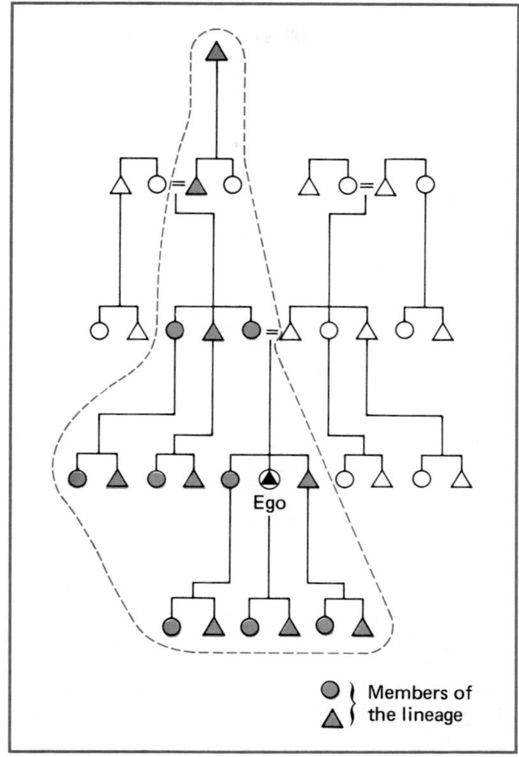

Figure 14.8 *COGNATIC LINEAGE*
Descent is traced to an apical ancestor through males and/or females.

UNILINEAL DESCENT GROUPS

When unilineal descent is systematically demonstrated with respect to a particular ancestor, the resultant kin group is called a *patrilineage* (Fig. 14.9) or a *matrilineage*. All lineages contain the same set of people regardless of the genealogical perspective from

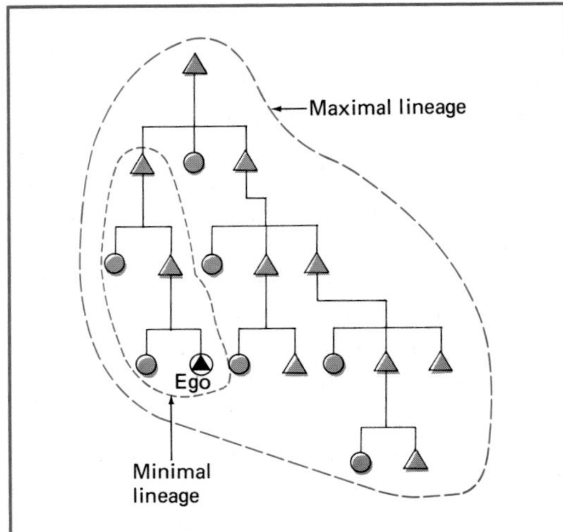

Figure 14.9 *PATRILINEAGES*
Everyone on the diagram belongs to the same maximal lineage.

which they are viewed. This makes them ideally suited to be coresident domestic groups and to hold joint interests in persons and property. Because of exogamy, however, both sexes cannot remain coresident beyond childhood. Some lineages include all the generations and collateral descendants of the first ancestor. These are *maximal* lineages. Sublineages that contain only three generations are *minimal* lineages (Fig. 14.9).

When unilineal descent from a specific ancestor is stipulated rather than demonstrated, the group that results is known as either a *patriclan* or a *matriclan* (the terms *patrisib* and *matrisib* are also in use). There are many borderline cases, however, in which it is difficult to decide whether one is dealing with a lineage or a clan. Just as lineages may contain lineages, clans may contain clans, which are usually called subclans. Finally, it should be noted that clans may also contain lineages.

POSTMARITAL LOCALITY PATTERNS

In order to understand the processes responsible for different varieties of domestic groups and different ideologies of descent, one additional aspect of domestic organization must be discussed. There is considerable agreement among anthropologists that an important determinant of descent rules is the pattern of residence after marriage. The principal postmarital locality practices are described in Table 14.1.

Postmarital residence practices influence descent rules because they determine who will enter, leave, or stay in a domestic group (Murdock 1949; Naroll 1973). They thus pro-

Table 14.1 PRINCIPAL VARIETIES OF POSTMARITAL RESIDENCE

Name of pattern	Place where married couple resides
Neolocality	Apart from either husband's or wife's kin
Bilocality	Alternately shifting from husband's kin to wife's kin
Ambilocality	Some couples with husband's kin, others with wife's kin
Patrilocality	With husband's father
Matrilocality	With wife's mother
Avunculocality	With husband's mother's brother
Amitalocality	With wife's father's sister (this pattern exists only as a theoretical possibility)
Uxorilocality	With the wife's kin (several of the above may be combined with uxorilocality)
Virilocality	With the husband's kin (several of the above may be combined with virilocality)

vide domestic groups with distinctive cores of relatives that correspond to the inclusions and exclusions produced by the movements of married couples. These movements themselves are influenced by the demographic, technological, economic, and ecological conditions in which people find themselves. Thus, in many societies descent rules and other kinship principles can be seen as organizing and justifying domestic group structures in relation to particular infrastructural conditions.

CAUSES OF BILATERAL DESCENT

Bilateral descent is associated with various combinations of neolocality, ambilocality, and bilocality. These locality practices in turn usually reflect a high degree of mobility and flexibility among nuclear families. Mobility and flexibility, as we have seen (Ch. 11), are useful for hunters and gatherers and are an intrinsic feature of band organization. The !Kung San, for example, are primarily bilateral, and this reflects in turn a predominant bilocal postmarital residence pattern. !Kung San camps contain a core of siblings of both sexes, plus their spouses and children and an assortment of more distant bilateral kin and affines. Each year, in addition to much short-time visiting, about 13 percent of the population makes a more or less permanent residential shift from one camp to another, and about 35 percent divide their time equally among two or three different camps (Lee 1979:54). This mobility and flexibility is advantageous for people who must rely on hunting and gathering for their livelihood.

North American bilaterality is associated with a similar flexibility and mobility of nuclear families. Bilaterality in this case reflects a neolocal pattern that is advantageous with respect to wage-labor opportunities and the substitution of price-market money exchanges for kinship-mediated forms of exchange. Whereas the !Kung San always live with relatives and depend on kindreds and extended families for their subsistence, North American nuclear families live apart from their kindreds. North American domestic groups consist predominantly of nuclear families that are geographically and socially isolated from both husband's and wife's relatives, except for rites of passage (see p. 442) and Christmas or Thanksgiving feasts.

DETERMINANTS OF COGNATIC LINEAGES AND CLANS

Cognatic lineages and cognatic clans are associated with *ambilocality*. This is a form of postmarital residence in which the married couple elects to stay on a relatively permanent basis with the wife's or the husband's domestic group. Ambilocality differs from the neolocality of the North American family, since residence is established with a definite group of kin. Ambilocality also differs from the bilocality of hunting and gathering bands in that the shifting from one domestic group to another occurs less frequently. This implies a relatively more sedentary form of village life and also a somewhat greater potential for developing exclusive "corporate" interests in people and property. Yet all cognatic descent groups, whether bilateral or ambilineal, have less potential for corporate unity than unilineal descent groups, a point to which we return in a moment.

One example of how cognatic lineages work has already been discussed. Such lineages occurred among the Pacific Northwest Coast potlatchers (see Ch. 12). The Kwakiutl potlatch chiefs sought to attract and to hold as large a labor force as they possibly could. The more people a village put to work during a salmon run, the more fish they would catch.

The core of each village consisted of a chieftain and his followers, usually demonstrably related to him through ambilineal descent and constituting a cognatic lineage known as a *numaym*. The chieftain claimed hereditary privileges and noble rank on the basis of ambilineal reckoning from his noble forebears. Validation of this status depended upon his ability to recruit and hold an adequate following in the face of competition from like-minded neighbor chieftains. The importance placed upon individual choice and the uncertainty surrounding the group's corporate estate is typical of cognatic lineages in other cultures as well.

DETERMINANTS OF UNILINEAL LINEAGES AND CLANS

Although there is no basis for reviving nineteenth-century notions of universal stages in the evolution of kinship (see p. 515), certain well-substantiated general evolutionary trends do exist. Hunting and gathering band societies tend to have cognatic descent groups and/or bilocal residence because their basic ecological adjustment demands that local groups remain open, flexible, and nonterritorial. With the development of horticulture and more settled village life, the identification between domestic groups or villages and definite territories increased and became more exclusive. Population density increased and warfare became more intense, for reasons to be discussed (Ch. 15), contributing to the need for emphasizing exclusive group unity and solidarity (Ember, Ember, and Pasternak 1974). Under these conditions, unilineal descent groups with well-defined localized membership cores, a heightened sense of solidarity, and an ideology of exclusive rights over resources and people become the predominant form of kinship group. Using a sample of 797 agricultural societies, Michael Harner (1970) has shown that a very powerful statistical association exists between an increased reliance on agriculture as opposed to hunting and gathering and the replacement of cognatic descent groups by unilineal descent groups.

This is not a one-way process, however. Reversion to cognatic forms can be expected if warfare is eliminated and/or population declines precipitously. Kwakiutl cognatic descent groups probably represent such reversions from formerly unilineal organizations. As will be recalled, the Kwakiutl population was decimated as a result of contagious diseases introduced by Euramerican and Russian traders. And the Canadian government suppressed the warfare characteristic of the early days of contact.

Horticultural village societies that are organized unilineally outnumber those that are organized cognatically, 380 to 111 in Harner's sample. Moreover, almost all the unilineal societies display signs of increased population pressure, as indicated by the depletion of wild plant and food resources.

Unilineal descent groups are closely associated with one or the other variety of unilocal residence: that is, patrilineality with patrilocality and matrilineality with matrilocality. In addition, there is a close correlation between avunculocality and matrilineality. With patrilineality, fathers, brothers, and sons form the core of the domestic group; and with matrilocality, mothers, sisters, and daughters form the core of the domestic group. The connections between these locality practices and descent rules should be clear, although the reason for the connection between avunculocality and matrilineality is more complex. With avunculocality, mother's brothers and sister's sons form the core of the domestic unit. Sister's son is born in her husband's mother's brother's household, but as a juvenile or adult, sister's son leaves this household and takes up residence with his own mother's brother (Fig 14.10). The way in which avunculocality works and the reason for its association with matrilineality will become clearer in a moment as we examine the infrastructural causes of matrilocality and patrilocality.

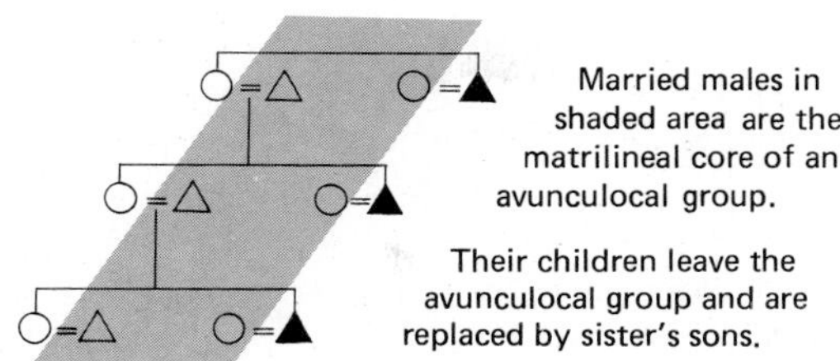

Figure 14.10 *AVUNCULOCALITY*

CAUSES OF PATRILOCALITY

The overwhelming majority of known societies has male-centered residence and descent patterns. Seventy-one percent of 1179 societies classified by George Murdock (1967) are either patrilocal or virilocal; and in the same sample, societies that have patrilineal kin groups outnumber societies that have matrilineal kin groups 558 to 164. Patrilocality and patrilineality are the statistically "normal" mode of domestic organization. They have been predominant not only, as was once thought, in societies that have plows and draft animals or that practice pastoral nomadism, but in simple horticultural and slash-and-burn societies as well (Divale 1974).

It is difficult to escape the conclusion that the underlying reason for the prevalence of patrilocality among village societies is that cooperation among males is more crucial than cooperation among females. Men are more effective in hand-to-hand combat than women, and women are less mobile than men during pregnancy and when nursing infants. As a consequence, men generally monopolize the weapons of war and the hunt, leading to male control over trade and politics. The practice of intense small-scale warfare between neighboring villages may be a crucial factor in promoting a widespread complex of male-centered and male-dominated institutions (see Ch. 24). By structuring domestic groups around a core of fathers, brothers, and sons, patrilocality facilitates military cooperation among males who have grown up together. It also avoids pitting fathers, sons, and brothers against each other in combat when one village attacks another (Divale and Harris 1976).

CAUSES OF MATRILOCALITY

It is generally agreed that matrilineal descent groups will not form independently—that is, in the absence of matrilineal neighbors—unless matrilocality is the postmarital residence practice. But why matrilocality? One theory holds that when women's role in food production became more important, as in horticultural societies, domestic groups would tend to be structured around a core of females. This theory, however, must be rejected, because there is no greater association between horticulture and matrilocality than between horticulture and patrilocality (Ember and Ember 1971; Divale 1974). Moreover, it is difficult to see why field labor would require a degree of cooperation so high that only women from the same domestic groups could carry it out efficiently, nor why it would require all brothers and sons to be expelled from the natal domestic group (see Burton et al. 1977; Sanday 1973; White et al. 1977).

The question that must be asked concerning the origin of matrilocality is this: What kinds of modifications in the male specialties of warfare, hunting, and trade would benefit from a shift to matrilocality? The most likely answer is that when warfare, hunting, and trade change from quick short-distance forays to long-distance expeditions lasting several months, matrilocality is more advantageous than patrilocality. When patrilocal males leave a village for extended periods, they leave behind their patrilineal kin group's corporate interests in property and people to be looked after solely by their wives. The allegiance of their wives, however, is to another patrilineal kin group. The local group's women are drawn from different kin groups and have little basis for cooperative activity when they are unsupervised by the male managers of the corporate domestic units into which they have married. There is no one home, so to speak, "to mind the store." Matrilocality solves this problem because it structures the domestic unit around a permanent core of resident mothers, daughters, and sisters who are trained in cooperative labor patterns from birth and who identify the "minding of the store" with their own material and sentimental interests. Thus, males reared in matrilocal domestic groups are less constrained to return to their villages and can remain on the trail or at sea for long periods.

The ability to launch and successfully complete long-distance expeditions implies that neighboring villages will not attack each other when the men are away. This is best assured by forming the expeditions around a core of males drawn from several neighboring villages or different households within a given village. Among patrilocal, patrilineal villages, the belligerent territorial teams consist of patrilineally related kin who constitute competitive "fraternal interest groups." These groups make shifting alliances with neighboring villages, exchange sisters, and raid each other. Most combat takes place between villages that are about a day's walk from each other. Matrilocal, matrilineal cultures, on the other hand, are bonded not by the exchange of women, but by the inmarrying of males from different domestic groups, and this prevents the formation of competitive and disruptive fraternal interest groups by scattering fathers and brothers into several different households in different villages.

Thus matrilocal, matrilineal societies like the Iroquois of New York and the Huron of Ontario enjoy a high degree of internal peace. But most matrilineal societies, like the Iroquois and the Huron, have a history of intense warfare directed outward against powerful enemies (Gramby 1977; Trigger 1978). The Nayar, for example, were a soldier caste in the service of the kings of Malabar. Among the matrilocal Mundurucu of the Amazon, conflict between villages was unheard of and interpersonal aggression was suppressed. But the Mundurucu launched raids against enemies hundreds of miles away, and unrelenting hostility and violence characterized their relations with the "outside world" (Murphy 1956).

An additional reason for the suppression of internal hostility among matrilocal groups is that matrilocality is incompatible with polygyny. The males who are in charge of the matrilineal estate are not interested in marrying several of their sisters to one male, and they themselves will not benefit from having many wives and children. Conflict over women, one of the major causes of war between neighboring villages, is thus reduced.

There remains the further question of why long-distance raiding-hunting-trading expeditions come to be important for some village societies and not others. The answer probably resides in increased population pressure brought about by intensification of production and depletion of local resources. Matrilineal, matrilocal societies tend to have larger villages and better-developed political institutions than patrilocal villages. We will return to this subject in Chapter 16.

CAUSES OF AVUNCULOCALITY

In matrilocal, matrilineal societies males are reluctant to relinquish control over their own sons to the members of their wives' kin groups, and they are not easily reconciled to the fact that it is their sons rather than their daughters who must move away from them at marriage. Because of this contradiction, matrilocal, matrilineal systems tend to revert to patrilocal, patrilineal systems as soon as the forces responsible for keeping males away from their natal village and domestic groups are removed or moderated.

One way to solve this contradiction is to loosen the male's marital obligations (already weak in matrilocal societies) to the point where he need not live with his wife at all. This is the path followed by the Nayar. As we have seen, Nayar men had no home other than their natal domestic unit; they were untroubled by what happened to their children—whom they were scarcely able to identify—and they had no difficulty keeping their sisters and their nephews and nieces under proper fraternal and avuncular control.

But the most common solution to the tension between male interests and matrilineality is the development of avunculocal patterns of residence. It is a remarkable fact that there are more matrilineal descent groups that are avunculocal than matrilineal descent groups that are matrilocal (Table 14.2).

Under avunculocality a male eventually goes to live with his mother's brothers in their matrilineal domestic unit. His wife will join him there. Upon maturity, a male ego's son will in turn depart for ego's wife's brother's domestic unit (ego's daughter, however, may remain resident if she marries her father's sister's son). Thus the core of an avunculocal domestic unit consists of a group of brothers and their sister's sons. The function of this arrangement seems to be to reinsert a male fraternal interest group as the residential core of the matrilineal descent group.

Avunculocality probably occurs so often because males continue to dominate the affairs of matrilineal groups when warfare has not been suppressed. This interpretation accords well with another remarkable fact: The logical opposite of avunculocality never occurs. The logical opposite of avunculocality is *amitalocality* (aunt-locality). Amitalocality would exist if brother's daughters and fa-

TABLE 14.2 RELATIONSHIP BETWEEN RESIDENCE AND DESCENT IN THE ETHNOGRAPHIC ATLAS

	Postmarital Residence				
Kin Groups	Matrilocal or uxorilocal	Avunculocal	Patrilocal or virilocal	Other	Total
Patrilineal	1	0	563	25	588
Matrilineal	53	62	30	19	164

SOURCE: Murdock 1967; Divale and Harris 1976.

ther's sisters constituted the core of a patrilineal domestic unit.* Women, however, have never been able to control patrilineal kin groups in the same way men have been able to control matrilineal kin groups. Hence males, not females, constitute the resident core of virtually all patrilineal kin groups as well as most of the known cases of matrilineal kin groups.

A rather thin line separates avunculocality from patrilocality. If the resident group of brothers decides to permit one or more of its sons to remain with them after marriage, the residential core will begin to resemble an ambilocal domestic group. If more sons than nephews are retained in residence, the locality basis for a reassertion of patrilineal descent will be present.

After a society has adopted matrilocality and developed matrilineal descent groups, changes in the original conditions may lead to a restoration of the patrilocal, patrilineal pattern. At any given moment many societies are probably in a transitional state between one form of residence and another and one form of kinship ideology and another. Since the changes in residence and descent may not proceed in perfect tandem at any given moment—that is, descent changes may lag behind residence changes—one should expect to encounter combinations of residence with the "wrong" descent rule. For example, a few patrilocal societies and quite a large number of virilocal societies have matrilineal descent, and one or two uxorilocal societies have patrilineal descent (see Table 14.2). But there is evidence for a very powerful strain toward consistency in the alignment between domestic groups, their ecological, military and economic adaptations, and their ideologies of descent.

*If patrilocal, patrilineal descent groups practice matrilaterāl cross cousin marriage, they will contain male ego's paternal aunts. But these women will not constitute the "core" of the domestic unit, since it is they and not their husbands who depart from their natal domicile to reside with their spouse (countra Ottenheimer 1984).

KINSHIP TERMINOLOGIES

Another aspect of domestic ideology that participates in the same strain toward functional consistency is kinship terminology. Every culture has a special set of terms for designating types of kin. The terms plus the rules for using them constitute a culture's *kin terminological system.*

Lewis Henry Morgan was the first anthropologist to realize that despite the thousands of different languages over the face of the globe and despite the immense number of different kinship terms in these languages, there is only a handful of basic types of kin terminological systems. These systems can best be defined by the way in which terms are applied to an abbreviated genealogical grid consisting of two generations, including ego's siblings of the same and opposite sex and ego's cross and parallel cousins. Here we will examine only three of the best-known systems in order to illustrate the nature of the causal and functional relationships that link alternative kinship terminologies to the other aspects of domestic organizations. (It should be emphasized that these are basic terminological *types*. Actual instances often vary in details.)

Eskimo Terminology

The kind of kin terminological systems with which North Americans are most familiar is known as Eskimo, shown in Figure 14.11. Two important features of this system are these: First, none of the terms applied to ego's nuclear relatives—1, 2, 6, 5—is applied outside the nuclear family; and second, there is no distinction between maternal and paternal sides. This means that

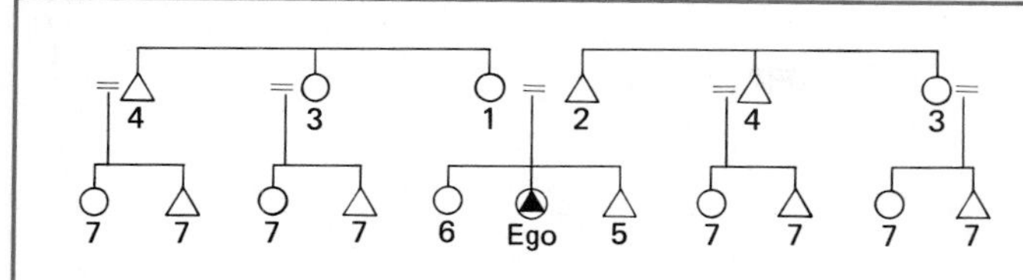

Figure 14.11 *ESKIMO TERMINOLOGY*

there is no distinction between cross and parallel cousins or between cross and parallel aunts or uncles. These features reflect the fact that societies using Eskimo terminology generally lack corporate descent groups. In the absence of such groups, the nuclear family tends to stand out as a separate and functionally dominant productive and reproductive unit. For this reason, its members are given a terminological identity separate from all other kin types. On the other hand, the lumping of all cousins under a single term (7) reflects the strength of bilateral as opposed to unilineal descent. The influence of bilateral descent is also reflected in the failure to distinguish terminologically between aunts and uncles on the mother's side as compared with aunts and uncles on the father's side. The theoretical predictions concerning Eskimo terminology are strongly confirmed by the tabulations of Murdock's *Ethnographic Atlas* (1967). Of the 71 societies having Eskimo terminology, only 4 have large extended families and only 13 have unilineal descent groups. In 54 of the 71 Eskimo terminology societies, descent groups are entirely absent or are represented only by kindreds.

Eskimo is the terminological system of modern North America. But as the name "Eskimo" implies, the same pattern is frequently found among hunters and gatherers. The reason is that any factors which isolate the nuclear family increase the probability that an Eskimo terminology will occur. As we have seen, among hunting and gathering groups, the determining factors are low population densities and the need for maximum geographical mobility in relationship to fluctuations in the availability of game and other resources. In the United States and Canada the same terminological pattern reflects the intrusion of price-market institutions into the domestic routine and the high level of wage-induced social and geographic mobility.

Hawaiian Terminology

Another common kin terminological system is known as Hawaiian. This is the easiest system to portray, since it has the least number of terms (Fig. 14.12). In some versions even the distinction between the sexes is dropped, leaving one term for the members of ego's generation and another for the members of ego's parents' generation. The most remarkable feature of Hawaiian terminology, as compared with Eskimo, is the application of the same terms to people inside and outside the nuclear family. Hawaiian is thus compatible with situations where the nuclear family is submerged within a domestic context dominated by extended families and other corporate descent groups. In Murdock's *Ethnographic Atlas*, 21 percent of the Hawaiian terminology societies do indeed have large extended families. In addition, well over 50 percent of Hawaiian terminology societies have some form of corporate descent group other than extended families.

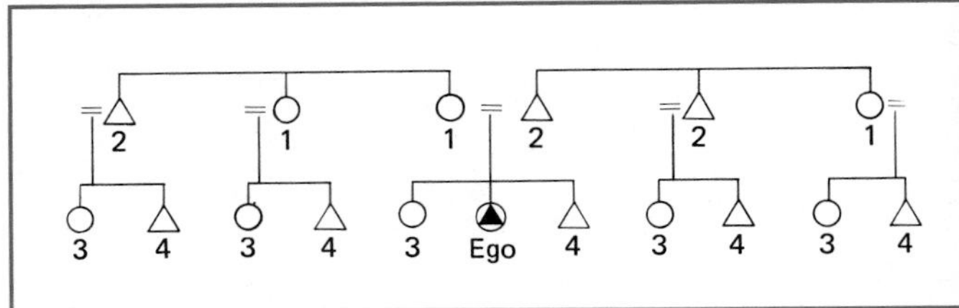

Figure 14.12 *HAWAIIAN TERMINOLOGY*

Theoretically, most of these descent groups should be cognatic rather than unilineal. The reason for this prediction is that the merging of relatives on the maternal side with those on the paternal side indicates an indifference toward unilineality, and an indifference toward unilineality is logically consistent with ambilineal or bilateral descent.

Data from Murdock's ethnographic sample only partially support this prediction: There are, indeed, many more Hawaiian terminology societies that have cognatic as opposed to unilineal descent. But there are many exceptions for which as yet no generally accepted explanation is available.

Iroquois Terminology

In the presence of unilineal kin groups, there is a worldwide tendency to distinguish parallel from cross cousins, as previously noted. This pattern is widely associated with a similar distinction in the first ascending generation, whereby father's brothers are distinguished from mother's brothers and father's sisters are distinguished from mother's sisters.

An Iroquois terminology exists where—in addition to these distinctions between cross and parallel cousins and cross and parallel aunts and uncles—mother's sister is terminologically merged with mother, father's brother is terminologically merged with father, and parallel cousins are terminologically merged with ego's brothers and sisters (Fig. 14.13).

This pattern of merging occurs in large part as a result of the shared membership of siblings in corporate unilineal descent groups and of the marriage alliances based on cross-cousin marriage between such groups. In Murdock's ethnographic sample there are 166 societies having Iroquois terminology. Of these, 119 have some form of unilineal descent group (70 percent).

We have only skimmed the surface of a few of the many fascinating and important problems in the field of kinship terminology (see box). But perhaps enough has been said to establish at least one point: Kin terminological systems possess a remarkable logical coherence. Yet like so many other aspects of culture, kin terminological systems are never the planned product of any inventive genius. Most people are unaware that such systems even exist. Clearly, the major features of these systems represent recurrent unconscious adjustments to the prevailing conditions of domestic life. Yet there are many details of kin terminologies, as well as of other kinship phenomena, that are as yet not well understood.

SUMMARY

To study kinship is to study the ideologies that justify and normalize the corporate structure of domestic groups. The basis of kinship is the tracing of relationships

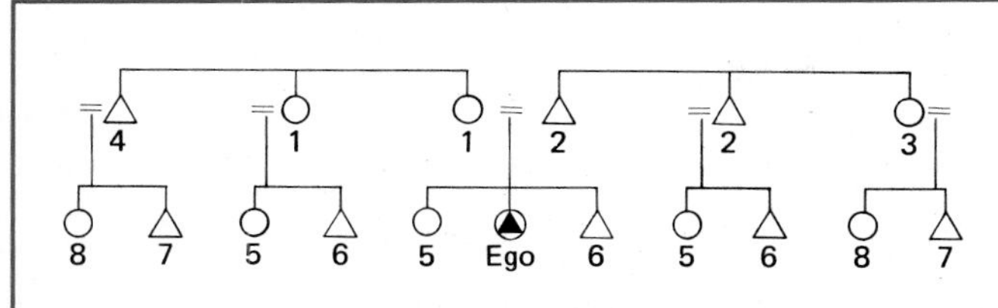

Figure 14.13 *IROQUOIS TERMINOLOGY*

FOR THE KINSHIP ENTHUSIAST: CROW TERMINOLOGY, MALE EGO

Many cultures have terminological systems in which the influence of lineality overwhelms generation criteria. These systems occur in both matrilineal and patrilineal versions. The matrilineal variety is known as Crow. These Crow systems involve the distinction between patrilateral and matrilateral cross cousins. Such "cousins" are not only distinguished from each other, but the patrilateral cross cousins are equated with father's sister, and father. There is also the curious fact that the matrilateral cross cousins are equated with ego's daughter and son.

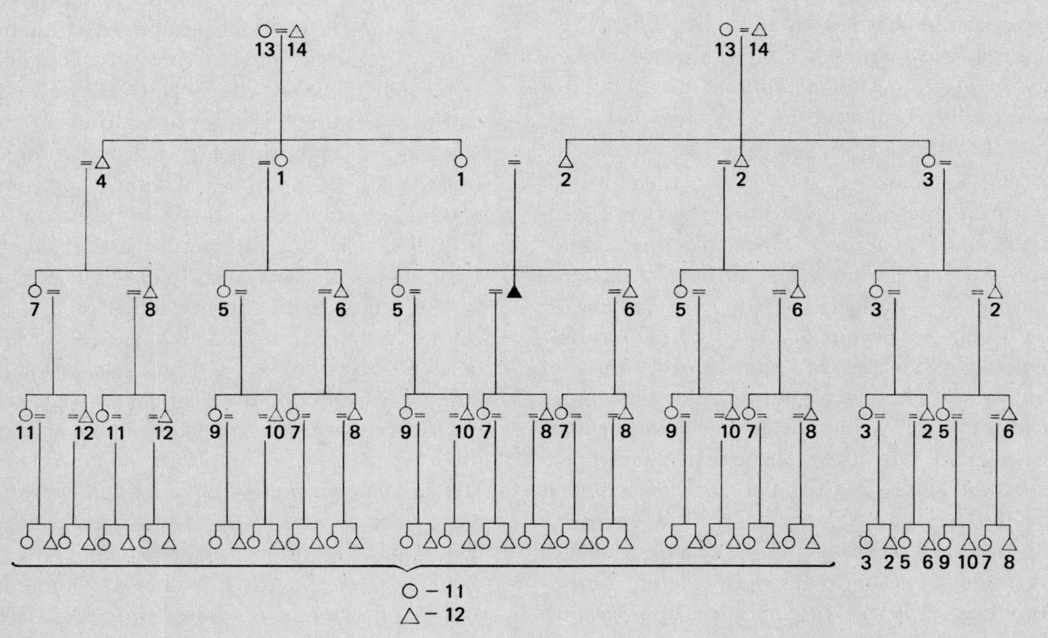

through marriage and descent. Descent is the belief that certain persons play a special ascribed role in the conception, birth, or nurturance of certain children. Many different folk theories of descent exist, none of which corresponds precisely to modern-day scientific understandings of procreation and reproduction.

The principal varieties of cognatic descent rules are the bilateral and the ambilineal; these are associated, respectively, with kindreds on the one hand, and with cognatic lineages and clans on the other. The principal varieties of unilineal descent are matrilineality and patrilineality. These are associated, respectively, with patri- and matrilineages or patri- and matriclans.

An important key to the understanding of alternative modes of descent and domestic organization is the pattern of postmarital residence. Bilateral descent and bilateral descent groups are associated with neolocality, bilocality, and ambilocality. More specifically, the flexible and mobile forms of band organization are facilitated by bilocality, whereas the greater isolation of nuclear familes in price-market economies gives rise to neolocality. Cognatic lineages and clans, on the other hand, give functional expression to ambilocality.

Unilineal domestic groups reflect unilocal patterns of residence. These in turn imply well-defined membership cores and an emphasis upon exclusive rights over resources and people. There is a strong correlation between patrilocality and patrilineality on the one hand, and between matrilineality, matrilocality, and avunculocality on the other. Patrilocal and patrilineal groups are far more common than matrilineal or avunculocal groups. A reason for this is that warfare, hunting, and trading activities among village societies are monopolized by males. These activities, in turn, are facilitated by stressing the coresidence of fathers, brothers, and sons and the formation of fraternal interest groups. Under conditions of increasing population density and pressure on resources, local groups may find it adaptive to engage in long-distance war-trade-hunting expeditions. Such expeditions are facilitated by breaking up the fraternal interest groups and structuring domestic life around a core of mothers, sisters, and daughters or, in other words, by developing a matrilocal, matrilineal organization. Since males in matrilineal, matrilocal societies continue to dominate military and political institutions, they are inclined to reinject the patrilineal principle into domestic life and to moderate the effects of matrilocality on their control over their sons and daughters. This accounts for the fact that as many matrilineal societies are avunculocal as are matrilocal. Thus the principal function of alternative rules of descent may be described as the establishment and maintenance of networks of cooperative and interdependent kinspeople aggregated into ecologically effective and militarily secure domestic production and reproduction units. In order for such units to act effectively and reliably, they must share an organizational ideology that interprets and validates the structure of the group and the behavior of its members. This interpretation of kinship rules can also be applied to the principal varieties of kin terminological systems. Such systems tend to classify relatives in conformity with the major features of domestic organization, locality practices, and descent rules. Eskimo terminology, for example, is functionally associated with domestic organizations in which nuclear families tend to be mobile and isolated; Hawaiian terminology is functionally associated with cognatic lineages and cognatic clans; and Iroquois terminology, with its emphasis on the distinction between cross and parallel cousins, is functionally associated with unilinear descent groups.

15 LAW, ORDER, AND WAR IN EGALITARIAN SOCIETIES

In this chapter we continue our discussion of the structural level of sociocultural systems. The focus now shifts from the structure of domestic groups to the regulation of interpersonal relationships and the maintenance of political cohesion and law and order within and between band and village societies. Conflict resolution through warfare will be shown to be present in both band and village societies, and theories of why this should be the case will be presented.

LAW AND ORDER IN BAND AND VILLAGE SOCIETIES

People in every society have conflicting interests (Fig. 15.1). Even in band-level societies, old and young, sick and healthy, men and women do not want the same thing at the same time. Moreover, in every society people want something that others possess and are reluctant to give away. Every culture, therefore, must have structural provisions for resolving conflicts of interest in an orderly fashion and for preventing conflicts from escalating into disruptive confrontations. There are marked qualitative and quantitative differences, however, between the kinds of conflicting interests found in band and village societies and those found in more complex societies. There are also marked differences in the methods employed to prevent disruptive confrontations.

The enormous apparatus of "law and order" associated with modern life is absent among village- and band-level cultures. Yet there is no "war of all against all." The Eskimo, the !Kung San of the Kalahari, the native Australians, and many other band and village peoples enjoy a high degree of personal security without having any rulers or law-and-order specialists. They have no kings, queens, dictators, presidents, governors, or mayors; police forces, soldiers, sailors, or marines; CIA, FBI, treasury agents, or federal marshals. They have no written law codes and no formal law courts; no lawyers, bailiffs, judges, district attorneys, juries, or court clerks; and no patrol cars, paddy wagons, jails, or penitentiaries. How do band and village peoples get along without these law enforcement specialists and facilities, and why are modern societies so dependent on them?

The basic reasons for these differences are to be found in (1) the small size of band and village societies; (2) the central importance of domestic groups and kinship in their social organization; and (3) the absence of marked inequalities in access to technology and resources. Small size means that everyone knows everyone else personally. Therefore, stingy, aggressive, and disruptive individuals can be identified by the group and exposed to the pressure of public opinion. The centrality of domestic group and kinship relations means that reciprocity can be the chief mode of exchange and that the collective interests of the domestic unit can be recognized by all of its members. Finally, equality of access to technology and natural resources means that food and other forms of wealth cannot be withheld by a wealthy few while others endure shortages and hardships.

"PRIMITIVE COMMUNISM"

Among band-level societies, all adults usually have open access to the rivers, lakes, beaches, oceans; all the plants and animals; and the soil and the subsoil. Insofar as these

Figure 15.1 *YANOMAMO CLUB FIGHT*
Egalitarin peoples are not without problems of law and order.

are basic to the extraction of life-sustaining energy and materials, they are communal "property."

Anthropologists have reported the existence of nuclear families and even individual ownership of hunting-and-gathering territories among native American band-level societies in Canada. But subsequent research has shown that these ownership patterns were associated with the fur trade and that such patterns did not exist aboriginally (Speck 1915; Knight 1974; Leacock 1973). In other cases, reports of family territories fail to distinguish between ideological claims and actual behavior. The fact that a nuclear family regards a particular area as its "own" must be weighed against the conditions under which others can use the area and the consequences of trespass. If permission to use the area is always freely granted and if use without permission results merely in some muttering or name-calling, the modern concept of "ownership" may be the wrong concept to use.

Among the !Kung San, waterholes and hunting and gathering territories are emically "owned" by the core groups of particular bands. But since neighboring bands contain many intermarried kin, there is a great deal of sharing of access to resources as a result of mutual visiting. Neighbors who ask for permission to visit and exploit the resources of a particular camp are seldom refused. Even people who come from distant bands and who lack close kin ties with the hosts are usually given permission to stay, especially for short periods, since it is understood that the hosts may return the visit at some future date (Lee 1979:337).

The prevalence of communal ownership of land, however, does not mean that hunter-gatherer bands lack private property altogether. There is little support for the theory of "primitive communism," which holds that there was a universal stage in the development of culture marked by the complete absence of private property (Epstein 1968). Many material objects of band-level societies are effectively controlled ("owned") by specific individuals, especially items the user has produced. The members of even the most egalitarian societies usually believe that weapons, clothing, containers, ornaments, tools, and other "personal effects" ought not to be taken away or used without the consent of the "owner." However, the chance is remote that theft or misappropriation of such objects will lead to serious conflict.

First of all, the accumulation of material possessions is rigidly limited by the recurrent need to break camp and travel long distances on foot. In addition, most utilitarian items may be borrowed without difficulty when the owner is not using them. If there are not enough such items to go around (arrows, nets, bark, or gourd containers), easy access to the raw materials and mastery of the requisite skills provide the have-nots with the chance of making their own. Moreover, among societies having no more than a few hundred people, thieves cannot be anonymous. If stealing becomes habitual, a coalition of the injured parties will eventually take action. If you want something, better to ask for it openly. Most such requests are readily obliged, since reciprocity is the prevailing mode of exchange. Finally, it should be pointed out that, contrary to the experience of the successful modern bank robber, no one can make a living from stealing bows and arrows or feather headdresses, since there is no all-purpose medium of exchange nor any regular markets at which stolen goods can be redeemed for other valuables (see Ch. 12).

MOBILIZING PUBLIC OPINION: SONG DUELS

The most important requirement for the control of disputes in band and village societies is the temporary insulation of the disputants from the corporate response of their respective kin. As long as the disputants feel they have the backing of their kin, they will continue to press their claims and counterclaims. The members of kin groups, however, never react mechanically. They are eager not to be caught in a situation in which they are opposed by a majority of people in the band or village. Public opinion, in other words, influences the support disputants can expect from their kin. Because of the importance of aligning potential kin group supporters with the drift of public opinion, band and village concepts of justice seem peculiar to Westerners. What matters is not so much who is morally right or wrong, or who is lying or telling the truth; the important thing is to mobilize public opinion on one side or the other decisively enough to prevent the outbreak of large-scale feuding.

A classic example of how such mobilization can be achieved independently of abstract principles of justice is the song contest of central and eastern Eskimo (Fig. 15.2). Here it frequently happens that one man claims another man has stolen his wife. The counterclaim is that she was not stolen but left voluntarily because her husband "was not man enough" to take good care of her. The issue is settled at a large public meeting that might be likened to a court. But no testimony is taken in support of either of the two versions of why the wife has left her husband. Instead, the "disputants" take turns singing insulting songs at each other. The "court" responds to each performance with differential degrees of laughter. Eventually one of the singers gets flustered, and the hooting and hollering raised against him becomes total—even his relatives have a hard time not laughing.

Something was whispered
Of a man and wife
Who could not agree
And what was it all about?
A wife who in rightful anger
Tore her husband's furs,
Took their boat
And rowed away with her son.
Ay-ay, all who listen,

Figure 15.2 *SONG CONTEST*
Eskimo "disputants" in "court" in eastern Greenland.

What do you think of him
Who is great in his anger
But faint in strength,
Blubbering helplessly?

He got what he deserved
Though it was he who proudly
Started this quarrel with stupid words.
(Rasmussen 1929:231–232).

The Eskimo have no police military specialists to see to it that the "decision" is enforced. Yet chances are that the man who has lost the song duel will give in, since he can no longer count on anyone to back him up if he chooses to escalate the dispute. Nonetheless, the defeated man may choose to go it alone.

Wife stealing does occasionally lead to murder. When this happens, the man who has lost public support may survive on the strength of his own vigilance and fighting skill. He will probably have to kill again, however, and with each transgression the coalition against him becomes larger and more determined, until finally he falls victim to an ambush.

MOBILIZING PUBLIC OPINION: WITCHCRAFT ACCUSATIONS

Among egalitarian band and village societies, part-time magico-religious specialists known as *shamans* frequently play an important role in mobilizing public opinion and in eliminating persistent sources of conflict. Most cultures reject the idea that misfortune can result from natural causes. If animals suddenly become scarce or if several people fall sick, it is assumed that somebody is practicing witchcraft. It is the shaman's job to identify the culprit. Normally this is done through the art of *divination* or clairvoyance. Putting themselves into trances with the aid of drugs, tobacco smoke, or monotonous drumming, shamans discover the name of the culprit. The people demand vengeance, and the culprit is ambushed or murdered.

It might be thought that this sequence of events would lead to more rather than less internal conflict. Even if the accused had actually been practicing witchcraft, the consequences of this form of symbolic aggression would seem to be considerably less disruptive than those resulting from actual murder. (The mechanisms responsible for death by witchcraft will be discussed in Ch. 22.) But the chances are that the murdered individuals never even attempted to carry out the witchcraft of which they were accused, or indeed any witchcraft at all! In other words, the witches are probably wholly "innocent" of the crime with which they have been charged. Nonetheless, the shaman's witchcraft accusations usually conserve rather then destroy the group's feeling of unity.

Consider the case reported by Gertrude Dole (1966) for the Kuikuru—an egalitarian, village-dwelling group of Brazilian Indians. Lightning had set fire to two houses. The shaman went into a trance and discovered that the lightning had been sent by a man who had left the village some years previously and had never returned. This man had only one male relative, who was also no longer living in the village. Before the accused witch had left the village, he had become engaged to a young girl. The shaman's brother had persuaded the girl's mother to break the betrothal and to permit him to marry the girl.

During the course of the divining ceremony, the shaman carried on dialogues with various interested members of the community. When he finally disclosed the identity of the culprit, it created considerable anxiety. One after another, several individuals stood apart in the plaza and spoke in long monologues. . . . In the heat of the excitement, the shaman's brother left with a few companions to kill the man suspected of witchcraft (1966:76).

The ethnographer points out that among the Kuikuru a change of residence from one village to another usually indicates that there is trouble brewing and that, in effect, the individual has been ostracized. (The Kuikuru suspected Dole and her anthropologist husband of having been "kicked out" of their own society.) Thus the man accused of sorcery was not a randomly chosen figure but one who fulfilled several well-defined criteria: (1) a history of disputes and quarrels within the village; (2) a motivation for continuing to do harm (the broken engagement); and (3) weak kinship backing.

Thus the shaman's accusation was not based on a spur-of-the-moment decision; there had been a long incubation period during which the shaman in or out of trance sounded out his fellow villagers on their attitude toward the accused. As Dole indicates, the supernatural authority of the shaman allows him to make public indictments. But shamans are not in control, as in late-night movie versions of the sinister medicine man turning the "natives" against the friendly European explorers. Rather, they are largely constrained by public opinion. Although the act of divination appears to put the onus of the judicial process on the shaman, clearly the shaman actually "deduces, formulates, and expresses the will of the people" (Dole 1966:76). Shamans abuse their supernatural gifts if they accuse people who are well liked and who enjoy strong kin group support. If they persist in making such mistakes, they themselves will be ostracized and eventually murdered.

The peculiar thing about witchcraft as a means of social control is that its practitioners, if they exist at all, can seldom be detected. The number of persons falsely accused of witchcraft probably far exceeds the number who are justly accused. It is clear, therefore, that nonpractice of witchcraft is no safeguard against an accusation of witchcraft. How then do you protect yourself from such false accusations? By acting in an amiable, open, generous manner; by avoiding quarrels; by doing everything possible not to lose the support of your kin groups. Thus the occasional killing of a supposed sorcerer results in much more than the mere elimination of a few actual or potential antisocial individuals. These violent incidents convince everyone of the importance of not being mistaken for an evildoer. As a result, as among the Kuikuru, people are made more amiable, cordial, generous, and willing to cooperate:

> The norm of being amiable deters individuals from accusing one another of delicts, hence in the absence of effective political or kin-group control, interpersonal relations have become a kind of game, in which almost the only restrictive rule is not to show hostility to one another for fear of being suspected of witchcraft (Dole 1966:74).

This system is not "fail-safe." Many cases are known of witchcraft systems that seem to have broken down, involving the community in a series of destructive retaliatory accusations and murders. These cases, however (especially in situations of intensive colonial contact, as in Africa and Melanesia), must be carefully related to the underlying conditions of communal life. In general, the incidence of witchcraft accusations varies with the amount of community dissension and frustration (Mair 1969; Nadel 1952). When a traditional culture is upset by exposure to new diseases, increased competition for land, and recruitment for wage labor, an epoch of increased dissension and frustration can be expected. This period will also be characterized by frenzied activity among those who are skilled in tracking down and exposing the malevolent effects of witches, as in the case of the breakup of feudal society in Europe and the great witch craze of the fifteenth to seventeenth centuries (Harris 1974).

HEADMANSHIP

To the extent that political leadership can be said to exist at all among band and village societies, it is exercised by headmen (or far less commonly, headwomen). The headman, unlike such specialists as king, president, or dictator, is a relatively powerless figure incapable of compelling obedience. He lacks sufficient force to do so. When he gives a command, he is never certain of being able to punish physically those who disobey. (Hence, if he wants to stay in "office," he gives few direct commands.) In contrast, the political power of rulers depends on their ability to expel or exterminate any readily foreseeable combination of nonconforming individuals and groups. Genuine rulers control access to basic resources and to the tools and weapons for hurting or killing people.

Among the Eskimo, leadership is especially diffuse, being closely related to success in hunting. A group will follow an outstanding hunter and defer to his opinion with respect to choice of hunting spots. But in all other matters, the "leader's" opinion carries no more weight than any other man's.

Similarly, among the !Kung San, each band has its recognized "leaders," most of whom are males. Such leaders may speak out more than others and are listened to with a bit more deference than is usual, but they "have no formal authority" and "can only persuade, but never enforce their will on others" (Lee 1979:333–334). When Richard Lee asked the !Kung San if they had "headmen" in the sense of a powerful chief, he was told: "Of course we have headmen! In fact we are all headmen . . . each one of us is headman over himself" (1979:348).

A similar pattern of leadership is reported for the Semai of Malaya. Despite recent attempts by outsiders to bolster up the power of Semai leaders, the headman is merely the most prestigious figure among a group of peers. In the words of Robert Dentan, who carried out fieldwork among these egalitarian shifting horticulturalists in 1962–1963:

> [The headman] keeps the peace by conciliation rather than coercion. He must be personally respected. . . . Otherwise people will drift away from him or gradually stop paying attention to him. Moreover, the Semai recognize only two or three occasions on which he can assert his authority: dealing as a representative of his people with a non-Semai; mediating a quarrel, if invited by the quarreling parties to do so but not otherwise; and . . . selecting and apportioning land for fields. Furthermore, most of the time a good headman gauges his general feeling about an issue and bases his decision on that, so that he is more a spokesman for public opinion than a molder of it (1968:68).

Somewhat confusingly, the term *chief* is often used to designate the kind of leadership embodied in the concept of headman. But the context usually clarifies the kind of leadership involved. For example, Claude Lévi-Strauss refers to the Nambikwara Indians of Brazil as having "chiefs." Yet he states:

> It should be said at once that the chief cannot seek support either in clearly defined powers or in publicly recognized authority. . . . One or two malcontents may throw the chief's whole programme out of joint. Should this happen, the chief has no powers of coercion. He can disembarrass himself of undesirable elements only in so far as all the others are of the same mind as himself (1963b:303).

Headmanship is likely to be a frustrating and irksome position. The cumulative impression given by descriptions of leadership among Brazilian Indian groups is that of an overzealous scoutmaster on an overnight cookout. The first one up in the morning, the headman tries to rouse his companions by standing in the middle of the village plaza and shouting. The headman seems to cajole, harangue, and plead from morning to night. If a task needs to be done, it is the headman who starts doing it; and it is the headman who works at it harder than anyone else. Moreover, not only must the headman set an example for hard work, but he must also set an example for generosity. After a fishing or hunting expedition, he is expected to give away more of the catch than anyone else; if trade goods are obtained, he must be careful not to keep the best pieces for himself.

Thomas Gregor, who studied the Mehinacu Indians of Brazil's Xingu National Park in 1967 (Fig. 15.3), describes the Mehinacu "chief" (i.e., headman) as follows:

The most significant qualifications for Mehinacu chieftainship are learned skills and personal attributes. The chief, for example, is expected to excel at public speaking. Each evening he should stand in the center of the plaza and exhort his fellow tribesmen to be good citizens. He must call upon them to work hard in their gardens, to take frequent baths, not to sleep during the day, not to be angry with each other, and not to have

Figure 15.3 *MEHINACU CHIEFTAINSHIP*
In front of the men's house the chief is redistributing presents given to him by the ethnographer.

sexual relations too frequently. . . . In addition to being a skilled orator, the chief is expected to be a generous man. This means that when he returns from a successful fishing trip, he will bring most of his catch out to the men's houses where it is cooked and shared by the men of the tribe. His wife must be generous, bringing manioc cakes and pepper to the men whenever they call for it. Further, the chief must be willing to part with possessions. When one of the men catches a harpy eagle, for example, the chief must buy it from him with a valuable shell belt in the name of the entire tribe. . . . A chief should also be a man who never becomes angry in public. . . . In his public speeches he should never criticize any of his fellow tribesmen, no matter how badly they may have affronted the chief or the tribe as a whole (Gregor 1969: 88–89).

It is pertinent at this point to recall the plight of the ungenerous Kapauku headman (Ch. 12). Even the most generous headman in good standing cannot force obedience to his decisions.

If the principals are not willing to comply, the authority [headman-chief] becomes emotional and starts to shout reproaches; he makes long speeches in which evidence, rules, decisions, and threats form inducements. Indeed, the authority may go as far as to start *wainai* (the mad dance), or change his tactics suddenly and weep bitterly about the misconduct of the defendant and the fact that he refuses to obey. Some native authorities are so skilled in the art of persuasion that they can produce genuine tears which almost always break the resistance of the unwilling party (Pospisil 1968:221).

One wonders if the Kapauku headman does not shed tears more because he is frustrated than because he is skilled.

BLOOD FEUD

The ever-present danger confronting band and village societies is that their kinship groups tend to react as units to real or alleged aggression against one of their members. In this way disputes involving individuals may escalate to include whole villages or groups of villages. The worst danger, of course, arises from disputes that lead to homicide. Among kinship-organized band and village peoples, there is intense adherence to the conviction that the only proper reaction to a murder is to kill the murderer or any convenient member of the murderer's kin group. Yet the absence of centralized political authority does not mean that blood feuds cannot be brought under control.

Among many decentralized societies, the formal mechanisms for preventing homicide from flaring into a protracted feud include the transference of substantial amounts of prized possessions from the slayer's kin group to the victim's kin group. This practice is especially common and effective among pastoral peoples whose animals are a concentrated form of material wealth and for whom bride-price is a regular aspect of kin group exogamy.

The prime ethnographic case is that of the Nuer, a pastoral and farming people who live amid the marshy grasslands of the Upper Nile in the Sudan. There is no doubt about the absence of centralized political leadership throughout Nuerland:

The lack of governmental organs among the Nuer, the absence of legal institutions of developed leadership, and generally, of organized political life is remarkable. . . . The ordered anarchy in which they live accords well with their character, for it is impossible to live among Nuer and conceive of rulers ruling over them. . . . The Nuer is a product of hard and egalitarian upbringing, is deeply democratic, and is easily roused to violence. This turbulent spirit finds any restraint irksome and no man recognizes a superior. Wealth makes no difference. A man with many cattle is envied but not treated differently from a man with few cattle. Birth makes no difference. . . . There is no master or servant in their society but only equals who regard themselves as God's noblest creation. . . . Among themselves even the suspicion of an order riles a man . . . he will not submit to any authority which clashes with his own interest and he does not consider himself bound to anyone. (Evans-Pritchard 1940:181–182)

Figure 15.4 *LEOPARD SKIN CHIEF*

The Nuer settle their feuds (or at least de-escalate them) by transferring 40 or more head of cattle to the victim's affines and kin. If a man has been killed, these animals will be used to "buy" a wife whose sons will fill the void left by his death. The dead man's closest kin are obliged to resist the offer of cattle, demanding instead a life for a life. However, more distant kin do their best to convince the others to accept the compensation. In this effort they are aided by certain semisacred arbitration specialists. The latter, known as leopard skin chiefs (Fig. 15.4), are usually men whose kin groups are not represented locally and hence who can more readily act as neutral intermediaries.

The leopard skin chief is the only one who can ritually cleanse a murderer. If a homicide takes place, the killer flees at once to the leopard skin chief 's house, which is a sanctuary respected by all Nuer. Nonetheless, the leopard skin chief lacks even the rudiments of political power; the most that he can do to the reluctant members of the slain man's relatives is to threaten them with various supernatural curses. Yet the determination to prevent a feud is so great that the injured relatives eventually accept the cattle as compensation (Verdon 1982).

NONKIN ASSOCIATIONS: SODALITIES

Although relations of affinity and descent dominate the political life of band and village peoples, nonkin forms of political organization also occur to a limited extent. Such groups are called *sodalities*. A common form of sodality is the exclusive men's or women's association or "club." These usually involve men and women drawn from different domestic groups who cooperate in secret ritual or craft performances. Age-grade associations are another common form of sodality, already mentioned with respect to the Masai warrior camps (p. 252). Among the Samburu, another group of East African pastoralists, all men initiated into manhood over a span of about 12 to 14 years comprised an age set whose members had a special feeling of solidarity that cut across domestic and lineage kin groups. The age-set members advanced as a group from junior to senior status. As juniors they were responsible for military combat and as seniors they were responsible for initiating and training the upcoming age sets (P. Spencer 1965; see Kertzer 1978).

A classic case of a sodality is the native North American military associations which developed on the Great Plains after the introduction of the horse. Among the Crow and the Cheyenne, these associations tried to outdo one another in acts of daring during combat and in horse-stealing expeditions. Although the members of each club did not fight as a unit, they met in their respective tepees to reminisce and sing about their exploits, and they wore distinctive insignia and clothing. Gretel and Perttie Pelto (1976:324) have aptly compared them to organizations like the Veterans of Foreign Wars and the American Legion because their main function was to celebrate military exploits and to uphold the honor and prestige of the "tribe." However, on the occasion of a long march to a new territory or large-scale collective hunts, the military clubs took turns supervising and policing the general population. For example, they prevented overeager hunters from stampeding the buffalo herds, and they suppressed rowdy behavior at ceremonials by fining or banishing disruptive individuals. But these were only seasonal functions, since it was only during the spring and summer that large numbers of unrelated people could congregate together at the same camp.

WARFARE AMONG HUNTERS AND GATHERERS

War is defined as armed combat between groups of people who constitute separate territoral teams or political communities (Otterbein 1973). Some anthropologists believe warfare was universally practiced, even among Paleolithic hunters and gatherers (Lizot 1979:151). Others hold that warfare was uncommon until the advent of state societies. It has been said that warfare was absent among the following hunter-gatherers: the Andaman Islanders, the Shoshoni, the Yahgan, the Mission Indians of California, and the Tasaday of the Philippines (Lesser 1968; MacLeish 1972). Even these groups, however, may have practiced warfare at some time in the past. On the other hand, William Divale (1972) lists 37 hunting-and-gathering cultures in which warfare is known to have been practiced. Some anthropologists attribute these cases to the shocks of contact with state-level colonial systems. Warfare was probably practiced by Paleolithic hunter-gatherers, but on a small scale and infrequently. Warfare probably increased in intensity during the Neolithic among village-organized farming cultures.

The archaeological evidence for warfare in the Paleolithic is inconclusive. Mutilated skulls found in Paleolithic caves have sometimes been interpreted as indicating prehistoric head-hunting and cannibalism. But no one really knows how the individuals died. Even if cannibalism was practiced, the cannibalized individuals were not necessarily enemies. For example, eating the brains of kin is a form of mortuary ritual. The earliest definite archeological evidence for warfare is found in Neolithic Jericho in the form of defensive walls, towers, and ditches (Roper 1969, 1975; Bigelow 1975).

After the development of permanent villages with large investments in crops, animals, and stored foods, the form of warfare changed. Among nonsedentary hunters and gatherers, warfare involved a higher degree of individualized combat directed toward the adjustment of real or imagined personal injuries and deprivations. Although the combat teams may have had a temporary territorial base, the organization of battle and the consequences of victory or defeat reflected the loose association between people and territory. The victors did not gain territory by routing their enemies. Warfare among village-dwelling cultivators, however, frequently involves a total team effort in which definite territories are fought over and in which defeat may result in the rout of a whole community from its fields, dwellings, and natural resources.

The slippery line between warfare and personal retribution among hunters and gatherers is well illustrated in the example of armed conflict among the Tiwi of Bathurst and Melville Islands, northern Australia (Fig. 15.5). As recounted by C. W. Hart and Arnold Pilling (1960), a number of men from the Tiklauila and Rangwila bands developed personal grievances against a number of men who were residing with the Mandiimbula band. The aggrieved individuals, together with their relatives, put on the white paint of war, armed themselves, and set off, some 30 members strong, to do battle with the Mandiimbula:

> On arrival at the place where the latter, duly warned of its approach, had gathered, the war party announced its presence. Both sides then exchanged a few insults and agreed to meet formally in an open space where there was plenty of room (1960:84).

During the night, individuals from both

Figure 15.5 *TIWI WARRIOR*
Tiwi man dressed in traditional dance body paint and feathers.

groups visited each other, renewing acquaintances. In the morning the two armies lined up at opposite sides of the battlefield. Hostilities were begun by elders shouting insults and accusations at particular individuals in the "enemy" ranks. Although some of the old men urged that a general attack be launched, their grievances turned out to be directed not at the Mandiimbula band, but at one or at most two or three individuals: "Hence when spears began to be thrown, they were thrown by individuals for reasons based on individual disputes" (ibid). Marksmanship was poor because it was the old men who did most of the spear-throwing.

> Not infrequently the person hit was some innocent noncombatant or one of the screaming old

women who weaved through the fighting men, yelling obscenities at everybody, and whose reflexes for dodging spears were not as fast as those of the men. . . . As soon as somebody was wounded . . . fighting stopped immediately until the implications of this new incident could be assessed by both sides (ibid).

Although hunters and gatherers seldom try to annihilate each other and often retire from the field after one or two casualties have occurred, the cumulative effect may be quite considerable. Remember that the average !Kung San band has only about 30 people in it. If such a band engages in war only twice per generation, and each time with the loss of only one adult male, casualties due to warfare would account for more than 10 percent of all adult male deaths. This is an extremely high figure when one realizes that less than 1 percent of all male deaths in Europe and the United States during the twentieth century have been battlefield casualties. In contrast, Lloyd Warner estimated that 28 percent of the adult male deaths among the Murngin, a hunting-and-gatherering culture of northern Australia, were due to battlefield casualties (Livingstone 1968).

WARFARE AMONG VILLAGE AGRICULTURALISTS

Although village peoples were not the first to practice warfare, they did expand the scale and ferocity of military engagements. Village houses, food-processing equipment, crops in the field, domestic animals, secondary-growth forests, and prime garden lands represent capital investments closely identified with the arduous labor inputs by specific groups of individuals. The defense of this investment laid the basis for the development of stable, exclusive territorial identities. Villages often oppose each other as traditional enemies, repeatedly attack and plunder each other, and often expropriate each other's territories. Archaeologically, the onset of territoriality is suggested by the practice of burying deceased villagers beneath the houses they occupied during life (Flannery 1972). Ethnologically, the intensification of local identities is suggested by the development of unilineal systems of reckoning descent. As we have seen (p. 280), the development of the concern with descent and inheritance is closely related to the degree to which agricultural populations cease to depend on hunting and gathering for their food supply.

Warfare among village cultivators is likely to be more costly in terms of battle casualties than among seminomadic hunters and gatherers. Among the Dani of West Irian, New Guinea, warfare has an open-field, ritualistic phase (which resembles the encounters described for the Tiwi) in which casualties are light. But there are also sneak attacks resulting in a hundred fatalities at a time and in the destruction and expulsion of whole villages. Karl G. Heider (1972) estimates that the Dani lost about 5 percent of their population per year to warfare and that 29 percent of the men and 3 percent of the women died as a result of battle injuries incurred primarily in raids and ambushes. Among the Yanomamo (Fig. 15.6) of Brazil and Venezuela, sneak raids and ambushes account for about 33 percent of adult male deaths from all causes and about 7 percent of adult female deaths from all causes (Chagnon 1974:160–161).

WARFARE AND THE REGULATION OF POPULATION GROWTH

It may seem obvious that since people kill each other in warfare, warfare restrains population growth. But the matter is not so sim-

Figure 15.6 *YANOMAMO WARRIORS*
Preparations for battle include body painting and "line-ups."

ple. War makers like the Yanomamo and Tsembaga Maring cannot control the growth of their population merely by killing each other at the rates reported above. The reason is that the individuals who are killed in battle are mostly males. Male deaths due to warfare among the Yanomamo have no long-run effect on the size of the population because, like most war-making preindustrial societies, the Yanomamo are polygynous. This means that any woman whose husband is killed is immediately remarried to another man. The reported female death rates from battle casualties is almost everywhere below 10 percent (see Polgar 1972:206), not enough to produce by itself a substantial lowering of population growth. Similar conclusions about the ineffectuality of combat deaths as a population control device have been reached with respect to warfare in industrial contexts. Catastrophes like World War II "have no effect on the population growth or size" (Livingstone 1968:5). This can be seen vividly in the case of Vietnam, where population continued to increase at a phenomenal 3 percent per year during the decade 1960 to 1970.

Among band and village peoples, however, warfare may achieve its major effect as a regulator of population growth through an indirect consequence. William Divale has shown that there is a strong correlation between the practice of warfare and high levels of female mortality in the age group from birth through 14 years (Divale and Harris 1976; see Hirschfeld et al. 1978; Divale et al. 1978). This is revealed by the ratio of males to females in the birth to 14-year age bracket among societies actively engaged in warfare when they were first censused (see Table 15.1).

It is generally accepted that slightly more boys than girls are born on a worldwide basis and that the average sex ratio at birth is about 105 males to 100 females. This imbalance, however, is much smaller than that found in the war-making societies. The discrepancy may be accounted for by a higher rate of death among female infants, children, and juveniles than among their male counterparts. This higher rate of female mortality probably reflects the practice of more female infanticide than male infanticide and the practice of various forms of neglect more often against young girls than against young boys. There is a strong correlation between societies which admit that they practice infanticide and those which were actively engaged in warfare when they were first censused; in these societies, at least, it is clear that female infanticide was more common than male infanticide.

Perhaps the reason for the killing and neglect of female children is that success in preindustrial warfare depends on the size of the male combat teams. When weapons are muscle-powered clubs, spears, and bows-and-arrows, victory will fall to the group that has the biggest and most aggressive males. Since there are ecological limits to the number of people who can be reared by band and village societies, war-making band and village societies tend to rear more males than females. This favoring of male over female children reduces the rate of growth of regional populations and, whether or not intended, may help to explain why warfare is so widely practiced by preindustrial peoples. According to this theory, slowing of regional population growth could not be achieved without warfare, since without the war-induced motivation to prefer male children to female children, each group would tend to reduce its postconception penalties, rear all its female children, and expand its population at its neighbor's expense. Warfare tends to equalize these costs or at least to spread them among all the bands and villages in the region in the form of both high rates of female mortality produced by infanticide and neglect and high rates of male mortality produced by combat. Although this system seems cruel and wasteful, the preindustrial alternatives for keeping population below the point of diminishing returns were equally if not more cruel and wasteful—abortion, malnutrition, and disease. The reader is warned that this theory remains highly controversial.

Table 15.1 SEX RATIOS AND WARFARE

	Young Males per 100 Females
Warfare present	128
Stopped 5–25 years before census	113
Stopped over 25 years before census	109

SOURCE: Divale and Harris 1976. Reproduced by permission of the American Anthropological Association from the *American Anthropologist* 78:527, 1976.

GAME ANIMALS AND WARFARE: THE YANOMAMO

The Yanomamo derive their main source of food calories with little effort from the plantains and banana trees that grow in their forest gardens. Like the Maring, they burn the forest to get these gardens started, but bananas and plantains are perennials that provide high yields per unit of labor input for many consecutive years. Since the Yanomamo live in the midst of the world's greatest tropical forest, the little burning they do scarcely threatens to "eat up the trees." A typical Yanomamo village has less than 100 people in it, a population that could easily grow enough bananas or plantains in nearby garden sites without ever having to move (Fig. 15.7). Yet the Yanomamo villages constantly break up into factions that move off into new territories.

It has been suggested that despite the apparent abundance of resources, the high level of Yanomamo warfare is caused by resource depletion and population pressure. The resource in question is meat. The Yanomamo lack domesticated sources of meat and must obtain their animal foods from hunting and collecting. Moreover, unlike many other inhabitants of the Amazon Basin, the Yanomamo traditionally did not have access to big river fish and other aquatic animals which elsewhere provided high-quality animal foods sufficient to supply villages that contained over 1000 people.

It is possible for human beings to remain healthy on diets which lack animal foods; however, meat, fish, and other animal products contain compact packages of proteins, fats, minerals, and vitamins which make them extremely valuable and efficient sources of nutrients.

Figure 15.7 *YANOMAMO VILLAGE*
This scene is more representative of everyday life among the Yanomamo, despite their warlike reputation. Note the plantains, the staple food of the Yanomamo, hanging from the rafters.

The theory relating meat to warfare among the Yanomamo is this: As Yanomamo villages grow, intensive hunting diminishes the availability of game nearby. Meat from large animals grows scarce and people eat more small animals, insects, and larva—the familiar broad-spectrum response (see p. 160). The point of diminishing returns is reached. Tensions within and between villages increases and this leads to villages breaking apart before they permanently deplete the animal resources. It also leads to the escalation of raiding, which disperses the Yanomamo villages over a wide territory, and this also protects vital resources by creating no-man's-lands, which function as game preserves (Harris 1984).

Some anthropologists with firsthand knowledge of the Yanomamo have rejected this theory. They point to the fact that there are no clinical signs of protein deficiencies among the Yanomamo. Also they have shown that in at least one village whose population is 35, daily per capita overall protein intake was 75 grams per day per adult, which is far higher than the minimum 35 grams recommended by the Food and Agricultural Organization. They have also shown that Yanomamo villages that have low levels of protein intake (36 grams) seem to engage in warfare just as frequently as those that have high protein intake (75 grams) per adult. Finally, they point out the other groups in the Amazon such as the Achuara enjoy as much as 107 grams of animal protein per capita and still go to war frequently (Chagnon and Hames 1979; Lizot 1977, 1979). Kenneth Good (1982), however, has shown that obtaining adequate supplies of meat is a constant preoccupation among the Yanomamo, and that meat is actually consumed only once or twice a week on the average. Good also points out that the efficiency of hunting declines in areas close to villages, necessitating frequent long distance hunts, some of which take the whole village on protracted treks.

Eric Ross (1979) also points out that the average daily amount of animal protein consumed is a misleading figure. Because of fluctuations in the number and size of animals captured there are actually many days during which there is little or no meat available. On days when a large animal such as a tapir is caught, the consumption rate may rise to 250 or more grams per adult; but for weeks at a time, the consumption rate may not rise above 30 grams per adult per day.

The absence of clinical signs of protein deficiency is not an argument against the theory, but rather supports the general point that band and village peoples can enjoy high standards of health as long as they control population growth (see Ch. 11) and that warfare protects the Yanomamo from diminishing returns and the effects of depletions. The fact that villages that have both high and low protein intake have the same level of warfare also does not test the theory because, as among the Maring and Mae Enga, warfare necessarily pits villages at different stages of growth against each other. Hence Yanomamo groups with little immediate ecological motivation to go to war may have no choice but to engage in counterraids against large groups that are depleting their game reserves and raiding their less populous neighbors in order to expand their hunting territory. The theory in question stresses that warfare is a regional phenomenon involving regional adjustments of population and resources.

The prepoderance of evidence strongly supports the view that Amazonian fauna are a fragile resource, readily depleted with consequent adverse costs and benefits and/or a decline in per capita meat consumption.

Michael Baksh (1982), for example, has

quantitatively documented the effect of the nucleation of despersed Machiguenga homesteads (see p. 219) into a village of 250 people in eastern Peru. Baksh concludes that faunal resources in the vicinity of the village "have been declining significantly in availability," that in "the attempt to maintain previous levels of intake men are working harder," that "there is more travel to distant hunting and fishing locations," and that "faunal resources are limited in availability and encourage the existence of small, mobile groups" (1982:12–13).

> Men frequently arrive home empty-handed, or perhaps with a few grubs, some wild fruits, palm nuts, or manufacturing materials. A successful day-long or overnight trip might yield a small monkey or a few birds. One tapir and six peccary were obtained . . . over a 17 month period (ibid.:13).

Michael Paolisso and Ross Sackett (1982:1) report "an extreme scarcity of high quality protein" among the (non-Amazonian) Yukpa of western Venezuela. Despite the fact that the Yukpa use shotguns for hunting (or because of it), daily animal protein consumption has fallen from some higher amount to a mere 4.8 to 11.3 grams per capita per day, as measured by different dietary and consumption methods (personal communication, Michael Paolisso).

Similarly, William Vickers (1980:17) reports that as the population of a Siona-Sicoya village in northeastern Ecuador grew from 132 persons in 1973 to 160 in 1979, yield per hunt fell by 44 percent, time spent in hunting increased by 12 percent, and caloric efficiency fell by 50 percent. These adverse effects were particularly strong in relation to the preferred larger animal targets.*

This evidence suggests that Yanomamo warfare is best understood as a means of keeping population growth rates down as a precondition for assuring the capture and consumption of high-quality game animals. Yet more data on the regional consequences of warfare on population growth and resource depletion are needed for a proper test of this theory.

*See Harris (1984) for further details.

SUMMARY

Orderly relationships between individuals and domestic groups in band and village societies are maintained without governments and law enforcement specialists. This is possible because of small size, predominance of kinship and reciprocity, and egalitarian access to vital resources. Public opinion is the chief source of law and order in these societies.

There is an absence of individual or nuclear family ownership of land among hunting-and-gathering bands and most village peoples. However, even in the most egalitarian societies there is private ownership of some items. The prevalence of the reciprocal mode of exchange and the absence of anonymous price markets renders theft unnecessary and impractical.

The major threat to law and order among band and village societies stems from the tendency of domestic and kinship groups to escalate conflicts in support of real or imagined injuries to one of their members. Such support is not dependent upon abstract principles of right and wrong, but upon the probable outcome of a particular course of action in the face of public opinion. The Eskimo song duel is an illustration of how public opinion can be tested and used to end conflicts between individuals who belong to different domestic and kinship groups.

Witchcraft accusations are another means of giving public opinion an opportunity to identify and punish persistent violators of the rules of reciprocity and other troublemakers. Shamans act as the mouthpiece of the community, but their position is precarious and they themselves are frequently identified as the source of misfortune and conflict. As among the Kuikuru, the fear of being accused of witchcraft encourages people to be amiable and generous. However, under stressful conditions witchcraft accusations may build to epidemic proportions and become a threat to the maintenance of law and order.

Headmanship reflects the pervasive egalitarian nature of the institutions of law and order in band and village societies. Headmen can do little more than harangue and plead with people for support. They lack physical or material means of enforcing their decisions. Their success rests on their ability to intuit public opinion. As exemplified by the Nuer, avoidance of blood feud can be facilitated by the payment of compensation and by appeal to ritual chiefs who lack political and economic power.

Other instances of nonkin political organization take the form of voluntary associations or sodalities such as men's and women's clubs, secret societies, and age-grade sets. However, all these nonkin modes of political organization remain rather rudimentary and are overshadowed by the pervasive networks of kinship alliances based on marriage and descent, which constitute the "glue" of band and village societies.

Although both hunter-gatherers and village farmers engage in warfare, there is reason to believe that warfare was less frequent in the Paleolithic than in the Neolithic and that village farmers are more likely to attempt to rout each other. It seems likely that warfare in some preindustrial contexts helped to restrain population growth and to protect resources from depletion. Warfare could have this effect through combat deaths, the encouragement of female infanticide and neglect, and the creation of no-man's-land game preserves. Evidence for this ecological interpretation of warfare consists of cross-cultural studies that correlate unbalanced sex ratios with active warfare.

The theory that warfare regulates population growth or prevents depletions is not accepted by many anthropologists. Others even deny that warfare is caused by population pressure and insist that the causes are mainly psychological. In the case of the Yanomamo, considerable controversy surrounds the role of game animals as a limiting factor in regional carrying capacities. It cannot be said that the Yanomamo suffer from a shortage of protein. Yet it seems likely that as their villages grow in size, the quality and quantity of animal resources decline and the costs of obtaining high-quality diets increase. It is useful to strive to maintain animal production and consumption at levels far higher than those minimally necessary to avoid malnutrition. More research encompassing long-range regional trends in population density, frequency of warfare, and changes in quantity and quality of animal capture and consumption is needed to resolve these controversies.

16 THE POLITICAL ECONOMY OF THE STATE

In this chapter we contrast the egalitarian forms of political life characteristic of band and village societies with the political life of chiefdoms and states. We will also examine a plausible theory of how the great transformations from bands and villages to chiefdoms and states took place. We will also discuss the role of coercive physical force and of more subtle forms of thought control in the maintenance of inequality and the status quo in ancient and modern states.

BIGMANSHIP

As discussed in Chapter 15 (p. 297), headmen often function as intensifiers of production and as redistributors. They get their relatives to work harder, and they collect and then give away the extra product. A village may have several headmen. Where technological and ecological conditions encourage intensification, a considerable degree of rivalry may develop among headmen living in the same village. They vie with each other to hold the most lavish feasts and to redistribute the greatest amount of valuables. Often, the most successful redistributors earn the reputation of being "big men."

Anthropologist Douglas Oliver (1955) carried out a classic study of "bigmanship" during his fieldwork among the Siuai on Bougainville in the Solomon Islands. Among the Siuai a "big man" is called a *mumi* (or chief, as they now prefer to be called) (Fig. 16.1) and to achieve *mumi* status is every youth's highest ambition. A young man proves himself capable of becoming a *mumi* by working hard and by carefully restricting his consumption of meat and coconuts. Eventually, he impresses his wife, children, and near relatives with the seriousness of his intentions, and they vow to help him prepare for his first feast. If the feast is a success, his circle of supporters widens and he sets to work readying an even greater display of generosity. He aims next at the construction of a men's clubhouse in which his male followers can lounge about and in which guests can be entertained and fed. Another feast is held at the consecration of the clubhouse, and if this is also a success, the circle of people willing to work for him grows still larger and he will begin to be spoken of as a *mumi*. Larger and larger feasts mean that the *mumi's* demands on his supporters become more irksome. Although they grumble about how hard they have to work, they remain loyal as long as their *mumi* continues to maintain or increase his renown as a "great provider."

Finally, the time comes for the new *mumi* to challenge the others who have risen before him. This is done at a *muminai* feast, where a tally is kept of all the pigs, coconut pies, and sago-almond puddings given away by the host *mumi* and his followers to the guest *mumi* and his followers. If the guest *mumi* cannot reciprocate in a year or so with a feast at least as lavish as that of his challengers, he suffers a great social humiliation and his fall from *mumi*hood is immediate. In deciding on whom to challenge, a *mumi* must be very careful. He tries to choose a rival whose downfall will increase his own reputation, but he must avoid one whose capacity to retaliate exceeds his own.

At the end of a successful feast, the greatest of *mumis* still faces a lifetime of personal toil and dependence on the moods and inclinations of his followers. *Mumi*hood does not confer the power to coerce others into doing one's bidding, nor does it elevate one's standard of living above anyone else's. In fact, since giving things away is the essence of *mumi*hood, great *mumis* may even consume

Figure 16.1 *SOLOMON ISLAND CHIEFS*
They prefer to be called chiefs rather than *mumis* as of old.

less meat and other delicacies than an ordinary, undistinguished Siuai. Among the Kaoka, another Solomon Island group reported on by H. Ian Hogbin (1964:66), there is the saying: "The giver of the feast takes the bones and the stale cakes; the meat and the fat go to the others." At one great feast attended by 1100 people, the host *mumi*, whose name was Soni, gave away 32 pigs plus a large quantity of sago-almond puddings. Soni and his closest followers, however, went hungry. "We shall eat Soni's renown," his followers said.

BIG MEN AND WARFARE

Formerly, the *mumis* were as famous for their ability to get men to fight for them as they were for their ability to get men to work for them. Warfare had been suppressed by the colonial authorities long before Oliver carried out his study, but the memory of *mumi* war leaders was still vivid among the Siuai. As one old man put it:

> In the olden times there were greater *mumi* than there are today. Then they were fierce and relentless war leaders. They laid waste to the countryside and their clubhouses were lined with the skulls of people they had slain (Oliver 1955:411).

In singing praises of their *mumis*, the generation of pacified Siuai call them "warriors" and "killers of men and pigs" (ibid.:399):

Thunderer, Earth-shaker
Maker of many feasts,
How empty of gong sounds with all the places be when you leave us!
Warrior, Handsome Flower,
Killer of men and pigs,
Who will bring renown to our places
When you leave us?

Oliver's informants told him that *mumis* had more authority in the days when warfare was still being practiced. Some *mumi* war leaders even kept one or two prisoners who were treated like slaves and forced to work in the *mumi's* family gardens. And people could not talk "loud and slanderously against their *mumis* without fear of punishment." This fits theoretical expectations, since the ability to redistribute meat and other valuables goes hand in hand with the ability to attract a following of warriors, equip them for combat, and reward them with spoils of battle. Rivalry between Bougainville's war-making *mumis* appeared to have been leading toward an islandwide political organization when the first European voyagers arrived. According to Oliver (ibid:420): "For certain periods of time many neighboring villages fought together so consistently that there emerged a pattern of war-making regions, each more or less internally peaceful and each containing one outstanding *mumi* whose war activities provided internal 'social cohesion.'" These *mumis* enjoyed regional fame, but their prerogatives remained rudimentary. This is shown by the fact that the *mumis* had to provide their warriors with prostitutes brought into the clubhouses and with gifts of pork and other delicacies. As one old warrior said:

> If the *mumi* didn't furnish us with women, we were angry. . . . All night long we would copulate and still want more. It was the same with eating. The clubhouse used to be filled with food, and we ate and ate and never had enough. Those were wonderful times (ibid:415).

Furthermore, the *mumi* who wanted to lead a war party had to be prepared personally to pay an indemnity for any of his men who were killed in battle and to furnish a pig for each man's funeral feast.

CHIEFS, WAR, AND REDISTRIBUTION: TROBRIANDERS AND CHEROKEE

Only a thin line separates a successful big man from a chief. Whereas big men must achieve and constantly validate their status by recurrent feasts, chiefs inherit their office and hold it even if they are temporarily unable to provide their followers with generous redistributions. Chiefs tend to live better than commoners; unlike big men, they do not always keep only the "bones and stale cakes for themselves." Yet in the long run, chiefs too must validate their title by waging successful war, obtaining trade goods, and giving away food and other valuables to their followers.

The Trobriand Islanders

The difference between big men and chiefs can be illustrated with the case of the Trobrianders (see pp. 233–234). Trobiander society was divided into several matrilineal clans and subclans of unequal rank and privilege through which access to garden lands was inherited. Bronislaw Malinowski (1920) reported that the Trobrianders were keen on fighting and that they conducted systematic and relentless wars, venturing across the open ocean in their canoes to trade—or, if need be, to fight—with the people of islands over 100 miles away. Unlike the Siuai *mumis*, the Trobriand chiefs occupied hereditary offices and could be deposed only through defeat in war. One of these, whom Malinowski considered to be the "paramount chief" of all the Trobrianders, held sway over more than a dozen villages, containing several thousand people all told. Chieftainships were hereditary within the wealthiest and largest subclans, and the Trobrianders attributed these inequalities to wars of conquest carried out long ago. Only the chiefs could wear certain shell ornaments as the insignia of high rank, and it was forbidden for any commoner to stand or sit in a position that put a chief's head at a lower elevation than anyone else's. Malinowski (1922) tells of seeing all the people present in the village of Bwoytalu drop from their verandas as if blown down by a hurricane at the sound of a drawn-out cry announcing the arrival of an important chief.

The Trobriand chief's power rested ultimately upon his ability to play the role of "great provider," which depended on customary and sentimental ties of kinship and marriage rather than on the control of weapons and resources. Residence among the Trobraind commoners was normally avunculocal (see p. 283). Adolescent boys lived in bachelor huts until they got married. They then took their brides to live in their mother's brother's household, where they jointly worked the garden lands of the husband's matrilineage. In recognition of the existence of matrilineal descent, at harvest time brothers acknowledged that a portion of the produce of the matrilineal lands was owed to their sisters and sent them presents of baskets filled with yams, their staple crop. The Trobriand chief relied on this custom to validate his title. He married the sisters of the headmen of a large number of sublineages. Some chiefs acquired several dozen wives, each of whom was entitled to an obligatory gift of yams from her brothers. These yams were delivered to the chief's village and displayed on special yam racks. Some of the yams were then distributed in elaborate feasts at which the chief validated his position as a "great provider," while the remainder were used to feed canoe-building specialists, artisans, magicians, and family servants who thereby became partially dependent on the chief's power. In former times the yam stores also furnished the base for launching long-distance Kula trading expeditions (see. p. 233) among friendly groups and raids against enemies (Malinowski 1935; Brunton 1975).

Figure 16.2 *CHEROKEE CHIEF*
Black Coat, painted by George Catlin at Fort Gibson in 1834.

The Cherokee

The political organization of the Cherokee of Tennessee (and of other southeastern woodland native Americans) bears striking resemblances to the Trobrianders' redistribution-warfare-trade-chief complex. The Cherokee (Fig. 16.2), like the Trobrianders, were matrilineal, and they waged external warfare over long distances. At the center of the principal settlements was a large, circular "council house" where the council of chiefs discussed issues involving several villages and where redistributive feasts were held.

The council of chiefs had a supreme chief who was the central figure in the Cherokee redistributive network. At harvest time a large crib, identified as the "chief's granary," was erected in each field. "To this each family carries and deposits a certain quantity according to his ability or inclination, or none at all if he so chooses." The chief's granaries functioned as "a public treasury . . . to fly to for succor" in the case of crop failure, as a source of food "to accommodate strangers, or travellers," and as a military store "when they go forth on hostile expeditions." Although every citizen enjoyed "the right of free and public access," commoners had to acknowledge that the store really belonged to the supreme chief who had "an exclusive right and ability . . . to distribute comfort and blessings to the necessitous" (Bartram in Renfrew 1973:234).

LIMITATIONS OF CHIEFLY POWER

Even though the Trobrianders feared and respected their "great provider" war chiefs, they were still a long way from a state society. Living on islands, the Trobrianders were not free to spread out, and their population density had risen in Malinowski's time to 60 persons per square mile. Nonetheless, the chiefs could not control enough of the production system to acquire great power. Perhaps one reason for this is that Trobriand agriculture lacked cereal grains. Since yams rot after 3 or 4 months (unlike rice or maize), the Trobriand "great provider" could not manipulate people through dispensing food year-round, nor could he support a permanent police-military garrison out of his stores. Another important factor was the open resources of the lagoons and ocean from which the Trobrianders derived their animal proteins. The Trobriand chief could not cut off access to these resources and hence could not exercise permanent coercive political control over subordinates. Only with more intense forms of agriculture and large harvests of grains could the power of the "great provider" evolve beyond that of the Trobriand chiefs.

Another classic illustration of the limited nature of chiefly power is that of the chiefs of Tikopia (Fig. 16.3), one of the smallest of the Solomon Islands. Here the chiefs' pretensions were even greater than those of the Trobriand chief, but their actual power was considerably less. The Tikopian chiefs claimed that they "owned" all the land and sea resources, yet the size of the redistributive network and of the harvests under their control made such claims unenforceable. Tikopian chiefs enjoyed few privileges. Nominally they claimed control of their cognatic kin group's gardens; but in practice they could not restrict their kin from any unused

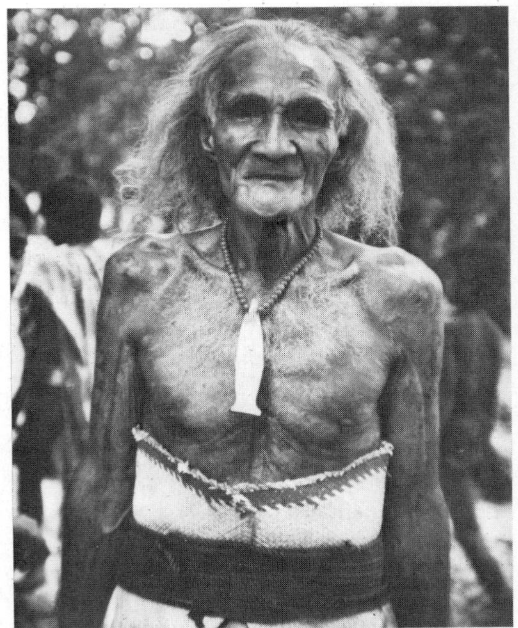

(a)

(b)

Figure 16.3 *TIKOPIA CHIEF AND HIS "HONOR GUARD"*
(a) Tikopia chief and *(b)* his hut. The two men standing outside the hut are the chief's "honor guard," but note unpretentious residence.

sites. Labor for their own gardens was in scarce supply, and they themselves worked like any "commoner" in the fields. To validate their positions, they were obliged to give large feasts, which in turn rested upon the voluntary labor and food contributions of their kin. Ties of kinship tended to efface the abstract prerequisites and etiquette of higher rank. Raymond Firth describes how a man from a commoner family, who in the kin terminology of the Tikopians was classified as a "brother," could exchange bawdy insults with the island's highest ranking chief:

> On one occasion I was walking with the Ariki (chief) Kafika . . . when we passed the orchard of Pae Sao . . . all the principals present were "brothers" through various ties, and with one accord they fell upon each other with obscene chaff. Epithets of "Big testicles!" "You are the enormous testicles!" flew back and forth to the accompaniment of hilarious laughter. I was somewhat surprised at the vigor of the badinage for the Ariki Kafika, as the most respected chief of the island, has a great deal of sanctity attached to him. . . . However, this did not save him and he took it in good part (Firth 1957:176–177).

Similar remarks pertain to the Cherokee chief. Outside the council, "He associates with the people as a common man, converses with them, and they with him in perfect ease and familiarity" (Bartram in Renfrew 1973:233).

FROM CHIEFDOM TO STATE

The larger and denser the population, the larger the redistributive network and the more powerful the redistributor war chief. Under certain circumstances, to be specified in a moment, the exercise of power by chiefs on the one hand and by ordinary food producers on the other becomes highly unbalanced. Contributions to the central store cease to be voluntary contributions. They become taxes. Access to the farmlands and natural resources cease to be rights. They become dispensations. Food producers cease being the chief's followers. They become peasants. Redistributors cease being chiefs. They become kings. And chiefdoms cease being chiefdoms. They become states.

The *state,* then, is a form of politically centralized society whose governing elites have the power to compel subordinates into paying taxes, rendering services, and obeying the law.

Mature states have several levels of *government;* that is administrative bureaucracies that coordinate the military, economic, legal, and ritual activities of a network of villages (Wright 1977). Archaeologically, the state can often be identified by *site stratification:* large villages with public buildings surrounded by smaller villages and hamlets (McEwan and Dickson 1978; Price 1977).

One of the conditions that probably contributed to the development of the first states was the concentration of population in restricted habitats such as narrow river valleys surrounded by deserts, mountain valleys surrounded by precipitous slopes, or as in the case of the Olmec (see p. 181), natural levee lands surrounded by tropical forests. These are said to be *circumscribed* habitats, because if people attempt to migrate away from them in order to escape from the burden of paying taxes, they will not be able to use the same mode of production and will have to endure hardships or accept a lower standard of living (Carnerio 1970). In large chiefdoms located in circumscribed environments, some people or even whole villages would be inclined to accept a permanently subordinate political status rather than migrate to an unfavorable habitat where they would have to change their whole way of life.

In circumscribed habitats, little direct physical coercion would be needed to keep the subordinate peasantry in line. Kinship would be used to justify the legitimacy of differential access to resources on the part of junior and senior lineages or of wife-giving–wife-taking alliance groups (those who gave wives would expect tribute and labor services in return). Access to stored crops might be made contingent upon rendering craft or military services. Warfare would increase, and defeated villages would be incorporated into the tax and tribute network. A growing corps of military, religious, and craft specialists would be fed out of the central food stores, supporting the image of the rulers as beneficent "great providers." And the social distance between the police-military-priestly-managerial elite and the class of food-producing peasants would widen still more as food production increased, as trade networks expanded, as population grew, and as production was intensified through taxation and labor conscription (see Fried 1978; Service 1975; Haas 1982).

On archaeological evidence it seems probable that some of the very earliest states arose in river and mountain valleys and other circumscribed environments of the ancient Middle East and Mesoamerica (Renfrew 1973). However, there is also considerable archaeological evidence that indicates some of the earliest states may have arisen in noncircumscribed environments (MacNeish 1972). Once the first states came into existence, they themselves constituted barriers against the flight of people who sought to preserve egalitarian systems. Moreover, with states as neighbors, egalitarian peoples found themselves increasingly drawn into warfare and were compelled to increase production and to give their redistributor–war chiefs more and more power in order to prevail against the expansionist tendencies of their neighbors. Thus most of the states of the world were produced by a great diversity of specific historical and ecological conditions (Fried 1967). But once states come into existence, they tend to spread, engulf, and overwhelm nonstate peoples (Carneiro 1978).

AN AFRICAN KINGDOM: BUNYORO

The difference between a chiefdom and a state can be illustrated with the case of the Bunyoro, a kingdom located in Uganda and studied by John Beattie (1960). Bunyoro had a population of about 100,000 people and an area of 5000 square miles. Supreme power over the Bunyoro territory and its inhabitants was vested in the Mukama, senior member of a royal lineage that reckoned its descent back to the beginning of time (Fig. 16.4). The use of all natural resources, but

Figure 16.4 *MUKAMA OF BUNYORO*
This is a King, not a chief.

especially of farming land, was a dispensation specifically granted by the Mukama to a dozen or more "chiefs" or to commoner peasants under their respective control. In return for these dispensations, quantities of food, handicrafts, and labor services were funneled up through the power hierarchy into the Mukama's headquarters. The Mukama in turn directed the use of these goods and services on behalf of state enterprises. The basic redistributive pattern was still plainly in evidence:

> In the traditional system the king was seen both as the supreme receiver of goods and services, and as the supreme giver. . . . The great chiefs, who themselves received tribute from their dependents, were required to hand over to the Mukama a part of the produce of their estates in the form of crops, cattle, beer or women. . . . But everyone must give to the king, not only the chiefs. . . . The Mukama's role as a giver was accordingly no less stressed. Many of his special names emphasize his magnanimity and he was traditionally expected to give extensively in the form both of feasts and of gifts to individuals (Beattie 1960:34).

However great the Mukama's reputation for generosity, it is clear that he did not give away as much as he received. He certainly did not follow the Solomon Island *mumis* and keep only the stale cakes and bones for himself. Moreover, much of what he gave away did not flow back down to the peasant producers. Instead, it remained in the hands of his genealogically close kin, who constituted a clearly demarcated aristocratic class. Part of what the Mukama took away from the peasants was bestowed on nonkin who performed extraordinary services on behalf of the state, especially in connection with military exploits. Another part was used to support a permanent palace guard and resident staff who attended to the Mukama's personal needs and performed religious rites deemed essential for the welfare of the Mukama and the nation, such as custodian of spears, custodian of royal graves, custodian of the royal drums, custodian of royal crowns, "putters-on" of the royal crowns, custodians of royal thrones (stools) and other regalia, cooks, bath attendants, herdsmen, potters, barkcloth makers, musicians, and others. And many of these officials had several assistants.

In addition, there was a loosely defined category of advisors, diviners, and other retainers who hung around the court, attached to the Mukama's household as dependents, in the hope of being appointed to a chieftainship. To this must be added the Mukama's extensive harem, his many children, and the polygynous households of his brothers and of other royal personages. To keep his power intact, the Mukama and portions of his court made frequent trips throughout Bunyoro land, staying at local places maintained at the expense of his chiefs and commoners.

FEUDALISM

As Beattie points out, there are many analogies between the Bunyoro state and the "feudal" system existing in England at the time of the Norman invasion (A.D. 1066). As in early medieval England, Bunyoro stratification involved a pledge of loyalty on the part of the district chiefs (lords) in return for grants of land and of the labor power of the peasants (serfs) who lived on these lands. The English king, like the Mukama, could call upon these chiefs to furnish weapons, supplies, and warriors whenever an internal or external threat to the king's sovereignty arose. The survival of the English feudal royal lineage, as in Bunyoro, was made possible by the ability of the king to muster larger coalitions of lords and their military forces than could be achieved by any combination of disloyal lords. But there are important differences in demographic scale and in the ruler's role as redistributor that must also be noted. While redistribution was continued through a system of royal taxation and tribute, the police-military function of the English king was more important than among the Bunyoro. The English sovereign was not the "great provider." He was, instead, the "great protector." With a population numbering over a million people and with agricultural and handicraft production organized on the basis of self-sustaining independent local estates, redistribution was wholly asymmetrical. It was not necessary for William the Conqueror to cultivate an image of generosity among the mass of peasants throughout his kingdom. Although he was careful to be generous to the lords who supported him, the display of generosity to the peasants was no longer important. A vast gulf had opened between the styles of life of peasants and overlords. And the maintenance of these differences no longer rested mainly on the special contribution the overlords made to production, but largely on their ability to deprive the peasants of subsistence and of life itself. But on the European medieval manorial estates, feudal lords were well advised not to push the exploitation (see p. 334) of their peasants beyond certain limits, lest they destroy the basis of their own existence.

In comparing African with European political development, it must be remembered that there were two periods of feudalism in western and northern Europe. The first, about which little is known, preceeded the growth of the Roman Empire and was cut off by the Roman conquest. The second followed the collapse of the Roman Empire. Although the latter period provides the standard model of feudalism, the Bunyoro type of polity is actually a much more widely distributed form and probably closely resembles the political systems the Romans encountered and overran in their conquest of western Europe (see Bloch 1964; Piggott 1966; Renfrew 1973).

Because of the Roman Empire, the feudalism of medieval Europe rested on a technology far in advance of the technology found in even the most populous kingdoms south of the Sahara. The product taxed away by the Bunyoro ruling class was small compared to what was taxed away by the English feudal aristocracy. Architecture, metallurgy, textiles, and armaments were far more advanced in medieval Europe.

A NATIVE AMERICAN EMPIRE: THE INCA

Alternative evolutionary steps led to state systems that were larger and more centralized than those of medieval Europe. In several regions, there arose state systems in which scores of former small states were incorporated into highly centralized superstates or empires. In the New World, the largest and most powerful of these systems was the Inca Empire.

At its prime the Inca Empire stretched 1500 miles from northern Chile to southern Colombia and contained possibly as many as 6 million inhabitants. Because of government intervention in the basic mode of production, agriculture was not organized in terms of feudal estates, but rather in terms of villages, districts, and provinces. Each such unit was under the supervision not of a feudal lord who had sworn loyalty to another lord slightly his superior and who was free to use his lands and peasants as he saw fit, but of appointed government officials responsible for planning public works and delivering government-established quotas of laborers, food, and other material (Morris 1976). Village lands were divided into three parts, the largest of which was probably the source of the workers' own subsistence; harvests from the second and third parts were turned over to religious and government agents who stored them in granaries. The distribution of these supplies was entirely under the control of the central administration. Likewise when labor power was needed to build roads, bridges, canals, fortresses, or other public works, government recruiters went directly into the villages. Because of the size of the administrative network and the density of population, huge numbers of workers could be placed at the disposal of the Inca engineers. In the construction of Cuzco's fortress of Sacsahuaman (Fig. 16.5), probably the greatest pre-Columbian masonry structure in the New World, 30,000 people were employed in cutting, quarrying, hauling, and erecting huge monoliths, some weighing as much as 200 tons. Labor contingents of this size were rare in medieval Europe but were common in ancient Egypt, the Middle East, India, and China.

Control over the entire empire was concentrated in the hands of the Inca. He was the first-born of the first–born, a descendant of the god of the sun and a celestial being of unparalleled holiness. This god-on-earth enjoyed power and luxury undreamed of by the poor Mehinacu chief in his plaintive daily quest for respect and obedience. Ordinary people could not approach the Inca face to face. His private audiences were conducted from behind a screen, and all who approached him did so with a burden on their back. When traveling he reclined on an ornate palanquin carried by special crews of bearers (Mason 1957:184). A small army of sweepers, water carriers, woodcutters, cooks, wardrobemen, treasurers, gardeners, and hunters attended the domestic needs of the Inca in his palace in Cuzco, the capital of the empire. If members of this staff offended the Inca, their entire village was destroyed.

The Inca ate his meals from gold and silver dishes in rooms whose walls were covered with precious metals. His clothing was made of the softest vicuña wool, and he gave away each change of clothing to members of the royal family, never wearing the same garment twice. The Inca enjoyed the ser-

Figure 16.5 *SACSAHUAMAN*
The principal fortress of the Inca Empire, near Cuzco, Peru.

Figure 16.6 *STRATIFICATION: THE KING OF MOROCCO*
Social inequality cannot endure without the use or threat of force.

vices of a large number of concubines who were methodically culled from the empire's most beautiful girls. His wife, however, to conserve the holy line of descent from the god of the sun, had to be a full or half sister. When the Inca died, his wife, concubines, and many other retainers were strangled during a great drunken dance in order that he suffer no loss of comfort in the afterlife. Each Inca's body was eviscerated, wrapped in cloth, and mummified. Women with fans stood in constant attendance upon these mummies, ready to drive away flies and to take care of the other things mummies need to stay happy.

THE STATE AND THE CONTROL OF THOUGHT

Large populations, anonymity, use of market money, and vast differences in wealth make the maintenance of law and order in state societies more difficult to achieve than in bands, villages, and chiefdoms. This accounts for the great elaboration of police and paramilitary forces, and the other state-level institutions and specialists concerned with crime and punishment (Fig. 16.6). Although every state ultimately stands prepared to crush criminals and political subversives by imprisoning, maiming, or killing them, most of the daily burdens of maintaining law and order against discontented individuals and groups is borne by institutions that seek to confuse, distract, and demoralize potential troublemakers before they have to be subdued by physical force. Therefore, every state, ancient and modern, has specialists who perform ideological services in support of the status quo. These services are often rendered in a manner and in contexts that seem unrelated to economic or political issues.

The main thought-control apparatus of preindustrial states consists of magico-religious institutions. The elaborate religions of the Inca, Aztecs, ancient Egyptians, and other preindustrial civilizations sanctified the privileges and powers of the ruling elite. They upheld the doctrine of the divine descent of the Inca and the pharaoh and taught that the entire balance and continuity of the universe required the subordination of commoners to persons of noble and divine birth. Among the Aztecs, the priests were convinced that the gods must be nourished with human blood; and they personally pulled out the beating hearts of the state's prisoners of war on top of Tenochtitlan's pyramids (see p. 440). In many states, religion has been used to condition large masses of people to accept relative deprivation as necessity, to look forward to material rewards in the afterlife rather than in the present one, and to be grateful for small favors from superiors lest ingratitude call down a fiery retribution in this life or in a hell to come. (Religion can also inspire reform and revolution—see pp. 448–453 and 454–458.)

To deliver messages of this sort and demonstrate the truths they are based on, state societies invest a large portion of national wealth in monumental architecture. From the pyramids of Egypt or Teotihuacán in Mexico to the Gothic cathedrals of medieval Europe, state-subsidized monumentality in religious structures make the individual feel powerless and insignificant. Great public edifices, whether seeming to float as in the case of the Gothic cathedral of Amiens, or to press down with the infinite heaviness of the pyramids of Khufu (Fig. 16.7), teach the futility of discontent and the invincibility of those who rule as well as the glory of heaven and the gods. (This is not to say that they teach nothing else.)

Figure 16.7 *THE GREAT PYRAMID OF KHUFU*

THOUGHT CONTROL IN MODERN CONTEXTS

A considerable amount of conformity is achieved not by frightening or threatening people, but by inviting them to identify with the governing elite and to enjoy vicariously the pomp of state occasions. Public spectacles such as religious processions, coronations, and victory parades work against the alienating effects of poverty and exploitation (Fig. 16.8). During Roman times, the masses were kept under control by letting them watch gladiatorial contests and other circus spectaculars. In the movies, television, radio, and organized sports, modern state systems possess powerful techniques for distracting and amusing their citizenry. Through modern media the consciousness of millions of listeners, readers, and watchers is often manipulated along rather precisely determined paths by government-subsidized specialists (Efron 1972; Ellul 1965; Key 1976). "Entertainment" delivered through the air or by cable directly into the shantytown house or tenement apartment is perhaps the most effective form of "Roman circus" yet devised. Television and radio not only prevent alienation through the spectator's powers of enjoyment, they also keep people off the streets.

(a)

(b)

Figure 16.8 *THOUGHT CONTROL IN TWO MODERN STATES*
(a) United States; *(b)* Soviet Union.

Yet the most powerful modern means of thought control may not lie in the electronic opiates of the entertainment industry, but in state-supported universal education. Teachers and schools obviously serve the instrumental needs of complex industrial civilizations by training each generation to provide the skills and services necessary for survival and well-being. But teachers and schools also devote a great deal of time to civics, history, citizenship, and social studies. These subjects are loaded with implicit or explicit assumptions about culture, people, and nature indicative of the superiority of the political-economic system in which they are taught. In the Soviet Union and other highly centralized Communist countries, no attempt is made to disguise the fact that one of the principal functions of universal education is political indoctrination. Western capitalist democracies are less open in acknowledging that their educational systems are also instruments of political control. Many teachers and students, lacking a comparative perspective, are not conscious of the extent to which their books, curricula, and classroom presentations uphold the status quo. Elsewhere, however, school boards, boards of regents, library committees, and legislative committees openly call for conformity to the status quo.

Modern universal educational systems from kindergarten to graduate school operate with a politically convenient double standard. In the sphere of mathematics and the biophysical sciences, every encouragement is given to students to be creative, persistent, methodical, logical, and independently inquisitive. On the other hand, courses dealing with social and cultural phenomena systematically avoid "controversial subjects" such as concentration of wealth; ownership of multinational corporations; nationalization of key industries; involvement of banks and real estate interests in urban blight; ethnic and racial minority viewpoints; control of the mass media; military defense budgets; viewpoints of underdeveloped nations; alternatives to capitalism; alternatives to nationalism; atheism; and so on. But schools do not merely avoid controversial subjects. Certain political viewpoints are so essential to the maintenance of law and order that they cannot be entrusted to objective methods of instruction; instead, the viewpoints are implanted in the minds of the young through appeal to fear and hatred. The reaction of North Americans to socialism and communism is as much the result of indoctrination as is the reaction of Russians to capitalism. Flag saluting, oaths of allegiance, patriotic songs, and patriotic rites (assemblies, plays, pageants) are some of the other familiar ritualized political aspects of public school curricula (Ramirez and Meyer 1980; Bowles and Gintis 1976).

Jules Henry, who went from the study of Indians in Brazil to the study of high schools in St. Louis, has contributed to the understanding of some of the ways by which universal education molds the pattern of national conformity. In his book *Culture Against Man,* Henry shows how even in the midst of spelling and singing lessons, there can be basic training in support of the competitive "free enterprise system." Children are taught to fear failure; they are also taught to be competitive. Hence they soon come to look upon each other as the main source of failure, and they become afraid of each other. As Henry (1963:305) observes: "School is indeed a training for later life not because it teaches the 3R's (more or less), but because it instills the essential cultural nightmare—fear of failure, envy of success."

Today in the United States, acceptance of economic inequality depends on thought control more than on the exercise of naked repressive force. Children from economically deprived families are taught to believe that the main obstacle to achievement of wealth and power is their own intellectual merit, physical endurance, and will to compete. The poor are taught to blame themselves for being poor, and their resentment is directed primarily against themselves or against those with whom they must compete and who stand on the same rung of the ladder of upward mobility. In addition, the economically deprived portion of the population is taught to believe that the electoral process guarantees redress against abuse by the rich and powerful through legislation aimed at redistributing wealth. Finally, most of the population is kept ignorant of the actual workings of the political-economic system and of the disproportionate power exercised by lobbies representing corporations and other special interest groups. Henry concludes that U.S. schools, despite their ostensible dedication to creative inquiry, punish the child who has intellectually creative ideas with respect to social and cultural life:

> Learning social studies is, to no small extent, whether in elementary school or the university, learning to be stupid. Most of us accomplish this task before we enter high school. But the child with a socially creative imagination will not be encouraged to play among new social systems, values, relationships; nor is there much likelihood of it, if for no other reason than that the social studies teachers will perceive such a child as a poor student. Furthermore such a child will simply be unable to fathom the absurdities that seem transparent *truth* to the teacher. . . . Learning to be an idiot is part of growing up or, as Camus put it, learning to be absurd. Thus the child who finds it impossible to learn to think the absurd truth . . . usually comes to think himself stupid (1963:287–288).

THE STATE AND PHYSICAL COERCION

Law and order in stratified societies depends upon an infinitely variable mixture of physical compulsion through police-military force and thought control based on the kinds of techniques discussed in the previous section. In general, the more marked the social inequalities and the more intense the labor exploitation, the heavier must be the contribution of both forms of control. The regimes relying most heavily on brutal doses of police-military intervention are not necessarily those that display the greatest amount of visible social inequality. Rather, the most brutal systems of police-military control seem to be associated with periods of major transformations, during which the governing classes are insecure and prone to overreact. Periods of dynastic upheaval and of prerevolutionary and postrevolutionary turmoil are especially productive of brutality.

The most enduring of the world's despotisms keep their powers of coercion coiled in readiness. For example, as long as the Chinese emperors felt politically secure, they needed to give only an occasional demonstration of physical destruction in order to repress disloyal factions. Karl Wittfogel (1957) has provided a vivid account of the coiled terrors at the disposal of ancient despotisms. He writes of "total loneliness in the hour of doom" awaiting those who gave the slightest cause for apprehension to the emperor. In the torture rooms and at the execution blocks, the vast power of the state, symbolized so perfectly in colossal public monuments and edifices, routinely obliterated potential trouble-makers.

Some of the most brutal episodes in the career of the state occurred in the aftermath of the Russian revolution, when millions of people suspected of "counterrevolutionary" thoughts and attitudes were executed or sent to slower deaths in a vast system of slave labor camps (Solzhenitsyn 1974). The Chinese revolution was also followed by waves of unrestrained attacks against millions of persons suspected of bourgeois sympathies (Bao and Chelminski 1973; Bettleheim 1978; London 1979).

Yet, according to Karl Marx, communism is not only antithetical to despotism, but to any form of the state whatsoever. Marx was convinced that the state had come into existence only to protect the economic interests of the ruling class. He believed that if economic equality could be restored, the state would "wither away." The very notion of a "Communist state" is a contradiction in terms from the point of view of Marxist theory (Marx and Engels 1948; Lichtheim 1961). The existence of the Communist state is officially attributed to the need to protect the people who are building a Communist order from the aggression of the capitalist states or the lingering threat of procapitalist citizens (Lenin 1965 [1917]). An equally plausible interpretation, however, is that the ruling classes in the Soviet Union and China will never voluntarily dissolve the still rapidly growing apparatus of thought control and physical coercion.

Although the ruling classes of Western parliamentary democracies rely more on thought control than on physical coercion to maintain law and order, in the final analysis they too depend on guns and jails to protect their privileges. Strikes by police in cities such as Montreal and blackouts such as occurred in New York City in 1977 (Fig. 16.9) quickly led to extensive looting and widespread disorder, proving that thought control is not enough and that large numbers of ordinary citizens do not believe in the system and are held in check only by the threat of physical punishment (Curvin and Porter 1978; Weisman 1978).

THE FATE OF PRESTATE BANDS AND VILLAGES

The career of state-level societies has been characterized by continuous expansion into and encroachment upon the lands and freedoms of prestate peoples. For advanced chiefdoms the appearance of state-level soldiers, traders, missionaries, and colonists often resulted in a successful transition to state-level organization. But over the vast regions of the globe inhabited by dispersed bands and villages, the spread of the state has resulted in the annihilation or total distortion of the way of life of thousands of once free and proud peoples. These devastating changes are aptly described as *genocide*—the extinction of whole populations—or as *ethnocide*—the systematic extinction of cultures.

The spread of European states into the Americans had a devastating effect upon the inhabitants of the New World. Many methods were employed to rid the land of its original inhabitants in order to make room for the farms and industries needed to support Europe's overflowing population. Native American peoples were exterminated during unequal military engagements that pitted guns against arrows; others were killed off by new urban diseases brought by the colonists—diseases such as smallpox, measles, and the common cold—against which people who lived in small, dispersed settlements lacked immunity. The colonists were also not above deliberately giving away infected clothing to hasten the spread of these diseases as a type of bacteriological warfare. Against the cultures of the natives there were other weapons. Their modes of production were destroyed by slavery, debt

Figure 16.9 *NEW YORK CITY, JULY 14, 1977*
Looting in the aftermath of a blackout.

forms of peonage, and wage labor; their political life was destroyed by the creation of chiefs and tribal councils who were puppets and convenient means of control for state administrators (Fried 1975); and their religious beliefs and rituals were demeaned and suppressed by missionaries who were eager to save their souls but not their lands and freedom (Ribeiro 1971; Walker 1972).

These genocidal attacks were not confined to North and South America. They were also carried out in Australia, on the islands of the Pacific, and in Siberia. Nor are they merely events that took place a long time ago and about which nothing can now be done. For they are still going on in the remote vastness of the Amazon Basin and other regions of South America where the last remaining New World free and independent band and village peoples have been cornered by the remorseless spread of colonists, traders, oil companies, teachers, ranchers, and missionaries (Bodley 1975; Davis 1977).

The tragic plight of the Aché Indians of eastern Paraguay is a case point. As documented by Mark Münzel (1973), these independent foragers are being systematically hunted, rounded up, and forced to live on small reservations in order to make room for ranchers and farmers. Aché children are separated from their parents and sold to settlers as servants. The manhunters shoot anyone who shows signs of resistance, rape the women, and sell the children. In March and April of 1972, about 171 "wild" Aché were captured and deliberately taken to the Aché reservation, where it was known that an influenza epidemic was already raging. By July, 55 Achés on the reservation had died. Concludes Münzel (1973:55): "Taking a large number of forest Indians there at this time, without providing for their health requirements, was indirect mass murder."

As Gerald Weiss points out, the last remaining "tribal" cultures are found in the remote regions of developing countries that often regard the survival of such independent peoples as a threat to their national unity.

> The last of the tribal cultures are in serious jeopardy. When they are gone, we will not see their like again. The nonindustrialized statal [i.e., state] cultures have joined forces with the industrialized states to eliminate them. The reason for this lies in the contrasting natures of statal and tribal cultures: the former are larger, more powerful, and expansionistic. Tribal cultures, representing an earlier cultural form, are denigrated as "savage" and viewed as an anachronism in the "modern world." The statal cultures have exercised their power by dividing all land on this planet among themselves. . . . This is as true for the Third World—where concerted efforts are made to destroy the last vestiges of tribalism as a threat to national unity—as it has been for the Western World (1977a:890).

Weiss argues it is probable but not inevitable that none of the tribal societies will survive. Yet he insists that anthropologists must not be defeatists and must strive to prevent that from happening:

> No biologist would claim that evolution in the organic realm makes either necessary or desirable the disappearance of earlier forms, so no anthropologist should be content to remain a passive observer of the extinction of the Tribal World (ibid:891).

SUMMARY

Societies with big men, chiefs, and ruling classes represent three different forms of political organization involved in the transformation of egalitarian into stratified state societies. The big man is a rivalrous form of headmanship marked by competitive redistributions that expand and intensify production. As illustrated by the *mumis* of the Solomon Islands, bigmanship is a temporary status requiring constant validation through displays of generosity that leave the big man poor in possessions but rich in prestige and authority. Since they are highly respected, big men are well suited to act as leaders of war parties, long-distance trading expeditions, and other collective activities that require leadership among egalitarian peoples.

Like big men, chiefs also play the role of great provider, expand and intensify production, give feasts, and organize long-distance warfare and trading expeditions. However, as illustrated by the Trobriand, Cherokee, and Tikopian chiefdoms, chiefs enjoy hereditary status, tend to live somewhat better than the average commoner, and can be deposed only through defeat in warfare. Nonetheless, the power of chiefs is distinctly limited because they lack support from a permanent group of police-military specialists and cannot permanently deprive significant numbers of their followers from access to the means of making a living.

In stratified state societies, the power of kings is the power of taxation. Failure of peasants to contribute to the redistributive system may result in their being cut off from the means of subsistence. The military, economic, and ritual activities of a network of villages is coordinated by an administrative bureaucracy, and the settlements themselves exhibit hierarchical differences known as site stratification.

The pristine forms of stratification and statehood were probably often linked to the development of dense populations in circumscribed habitats. Peasantries arose when subordinate villages and lineages could not avoid taxation by fleeing to other habitats without changing their whole way of life. Secondary states, however, arose under a variety of conditions related to the spread of the pristine states.

The difference between chiefdoms and states is illustrated by the case of the Bunyoro. The Mukama was a great provider for himself and his closest supporters but not for the majority of the Bunyoro peasants. The Mukama, unlike the Trobriand chief, maintained a permanent court of personal retainers and a palace guard. There are many resemblances between the Bunyoro and the "feudal" kingdoms of early medieval Europe. But the power of the early English kings was greater and depended less on the image of the great provider than on that of the great protector.

The most developed and highly stratified form of statehood is that of empire. As illustrated by the Inca of Peru, the leaders of ancient empires possessed vast amounts of power and were unapproachable by ordinary citizens. Production was supervised by a whole army of administrators and tax collectors. While the Inca was concerned with the welfare of his people, they viewed him as a god to whom they owed everything rather than as a headman or chief who owed everything to them.

Since all state societies are based on marked inequalities between rich and poor and rulers and ruled, maintenance of law and order presents a critical challenge. In the final analysis it is the police and the military with their control over the means of physical coercion that keep the poor and the exploited in line. However, all states find it more expedient to maintain law and order by controlling people's thoughts. This is done in a variety of ways, ranging from state religions to public rites and spectacles and universal education.

The plight of the remaining prestate band and village societies must not be overlooked. As in the case of the Aché, civilization and modernization lead to slavery, disease, and poverty for such people.

17 STRATIFIED GROUPS: CLASS, CASTE, MINORITY, ETHNICITY

This chapter examines the principal varieties of stratified groups found in state-level societies. We will see that people who live in such societies think and behave in ways that are determined to a great extent by their membership in stratified groups and by their position in a stratification hierarchy. The values and behavior of such groups are in turn often related to a struggle for access to the structural and infrastructural sources of wealth and power.

CLASS AND POWER

All state-level societies are organized into a hierarchy of groups known as classes. A *class* is a group of people who have a similar relationship to the apparatus of control in state-level societies and who possess similar amounts of power (or lack of power) over the allocation of wealth and privileges and access to resources and technology (Fig. 17.1).

Figure 17.1 *POVERTY AND POWER* This man is not only poor, he is also relatively powerless.

All state societies necessarily have at least two classes arranged hierarchically—rulers and ruled. But where there are more than two classes, they are not necessarily all arranged hierarchically with respect to each other. For example, fishermen and neighboring peasant farmers are usefully regarded as two separate classes because they relate to the ruling class in distinctive ways, have different patterns of ownership, rent, and taxation, and exploit entirely different sectors of the environment. Yet neither has a clear-cut power advantage or disadvantage with respect to the other. Similarly, anthropologists often speak of an urban as opposed to a rural lower class, although the quantitative power differentials between the two may be minimal.

Before proceeding any further, the nature of power involved in class hierarchies should be made as explicit as possible. *Power* in human affairs, as in nature, consists of the ability to control energy. Control over energy is mediated by the tools, machines, and techniques for applying that energy to individual or collective enterprises. To control energy in this sense is to possess the means for making, moving, shaping, and destroying minerals, vegetables, animals, and people. Power is control over people and nature (R. Adams 1970).

The power of particular human beings cannot be measured simply by adding up the amount of energy they regulate or channel. If that were the case, the most powerful people in the world would be the technicians who turn the switches at nuclear power plants, or the pilots who fly jet aircraft. Military field officers in the armed forces, with their enormous capacity for killing and maiming, are not necessarily powerful people. The crucial question in all such cases is this: Who controls these technicians, civil servants, and generals, and makes them turn their "switches" on or off? Who tells them when, where, or how to fly? Who and when to shoot and kill? Or, equally important, who has the power to determine where and when a nuclear power plant or a space shuttle will be built, or how large a police-military force is to be recruited and with what machinery of destruction it is to be equipped?

One cannot simply add up all the energy in the form of food, chemicals, and kinetic forces that flow through the masses of the Inca commoners as compared with the Inca nobility and arrive at an assessment of their relative power positions. Nonetheless, there is a correspondence between control over energy flow and the rate at which energy is "consumed" by individuals and households. Wealthier and more powerful countries consume more energy; wealthier and more powerful individuals and households also consume more energy (Bodley 1981:185). Thus, not only do subordinate classes consume less energy per capita, but they do so under conditions that are stipulated or constrained by the ruling class.

SEX, AGE, AND CLASS

Sex hierarchies are conventionally distinguished from class hierarchies. We will do the same and postpone the discussion of sex hierarchies to Chapter 24. This distinction rests on the fact that class hierarchies include both sexes, whereas sex hierarchies refer to the domination of one sex by another within and across classes. Moreover, unlike class hierarchies, sex hierarchies occur in bands, villages, and chiefdoms as well as in states.

It should also be noted that age groups within both state and prestate societies are usually associated with unequal distributions of power. Indeed, hierarchical differences between mature adults and juveniles and infants are virtually universal. Moreover, the treatment of children by adults sometimes involves highly exploitative and physically and mentally punitive practices. One might argue that age hierarchies are fundamentally different from class and sex hierarchies because the maltreatment and exploitation of children is always "for their own good." Superordinate groups of all sorts, however, usually say this of the subordinate groups under their control. The fact that some degree of subordination of juveniles and infants is necessary for enculturation and population survival does not mean that such hierarchies are fundamentally different from class and sex hierarchies. As discussed above (p. 223), brutal treatment of children can result in death or permanent damage to their health and well-being. The resemblance between age hierarchies and class hierarchies is also strong in the cases in which old people constitute a despised and powerless group. In many societies senior citizens are victims of punitive physical and psychological treatment comparable to that meted out to criminals and enemies of the state. Descriptions of class structure, therefore, must never lose sight of the differences in power and life-style associated with sex and age groups within each class.

EMICS, ETICS, AND CLASS CONSCIOUSNESS

Class is an aspect of culture in which there are sharp differences between emic and etic points of view (Berreman 1982:18). Many social scientists accept class distinction as real and important only when consciously perceived and acted upon by the people involved. They hold that in order for a group to be considered a class, its members must have a consciousness of their own identity, exhibit a common sense of solidarity, and engage in organized attempts to promote and protect collective interests (T. Parsons 1970; Fallers 1977). Moreover, some social scientists (see Bendix and Lipset 1966) believe that classes exist only when persons with similar forms and quantities of social power organize into collective organizations such as political parties or labor unions. Other social scientists believe that the most important features of class hierarchies are the actual concentrations of power in certain groups and the powerlessness of others, regardless of any conscious or even unconscious awareness of these differences on the part of the people concerned and regardless of the existence of collective organizations (Roberts and Brintnall 1982:195–217).

From an etic and behavioral viewpoint, a class can exist even when the members of the class deny that they constitute a class, and even when instead of collective organizations they have organizations (such as rival business corporations or rival unions) that compete. The reason for this is that subordinate classes which lack class consciousness are obviously not exempt from the domination of ruling classes. Similarly, ruling classes containing antagonistic and competitive elements nonetheless dominate those who lack social power. Members of ruling classes need not form permanent, hereditary, monolithic, conspiratorial organizations in order to protect and enhance their own interests. A struggle for power within the ruling class does not necessarily result in a fundamentally altered balance of power between the classes. The struggle for control of the English crown, the Chinese dynasties, the Soviet Party apparatus (Fig. 17.2), and rivalrous modern multinational corporations all testify to the fact that the members

Figure 17.2 *THE SOVIET RULING CLASS*
Looking down from the top of Lenin's tomb, these powerful men are watching the May Day parade in Moscow, May 1, 1984. Where once the Czar ruled in the name of God, generals and bureaucrats now rule in the name of the proletariat.

of a ruling class may fight among themselves at the same time that they dominate or exploit subordinates.

Of course, there is no disputing the importance of a people's belief about the shape and origin of their stratification system. Consciousness of a common plight among the members of a downtrodden and exploited class may very well lead to the outbreak of organized class warfare. Consciousness is thus an element in the struggle between classes, but it is not the cause of class differences.

ECONOMIC EXPLOITATION

The control over large amounts of power by one class relative to another permits the members of the more powerful class to exploit the members of the weaker class. There is no generally accepted meaning of the term *exploitation,* but the basic conditions responsible for economic exploitation can be identified by reference to the previous discussion of reciprocity and redistribution (Ch. 16). When balanced reciprocity prevails or when the redistributors keep only the "stale cakes and bones" for themselves, there is no economic exploitation. But when there is unbalanced reciprocity or when the redistributors start keeping the "meat and fat" for themselves, exploitation may soon develop.

In the theories of Karl Marx, all wage laborers are exploited because the value of what they produce is always greater than what they are paid. Similarly, some anthropologists take the view that exploitation begins as soon as there is a structured flow of goods and services between two groups (Newcomer 1977; Ruyle 1973, 1975). Against this view it can be argued that the activities of employers and of stratified redistributors may result in an improvement in the well-being of the subordinate class and that without entrepreneurial or ruling class leadership everyone would be worse off (Dalton 1972, 1974). One cannot say, therefore, that every inequality in power and in consumption standards necessarily involves exploitation. If, as a result of the rewards given to or taken by the ruling class, the economic welfare of all classes steadily improves, it would seem inappropriate to speak of the people responsible for that improvement as exploiters.

Exploitation may be said to exist when the following four conditions exist: (1) The subordinate class experiences deprivations with respect to basic necessities such as food, water, air, sunlight, leisure, medical care, housing, and transport; (2) the ruling class enjoys an abundance of luxuries; (3) the luxuries enjoyed by the ruling class depend upon the labor of the subordinate class; and (4) the deprivations experienced by the subordinate class are caused by the failure of the ruling class to apply its power to the production of necessities instead of luxuries and to redistribute these necessities to the subordinate class (Boulding 1973). The fulfillment of these conditions indicates the existence of an etic and behavioral form of exploitation.

Because of the relationship between exploitation and human suffering, the study of exploitation is an important responsibility of social scientists who are concerned with the survival and well-being of our species. We must see to it that the study of exploitation is conducted empirically and with due regard to mental and emic as well as to etic and behavioral components.

PEASANT CLASSES

The majority of people alive today are members of one kind or another of peasant class.

Peasants are the subordinate food-producing classes of state societies who use preindustrial technologies of food production. Many different types of rent and taxes are extracted from peasants. But "peasants of all times and places are structured inferiors" (Dalton 1972:406). The kind of rent or taxes extracted from peasants defines the essential features of their structured inferiority.

Each major type of peasant is the subject of vast research literature. Anthropological studies of peasants have usually taken the form of "community studies." Anthropologists have studied peasant communities more than they have studied village peoples or hunter-gatherers (Pelto and Pelto 1973), primarily because the latter groups are less abundant and are disappearing rapidly. Three major types of peasant classes can be distinguished: feudal, agromanagerial state, and capitalist.

1. **Feudal Peasants** These peasants are subject to the control of a decentralized hereditary ruling class whose members provide military assistance to one another but do not interfere in one another's territorial domains. Feudal peasants, or "serfs," inherit the opportunity to utilize a particular parcel of land; hence they are said to be "bound" to the land. For the privilege of raising their own food, feudal peasants render unto the lord rent in kind or in money. Rent may also take the form of labor service in the lord's kitchens, stables, or fields.

Some anthropologists, following the lead of historians of European feudalism, describe feudal relationships as a more or less fair exchange of mutual obligations, duties, privileges, and rights between lord and serf. George Dalton (1969:390–391), for example, lists the following European feudal lord's services and payments to peasants:

1. Granting peasants the right to use land for subsistence and cash crops
2. Military protection (e.g., against invaders)
3. Police protection (e.g., against robbery)
4. Juridical services to settle disputes
5. Feasts to peasants at Christmas, Easter; also harvest gifts
6. Food given to peasants on days when they work the lord's fields
7. Emergency provision of food during disaster

Dalton denies that feudal peasants are exploited because it is not known if "the peasant paid out to the lord much more than he received back." Other anthropologists point out that the reason feudal peasants are "structured inferiors" is that the feudal ruling class deprives them of access to the land and its life-sustaining resources, which is antithetical to the principle of reciprocity and egalitarian redistribution. The counterflow of goods and services listed by Dalton merely perpetuates the peasant's structured inferiority. The one gift which would alter that relationship—the gift of land, free of rent or taxes—is never given.

History suggests that the structured inferiority of feudal peasants is seldom acceptable to the peasants. Over and over again the world has been convulsed by revolutions in which peasants struggled in the hope of restoring free access to land (E. Wolf 1969).

Many feudal peasantries owe their existence to military conquest, and this further emphasizes the exploitative nature of the landlord-serf relationship. For example, the Spanish crown rewarded Cortez and Pizarro and the other *conquistadores* (conquerers) with lordships over large slices of the territories they had conquered in Mexico and Peru. The heavy tax and labor demands placed on the conquered native Americans thereafter contributed to a precipitous decline in their numbers (Dobyns 1966; C. Smith 1970).

2. Agromanagerial State Peasantries

Where the state is strongly centralized, as in ancient Peru, Egypt, Mesopotamia, and China, peasants may be directly subject to state control in addition to, or in the absence of, control by a local landlord class. Unlike the feudal peasants, agromanagerial peasants are subject to frequent conscription for labor brigades drawn from villages throughout the realm to build roads, dams, irrigation canals, palaces, temples, and monuments. In return the state makes an effort to feed its peasants in case of food shortages caused by droughts or other calamities. The pervasive bureaucratic control over production and life-styles in the ancient agromanagerial states has often been compared with the treatment of peasants in modern socialist and communist societies such as China, Albania (Fig. 17.3), Vietnam, and Cambodia. The state in these countries is all-powerful—setting production quotas, controlling prices, extracting taxes in kind and in labor.

In Communist China (Fig. 17.4), a considerable effort was made under Mao Tse-tung to destroy the class nature of peasant identity and to merge all labor—intellectual, industrial, and agricultural—in a single working class. But some analysts hold that the political economy of China amounts to little more than the restoration

Figure 17.3 *ALBANIAN PEASANTS*
Commune members plowing.

Figure 17.4 *CHINESE PEASANTS*
Lack of modern machinery has been acknowledged as a source of underdevelopment by China's post-Mao leaders.

of the despotic agromanagerial state socialism that had existed for thousands of years under the Ming, Han, and Chou dynasties (Wittfogel 1960, 1979).

3. **Capitalist Peasants** In Africa, Latin America (Fig. 17.5), India, and Southeast Asia, feudal and agromanagerial types of peasantries have been replaced by peasants who enjoy increased opportunities to buy and sell land, labor, and food in competitive price markets. Most of the existing peasantries of the world outside of the Communist block belong to this category. The varieties of structured inferiority within this group defy any simple taxonomy. Some capitalist peasants are subordinate to large landowners; others are subordinate to banks that hold mortgages and promissory notes.

When the crops in production enter the international market, holdings are of the large or *latifundia*, type and the real landowners tend to be the commercial banks. Elsewhere, in more isolated or unproductive regions, holdings may be very small, giving rise to postage-stamp farms known as *minifundia* (Fig. 17.6) and to the phenomenon Sol Tax has aptly called "penny capitalism."

Capitalist peasants correspond to what Dalton calls "early modernized peasants." They display the following features:

1. Marketable land tenure

Figure 17.5 *PERUVIAN PEASANTS*
Man's wife is planting potatoes as he plows.

2. Predominance of production for cash sale
3. Growing sensitivity to national commodity and labor price markets
4. Beginnings of technological modernization

Although many capitalist peasants own their own land, they do not escape payment of rent or its equivalent. Many communities of landowning peasants constitute labor reserves for larger and more heavily capitalized plantations and farmers. Penny capitalists are frequently obliged to work for wages paid by these cash-crop enterprises. Penny capitalist peasants cannot obtain enough income to satisfy subsistence requirements from the sale of their products in the local market.

Figure 17.6 *ECUADORIAN PEASANTS*
Note the postage stamp minifundia on the steep hillsides.

RULING CLASSES: THE SOVIET UNION

The class structures of the Soviet Union and the United States are test cases for the proposition that all state societies have a ruling class. Both the United States and the Soviet governments, for example, foster the belief that they do not have ruling classes. The governing elites of both countries claim that the people are the source of all power. Both countries claim to be democratic. The mass of Soviet and U.S. citizens appear to accept these propositions as accurate accounts of actual conditions in their own but not the other country.

According to Soviet ideology, classes in the Soviet Union begin to disappear after 1917 as a result of the transfer of the ownership of the means of production to the people under the leadership of the Communist party [Lenin 1965 (1917)]. The Communist party was to organize the productive resources of the nation allegedly in order to maximize the material and spiritual well-being of the entire population. In the newly created government, all of the leaders were also Communist party members. The party elected its own top leadership. This leadership then filled out the top posts in government through appointments and sham elections. Despite the fact that the entire apparatus of party government had quickly fallen under the control of a single man (or small group, after Stalin's death), the party's theoreticians insisted that there was no ruling class (Djilas 1957). During the Stalinist period, citizens who were suspected of believing that the party and its government bureaucracy were indeed a ruling class suffered banishment, forced labor, torture, intimidation, and loss of life. Yet today, despite systematic censorship of artistic, literary, and scholarly work, despite direct state control over all communications media, and despite the complete absence of opposition parties, the Soviet Union continues to represent itself as a socialist democracy (Rothberg 1972). Although it is easy enough for Westerners to "see through" this charade, it is very difficult to adjust to the fact that large numbers of Soviet citizens probably do not (cf. Inkeles 1966; Feldmersen 1966; Fainsod 1967; Sweezy 1978; Shipler 1977; Connor 1979).

IS THERE A RULING CLASS IN THE UNITED STATES?

From both a practical and a theoretical point of view, the most important question that can be asked about class in the United States is whether or not there is a ruling class. Paradoxically, this is a subject about which relatively little is known.

The existence of a ruling class in the United States seems to be negated by the ability of the people as a whole to vote political power-holders in or out of office by secret ballot. Yet the fact that less than half of the voting-age population votes in presidential elections suggests that the majority of citizens distrusts the candidates' promises or doubts that one candidate can do anything more than any other to make life significantly better (Hadley 1978; Ladd 1978).* Moreover, it is well known that the actual selection of political candidates and the financing and conduct of election campaigns are controlled through special interest groups and political action committees rather than by the "people." Small coalitions of powerful individuals working through lobbyists, law firms, legislatures, the courts, executive and administrative agencies, and the mass media can decisively influence the course of elections and of national affairs. A great part of the decision-making process consists of responses to pressures exerted by special interest groups (Aron 1966; Dahl 1961; Domhoff 1970; Lundberg 1968). In the campaigns for election to Congress, the

*In the 1984 presidential election, 53 percent of the voting-age population voted. This means that President Reagan, who received 59 percent of the popular vote, was actually elected by only 31 percent of the voting-age population (*The New York Times*, 8 November 1984).

candidate who spends the most money usually wins. In 1978, for example, the candidates who spent more than their rivals won 87 percent of the time in the House of Representatives and 85 percent of the time in the Senate (*The New York Times*, 19 January 1979).

Those who reject the notion that there is a ruling class in the United States base their claim on the multiplicity of special interest groups. They argue that power in the United States is dispersed among so many different contending blocs, lobbies, associations, clubs, industries, regions, income groups, ethnic groups, states, cities, age groups, legislatures, courts, and unions that no coalition powerful enough to dominate all the others can form. In the terminology of the economist John Kenneth Galbraith (1958, 1967), there is no ruling class; there is only "countervailing" power (Roach et al. 1969). But the crucial question is this: Is there a category of people who share a common set of underlying interests in the perpetuation of the status quo and who by virtue of their extreme wealth are able to set limits to the kinds of laws and executive policies that are enacted and followed out? The evidence for the existence of such a category of people consists largely of studies of the degree of concentration of wealth in giant corporations and wealthy families. This kind of data alone cannot prove the existence of a ruling class, since there remains the problem of linking the boards of directors of these powerful corporations and leaders of wealthy families with decisions on crucial matters such as the rate of inflation, unemployment, national health service, energy policy, tax structure, resource depletion, pollution, military spending, urban blight, and so forth. Nonetheless, as we will see in the next section, the extraordinary concentration of wealth and economic power in the United States strongly suggests that such linkages do exist (Roberts and Brintnall 1982:259; Domhoff 1980).

THE CONCENTRATION OF WEALTH IN THE UNITED STATES

In a study of the concentration of wealth based on estate inheritance taxes filed with the Internal Revenue Service (Smith, Franklin, and Wion 1973), it was found that the less than 5 percent of individual adults who have a net worth of $60,000 or more possess 35.6 percent of the nation's wealth. Average wealth per individual was $200,000. In contrast, 53 percent of the adult population would have been worth less than $3000 if they sold all their possessions and paid all their debts:

> Four percent of the population owned over a quarter of the nation's real estate, three-fifths of all privately held corporate stock, four-fifths of the business assets (excluding business, real estate), a third of the cash and virtually all of the notes, mortgages and foreign and corporate bonds. After subtracting their debts, they were worth over a trillion dollars, enough to have purchased the entire national output of the United States plus the combined output of Switzerland, Denmark, Norway and Sweden in 1969 (J. Smith 1973:44).

The same study also showed that 1 percent of the richest adults—about 550,000 individuals—owned 21.2 percent of all the wealth, and that there were about 2500 individuals who possessed more than $10 million, with an average of almost $20 million per head! Although these figures reveal more about class in the United States than do income studies, they still leave the structural significance of the concentration of wealth in doubt because they do not show the extent to which the top 1 percent of wealthy individuals are actually members of the same households, families, or personal networks. In 1975, the top 1 percent of wealth holders held 19.5 percent of all personal wealth (J. Smith 1981). Since then, with the rise in the value of stocks in 1983, this percentage has increased markedly.

Where the holdings of very rich families are identified as a unit, the degree of concentration of wealth can be quite astonishing. For example, the value of assets held by descendants of Thomas Mellon exceeds $5 billion. Although this wealth is held in separate trusts and accounts of about 50 living descendants (giving them an average of $100 million a head), a large block of it is managed by a single group of investment companies located in a skyscraper in Pittsburgh (Hersh 1978; Koskoff 1978). Mellon family interests controlled 23 percent of Mellon National Corporation, which controlled 15 percent of the Gulf Oil Corporation, the tenth largest company in the world. This does not mean that all the Mellons think alike or conspire to influence corporate or public decisions as a unit. It does mean, however, that active key members of the family were able to forestall decisions adverse to their interests in the affairs of companies like Gulf Oil, Alcoa Aluminum, and the Mellon National Bank.

The question of who controls the corporations in the United States is difficult to answer. The average individual stockholder owns only trivial amounts of stock compared with the top managers and the major stockholders. Fewer than 90,000 individuals—0.3 percent of all stockholders—own over 25 percent of all the stock in private hands. Fewer than 23,000 individuals—0.1 percent—own all the tax-free state and municipal bonds in private hands. The same top 1 percent of wealthy individuals own 40 percent of all treasury bills, notes, and mortgages. But about half of stocks and bonds are no longer owned by individuals; they are owned by so-called institutional investors who administer pension funds, trust funds, and insurance companies. It is the corporations, families, and people who control these institutional investors who have the greatest economic power.

According to a study carried out on voting rights in major corporations by the U.S. Senate Committee on Governmental Affairs (1978), power to vote stock in 122 of the largest corporations in America was concentrated in 21 institutional investors. These 122 corporations had a market value of about $500 billion, and they had 2259 subsidiaries and affiliates comprising the largest industrial, financial, transportation, insurance, utility, and retail firms in the country. The 21 top institutional investors consist mostly of banks and insurance companies such as Morgan Guaranty, Citicorp, Prudential Insurance, Bankamerica, Manufacturers Hanover, Bankers Trust, Equitable Life, and Chase Manhattan. Each of these banks is not only one of the five largest stockvoters in anywhere from 8 to 56 of the largest corporations, but as a group they are one another's largest stockvoters. Morgan Guaranty, which is the top stockvoter in 27 of the largest corporations, is also the top stockvoter in Citicorp, Manufacturers Hanover, Chemical New York, Bankers Trust, and Bankamerica. But the controllers and the controlled are really one and the same, because the largest institutional stockvoters in Morgan Guaranty are none other than Citicorp, Chase Manhattan, Manufacturers Hanover, and Bankers Trust (U.S. Senate Committee on Governmental Affairs 1978:3).

It is entirely possible, therefore, that a small group of individuals and families may in fact exert a decisive influence over the policies of this small but immensely power-

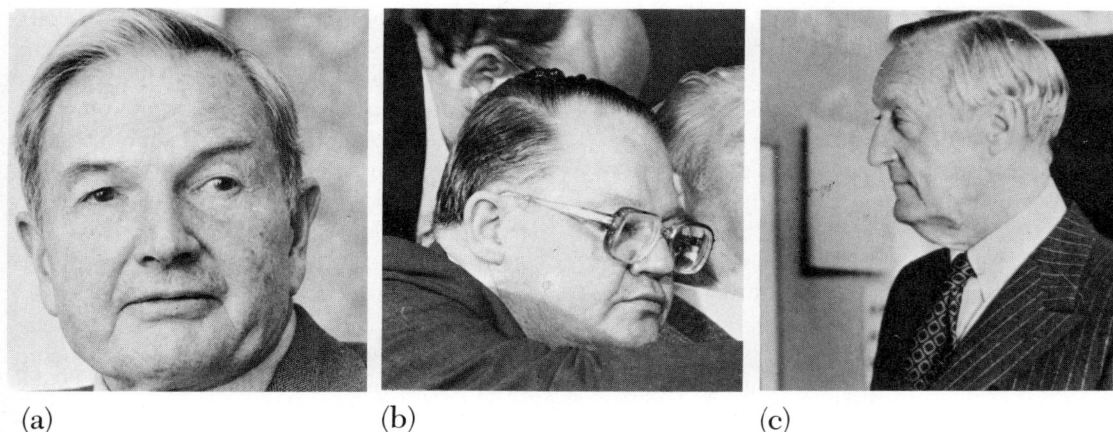

(a) (b) (c)

Figure 17.7 *MEMBERS OF THE RULING CLASS?*
David Rockefeller *(a)*, Nelson Bunker Hunt *(b)*, and Paul Mellon *(c)*.

ful group of corporations. Some of the individuals and families involved are well known. Besides the Mellons, they include Rockefellers, Du Ponts, Fords, Hunts, Pews, and Gettys (Fig. 17.7). But it is a testament to the ability of the super-rich to live in a world apart that the names of many other powerful families are unknown to the general public. Anthropologists, with their many studies of people in poverty, have been remiss in not studying the corresponding patterns of thoughts and actions among the super-rich (Nader 1972; Riner 1981).

CLASS AND LIFE-STYLE

Classes differ from one another not only in amount of power per capita, abut also in broad areas of patterned thought and behavior called *life-style* (Fig. 17.8). Peasants, ur-

Figure 17.8 *CLASS AND LIFE-STYLE*
South Bronx.

ban industrial wage workers, middle-class suburbanities, and upper-class industrialists have different life-styles (Fig. 17.9). Cultural contrasts among class-linked life-styles are as great as contrasts between life in an Eskimo igloo and life in a Mbuti village of the Ituri forest. For example, the former Mrs. Seward Prosser Mellon had a household budget of $750,000 a year, not including a $20,000 budget for the family dog (Koskoff 1978:467).

Classes, in other words, have their own *subcultures* made up of distinctive work patterns, architecture, home furnishings, diet, dress, domestic routines, sex and mating practices, magico-religious rituals, art, ideology. In many instances, classes even have accents that make it difficult for them to talk to one another. Because of exposure of body parts to sun, wind, and callus-producing friction, working-class people tend to look different from their "superiors." Further distinctions are the result of dietary specialties—the fat and the rich were once synonymous. Throughout almost the entire evolutionary career of stratified societies, class

Figure 17.9 *CLASS AND LIFE-STYLE*
Miami Beach.

identity has been as explicit and unambiguous as the distinction between male and female. The Chinese Han dynasty peasant, the Inca commoner, or the Russian serf could not expect to survive to maturity without knowing how to recognize members of the "superior" classes. Doubt was removed in many cases by state-enforced standards of dress: Only the Chinese nobility could wear silk clothing; only the European feudal overlords could carry daggers and swords; only the Inca rulers could wear gold ornaments. Violators were put to death. In the presence of their "superiors," commoners still perform rituals of subordination, among which lowering the head, removing the hat, averting the eyes, kneeling, bowing, crawling, and maintaining silence unless spoken to occur almost universally.

Throughout much of the world, class identity continues to be sharp and unambiguous. Among most contemporary nations, differences in class-linked life-styles show little prospect of diminishing or disappearing. Indeed, given the increase in luxury goods and services available to contemporary elites, contrasts in life-styles between the rich and powerful and the people of peasant villages or urban shantytowns (Fig. 17.10) may be reaching an all-time high.

Figure 17.10 *CARACAS SHANTYTOWN*
Squatters in Latin American cities often enjoy the best views, since apartment houses were not built on hilltops due to lack of water. But this means that the squatters have to carry their water up the hill in cans.

During the recent epochs of industrial advance, governing classes throughout the world have gone from palanquins to Cadillacs to private jets, while their subordinates find themselves without even a donkey or a pair of oxen. The elites now have their medical needs taken care of at the world's best medical centers, while vast numbers of less fortunate people have never even heard of the germ theory of disease and will never be treated by modern medical techniques. Elites attend the best universities, while half of the people in the world remain illiterate (Fig. 17.11).

CLASS MOBILITY

Classes differ greatly in the manner in which membership is established and in the rate at which membership changes. When class membership is established exclusively through hereditary *ascription*—through the inheritance of durable power in the form of money, property, or some other form of wealth—there is necessarily a low rate of *mobility* in or out. Such a class is spoken of as being "closed" (it is also sometimes referred to as being a *caste* or being "caste like"; see below). The ruling classes of despotic states, the nobility of seventeenth-century Europe, and the highest echelons of contemporary billionaire elites in the United States and Canada are examples of superordinate closed classes.

Closed classes tend to be endogamous. Among superordinate groups, endogamy is practiced as a means of preventing the dispersal of power; marriage alliances among

Figure 17.11 *SQUATTERS IN LIMA*
Life on a garbage heap.

families consolidate and concentrate lines of control over the natural and cultural sources of power (see p. 267). For the subordinate classes, endogamy is almost always an imposed condition that prevents men and women of humble birth from changing their class identity and from sharing in the power prerogatives of the superordinate segments.

Will it ever be possible to produce a completely open class structure? What would such a system look like? If there were only two classes, complete mobility could be achieved if each person spent half a lifetime in the upper group and half in the lower group. Aside from the incredible confusion this transfer of wealth, power, and leadership would create, there is another reason intrinsic to the nature of class stratification that makes a completely open system improbable. For a class system to be completely open, the members of the ruling class must voluntarily abdicate their powerful positions. But in the entire evolutionary career of state-level societies, no ruling class has been known voluntarily to surrender its power simply out of a sense of obligation to ethical or moral principles. Of course individuals may do so, but there will always be a residue who will use their power to stay in power. One interpretation of the recurrent upheavals in China, known as "cultural revolutions," is that they are designed to prevent government bureaucrats from showing favoritism to their own children with respect to educational opportunities and exemptions from labor battalions. These cultural revolutions, however, are obviously not designed to destroy the power of those who command each successive upheaval to start and stop. Perhaps a completely open class system is a contradiction in terms; the best that can be hoped for are relatively high rates of mobility.

In the great world museum of exotic ethnographic forms, at least one society made an ingenious attempt to create a maximally open class system through special rules of marriage and descent. The Natchez of the lower Mississippi were organized into two classes—rulers and commoners. The early French explorers called the latter *stinkards*. The members of the ruling group were obliged to marry commoners (but since there were more commoners than rulers, most commoners married commoners). Children of female members of the ruling class inherited the positions of their mothers, but children of the male members of the ruling class dropped down a grade with each marriage. Thus a male *sun* had a *noble* male child, who in turn had a *stinkard* male child. The female *sun*'s children, however, remained *suns;* the female *noble*'s children remained *nobles*, and so on. This system might be compared to a custom that would oblige all male millionaires to marry paupers; it would not put an end to the distinction between millionaires and paupers, but it would certainly reduce the social distance between them. The exogamy of the Natchez ruling class probably indicates a fairly recent emergence from an unstratified form of organization (C. Mason 1964). Under other circumstances, however, there are no structural reasons for expecting a ruling class to accept power-dispersing, exogamic marriage rules.

MINORITIES AND MAJORITIES

In addition to classes, most state societies are also stratified into so-called racial, ethnic, and cultural groups (R. Cohen 1978a and b). These groups—often called *minorities* or *majorities*—differ from classes in three ways: (1) They have distinctive lifestyles that can be traced to the cultural traditions of another society; (2) their members often belong to different classes; (3) their members are conscious of their existence as a group set apart from the rest of the population.

The separation into racial, ethnic, or cultural minorities is based upon whether the criteria of group membership are primarily physical appearance, common origin in another country or region, or possession of a distinctive life-style. In reality, however, all three criteria occur in a bewildering number of combinations. Racial and cultural differences and common ancestry are often claimed by or attributed to groups that lack them, giving rise to sharp discrepancies between emic and etic versions of group identity (Fig. 17.12).

Racial, ethnic, and cultural *minorities* are

Figure 17.12 *ETHNIC IDENTITY*
All of these people identify themselves as Jews. The man *(a)* was born in Yemen and the girl *(b)* in India. The young woman *(c)* was born in Morocco and both boys *(d)* in Israel.

groups that are subordinate or whose position is vulnerable to subordination. The term *majority* refers to the higher-ranking and more secure racial, ethnic, or cultural segments of the population. Minority and majority are unsatisfactory terms because "majorities" like the whites in South Africa are sometimes vastly outnumbered by the "minorities" whom they oppress and exploit (Fig. 17.13). No satisfactory substitute for these terms has been devised, however (Simpson and Yinger 1962).

The most important point to bear in mind about minorities and majorities is that they are invariably locked into a more or less open form of political, social, and economic struggle to protect or raise their position in the stratification system (Despres 1975; Schermerhorn 1970; Wagley and Harris 1958; Abruzzi 1982). Depending on their respective numbers, their special cultural strengths and weaknesses, and their initial advantages or disadvantages during the formation of the stratification system, their status as a group may rise or fall in the hierarchy. Thus, although many minorities are subject to excruciating forms of discrimination, segregation, and exploitation, others may actually enjoy fairly high although not dominant positions.

Figure 17.13 *APARTHEID*
Pretoria, South Africa

ASSIMILATION VERSUS PLURALISM

Like classes, minorities occur in both relatively open and closed versions. Some minorities are almost completely endogamous, and of these many are endogamous by "choice." The Jews, Chinese, and Greeks in the United States, the Hindus in Guyana, the Muslims in India, and the Japanese in Brazil are examples of groups for whom endogamy is a practice valued as much by the minority as by the rest of the population. Other minorities, such as the blacks of the United States and the coloreds of South Africa, have no strong motivation to be endogamous but find intermarriage blocked largely by the hostility of the rest of the population. Still other minorities neither possess internal barriers to exogamy nor encounter external resistance. Such groups (e.g., the Germans or Scots in the United States and the Italians in Brazil) usually move toward *assimilation*—the loss of separate identity as a minority group.

Where endogamy prevails, either by choice of the minority or by imposition of the "majority," a *pluralistic* condition may endure for centuries or even millennia. Assimilation may also fail to take place even when a certain amount of intermarriage occurs if there is a form of descent rule, as in the United States, that assigns the mixed offspring to the minority or if the rate of intermarriage is not very high relative to the rate of population increase.

What accounts for these variations? The attempt to explain why a minority will develop along pluralistic rather than assimilationist lines requires a broad evolutionary and comparative approach. The most important fact to consider is this: Minorities enter a particular state society under disadvantageous circumstances. They enter as migrants seeking relief from exploitative class systems in their native lands; they enter as defeated people who have been overrun during wars of conquest and expansion; or they enter as defeated peoples transferred from colonial outposts as indentured servants or slaves.

Each minority has a unique *adaptive capacity* to survive and prosper in the particular situation in which it finds itself. This capacity is based on its prior experiences, history, language, and culture. If the class structure of the majority's social system is marked by individualized competition for upward mobility and a corresponding lack of class identity or class solidarity, the minority may derive advantages from the practice of endogamy, settlement in restricted regions or neighborhoods, and pursuit of pluralistic goals.

The reasons for the development of pluralistic goals are as diverse as the adaptive capacities in the world inventory of minorities and the structure of state societies in which they live. Some groups appear to be more likely than others to benefit from the preservation of their traditional culture patterns because these patterns have a high adaptive capacity. Jews, for example, long excluded from land-based means of earning a living in Europe, arrived in the rapidly urbanizing society of the late nineteenth-century United States "preadapted" to compete for upward mobility in urban occupations requiring high levels of literacy. Contemporary Japanese migrants to Brazil bring with them special skills related to intensive agriculture and truck farming. Chinese migrants in many parts of the world achieve outstanding success by adhering to traditional family-based patterns of business activity.

The emphasis upon differences in language, religion, and other aspects of lifestyles can increase the minority's sense of solidarity and may help its members to compete in impersonalized, class-structured, competitive societies such as those of the United States and Canada. Jewish, Chinese, Japanese, Greek, Syrian, Hindu, or Muslim merchants and businesspeople, for example, frequently enjoy important commercial advantages in highly competitive situations. Based on his study of the relations between Afro-Americans and Hindus in Guyana, Leo Despres (1975) suggests that ethnic, cultural, and racial identities confer competitive advantages with respect to environmental resources. The Hindu segment of Guyana society, for example has a firmer grip on the land than the black segment.

In many situations, however, strong minority solidarity carries with it the danger of overexposure and reaction. In maintaining and increasing their own solidarity, minorities run the risk of increasing the sense of alienation of the larger population and hence of becoming the scapegoats of genocidal policies. The fate of the Jews in Germany and Poland, the Hindu Indians in east and southern Africa, the Chinese in Indonesia, and the Muslims in India are some of the better-known examples of "successful" minority adaptations that were followed by mass slaughter and/or expulsion.

Moreover, it is well to keep in mind that minorities are themselves stratified and that, therefore, the upper classes and elites within the minority may stand to gain more from the perpetuation of the minority than the average member. One important reason for the perpetuation of pluralist aims and symbols is that the wealthier and more powerful segments of both the minority and majority often derive economic and political strength from the maintenance of a separate identity for their subordinates. Roger Sanjek (1972, 1977) studied the relationship among 23 different "tribal" groups who live in the city of Accra, Ghana, and found that in terms of language, behavior, dress, residence, and facial markings there was little to distinguish one group from another. Nonetheless, politicians relied heavily on their "tribal" identities in competing for political office. Similarly, the tragic history of Lebanon cannot be understood apart from the private fortunes that both Christian and Muslim elites have been able to amass as a result of drawn-out communal strife (Joseph 1978).

CASTES IN INDIA

Indian castes are closed, endogamous, and stratified descent groups. They bear many resemblances to both endogamous classes and racial, ethnic, and cultural minorities. No sharp line can be drawn between groups such as the Jews or blacks in the United States or the Inca elite and the castes of India. However, some features of the Indian caste hierarchy are unique and deserve special attention.

The unique features of Indian castes have to do with the fact that the caste hierarchy is an integral part of Hinduism, which is the religion of most of the people of India. It is a matter of religious conviction in India that all people are not spiritually equal and that the gods have established a hierarchy of groups (Bose 1975). This hierarchy consists of the four major *varnas*, or grades of being. According to the earliest traditions (e.g., the Hymns of Rigveda), the four *varnas* correspond to the physical parts of Purusa, who gave rise to the human race through dismemberment. His mouth became the *Brahmans* (priests), his arms the *Kshatriyas* (warriors), his thighs the *Vaishyas* (merchants and craftsmen), and his feet the *Shudras* (menial workers) (Gould 1971). According to Hindu scripture, an individual's *varna* is determined by a descent rule; that is, it corresponds to the *varna* of one's parents and is unalterable during one's lifetime.

The basis of all Hindu morality is the idea that each *varna* has its appropriate rules of behavior, or "path of duty" (*dharma*). At the death of the body, the soul meets its fate in the form of a transmigration into a higher or lower being (*karma*). Those who follow the "path of duty" will find themselves at a higher point on Purusa's body during their next life. Deviation from the "path of duty" will result in reincarnation in the body of an outcaste or even an animal.

One of the most important aspects of the "path of duty" is the practice of certain taboos regarding marriage, eating, and physical proximity. Marriage below one's *varna* is generally regarded as a defilement and pollution; acceptance of food cooked or handled by persons below one's *varna* is also a defilement and pollution; any bodily contact between Brahman and Shudra is forbidden (Fig. 17.14). In some parts of India there were not only untouchables but unseeables—people who could come out only at night.

Although the general outlines of this system are agreed upon throughout Hindu India, there are enormous regional and local differences in the finer details of the ideology and practice of caste relationships. The principal source of these complications is the fact that it is not the *varna* but thousands of internally stratified subdivisions known as

Figure 17.14 *UNTOUCHABLES* Caste in India must be seen from the bottom up to be understood.

jatis (or subcastes) that constitute the real functional endogamous units. Moreover, even *jatis* of the same name [e.g., "washermen" (Fig. 17.15), "shoemakers," "herders," and so on] further divide into local endogamous subgroups and exogamous lineages (Klass 1979).

CASTE FROM THE TOP DOWN AND BOTTOM UP

There are two very different views of the Hindu caste system. The view that predominates among Westerners is that which conforms largely to the emics of the top-ranking Brahman caste. According to this view, each caste and subcaste has a hereditary occupation that guarantees its members basic subsistence and job security. The lower castes render vital services to the upper castes. Hence the upper castes know they cannot get along without the lower castes and do not abuse them. And in times of crisis, the upper castes will extend emergency assistance in the form of food or loans. Moreover, since the Hindu religion gives every-

Figure 17.15 *BOMBAY LAUNDRY* Members of the washerman subcaste have privileged access to these facilities.

one a convincing explanation of why some are inferior and others superior, members of lower castes do not resent being regarded as a source of pollution and defilement and have no interest in changing the status of their caste in the local or regional hierarchy (Dumont 1970).

The other view—the view from the bottom up—makes the Indian caste system hard to distinguish from the racial, ethnic, and cultural minorities with which Westerners are familiar. Critics of the top-down view point out that whites in the United States once insisted that the Bible justified slavery, that blacks were well treated, contented with their lot in life, and not interested in changing their status. According to Joan Mencher, who has worked and lived among the untouchable castes of southern India, the error in the top-down view is just as great in India as in the United States. Mencher (1980) reports that the lowest castes are not satisfied with their station in life and do not believe they are treated fairly by their caste superiors. As for the security allegedly provided by the monopoly over such professions as smiths, washermen, barbers, potters, and so on, such castes taken together never constituted more than 10 to 15 percent of the total Hindu population. And even within such castes, the caste profession never provided basic subsistence for the majority of people. Among the Chamars, for example, who are known as leatherworkers, only a small portion of the caste engages in leatherwork. In the countryside almost all Chamars are a source of cheap agricultural labor. When questioned about their low station in life, many of Mencher's low-caste informants explained that they had to be dependent on the other castes since they had no land of their own. Did landowners in times of extreme need or crisis actually give free food and assistance to their low-caste dependents? "To my informants, both young and old, this sounds like a fairytale" (Mencher 1974b).

Anthropological studies of actual village life in India have yielded a picture of caste relationships drastically opposed to the ideals posited in Hindu theology (Carrol 1977). One of the most important discoveries is that local *jatis* recurrently try to raise their ritual status. Such attempts usually take place as part of a general process by which local ritual status is adjusted to actual local economic and political power. There may be low-ranking subcastes that passively accept their lot in life as a result of their *karma* assignment; such groups, however, tend to be wholly lacking in the potential for economic and political mobility. "But let opportunities for political and economic advance appear barely possible and such resignation is likely to vanish more quickly than one might imagine" (Orans 1968:878).

One of the symptoms of this underlying propensity for *jatis* to redefine their ritual position to conform with their political and economic potential is a widespread lack of agreement over the shape of local ritual hierarchies as seen by inhabitants of the same village, town, or region.

As the sociologist Bernard Barber (1968) has noted, the study of caste "dissensus" is a central concern of village Indian research. Kathleen Gough (1959) indicates that in villages of South India, the middle reaches of the caste hierarchy may have as many as fifteen castes whose relative ritual ranks are ambiguous or in dispute. Different individuals and families even in the same caste give different versions of the rank-order of these groups. Elsewhere, even the claims of Brahman subcastes to ritual superiority are openly contested (Srinivas 1955). The conflict among *jatis* concerning their ritual position may involve prolonged litigation in the local courts and if not resolved may, under certain circumstances, lead to much violence and bloodshed (see Berreman 1975; Cohn 1955).

Contrary to the view that these features of caste are a response to the recent "modernization" of India, Karen Leonard (1978) has shown that similarly fluid and flexible individual, family, and subcaste strategies date back at least to the eighteenth century. According to Leonard, the internal organization and external relationships of the Kayastks, originally a caste of scribes and record keepers, shifted continuously to adapt to changing economic, political, and demographic circumstances. Kayastks attempted to better their lot in life as individuals, as families, and as subcastes as opportunities changed. Marriage patterns and descent rules were continually modified to provide maximum advantages with respect to government and commercial employment, and even the rule of endogamy was broken when alliances with other subcastes became useful: "Adaptability, rather than conformity to accepted Brahmanical or scholarly notions about caste, has always characterized the Kayastk marriage networks and kin groups" (Leonard 1978:294).

In comparing Indian castes with minorities in other parts of the world, it should be emphasized that substantial cultural differences are frequently associated with each local *jati*. Subcastes may speak different languages or dialects, have different kinds of descent and locality rules, different forms of marriage, worship different gods, eat different foods, and altogether present a greater contrast in life-style than that which exists between New Yorkers and the Zuni Indians. Moreover, many castes of India are associated with racial differences comparable to the contrast between whites and blacks in the United States. In view of all these resemblances, it might very well be argued that we could dispense with either the term *caste* or the term *minority*.

The stratification system of India is not noteworthy merely for the presence of endogamous descent groups possessing real or imagined racial and cultural specialties. Every state-level society has such groups. It is, rather, the extraordinary profusion of such groups that merits our attention. Nonetheless, the caste system of India is fundamentally similar to that of other countries that have closed classes and numerous ethnic and racial minorities: Like the blacks in the United States or the Catholics in Northern Ireland, low castes in India resist the status accorded them, with its concomitant disabilities and discrimination, and strive for higher accorded status and its attendant advantages. High castes attempt to prevent such striving and the implied threat to their position. In this conflict of interests lies the explosive potential of all caste societies (Berreman 1966:318).

SUMMARY

All state societies are organized into stratified groups such as classes, minorities, and castes. Stratified groups consist of people who relate to the apparatus of control in similar ways and who possess similar amounts of power over the allocation of wealth, privileges, resources, and technology. Power, in this context, means control over energy or the ability to move and shape people and things. All state societies have at least two classes—rulers and ruled. Theoretically, ruling classes may voluntarily act in the best interests of commoners, but only if ruling class power is not thereby diminished.

Sex and age hierarchies are also important forms of stratification, but they are not confined to state societies. Class differences involve both differential access to power and profound differences in life-styles. The understanding of class and all other forms of social stratification is made difficult by the failure to separate emic and etic versions of stratification hierarchies. From an etic and behavioral point of view, classes can exist even if there is no emic recognition of their existence and even if segments of the same class compete. Ruling classes need not form permanent, hereditary, monolithic, conspiratorial organizations. Their membership can change rapidly and they may actively deny that they constitute a ruling class. Similarly, subordinate classes need not be conscious of their identity and may exist only in an etic and behavioral sense.

The understanding of the phenomenon of exploitation also depends on the distinction between emic and etic perspectives. It cannot be maintained that the mere existence of differential power, wealth, and privilege guarantees the existence of exploitation; nor that exploitation exists only when or as soon as people feel exploited. Etic criteria for exploitation focus on the acquisition of luxuries among elites based on the deprivation of necessities among commoners and perpetuation or intensification of misery and poverty.

The majority of the people in the world today are members of peasant classes. Peasants are structured inferiors who farm with preindustrial technologies and pay rent or taxes. Three major varieties of peasants can be distinguished: feudal, agromanagerial, and capitalist. Their structured inferiority depends in the first case on the inability to acquire land; in the second, on the existence of a powerful managerial elite that sets production and labor quotas; and in the third, on the operation of a price market in land and labor controlled by big landlords, corporations, and banks.

The question of the existence of an etic ruling class in the Soviet Union and the United States provides an important test case of the proposition that all state societies have at least two classes—rulers and ruled. Westerners readily reject the claim that the Soviet Communist party bosses are not part of a ruling class, given the absence of opposition parties and genuine national elections. But the case of the United States is more perplexing. Elections are held, but the choice of candidates is small and about half the electorate abstains from voting. Legislation is controlled by lobbies through which the interests of corporate managers and the superrich are advanced and protected more readily than those of ordinary individuals. Despite the considerable number of countervailing foci of power, there is an enormous concentration of wealth and hence power in a small number of superrich families and a handful of institutional investors and giant corporations.

Systems of class stratification differ widely in the amount of upward mobility they permit. If classes were exogamous and if children of the very rich were disinherited, mobility would be much higher. One of the most fluid systems of social stratification known is that of the Natchez.

Racial, ethnic, and cultural minorities and majorities are present in virtually all state societies. These groups differ from classes in having distinctive life-styles derived from another society; internal class differences; and a high degree of group consciousness. Minorities and majorities struggle for access to and control over the sources of wealth and power, aided or hindered by their adaptive strengths and weaknesses in relation to specific arenas of competition. It is the specific nature of this struggle in the history of each minority-majority relationship that determines whether assimilation or pluralism will be emphasized by the minority and/or the majority. Advantages and disadvantages are associated with both options. Neither assimilationist nor pluralist commitments may suffice to overcome the effects of segregation, discrimination, and exploitation. It can be argued that racial and ethnic chauvinism benefits the ruling class more than the ordinary members of either the minority or majority.

Social scientists usually identify a third type of stratified group known as castes. Castes are epitomized by the case of Hindu India. Traditional views of Indian castes have been dominated by top-down idealizations in which the lower castes are represented as voluntarily accepting their subordinate status. Bottom-up studies show that Indian castes struggle for upward mobility in a flexible and adaptive fashion and that they closely resemble cultural, ethnic, and racial minorities in other societies.

18 UNDERDEVELOPMENT AND CULTURAL CHANGE

This chapter deals with inequalities that stem from levels of economic development and underdevelopment in the world today. We shall attempt to analyze the causes of development and of underdevelopment in relation to the heritage of colonial empires and to describe and evaluate some of the proposals for stimulating development as well as for alternative solutions involving "appropriate" technologies. We shall also focus on the plight of the rural poor in societies that are undergoing rapid change in a variety of economic and political contexts characteristic of modern times. We shall pay special attention to the role of values and ideology in mediating adjustments to the stresses of modern life and to the relationship between population growth and development.

COLONIALISM AND UNDERDEVELOPMENT

To a considerable extent the unequal development of the industrial and nonindustrial countries today is a heritage of recent economic and political imperialism. The capitalist countries were involved in a ceaseless quest for new sources of raw materials, cheap labor, and new markets for their manufactures (Wallerstein 1974; E. Wolf 1982). The profits from these far-flung enterprises benefited the industrial powers and helped to accelerate their growth; but they had a generally negative effect on the dependent nations (Fig. 18.1). For example, starting with the sixteenth century, colonies in the tropics and semitropics were used to grow plantation crops such as sugar, cotton, tea, tobacco, sisal, hemp, and copra. Although these crops were a source of great wealth for the foreigners who controlled the plantations, the workers were paid very low wages relative to the costs of manufactured items and they could not accumulate any capital. Instead of substituting machines for labor, colonial entrepreneurs remained competitive by keeping labor costs down to the barest possible minimum. Protected colonial landowners did not need to invest in improved production facilities in order to stay in business. With the assistance of police-military forces, they merely lowered the price of labor. Slavery was one means of doing this. *Corvée* was another. Corvée workers spent most of their time earning their own subsistence on small farms. Through the imposition of tax per number of people in a household (head tax), which had to be paid in cash, or through a law that specified that every man had to work so many months of the year for wages or through outright impressment into labor crews, cheap labor was forced into the production of the export commodities (Amin 1976).

These arrangements were prevalent in Africa after the period of slavery came to an end and before independence. They flourished most recently in the Portuguese colonies of Mozambique and Angola and are still found in the Reserve and "Bantustan" areas of the Republic of South Africa (Chilcote 1972; Magubane 1979). In Mozambique, Africans who were unable to prove that they had worked for wages on European plantations or in other European-dominated businesses were conscripted into labor brigades and put to work on the docks and roads. Their salaries were lower than the already below-subsistence salaries they would have obtained had they dutifully "volunteered" for work. Another common colonial solution to the problem of making inefficient tropical agriculture profitable was to award buying

Figure 18.1 *UNDERDEVELOPMENT*
In absolute numbers, there are more children like this in the world than ever before.

concessions to protected companies and then to force every "native" in a given area to grow a fixed minimum of a designated crop. In many parts of Africa, hundreds of thousands of people were forced to divert a portion of their subsistence plots to the cultivation of cotton and other cash crops, even in areas where such cultivation was ecologically risky and prone to complete failure. Such experiments cost the concessionaires nothing; only the peasant family paid in the form of malnutrition and drudgery (Harris 1958, 1972, 1974a; Mondlane 1969).

INDONESIA AND JAPAN

The magnitude of the economic disaster inherent in colonialism can best be understood by comparing areas that experienced colonial rule with those that partially or totally escaped it. The comparison between Japan and Java is especially instructive in this regard.

Java, the most populous island in the modern Republic of Indonesia, resembles the larger Japanese islands in certain important ecological and political respects. When first contacted by Europeans, both Japan and Java had feudal organizations based on wet-rice agriculture. Irrigation was essential in both instances. Both Java and Japan have relatively small land-masses, broken into small valleys by numerous volcanic peaks and mountains. In the early sixteenth century, when European influence first began to spread into the western Pacific, Java was the more appealing colonial target because of its tropical products. Moreover, the conquest of Java was easier than the conquest of Japan. Java was fragmented into warring kingdoms, each of which was fragmented into feudal holdings. Japan, on the other hand, was nominally a single kingdom, headed by an emperor; the Japanese feudal subdivisions thus tended to be larger and militarily better organized than those of the independent Javanese kingdoms. The first attempts at European penetration were carried out in both cases by Portuguese and Spanish merchants and priests.

Spain and Portugal soon established regular trade relations with Japan. The Portuguese gained entrance to the Japanese markets through the missionary work of the Jesuit order under the leadership of the Italian, Francis Xavier. The vanguard of the Spanish penetration, on the other hand, were missionaries of the Franciscan order. The missionaries, European traders, rival Japanese feudal princes, and rebellious peasants all began fighting with each other, until in 1614, the Europeans were thrown out of the country. We shall return to this important event in a moment.

In Java the early missionary work of the Portuguese was impeded by the spread of Islam, and it seemed for a while as if the Europeans were also about to be driven from the East Indies. Under Islamic influence a vigorous class of Indonesian traders and businessmen held their own in competition with the Portuguese. However, the Dutch, newly emancipated from Spanish tutelage, formed the United East India Company in 1602 and pursued a policy of armed conquest intended to assure monopoly control over the entire East Indies trading area. Maneuvering between the rival Javanese kingdoms, the Dutch steadily expanded their domination of Java and the Outer Islands (Sumatra, Borneo, and Celebes).

As the conquest was enlarged, the defeated ruling families were converted into agents of the "Company." Profits were made in a variety of ways: by forced planting of export crops (indigo, coffee, sugar) over which the Company exercised monopoly privileges; by simple tribute taxation in kind (rice, timber, cotton thread, beans); by money taxes; and by exports from sugar and coffee plantations worked by forced laborers. This phase of Dutch colonial rule lasted from 1602 to 1798. Its main economic consequence was the destruction of the Javanese trader class, which had almost succeeded in getting the upper hand over the Portuguese.

Between 1798 and 1825 there was an interlude during which the East India Company went bankrupt from paying dividends at an annual rate of 40 percent. The English took over temporarily during the Napoleonic Wars. The Dutch returned in 1816, but there was mounting unrest among the Javanese peasants. A bloody war for independence broke out in 1825 in which some 200,000 Javanese lost their lives to no avail. (In contrast, 4000 deaths had secured the freedom of the 13 American colonies.) At the end of this war in 1830 the Dutch intensified their efforts to make profits from compulsory crop quotas. Through massive corvées they planted a large proportion of Java's remaining nonirrigated lands with coffee—300 million trees between 1837 and

1850 (enough to make the phrase "a cup of Java" a household substitute for "a cup of coffee" in many parts of the world). At the same time, in order to encourage the villagers to plant sugarcane in their paddy fields, the Dutch authorities undertook a vast expansion of irrigation facilities, again through the use of forced labor. The official policy forced the peasants to rotate the planting of sugar and rice in their own paddy fields (Fig. 18.2). The heavy labor demand on the peasants was met by an increase in child labor and rapid population growth (from 4 to 30 million). Much capital was accumulated out of sugar and coffee, but the capital remained wholly under the control of Dutch rather than Indonesian entrepreneurs.

The Dutch wanted to preserve the peasant economy, while continuing to guarantee profits to the Dutch corporations. Hence the government prohibited the sale of village paddy lands. Sugar was cultivated on lands leased by the private corporations. Given the enormous population increase, the sugar corporations never lacked for labor to plant and cut the cane. Yet the system of leasing

Figure 18.2 *JAVA RICE TERRACES*
Intensive labor input into irrigation agriculture under colonial conditions yielded population growth without economic development.

preserved the illusion of ownership and thus reduced the political hazards of creating an agroindustrial class of landless laborers.

The net result of all this "development" is that when independence finally came in 1949, the Javanese peasants were demonstrably worse off than they had been at the beginning of the 350 years of Dutch rule. No significant beginnings had been made toward industrialization; the population had swollen from 4 million to 60 million; food consumption had never risen above 2000 calories a day; the entire island, with its millions of tiny holdings, had been converted into "one vast rural slum." Practically all its capital had been drained off to build the economy of Holland and Europe (Geertz 1963; White 1983).

JAPAN

Momentarily, toward the end of the sixteenth century, it appeared that Japan would not escape the fate of Java. Missionization under Francis Xavier had been successful; but Japanese feudalism was more centralized than the Javanese counterpart. Under the threat of a European takeover, the Japanese feudal lords united under the emperor and dedicated themselves to the task of evicting the missionaries, stamping out Christianity, and controlling their own trade. The Jesuits and their Japanese allies fought back but were defeated; large numbers of Christians were massacred, and trade with Europe was cut off.

In 1614, under the victorious warlord Tokugawa Ieyasu, the process of consolidating Japanese nationhood was accelerated. Foreign commercial interests were vigorously combated; soon even the Japanese themselves were forbidden to build ships for foreign trade. By 1637, except for a small group of Dutch traders maintained in quarantine on an island in Nagasaki harbor—Japan's "window on the west"—Japan became totally cut off from the "assistance" of European administrators, missionaries, and businessmen. This state of affairs lasted until 1853. During the 250 years of "isolation," however, Japan evolved in a direction convergent with the European transition from feudalism to capitalism. Entrepreneurial activity expanded at the expense of feudal privileges, and by the time Commodore Perry arrived in 1853 to force Japan to open its doors to international trade, a vigorous class of capitalist entrepreneurs was ready to receive him (Hanley and Yamamura 1977).

Moreover, despite their "isolation," the Japanese had assiduously been studying the development of Western technology as depicted in Dutch books passed through the "window" in Nagasaki harbor. Even before Perry's arrival they had been experimenting with everything from the telegraph to steel mills by following the directions in these books. Special laboratories had been established to explore the practical application of all branches of "Dutch" learning—photography, cotton spinning, sugar refining, metal plating, and the manufacture of acids, alcohol, and glass (T. Smith 1955:3).

Most importantly, the opening of Japan to the West began only after Japan had succeeded in casting its own large-bore cannon in its own foundries. Of course, after the restoration of international trade, Japanese government officials and businessmen turned increasingly to foreign technological advice. They imported technicians and engineers and went on countless overseas inspection tours. But the decisive difference between this kind of technological assistance and many modern aid programs to underdeveloped nations is that the beneficiaries were Japanese industries, protected by a Japanese government relying on Japanese armaments.

With the establishment of the Meiji government in 1868, the protection of Japanese entrepreneurial activity was guaranteed by an emerging centralized state committed to rapid industrialization and the encouragement of all forms of capital accumulation as long as the beneficiaries were Japanese.

Japan today is the world's third-ranking industrial power. Its automotive, steel, optical, electronic, textile, and plastics industries are envied even in the United States. In comparing Japan's emergence as a developed nation with what Geertz has called the "anthology of missed opportunities" and the "conservatory of missed possibilities" represented by Java, it is difficult to avoid the conclusion that the difference lies in Japan's unique exemption from colonial bondage. As Geertz (1963:141) states: "The existence of colonial government was decisive because it meant that the growth potential inherent in the traditional Javanese economy . . . was harnessed not to Javanese (or Indonesian) development but to Dutch."

THE GREEN REVOLUTION

All too often development has been viewed as a narrow problem that can be solved simply by technological change. In fact, however, development is a problem that requires an understanding of politico-economic and ecological processes. The Green Revolution well illustrates the calamitous possibilities inherent in development approaches that disregard the relationship between technology and environment, on the one hand, and between politics and economy, on the other (Miller 1977; Gough 1978; Harding 1975).

The Green Revolution had its origin in the late 1950's in the dwarf varieties of "wonder wheat" developed by Nobel prizewinner plant geneticist Norman Borlaug at the Rockefeller Foundation's Ciudad Obregón research center in northwest Mexico. Designed to double and triple yields per acre, wonder wheat was soon followed by dwarf varieties of "miracle rice" engineered at a joint Rockefeller and Ford Foundation research center in the Philippines. The significance of the dwarfed forms is that short, thick stems can bear heavy loads of ripe grain without bending over. On the basis of initial successes in Mexico and the Philippines, the new seeds were hailed as the solution to the problem of feeding the expanding population of the underdeveloped world and were soon planted in vast areas of Pakistan, India, and Indonesia (Cloud 1973).

Although the new seeds have resulted in a definite increase in output per area, they have done so only at considerable economic and social cost. Moreover, this rate of increase has not been large enough to offset the rate of population growth, and hence per capita production of wheat and rice in most of Asia has remained stagnant (Wade 1973; McNamara 1984). The main problem with the miracle seeds is that they were engineered to outperform native varieties of rice and wheat only if grown in fields that have been heavily irrigated and treated with inputs of chemical fertilizers, pesticides, insecticides, and fungicides. Without such inputs the high-yield varieties perform little better, and sometimes worse, than the native varieties, especially under adverse soil and weather conditions.

The question of how these inputs are to be obtained and how and to whom they are to be distributed immediately raises profound ecological and politico-economic issues. Irrigated croplands form only 30 percent of Asian croplands (Wade 1973). Most peasants in the underdeveloped world not only lack access to adequate amounts of irrigation water, but they are unable to pay for expensive chemical fertilizers and the other chemical inputs. This means that unless counterefforts are made by the governments of countries switching to the miracle seeds, the chief beneficiaries of the Green Revolution will be the richest farmers and merchants who already occupy the irrigated lands and who are best able to pay for the chemical inputs (Mencher 1974a, 1978).

Richard Franke (1973, 1974) studied the Green Revolution in a village in central Java. He describes the Indonesian government's attempt to distribute miracle rice. Despite the fact that yield increases of up to 70 percent were being obtained, only 20 percent of the farming households had joined the program. The chief beneficiaries were the farmers who were already better off than average, owned the most land, and had adequate supplies of water. The poorest families did not adopt the new seeds. They make ends meet by working part-time for well-to-do farmers who lend them money to buy food (Fig. 18.3). The rich farmers prevented their part-time workers from adopting the new seeds. The rich farmers feared that they would lose their supply of cheap labor, and the poor farmers feared that if they cut themselves off from their patrons, they would have no one to turn to in case of sickness or drought. Franke concludes that the theories behind the Green Revolution are primarily rationalizations for ruling elites which are trying to find a way to achieve economic development without the social and political transformation which their societies need.

Why has there been so much public enthusiasm for miracle seeds that cannot be used by the great mass of ordinary peasants? From the point of view of the poor peasant farmer, these seeds, with their tremendous water and chemical input requirements, are often antimiracles. If the seeds were miracles, they would require less water and fertilizer, not more. But the authorities and technicians responsible for promoting the Green Revolution originally sought to convert peasant farming into agribusiness systems modeled after high-energy agriculture in the developed countries (Cleaver 1975). It was hoped that by stimulating the development of agribusiness in the tropics the productivity of agriculture would be raised fast enough to catch up with the rate of population growth. This transformation obviously requires the virtual destruction of small peasant holdings—just as it has meant the destruction of the small family farm in the United States. There are grave penalties associated with this transformation even in the industrial nations, where the former farm population can be employed as truck drivers, fast-food servers, clerks, and programmers. But in the underdeveloped countries, where there are few jobs in the manufacturing and service sectors of the economy, migration to the cities cannot result in higher standards of living for hundreds of millions of underemployed peasants (Raj 1977).

MEXICAN WONDER WHEAT

The association between the miracle seeds and agribusiness was present at the start of the Mexican wheat experiment. Ciudad Obregón in Sonora was the center of huge wheat farms that depended upon extensive government irrigation projects in the Yaqui River Valley. The former peasant inhabitants of this valley—the Yaqui Indians—had been evicted from their lands in a series of military engagements, the last of which occurred in 1926 when the Yaquis tried unsuccessfully to kidnap Mexico's President Obregón (Spicer 1954). The Yaquis were replaced by medium- and large-scale farm-

(a)

(b)

Figure 18.3 *RICE HARVEST, JAVA*
Harvesting *(a)* is done with a small hand-knife, known as the ani-ani. Each stalk is individually cut, but with the large supply of labor, a single morning is enough for all but the very largest plots to be harvested. The paddy is bound in bundles *(b)* and carried to the home of the owner where one-tenth portions are given to the harvesters. No other wage is paid.

ers who were the beneficiaries of $35 million of public funds expended on dams alone. The Mexican government subsidized the growth of the petrochemical industry, which supplied the fertilizers for the new seeds. Further subsidies were given to the wonder wheat producers in the form of government support prices pegged 33 percent above world market prices. It is true that the wonder wheat made Mexico into a wheat-exporting nation. Yet the price of Mexican wheat is so high that it must be exported—the average Mexican peasant cannot afford to eat it. Poor Mexicans eat corn and beans, which remain the basic Mexican staples. Meanwhile, in 1969 miracle wheat that had been produced at a cost of $73 a ton, the support price, was being sold at $49 a ton to foreign buyers. "Mexico thus lost $30.00 a ton, or 80¢ on each bushel exported" (Paddock and Paddock 1973:218). Cynthia Hewitt de Alcantara (1976:320) has characterized the Green Revolution in Mexico as highly wasteful of natural and human resources and of the wealth created by government investments in irrigation facilities. "The ability of most rural people to satisfy their basic needs after thirty years of agricultural modernization is still in fact extraordinarily limited" (Hewitt de Alcantara 1976:135). This analysis of Mexican agriculture is confirmed by the fact that in 1982–1983 Mexico was obliged to import over 9 million metric tons of grain, mostly corn, from the United States (Walsh 1983:825).

THE GREEN REVOLUTION IN BANGLADESH

The influence of multinational agribusiness interests has had similar paradoxical effects in Bangladesh. Traditionally, Bangladesh was a land whose staple was rice. Wheat was virtually unknown until famine struck in the mid-1970s and the United States sent surplus wheat to meet the emergency. This wheat was sold by the Bangladesh government to the people at prices lower than those for rice. With a market established for wheat, national and international development agencies and banks saw the further increase in dependence on wheat as a source of government revenues and private profit. The purchase of seeds, fertilizer, and other agribusiness inputs was subsidized by the government, encouraging farmers to grow high-yield varieties of wheat instead of the traditional protein-rich winter crop of legumes. (Lindenbaum 1983). Consequently, wheat production skyrocketed from 35,000 to 1.1 million metric tons between 1975 and 1981 (Fig. 18.4).

Meanwhile, per capita production of pulses and rice declined. By 1983, wheat in one form or another was being eaten at least once a day by most Bangladesh families. Yet continuing subsidies have led to an increase rather than decrease in wheat imports. And in spite of $2 billion worth of food shipments, technical aid, loans, and other development assistance, the nutritional status of the population has continued to deteriorate. By 1983, 60 percent of rural households were deficient in calories and 30 percent were deficient in proteins, while 78 percent of children under 10 years of age were judged to be suffering from some degree of malnutrition. Part of the problem is that profits from wheat production have been distributed unequally in favor of the better-off farmers. This has increased the sale of

Figure 18.4 *PLANTING WHEAT IN BANGLADESH*
International aid programs have fostered a switch from rice to wheat. Rice is a more efficient crop in this habitat.

lands belonging to the poorer farmers. Landlessness reached over 50 percent in 1983 and there has been a marked increase in the number of migrant laborers and in the substitution of cheaper female and child labor for male workers. The biggest winners in the Green Revolution of Bangladesh thus far appear to be the multinational grain and seed dealers and U.S. farmers whose surplus production costs the U.S. taxpayers about $20 billion a year (Lindenbaum 1983).

Recently, some governments and foundations have recognized the importance of concentrating on helping poor farmers who depend on rainfall. For example, the International Crops Research Institute for the Semi-Arid Tropics located in Hyderabad, India, has embarked upon a program to increase production of such dry farming crops as sorghum, millet, chick-peas, and peanuts, which are the staple foods of 500 million people in Asia and Africa (ICRISAT n.d.). It remains to be seen whether substantial improvements in the yields of these crops can be achieved without expensive inputs.

LIMITS TO TECHNIFICATION AND INDUSTRIAL GROWTH

During the last two decades many anthropologists and economists have become disillusioned with the possibility and desirability of achieving development by means of advanced industrial technologies and production methods. Rather than emulate the experience of the industrial nations, greater consideration is now being given to raising living standards by means of "intermediate" or "appropriate" types of technologies. Such technologies use local materials and preexisting skills, have high labor demand and low-energy budgets, and raise production efficiency without destroying the continuity of the local culture.

This approach has been stimulated by the recognition that the prosperity of the developed countries is threatened by the side effects of industrialization, such as pollution, and by the increasing costs of fossil fuels (Lovins 1976). Energy considerations alone show that U.S. agribusiness cannot be exported intact to the rest of the world. This system, as discussed in Chapter 11, is the most energy-expensive mode of food production that has ever been devised. If it were used to feed the entire world, it would absorb almost 80 percent of the current global total annual expenditure of energy (Steinhart and Steinhart 1974:312). David Pimentel and his associates have calculated that if petroleum were the source of energy for a world agricultural system modeled after the U.S. agricultural system, the known oil reserve of the entire world would be used up in 13 years (Pimentel et al. 1975:758) (see Table 18.1).

Moreover, there is considerable evidence that the entire system of industrialized food production is growing more inefficient as a result of the overexploitation of natural resources and the lack of additional prime agricultural lands. Lester Brown (1978) has shown that the law of diminishing returns (less produced for the same effort) is now operating with respect to such diverse activities as grain production, ocean fishing, and petroleum production (see p. 209). An alarming example is the grain fertilizer-response curve, which describes the average annual increment in grain production per unit of fertilizer applied to grain production. Despite the Green Revolution, this has declined steadily from 14.8 in 1948–1952 to 5.8 in 1974–1976. The reason for the decline is that practically all the land having optimum soil and climate conditions for applying fertilizer has already been put into production; what remains is agriculturally

Table 18.1 INEQUALITIES IN SOCIAL AND ECONOMIC DEVELOPMENT

	Life expectancy at birth	GNP ($)	Energy consumption (kilowats per capita)	Literate adults (%)	Population (millions)
Low-Income Countries	57	260	421	50	2,160
China and India	59	270	514	54	1,649
Other Low-Income Countries	48	230	87	34	511
Middle Income Countries	60	1,400	965	65	1,138
Oil Exporters	56	1,160	658	57	496
Oil Importers	63	1,580	1,204	73	642
High Income Oil Exporters	57	12,630	2,609	25	14
Industrial Market Countries	74	10,320	7,293	99	714
Industrial Non-Market Countries	71	4,640	5,822	100	353

SOURCE: World Bank.

marginal land (Jensen 1978). Similarly, the total gross tonnage of the world's large-vessel fishing fleet grew by more than 50 percent from 1970 to 1975, but the total fish catch remained the same, which means that the catch per dollar invested declined precipitously. The reason for this is that all the close-to-shore and shallow-water fish stocks have already reached maximum sustained yield levels or have actually been fished out. Indeed, world per capita fish production has actually begun to decline. Finally, as everyone now realizes, petroleum, which once oozed up out of the ground practically for the taking, is being sought at enormous expense in the midst of arctic wastelands and thousands of feet under the oceans.

Another important consideration weighing against the technification of production is that in wage-labor economies the replacement of human labor by machines merely swells the ranks of the vast armies of unemployed workers. For example, according to Collin Norman (1978), when the World Bank loaned Pakistan money to buy 18,000 tractors, labor needs dropped by 40 percent, creating great suffering among small farmers who had relied on wage labor on the large farms to balance their household budgets. The introduction of agricultural and manufacturing machinery in developing countries is not only wasting energy and depleting the environment, but it is making it impossible to find work for the rapidly growing labor force. Norman estimates that 30 million new jobs per year will be necessary merely to keep pace with Third World population growth and that 1 billion new jobs must be created by the year 2000 in order to achieve full employment.

BULLOCK VERSUS TRACTOR

Reliance on appropriate or intermediate technology for development involves a commitment to low-energy rather than high-energy production processes, recycled rather than new materials, and renewable rather than nonrenewable resources. An example of an appropriate technology that is currently being considered as an alternative to technification in India is the use of bullock (oxen) power instead of tractors. Some 83 million bullocks are already in use. They are fed mainly on renewable agricultural by-products such as straw from grains supplemented with cotton seed or sesame seed oil cakes. Unlike tractors, bullocks recycle their fuel by producing dung which is used as fertilizer. They can be produced and maintained by traditional means right in the countryside, whereas tractors make farmers dependent on distant factories and urban specialists in India and abroad for maintenance and replacement. But what about the relative efficiency of bullocks and tractors? Surprisingly enough, it is very difficult to show that if tractors replaced bullocks, the average farmer would be any better off. While a 35-horsepower tractor can plow a field almost ten times faster than a pair of bullocks, the initial investment in the tractor is over 20 times greater than the investment in the bullocks. Moreover, the cost per hour of tractors remains above the cost per hour of bullocks, unless the tractor is used over 900 hours per year. This implies that tractors are cheaper than bullocks only on very large farms. But the majority of Indian farms are very small and the use of tractors could only be justified if elaborate provisions were made to lease or rent the machines. Similar provisions, however, could also easily lower the cost of using bullock power. Hence, given the enormous initial expense in converting from bullocks to tractors, it may be more economical to concentrate on ways of improving bullock power by breeding programs, changes in cropping patterns, and land tenure, thereby increasing bullock working hours and lowering costs still further (Subrahmanyam and Ryan 1975; Binswanger 1977; Dolberg 1982).

This example suggests that in countries poorly endowed with industrial sources of energy, much of the development process will have to be carried out by socially more efficient and more equitable management of existing infrastructures rather than by the introduction of a new technological base. The recent decision by the Chinese to attempt a thoroughgoing modernization of production reflects the hope that vast untapped reserves of oil and gas will become available to the Chinese people in the near future. India does not have this hope.

POPULATION AND DEVELOPMENT

Behind all the failures of development efforts in both the socialist and capitalist countries, there looms the pervasive influence of rapid population growth (see Table 18.2). Despite the burden of poverty, the population of the less developed countries is increasing at the rate of 2.1 percent per year (Fig. 18.5). If the increase continues at the present rate, their population will rise from the current 3.5 billion to 4.9 billion by the year 2000, and 7 billion by 2025. Within 45 years from 1984, India's population will double, Bangladesh's will triple, and Kenya's will quintuple (McNamara 1984). There is no doubt that rapid population growth makes the task of raising per capita consumption standards immensely more difficult. If world population had stabilized at 1950 levels, the food that is now being produced globally would be sufficient to provide everyone with U.S. standards of proteins and calories. (Of course, producing the food is only part of the problem—getting it distributed fairly is the other part.)

Up until recently, the solution to the problem of the population explosion was sought primarily through the development and dissemination of cheap contraceptive devices. Use of these devices has generally been left to the discretion of domestic units and so-called family planning programs. It is now generally recognized, however, that

Table 18.2 WORLD POPULATION ESTIMATES

	Population now (millions)	Growth rate (% per year)	Population by year 2000 (millions)
World	4,677	1.8	6,130
More developed	1,158	0.6	1,273
Less developed	3,519	2.1	4,857

SOURCE: The Population Reference Bureau, Inc., 1983 World Population Data Sheet.

family planning programs by themselves are an ineffectual means of population control. As Kingsley Davis foresaw:

> Current programs will not enable a government to control population size. In countries where couples have numerous offspring that they do not want, such programs may possibly accelerate a birth-rate decline that would occur any way, but the conditions that cause births to be wanted or unwanted are beyond the control of family planning, hence beyond the control of any nation which relies on family planning alone as its population policy (1967:734).

The emphasis on contraceptive technology fails to take into consideration the fact that human beings have been able to raise and lower population growth rates throughout prehistory and history (Handwerker 1983). Even without resorting to infanticide (which was generally repressed during the colonial period), neglect of unwanted children is sufficient to slow growth rates. Indeed, many instances of high infant and childhood mortality in the world today can be interpreted as etic forms of population control (Scrimshaw 1983). It should also be

Figure 18.5 *CROWDED THIRD WORLD*
This market scene in Jakarta is typical of many less developed countries.

kept in mind that the decline in the European rate of increase began in the middle of the nineteenth century before effective contraceptive devices were cheap enough to be widely used. A similar decline in the rate of population growth lies behind Japan's industrialization in the nineteenth century (see above). In Japan, however, infanticide was openly practiced (Hanley and Yamamura 1977).

Another explanation for the current population explosion that has lost much of its credibility is that the high rate of increase is due to the introduction of improved health care. Modern medicine, it is often said, has lowered infant mortality and promoted longevity. People continue to have children at the former rate, and the widened gap between birthrate and death rate produces the explosion. This explanation fails to take into account the fact that the population explosion began in most countries before the introduction of improved medical care. The population of India, Indonesia, Egypt, and Mexico, for example, began to zoom during the nineteenth century, and the increment may even have been associated with an average shortened life span and deteriorating health conditions. Even today some of the highest fertility and growth rates are found in areas that have the highest death rates and the least medical care. Indeed, there is considerable evidence indicating that where other factors are favorable, improved public health measures bring about a rapid decline in numbers of children born per woman. This results from the fact that the level of childbirths is often geared to the level of survivorship. Parents want to assure themselves that at least some of their children will live long enough to take care of them in their old age (Polgar 1972:211). There is considerable evidence that when death rates come down far enough and parents have good odds that most of their children will survive to adulthood, then they have fewer children. Thus, contrary to popular opinion, improving the diet and health of infants and children is not necessarily a self-defeating activity that results in greater suffering for all (Brown and Wray 1974).

There is now also considerable evidence that families in many underdeveloped countries want more children to improve their economic position or to prevent its deterioration. The fact that this behavior leads in the aggregate to a declining per capita income puzzles many outsiders. It seems irrational for poor people to have so many children. Yet from the point of view of each domestic unit, the only hope of improving one's standard of living or even of holding on to what one has, meager as it may be, often depends on increasing the size of the domestic work force (Mamdani 1973).

Seeking an explanation for the tenfold increase in the population of Java between 1820 and 1920, Benjamin White (1973, 1983) has suggested that peasant families were responding to imposed needs and opportunities for greater labor input into agriculture per household. The Dutch, as described earlier in this chapter, established sugar plantations, expanded the irrigation networks, and enlarged the sphere of commercial agriculture. At the same time they imposed various forms of rents, taxes, and corvée. Peasant families responded by rearing more children and putting them to work at an early age. They reared extra children as long as the cost of raising each child was more than compensated for by the value of the food and handicrafts that each child produced. In a study of the labor contribution of Javanese children to the domestic economy White (1975) has provisionally shown that the cost of rearing children is still a major determinant of family size in rural Java.

The more children a family has, the more children it can free from household chores and put to work weaving mats or working for wages in the fields (Nag, White, and Peet 1978; B. White 1982).

This theory helps to explain why middle-class families in Europe, Japan, and the United States are more likely to want fewer children than do peasant families in underdeveloped parts of the world. The more children a modern middle-class couple have, the closer to bankruptcy they must live. In the developed countries children are prohibited from entering the labor force until they are 14 or 16; their lifetime economic contribution to their parents consists largely of occasional household chores and small income tax deductions. The drain for child support may last for as much as 30 years in the case of students educated for professional specialties, and most modern parents have no expectation of a return flow of support for their old age. We shall return to the decline in fertility rates in the developed countries in Chapter 24 as part of the discussion of changing sex roles.

Based on the insights gained from anthropological studies of population trends, a maximally effective (and humane) program for rapid reduction in the rate of population growth should include the following provisions:

1. Improved public health facilities especially for infants and children
2. National old age social security
3. Compulsory education through age 16 for both girls and boys and antichild labor legislation
4. Cheap and readily available contraceptive devices, medical abortions, and medical sterilization

As summed up by Steven Polgar (1975:22), "Population growth will level off when opportunities for economic survival and advance are no longer tied to having four or five children per family."

THE IMAGE OF LIMITED GOODS

A recurrent question concerning the plight of contemporary peasant communities is the extent to which they are victims of their own values. It has often been noted, for example, that peasants are very distrustful of innovations and cling to their old ways of doing things. Based on his study of the village of Tzintzuntzan in the state of Michoacán, Mexico, George Foster (1967) has developed a general theory of peasant life based on the concept of the "image of limited good." According to Foster, the people of Tzintzuntzan, like many peasants throughout the world, believe that life is a dreary struggle, that very few people can achieve "success," and that they can improve themselves only at the expense of other people. If someone tries something new and succeeds at it, the rest of the community resents it, becomes jealous, and snubs the "progressive" individual. So, many peasants are afraid to change their way of life because they do not want to stir up the envy and hostility of friends and relatives.

Although there is no doubt that an image of limited goods exists in many peasant villages in Mexico and elsewhere, the role it plays in preventing economic development is not clear. Foster provides much evidence for doubting the importance of the image of limited good in Tzintzuntzan (Fig. 18.6). He tells the story of how a community development project sponsored by the United Nations achieved success initially, only to end in disasters that had little to do with the values held by the villagers. Also, most of the community's cash income was derived by working as *braceros* (migrant laborers) in

Figure 18.6 *IMAGE OF LIMITED GOODS*
Peasant women of Tzintzuntzan with their homemade pottery.

the United States. To get across the border, the *braceros* must bribe, scheme, and suffer great hardships. Yet 50 percent of them had succeeded in getting through, "many of them ten times or more" (Foster 1967:277).

As Foster suggests, the "image of limited good" is not a crippling illusion, but rather a realistic appraisal of the facts of life in a society where economic success or failure is capricious and hinged to forces wholly beyond one's control or comprehension (as, for example, when the United States unilaterally terminated the *bracero* program).

> For the underlying, fundamental truth is that in an economy like Tzintzuntzan's, hard work and thrift are moral qualities of only the slightest functional value. Because of the limitations on land and technology, additional hard work does not produce a significant increment in income. It is pointless to talk of thrift in a subsistence economy, because usually there is no surplus with which to be thrifty. Foresight, with careful planning for the future, is also a virtue of dubious value in a world in which the best-laid plans must rest on a foundation of chance and capriciousness (1967:150–151).

With the passage of time it has become clear that many of the heavily staffed development schemes in Mexico have been less successful than development efforts made by the people themselves with capital accumulated from working as *braceros*. James Acheson (1972), who studied a community near Tzintzuntzan, has argued that without realistic economic opportunities, development will not occur. If opportunities present themselves, some individuals will always take advantage of them, regardless of the image of limited good.

> It is one thing to say that Tarascans [the people of the region of Tzintzuntzan] are suspicious, distrustful, and uncooperative; it is another to assume that this lack of cooperation precludes all possibility for positive economic change (Acheson 1972:1165; cf. Foster 1974; Acheson 1974).

SISAL IN BRAZIL

Anthropologists have written about many other cases in which peasant communities undergo rapid change only to find themselves no better off or even worse off than they had been earlier. One such case studied by David Gross (1970) concerns the shift from subsistence farming to sisal farming in northeastern Brazil.

In the great hinterland of Brazil's Atlantic bulge, there is an underdeveloped, drought-ridden region known as the *Nordeste*, inhabited by some 30 million people. During the droughts, hundreds of thousands of refugees trek along the dusty roads seeking temporary shelter and employment. When the rains come, they trek back to plant 2 or 3 acres of corn, beans, and manioc.

Sisal, a plant that yields a high-quality fiber suitable for twine, was not widely cultivated in Brazil until World War II. During World War II, however, Asian sources of natural fiber were cut off and Brazilian sisal came into great demand. During the 1950s sisal prices climbed steadily in response to the worldwide spread of hay-baling machinery for which natural twine has certain advantages over wire. (If an animal accidentally swallows the twine along with the hay, no damage results.) In a few years millions of sisal plants stood where previously there had been nothing but shrubs and cactus.

The large-scale planters benefited from this conversion. So did the sisal buyers and truckers who financed and distributed the diesel-driven machines that strip away the green portion of the sisal leaf leaving the useful fibers (Fig. 18.7).

Between 1955 and 1965 some 800 of these machines were introduced into Gross's study area, a typical sisal county in the state of Bahia. Small farmers also began to plant sisal. In fact, the smaller the farm, the higher percentage of land planted in sisal. Yet the income from sisal for the small farmer was not enough to live on. Many of them had to work for wages on the sisal machines. They cut and stacked the leaves, put them through the dangerous stripper, cleaned away the debris, and dried and weighed the fibers, all for less than 50 cents a day. Like the peasants of Tzintzuntzan, the farmers of the *Nordeste* were eager to change. But there were things about sisal that they did not know until it was too late. Between 1951 and 1969 the world market price of sisal declined from $600 per metric ton to $170 per metric ton, largely as a result of overproduction and the appearance of artificial fiber substitutes for use in the hay-bailing machines.

By 1968 the value of the output of an eight-man sisal machine crew working from dawn to dusk had sunk to about $16 on the world market. Yet production continued, since the machines had not yet been paid off, and the erstwhile subsistence farmers could not get rid of the virtually indestructible plants. (Sisal is a hardy plant with extensive roots and thorny leaves.) Gross timed the men who fed the sisal into the machine and calculated that they were expending as much as 5000 calories per day. The only way that a man could feed himself well enough to work at the required rate was to keep his wife and children malnourished. As a result, the average physical condition of the poor farmers deteriorated rather than improved (Gross and Underwood 1969; Gross 1970).

SAN PEDRO: A SUCCESS STORY

Despite the many failures and misfortunes experienced by rural and peasant societies in their attempt to improve their position in the modern world, there have also been a few success stories. One such case was stud-

Figure 18.7 *SISAL WORKER*
Five thousand calories to make fifty cents.

ied by Waldemar Smith (1977). It concerns the Maya Indian community of San Pedro, which is located in the western highlands of Guatemala (Fig. 18.8). This case is extremely interesting because it reveals that in certain contexts traditional features of family life and ethnic subordination contain a hidden strength which can give "backward" Indian communities a competitive advantage over the usually more "progressive" *ladino* (i.e., non-Indian) communities.

"Welcome to the modern and progressive *pueblo* of San Pedro" says the sign at the entrance to town. The sign tells the truth according to Smith, who regards San Pedro as a "unique Indian community . . . of over 10,000 people with a dynamic, developing economy, an evolving class structure, and a modernizing culture" (W. Smith 1977:54–55). Since the 1940s San Pedro's economy has been expanding at a rapid rate. All the major stores are Indian-owned; it manufactures textiles and other products that are exported on 42 locally owned heavy 8- or 10-ton trucks that have replaced the mules formerly used for transport. Emphasizing education, the town has already produced one doctor, a handful of lawyers, and several hundred teachers. It is "alive with energy . . . even late at night looms slam, sewing machines clatter, and diesel trucks pull in and out" (ibid.: 104). The life history of An-

Figure 18.8 *SAN PEDRO, GUATEMALA*

selmo, who was born landless and poor but is now one of the region's richest merchants, shows little resemblance to stereotypes about tradition-bound Guatemalan Indians. With only 2 years of schooling behind him, Anselmo and his wife opened a soap-making business. He purchased tallow in large drums, collected ashes needed for soap making from his neighbors' kitchens, made 400 pounds of soap a week, and then took it to be sold in the regional markets. After a while he bought a one-eyed horse to help in collecting the ashes. By living frugally, Anselmo saved enough money to go into partnership with his brother in the purchase of a used 4-ton truck. Through more hard work and savings, Anselmo became the owner of a 10-ton diesel, a pickup, and a townhouse and warehouse. His children are all being educated through high school and beyond.

Smith points to the interplay between national and local conditions as furnishing the key to the success of Anselmo and the many others like him in San Pedro. Roads, trucks, markets, and schools had to be provided from outside—by means of national development plans and public investments. But many other highland communities have access to similar facilities and still remain tradition-bound and economically dependent. An important difference is that San Pedro had long been a center of handicrafts and transport services rather than of subsistence agriculture. In addition, San Pedro was a much larger town than most predominantly Indian settlements. Under these conditions the Indian entrepreneurs were aided by the image of limited good. In order to avoid the envy of their neighbors, they lived frugally and did not display their wealth. This helped them to save and reinvest their profits. Moreover, their family-oriented social life gave them access to a large pool of relatives who would work long hours for little pay on behalf of the family's business:

Ladino businessmen uniformly fear their Indian competitors because . . . of the Indians' willingness to live "below their means." . . . Indian entrepreneurs commonly maintain their customary standard of living, deferring improvements in diet, clothing, and housing in favor of reinvestment. Compared to Ladinos, furthermore, Indian children became productive at a tender age, and Indian wives—unlike their Ladina counterparts, who are commonly unemployed and demand household help besides—strap their babies on their backs and set about their trades and crafts. Indian families also tend to keep in close touch with their operations, rather than allocating the harder and more routine tasks to unreliable help. . . . The dynamic Indian household thus generates more income, allocates a greater proportion to capital investment, and can undercut its Ladino competition at will (W. Smith 1977:178).

Finally, it must be emphasized that none of these advantages would actually be effective were it not for the ability of the Indians to elect their own officials and to control local politics. The fact that San Pedro is a large settlement gives it considerably more political clout than the typical small Indian villages scattered about the Guatemalan highlands.

SUMMARY

An important source of inequality in the world today is the disparity in living standards between the developed industrialized countries and the underdeveloped or less developed nonindustrialized countries. To understand the causes of this situation anthropological perspective is essential. In its ceaseless search for raw materials, cheap labor, and new markets for their products, Europe created vast systems of colonized and dependent countries. Because of political and economic restrictions and exploitation, these countries could not accumulate capital nor develop their own forms of industrial production and, as in the case of China, many even have regressed to earlier levels of productivity.

That much of the phenomenon of underdevelopment is a legacy of colonialism and imperialism can be seen from the case of Japan. The comparison of Japan with Java is especially illuminating because in precolonial times both countries enjoyed decentralized feudal political and economic conditions well suited for the growth of capitalism and for industrialization. Japan, which isolated itself from direct European influence, made a successful transition to industrial capitalism, whereas Java, directly ruled by the Dutch, remained rural, agrarian, and impoverished.

With the approaching end of the era of direct colonial rule, the underdeveloped countries have yet to find an easy or certain path toward improving their lot. The development process has increasingly come to be seen as involving a complex interplay between infrastructural and structural components. Narrow technological solutions such as those embodied in the Green Revolution have fallen into disrepute. As in the case of Java, Mexico, and Bangladesh, it is generally recognized that expensive new production techniques tend to benefit the well-to-do farmers more than the rural poor. Further disillusionment with mere technification stems from the adverse consequences which the substitution of machines for human labor have had upon the employment situation.

There is growing recognition in both the developed and less developed countries that a considerable share of the development process will have to depend on appropriate technologies such as bullock power that utilize local skills and resources in combination with more efficient and equitable social management policies. Transfer of the present system of industrial agriculture to the rest of the world does not seem feasible or desirable in the light of the current rate of depletion of fossil fuels, the high rate of world population growth, and the many unpleasant side effects of industrialism.

There is no doubt that, in general, high rates of population growth have an adverse effect on the development process. Yet, there is no purely technological solution to the population problem. Current rates of rearing children reflect the importance of children for economic security and advance under conditions where survivability is uncertain, there are no alternative provisions for the aged, and children constitute a large part of the labor force. Cheap contraceptive techniques will not substantially reduce the rate of increase as long as these social, political, and economic conditions prevail.

Underdevelopment can seldom be attributed primarily to values and other superstructural components of sociocultural systems. Among peasants, an "image of limited good" is widespread. However, there are also contradictory values and attitudes that lead to innovations under appropriate structural and infrastructural conditions. In Tzintzuntzan, despite the image of limited good, men struggled for a chance to work as migrant laborers, and both men and women participated in a series of ill-fated development experiments in the hope of bettering their lives.

The case of the sisal experiment in northeastern Brazil leads to a similar conclusion. While the Brazilian peasants can be described as suspicious, distrustful, and uncooperative, that did not prevent them from being gullible, shortsighted, and too compliant in giving up their traditional system of subsistence agriculture in order to experiment with a cash crop.

As the case of San Pedro illustrates, traditional values and organizations may actually contain hidden strengths that can confer competitive advantages on subordinate groups seeking to improve their lot. Much depends on the mix of local, national, and even international infrastructural and structural conditions. Thus, the success of San Pedro was made possible by its traditional inclination to save, to use family labor, and to work hard, combined with the existence of roads, schools, markets, plus the large size of the community which gave it political security.

19 POVERTY AND CULTURE

This chapter adds another dimension to the study of inequality. It focuses on the plight of the urban poor. We shall pay special attention to the role of the "culture of poverty" in perpetuating the plight of the urban poor. We shall draw on the unique experiences of anthropologists who have done fieldwork among the unemployed and who have lived in the slums and blighted neighborhoods of the world's great cities.

THE CULTURE OF POVERTY

In studying the problems of people living in urban slums and shantytowns, Oscar Lewis found evidence for a distinct set of values and practices he called the "culture of poverty." Although not exactly comparable point by point, the concepts of the culture of poverty and of the image of limited good resemble each other in many respects and represent similar attempts to explain the perpetuation of poverty by focusing on the traditions and values of the underprivileged groups. Lewis (1966) pictures the poor in cities like Mexico City, New York, and Lima (Fig. 19.1) as tending to be fearful, suspicious, and apathetic toward the major institutions of the larger society, as hating the police and being mistrustful of government, and "inclined to be cynical of the church." They are also supposed to have "a strong present-time orientation with relatively little disposition to defer gratification and plan for the future." This implies that poor people are less willing to save money and are more interested in "getting mine now" in the form of stereos, color television, the latest style of clothing, and flashy automobiles. It also implies that the poor squander their earnings by getting drunk or going on buying sprees. Like George Foster, Lewis recognizes that in some measure the culture of poverty is partly a rational response to the objective conditions of powerlessness and poverty: "an adaptation and a reaction of the poor to their marginal position in a class-stratified society" (Lewis 1966:21). But he also states that once the culture of poverty comes into existence, it tends to perpetuate itself:

> By the time slum children are six or seven they have usually absorbed the basic attitudes and values of their subculture. Thereafter they are psychologically unready to take full advantage of changing conditions or improving opportunities that may develop in their lifetime (1966:21).

Lewis proposes that only 20 percent of the urban poor actually have the culture of poverty, implying that 80 percent fall into the category of those whose poverty results from infrastructural and structural conditions, rather than from the traditions and values of a culture of poverty.

The concept of the culture of poverty has been criticized on the grounds that the poor have many values other than those stressed in the culture of poverty which they share in common with other classes (Leeds 1970; Valentine 1970; cf. Parker and Kleiner 1970).

Although the poor may have some values different from those of members of other classes, they are not necessarily harmful. Helen Icken Safa (1967) has shown, for example, that developed patterns of neighborly cooperation frequently exist in established slums and shantytowns. And Oscar Lewis himself (1961, 1966) has shown in the tape-recorded words of the people themselves that many individuals who are trapped in poverty nonetheless achieve great nobility of spirit.

Figure 19.1 *MOTHER-CENTERED FAMILY*
Roxbury, Massachusetts

Values said to be distinctive of the urban poor are actually shared equally by the middle class. For example, being suspicious of government, politicians, and organized religion is not an exclusive poverty class trait; nor is the tendency to spend above one's means. There is little evidence that the middle class as a whole lives within its income more effectively than poor people do. But when the poor mismanage their incomes, the consequences are much more serious. If the male head of a poor family yields to the temptation to buy nonessential items, his children may go hungry or his wife may be deprived of medical attention. But these consequences result from being poor, not from any demonstrable difference in the capacity to defer gratification.

The stereotype of the improvident poor masks an implicit belief that the impoverished segments of society ought to work harder and to be more thrifty and more patient than the members of the middle class. This belief is spelled out by George Gilder (1981:256): "the poor must not only work, they must work harder than the classes above them." Most people, however, find it difficult to place this additional burden on the poor. It is conscience-saving to be able to attribute poverty to values for which the poor themselves can be held responsible (Piven and Cloward 1971).

DEFERRED GRATIFICATION AND THE FUTILITY OF WORK

The view that the poor refuse to work hard and to save because of a culture of poverty fails to take into account the type of work and opportunities for advancement that are open to them. In his book *Tally's Corner* (1967), Elliot Liebow, an ethnographer who has studied the black streetcorner men of Washington, D.C., provides a vivid account of the infrastructural and structural conditions shaping the work patterns of the unskilled black male. The streetcorner men are full of contempt for the menial work that they must perform, but this is not a result of any special tradition that they acquire from the culture of poverty. Historically, the bottom of the job market in the United States has been left for blacks and other minorities: jobs whose conditions and prospects are the mark of failure, which are demeaned and ridiculed by the rest of the labor force and which do not pay enough for a man to get married and have a family; jobs that are dull (as in dishwashing or floor polishing), dirty (as in garbage collecting and washroom attending), or backbreaking (as in truck loading or furniture moving) (Fig. 19.2).

The duller, dirtier, and more exhausting the work, the less likely the extra diligence and effort will be rewarded by anything but more of the same. There is no "track" leading from the night maid who cleans the ex-

Figure 19.2 *DEAD-END JOB*
Nonunion employment in construction in Washington, D.C.

ecutive's office to the executive; from the dishwasher to the restuarant owner; from the unskilled, unapprenticed construction worker to journeyman electrician or bricklayer. These jobs are dead ends from the beginning. To expect people not to be apathetic, lethargic, and uninterested under such conditions is to expect more of the poor than of the affluent. As Liebow points out, no one is more explicit in expressing the worthlessness of the job than the boss who pays for it. The boss pays less than what is required to support a family. The rest of society, contradicting its professed values concerning the dignity of labor, also holds the job of dishwasher or janitor in low esteem.

> So does the streetcorner man. He cannot do otherwise. He cannot draw from a job those social values which other people do not put into it (Liebow 1967:59).

According to Liebow, an additional mark of the degradation involved in these jobs is that wages for menial work in hotels, restaurants, hospitals, office and apartment buildings take into account the likelihood that the workers will steal food, clothing, or other items in order to bring their take-home pay above subsistence. The employer then sets the wages so low that stealing must take place. While implicitly acknowledging the need for theft, the employer, nonetheless, tries to prevent it and will call the police if someone is caught stealing.

Many young men are apathetic at the outset of their employment careers and quickly gravitate toward the streetcorner life: occasional jobs, borrowing from girl friends, short-lived marriages followed by abandonment of wife and children, drugs, crime. Many others, however, struggle toward the vision of a better life.

Liebow tells the story of Richard, a black man in his twenties who had tried to support his family by extra jobs ranging from shoveling snow to picking peas and who had won the reputation of being one of the hardest working men on the street. "I figure you got to get out there and try. You got to try before you can get anything," said Richard. After 5 years of trying, Richard pointed to a shabby bed, a sofa, a couple of chairs, and a television set, and gave up:

> I've been scuffling for five years from morning till night. And my children still don't have anything, my wife don't have anything, and I don't have anything (1967:67).

At one point along the road leading to his entry into the ranks of the streetcorner men, Richard took a job with a fence company in Virginia. Like many of the nonunion construction jobs, the work required was greater than most of the streetcorner men could physically manage. Richard, crying out in his sleep about the "Goddamn digging," could not keep it up long enough to save any money. Construction jobs, whose high hourly wage would seem to be a way out for at least some of the streetcorner men, also tend to be seasonal and are subject to interruption by rain or snow. Moreover, most of the nonunion jobs offered in construction are located far outside of town and can seldom be reached by public transportation. Liebow sums up the etic conditions regulating the work pattern of the streetcorner men as follows:

> The most important fact is that a man who is able and willing to work cannot earn enough money to support himself, his wife and one or more children. A man's chances for working regularly are good only if he is willing to work for less than he can live on, and sometimes not even then. On some jobs, the wage rate is deceptively higher than on others, but the higher the wage rate, the more difficult it is to get the job, and the less the job security. Higher paying construction work tends to be seasonal and, during the season, the

amount of work available is highly sensitive to business and weather conditions and to the changing requirements of individual projects. Moreover, high-paying construction jobs are frequently beyond the physical capacity of some of the men, and some of the low-paying jobs are scaled down even lower in accordance with . . . the assumption that the man will steal part of his wages on the job (1967:50–52).

NOW WHOSE FAULT IS THAT?

The tendency to blame the poor for being poor is not confined to relatively affluent members of the middle class. The poor or near-poor themselves are often the staunchest supporters of the view that people who really want to work can always find work. This attitude forms part of a larger world view in which there is little comprehension of the structural conditions that make poverty for some inevitable. What must be seen as a system is seen purely in terms of individual faults, individual motives, individual choices. Hence the poor turn against the poor and blame one another for their plight.

In a study of a Newfoundland community called Squid Cove, Cato Wadel (1973) has shown how a structural problem of unemployment caused by factors entirely beyond the control of the local community can be interpreted in such a way as to set neighbor against neighbor. The men of Squid Cove earn their living from logging, fishing, and construction (Fig. 19.3). Mechanization in logging, depletion of the fishing grounds, and upgrading of construction skills have left most of the men without a steady, year-round means of making a living. A certain number of men, especially those who have large families and who are past their physical prime, place themselves on the able-bodied welfare rolls. In doing so they must be prepared to wage a desperate struggle to preserve their self-esteem against the tendency of their neighbors to regard them as shirkers who "don't do nothin' for the money they get." What makes the plight of the Squid Cove welfare recipients especially poignant is that Newfoundlanders have long been noted for their intense work ethic. Many welfare recipients formerly worked at extremely arduous unskilled jobs. For example, Wadel's principal informant, George, was a logger for 29 years. George stopped logging because he injured a disk in his spine. The injury was sufficient to prevent him from competing for the better-paying unskilled jobs but insufficient to place him on the welfare roles as a disabled worker. George says he is willing to work, provided it is not too heavy and does not require him to move out of the house he owns in Squid Cove. "I'm willin' to work but there's no work around." "Now whose fault is that?" he asks. Others disagree. In Squid Cove welfare is thought of as something "we," the taxpayers, give to "them," the unemployed. There is no generally accepted feeling that it is the responsibility of the government or the society to secure appropriate work; the responsibility for finding a job falls upon the individual and no one else:

> For a welfare recipient to say outright that if work is not available, it is only proper for the government to provide adequate assistance, is not approved. Recipients thus have to be careful not to talk about their "rights" . . . On the other hand, if a recipient does not complain at all, this might be taken as a sign that he is satisfied with being on welfare, that he, in fact, is unwilling to work. Whatever the recipient does, complain or not, he is likely to be sanctioned (Wadel 1973:38).

In explaining why he chose to study the plight of people on welfare, Cato Wadel writes:

Figure 19.3 *NEWFOUNDLANDERS*

From what has been said so far, it should be clear that I am not much in doubt about "whose fault it is." It is *not* the fault of the unemployed individual. If this study were summarized into a simple and clear statement, it would be that it is unemployment itself which produces behavior on the part of the unemployed which makes people blame the unemployment on the individual, and *not* the other way around: that a special attitude or personal defect produces unemployment (1973:127).

GETTING DRUNK IN DENVER

One of the few quantitative studies of the relationship found in the culture of poverty between personal values and economic success has yielded some surprising results. Theodore Graves (1974) selected three personality attributes that occupy a central place in discussions of the culture of poverty: (1) future-time perspective and delayed gratification, (2) control over one's destiny (internal locus of control), and (3) drive for achievement. Graves attempted to measure the extent to which these attributes contributed to the success or failure of Navajo men who had migrated to Denver in search of work. Graves formulated a specific hypothesis: Those migrants who possess the above attributes will do significantly better economically in the city than those who do not possess them (Fig. 19.4).

To determine the strength of each of the three attributes in a sample of Navajo migrants, Graves had them take three tests. The first test measured their future-time ori-

Figure 19.4 *NAVAJO YOUTH*
Times are changing. We must be careful to avoid stereotyping of Native Americans.

entation by asking them to name things that they expected to do or expected to happen to them. They were then asked to say when they thought these events were going to occur—the average time cited in the future being the measure of their future-time orientation. The second test measured their belief in their ability to control their own destiny by asking the migrants to choose from among paired statements that expressed feelings of fatalism or personal control. (For example: "When I make plans, I am almost certain that I can make them work" versus "I have usually found that what is going to happen will happen regardless of my plans.") Finally, in the third test, to measure the drive for achievement, the migrants were shown drawings of Navajos in everyday scenes and asked to tell what was happening in the pictures. The answers were then rated for the extent to which they revealed a concern with getting things done and overcoming obstacles.

The results of all three tests were then compared with data about how successful the migrants had actually been in getting jobs at various wage levels and at holding on to them. Contrary to popular stereotypes, there was no significant correlation between having a culture of poverty mentality and getting and holding a decent job. Writes Graves (1974:76): ". . .our data provide *no* empirical support for the thesis that an absence of middle-class personality traits is contributing to Navajo marginality in the economic sphere."

Graves also tested a second hypothesis. Many of the Navajo migrants to Denver get arrested for drunk and disorderly conduct. One might suppose that those Navajos whose values more closely resembled middle-class values would get drunk and get arrested less often than those Navajos who had the culture of poverty values. But Navajos strong in future-time orientation and achievement motivation got drunk and were arrested more, not less, frequently! Graves suggests that migrants who do poorly and have a future-time orientation tend to berate themselves and to be more anxious than those who live from day to day. Similarly, migrants who do poorly and have a high achievement drive feel their economic failure more keenly. Both types drink more often, which causes them to be arrested more often. Graves concludes:

A middle-class personality is adaptive only within a structural setting which permits the attainment of middle-class goals. Otherwise such psychological traits tend to be *maladaptive* and to create additional adjustment problems for those who have acquired them (1974:83).

VALUES AND THE MATRIFOCAL FAMILY: THE FLATS

One of the explanations for poverty in the urban ghettos focuses attention on the problem of so-called "fatherless," or *matrifocal*, families (see p. 257). In 1965, with the release of a report by Daniel P. Moynihan, then U.S. Assistant Secretary of Labor, matrifocality received official recognition as the prime cause of the perpetuation of poverty among blacks in the United States. According to Moynihan, black youths are not properly motivated to take jobs that are actually available because of the absence of a male father figure in their family. They are reared in households where only the women are regularly employed. Adult males drift in and out of these households, and thus black youths grow up without the aid and inspiration of a stable male figure holding a steady job and providing comfort and security for his wife and children. Moynihan proposed that matrifocality not only was a cause of poverty but of crime and drug addiction as well.

Explanations of poverty that appeal to the enculturation experience within the matrifocal household must be rejected because the phenomenon of matrifocality is itself an adaptive response to poverty. The main structural features of matrifocality are as follows: The domestic unit consists of a mother and her children by several different men. Some of the woman's coresident adult daughters may also have children. The fathers provide only temporary and partial support. Men who move in and out of the domestic unit are etically "married" to the mothers—they act out all the typical husband/father roles. Yet emically the relationship is distinguished from "true marriage," and the children are legally regarded as "illegitimate" (González 1970).

Like all domestic arrangements, the matrifocal family represents an adaptive achievement that is no more or less "pathological" than any other family form. The conditions in question are: (1) Both men and women lack access to strategic resources; that is, they own no significant property; (2) wage labor is available to both men and women; (3) women earn as much as or more than men; and (4) a man's wages are insufficient to provide subsistence for a dependent wife and children.

In the United States a high incidence of matrifocal families among the poor is assured by the structure and ideology of the welfare system (Figs. 19.5, 19.6). In many states poor households that seek welfare support cannot contain able-bodied "fathers." Mothers whose husbands or children's fathers do not earn enough money to support the household can claim Aid to Families with Dependent Children (AFDC) welfare allotments, provided the fathers are not coresident with their children. The reason for this provision is that it is far cheaper for the government to provide such payments than to establish a high-quality system of child day-care centers that would free mothers to help their husbands by going to work. Since fathers cannot stay home with their children and claim AFDC allotments, the law confers upon women an extra economic value that makes it inevitable that they will become the center of domestic organization as long as the men cannot earn enough to make the AFDC allotments unnecessary. Since it is the woman who is fa-

Figure 19.5 *PRUITT-IGOE*
To avoid charges of coddling the poor for whom this huge high-rise project was built in St. Louis, elevator exits were installed only on alternate floors and water pipes were run through the corridors. Vandals broke the corridor windows, the pipes froze and burst, water cascaded down the stairwells and then froze. This rendered the stairwells unusable and trapped hundreds of people on alternate floors in waterless and heatless apartments. Plagued by vandalism and crime and unable to obtain funds for security and maintenance, the housing authority decided to dynamite the buildings and level the entire project despite the acute shortage of low-income housing.

Figure 19.6 *ANOTHER SOLUTION*
One of hundreds of buildings gutted by fire in New York's South Bronx. To overcome the impression of ruin and despair, the city began a $350,000 program in 1983 to cover up the empty windows with cheerful decals.

vored for AFDC payments, it is she who gets the lease in public housing projects and who controls (but does not own) the family's dwelling space.

In her study of the Flats (Fig. 19.7), a black ghetto in a midwestern city, Carol Stack (1974) provides a vivid account of the adaptive strategies that poverty-level families follow in attempting to maximize their security and well-being in the face of the AFDC laws and the inadequate wages of the unskilled male. Nuclear families on the middle-class model do not exist because the material conditions necessary for such families do not exist. Instead, the people of the Flats are organized into large female-centered networks of kinfolk and neighbors. The members of these networks engage in reciprocal economic exchanges, take care of each other's children, provide emergency shelter, and help each other in many ways not characteristic of middle-class domestic groups.

In the Flats the most important single factor which affects interpersonal relationships between men and women is unemployment.

Figure 19.7 *CHILDREN OF THE FLATS*
Area of Carol Stack's study.

> Losing a job, or being unemployed month after month, debilitates one's self-importance and independence, and for men, necessitates that they sacrifice their role in the economic support of their families. Then they become unable to assume the masculine role as defined by American society (Stack 1974:112).

Ironically, as Stack points out:

> Attempts by those on welfare to form nuclear families are efficiently discouraged by welfare policy. In fact, welfare policy encourages the maintenance of non-coresidential cooperative domestic networks (1974:127).

A woman can be cut off from welfare rolls as soon as her husband gets out of the army, comes home from prison, or if she gets married. Thus, "Women come to realize that welfare benefits and ties with kin networks provide greater security for them and their children" (Stack 1974:113).

THE WELFARE CONNECTION

A disproportionate share of violent urban crime in the United States is committed by black and Hispanic juveniles brought up in matrifocal families that receive AFDC allotments. This connection between juvenile delinquency and matrifocality reflects the fact that AFDC benefits are set below poverty-level incomes. Almost all inner-city AFDC women therefore count on supplementary incomes from husbands-in-hiding, coresident male consorts, or former consort fathers of their children.

Anthropologist Jagna Sharff (1981) found that all the mothers in a group of 24 Hispanic AFDC families living in New York City's Lower East Side had some kind of male consort. While few of the men in the house held regular full-time jobs (Fig. 19.8), even those who were unemployed chipped in something toward food and rent from selling stolen goods, dealing in marijuana or cocaine, and from an occasional burglary or mugging. Some women had more than one consort, while others picked up money and gifts through more casual relationships.

In their early teens, young inner-city boys make substantial contributions to their household's economic balance through their involvement in street crime and dope peddling. In addition, they confer an important benefit upon their mothers in the form of protection against the risk of rape, mugging, and various kinds of ripoffs to which the ghetto families are perpetually exposed.

Figure 19.8 *LOWER EAST SIDE* In the vicinity of Jagna Sharff's study.

Sharff found that AFDC mothers value sons for streetwise *macho* qualities, especially their ability to use knives or guns, which are needed to protect the family against unruly or predatory neighbors. While the AFDC mothers did not actively encourage their sons to enter drug trade, everyone recognized that a successful drug dealer could become a very rich man. To get ahead in the drug business, one needs the same *macho* qualities that are useful in defending one's family. When a young man brings home his first drug profits, mothers have mixed feelings of pride and apprehension. Since young ghetto males have a 40 percent chance of dying by age 25, a ghetto mother has to have more than one son if she hopes to enjoy the protection of a streetwise male. In her sample of 24 AFDC families, Sharff compiled this record of male homicides in the 3-year period 1976 to 1979:

Victim's Age	*Immediate Case of Death*
25	Shot in drug-related incident
19	Shot in dispute in grocery store
21	Shot in drug-related incident
28	Stabbed in drug-related incident
32	"Suicide" in a police precinct house
30	Stabbed in drug-related incident
28	Poisoned by adulterated heroin
30	Arson victim
24	Shot in drug-related incident
19	Tortured and stabbed in drug-related incident

One must be careful not to conclude that every family on AFDC conforms to this pattern. For some mothers, AFDC represents a one-time emergency source of funds used in the aftermath of divorce or separation until they can find a job and arrange for child care. But several million inner-city women, mostly black and Hispanic, use AFDC not as a temporary crutch, but as a regular or recurrent source of subsistence. A hard core of such women—estimated by sociologists Martin Rein and Lee Rainwater (1977) to number about 750,000—stay on AFDC for as many as 12 years at a stretch. And a far larger number of inner-city women follow a pattern of going on and off AFDC as they move in and out of the labor market between pregnancies.

"THE BROKEN FOUNTAIN"

Thomas Belmonte lived for a year in a slum neighborhood in Naples, Italy, a city which is known as the "Calcutta of Europe." Belmonte describes the neighborhood, Fontana del Re (Fig. 19.9), as being inhabited by a sub-proleteriat, or underclass, who lacked steady employment and who produced so little that they could not even be said to be exploited because there was nothing to be taken away from them. There were people like Gabriele, who collected metal junk and broke it into pieces with the help of his four children but who also ran a little store during the day and drove a taxi for prostitutes at night. Others were part-time sailors, waiters, bartenders, dockworkers, scavengers, and movers. Some groomed dogs, others were jacks-of-all-trades. Some were full-time smugglers, dope dealers, pickpockets, purse-snatchers and burglars. There were also dressmakers, flower vendors, beggars, and old women who added to their small pensions "by selling contraband cigarettes

Figure 19.9 *NAPLES*
Children from a poor neighborhood.

and condoms, and greasy sandwiches and wine so bad it burned a hole through your gut." The children of Fontana del Re did odd jobs which earned them about 33 cents an hour. Pepe, the 11-year-old son of a cobbler, had a job in a TV repair shop; his face and chest were scarred from defective tubes that blew up when he tested them. Several neighborhood children made daily forays to pry open the trunks of parked cars. Other children carried trays of espresso to offices and shops.

The people of Fontana del Re have many of Oscar Lewis's culture of poverty traits. But Belmonte traces most of these traits to being broke and lacking steady employment:

> The poor hesitate to plan for the future because they are hard-put to stay afloat in the present, and not because of a "present-time orientation." They have no trouble recalling the high and low points of their past. Their avoidance of banks relates to a realistic fear of inflation and a realistic mistrust of the literate officialdom. They do not patronize department stores because they prefer

to cultivate their own, more personalized networks of local credit, marketing, and exchange. In direct contradiction to Lewis's formulation, the poor of Naples purchase vital supplies wisely and in bulk. They place numerous cultural controls on consumption, wasting nothing. They are habituated to delaying gratifications in terms of clothing, housing, plumbing, heating, travel, transportation, and entertainment. If in good times they allow themselves the one luxury of channeling surplus funds into good, abundant food, I think it ethnocentric to label them irrational or immature, since this is how they sublimate a historically inherited and confirmed terror of hunger.

Confronted by a scarcity of opportunities, they become resigned, to preserve their sanity, and do not think to transcend their condition so long as they remain in underdeveloped Naples. . . . They have a culture that is simultaneously against poverty, adapted to the stresses of poverty, and mangled by poverty. But they have a culture which is also fashioned out of a great Mediterranean tradition, in the crucible of a great Mediterranean city. Their culture reflects their various and ingenious strategies for survival and their low position in a hierarchy, in other words, it is a class culture as well as a regional one. . . .

The Neapolitan urban poor are fashion-wise, street-wise, and urbane. They are not provincial. They live close to the gates of power in the wards of a great city, but unlike proletarians they are not integrated into the political and ideological currents of mass culture. They inhabit a world connected and apart from the main, a dense and crowded urban world, submerged; a crude, loud, pushy world where the moral order is exposed as a fraud which conceals the historical ascendancy of cunning and force (Belmonte 1979:144).

SUMMARY

Among the urban poor, the counterpart of the image of limited good is the culture of poverty. This concept focuses on the values and the traditions of the urban poor as an explanation for poverty. However, many of the values in the culture of poverty, such as distrust of authority, consumerism, and im-

LIFE IN FONTANA DEL RE

At Fontana del Re in a corner strewn now with rubble, beneath the bruised, shattered visage of a lion, the eroded figure of a sculpted stone sea shell recedes into a wall.

"This was our fountain," they told me. "Oh you should have seen it, Tommaso. The water played night and day. In summer, the children scampered about in it. At night, falling asleep, you heard it, and it was like music." The young men told me it was they who had destroyed it. As children, many years before, with iron rods, they had gone every day to hammer and smash it, until they were satisfied and there was nothing left to break.

Thereafter, whenever I passed that ruined corner, I tried to imagine what the fountain had once been like, and thought and wondered and sorrowed the more as I understood how it came to be broken.

SOURCE: Belmonte 1979:144.

providence, are also found in the middle class and in the inflationary economy of the United States as a whole. Moreover, in order to understand the attitude of the urban poor toward work, it is necessary to consider the tedious and unrewarding nature of the work they must do. As *Tally's Corner* demonstrates, it is unrealistic for most poor black youths to believe that they will be able to achieve middle-class status by working at menial jobs.

The irrelevance of the emphasis people place on the value of work for understanding the genesis of poverty can be seen in the case of Squid Cove. Newfoundlanders are known the world over for their work ethic, yet when mechanization and resource depletion left them without year-round jobs, they had no alternative but to accept welfare assistance.

The relationship between middle-class values and economic and social success is also clarified by the case of the Navajo in Denver. Navajo men with strong middle-class values were no more likely to hold good jobs than those with strong culture of poverty values.

Returning to the causes of poverty in the United States, the prevalence of matrifocal organization in the Flats again shows the essentially adaptive nature of the subcultures of the urban poor. Matrifocality is not the cause of poverty, but a result of such factors as male unemployment and welfare regulations that make women the homebodies and men the breadwinners. Further evidence for the adaptiveness, resiliency, and resourcefulness of members of the urban underclass can be found in studies of Hispanic neighborhoods in New York's Lower East Side and in the study of Fontana del Re in Naples. As Thomas Belmonte concludes, the underclass has a culture that is simultaneously against poverty, adapted to the stresses of poverty, and mangled by poverty.

20 LANGUAGE AND CULTURE

This chapter concerns the distinctive aspects of human languages. Human and infrahuman communication systems are compared, and the basic components of human languages are identified. We discover the root of the emic/etic distinction in the distinction between phonetics and phonemics. The reasons for the diversity of human languages are investigated. Then the relationship between language and culture is explored and, finally, the significance of consciousness for cultural change is illustrated by the nature of the processes of language change.

SEMANTIC UNIVERSALITY

As stated earlier (Ch. 7), the human capacity for culture, from technology to religion, is based on the uniquely human development of language and of systems of thought based on language. While other primates use complex signal systems to facilitate their social behavior, human signal systems are quantitatively, if not qualitatively, different from all other animal modes of communication. The unique features of human languages undoubtedly arise from genetic adaptations related to the increasing reliance of the early hominids on social cooperation and cultural rather than genetically determined modes of subsistence. Human babies are born with the kind of neural circuitry that makes learning to talk and to use language as natural for them as learning to walk.

One way to sum up the special characteristics of human language is to say that we have achieved what Joseph Greenberg (1968) calls "semantic universality." A communication system that has *semantic universality* can convey information about aspects, domains, properties, places, or events in the past, present, or future, whether actual or possible, real or imaginary, near or far.

Human languages achieve their semantic universality in part by possessing the feature known as *productivity* (Hockett and Ascher 1964). In fact, human languages are infinitely productive. This means that to every message that we send, we can always add another whose meaning cannot be predicted from the information in previous messages, and that we can continue to expand such messages without any loss in the efficiency with which such information is encoded (although the "decoding"—the understanding of the message—may get progressively more difficult, as in this sentence).

Nonhuman languages have only limited powers of productivity, C. R. Carpenter's (1940) classic study of gibbon language shows the limits of the productivity of nonhuman primate languages. Carpenter found that gibbons have nine major types of calls. These calls convey socially useful information such as: "I am here"; "I am angry"; "Follow me"; "Here is food"; "Danger!"; "I am hurt." Because each call can be repeated at different volumes and durations, the gibbon system possesses a small amount of productivity. For example, the gibbon can say "Danger!" with different degrees of emphasis roughly equivalent to the series: "Danger!"; "Danger! Danger!"; "Danger! Danger! Danger!"; and so on. But this series exhibits little productivity because the amount of information conveyed does not increase at the same rate that the length of the message increases. A "danger" call repeated 20 times in succession is informationally not much different from "danger" repeated 19 times. In contrast, the productivity of human language is extremely efficient. In order to convey more and more specific information in a particular domain, our messages do not have to keep getting longer. We can say: "Be careful, there's a strange movement over there"; "I think I see a leopard"; "It's in that tree." Moveover, these unique powers of productivity are not constrained to the small set of domains that gibbons and other primates "talk about." Rather, we are capable of producing an infinite number of messages in an infinite number of domains.

Another component in the concept of semantic universality is the feature known as *displacement* (Hockett and Ascher 1963). A message is displaced when either the sender or the receiver has no immediate direct sensory contact with the conditions or events to which the message refers. We have no difficulty, for example, in telling each other about events like football games after they are over or about events like meetings and appointments before they take place. Human language is capable of communicating an infinity of details about an infinity of displaced domains. This contrasts with all other infrahuman communication systems. Among anthropoids, for example, usually only the listener exhibits some degree of displacement, as when a "danger" message is understood at a distance. But the sender must be in sensory contact with the source of danger in order to give an appropriate warning. A gibbon does not say, "Danger! There may be a leopard on the other side of this hill." On the other hand, in human communication both sender and receiver are frequently displaced. We talk routinely about people, places, and things seen, heard, or felt in the past or future; or that others have told us about; or that enjoy a completely imaginary existence.

Displacement is the feature usually in mind when human language is referred to as having the capacity to convey "abstract information." Some of the greatest glories of human life—including poetry, literature, and science—depend upon displacement; but so too do some of our species' most shameful achievements—lies and false promises. As St. James put it:

> But the tongue can no man tame; it is an unruly evil, full of deadly poison. . .Out of the same mouth proceedeth blessing and cursing (James 3:6–11).

ARBITRARINESS

Another striking feature of human languages is the unprecedented degree to which they are constructed out of sounds whose physical shape and meaning have not been programmed in our genes. Most infrahuman communication systems consist of genetically stereotyped signals whose meaning depends on genetically stereotyped decoding behavior. For example, in communicating its sexual receptivity, a female dog emits chemical signals whose interpretation is genetically programmed into all sexually mature male dogs. Primate call patterns, like those of Carpenter's gibbons, are somewhat less tied to specific genetic programs and are known to vary among local groups of the same species. But the basic signal repertory of primate communication systems is species-specific. The facial expressions, hand gestures, cries, whimpers, and shrieks of chimpanzees constitute a genetically controlled repertory that is shared by all chimpanzees.

Not so with human languages. True enough, the general capacity for human language is also species-specific. That is, the ability to acquire semantic universality is genetically determined. Nonetheless, the actual constituents of human language codes are virtually free of genetic constraints (not counting such things as the physiology of the ear and of the vocal tract). Take as an example the languages of England and France. There are no genes which make the English say "water," "dog," or "house." These words are arbitrary because (1) they do not occur in the language behavior of most human beings; (2) neighboring populations in France with whom there is considerable gene flow utilize "eau," "chien," and "maison" to convey similar meanings; and (3) all normal human infants drawn from any population will acquire that English or French words with equal facility depending upon whether they are *enculturated* (see p. 115) in England or in France.

There is another important sense in which human language is arbitrary. Human language code elements lack any physically regular relationship to the events and properties that they signify. That is, there is no inherent physical reason why "water" designates water. Many infrahuman communication systems, on the other hand, are based on code elements that resemble, are part of, or are analogous to the items they denote. Bees, for example, trace the location of sources of nectar by smelling the pollen grains that cling to the feet of their hive mates. Chimpanzees communicate threats of violence by breaking off branches and waving or throwing them. Although we humans also frequently communicate by means of similar *iconographic symbols*—like shaking our fist or pointing to a desired object—the elements in spoken language seldom bear anything other than an arbitrary relationship to their meaning. Even words like "bow-wow" or "hiss" are arbitrary. "Ding-dong" may sound like a bell to speakers of English but not to Germans, for whom bells say "bim-bam."

DUALITY OF PATTERNING

The "miracle" of human semantic universality is that it is achieved by means of a very small number of arbitrary sounds called *phonemes*. Phonemes are sounds that native speakers perceive as being distinct—that is, as contrasting with other sounds. Phonemes are meaningless in isolation, but when phonemes are combined into prescribed sequences, they convey a definite meaning. The contrastive sounds in the utterance "cat" by themselves mean nothing; but combined they signify a small animal. In reverse order the same sounds signify a small nail or a sailing maneuver. Thus the basic elements in human language have *duality of patterning:* The same contrastive sounds combine and recombine to form different messages.

Theoretically, semantic universality could be achieved by a code that has duality of patterning based upon only two distinctive elements. This is actually the case in the dots and dashes of Morse Code and the binary 0 and 1 of digital computers. But a natural language having only two phonemes would require a much longer string of phonemes per average message than one having several phonemes. The smallest number of phonemes known in a natural language is 13 in Hawaiian. English has between 35 and 40 (depending on which authority is cited). Once there are more than ten or so phonemes, there is no need to produce exceptionally long strings per message. A repertory of ten phonemes, for example, can be combined to produce 10,000 different words consisting of four phonemes each. Let us now take a closer look at how phonemes can be identified and at how they are combined to form meaningful utterances.

PHONEMIC SYSTEMS

Phonemes consist of etic sounds called *phones*. In order to be effective as code elements, the phones of a language must be clearly distinguishable. One way to achieve a well-defined set of phones is to make each phone contrast as much as possible with every other phone. But when does one phone contrast with another? No two phones "naturally" contrast with each other. If we are able to distinguish one phoneme from another it is only because as native speakers we have learned to accept and recognize certain phones and not others as being contrastive. For example, the [t] in "ten" and the [d] in "den" are automatically regarded by speakers of English as contrastive sounds. (A symbol between brackets denotes a phone.) Yet these two sounds actually have many *phonetic,* that is, acoustical, features in common. It is culture, not nature, that makes them significantly different.

What is the critical difference between [t] and [d] for speakers of English? Let us examine the *articulatory features,* that is, the manner in which they are produced by the vocal tract (Fig. 20.1). Notice that when you produce either sound, the tip of your tongue presses against the *alveolar ridge* just behind the top of your teeth. Notice, in addition, that when either sound is made, the flow of the column of air coming from the lungs is momentarily interrupted and then released only in order to form the rest of the sounds in the utterance. In what way, then, are they different? The major articulatory difference between [t] and [d] consists of the way the column of air passes through the vocal chords. The vibration of the vocal chords produces a *voiced* effect in the case of [d] but not in the case of [t]. Both [t] and [d] are described phonetically as *alveolar stops,* but [d] is a *voiced alveolar stop,* whereas [t] is an *unvoiced alveolar stop.* The use of a voiced and unvoiced alveolar stop to distinguish utterances such as "ten"–"den," "tock"–"dock," "to"–"do," or "train"–"drain" is an entirely arbitrary device that is characteristic of English but that is absent in many other languages. The phonemic system of a given language thus consists of sets of phones that are arbitrarily and unconsciously perceived by the speakers as contrastive.

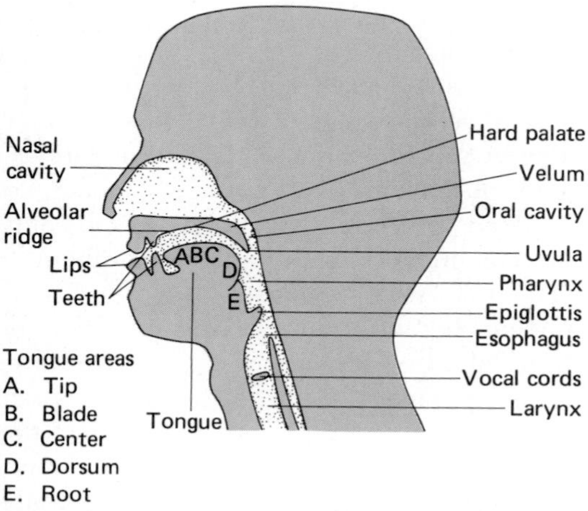

The structure of a given language's *phonemic system*—its system of sound contrasts—is discovered by testing observed phonetic variations within the context of pairs of words that sound alike in all but one respect. The testing consists in part of asking native speakers if they detect a change in meaning. This is what is achieved in the comparison between "ten" and "den." By asking native speakers to compare similar *minimal pairs* of words, we can detect most of the phonemic contrasts in English. For example, another instance in which voicing sets up a phonemic contrast is found in "bat"–"pat." Here the initial sounds are also stops. But this time they are made by pressing both lips together and are called *bilabial stops.* Again one of the stops, [b], is voiced, whereas the other, [p], is unvoiced. It is only the fact that these phones are contrastive from the native speaker's point of view

Figure 20.1 *PARTS OF ORAL PASSAGE*

that validates the classification of these two sounds as different phonemes. It is this fact that is generalized when the terms *emic* from phonemic and *etic* from phonetic are applied to other domains of culture (see p. 123).

To the linguist's trained ear, many sound differences that escape the notice of the native speaker will appear as possible contenders for phonemic status. For example, the removal of the labial obstruction in the utterance "pat" is accompanied by a slight puff of air that is not found at the beginning of "bat." This phonetic feature is known as *aspiration* and can easily be detected by placing your hand close to your lips and pronouncing first "pat" and then "bat" several times in succession. A more precise phonetic description of the [p] in "pat," therefore, is that it is an *aspirated bilabial unvoiced stop,* for which the phonetic symbol is [p^h]. Both aspirated and nonaspirated /p/s occur in English. (A symbol between slant lines indicates a phoneme.) Thus the bilabial stops in "sap," "flip," and "hip" are nonaspirated. Hence the question arises as to whether [p] and [p^h] constitute separate phonemes. A search for a minimal-pair contrast between [p] and [p^h] in English will fail. There are no meaningful English utterances in which the substitution of [p] for [p^h] alters the meaning of an utterance. Instead, [p] and [p^h] are in *complementary distribution;* that is, they occur regularly in different sound environments. Closely resemblant but nondistinctive sounds like [p] and [p^h] are called *allophones.* In a sense every specific instance of any given phoneme is an allophone since no two utterances are ever exactly the same in terms of either articulation or acoustic effect. A given phoneme, then, designates a range or class of allophones.

Phones that regularly occur in one language may not occur at all in another. When the same phone does occur in two languages, it may be phonemic in one but not the other. When similar phones are phonemic in two languages, they may have a different set of free and conditioned allophones.

In Chinese, for example, the nonphonemic aspirated and nonaspirated [t] of English "tick" and "stick" are phonemic. Also, Chinese uses "sing-song" tonal differences for phonemic contrasts in ways that English does not. On the other hand, in English the initial sound difference in "luck" and "rot" are phonemic, whereas in Chinese they are not (in an initial position). Hence "rots of ruck" sounds the same as "lots of luck" to a Chinese learning English.

MORPHEMES

The smallest units of language that have a definite meaning are called *morphemes.* Like each phoneme, each morpheme designates a class of basic units. In this case the constituents of the class are called *morphs.* Hence, just as phonemes are a class of allophones, so morphemes are a class of *allomorphs.* For example, the prefix *in-* as in "*in*sane" and the prefix *un-* as in "*un*safe" are morphs that belong to a morpheme meaning *not.*

Morphemes may consist of single phonemes or of strings of phonemes in many different combinations and permutations. Some morphemes can occur as isolates, as opposed to those which can occur only in conjunction with other morphemes. "Hello," "stop," "sheep" are *free* morphemes because they can constitute the entirety of a well-formed message. ("Are those goats or sheep?" "Sheep.") But the past-forming /-ed/ of "talked" or "looked" and the /-er/ of "speaker" or "singer" are *bound* morphemes because they can never constitute well-formed messages on their own. Languages vary widely in their reliance on free or bound morphemes. Chinese, for example, has many free morphemes while Turkish has many bound morphemes. Words are free morphemes or combinations of morphemes that can constitute well-formed messages. ("The" by this definition is not a word but a bound morpheme.)

GRAMMAR: RULES GOVERNING THE CONSTRUCTION OF MORPHEMES

Grammar consists of sets of unconscious rules for combining phonemes into morphemes and morphemes into appropriate sentences. Some linguists also include the rules for interpreting the meaning of words and the rules for speaking in ways that are appropriate in particular contexts as part of grammar. The existence of rules governing the formation of permitted sequences of phonemes can be seen in the reaction of speakers of English to the name of former President Carter's security advisor, Zbigniew Brzynzki. The rules of English, unlike the rules of Polish, do not permit sound combinations such as *zb*. Similarly, speakers of English know by unconscious rule that the words "btop" and "ndak" cannot exist in English since they involve prohibited sound combinations.

GRAMMAR: SYNTAX

Similar unconscious rules govern the combination of morphemes into sentences. This branch of grammar is called *syntax*. Native speakers can distinguish between grammatical and nongrammatical sentences even when particular combinations have never been heard before. The classic example is the following:

a. Colorless green ideas sleep furiously.
b. Furiously sleep ideas green colorless.

Most speakers of English will recognize sentence *a* as a grammatical utterance but reject *b* as ungrammatical even if both seem equally nonsensical.

Native speakers can seldom state the rules governing the production of grammatical utterances. Even so simple a transformation as that from singular to plural nouns is hard to formulate as a conscious rule. As has been seen, adding an *s* converts "cat" into "cats," "slap" into "slaps," "fat" into "fats"; but something else happens in "house"–"houses," "rose"–"roses," "nose"–"noses"; and something else again in "crag"–"crags," "flag"–"flags," "hand"–"hands." (Three different allomorphs—/-s/, /-ez/, and /-z/—are employed according to a complex rule that most native speakers of English cannot put into words.)

It is the set of unconscious structural rules, and the sharing of these rules by the members of a speech community, that makes it possible for human beings to produce and interpret a potentially infinite number of messages, none of which need precisely replicate any other previous message.

Noam Chomsky described this behavior as follows:

> Normal linguistic behavior . . . as speaker or reader or hearer, is quite generally with novel utterances, with utterances that have no physical or formal similarity to any of the utterances that have ever been produced in the past experience of the hearer or, for that matter, in the history of the language, as far as anyone knows (1973:118).

DEEP STRUCTURE

How is it possible for us to create so many different messages and still be understood?

No one is quite sure of the answer to this question. One of the most popular theories is that proposed by Chomsky. According to Chomsky, every utterance has a *surface structure* and a *deep structure*. Surface structures may appear dissimilar, yet deep structure may be identical. For example, "Meat and gravy are loved by lions" is superficially dissimilar to the sentence "Lions love meat and gravy." Yet both sentences take as their model a third sentence: "Lions love meat and lions love gravy." This third sentence more closely reflects the "deep structure" which can be transformed into various superficially different variatons.

What is the deep structure of a sentence like "John knows a kinder person than Bill"? Note that the meaning of this sentence is ambiguous. Does John know a kinder person than Bill knows, or does John know a kinder person than Bill is? There must be two different deep structures that have gotten confused in the single ambiguous surface structure. Working backward through a number of inferences, the linguist arrives at the two distinctive deep structures:

> John knows a person/a person is kind/more than Bill is kind. John knows a person/a person is kind/more than a person Bill knows (Katz 1971:79 – 81).

Theoretically, a knowledge of the transformation rules should also lead to the identification of the deep structures that underlie apparently dissimilar ways of saying the same thing. Unfortunately, it has not yet proved feasible to identify all the transformation rules in any given language, and many linguists are convinced that there is a difference in meaning between deep structure sentences and their surface structure transforms (Silverstein 1972:376).

An essential feature of Chomsky's notion of grammar is that at the deepest levels all human languages share a common inborn species-specific structure. It is the existence of this inborn structure that makes it possible for children to learn to speak at an early age and that makes it possible to translate any human language into any other human language. Other authorities, however, doubt the existence of inborn grammar and attribute the acquisition of language skills by children to ordinary learning processes. One test of the uniqueness and innateness of human language is to see whether or not animals can learn to use language the way humans do. And it is to this question that we now turn.

APES AND LANGUAGE

In recent years a revolutionary series of experiments have shown that the gaps between human and ape capacities for symbolizing and grammar are not as great as had previously been supposed. Many futile attempts had been made to teach chimpanzees to speak in human fashion. But after 6 years of intensive training, the chimpanzee Viki only learned to say "mama," "papa," and "cup." With the demonstration that the vocal tract of apes renders it anatomically impossible for them to produce phones necessary for human speech (see p. 90), attention shifted toward attempting to teach apes to use sign languages and to read and write. Washoe, a female chimpanzee, learned 160 different standard signs of Ameslan (American Sign Language). Washoe used these signs productively (Fig. 20.2). She first learned the sign for "open" with a particular door and later spontaneously extended its use beyond the initial training context to all closed doors, then to closed containers such as the refrigerator, cupboards, drawers, briefcases, boxes, and jars. When Susan, a research assistant, stepped on Washoe's doll, Washoe had many ways to tell her

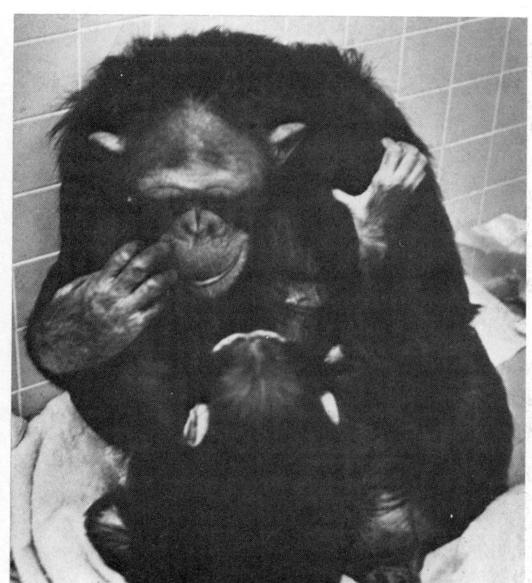

Figure 20.2 *WASHOE SIGNING "FUNNY"*

what was on her mind: "Up Susan; Susan up; mine please up; gimme baby; please shoe; more mine; up please; please up; more up; baby down; shoe up; baby up; please move up" (Gardner and Gardner 1971, 1975).

David Premack (1971, 1976) used a set of plastic chips to teach a chimpanzee named Sarah the meaning of a set of 130 symbols with which they could communicate with each other. Premack could ask Sarah rather abstract questions such as "What is an apple the same as?" Sarah could respond by selecting the chips that stood for "red," "round," "stem," and "less desirable than grapes." Premack made a special effort to incorporate certain rudimentary grammatical rules into his human-chimp language. For example, Sarah could respond appropriately to the plastic-chip command: "Sarah put the banana in the pail and the apple in the dish." Sarah herself, however, did not make such complex demands of Premack.

Another approach with a chimpanzee named Lana utilized a keyboard controlled by a computer and a written language known as Yerkish (Fig. 20.3). Lana could read and write such sentences as "Please machine make the window open," correctly distinguishing between sentences that begin appropriately and inappropriately and that have permitted and prohibited combinations of Yerkish words in permitted and prohibited sequence (Rambaugh 1977).

With each passing year, more apes and experimenters have been exchanging more and more complex messages showing

Figure 20.3 *LANA USING YERKISH TO COMMUNICATE WITH A COMPUTER*
She can read and "write" 71 cards.

greater and greater resemblance to the language capabilities of human children. The new strategy has been to use Ameslan from the animal's infancy onward and to make the ape part of a human family. Francine Patterson has had spectacular success with Koko, a female gorilla who holds the record thus far of 600 Ameslan words (Fig. 20.4). Nim Chimpsky (the resemblance to the name Noam Chomsky was not accidental) had a vocabulary of 125 signs at age 4 in combinations of up to four signs per message (Fig. 20.5). Both Washoe and Lucy, a chimpanzee raised by Roger Fouts, learned to generalize the sign for dirty from feces. Lucy applied it to Fouts when he refused her requests! Lucy also invented the combinations "cry hurt food" to name radishes and "candy fruit" for watermelon. Koko signed "finger bracelet" for ring; "white tiger" for zebra; "eye hat" for mask. Koko has also begun to talk about her inner feelings, signaling happiness, sadness, fear, and shame (Hill 1978:98–99).

Despite these apparent successes, the experimenters remain divided as to the extent to which their apes have actually demonstrated a capacity for using language the way humans do. According to Terrace (1981), Nim did not form sentences based on word order the way human children do. Nim's utterances were therefore much less productive (see above) than a child's. Most sequences were short; the longer ones, for example, "play me Nim play" were merely redundant; there was no marked tendency for utterances to increase in length and become less redundant as Nim grew older; and most signing episodes were initiated by Nim's trainers with Nim incorporating the signs used by them in response.

Francine Patterson (1981), on the other hand, insists that Koko has learned to sign in an open creative way. Koko's utterances average 2.7 signs versus Nim's 1.5. While word order is not important for Koko, Patterson attributes this to the peculiarities of Ameslan, which permits one to sign different words simultaneously and to create new meanings by slight changes in the way the signs are made. Thus, Koko expresses grammatical rules by modifying the signs rather

Figure 20.4 *KOKO*
Koko is giving the sign "Pour-Drink" to her teacher Francine Patterson.

than their order: "When she moves the *sip* sign away from her mouth toward me, Koko is actually saying 'you sip'" (ibid.:117).

It is clear that the genetically determined symboling and metaphorical capabilities of apes are much closer to human capacities than most anthropologists were previously willing to concede. As the experiments continue, it would seem rash for anyone to predict exactly how far the conversation between people and apes will go before some absolute limit is found.

Noam Chomsky, however, does not agree:

> Perhaps some hopelessly confused observer might argue . . . that the distinction between jumping and flying is arbitrary, a matter of degree. People can really fly, just like birds, only less well. Analogous proposals in the case of language seem to me to have no greater force or significance (Chomsky 1975:41).

LANGUAGE ACQUISITION

Great strides have also recently been made in the study of how children acquire their native languages. These studies have also narrowed the gap between humans and apes (without, however, eliminating the differences). They have shown that the acquisition of language proceeds step by step from the acquisition of phonemes to simple morphemes and grammatical rules to more and more complex vocabularies and structural rules. It has been found that children will not learn to speak merely if they hear others speak. A boy with normal hearing and comprehension, but with deaf parents who communicated in Ameslan, watched and listened to television every day. His parents hoped that he would learn English. Because the boy was asthmatic he was kept at home and interacted only with people who communicated in sign language. By the age of 3 he was fluent in Ameslan but neither understood nor spoke English. This shows that in order to learn a language, children must be able to test out and improve their tentative knowledge of phonemes, morphemes, and grammar by interacting with other people. In other words, although human beings have a uniquely developed species-specific

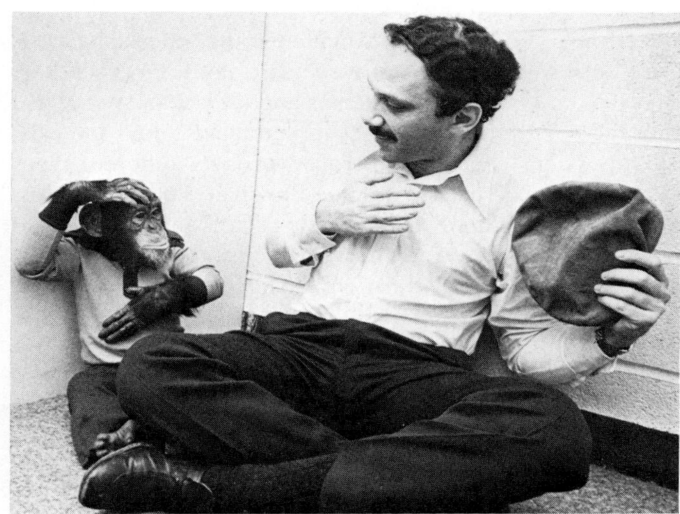

Figure 20.5 *NIM CHIMPSKY SIGNING "ME HAT" TO HERBERT TERRACE*

capacity for language, we will not automatically begin to speak as soon as we hear others doing it. We learn our languages by using them to make requests and by responding to the requests that others make (Moscowitz 1978:94b).

THE EQUIVALENCE OF ALL GRAMMARS

European linguists of the nineteenth century were convinced that the languages of the world could be arranged in a hierarchical order. They invariably awarded the prize for efficiency, elegance, and beauty to Latin, the mastery of whose grammar was long a precondition of scholarly success in the West.

One of the more influential schemes for evaluating the relative worth of different languages postulated that grammars evolve through *isolating*, *agglutinative*, and *inflective* stages. In the isolating stage there are few bound morphemes and few changes in roots in conformity with grammatical rules. Chinese is such a language. In the agglutinative stage, as in Turkish or Finnish, *affixes* or bound morphemes are attached to roots in long strings. Finally, in the inflective stage, as represented by Latin, there are numerous bound morphemes that themselves undergo regular variations in conformity with their semantic and grammatical function within an utterance.

Regardless of the appropriateness of the isolative-agglutinative-inflective distinction, there are neither functional nor historical reasons for rating one type as superior to the others. To classify Chinese as a "primitive" language is not only to ignore the complete and efficient nature of Chinese as a communication system, but also the fact that both Chinese and English are today less inflective than they were in former times. Over thousands of years several alternations between isolative and inflective tendencies have probably occurred among most of the world's language families. Furthermore, if complexity is to be the criterion of superiority, then Latin can scarcely hold its own in comparison with many American Indian and other "primitive" languages that possess noun cases and verb tenses undreamed of by Cicero.

Beginning with the study of American Indian languages, anthropological linguists led by Franz Boas (see Ch. 25) showed that the belief in the superiority of "civilized" grammars was untenable. It was found that grammatical rules run the full gamut from relatively simple to relatively complex systems among peoples on all levels of technological and political development. The conclusion of the great anthropological linguist Edward Sapir (1921:234) stands unchallenged: "When it comes to linguistic form, Plato walks with the Macedonian swineherd, Confucius with the head-hunting savages of Assam."

GENERALITY AND SPECIFICITY

Two other kinds of language differences are often cited as evidence that one language is more "primitive" than another: (1) lack of generalizing terms and (2) lack of specialized terms. Many observers have noted the existence of numerous words for different types of parrots in the Brazilian Tupi languages, and yet no term for parrots in general. This has led to the assumption that the lack of a general term is associated with a primitive intellectual and primitive linguistic capacity. The opposite side of this coin is the comparison that emphasizes a lack of specific terms. Thus, many languages have no specific terms for numbers higher than five. Larger quantities are simply referred to as "many." From this it is concluded that the lack of specific terms is associated with a primitive intellect and primitive linguistic capacity.

These evaluations fail to take into account the fact that the extent to which discourse is specific or general reflects the culturally defined need to be specific or general, not the capacity of one's language to transmit messages about specific or general phenomena. For a Brazilian Indian there is little need to distinguish parrots in general from other birds, but there is a need to distinguish one parrot from another since each type is valued for its plumage. The ordinary individual in a small-scale band or village society can name and identify 500 to 1000 separate plant species, but the ordinary modern urbanite can usually name only 50 to 100 such species. Paradoxically, urbanites usually have a more complex set of general terms, such as *plant, tree, shrub,* and *vine,* than band and village peoples for whom such generalities are of little practical use (Witowski and Brown 1978:445–446). English, which has terms for many special vehicles—*cart, stretcher, auto, sled, snowmobile*—lacks a general term for wheeled vehicles. Yet this does not prevent one from communicating about wheeled vehicles as distinguished from sleds and helicopters when the need arises. Similarly, the absence of higher-number terms usually means that there are few occasions in which it is useful to specify precisely large quantities. When these occasions become more common, any language can cope with the problem of numeration by repeating the largest term or by inventing new ones.

It has been found that band and village societies tend to have languages with fewer color terms than more complex societies. Some languages only have separate terms for brightness contrasts such as those designated by black and white. With the evolution of chiefdoms and states, languages tend to add additional color distinctions in a regular sequence: red → green or blue → brown → pink, orange, purple. The emergence of these distinct color terms is probably linked with increasing technological control over dyes and paints (Witowski and Brown 1978).

These differences, in any event, are necessarily superficial. Semantic productivity is infinite in all known languages. When the social need arises, terms appropriate to industrial civilization can be developed by any language. This can be done either through the direct borrowing of the words of one language by another (*sputnik, blitzkrieg, garage*) or by the creation of new words based on new combinations of the existing stock of morphemes (*radiometric, railroad, newspaper*). We humans are never at a loss for words—not for long, that is.

LANGUAGE, SOCIAL CLASS, AND ETHNICITY

A final form in which the claim for language superiority appears is associated with the dialect variations characteristic of stratified societies. One hears of the "substandard" grammar or "substandard" pronunciation of a particular ethnic group or social class. Such allegations have no basis in linguistic science except insofar as one is willing to accept all contemporary languages as corrupt and "substandard" versions of earlier languages (Fig. 20.6) (and see below).

When the dialect variant of a segment of a larger speech community is labeled "substandard," what is usually being dealt with is a political rather than a linguistic phenomenon (Hertzler 1965; Southworth 1969). The demotion of dialects to inferior status can only be understood as part of the general process by which ruling groups attempt to maintain their superordinate position (see

Figure 20.6 *CLASS AND SPEECH*
Henry Higgins teaching Eliza Doolittle how to speak like an upper-class person. From *My Fair Lady,* an adaptation of George Bernard Shaw's *Pygmalion,* featuring Rex Harrington and Julie Andrews.

Ch. 17). Linguistically, the phonology and grammar of the poor and uneducated classes are as good as those of the rich, educated, and powerful classes.

This point should not be confused with the problem of functional vocabulary differences. Exploited and deprived groups often lack key specialized and technical words and concepts as a result of their limited educational experience. This constitutes a real handicap in competing for jobs. But this has nothing to do with the question of the adequacy of the phonological and grammatical systems of working class and ethnic dialects.

Well-intentioned educators often claim that the poor and ghetto children are reared in a "linguistically deprived" environment. In a detailed study of the actual speech behavior of blacks in northern ghettos, William Labov (1972a and b) has shown that this belief reflects the ethnocentric prejudices of middle-class teachers and researchers rather than any deficit in the grammar or logical structure of the ghetto dialect. The nonstandard English of the black ghetto—black vernacular English—contains certain forms that are unacceptable in white middle-class settings. Among the most common are negative inversion ("don't nobody know"); negative concord ("you ain't goin' to no heaven"); invariant "be" ("when they be sayin"); dummy "it" instead of "there" ("it ain't no heaven"); and copula deletion ("if you bad"). Yet the utilization of these forms in no way prevents or inhibits the expression of complex thoughts in concise and logically consistent patterns, as exemplified in a black teenager's discussion of life after death:

> Soon as you die, your spirit leaves you. (And where does the spirit go?) Well, it all depends. (On what?) You know, like some people say if you're good an' shit, your spirit goin't'heaven . . . 'm' if you bad, your spirit goin' to hell. Well, bullshit! Your spirit goin' to hell anyway, good or bad. (Why?) Why? I'll tell you why. 'Cause, you see, doesn' no body really know that it's a God, y'know, 'cause, I mean I have seen black gods, pink gods, white gods, all color gods, and don't nobody know it's really a God. An' when they be saying' if you good, you goin' t'heaven, tha's bullshit, 'cause you ain't goin' to no heaven, 'cause it ain't no heaven for you to go to (Labov 1972a:214–215).

The grammatical properties of nonstandard language are not haphazard and arbitrary variations. On the contrary, they conform to rules that produce regular differences with respect to the standard grammar. All the dialects of English possess equivalent means for expressing the same logical content:

> Whatever problems working-class children may have in handling logical operations are not to be blamed on the structure of their language. There is nothing in the vernacular which will interfere with the development of logical thought, for the logic of standard English cannot be distinguished from the logic of any other dialect of English by any test that we can find (Labov 1972a:229).

LANGUAGE, THOUGHT, AND CAUSALITY

A question that has been investigated by linguists for many years is the extent to which different word categories and grammars produce habitually incompatible modes of thought among peoples who belong to different language communities (Hymes 1971; Kay and Kempton 1984). At the center of this controversy is the comparison made by the anthropological linguist Benjamin Whorf between native American languages and the Indo-European family of languages, to which English belongs. According to Whorf, when two language systems have radically different vocabularies and grammars, their respective speakers live in wholly different thoughtworlds. Even such fundamental categories as space and time are said to be experienced differently as a result of the linguistic "molds" that constrain thought.

> The forms of a person's thoughts are controlled by inexorable laws of pattern of which he is unconscious. These patterns are the unperceived intricate systematizations of his own language—shown readily enough by a candid comparison and contrast with other languages, especially those of a different linguistic family. His thinking itself is in a language—in English, in Sanskrit, in Chinese. And every language is a vast pattern-system, different from others, in which are culturally ordained the forms and categories by which the personality not only communicates, but also analyzes nature, notices or neglects types of relationship and phenomena, channels his rea-

soning, and builds the house of his consciousness (1956:252).

According to Whorf, English sentences are constructed in such a way as to indicate that some substance or matter is part of an event that is located at a definite time and place. Both time and space can be measured and divided into units. In Hopi sentences, however, events are not located with reference to time but, rather, to the categories of "being" as opposed to "becoming." English encourages one to think of time as a divisible rod that starts in the past, passes through the present, and continues into the future; hence, the English language's past, present, and future tenses. Hopi grammar, however, merely distinguishes all events that have already become manifest from all those still in the process of becoming manifest; it has no equivalent of past, present, and future tenses. Does this mean that a Hopi cannot indicate that an event happened last month or that it is happening right now or that it will happen tomorrow? Of course not. But Whorf's point is that the English tense system makes it easier to measure time, and he postulated some type of connection between the tense system of Indo-European languages and the inclination of Euro-Americans to read timetables, make time payments, and punch time clocks.

In rebuttal, other linguists have pointed out that the three-tense system that is supposed to color thinking about time really does not exist in English. First, there is no specific verb form indicating the future tense in English; one uses auxiliaries like "will" and "shall." Second, English speakers frequently use the present tense and even the past tense to talk about the future: "*I'm eating* at six this evening"; "If I *told* you, would you do anything?" This means that the use of tenses in English is a good deal more relaxed and ambiguous than high school grammars indicate. If one needed an opportunity to become confused about time, English provides no unusual obstacles (Haugen 1975).

A more important objection to Whorf's point of view is that it implicitly distorts the fundamental causal relationships between language and culture. No one would deny that the absence of calendars, clocks, and timetables must have given preindustrial societies like the Hopi an orientation to time very different from that of industrial-age societies. But there is no evidence to support the view that industrialization is in any way facilitated or caused by having one kind of grammar rather than another (see ch. 18).

An interest in calendars and other time-reckoning devices is a recurrent feature of social and political development associated with peoples whose languages are as diverse as Egyptian and Maya. Indeed, the Chinese contributed as much to the invention of modern mechanical clocks as did the Europeans. On the other hand, a lack of concern with counting time is a characteristic of preindustrial peoples in general, from Patagonia to Baffin Land and from New Guinea to the Kalahari desert—peoples who speak a thousand different tongues.

As it is with time reckoning, so it is with other aspects of culture. The Aztecs, whose powerful state marks the high point of political development in aboriginal North America, spoke a language closely related to that of the hunting and food-gathering Utes. Religions as different as Hinduism, Christianity, and Buddhism have flourished among peoples all of whom speak Indo-European languages. Malayo-Polynesian, Bantu, and Arabic have served equally well as media for the spread of Islam, whereas Chinese, Russian, and Spanish have served equally well for the spread of Marxism. Industrial capitalism in Japan and the United States share much in common, although the Japanese and English languages show few resemblances.

OBLIGATORY ELITISM AND SEXISM

Languages differ in having certain obligatory categories built into their grammatical rules. English requires us to specify number. Speakers of the Romance languages must indicate the sex (gender) of all nouns. Certain American Indian languages (for example, Kwakiutl) must indicate whether or not an object is near or far from the speaker and whether or not it is visible or invisible. These obligatory categories in all probability are not indicative of any active psychological tendency to be obsessed with numbers, sex, or the location of people or objects.

It should not be concluded, however, that grammatical conventions are always trivial. Certain obligatory grammatical categories do mirror social life quite faithfully. Consider the pronouns and verb forms for peers versus subordinates in the Romance languages. Because of the existence of a second person "familiar" form in the conjugation of Romance verbs, the speaker of French or Spanish is frequently obliged to evaluate and express the relative social standing of persons engaged in a conversation. Today these second person familiar forms (e.g., *tu hablas, tu parles*—in Spanish and French; roughly, "thou speaketh") are primarily applied to children, pets, very close friends, and loved ones. But another usage persists, especially in parts of Latin America, where landlords and officials apply the *tu* forms to servants, workers, and peasants as well as to children and pets. These forms clearly reflect an active consciousness of class and rank distinctions and bear a social significance that is far from trivial or merely conventional (Southworth 1974; Brown and Gilman 1960).

Similarly, certain obligatory categories in standard English seem to reflect a pervasive social bias in favor of male-centered viewpoints and activities. Many nouns that refer to human beings lack a sex gender—*child, everybody, everyone, person, citizen, American, human,* and so on. Teachers of standard English prescribe masculine rather than feminine pronouns for these nouns. Thus it is considered "correct" to say: "Everyone must remember to take *his* toothbrush," even though the group being addressed consists of both males and females. Newspaper columnists are fond of writing: "The average American is in love with *his* car." And high school grammars insist that one must say: "All the boys and girls were puzzled but no one was willing to raise *his* hand" (Roberts 1964:382). Obviously a perfectly intelligible and sexually unbiased substitute is readily available in the plural possessive pronoun "their." In fact, almost everybody uses "their" in their [sic] everyday conversation (cf. Newmeyer 1978). So why bother to insist that "his"is correct?

Anthropologists face a particularly acute form of this problem in their dependence upon *man* as the vernacular term for *Homo sapiens*. Consider the following excerpt from a popular textbook:

> A million or more years ago, man had become sufficiently differentiated from the other animals so that we can now look back on *him* as representing a new form of life. A feature of this differentiation was the elaboration of *his* nervous system . . . to the point where he could not only see, smell, and act but also symbolically represent a wide range of experience. *He* acquired the capacity to think and to speak. *He* could experience things and situations vicariously. . . .*He* learned how to communicate experience to *him-*

self and to others. . . .*He* began a process of self-organization. *He* began to see the universe about him. . . .*He* acquired the capacity. . . .*He* learned to create. . . .*He* began to shape. . . .*He* became imaginative.

It seems likely that the grammar of this passage reflects the fact that anthropology, like other learned professions in Western society, has been dominated by men. It seems just as likely that the use of *Him* and *He* as pronouns for God reflects the fact that men are the priests of Judaism and Christianity (see p. 503). The male-centered conventions of the English language may not be as benign and trivial as male anthropologists believe them to be (Lakoff 1973; Philips 1980:531). But it is not my intention to imply that anthropologists who persist in the more conventional usage are dominated by unconscious sexist stereotypes. As Franklin Southworth has shown in his study of changes in the use of obligatory forms of address in India (1974), mere linguistic changes are easy to make. So easy, in fact, that they sometimes function as "masks for power" by creating the superficial impression of democratization. One must certainly guard against trying to change the world by mere word magic. Yet if a particular word or grammatical rule hurts and offends people, why continue to use it?

LINGUISTIC CHANGE

Language like all other parts of culture is constantly undergoing change. These changes result from slight phonological, morphemic, or grammatical variations. They are often identifiable at first as "dialect" differences such as those which distinguish the speech of American southerners from the speech of New Englanders or the speech of Londoners. If groups of southerners, New Englanders, and Londoners were to move off to separate islands and lose all linguistic contact with each other and their homelands, their speech would eventually cease to be mutually intelligible. The longer the separation, the less resemblance there would probably be among them.

The process of dialect formation and geographical isolation is responsible for much of the great diversity of languages. Many mutually unintelligible languages of today are "daughter" languages of a common "parent" language. This can be seen by the regular resemblances which languages display in their phonological features. For example, English /t/ corresponds to German /z/, as in the following words (after Sturtevant 1964:64–66):

tail	Zagel	tin	Zinn
tame	zahm	to	zu
tap	zapfen	toe	Zehe
ten	zehn	tooth	Zahn

These correspondences result from the fact that both English and German are daughter languages of a common parent language known as Proto-West Germanic.

In the 2000 years that have elapsed since the Roman conquest of western Europe, Latin has evolved into an entire family of languages of which French, Italian, Portuguese, Rumanian, and Spanish are the principal representatives. If linguists did not know of the existence of Latin through the historical records, they would be obliged to postulate its existence on the basis of the sound correspondences within the Romance family. It is obvious that every contemporary spoken language is nothing but a transformed version of a dialect of an earlier language, and even in the absence of written records, languages can be grouped together on the basis of their "descent" from a common ancestor. Thus, in a more remote period, Proto-West Germanic was undifferentiated from Latin and a large number of additional languages including the ancestral forms of Hindi, Persian, Greek, Russian, and Gaelic. This group of languages constitutes the *Indo-European family* of languages. Inferences based upon the sound correspondences among the Indo-European languages have led linguists to reconstruct the sound system of the parent from which they all ultimately derive. This language is called *Proto-Indo-European* (Fig. 20.7).

Languages may also change without any geographical separation of different portions of a speech community. Within 1000 years, English, for example, changed from Old English to its modern form as a result of shifts in pronunciation and the borrowing of words from other languages. The following passage from the Anglo-Saxon *Chronicle* written in A.D. 1066 shows how far the change has gone—the two languages are actually mutually unintelligible:

> *On bissum eare . . . be he cyning waes, he for ut mid scrip-here to eanes Willelme; and ba hwile com Tosti eorl into Humbran mid 60 scipum. Eadwine eorl com mid land-fierde and draf hine ut; and ba butse-carlas hine forsocon, and he for to Scotlande mid 12 snaccum, and hine emette Harald se Norrena cyning mid 300 scipum, and Tosti him tobeag. And man cyode Harolde cyning hu hit waes baer edon and eworden, and he com mid miclum here Engliscra manna and emette hine aet Staengfordes brycge and hine ofslog, and bone eorl Tosti, and eallne bone here ehtlice ofercom.*
>
> *In this year when he [Harold] was king, he went out with a fleet against William; and meanwhile Earl Tosti came into the Humber with sixty ships. Earl Edwin came with a land force and drove him out; and then the sailors forsook him [Tosti], and he went to Scotland with twelve small boats, and Harald, the Norwegian king, met him with three hundred ships, and Tosti submitted to him. And they told King Harold what had been done and had befallen there, and he came with a large army of Englishmen and met him [Harald III Hardraade, the Norwegian king] at Stamford Bridge and slew him and Earl Tosti, and courageously overcame the whole army.*

As these changes illustrate, Modern English can be regarded as a "corruption" of Old English. Indeed, all modern languages are "corruptions" of older languages. This does not prevent people from forming committees to save the "King's English" or to protect the "purity" of French. However, the expectation of linguistic change is so great that linguists have developed a technique for dating the separation of one language from another, called *glottochronology*. This technique is based on the assumption that due to borrowing and internal changes, about 14 percent of the most basic words in a language's vocabulary will be replaced every 1000 years.

LANGUAGE AND CONSCIOUSNESS

Language and language change illustrate the remarkable forms that can emerge in human culture without the conscious design of the participants. As pointed out by Alfred Kroeber,

> The unceasing processes of change in language are mainly unconscious or covert, or at least implicit. The results of the change may come to be recognized by speakers of the changing languages; the gradual act of change, and especially the causes, mostly happen without the speaker being aware of them. . . .When a change has begun to creep in, it may be tacitly accepted or it may be observed and consciously resisted on the ground of being incorrect or vulgar or foreign. But the underlying motives of the objectors and the impulses of the innovator are likely to be equally unknown to themselves (1948:245).

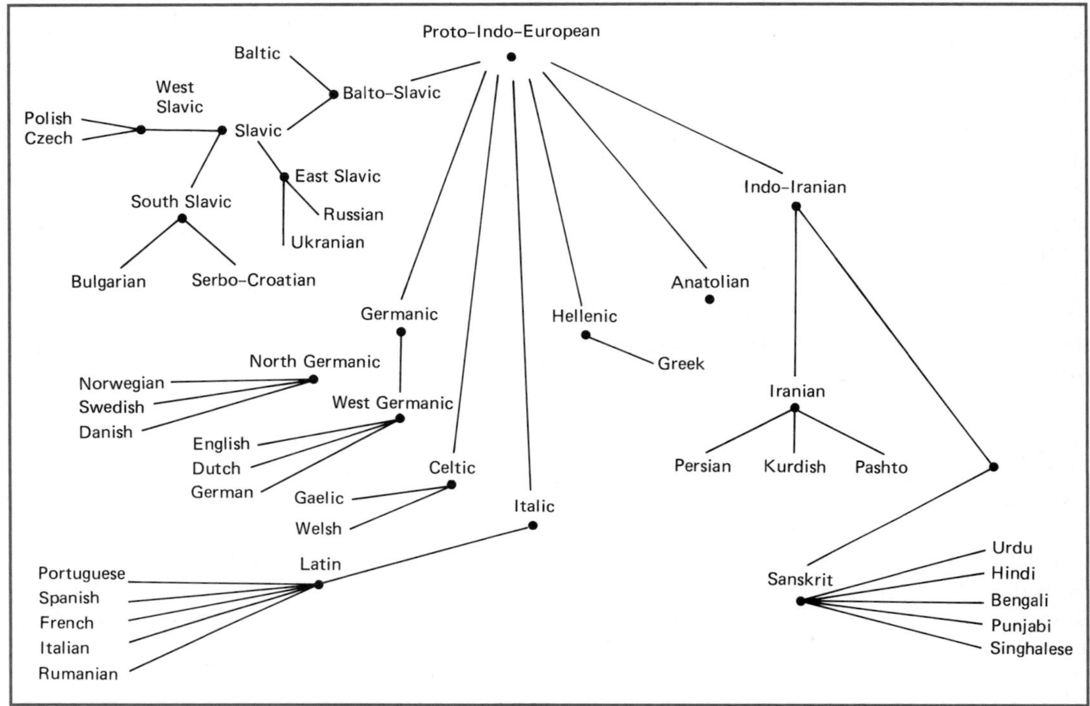

Figure 20.7 *INDO-EUROPEAN FAMILY OF LANGUAGES*

This aspect of language change can be generalized to changes in all of the other sectors of sociocultural systems. As stated long ago by Adam Fergusson, a great eighteenth-century Scottish philosopher, the forms of society "even in what are termed enlightened ages are made with equal blindness toward the future." Cultural systems are "indeed the result of human action, but not the execution of any human design."

It is true that we are the only animals capable of talking about ourselves and of consciously analyzing our problems. We alone have conscious self-awareness, which many people regard as the most important attribute of human nature. Yet there is something that is usually overlooked when consciousness is celebrated as our species' crowning glory. What is overlooked is that our minds are subject to restraints that do not affect the mental life of other organisms. Since we live by culture, our minds are shaped and channeled by culture. Hence the gift of semantic universality has many strings attached to it. Language does not necessarily give us freedom of thought; on the contrary, it often traps us into delusions and myths. Because we live by culture and because our minds are molded by culture, we have more to become aware of than other creatures. We alone must struggle to understand how culture controls what goes on inside our heads. Without this additional level of awareness, the human mind cannot be said to be fully conscious.

SUMMARY

Human language is unique in possessing semantic universality or the capacity to produce unlimited numbers of novel messages without loss of informational efficiency. In contrast to gibbon calls, for example, human language has unrestricted powers of productivity. One of the most important means of achieving this productivity is the arbitrariness of the elements that convey the information. Despite the importance of the genetic heritage for acquiring speech, the actual languages spoken depend entirely on enculturation; moreover, words in general lack any physical or iconographic resemblance to their referents.

Another important component in the achievement of semantic universality is duality of patterning. This refers to the use of arbitrary code elements in different combinations to produce different messages. The basic code elements of human languages are the phonemes or classes of contrastive phones. A phoneme consists of a bundle of allophones which are contrastive with respect to the allophones of other phonemes. Different languages have widely different repertories of phones, phonemes, and allophones. None of these elements carry meaning in themselves.

Duality of patterning is further exemplified by the combination of phonemes into morphemes, which are the minimal units of meaningful sound. Morphemes are classes of phonemes and contain variant forms called allomorphs. Morphemes can be free or bound depending on whether they can occur alone and constitute well-formed utterances.

The ability to send and receive messages in a human language is dependent on the sharing of rules for combining phonemes into morphemes and morphemes into sentences. These rules are part of a language's grammar. They are usually held unconsciously. On the phonemic level they specify the permitted and prohibited combinations of phonemes; on the morphemic level they specify the sequences of morphemes and allomorphs required for well-formed utterances. Such rules are called syntax. Knowledge of the rules of syntax makes it possible to produce completely novel utterances and yet be understood. A theory which accounts for this property of syntax is that there is a deep structure to which various superficially dissimilar utterances can be reduced. Novel sentences are transformations of these deep structures and can be understood by tracing them back to their underlying components.

Recent experiments with apes have helped to clarify what aspects of human semantic universality are primarily genetically determined and what aspects are due to the use of learning capacities that are shared with other hominoids. Training with Ameslan has been especially revealing and has narrowed the gap between apes and humans. Chimps and gorillas are displaying unexpected capacities for arbitrariness, productivity, and grammatical rule learning. Studies of human infants show that broad general capacity for learning rather than narrow instinctual programming determines the steps taken in the acquisition of language.

All human languages are mutually translatable and there is no evidence that some languages have more efficient grammars than others. Categories and vocabularies differ widely, but these differences do not indicate any inherent defect in a language nor any intellectual inferiority on the part of the speakers. General and specific categorizations as in numbers, plant classifications, and color terms reflect the practical need for making general or specific distinctions under particular cultural and natural conditions.

The view that certain dialects of standard languages are "inferior" forms of speech reflects class and ethnic biases. Dialects such as black vernacular English in and of themselves do not inhibit clear and logical thought.

Attempts to show that differences in grammar determine how people think and behave in different cultures have not been successful. There are very few if any correlations other than vocabulary that can be shown between language and the major forms of demographic, technological, economic, ecological, domestic, political, and religious adaptations. This does not mean that obligatory linguistic categories such as those concerned with sex, age, and class differences are trivial aspects of sociocultural life. These aspects of language must be regarded seriously and examined for their possible harmful effects.

Languages, like all other aspects of culture, are constantly being changed as a result of both internal and external processes. All languages are "corruptions" of earlier parent languages. Glottochronology is based on the premise that not only do all languages change but that they change at a predictable rate.

The study of language change, as well as the study of the other aspects of linguistics, shows the predominance of unconscious factors in sociocultural life. Although semantic universality is a great and uniquely human gift, it does not automatically bestow on us full consciousness and genuine freedom of thought. To become fully conscious, we must strive to understand how culture controls what we think and do.

21 VARIETIES OF RELIGIOUS EXPERIENCE

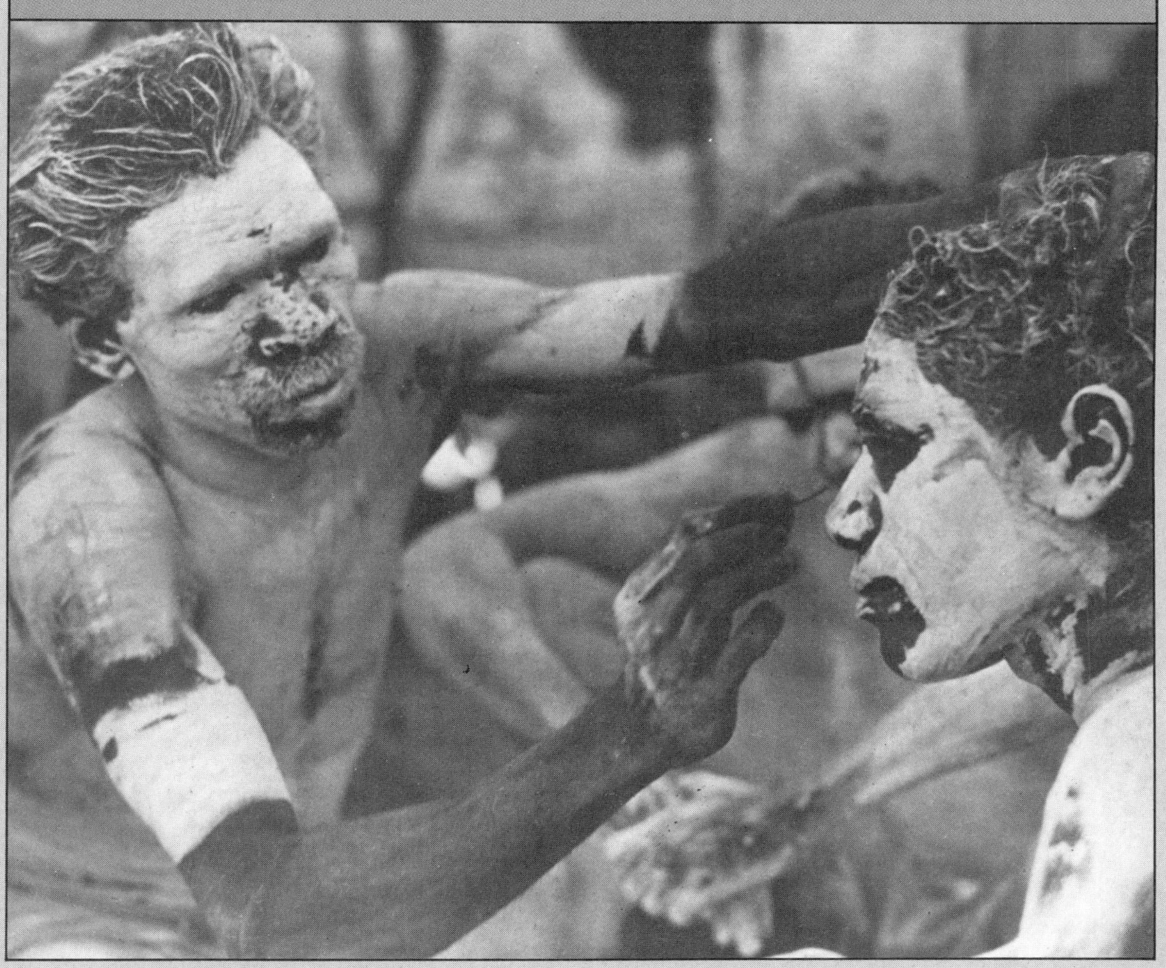

This chapter shifts the focus of our inquiry to the superstructure. It surveys general aspects of culturally patterned ideas that are conventionally known as religion, myth, and magic. It also surveys the patterns of behavior that are called ritual and that are intended to mediate between human beings and natural forces, on the one hand, and supernatural beings and supernatural forces, on the other. This chapter is primarily descriptive. It defines basic concepts such as religion and magic and sets forth the basic types of religious organizations and rituals. Theories that attempt to explain varieties of religious experiences will be presented in the chapter that follows.

ANIMISM

What is religion? The earliest anthropological attempt to define religion was that of E. B. Tylor. For Tylor the essence of religion was belief in the idea of "god." Most Western peoples would probably still find such a belief an essential ingredient in their own conception of what constitutes religion. The Victorian Age in which Tylor lived, however, tended to regard religion in even narrower terms, often restricting the concept to Christianity. Other people's beliefs in god were relegated to the realm of "superstition" and "paganism." Tylor's principal contribution was to show that the Judeo-Christian concept of god was essentially similar to beliefs about supernatural beings found the world over.

Tylor attempted, with considerable success, to show that the idea of god was an elaboration of the concept of "soul." In his book *Primitive Culture*, Tylor (1871) demonstrated that belief in "the doctrine of souls" occurs to some extent and in one form or another in every society. He gave the name *animism* to this belief. Animism is the belief that inside ordinary visible tangible bodies there is a normally invisible, normally intangible being: the soul. Throughout the world souls are believed to appear in dreams, trances, visions, shadows, and reflections, and to be implicated in fainting, loss of consciousness, and birth and death. Tylor reasoned that the basic idea of soul must have been invented in order to explain all these puzzling phenomena. Once established, the basic idea of soul was embroidered upon and ultimately gave rise to a variety of supernatural beings including the souls of animals, plants, and material objects, as well as of gods, demons, spirits, devils, ghosts, saints, fairies, gnomes, elves, angels, and so forth.

Tylor has been criticized by twentieth-century anthropologists for his suggestion that animism arose merely as a result of the attempt to understand puzzling human and natural phenomena. Today we know that religion is much more than an attempt to explain puzzling phenomena. Like other aspects of superstructure, religion serves a multitude of economic, political, and psychological functions.

Another important criticism of Tylor's stress on the puzzle-solving function of religion concerns the role of hallucinations in shaping religious beliefs. During drug-induced trances and other forms of hallucinatory experience, people "see" and "hear" extraordinary things which seem even more "real" than ordinary people and animals. One can argue, therefore, that animistic theories are not intellectual attempts to explain trances and dreams, but direct expressions of extraordinary psychological experiences. Nonetheless, it cannot be denied that religion and the doctrine of souls also have the function of providing people with answers to fundamental questions about the meaning of life and death and the causes of events.

THE THREE SOULS OF THE JÍVARO

Although there are certain animistic beliefs that are universal, each culture has its own distinctive animistic beings and its own specific elaboration of the soul concept. Some cultures insist that people have two or more souls; and some cultures believe that certain individuals have more souls than others. Among the Jívaro of eastern Ecuador, for example, three kinds of souls are recognized: an ordinary, or "true," soul; an *arutam* soul; and a *muisak* soul (Harner 1972b).

The Jívaro believe that the true soul is present from birth inside every living Jívaro, male and female. Upon a person's death, this soul leaves the body and undergoes a series of changes. During the first phase of its afterlife, the true soul returns to its body's birthplace and relives its former life in an invisible form. The major difference between the two existences is that after death the true soul cannot eat real food and thus remains perpetually hungry. Needless to say, the Jívaro do not look forward to this experience. After the true soul has relived the entire life of its deceased owner, the second phase begins. It changes into a demon. This demon roams the forest, solitary, hungry, and lonely. The second phase lasts for the equivalent of another lifetime. The true soul then dies again and enters its third phase. It changes into a *wampang*, a species of giant moth that is occasionally seen flitting about. The living try to feed it because it too is perpetually hungry. In its fourth and final phase the true soul turns to mist:

> After a length of time about which the Jívaro are uncertain, the *wampang* finally has its wings damaged by raindrops as it flutters through a rainstorm, and falls to die on the ground. The true soul then changes into water vapor amidst the falling rain. All fogs and clouds are believed to be the last form taken by true souls. The true soul undergoes no more transformations and persists eternally in the form of mist (Harner 1972b:151).

No one is born with the second Jívaro soul—the *arutam*. It must be acquired. All men and occasionally some women try to acquire one. The possessor of an arutam feels great power and cannot be killed. To obtain an arutam, one must fast, bathe in a sacred waterfall, and drink tobacco water or the juice of a plant containing the hallucinogenic substance *datura*. The arutam comes out of the depths of the forest in the form of a pair of giant jaguars or a pair of huge snakes rolling over and over toward the soul-seeker. When the apparition gets close, the terrified soul-seeker must run forward and touch it. If this is done, when the soul-seeker goes to sleep, the arutam will enter the body and lodge in the chest. People who possess an arutam soul are different from other men and women. They speak and act with great confidence, and they feel an irresistible craving to kill their enemies. Great warriors and other exceptionally powerful individuals may possess more than one arutam soul at a time. Unfortunately, arutam souls cannot be kept forever. They leave their temporary abode just before their possessor kills someone. Eventually, wandering in the forest, they will be captured by other soul-seekers brave enough to touch them.

The third Jívaro soul is the *muisak*—the avenging soul. The muisak comes into existence when people who formerly possessed an arutam are killed by their enemies. The muisak develops inside the victim's head and tries to get out and attack the killer. To prevent this from happening, the best thing to do is to cut off the victim's head, "shrink" it, and bring it back home. If it is handled properly in various rituals and dances, the muisak can make the killer strong and happy. After the muisak has been used to the killer's advantage, a ritual is performed to send it back to the village from which it came. To get it to go back, the women sing this song:

Now, now, go back to your house where you lived.
Your wife is there calling from your house.
You have come here to make us happy.
Finally we have finished.
So return (Harner 1972b:146).

ANIMATISM AND MANA

Tylor's definition of religion as animism was quickly seen as too narrow. As Robert Marett (1914) pointed out, when people attribute lifelike properties to rocks, pots, storms, and volcanoes, they do not necessarily believe that souls are the cause of the lifelike behavior of these objects. Hence there is a need to distinguish a concept of a supernatural force that does not derive its effect from souls. Marett introduced the term *animatism* to designate the belief in such nonsoul forces. Possession of concentrated animatistic force can give certain objects, animals, and people extraordinary powers independent of power derived from souls and gods. To label this concentrated form of animatistic power, Marett introduced the Melanesian word *mana*. An adze that makes intricate carvings, a fishhook that catches large fish, a club that kills many enemies, or a rabbit's foot that brings "good luck" have large amounts of mana. People, too, may be spoken of as having more or less mana. A woodcarver whose work is especially intricate and beautiful possesses mana, whereas a warrior captured by the enemy has obviously lost his mana.

In its broadest range of meaning, mana simply indicates belief in a powerful force. Many vernacular relationships not normally recognized as religious beliefs in Western cultures can be regarded as mana. For example, vitamin pills are consumed by many millions of people in expectation that they will exert a powerful effect on health and well-being. Soaps and detergents are said to clean because of "cleaning power"; gasolines provide engines with "starting power" or "go-power"; salespeople are prized for their "selling power"; and politicians are said to have *charisma* or "vote-getting power." Many people fervently believe that they are "lucky" or "unlucky"—which could easily be translated as a belief in control over varying quantities of mana.

NATURAL AND SUPERNATURAL

One way to prevent the definition of religion from getting so broad as to include virtually every belief is to distinguish between natural and supernatural beings and natural and supernatural forces. It must be emphasized, however, that few cultures neatly and conveniently divide their beliefs into natural and supernatural categories. In a culture where people believe that ghosts are always present, it is not necessarily either natural or supernatural to provide dead ancestors with food and drink. The culture may simply lack the emic categories "natural" and "supernatural." Similarly, when a shaman blows smoke over a patient and triumphantly removes a sliver of bone allegedly inserted by the patient's enemy, the question of whether the performance is natural or supernatural may have no emic meaning.

Writing of the Gururumba (Fig. 21.1) of the highlands of western New Guinea, Philip Newman notes that they "have a series of beliefs postulating the existence of entities and forces we would call supernatural." Yet the contrast between natural and supernatural is not emically relevant to the Gururumba themselves:

> It should be mentioned . . . that our use of the notion "Supernatural" does not correspond to any Gururumba concept: they do not divide the world into natural and supernatural parts. Certain entities, forces, and processes must be controlled partially through *lusu,* a term denoting rituals relating to growth, curing, or the stimulation of strength, while others need only rarely be controlled in this way. . . .However, *lusu* does not contrast with any term denoting a realm of control where the nature of the controls differ from *lusu.* Consequently *lusu* is simply part of all control techniques and what it controls is simply part of all things requiring human control (Newman 1965:83).

SACRED AND PROFANE

Some anthropologists have suggested that the true hallmark of a religious belief or religious practice is the emotional state of the participant. Robert R. Marett, Alexander Goldenweiser, and Robert Lowie were among those who sought the essence of religion in the "religious experience." Lowie (1948:339) characterized this experience as consisting of "amazement and awe," a feeling that one is in the presence of something extraordinary, weird, sacred, holy, divine. Lowie was even willing to rule that beliefs about gods and souls were not religious beliefs if the existence of these beings was taken for granted and if, in contemplating them, the individual did not experience awe or amazement.

The theoretician who made the greatest contribution to this way of looking at religion was Emile Durkheim. Like many others, Durkheim proposed that the essence of religious belief was that it evoked a mysterious feeling of communion with a sacred

Figure 21.1 *GURURUMBA MEDICINE* This man is inducing vomiting by swallowing a 3-foot length of cane. After he has pushed it all the way into his stomach he will work it up and down until he vomits. It is thought to be necessary to do this to rid the individual of contaminating influences gotten through contact with women.

realm. Every society has its *sacred* beliefs, symbols, and rituals, which stand opposed to ordinary or *profane* events (Fig. 21.2). Durkheim's distinctive contribution was to relate the realm of the sacred to the control exercised by society and culture over each individual's consciousness. When people feel that they are in communion with occult and mysterious forces and supernatural beings, what they are really experiencing is the force of social life. For Durkheim, the essence of being human was to be born into and sustained by society and culture. In our awe of the sacred, we express our dependence on society in symbolic form. Thus, according to Durkheim, the idea of "god" is but one form of the worship of society.

It seems likely that every culture does make a distinction between sacred and profane realms and that there is some element of truth in Durkheim's idea that the sacred represents the worship of collective life. As we shall see in the next chapter, the ability to appeal to the sacred character of certain beliefs and practices has great practical value in diminishing dissent, compelling conformity, and resolving ambiguities (cf. Rappaport 1971 a and b).

Figure 21.2 *SACRED AND PROFANE*
Shoes are left outside the Mosque, symbolizing the transition from ordinary, mundane affairs to the realm of the holy and extraordinary.

MAGIC AND RELIGION

Sir James Frazer attempted to define religion in his famous book *The Golden Bough.* For Frazer the question of whether a particular belief was religious or not centered on the extent to which the participants felt that they could make an entity or force do their bidding. If the attitude of the participants was one of uncertainty, if they felt humble and were inclined to supplicate and request favors and dispensations, then their beliefs and actions were essentially religious. If they thought they were in control of the entities and forces governing events, felt no uncertainty about the outcome, and experienced no need for humble supplication, then their beliefs and practices were examples of magic rather than of religion.

Frazer regarded prayer as the essence of religious ritual. But prayers are not always rendered in a mood of supplication. For example, prayers among the Navajo must be letter-perfect to be effective. Yet the Navajo do not expect that letter-perfect prayers will always get results. Thus, the line between prayers and "magical spells" is hard to draw. Supplication cannot be taken as characteristic of verbal communication between people and their gods. As Ruth Benedict (1938:640) pointed out, "cajolery and bribery and false pretense are common means of influencing the supernatural." Thus, the Kai of New Guinea swindle their ancestral ghosts as they swindle each other. Some cultures try to outwit the spirits by lying to them. The Tsimshian of the Canadian Pacific Coast stamp their feet and shake their fists at the heavens and call their gods "slaves" as a term of reproach. The Manus of the Bismarck Archipelago keep the skulls of their ancestors in a corner of the house and try their best to please "Sir Ghost." However, if someone gets sick, the Manus may angrily threaten to throw Sir Ghost out of the house. This is what they tell Sir Ghost:

> This man dies and you rest in no house. You will but wander about the edges of the island (used for excretory purposes) (Fortune 1965:216).

An additional important part of Frazer's scheme was his attempt to distinguish magic from science. The magician's attitude, he claimed, was precisely that of the scientist. Both magician and scientist believe that if A is done under the proper set of conditions, then B will follow regardless of who the practitioner is or what the attitude toward the outcome may be. A piece of an intended victim's fingernail tossed into the fire or pins stuck into an effigy doll are believed to accomplish their results with the automatic certainty characteristic of the release of an arrow from a bow or the felling of a tree with an ax. Frazer recognized that if this was going to be the essence of the distinction between magic and religion, then magic differed little from science. Indeed, he called magic "false science" and postulated a universal evolutionary sequence in which magic with its concern about cause and effect relationships gave birth to science, whereas religion evolved along completely independent lines.

Frazer's scheme has not withstood the test of fieldwork. The attitudes with which fearful Dobuan magicians dispose of fingernails and confident Zuñi priests whip up yucca suds to bring rain do not conform to Frazer's neat compartments. Human behavior unfolds as a complex mixture in which awe and wonder, boredom and excitement, power and weakness are all present at the same time.

The degree of anxiety and supplication associated with any sequence of behavior is probably regulated more by the importance of the outcome to the participants than by their philosophy of cause and effect. Not enough is known about the inner psychological state of priests, magicians, shamans, and scientists to make any firm pronouncements in this field.

THE ORGANIZATION OF RELIGIOUS BELIEFS AND PRACTICES

As we have just seen, religious beliefs and rituals involve a great variety of thoughts, feelings, and practices. Yet in this domain, as in all others, there are orderly processes. A good way to begin to understand the diversity of religious phenomena is to inquire if there are beliefs and practices associated with particular levels of political and economic development.

Anthony Wallace (1966) has distinguished four principal varieties of religious "cults"—that is, forms of organization of religious doctrines and activities—that have broad evolutionary implications. The four principal forms are: (1) *individualistic cults,* (2) *shamanistic cults,* (3) *communal cults,* and (4) *ecclesiastical cults,* defined as follows:

1. Individualistic Cults The most basic form of religious life involves individualistic (but culturally patterned) beliefs and rituals. Each person is a specialist; each individual enters into a relationship with animistic and animatistic beings and forces as each personally experiences the need for control and protection. One might call this "do-it-yourself" religion.

2. Shamanistic Cults As Wallace points out, no culture known to anthropology has a religion that is completely individualistic, although the Eskimo and other hunters and food-gatherers lean heavily in this direction. Every known society also exhibits at least the *shamanistic* level of religious specialization (Fig. 21.3). The term shaman derives from the word used by the Tungus-speaking peoples of Siberia to designate the part-time religious specialist consulted in times of stress and anxiety. In cross-cultural applications, however, the term shaman may refer to individuals who act as diviners, curers, spirit mediums, and magicians for other people in return for gifts, fees, prestige, and power.

3. Communal Cults At a more complex level of political economy, communal forms of beliefs and practices become more elaborate. Groups of nonspecialists

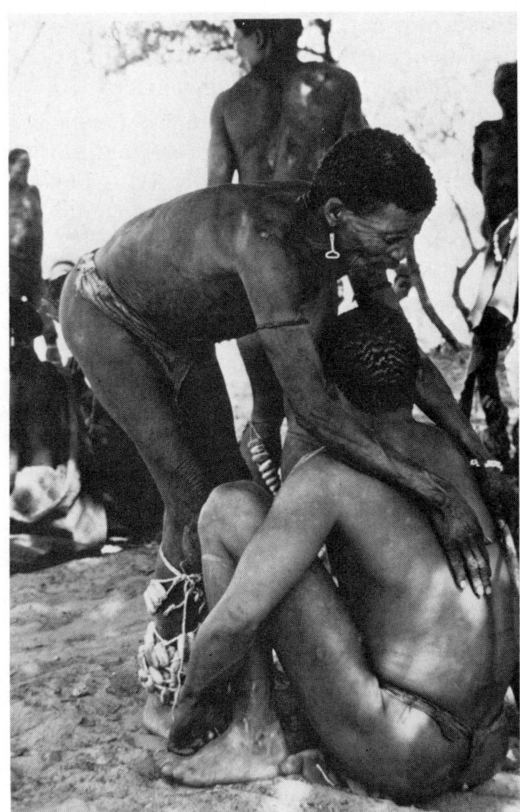

Figure 21.3 *SAN CURING*
Shaman in trance.

organized in terms of age grades, men's societies, clans, or lineages assume responsibility for regular or occasional performances of rituals deemed essential for their own welfare or for the survival of the society. While communal rituals may employ specialists such as shamans, orators, and highly skilled dancers and musicians, once the ritual performance is concluded, the participants revert to a common daily routine. There are no full-time religious specialists.

4. **Ecclesiastical Cults** The ecclesiastical level of religious organization involves a full-time professional clergy or priesthood. These professionals form a bureaucracy that monopolizes the performance of certain rites on behalf of individuals, groups, and the whole society. Ecclesiastical bureaucracies are usually closely associated with state-level political systems. In most instances the leaders of the ecclesiastical hierarchy are members of the ruling class and, in some instances, a state's political and ecclesiastical hierarchies are indistinguishable. It should be emphasized, however, that at particular moments in history ecclesiastical hierarchies may come into conflict with prevailing political and economic policies and take sides with and organize classes and movements directed against the ruling class.

Wallace notes that the individualistic, shamanistic, communal, and ecclesiastical forms of beliefs and rituals constitute a *scale*. That is, each of the more complex levels contains the beliefs and practices of all the less complex levels. Consequently, among societies with ecclesiastical cults, there are also communal cults, shamanistic cults, and strictly individualistic beliefs and rituals (Fig. 21.4). In the following sections, examples of each of these forms of religion will be given.

INDIVIDUALISTIC BELIEFS AND RITUALS: THE ESKIMO

The individualism of much of Eskimo belief and ritual parallels the individualism of the Eskimo mode of production. Hunters alone or in small groups constantly match their wits against the cunning and strength of animal prey and confront the dangers of travel over the ice and the threat of storms and month-long nights. The Eskimo hunter was equipped with an ingenious array of technological devices that alone made life possible in the Arctic. But the outcome of the daily struggle remained in doubt. From the Eskimo's point of view, it was not enough to be well equipped with snow goggles, fur parkas, spring-bone traps, harpoon points, and powerful compound bows. One also had to be equipped to handle unseen spirits and forces that lurked in all parts of nature and that, if offended or not properly warded off, could reduce the greatest hunter to a starving wretch. Vigilant individual effort was needed to deal with wandering human and animal souls, place spirits, Sedna (the Keeper of the Sea Animals), the Sun, the Moon, and the Spirit of the Air (Wallace 1966:89). Part of each hunter's equipment was his hunting song—a combination of chant, prayer, and magic formula—which he inherited from his father or father's brothers or purchased from some famous hunter or shaman. This he would sing under his breath as he prepared himself for the day's activities. Around his neck he wore a little bag filled with tiny animal carvings, bits of claws and fur, pebbles, insects, and other items, each corresponding to some Spirit Helper with whom he maintained a special relationship. In return for protection

(a)

(b)

Figure 21.4 *LEVEL OF RELIGIOUS ORGANIZATION*
(a) A Guatemalan shaman obtaining personal power at a shrine. This does not prevent him from participating in the ecclesiastical cult of the Catholic church *(b)*.

and hunting success given by his Spirit Helpers, the hunter had to observe certain taboos, refrain from hunting or eating certain species, or avoid trespassing in a particular locale. For example, a hunter should never sleep out on the ice-edge. Every evening he had to return either to land or to the old firm ice that lies some distance back from the open sea, because the Sea Spirit does not like her creatures to smell human beings while they are not hunting (Rasmussen 1929:76). Care must also be taken not to cook land and sea mammals in the same pot; fresh water must be placed in the mouth of recently killed sea mammals, and fat must be placed in the mouth of slain land mammals (Wallace 1966:90). Note that some of these "superstitions" may have alleviated psychological stress or have had a practical value. For example, sleeping out on the ice would expose the hunter to the danger of going adrift or being cut off from land.

THE PATTERNING OF INDIVIDUALISTIC BELIEFS AND RITUALS

It is apparent in cross-cultural perspective that religious beliefs and practices always exhibit a great deal of cultural patterning. Religious "do-it-yourselfers" never invent the major part of their religions. This is true even under the influence of drugs, during trance states, and in dreams and visions. For example, a form of individualistic religion common in North and South America involves the acquisition of a personal *guardian spirit* or supernatural protector. Typically this spirit protector is acquired by means of a visionary experience induced by fasting, self-inflicted torture, or hallucinogenic drugs. The Jívaro youth's search for an arutam soul described earlier is one variant of this widespread complex. Although each arutam vision is slightly different from the next, they all follow a similar pattern.

For many native North Americans the central experience of life was also an hallucinatory vision (Fig. 21.5). Young men needed this hallucinatory experience to be successful in love, warfare, horsestealing, trading, and all other important endeavors. In keeping with their code of personal bravery and endurance, they sought these vi-

(a)

(b)

Figure 21.5 *SIOUX VISION*
Section of pictographic biography done by Rain in The Face. In a dream *(a)*, the lightning tells him that unless he gives a buffalo feast, the lightning will kill him. He gives the feast, one part of which consists of filling a kettle with red hot buffalo tongues, of which he eats in order to save his life. He dreams *(b)* of buffalo again. While dancing, he is shot by an arrow which enters the feathers. In removing it, he soon vomits and grabbing a handful of earth, rubs it into the wound, healing it rapidly.

sions primarily through self-inflicted torture.

Among the Crow, for example, a youth who craved the visionary experience of his elders, went alone into the mountains, stripped off his clothes, and abstained from food and drink. If this was not sufficient, he chopped off part of the fourth finger of his left hand. Coached from childhood to expect that a vision would come, most of the Crow vision-seekers were successful. A buffalo, snake, chicken hawk, thunderbird, dwarf, or mysterious stranger would appear; miraculous events would unfold; and then these strange beings would "adopt" the vision-seeker and disappear. Scratches-face, who was one of Robert Lowie's informants, prayed to the morning star:

> Old woman's grandson, I give you this (finger-joint). Give me something good in exchange . . . a good horse . . . a good-natured woman . . . a tent of my own to live in (Lowie 1948:6).

Lowie reports that after cutting off his finger, Scratches-face saw six men riding horses. One of them said, "You have been poor, so I'll give you what you want." Suddenly the trees around them turned into enemy warriors who began to shoot at the six horsemen. The horsemen rode away but returned unscathed. The spokesman then said to Scratches-face, "If you want to fight all the people on earth, do as I do, and you will be able to fight for 3 days or 4 days and yet not be shot." The enemy attacked again, but Scratches-face's benefactor knocked them down with a spear. According to Lowie (1948:6), "In consequence of his blessing Scratches-face struck and killed an enemy without ever getting wounded. He also obtained horses and married a good-tempered and industrious woman."

Although each Crow's vision had some unique elements, they were usually similar in the following regards: (1) Some revelation of future success in warfare, horseraiding, or other acts of bravery was involved. (2) The visions usually occurred at the end of the fourth day—four being the sacred number of the native North Americans. (3) Practically every vision was accompanied by the acquisition of a sacred song. (4) The friendly spirits in the vision adopted the youth. (5) Trees or rocks often turned into enemies who vainly shot at the invulnerable spirit being. Lowie concludes:

> He sees and hears not merely what any faster, say in British Columbia or South Africa, would see and hear under like conditions of physiological exhaustion and under the urge of generally human desires, but what the social tradition of the Crow tribe imperatively suggests (1948:14).

SHAMANISTIC CULTS

Shamans, as discussed in Chapter 15, are people who are socially recognized as having special abilities for entering into contact with spirit beings and for controlling supernatural forces. The full shamanistic complex includes some form of trance experience during which the shaman's powers are increased. *Possession,* the invasion of the human body by a god or spirit, is the most common form of shamanistic trance. The shaman goes into a trance by smoking tobacco, taking drugs, beating on a drum, dancing monotonously, or simply by closing the eyes and concentrating. The trance begins with rigidity of the body, sweating, and heavy breathing. While in the trance the shaman may act as a *medium,* transmitting messages from the ancestors. With the help of friendly spirits shamans predict future events, locate lost objects, identify the cause of illness, prescribe cures, and give advice on how clients can protect themselves against the evil intentions of enemies.

There is a close relationship between shamanistic cults and individualistic vision quests. Shamans are usually personalities who are psychologically predisposed toward hallucinatory experiences. In cultures that use hallucinogenic substances freely in order to penetrate the mysteries of the other world, many people may claim shamanistic status. Among the Jívaro, one of every four men is a shaman, since the use of hallucinogenic vines makes it possible for almost anyone to achieve the trance states essential for the practice of shamanism (Harner 1972b:154). Elsewhere, becoming a shaman may be restricted to people who are prone to having auditory and visual hallucinations.

An important part of shamanistic performance in many parts of the world consists of simple tricks of ventriloquism, sleight of hand, and illusion. The Siberian shamans, for example, signaled the arrival of the possessing spirit by secretly shaking the walls of a darkened tent. Throughout South America the standard shamanistic curing ceremony involves the removal of slivers of bone, pebbles, bugs, and other foreign objects from the patient's body. The practice of these tricks should not be regarded as evidence that the shaman has a cynical or disbelieving attitude toward the rest of the performance. The human mind is fully capable of blocking out and compartmentalizing contradictory or inconvenient information both through suppression into unconsciousness and through rationalization ("it's a trick but it's for their own good"; or "it's a trick but it works").

Although trance is part of the shamanistic repertory in hundreds of cultures, it is not universal. Many cultures have part-time specialists who do not make use of trance but who diagnose and cure diseases, find lost objects, foretell the future, and confer immunity in war and success in love. Such persons may be referred to variously as magicians, seers, sorcerers, witch doctors, medicine men, and curers. The full shamanistic complex embodies all of these roles.

TAPIRAPÉ SHAMANISM

The Tapirapé who are village people of central Brazil have a typical shamanistic cult (Wagley 1977). Tapirapé shamans (Fig. 21.6) derive their powers from dreams in which

Figure 21.6 *TAPIRAPÉ SHAMAN*
The shaman has fallen into a tobacco-induced trance and cannot walk unaided.

they encounter spirits who become the shaman's helpers. Dreams are caused by souls leaving the body and going on journeys. Frequent dreaming is a sign of shamanistic talent. Mature shamans, with the help of the spirit familiars, can turn into birds or launch themselves through the air in gourd "canoes," visit with ghosts and demons, or travel to distant villages forward and backward through time. Here is an account of how the shaman Ikanancowi acquired his powers:

In his dream [Ikanancowi] walked far to the shores of a large lake deep in the jungle. There he heard dogs barking and ran in the direction from which the noise came until he met several forest spirits of the breed called *munpí anká*. They were tearing a bat out of a tree for food. [The spirits] talked with Ikanancowi and invited him to return to their village, which was situated upon the lake. In the village he saw *periquitos* [paraqueets] and many socó . . . birds which they keep as pets. [They] had several pots of *kauí* [porridge] and invited Ikanancowi to eat with them. He refused for he saw that their *kauí* was made from human blood. Ikanancowi watched one spirit drink of the *kauí* and saw him vomit blood immediately afterwards; the shaman saw a second spirit drink from another pot and immediately spurt blood from his anus. He saw the *munpí anká* vomit up their entrails and throw them upon the ground, but he soon saw that this was only a trick; they would not die, for they had more intestines. After this visit the *munpí anká* called Ikanancowi father and he called them his sons; he visited them in his dreams frequently and he had *munpí anká* near him always (Wagley 1943:66 – 67).

Tapirapé shamans are frequently called upon to cure illness. This they do with sleight of hand and the help of their spirit familiars while in a semitrance condition induced by gulping huge quantities of tobacco. Here is Charles Wagley's classic account of cure by vomit:

Unless the illness is serious enough to warrant immediate treatment, shamans always cure in the late evening. A shaman comes to his patient, and squats near the patient's hammock; his first act is always to light his pipe. When the patient has a fever or has fallen unconscious from the sight of a ghost, the principal method of treatment is by massage. The shaman blows smoke over the entire body of the patient; then he blows smoke over his own hands, spits into them, and massages the patient slowly and firmly, always toward the extremities of the body. He shows that he is removing a foreign substance by quick movement of his hands as he reaches the end of an arm or leg.

The more frequent method of curing, however, is by the extraction of a malignant object by sucking. The shaman squats alongside the hammock of his patient and begins to "eat smoke"—swallow large gulps of tabacco smoke from his pipe. He forces the smoke with great intakes of breath deep down into his stomach; soon he becomes intoxicated and nauseated; he vomits violently and smoke spews from his stomach. He groans and clears his throat in the manner of a person gagging with nausea but unable to vomit. By sucking back what he vomits he accumulates saliva in his mouth.

In the midst of this process he stops several times to suck on the body of his patient and finally, with one awful heave, he spews all the accumulated material on the ground. He then searches in this mess for the intrusive object that has been causing the illness. Never once did I see a shaman show the intrusive object to observers. At one treatment a Tapirapé [shaman] usually repeats this process of "eating smoke," sucking, and vomiting several times. Sometimes, when a man of prestige is ill, two or even three shamans will cure side by side in this manner and the noise of violent vomiting resounds throughout the village (Wagley 1943:73–74).

It is interesting to note in conjunction with the widespread use of tobacco in native American rituals that tobacco contains hallucinogenic alkaloids and may have induced visions when consumed in large quantities.

SHAMANS, WITCHCRAFT, AND WITCH-HUNTS

Only a thin line separates shamans from witches. Since shamans have the power to cure, they also have the power to kill. Much shamanic activity is devoted to the problem of identifying who is responsible for the sickness and death that occurs in the band or village. As we saw in Chapter 15, shamans play an important role in the maintenance of law and order in prestate societies by blaming misfortunes on scapegoats who can be killed or ostracized without damaging the fabric of social unity. Under conditions of continuing stress caused by repeated defeats in warfare, floods, droughts, or epidemics, people often lose faith in their shamans, decide that the shamans are really witches, and execute them.

With the development of ecclesiastical forms of religion and bureaucratized hierarchies of priests, shamans outside the ecclesiastical structure tend to be regarded as antisocial witches and "magicians." As in band and village cultures, the established ecclesiastical and civil authorities still find it convenient to blame misfortunes on scapegoats. In fact, the urgency to find some human being upon whom rampant misery, disease, and death can be blamed is probably greater in stratified than in egalitarian cultures. Witch-hunting often serves the function of befuddling people concerning the extent to which they are being exploited by a ruling class. The authorities try to find their witches by techniques that they themselves control; hence the prevalence of such techniques as throwing persons accused of witchcraft into the water to see if they will sink, or giving poisons to the accused to see if they will throw up, or handing them hot irons to see if they will burn. Some societies that have ecclesiastical hierarchies torture people into confessing that they are witches.

Church and state in Renaissance Europe (both Catholic and Protestant) made extensive use of torture as a means of identifying witches. It was widely believed that witches flew through the air to attend weekly meetings called *sabbats* (Fig. 21.7). Inquisitors insisted that each witch not only confess to being a witch, but that he or she also name the other persons who went to these meetings. Failure to confess and name names meant that the accused would be returned repeatedly to the torture chamber. Those who confessed were strangled before they were burned. The first people to be accused were defenseless or homeless women and children.

Initially no one named members of the clergy or nobility out of fear of being tortured until they recanted. As those being

Figure 21.7 *SABBAT*
Francisco Goya's rendering of witches' clandestine cult activities. Note the predominance of women.

tortured began to name prominent and protected individuals, however, the "witch craze" would suddenly cease, and the inquisitors would move off to the next town. Altogether about half a million people were burned to death during the two centuries when this system was at its peak (Harris 1974b).

It seems likely that few of the people who were executed had any knowledge of witches' meetings. As Michael Harner (1972a) has shown, some of the accused rubbed themselves with an ointment manufactured from nightshade, henbane, belladonna, and other plants that contain the skin-penetrating hallucinogenic substance atropine. Application of these substances to the feet and to the genitals produces a comatose condition for as much as 48 hours, during which vivid sensations of flying are experienced. People who rubbed themselves with such an ointment could scarcely have gotten to a sabbat on two feet, much less on a broomstick.

COMMUNAL CULTS

No culture is completely without communally organized religious beliefs and practices. Even the Eskimos have group rites. Frightened and sick Eskimo individuals under the cross-examination of shamans publicly confess violations of taboos, which have made them ill and which have endangered the rest of the community.

Among the native Americans of the west plains there were annual public rites of self-torture and vision quest known as the Sun Dance (Fig. 21.8). Under the direction of shaman leaders the sun dancers tied themselves to a pole by means of a cord passed through a slit in their skin. Watched by the assembled group, they walked or danced around the pole and tugged at the cord, until they fainted or the skin ripped apart. These public displays of endurance and bravery were part of the intense marauding and warfare complex that developed after the coming of the Europeans.

Communal rites fall into two major categories: (1) *rites of solidarity* and (2) *rites of passage*. In the rites of solidarity, participation in dramatic public rituals enhances the sense of group identity, coordinates the actions of the individual members of the group, and prepares the group for immediate or future cooperative action. Rites of passage celebrate the social movement of individuals into and out of groups or into or out of statuses of critical importance both to the individual and to the community. Reproduction, the achievement of manhood and womanhood, marriage, and death are the principal worldwide occasions for rites of passage. Examples follow.

COMMUNAL RITES OF SOLIDARITY: TOTEMISM

Rites of solidarity are common among clans and other descent groups. Such groups usually have names and emblems that identify group members and set one group off from another. Animal names and emblems predominate, but insects, plants, and natural phenomena such as rain and clouds also occur. These group-identifying objects are known as totems. Many totems such as bear, breadfruit, or kangaroo are useful or edible species, and often there is a stipulated descent relationship between the members of the group and their totemic ancestor. Sometimes the members of the group must refrain from harming or eating their totem. There are many variations in the specific forms of totemic belief, however, and no single totemic complex can be said to exist. Lévi-Strauss (1963a) has suggested that the

Figure 21.8 *DAKOTA SUN DANCE*
Painted by Short-Bull, chief of the Oglala Dakota (Sioux), this painting represents the Sun Dance of 90 years ago. The circle in the center represents a windbreak formed of fresh cottonwood boughs. In the center is the Sun Dance pole and hanging from it the figure of a man and a buffalo. Outside of the Sun Dance enclosure, devotees perform. One of them is dragging four buffalo skulls by cords run through openings in the skin on his back. He will continue to drag these until they tear loose.

unity of the concept of totemism consists not in any specific belief or practice, but in certain general logical relationships between the named groups and their names. No matter what kind of animal or thing serves as totem, it is the contrast with other totems rather than their specific properties that renders them useful for group identification.

The Arunta of Australia provide one of the classic cases of totemic ritual (Fig. 21.9). Here an individual identifies with the totem of sacred place near which one's mother passed shortly before becoming pregnant (see p. 273). These places contain the stone objects known as *churinga*, which are the visible manifestations of each person's spirit. The churinga are believed to have been left behind by the totemic ancestors as they traveled about the countryside at the beginning of the world. The ancestors later turned into animals, objects, and other phenomena constituting the inventory of totems. The sacred places of each totem are visited annually during rites known as *Intichiuma*.

Here is a description of the Intichiuma of the witchetty-grub men: They slip away from camp. Under the direction of their headman they retrace the trail taken by Intwailiuka, the dawn-time witchetty-grub leader. All along this trail they come upon the churinga and other mementos of Intwailiuka's journey. One sacred place consists of a shallow cave, inside of which is a large rock surrounded by small rounded stones. The headman identifies the large rock as the body of the witchetty-grub and the small stones as the witchetty-grub's eggs. The headman begins to sing, tapping the rocks with a wooden bough while the others join

Figure 21.9 *TOTEMIC SOLIDARITY*
Arunta men preparing themselves for totemic ritual.

in, tapping with twigs. The song asks the witchetty-grub to lay more eggs. The headman then strikes each man in the stomach with one of the "egg stones" saying, "You have eaten much food."

The party then moves on to the next sacred place underneath a large rock where Intwailiukas used to cook and eat. The men sing, tap with their twigs, and throw egg stones up the cliff, as Intwailiuka did. Then they march on to the next sacred place, which is a hole 4- or 5-feet deep. The headman scrapes away the dirt at the bottom of this hole, turning up more witchetty-grub churinga. The stones are carefully cleaned, handed about, and then replaced. The party stops at a total of ten such spots before returning to camp. In preparation for their return the men decorate themselves with strings, nose bones, rattails, and feathers. They also paint their bodies with the sacred design of the witchetty-grub. While they have been gone, one of the witchetty-grub men has constructed a brush hut in the shape of the witchetty-grub chrysalis. The men enter the hut and sing of the journey they have made. Then the headman comes shuffling and gliding out, followed by all the rest, in imitation of adult witchetty-grubs emerging from their chrysalis. This is repeated several times. During this phase of the ceremony all nonwitchetty-grub spectators are kept at a distance and obliged to follow the orders of witchetty-grub men and women (Spencer and Gillen 1968).

These rituals have many meanings and

functions. Witchetty-grub people are earnestly concerned with controlling the reproduction of witchetty-grubs, which are considered a great delicacy. But the exclusive membership of the ritual group also indicates that they are acting out the mythological dogma of their common ancestry. The witchetty-grub totem ceremonies reaffirm and intensify the sense of common identity of the members of a regional community. The ceremonies confirm the fact that the witchetty-grub people have "stones" or, in a more familiar metaphor, "roots" in a particular land.

COMMUNAL RITUALS: RITES OF PASSAGE

Rites of passage accompany changes in structural position or statuses that are of general public concern. Why are birth, puberty, marriage, and death so frequently the occasions for rites of passage (Fig. 21.10)? Probably because of their public implications: The individual who is born, who reaches adulthood, who takes a spouse, or who dies is not the only person implicated in these events. Many other people must adjust to these momentous changes. Being born not only defines a new life, but it also brings into existence or modifies the position of parent, grandparent, sibling, heir, age-mate, and many other domestic and political relationships. The main function of rites of passage is to give communal recognition to the entire complex of new or altered relationships and not merely to the changes experienced by the individuals who get born, married, or who die.

Rites of passage conform to a remarkably similar pattern among widely dispersed cultures (Eliade 1958; cf. Schlegel and Barry 1979). First, the principal performers are separated from the routines associated with their earlier life. Second, decisive physical and symbolic steps are taken to extinguish the old statuses. Often these steps include the notion of killing the old personality. To promote "death and transfiguration," old clothing and ornaments are exchanged for new and the body is painted or mutilated. Finally, the participants are ceremoniously returned to normal life.

CIRCUMCISION

The pattern of rites of passage can be seen in the male initiation ceremonies of the Ndembu of northern Zambia. Here, as among many African and Middle Eastern peoples, the transition from boyhood to manhood involves the rite of circumcision. Young boys are taken from their separate villages and placed in a special bush "school." They are circumcised by their own kinsmen or neighbors, and after their wounds heal, they are returned to normal life. Among the Ndembu the process of publicly transforming boys to men takes four months and is known as *mukanda*. Victor Turner (1967) has given a detailed account of a mukanda that he was permitted to witness in 1953. It began with the storage of food and beer. Then a clearing was made in the bush and a camp was established. This camp included a hearth at which the mothers of the boys undergoing circumcision cooked for them. On the day preceding the circumcision the circumcisers danced and sang songs in which they expressed antagonism to the boys' mothers and made reference to the "killing" that was about to take place. The boys and their families assembled at the campsite, fires were lit, and a night of dancing and sexual license was begun.

Suddenly the circumcisers entered in procession, carrying their apparatus. . . .All the rest of the gathering followed them as they danced crouch-

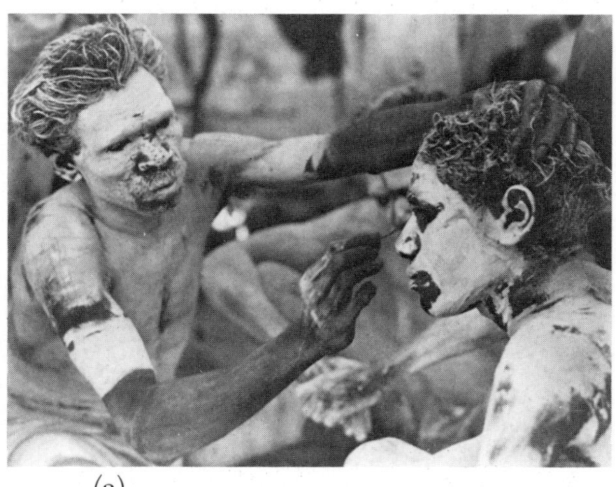

(a)

ing, holding up different items of apparatus, and chanting hoarsely. In the firelight and moonlight the dance got wilder and wilder (Turner 1967:205).

Meanwhile, "those who were about to die" sat in a line attended by their mothers and fathers. During the night they were repeatedly awakened and carried about by their male relatives. The next morning they were given a "last supper" (i.e., a last breakfast) by their mothers, "each mother feeding her son by hand as though he were an infant." The boys tried not to look terrified as, after breakfast, the circumcisers, their brows and foreheads daubed with red clay, danced about brandishing their knives.

The actual circumcision took place in another clearing some distance away from the cooking camp. The boys remained in seclusion at this site, which is known as the "place of dying." They slept in a brush lodge watched over and ordered about by a group of male "guardians" (Fig. 21.11). After their "last breakfast" the boys weie marched down the trail toward the "place of dying."

(b)

Figure 21.10 *RELIGION AND LIFE CRISES*
(a) Male puberty initiate in Arnhemland, Australia, being painted with white clay. *(b)* Dogon funeral dancers. The Crow scaffold burial *(c)* shows a common means of disposing of the dead in sparsely inhabited regions; the Peruvian mummies *(d)* show another method, which is common in arid climates.

(c)

The guardians came rushing out, seized them, and tore off their clothes. The mothers were chased back to the cooking camp where they began to wail as at the an-

(d)

Figure 21.11 *NDEMBU CIRCUMCISION CAMP*
"The place of dying."

nouncement of a death. The boys were held by the guardians while circumcisers

> stretch out the prepuce, make a slight nick on top and another underneath as guides, then cut through the dorsal section with a single movement and follow this by slitting the ventral section, then removing sufficient of the prepuce to leave the glans well exposed (Turner 1967:216).

During the seclusion at the place of dying, the boys were subject to the strict discipline of their guardians. They had to maintain a modest demeanor, speak only when spoken to, do errands, and fetch and carry everything on the run. In former times they were sent on dangerous hunting missions and subjected to severe beating for breaking discipline or displaying cowardice, and terrorized at night by the sound of the *bull roarer*—a flat disk that makes a howling noise as it is whirled about on the end of a string (Fig. 21.12). Masked dancers whom they believed to be "red grave people" appeared suddenly and beat them with sticks.

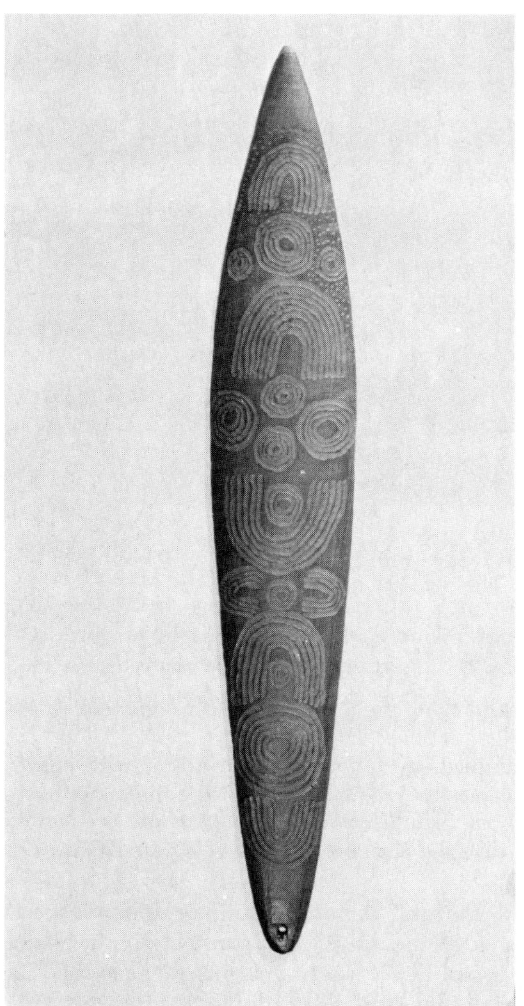

Figure 21.12 *BULL ROARER*
String is tied through hole and used to whirl bull roarer around head. This specimen is from Australia.

These same monsters visited the cooking camp, danced before the women, and terrorized the little children (Fig. 21.13). Throughout their seclusion the boys were taught the rules of manhood, how to be brave and sexually potent. They were lectured to, harangued, and made to answer riddles rich in symbolic meanings.

For their "rebirth" the boys were daubed all over with white clay, signifying their new being. Then they were brought into the cooking camp and shown to their mothers.

> At first the mothers wailed, then their mourning turned to songs of rejoicing as each realized that her son was safe and well. It is impossible to describe adequately the ensuing scene of complete, uninhibited jubilation. The guardians ran around in an inner circle, the mothers danced beside them . . . while other female relatives and friends made up an outer ring of joyful chanting and dancers. The men stood outside the whirl, laughing with pure pleasure. Dust rose in clouds (Turner 1967:255).

The next morning the seclusion ledge was

Figure 21.13 *NDEMBU MONSTER*
Although the women are supposed to be terrified, they are amused and skeptical.

burned, the boys were washed in the river and given new clothes, and then each performed the dance of war as a sign of manhood.

In many cultures girls are subject to similar rites of separation, seclusion, and return in relationship to their first menses and their eligibility for marriage. Genital mutilation is also common for girls, and there is a widely practiced operation known as *clitoridectomy*. In this operation the external tip of the clitoris is cut off. Among many Australian groups both circumcision and clitoridectomy were practiced. In addition, the Australians knocked out the pubescent child's front tooth. Males were subject to the further operation of *subincision*, in which the underside of the penis is slit open to the depth of the urethra.

The pattern of the rites of passage characterizes many modern rituals, although the phases of separation, seclusion, and return may appear in rapid succession. At high school and college graduation ceremonies, for example, the graduates are assembled somewhere offstage. They put on special costumes. When they march in they remain segregated from their relatives and friends. They are given advice by the equivalent of the Ndembu guardians and are handed a ceremonial document. Then they return to their joyous relatives and friends to mingle freely with them once again.

ECCLESIASTICAL CULTS

As stated above, ecclesiastical cults have in common the existence of a professional clergy or priesthood organized into a bureaucracy. This bureaucracy is usually associated with and under the control of a central temple. At secondary or provincial temple centers the clergy may exercise a considerable amount of independence. In general, the more highly centralized the political system, the more highly centralized the ecclesiastical bureaucracy.

The ecclesiastic specialists are different from both the Tapirapé shamans and the Ndembu circumcisers and guardians. They are formally designated persons who devote themselves full time to the rituals of their office (Fig. 21.14). These rituals usually include a wide variety of techniques for influencing and controlling animistic beings and animatistic forces. The material support for these full-time specialists is usually closely related to power and privileges of taxation. As among the Inca (p. 318), the state and the priesthood may divide up the rent and tribute exacted from the peasants. Under feudalism (see p. 319), the ecclesiastical hierarchy derives its earnings from its own estates and from the gifts of powerful princes and kings. High officials in feudal ecclesiastical hierarchies are almost always kin or appointees of members of the ruling class. In the case of modern ecclesiastical hierarchies, tax support may be indirect but, nonetheless, vital. In the United States, for example, church-owned real estate and church earnings on stocks and other investments are tax exempt and gifts to religious groups are tax deductible.

The presence of ecclesiastical organizations produces a profound split among those who participate in ritual performances. On the one hand, there is an active segment, the priesthood and, on the other, the passive "congregation," who are virtual spectators. The members of the priesthood must acquire intricate ritual, historical, calendrical, and astronomical knowledge. Often they are scribes and learned persons. It must be stressed, however, that the "congregation" does not altogether abandon their individualistic shamanistic and communal beliefs and rituals. These are all continued, some-

Figure 21.14 *ECCLESIASTICAL CULT*
Ordaining the Episcopalian bishop in the Cathedral of St. John the Divine.

times secretly, in neighborhoods, villages, or households side by side with the "higher" rituals, despite more or less energetic efforts on the part of the ecclesiastical hierarchy to stamp out what it often calls idolatrous, superstitious, pagan, heathen, or heretical beliefs and performances.

THE RELIGION OF THE AZTECS

Many of the principal characteristics of belief and ritual in stratified contexts can be seen in the ecclesiastical organizations of the Aztecs of Mexico. The Aztecs held their priests responsible for the maintenance and renewal of the entire universe. By performing annual rituals, priests could obtain the blessing of the Aztec gods, ensure the well-being of the Aztec people, and guard the world against collapse into chaos and darkness. According to Aztec theology, the world had already passed through four ages, each of which ended in cataclysmic destruction. The first age ended when the reigning god, Tezcatlipoca, transformed himself into the sun and all the people of the earth were devoured by jaguars. The second age, ruled over by the feathered serpent Quetzalcoatl

Figure 21.15 *TEMPLE OF QUETZALCOATL*
The plumed Serpent, Mexico City (formerly Tenochtitlán).

(Fig. 21.15) was destroyed by hurricanes that changed people into monkeys. The third age, ruled over by Tlaloc, god of rain, was brought to a close when the heavens rained fire. Then came the rule of Chalchihuitlicue, goddess of water, whose time ended with a universal flood, during which people turned into fish. The fifth age is in progress, ruled over by the sun god Tonatiuh, and doomed to destruction sooner or later by earthquakes.

The principal function of the 5000 priests living in the Aztec capital was to make sure the end of the world came later rather than sooner. This could be assured only by pleasing the legions of gods reputed to govern the world. The best way to please the gods was to give them gifts, the most precious being fresh human hearts. The hearts of war captives were the most esteemed gifts since they were won only at great expense and risk.

Aztec ceremonial centers were dominated by large pyramidal platforms topped by temples (Fig. 21.16). These structures were vast stages upon which the drama of human sacrifice was enacted at least once a day throughout the year. On especially critical days there were multiple sacrifices. The set pattern for these performances involved first the victim's ascent of the huge staircase to the top of the pyramid; then, at the summit, the victim was seized by four priests, one for each limb, and bent face up, spread-eagled over the sacrificial stone. A fifth priest cut the victim's chest open with an obsidian knife and wrenched out the beating heart. The heart was smeared over the statue of the god and later burned. Finally, the lifeless body was flung over the edge of the pyramid where it rolled back down the steps.

All aspects of Aztec ritual were regulated by intricate calendrical systems understood only by the priests. By means of their calendars, the priests kept track of the gods who had to be appeased and of the dangerous days, neglect of which might have occasioned the end of the world.

The Aztecs calculated the year as having 365 days. They divided this period into 18 months of 20 days each ($18 \times 20 = 360$), leaving 5 days over as an annual unlucky period. Each of the 20 days had a name, and each was numbered consecutively from 1 to 13. Every $13 \times 20 = 260$ days, the number 1 occurred at the beginning of a month. This period of 260 days was meshed with the 365-day year. Every 52 years the beginning of the 260-day and 365-day cycles coincided. The most holy days were those associated with the end of each 52-year cycle. At this time the priests struggled mightily to prevent the end of the world. The altar fires, which had burned perpetually for 52 years, were extinguished along with all the fires throughout the kingdom. The people destroyed their household furnishings, fasted, and prayed, awaiting the ultimate catastrophe. Pregnant women were hidden away and children were prevented from falling

Figure 21.16 *TENOCHTITLÁN*
A reconstructed view of the Aztec capital with its numerous temple-topped pyramids.

asleep. At sunset on the last day, the priests ascended an extinct volcanic crater at the center of the Valley of Mexico and anxiously watched the skies for signs that the world would continue. When certain stars passed the meridian, they sacrificed a captive and kindled a new fire in the victim's breast. Runners bore torches lit from this sacred fire throughout the kingdom.

It is believed that during a 4-day dedication ceremony of the main Aztec temple in Tenochtitlán, 20,000 prisoners of war were sacrificed in the manner described above. A yearly toll estimated to have been as high as 15,000 people were sent to their deaths to placate the bloodthirsty gods. Most of these victims were prisoners of war, although local youths, maidens, and children were also sacrificed from time to time (Vaillant 1966; Soustelle 1970). The bodies of most of those who were sacrificed were rolled down the pyramid steps, dismembered, cooked, and eaten. In the next chapter we shall discuss Michael Harner's (1977) controversial explanation of this unusual feature of the Aztec's ecclesiastical complex.

SUMMARY

Edward Tylor defined religion as animism or the doctrine of souls. According to Tylor, from the idea of the soul the idea of all godlike beings arose, while the idea of the soul itself arose as an attempt to explain phenomena such as trances, dreams, shadows, and reflections. Tylor's definition has been criticized for failing to consider the multifunctional nature of religion and for overlooking the compelling reality of direct halluncinatory contact with extraordinary beings. As the Jívaro's belief in three souls demonstrates, each culture uses the basic concepts of animism in its own distinctive fashion.

Tylor's definition of religion was supplemented by Marett's concepts of animatism and mana. Animatism refers to the belief in an impersonal, nonsoul-like life force in people, animals, and objects. The concentration of this force gives people, animals, and objects mana, or the capacity to be extraordinarily powerful and successful.

It should also be noted that the Western distinction between natural and supernatural is of limited utility for defining religion emically. As the case of the Gururumba indicates, the need for rituals to control certain entities, processes, or forces does not mean that other entities, processes, or forces can be controlled by a contrastive set of rituals. In other words, in many cultures there are no supernatural versus natural controls, only controls.

The distinction between sacred and profane realms of human experience may have greater universal validity than that between natural and supernatural. According to Durkheim, the feeling that something is sacred expresses the awe in which the hidden force of social consensus is held. Thus, although the content of the realm of the sacred may vary from one culture to another, the contrast between sacred and profane matters probably occurs universally.

Frazer tried to cope with the enormous variety of religious experience by separating religion from magic. Humility, supplication, and doubt characterize religion; routine cause and effect characterize magic. This distinction is difficult to maintain in view of the routine and coercive fashion in which animistic beings are often manipulated. There is no sharp difference between prayers and magic spells. Religion is a mix of awe and wonder, boredom and excitement, power and weakness.

The principal varieties of beliefs and rituals show broad correlations with levels of political economic organization. Four levels of religious organizations or cults can be distinguished: individualistic, shamanistic, communal, and ecclesiastical.

Eskimo religion illustrates the individualistic or do-it-yourself level. Each individual carries out a series of rituals and observes a series of taboos that are deemed essential for survival and well-being, without the help of any part-time or full-time specialist. Do-it-yourself cults, however, are not to be confused with "anything goes." As the example of Crow vision quests demonstrates, individualistic beliefs and rituals always follow definite culturally determined patterns.

No culture is completely devoid of shamanistic cults defined by the presence of part-time magicoreligious experts or shamans who have special talents and knowledge, usually involving sleight of hand, trances, and possession. As the case of Tapirapé shamanism indicates, shamans are frequently employed to cure sick people, as well as to identify and destroy evildoers. Many shamans think they can fly and move backwards and forwards through time.

Because of their extraordinary powers and unusual personalities, shamans are often blamed for misfortunes. The line between being a shaman and being a witch is very thin, as the case of the European witch-hunts illustrates. In societies with ecclesiastical cults, individuals who would be highly respected in band and village societies for their ability to have visions and dreams are condemned as witches or magicians and more or less actively persecuted.

Communal cults—involving public rituals deemed essential for the welfare or survival of the entire social group—also occur to some extent at all political-economic levels. Even in cultures such as the Eskimo and the Crow where individualistic and shamanistic rituals predominate, communal rituals such as confession and the Sun Dance also take place. Two principal types of communal rituals can be distinguished, rites of solidarity and rites of passage. As illustrated by the Arunta totemic rituals, rites of solidarity reaffirm and intensify a group's sense of common identity and express in symbolic form the group's claims to territory and resources. As illustrated in the Ndembu circumcision rituals, rites of passage symbolically and publicly denote the extinction or "death" of an individual's or group's socially significant status and the acquisition or "birth" of a new socially significant status.

Finally, ecclesiastical cults are those that are dominated by a hierarchy of full-time specialists or "priests" whose knowledge and skills are usually commanded by a state-level ruling class. To preserve and enhance the well-being of the state and of the universe, historical, astronomical, and ritual information must be aquired by the ecclesiastical specialists. Ecclesiastical cults are also characterized by huge investments in buildings, monuments, and personnel and by a thoroughgoing split between the specialist performers of ritual and the great mass of more or less passive spectators who constitute the "congregation." The religion of the Aztecs illustrates all of these aspects of ecclesiastical cults.

22 RELIGION AS ADAPTATION

This chapter is concerned with explanations of the varied content and form of religious beliefs and rituals. It explores the possibility that specific religious beliefs and rituals are determined by the combined influence of infrastructural and structural factors. Religion is not a mere passive "reflex" of the other parts of the cultural system. Religious beliefs and rituals frequently play a crucial role in organizing the impulses leading toward major transformations of social life. Yet infrastructural and structural conditions often provide a means for understanding the origin of beliefs and rituals, whereas beliefs and rituals seldom explain the origin of infrastructural and structural conditions.

RELIGION AND POLITICAL ECONOMY: HIGH GODS

The importance of political economy as a determinant of religious ritual and belief is clearly evident in ecclesiastical religions. Full-time specialists, monumental temples, dramatic processions, and elaborate rites performed for spectator congregations are incompatible with the infrastructure and political economy of hunters and food-gatherers. Similarly, the complex astronomical and mathematical components of ecclesiastical beliefs and rituals are never found among band or village peoples (although, as was seen in Ch. 8, the rudimentary beginnings of astronomy and mathematics can be traced back to paleolithic times).

The level of political economy also influences the way in which gods are thought to relate to each other and to human beings. For example, the idea of a single "high" or supreme god who creates the universe is found among cultures at all levels of economic and political development. These high gods, however, play different kinds of roles in running the universe after they have brought it into existence. Among hunter-gatherers and other prestate peoples, the high gods tend to become inactive after their creation task is done. It is to a host of lesser gods, demons, and ancestor souls that one must turn in order to obtain assistance. On the other hand, in stratified societies the high god bosses the lesser gods and tends to be a more active figure to whom priests and commoners address their prayers (Swanson 1960).

A plausible explanation for this difference is that prestate cultures have no need for the idea of a central or supreme authority. Just as there is an absence of centralized control over people and strategic resources in life, so in religious belief, the inhabitants of the spirit world lack decisive control over each other. They form a more or less egalitarian group. On the other hand, the belief that superordination and subordination characterizes relationships among the gods helps to obtain the cooperation of the commoner classes in stratified societies (Fig. 22.1).

One way to achieve conformity in stratified societies is to convince commoners that the gods demand obedience to the state. Disobedience and nonconformity result not only in retribution administered through the state's police-military apparatus, but also in punishments in present or future life administered by the high gods themselves. In prestate societies, for reasons discussed in Chapter 15, law and order are rooted in common interest. Consequently, there is little need for high gods to administer punishments for those who have been "bad" and

Figure 22.1 *RELIGION AND STRATIFICATION*
Bishops and other high prelates of the Corpus Christi Cathedral in Cuzco, Peru, are an awe-inspiring sight to an Indian peasant.

rewards for those who have been "good." However, as Table 22.1 shows, where there are class differences the gods are believed to take a lively interest in the degree to which each individual's thoughts and behavior are immoral or ethically subversive.

Table 22.1 RELIGION, CLASS, AND MORALITY

	Societies	
Gods interested in morality	With social classes	Without social classes
Present	25	2
Absent	8	12

SOURCE: Adapted from Swanson 1960:166.

IMPERIAL RELIGION

One of the most interesting contrasts between ecclesiastical religions and those found among bands, villages, and chiefdoms is their tendency to become *universalistic*, that is, to make their sacraments and moral standards applicable to people all over the world. Thus an important ingredient in the ecclesiastical religions of Buddhism, Hinduism, Christianity, and Islam is that they emphasize the need for human beings to be charitable and merciful toward people who are weak and poor. They also have in common the prohibition of human sacrifice, a prohibition on the consumption of human flesh, and a general reverence of human life.

The origin of these universalistic and charitable tendencies probably lies in the expansionist nature of the state. Prior to the evolution of the state, religions tended to be closely associated with the traditions and history of particular chiefdoms, villages, or bands. As discussed above (Ch. 15), prestate warfare seldom resulted in the incorporation of enemy populations into the victor's own social organization. Under prestate conditions, the incorporation of the enemy population would simply have meant lower living standards for everybody. Hence the enemy was merely driven away and few captives were taken. Moreover, there was a widespread pattern of making trophies of human skulls and bones as well as of bringing back a few captives, torturing them, and eating them.

With the development of the state, however, enemy populations could be left in their territories and made to contribute additional taxes, tribute, and labor which strengthened the power of the state and permitted it to expand still further and incorporate more and more chiefdoms and kingdoms until it finally reached the dimensions of an empire. Under these conditions it was no longer useful to terrorize one's enemies by threatening to kill them all and eat them if they did not run away. Rather, it became much more useful to promise that life would be better under the new rulers once the enemy accepted the political domination of the state and adopted its values and religion. Hence, even before the development of the modern universalistic religions, state religions tended to outlaw the sacrifice and eating of enemy soldiers.

The final step in the development of the values of love, mercy, and charity as aspects of universal ecclesiastical religions probably relates to the breakdown in the ability of imperial states to deliver on their promise to provide a better life on earth to the increasingly hard-pressed and exploited populations under their control. Christianity, Hinduism, Buddhism, and Islam advocate kindness and reverence toward one's fellows, but they do not blame the misery of the poor on the rich nor promise an end to poverty in one's lifetime. God or the devil or the poor themselves, rather than the emperor or king, are made responsible for the misery which accompanied the succession of empires and depletion of resources in India and the Near and Middle East, North Africa, and southern Europe. It is no accident, therefore, that although Christianity, Islam, Hinduism, and Buddhism all preach reverence for human life, they were all spread by the warfare of expansionist empires (Harris 1977).

HUMAN SACRIFICE AND CANNIBALISM AMONG THE AZTEC

As mentioned in the previous chapter, the Aztecs' ecclesiastical cult did not conform to the common pattern of tabooing human sacrifice and cannibalism and of encouraging charity and kindness toward enemy peoples. In the Aztec case, the state itself took over an earlier human sacrifice and cannibalism complex and made it the main focus of ecclesiatical beliefs and rituals (Fig. 22.2). As the Aztec evolved from a chiefdom to a state and as they became more powerful, they became more rather than less cannibalistic. Since the skulls of the victims were placed side by side on tall wooden racks after the brains were taken out and eaten, it was possible for members of Cortez's expedition to count at least one category of victim (Fig. 22.3). They reported that one of these skull racks at the center of Tenochtitlán held 136,000 heads, but they were unable to count another group of victims whose heads were heaped into two tall towers made entirely of crania and jawbones (Tápia 1971:583), nor did they count the skulls displayed on five smaller racks which were located in the same central area. According to calculations performed by Ortiz de Montellano (1983:404), the principal rack could not have held more than 60,000 skulls. Even if this lower figure is more accurate, the amount of human sacrifice and cannibalism practiced in Tenochtitlán remains unique in human history.

Although it is considered controversial, Michael Harner's (1977) explanation of the Aztec state's unique cannibal religion deserves serious consideration. Harner starts from the fact that as a result of millennia of intensification and population growth, the central Mexican highlands had lost their domesticable herbivores and swine (see Ch. 10). Unlike the Inca, who obtained animal foods from llama, alpaca, and guinea pigs—or the Old World states that had sheep, goats, pigs, and cattle—the Mesoamericans raised only semidomesticated ducks and turkeys and hairless dogs. Wild fauna, such as deer and migrating waterfowl, were not abundant enough to provide the Aztecs with more than 1 or 2 grams of animal protein

Figure 22.2 *AZTEC SACRIFICIAL KNIFE*

per capita per day (compared with over 60 grams in the United States). The depleted condition of the natural fauna is shown by the prominence in the Aztec diet of bugs, worms, and "scum cakes," which were made out of algae skimmed off the surface of Lake Texcoco (cf. Sahlins 1978; Harris 1979a).

Harner's theory is that the severe depletion of animal resources made it uniquely difficult for the Aztec state to prohibit the consumption of human flesh in order to facilitate its expansionist aims. Due to the severe depletion of animal resources, it was especially difficult to prevent the Aztec army from eating prisoners of war. Moreover, to have made serfs or slaves out of such captives would only have worsened the animal food shortage and lowered everybody's standard of living still further. There was thus much to lose by prohibiting cannibalism and little to gain. Human sacrifice and cannibalism, therefore, remained for

Figure 22.3 *SKULL RACK*
One of the smaller racks in the Aztec capital. The skulls in the photograph are sculpted in stone; during Aztec times real skulls were exhibited on wooden structures raised on the sculpted base. Part of the ongoing excavation in Mexico City.

the Aztecs irresistible temptations. Their ecclesiastical cult tipped over to favor an increase rather than a decrease in the ritual sacrifice of captives and the redistribution of human flesh as a means of rewarding bravery and loyalty in combat. The Aztec state, therefore, found itself waging war not to conquer new lands and absorb more chiefdoms and kingdoms, but to increase the flow of edible captives.

As discussed above with reference to game depletion and Yanomamo warfare (p. 306), animal foods are an extremely valuable compact package of nutrients essential for human growth, health, and vigor. Meat and other animal products are widely valued by human beings not only for the high-quality proteins they contain but for their fats, minerals, and vitamins. Hence, Harner's theory cannot be disproved by showing that the Aztecs could have obtained all of the essential amino acids (the nine building blocks of proteins that cannot be synthesized by the human body) from worms and insects, from algae, and from corn and beans and other plant foods (Ortiz de Montellano 1978). Worms and insects are small, dispersed food packages that occupy a position low in the food chain. It is more efficient to let higher organisms such as birds, fish, and mammals hunt and collect worms and insects and to eat the higher species instead of their prey. Also it is much more efficient to let fish eat algae and to eat the fish than it is to gather and process the algae and deprive the fish of their food.

Nutritionists are now of the opinion that a healthy adult can obtain all essential amino acids by eating large quantities of cereals alone (Pellet 1983). But such diets remain deficient in minerals (e.g., iron) and vitamins (e.g., vitamin A). Moreover, the protein levels that are adequate for normal adults and that can be obtained from cereals alone or from combinations such as corn and beans become hazardous when considering the needs of children, pregnant and lactating women, and anybody suffering from parasitical or viral infections or other diseases and body trauma caused by accidents or wounds (Scrimshaw 1977). Hence, the high value that the Aztecs placed upon the consumption of human flesh was not a purely arbitrary consequence of their religious beliefs. Rather, their religious beliefs (i.e., the cravings of their gods for human blood) reflect the extreme importance of animal foods in relation to human dietary needs and the extremely depleted supply of nonhuman animals in their habitat. (Note that most so-called "vegetarian cultures" are lactovegetarians or ovovegetarians, that is, they spurn meat but eat dairy products and eggs.)

REVITALIZATION

The relationship between religious belief and ritual and political and economic conditions can also be seen in the process known as *revitalization*. Under the severe stresses associated with colonial conquest and intense class or minority exploitation, beliefs and rituals tend to be concerned with achieving a drastic improvement in the immediate conditions of life and/or in the prospects for an afterlife. These beliefs and rituals are sometimes referred to as *nativistic*, *revivalistic*, *millenarian*, or *messianic* movements. The term "revitalization" is intended to embrace all the specific cognitive and ritual variants implied by these terms (cf. A. Wallace 1966).

Revitalization is a process of political and religious interaction between a depressed caste, class, minority, or other subordinate social group and a superordinate group. Some revitalization movements emphasize passive attitudes, the adoption of old rather than new cultural practices, or salvation through rewards after death; others advocate more or less open resistance or aggressive political or military action. These differences largely reflect the extent to which the superordinate groups are prepared to cope with the challenge to their power and authority. Direct challenges to political authority, as, for example, in a Joan of Arc type vision, are not to be expected where there is no possibility of military action. If the revitalization is sufficiently passive, the superordinate group may find it advantageous to encourage, or at least not to suppress, the revitalization movement. Many fundamentalist and revivalist Christian sects are politically conservative revitalizations that throw the onus of sickness, poverty, and psychological distress back onto the individual. Disciples are urged to stop smoking, drinking, lying, cheating, and fornicating in order to achieve a new identity free from sin that will entitle them to eternal life. In some cases Christian fundamentalist revitalization is explicitly linked with conservation of the political status quo through patriotic sermons and devotion to the struggle against atheism and "godless communism." Many revitalizations, however, lack an overt political theme, whether conservative or revolutionary. This does not mean that the political functions of revitalization can be disregarded but, rather, that the particular circumstances may not be appropriate for a mature phase of political struggle. As Peter Worsley (1968) has shown, revitalizations that take place under conditions of massive suffering and exploitation sooner or later result in political and even military confrontations, although both sides may overtly desire to avoid conflict.

NATIVE AMERICAN REVITALIZATIONS

Widespread revitalizations were provoked by the European invasion of the New World and the conquest and expulsion of the native American peoples and the destruction of their natural resources.

As early as 1680 the Pueblos of New Mexico underwent a violent politico-religious conversion led by the prophet Popé. According to Popé's visions, the Christian God had died. Under his direction the Catholic missionaries were burned at the altars of their churches and all European artifacts were destroyed.

Other parts of the United States experienced armed or passive revitalization organized around visions and prophecies stimulated by the European expansion. A common theme of these revitalizations concerned the defeat and expulsion of the white invaders. In the Great Lakes region the chief, Pontiac, attacked the whites as foretold in a prophetic vision.

Later there arose the Shawnee prophet Tenskwatawa, who foresaw the expulsion of the whites if the native Americans would give up alcohol and depose their peace chiefs. The prophet's twin brother, Tecumseh, formed a military alliance among tribes as far apart as Florida and the Rocky Mountains. Tenskwatawa himself was killed at Tippecanoe on the Wabash River during an attack against forces led by William Henry Harrison. This battle made Harrison famous. He and John Tyler successfully campaigned for president and vice-president under the slogan "Tippecanoe and Tyler Too" as heroes responsible for the suppression of the rebellious "savages."

As the more openly political and militaristic revitalizations were crushed by disease, starvation, and military defeat, they were replaced by more passive forms of revitalization. Thus the successor to Tenskwatawa was Kanakuk, who prophesied that if the Kickapoo would give up warfare, lying, stealing, and alcohol, they would find vast green lands to replace those stolen from them by the whites. Kanakuk's prophecies were as inaccurate as Tenskwatawa's, since the obedient Kickapoo were forced farther and farther west onto smaller and smaller reservations.

Revitalization in the northwest territories was led by the prophet Smohalla, known as the "Dreamer." Conversations with the Great Spirit had convinced Smohalla that the native Americans must resist the white man's attempt to convert them to farmers. His visions and prophecies inspired Chief Joseph of the Nez Percé, who led an unsuccessful rebellion in 1877.

Figure 22.4 *WOVOKA*
Leader of the Ghost Dance.

The most famous of the nineteenth-century revitalization movements was the Ghost Dance, also known as the Messiah craze. This movement originated near the California-Nevada border and roughly coincided with the completion of the Union Pacific Railroad. The Paviotso prophet Wodziwob envisioned the return of the dead from the spirit world in a great railroad train whose arrival would be signaled by a huge explosion. Simultaneously the whites would be swept from the land, but their buildings, machines, and other possessions would be left behind. (The resemblance to the neutron bomb is worth noting.) To hasten the arrival of the ancestors, there was to be ceremonial dancing accompanied by the songs revealed to Wodziwob during his visions.

A second version of the Ghost Dance was begun in 1889 under the inspiration of Wovoka (Fig. 22.4). A vision in which all the dead had been brought back to life by the Ghost Dance was again reported. Ostensibly Wovoka's teachings lacked political content, and as the Ghost Dance spread eastward across the Rockies, its political implications remained ambiguous. Yet for the native Americans of the plains, the return of the dead meant that they would outnumber the whites and hence be more powerful.

Among the Sioux, there was a version that included the return of all the bison and the extermination of the whites under a huge landslide. The Sioux warriors put on Ghost Dance shirts, which they believed would make them invulnerable to bullets. Clashes between the U.S. Army and the Sioux became more frequent, and the Sioux leader Sitting Bull was arrested and killed.

(a)

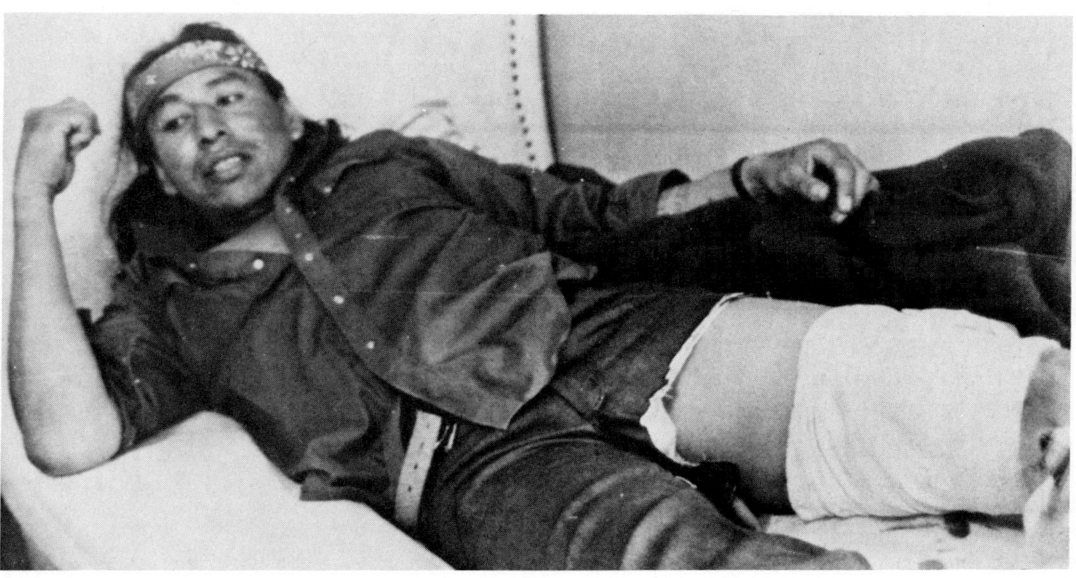

(b)

Figure 22.5 *WOUNDED KNEE*
In the first battle *(a)*, 1890, 200 Sioux Indians were killed by the U.S. Army. In the second battle *(b)*, 1973, militant Indians occupied the village of Wounded Knee, South Dakota, and exchanged gunfire with U.S. Marshalls.

The militant phase of the second Ghost Dance movement came to an end with the massacre of 200 Sioux at Wounded Knee, South Dakota (Fig. 22.5), on December 29, 1890 (Mooney 1965).

After all chance of military resistance was crushed, the native American revitalization movement became more introverted and passive. Visions in which all the whites are wiped out cease to be experienced, confirming once again the responsiveness of religion to political reality. The Ghost Dance, for example, lingered on in Saskatchewan as a religion which stressed obedience to the Creator and to Indian ways as a means of becoming reunited with one's tribe in the afterlife (Kehoe 1968:301).

The development and spread of beliefs and rituals centering upon peyote, mescal, and other hallucinogenic drugs are characteristic of many twentieth-century native American revitalizations. Peyote ritual involves a night of praying, singing, peyote eating, and ecstatic contemplation followed by a communal breakfast (Fig. 22.6). The peyote eaters are not interested in bringing

Figure 22.6 *PEYOTE CEREMONY*
Delaware Indians of Oklahoma spend the night in prayer and meditation. At right, they emerge to greet the dawn.

back the buffalo or making themselves invulnerable to bullets. They seek, rather, self-knowledge, personal moral strength, and physical health (Le Barre 1938; Stewart 1948).

> The peyote religion is a syncretistic cult, incorporating ancient Indian and modern Christian elements. The Christian theology of love, charity, and forgiveness has been added to the ancient Indian ritual and aboriginal desire to acquire personal power through individual visions. Peyotism has taught a program of accommodation for over 50 years and the peyote religion has succeeded in giving Indians pride in their native culture while adjusting to the dominant civilization of the whites (Stewart 1968:108).

Peyotism and allied cult movements do not, of course, signal the end of political action on the part of the native Americans. With the emergence of the "Red Power" movement, the native Americans' attempt to hold on to and regain their stolen lands is now being carried out through lawyers, politicians, novelists, Washington lobbyists, sit-ins, and land-ins (Deloria 1969; Walker 1972).

CARGO CULTS

In New Guinea and Melanesia, revitalization is associated with the concept of *cargo* (Fig. 22.7). The characteristic vision of the Melanesian revitalization prophets is that of a ship bringing back the ancestors and a cargo of European goods. In recent times airplane and spaceships have become the favorite means of delivering the cargo (Worsley 1968).

As a result of the abundance of goods displayed by U.S. military forces during the Pacific island campaigns of World War II, some revitalizations stressed the return of the Americans. In Espiritu Santo in 1944, the prophet Tsek urged his people to destroy all trade goods and throw away their clothes in preparation for the return of the mysteriously departed Americans. Some of the American-oriented revitalizations have placed specific American soldiers in the role of cargo deliverers. On the island of Tana in the New Hebrides, the John Frumm cult cherishes an old GI jacket as the relic of one John Frumm, whose identity is not other-

Figure 22.7 *JOHN FRUMM* Members of the Tana, New Hebrides, cargo cult.

wise known. The prophets of John Frumm build landing strips, bamboo control towers, and grass-thatched cargo sheds. In some cases beacons are kept ablaze at night and radio operators stand ready with tin-can microphones and earphones to guide the cargo planes to a safe landing.

An important theme is that the cargo planes and ships have been successfully loaded by the ancestors at U.S. ports and are on their way, but the local authorities have refused to permit the cargo to be landed. In other versions, the cargo planes are tricked into landing at the wrong airport. In a metaphorical sense these sentiments are applicable to the actual colonial contexts. The peoples of the South Seas have indeed often been tricked out of their lands and resources (Harris 1974).

In 1964 the island of New Hanover became the scene of the Lyndon Johnson cult. Under the leadership of the prophet Bos Malik, cult members demanded that they be permitted to vote for Johnson in the village elections scheduled for them by the Australian administration. Airplanes passing overhead at night were said to be President Johnson's planes searching for a place to land. Bos Malik advised that in order to get Johnson to be their president, they would have to "buy" him. This was to be done by paying the annual head tax to Malik instead of to the Australian tax collectors. When news reached New Hanover that an armed force had been dispatched to suppress the tax revolt, Malik prophesied that the liner *Queen Mary* would soon arrive bearing cargo and U.S. troops to liberate the islanders from the Australian oppressors. When the ship failed to materialize, Malik accused the Australian officials of stealing the cargo.

The confusion of the Melanesian revitalization prophets is a confusion about the workings of cultural systems. They do not understand how modern industrial wage-labor societies are organized, nor comprehend how law and order are maintained among state-level peoples. To them, the material abundance of the industrial nations and the penury of others constitute an irrational flaw, a massive contradiction in the structure of the world.

The belief system of the cargo cults vividly demonstrates why the assumption that all people distinguish between natural and supernatural categories is incorrect (see p. 418). Cargo prophets who have been taken to see modern Australian stores and factories in the hope that they would give up their beliefs return home more convinced than ever that they are following the best prescription for obtaining cargo. With their own eyes they have observed the fantastic abundance the authorities refuse to let them have (Lawrence 1964).

CHRISTIANITY AND REVITALIZATION

Revitalization also lies at the root of the fundamental religions of Western civilization. Judaism and Christianity are messianic religions born out of the struggles against poverty, colonialism, and imperialism in the ancient Middle East. The ancient Jewish state, founded by David and his son Solomon, was conquered and ruled over by a succession of powerful empires: Egyptian, Assyrian, Babylonian, Persian, Greek, and Roman, in that order. Each successive conquest only strengthened the hope of the Jews themselves that they would eventually achieve an empire of their own. This hope was nourished by the principal post-Babylonian prophets of the Old Testament—Isaiah, Jeremiah, Zechariah, and Ezekiel—all of whom predicted that God would eventually send a divine liberator—a messiah—to establish the ultimate, one, true, just, holy, and everlasting empire (Fig. 22.8). During the period of Roman rule, there were many messianic cults and messiahs. As in most revitalization movements, the civil authorities and the cultists eventually came into direct military-political conflict. In the year that Jesus was born, 2000 messianic cultists were crucified by the Roman governor Varus. A continuous series of military-messianic uprisings preceded and followed the messianic episodes involving John the Baptist and Jesus. According to the Jewish-Roman eyewitness and historian, Flavius Josephus, revolutionary cultists led by "religious frauds" ranged over the countryside, "plundering the houses of the well-to-do, killing the occupants, and setting fire to the villages, till their raging madness penetrated every corner of Judea" (Josephus 1970). These uprisings culminated in two full-scale messianic wars, both of which came close to defeating the Roman forces. In the first, which lasted from A.D. 68 to 73, the Roman army was led by Vespasian and his son Titus. These generals became emperors of Rome because of their success in repressing the messianic "bandits." Among the Jewish messiahs and prophets who kept the war going, the most famous was Manahem. Josephus blamed the million deaths suffered by the Jews on Manahem and the other messiahs—"false messengers [who] beguiled the people into believing that supernatural deliverance would yet be theirs."

The second and final great uprising against Rome occurred in A.D. 132–136. It

Figure 22.8 *TEMPLE OF JERUSALEM*
Lower walls in this photo were part of the monumental temple built by King Herod and the scene of events recounted in the New Testament. El Aksa mosque, whose dome appears at right, was built on top of the Herodian walls, left in ruins by the Roman conquest of Jerusalem in 70 A.D.

was led by Bar Kochva—Son of a Star—who, because of his miraculous victories, was identified by the chief rabbi of Jerusalem as the long-awaited messiah. The people reported seeing Bar Kochva mounted on a lion. After Bar Kochva was killed in battle, the Romans leveled a thousand villages, executed one-half million cultists, and shipped thousands more abroad as slaves (W. Wallace 1943).

It is clear that the spread of the peaceful Jewish messianic cult that eventually became Christianity was closely related to the unsuccessful attempts of the Jewish military messiahs to topple the Roman Empire. Although Jesus was crucified in A.D. 30 or 33, it was not until after Jerusalem was destroyed by Titus that the first Gospel was written. With the generals who had conquered Israel sitting on the imperial throne, many Jews and other minorities living under Roman rule rejected the idea of a military salvation and, like many native American cultists, turned instead to the dream of redemption in a "kingdom" that was not of this world. There is considerable evidence that the image of Jesus as the "Prince of Peace" may not have been formed until after the fall of Jerusalem (Brandon 1968a and b; Harris 1974b). One thing seems certain: Regardless of Jesus's intentions, the Roman governor treated him as if he were guilty of a political crime. Crucifixion was the common fate of all convicted military messiahs and their followers.

REVITALIZATIONS IN EUROPE

Starting with the tenth century, Europe was wracked by a continuous series of messianic revitalizations. The fundamental cause of these upheavals was the development of trade, markets, and banking which forced the feudal ruling class into enterprises aimed at maximizing profits. As a result, the paternalistic relationships characteristic of feudal manors and castle barons were undermined. Landholdings were divided, and serfs and servants gave way to renters and sharecroppers. Peasants lost their land, and great numbers of people began to drift about looking for jobs in the towns. People thought they saw the end of the world unfolding before their eyes. The sin and luxury of the clergy, the polarization of wealth, famines, plagues, threat of Islam, and incessant wars between rival factions of the nobility gave rise to one messianic revitalization after another.

The Protestant reformation was closely linked to these movements. Martin Luther was convinced that he was living in the Last Days, and that the return of Jesus was imminent. Luther's condemnation of radical peasant communitarian movements which were aimed at the redistribution of land and wealth, gave rise to a revitalization led by Thomas Müntzer. Müntzer accused Luther of being in league with those responsible for the misery of the peasants. He characterized the lords and princes who supported Luther as "ungodly scoundrels," "the seedbeds of usury, theft, and robbery," and "robbers who use the law to forbid others to rob." Convinced that the great peasant revolt of 1525 was the beginning of the new kingdom, Müntzer took command of the peasant army. God spoke to him and promised him victory. He told his followers that he would protect them by catching the enemy's cannonballs in his coatsleeve. Five thousand of Müntzer's followers were killed in battle, and he himself was captured, tortured, and beheaded. Similar messianic movements continued all during the sixteenth and seventeenth centuries, of which those associated with the Anabaptists are best known.

Modern-day communitarian movements, such as the People's Temple headed by the Reverend Jim Jones, perpetuate this tradition of messianic struggle against overwhelming odds. About 900 members of this communitarian movement poisoned themselves to death in 1978 in Jonestown, Guyana, in the hope of finding a better life in heaven than in the militarized and tension-ridden jungle settlement named after their psychotic messianic leader (Fig. 22.9).

Although most revitalization movements end in failure, established governments and colonial garrisons ignore the political potential of such movements at great peril to themselves. This is vividly demonstrable in the recent Shiite Moslem revitalization movement led by Ayatollah Khomeini (Fig. 22.10). Against seemingly invincible odds, Khomeini's followers deposed Iran's Shah and humiliated the United States by holding 52 U.S. citizens hostage for 444 days. Khomeini gave a religious interpretation of Iran's subordination to foreign military and oil interests. He combined a forward-looking program to end economic exploitation with a backward-looking insistence on making women wear veils, banning alcohol, and prohibiting radio and TV entertainment, which he characterized as "no different than opium."

Figure 22.9 *JONESTOWN, GUYANA*
Urged on by their cult leader Jim Jones, some 900 members of this cult drank Kool-Aid laced with poison and died.

Figure 22.10 *REVITALIZATION IN IRAN*
Ayatollah Khomeini addressing crowds in Teheran.

It is ironic, therefore, that Karl Marx (1973:14) should have characterized religion as the "opium of the people." Under conditions appropriate for the development of messianic leadership, religion again and again has proved itself capable of mobilizing downtrodden and exploited masses into powerful revolutionary armies, as well as into Jonestownlike *zombies*. Depending on the underlying conditions, therefore, religion may be a conservative or radical force (Cohn 1962; Thrupp 1962; Lanternari 1963; Hobsbawm 1965; E. Wolf 1969).

TABOO, RELIGION, AND ECOLOGY

As discussed in the previous chapter, religion can be seen as the concentration of the sense of the sacred. In the theories of Emile Durkheim, the sacred is the sense of awe evoked by the power of social life. It follows that an appeal to the sacred nature of a rule governing interpersonal relations or of a rule governing the relationship between a population and its environment will be useful in resolving the uncertainties that people may experience concerning what they ought to do.

For example, the prohibition on incest within the nuclear family is widely seen as a sacred obligation. The violation of an incest taboo is looked upon as a dirty or antisacred act. One plausible explanation for these powerful sentiments is that people are strongly tempted to commit incest, but that the short-run satisfactions they might receive from such acts would have long-run negative consequences for them and for the continuity of social life because of the reduced ability of individuals and local groups to establish adaptive intergroup relationships (see p. 267). By surrounding incest prohibitions with the aura of sacredness, the long-term individual and collective interest comes to prevail, and the ambiguities and doubts that individuals feel about renouncing the prohibited sexual relationships are resolved more decisively than would otherwise be possible. This does not mean that incest ceases to occur or that all psychological doubts are removed, but merely that such doubts are brought under effective social control.

A similar tension between short-run and long-run costs and benefits may explain the origin of certain food taboos that are regarded as sacred obligations. For example, it seems likely that the ancient Israelite prohibition on the consumption of pork reflects the contradiction between the temptation to rear pigs and the negative consequences of raising animals that are useful only for meat. Pigs require shade and moisture to regulate their body temperature. With the progressive deforestation and desertification of the Middle East caused by the spread and intensification of agriculture and stock raising and by population growth, habitat zones suitable for pig rearing became scarce. Hence, an animal that was at one time reared and consumed as a relatively inexpensive source of fat and protein could no longer be reared and consumed by large numbers of people without reducing the efficiency of the main system of food production (Harris 1979c; cf. Diener and Robkin 1978). The temptation to continue the practice of pig raising persisted, however; hence, the invocation of sacred commandments in the ancient Hebrew religion. Note that the explanation of the ancient origins of this taboo does not account for its perpetuation into the present. Once in existence, the taboo against pork (and other foods) acquired the function of demarcating or bounding Jewish ethnic minorities from other groups and of increasing their sense of identity and solidarity (see p. 348). Outside of the Middle East it no longer served an ecological function, but it continued to be useful on the level of structural relationships.

The general ecological adaptiveness of taboos regulating potentially important sources of animal protein in the Amazon basin has been studied by Eric Ross (1978). Ross holds that certain large animals such as deer, the tapir, and the white-lipped peccary are not hunted or eaten by the Achuara because to do so would be to misdirect the hunting effort away from gregarious, abundant, relatively accessible, and less costly species such as monkeys, birds, and fish. The costs of obtaining species such as deer and tapir among the Achuara are prohibitive because the Achuara live in very small dispersed villages and cannot form hunting parties with enough men to pursue, kill, and bring back the bigger animals.

Ross emphasizes the need to think about food taboos in dynamic long-term perspective. Species that at one time are abundant and easily accessible may later become scarce and even endangered. Taboos may shift from casual indifference to a particular scarce or hard to find animal, to a sacred prohibition against consuming its flesh. If the animal then becomes abundant again, it is possible that the taboo may be relaxed or it may disappear entirely. This raises the possibility that some band and village food taboos actually function as conservation measures that help to prevent the extinction of endangered food resources (Ross 1978 [cf. Lizot 1979] 1979, 1983; McDonald 1977).

It is interesting to note in this connection the origin of the word *taboo*. This is a Polynesian word which denotes the practice followed by Polynesian chiefs in limiting access to certain depleted agricultural lands or overfished portions of the seacoast. Anyone violating such taboos was subject to both natural and supernatural punishment.

THE SACRED COW

The case of the sacred cow of India conforms to the general theory that the flesh of certain animals becomes taboo when it becomes very expensive as a result of ecological changes. Like pigs in the Middle East, cattle were sacrificed and eaten quite freely in India during the Neolithic. With the rise of the state and of dense rural and urban populations, however, cattle could no longer be raised in sufficient numbers to be used both as a source of meat and as the principal source of traction power for pulling plows (Fig. 22.11). But as the taboo on cattle use developed, it took a form that was quite different from the Israelite taboo on the pig. Whereas the pig was valued almost exclusively for its flesh, cattle were also valued for their milk and especially for their traction power (see p. 367). Thus when pigs became too costly to be raised for meat, the whole animal became taboo and an abomination. But as cattle became too costly to be raised for meat, their value as a source of traction power increased (the land had to be plowed more intensively as population increased). Therefore, they had to be protected rather than abominated, and so the Hindu religion came to emphasize everyone's sacred duty to refrain from killing cattle or eating beef. Interestingly enough, the Brahmans, who at one time were the caste responsible for ritually slaughtering cattle, later became the caste most concerned with their protection and most opposed to the development of a beef slaughter industry in India (Harris 1977; cf. Simoons 1979; Harris 1979b).

Figure 22.11 *PLOW ANIMALS IN RAJASTAN, INDIA*
These small, humped breeds are adapted to the arid climate.

What about the sacred cow today? Is the religious ban on the slaughter of cattle and the consumption of beef an adaptive or maladaptive feature of modern Hinduism? Everyone agrees that the human population of India needs more calories and proteins. Yet the Hindu religion bans the slaughter of cattle and taboos the eating of beef. These taboos are often held responsible for the creation of large numbers of aged, decrepit, barren, and useless cattle. Such animals are depicted as roaming aimlessly across the Indian countryside, clogging the roads, stopping the trains, stealing food from the marketplace, and blocking city streets (Fig. 22.12). A closer look at some of the details of the ecosystem of the Indian subcontinent, however, suggests that the taboo in question does not decrease the capacity of the present Indian system of food production to support human life.

As discussed in Chapter 18, the basis of traditional Indian agriculture is the ox-drawn plow. Each peasant farmer needs at least two oxen to plow the fields at the proper time of year. Despite the impression of surplus cattle, the central fact of Indian rural life is that there is a shortage of oxen, since one-third of the peasant households own less than the minimum pair. Many cows are too old, decrepit, and sick to do a proper job of reproducing. At this point the ban on slaughter and beef consumption is thought to exert its harmful effect. For rather than kill dry, barren, and aged cows, the Hindu farmer is depicted as ritually obsessed with preserving the life of each sacred beast, no matter how useless it may become. From the point of view of the poor farmer, however, these relatively undesirable creatures may be quite essential and useful. The farmer would prefer to have more vigorous cows, but is prevented from achieving this goal not by the taboos against slaughter but by the shortage of land and pasture.

Even barren cows, however, are by no means a total loss. Their dung makes an essential contribution to the energy system as fertilizer and as cooking fuel. Millions of tons of artificial fertilizer at prices beyond the reach of the small farmer would be required to make up for the loss of dung if substantial numbers of cattle were sent to slaughter. Since cattle dung is also a major source of cooking fuel, the slaughter of substantial numbers of animals would also require the purchase of expensive dung substitutes, such as wood, coal, or kerosene. Cattle dung is relatively cheap because the cattle do not eat foods that can be eaten by people. Instead, they eat the stubble left in the fields and the marginal patches of grass on steep hillsides, roadside ditches, railroad embankments, and other nonarable lands. This constant scavenging gives the impression that cows are roaming around aimlessly devouring everything in sight. But most cows have an owner, and in the cities, after poking about in the market refuse and nibbling on neighbors' lawns, each cow returns to its stall at the end of the day.

In a study of the bioenergetic balance involved in the cattle complex of villages in West Bengal, Stuart Odend'hal (1972) found that "basically, the cattle convert items of

(a)

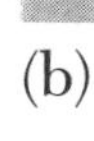

(b)

Figure 22.12 *SACRED COWS*
This resident of Calcutta *(a)* is not wandering aimlessly. Its owner knows where it is. These cows *(b)* are "parked," not blocking traffic. Cattle are ecologically more valuable than cars in India.

little direct human value into products of immediate human utility." Their gross energetic efficiency in supplying useful products was several times greater than that characteristic of agroindustrial beef production. He concludes that "judging the productive value of Indian cattle based on western standards is inappropriate."

Although it might be possible to maintain or exceed the present level of production of oxen and dung with substantially fewer cows of larger and better breeds, the question arises as to how these cows would be distributed among the poor farmers. Are the farmers who have only one or two decrepit animals to be driven from the land?

Aside from the problem of whether present levels of population and productivity could be maintained with fewer cows, there is the theoretically more crucial question of whether it is the taboo on slaughter that accounts for the observed ratio of cattle to people. This seems highly unlikely. Despite the ban on slaughter, the Hindu farmers cull their herds and adjust sex ratios to crops, weather, and regional conditions. The cattle are killed by various indirect means equivalent to the forms of benign and malign neglect discussed in Chapter 11 with respect to human population controls. The effectiveness of this form of control may be judged from the following fact. In the Gangetic plain, one of the most religiously orthodox regions of India, there are over 200 oxen for every 100 cows (Vaidyanathan, Nair, and Harris 1982).

Stepping away from the point of view of the individual farmer, there are a number of additional reasons for concluding that the Hindu taboos have had a positive rather than a negative effect upon Indian agriculture. The ban on slaughter, whatever its consequences for culling the herds, discourages the development of a meat-packing industry. Such an industry would be ecologically disastrous in a land as densely populated as India (Dolberg 1982:149–150). In this connection it should be pointed out that the nutritional output of the existing system is not unimportant. Although Indian cows are very poor milkers by Western standards, they, nonetheless, contribute critical if small quantities of protein, fats, and vitamins to the diets of millions of people. Moreover, a considerable amount of beef does get eaten during the course of the year, since the animals that die a natural death are consumed by carrion-eating outcastes. Finally, the critical function of the ban on slaughter during famines should be noted. When hunger stalks the Indian countryside, the slaughter taboo helps the peasants to resist the temptation to eat their cattle. If this temptation were to win out over religious scruples, it would be impossible for them to plant new crops when the rains began. Thus, the intense resistance among Hindu saints to the slaughter and consumption of beef takes on a new meaning in the context of the Indian ecosystem. In the words of Mohandas Gandhi:

> Why the cow was selected for apotheosis is obvious to me. The cow was in India the best companion. She was the giver of plenty. Not only did she give milk but she also made agriculture possible (1954:3).

THE SECRET OF VOODOO

Haitian voodoo cult rituals will serve as a final example of how seemingly irrational and wasteful religious beliefs and practices often serve hidden adaptive functions. When most of us hear the word *voodoo*, we think of witch doctors sticking pins in dolls and performing other kinds of black magic.

Gerald Murray (1980) however, reports that black magic is only a minor aspect of the folk religions he studied in Haiti. Voodoo according to Murray denotes an elaborate communal cult which has three major ritual foci: propitiating the *loua* or gods; "calling back" and honoring one's dead parents or grandparents; and warding off village vampires (people who turn into birdlike animals at night and suck the blood of children). To conduct voodoo rituals, considerable sums of money must be extended on hiring specialists and buying materials. For example, villagers say that it is shameful to bury one's parents underground; hence, they strive to build elaborate multichambered tombs

Figure 22.13 *HAITIAN CEMETERY*
To build these large structures, Haitian peasants must sell land.

which cost more than the simple stick-and-mud houses of the living (Fig. 22.13). Individuals who try to cut back on voodoo expenses are stigmatized by their neighbors and suspected of being vampires.

Murray remained puzzled by all this pressure to spend money on rituals until he began to investigate how the villagers raised the funds in question. He soon discovered that the most successful ceremonies (in the eyes of one's neighbors) were those financed by the sale of land to other members of the village. Indeed, about 75 percent of all land sales within the village were motivated by the need to pay for voodoo curing ceremonies, funerals, or other voodoo rituals. Although a villager could theoretically raise the necessary funds by selling off farm animals or surplus crops, neighbors tended to bad-mouth ceremonies which were not accompanied by the sale of a piece of land as a token of earnest devotion. Murray suggests that without the socioreligious pressure to sponsor voodoo rituals, village land would seldom be put on the market, many families would become or remain landless, and landholdings would become consolidated in the hands of a few wealthy peasants.

> It is in short, the folk religion of its members that keeps the community's land in circulation . . . (ibid.:313). It is this land release that constitutes the major payoff for other members of the community and it is this land-circulating phenomenon that I believe helps place the otherwise enigmatic pressure for expensive rituals in an intelligible context (ibid.:316).

The student should be warned that all of the theories presented in this chapter are considered controversial and are the object of continuing debate, discussion, and field research. They are not to be taken as final truths. Like all scientific theories, they can only be held tentatively and provisionally, and they are likely to be changed and improved, if not overthrown, by future research.

SUMMARY

Varieties of religious beliefs and practices are influenced by and adapted to structural and infrastructural conditions. For example, a close correlation exists between ecclesiastical religions and the state. The organization of the gods reflects the organization of society as in the occurrence of supreme beings who punish transgressions. Supernatural morality correlates with social classes.

The tendency of ecclesiastical religions to advocate universalistic creeds also shows the relationship between political economy and superstructure. With the development of the state, the objective of warfare shifted from that of routing the enemy population to incorporating them within imperial systems. This brought an end to the practice of torturing and eating prisoners of war and led to the development of universalistic religions of love and mercy. Aztec ecclesiastical religion did not conform to this pattern. Human sacrifice and cannibalism became more prominent as the state became more powerful, and wars were waged not to incorporate conquered populations but to obtain more sacrificial victims. A theory that explains the unique features of Aztec religion is that the animal resources of central Mexico had been uniquely depleted. It was difficult for the Aztec state to refrain from rewarding its armies with the flesh of enemy soldiers in its effort to justify, expand, and consolidate ruling-class power. The depleted nature of Aztec animal resources is shown by the prominence of insects, worms, and algae in their diet. While balanced protein rations can be obtained from such foods as well as from corn and beans, the emphasis upon obtaining and consuming vertebrate flesh and dairy products reflects a universal adaptive strategy for maximizing protein, fat, mineral, and vitamin consumption. The Aztec's search for human flesh was an expression of this adaptive strategy; it could not be suppressed because of the depletion of alternative sources of animal foods.

Revitalization is another category of religious phenomena that cannot be understood apart from political-economic conditions. Under political-economic stress, subordinate castes, classes, minorities, and ethnic groups develop beliefs and rituals concerned with achieving a drastic improvement in their immediate well-being and/or their well-being in a life after death. These movements have the latent capacity to attack the superordinate groups directly or indirectly through political or military action; on the other hand, they may turn inward and accommodate by means of passive doctrines and rituals involving individual guilt, drugs, and contemplation.

Native American revitalizations were initially violent protests against genocide and ethnocide. Prophets predicted the expulsion of the whites if native Americans gave up drinking and fighting among themselves. Later, there were visions of the whites being swept back into the sea after the arrival of a great train filled with ancestors brought back to life. The Sioux put on Ghost Dance shirts to protect themselves against bullets. After the suppression of the Ghost Dance movement, revitalization returned to contemplative renewal of native traditions as in the Peyote religion. More recently, the struggle of native Americans has become more secular and legalistic.

Melanesian and New Guinea cargo revitalizations foresaw the ancestors returning in ships laden with European trade goods. Later, airplanes and spaceships were substituted for sailing ships and steamboats. Cargo cults reflected a misunderstanding of industrial state systems by peoples who were living on the village level of political evolution when they were brought into the wage labor system.

Revitalization is also a fundamental theme of early Judaism and Christianity. During the period of the Roman rule in Palestine, there were many messianic movements that sought the overthrow of the Roman Empire and the establishment of a heaven on earth. Similar movements played an important role in European history and were closely associated with the Protestant Reformation. Revitalization themes continue to characterize many contemporary cults in the United States as well as abroad in countries such as Iran.

Religious beliefs and rituals also exhibit adaptive relationships in the form of taboos. Taboos often take the form of sacred injunctions that resolve ambiguities and control the temptation to engage in behavior, such as incest, that has short-term benefits but that is socially disruptive in the long run. Many taboos on animals whose exploitation leads to ambiguous ecological and economic consequences can be seen in the same light. The ancient Israelite pig taboo, for example, can be understood as an adaptation to the changing costs and benefits of pig rearing brought about by population increase, deforestation, and desertification. Similar short-term versus long-term costs and benefits among villages of different sizes in the Amazon tropical forest may also account for the pattern of animal use and nonuse and taboos associated with various intensities of sacredness. As the case of the sacred cow in India shows, taboos and whole religions adapt to changing political, economic, and ecological contexts. A final example of how seemingly irrational and wasteful religious beliefs and rituals often serve hidden adaptive functions is the relationship between Haitian voodoo and the circulation of land.

All of these theories are controversial and the subject of ongoing debate and research.

23 THE ARTISTIC ANIMAL

This chapter is concerned with finding the common element that underlies the thought and behavior associated with painting, music, poetry, sculpture, dance, and other media of artistic creation. At the same time, it is concerned with explaining why the specific forms and styles of artistic expression vary from one culture to another. We will see that art is not an isolated sector of human experience; it is intimately connected with and embedded in other aspects of sociocultural systems.

WHAT IS ART?

Alexander Alland (1977, p. 39) defines *art* as "play with form producing some aesthetically successful transformation-representation." The key ingredients in this definition are "play," "form," "aesthetic," and "transformation." *Play* is an enjoyable, self-rewarding aspect of activity that cannot be accounted for simply by the utilitarian or survival functions of that activity. *Form* designates a set of restrictions on how the art play is to be organized in time and space—the rules of the game of art. *Aesthetic* designates the existence of a universal human capacity for an emotionally charged response of appreciation and pleasure when art is successful. *Transformation-representation* refers to the communicative aspect of art. Art always represents something—communicates information—but this something is never represented in its literal shape, sound, color, movement, or feeling. To be art, as distinct from other forms of communication, the representation must be transformed into some metaphoric or symbolic statement, movement, image, or object which stands for that which is being represented. A portrait, for example, no matter how "realistic," can only be a transformation of the individual it depicts.

As Alland points out, play, adherence to form, and an aesthetic sense are found in many nonhuman animals. Chimpanzees, for example, like to play with paints (Fig. 23.1). Their adherence to form can be demonstrated by their placement of designs in the center of blank spaces or by their balancing of designs on different parts of a page. (They don't simply paint right off the page.) And an aesthetic sense can be inferred by their repeated attempts to copy simple designs such as circles and traingles accurately.

What about transformation-representation? This criterion of art can also be found among chimpanzees. As was seen in Chapter 20, the capacity to use symbols and to learn rules of symbolic transformation is not entirely confined to human beings. The 3-year-old chimp Moja drew a bird and gave the sign for it. The trainer tried to make sure that it was a bird rather than a berry, so he asked her to draw a berry, which she promptly did (Hill 1978:98).

Nonetheless, just as grammatical language remains rudimentary among apes in nature, so too does their artistry. Although the rudiments of art can be found in our primate heritage, only *Homo sapiens* can justly be called the artistic animal.

ART AS A CULTURAL CATEGORY

Although it is possible to identify art as an etic category of thought and behavior in all human cultures, an emic distinction between art and nonart is not universal (just as the distinction between natural and super-

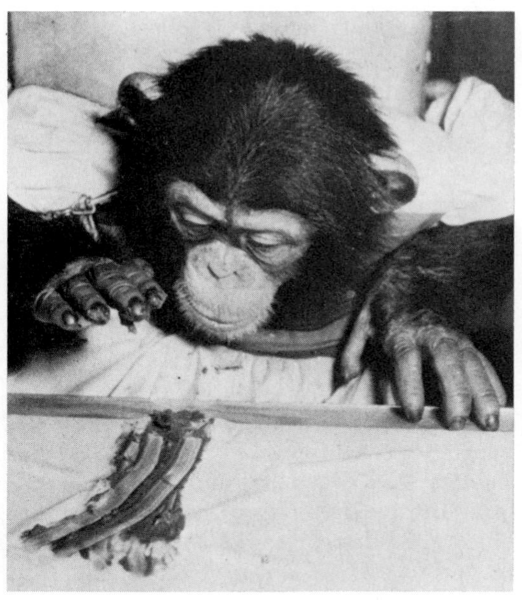

(a)

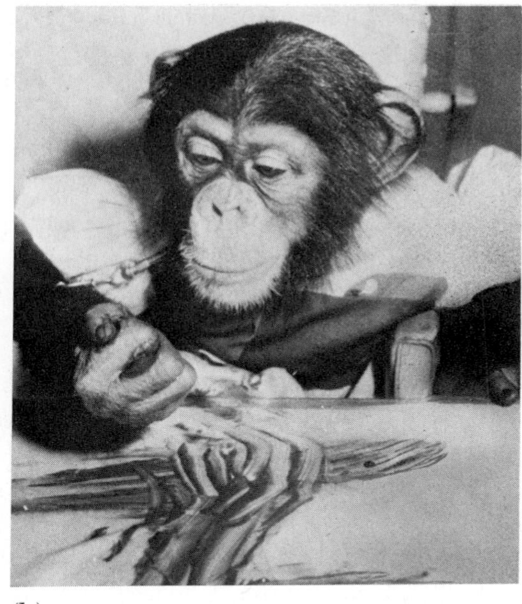

(b)

(c)

Figure 23.1 *CHIMPANZEE ARTISTS*
A 2-year-old chimpanzee *(a)*, *(b)* finger painting at the Baltimore, Md., Zoo. Note attempt to center painting. A chimpanzee named Candy *(c)* exhibits her artwork at the San Francisco Zoo.

natural is not universal). What most Westerners mean by art is a particular emic category of modern Euramerican civilization. Euramerican schoolchildren are enculturated to the idea that art is a category of activities and products that stands opposed to the category of nonart. We learn to believe, in other words, that some paintings, carvings, songs, dances, and stories are not art. In Western civilization a particular performance is deemed artistic or not by a distinct group of authorities who make or judge art and who control the museums, conservatories, critical journals, and other organizations and institutions devoted to art as a livelihood and style of life. Most cultures lack any semblance of an art establishment. This does not mean they lack art or artistic standards. A painted design on a pot or a rock, a carved mask or club, or a song or chant in a puberty ordeal are subject to critical evaluation by both performers and spectators. All cultures distinguish between less satisfactory and more satisfactory aesthetic experiences in decorative, pictorial, and expressive matters.

Basic to the modern Western idea of an opposition between art and nonart is the lack of artistic value placed on designs, stories, and artifacts that have a definite use in day-to-day subsistence activities and that are produced primarily for practical purposes or for commercial sale. Carpenters are distinguished from people who make wooden sculptures; bricklayers from architects; house painters from those who apply paint to canvas; and so forth, one group being labled *artists*, the other *artisans*. A similar opposition between art and practicality is seldom found in other cultures. Many works of art are produced and performed in complete harmony with utilitarian objectives. People everywhere, whether specialists or nonspecialists, derive pleasure from playfully embellishing and transforming the contours and surfaces of pots, fabrics, wood, and metal products (Fig. 23.2). All cultures, however, recognize that certain individuals are more skilled than others in making utilitarian objects and in embellishing them with pleasurable designs. Most anthropologists regard the skilled woodcarver, basketmaker, potter, weaver, or sandalmaker as an artist as well as an artisan.

ART AND INVENTION

As Alland (1977:24) suggests, play is a form of exploratory behavior that permits human beings to try out new and possibly useful responses in a controlled and protected context. The playful creative urge that lies behind art, therefore, is probably closely related to the creative urge that lies behind the development of science, technology, and new institutions. Art and technology often interact. For example, throughout the Paleolithic period it is difficult to say where technology ends and art begins, or where art ends and technology begins. A Solutrean laurel leaf blade is as much an aesthetic expression as it is a device for cutting flesh (Fig. 23.3). The beautiful symmetry of nets, baskets, and woven fabrics is essential for their proper functioning. Even in the devel-

Figure 23.2 *ART HAS MANY MEDIA* Native American cultures produced these objects. Gold mummy mask with green stone eyes, Chimu, Peru *(a)*. Globular basket with coiled weave, Chumash, California *(b)*. Feathers of blue and yellow form design of Tapirapé mask, Brazil *(c)*. Painted wooden kero, or beaker, representing ocelot head, Inca, Peru *(d)*. Ceramic jar, Nazca, Peru *(e)*. Blanket, in blue, black, and white, with stripes and frets, Navajo *(f)*.

(a)
(b)
(c)
(d)
(e)
(f)

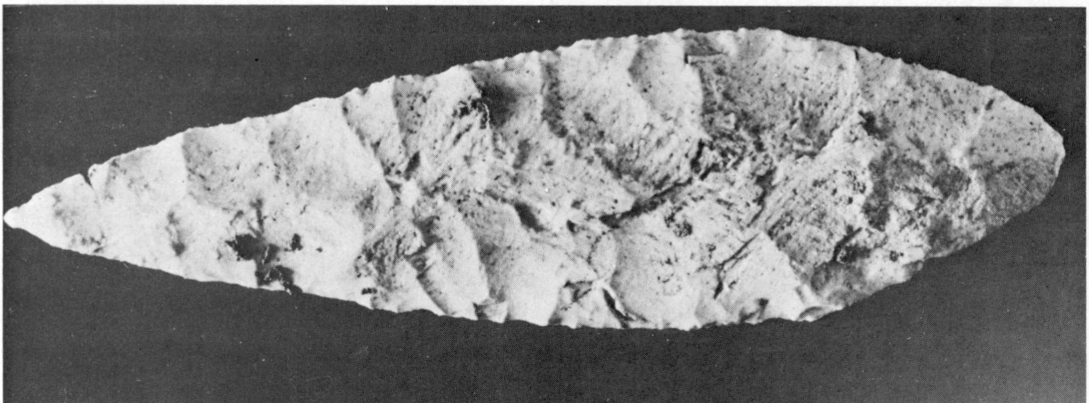

Figure 23.3 *SOLUTREAN LAUREL LEAF BLADE*
An Upper Paleolithic utilitarian art form from prehistoric France.

opment of media of musical expression there may be technological benefits. For example, there was probably some kind of feedback between the invention of the bow as a hunting weapon and the twanging of taut strings for musical effect. No one can say which came first, but cultures with bows and arrows invariably have musical strings. Wind instruments, blowguns, pistons, and bellows are all related. Similarly, metallurgy and chemistry relate to experimentation with the ornamental shape, texture, and color of ceramic and textile products. Thus, it is practical to encourage artisans and craftworkers to experiment with new techniques and materials. Small wonder that many cultures regard technical virtuosity as *mana*. Others regard it as the gift of the gods, as in the classical Greek idea of the Muses—goddesses of orators, dancers, and musicians whose asssistance was needed if an artistic performance was to be successful.

ART AND CULTURAL PATTERNING

Most artwork is deliberately fashioned in the image of preexisting forms. It is the task of the artist to replicate these forms by original combinations of culturally standardized elements—familiar and pleasing sounds, colors, lines, shapes, movements, and so on. Of course, there must always be some playful and creative ingredient, or it will not be art. On the other hand, if the transformation-representation is to communicate something—and it must communicate something if it is to be a successful work of art—the rules of the game cannot be the artist's own private invention. Complete originality, therefore, is not what most cultures strive for in their art.

It is the repetition of traditional and familiar forms that accounts for the major differences between the artistic products of different cultures. For example, Northwest Coast native American sculpture is well known for its consistent attention to animal and human motifs rendered in such a way as to indicate internal as well as external organs. These organs are symmetrically arranged within bounded geometrical forms (Fig. 23.4). Maori sculpture, on the other hand, requires that wooden surfaces be broken into bold but intricate filigrees and

(a)

(b)

Figure 23.4 *MASKS*
(a) Mask within mask. Wearer of this Kwakiutl mask uses strings to pull eagle apart revealing human face. *(b)* Mask within mask within mask. Whale conceals bird, which conceals human face, which conceals face of wearer. Another Kwakiutl masterpiece.

whorls (Fig. 23.5). Among the Mochica of ancient Peru, the sculptural medium was pottery, and the Mochica pots are famous for their representational realism in portraiture and in depictions of domestic and sexual behavior (Fig. 23.6). Hundreds of other easily recognizable and distinctive art styles of different cultures can be identified. The

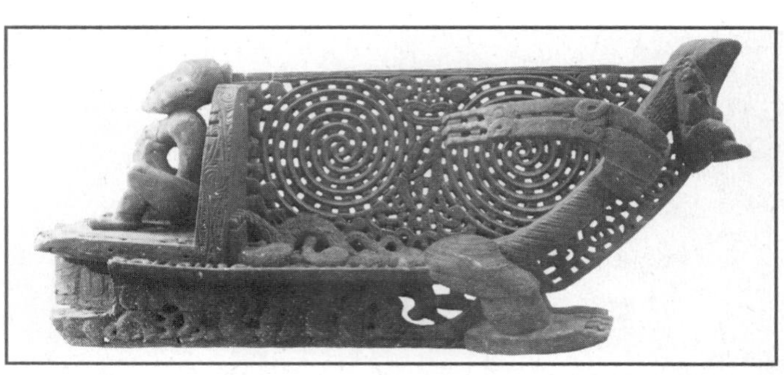

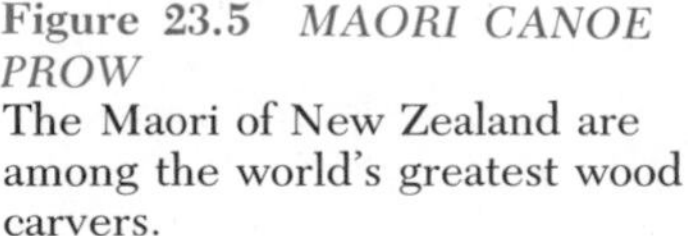

Figure 23.5 *MAORI CANOE PROW*
The Maori of New Zealand are among the world's greatest wood carvers.

Figure 23.6 *MOCHICA POT*
A Precolumbian portrait made by the Mochica of Northern Peru.

continuity of these styles is linked to the cultural rules of artistic play. It is enculturation for the appreciation of these forms that determines a people's likes and dislikes in art.

Establishment art in modern Western culture is unique in its emphasis upon formal originality. Western cultures regard it as natural that art must be interpreted and explained by experts in order to be understood and appreciated. Since the end of the nineteenth century, the greatest artists for Western art establishments are those who break with tradition, introduce new formal rules, and at least for a time render their work incomprehensible to a large number of people. Joined to this de-emphasis of tradition is the peculiar recent Western notion of artists as lonely people struggling in poverty against limitations set by the preexisting capability of their audience to appreciate and understand the true artistic genius.

Thus the creative, playful, and transformational aspects of modern art have gotten the upper hand over the formal and representational aspects (Fig. 23.7). Contemporary Euramerican artists consciously strive to be the originators of entirely new formal rules. They compete to invent new transformations to replace the traditional ones. Modern aesthetic standards hold that originality is more important than intelligibility. Indeed, a work of art that is too easily understood may be condemned. Many art critics more or less consciously take it for granted that novelty must result in a certain

Figure 23.7 *WHAT DOES IT MEAN?* Fur-covered cup, saucer, and spoon by Méret Oppenheim. (Cup 4⅜″ diameter; saucer 9¾″ diameter; spoon 8″ long.)

amount of obscurity. What accounts for this obsession with being original?

One important influence is the reaction to mass production. Mass production leads to a downgrading of technical virtuosity. It also leads to a downgrading of all artwork that closely resembles the objects or performances others have produced. Another factor to be considered is the involvement of the modern artist in a commercial market in which supply perennially exceeds demand. Part-time band- and village-level artists are concerned with being original only to the extent that it enhances the aesthetic enjoyment of their work. Their livelihood does not depend on obtaining an artistic identity and a personal following. Still another factor to be considered is the high rate of cultural change in modern societies. To some extent, the emphasis upon artistic originality merely reflects this rate of change. Finally, the alienating and isolating tendencies of modern mass society may also play a role. Much modern art reflects the loneliness, puzzlement, and anxiety of the creative individual in a depersonalized and hostile urban, industrial milieu.

ART AND RELIGION

The history and ethnography of art are inseparable from the history and ethnography of religion. As discussed in Chapter 8, art as an aspect of supernatural belief and ritual goes back at least 40,000 years on the walls and ceilings of deep caves throughout the European Paleolithic.

Art is intimately associated with all four organizational levels of religion. For example, at the individualistic level, magical songs are often included among the revelations granted the vision seekers of the Great Plains (p. 425). Even the preparation of trophy heads among the Jívaro must meet aesthetic standards (p. 417), and singing and chanting are widely used during shamanistic performances. There are many aesthetic components in the Tapirapé shaman's description (p. 427) of how he met the *munpi anka* forest spirits.

On the communal level, puberty rituals as among the Ndembu (p. 433) provide occasions for dancing and myth and storytelling. Body painting is also widely practiced in communal ceremonies, as among the Arunta. Singing, dancing, and the wearing of masks are common at both puberty and funeral rituals. Much artistic effort is expended in the preparation of religiously significant funeral equipment such as coffins and graveposts (Figs. 23.8 and 23.9). Many cultures include ceremonial artifacts like pottery and clubs, points, and other weapons among a deceased person's grave goods. Ancestors and gods are often depicated in statues and masks that are kept in men's houses or in shrines (Fig. 23.10). *Churingas* (p. 432), the Arunta's most sacred objects, are artfully incised with whorls and loops depicting the route followed by the ancestors during the dream time.

Finally, on the ecclesiastical level, art and

(a)

(b)

Figure 23.8 *BA KOTA FUNERARY FIGURES*
The Ba Kota of the Gabon Republic place the skeletal remains of dead chiefs in bark boxes or baskets surmounted by Mbulu-ngulu guardian figures of wood faced with brass or copper sheets or strips. Although each figure expresses the creative individuality of the artist, they each conform to the same stylistic pattern.

religion are fused in pyramids, monumental avenues, stone statuary, monolithic calendar carvings, temples, altars, priestly garments, and a nearly infinite variety of ritual ornaments and sacred paraphernalia.

It is clear that art, religion, and magic satisfy many similar psychological needs in human beings. They are media for expressing sentiments and emotions not easily expressed in ordinary life. They impart a sense of mastery over or communion with unpredictable events and mysterious unseen powers. They impose human meanings and values upon an indifferent world—a world that has no humanly intelligible meanings and

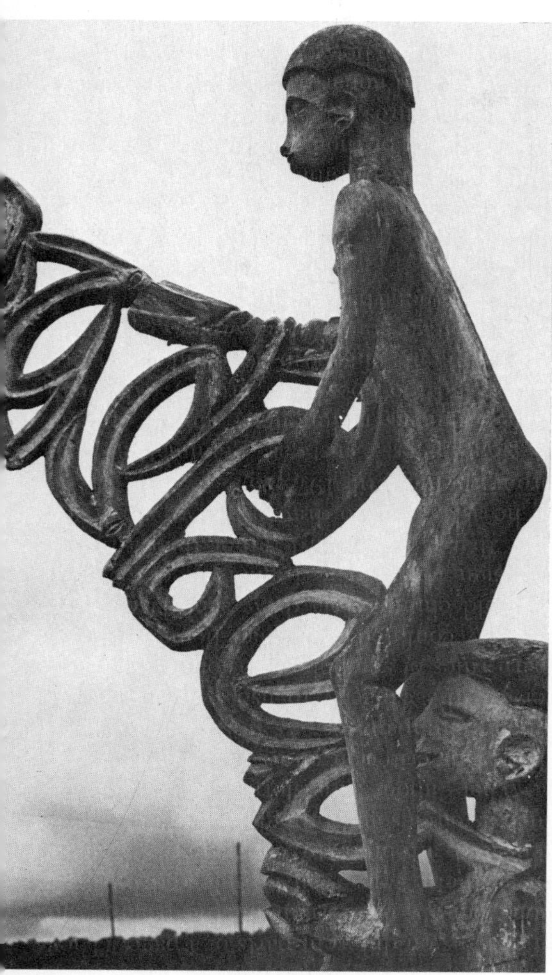

Figure 23.9 *ASMAT GRAVEPOST*
Around the world much talent has been lavished on commemorating the dead. But styles and media vary enormously. [Eugene Gordon]

Figure 23.10 *ART AND ARCHITECTURE*
Brightly painted faces on a men's house in the Sepik River basin, New Guinea.

values of its own. They seek to penetrate behind the façade of ordinary appearance into the true, cosmic significance of things. And they use illusions, dramatic tricks, and sleight of hand to get people to believe in them.

ART AND POLITICS

Art is also intimately related to politics. This is especially clear in the context of state-sponsored art. As we have seen, in stratified societies religion is a means of social control. The skills of the artist are harnessed by the ruling class to implant religious notions of obedience and to sanctify the status quo (Fig. 23.11). Contrary to the popular modern image of the artist as a free spirit disdainful of authority, most state-level art is politically conservative. Ecclesiastical art often interprets the world in conformity with prevailing myths and ideologies justifying inequities and exploitation. Art makes the gods visible as idols. Gazing upon massive

Figure 23.11 *GOLD DEATH MASK OF TUT* Another example of the interrelationship of art, religion, and politics.

stone blocks carved as if by superhuman hands, commoners comprehend the necessity for subservience. They are awed by the immense size of pyramids and fascinated and befuddled by processions, prayers, pomp, and the sacrifices of priests in dramatic settings—golden altars, colonnaded temples, great vaulted roofs, huge ramps and stairways, windows through which only the light from heaven passes (Fig. 23.12).

The church and state have been the greatest patrons of the arts in all but the last few hundred years of history. With the rise of capitalism, ecclesiastical and civil institutions in the West became more decentralized, and wealthy individuals to a considerable extent replaced church and state as the patrons of the arts. Individualized sponsorship promoted greater flexibility and freedom of expression. Politically neutral, secular, and even revolutionary and sacrilegious themes became common. The arts became established as individualistic, secular forms

Figure 23.12 *ART AND RELIGION* Notre Dame Cathedral, Paris. No one ever had to ask what it meant, but how it was built remains a mystery.

of expression and entertainment. To protect and preserve their new-found autonomy, the art establishment adopted the doctrine of "art for art's sake." But once they were free to express themselves as they saw fit, artists were no longer sure what they wanted to express. They devoted themselves more and more to idiosyncratic and obscure symbols organized into novel and unintelligible patterns, as noted earlier in this chapter. And the patrons of art, concerned less and less with communication, increasingly looked toward the acquisition and sponsorship of art as a prestigious commercial venture that yielded substantial profits, tax deductions, and a hedge against inflation. In contrast, art in the Communist countries has been returned to state sponsorship and is deliberately used as a means of convincing citizens that the postrevolutionary status quo is equitable and inevitable (Fig. 23.13). Thus it has come about that artists in both the East and West, and in the Third World, have found themselves embroiled in political controversy as well as in creative transformation-representations designed to satisfy our human craving for aesthetic pleasure. For every artist in the world today who places art before politics, there is at least one other who places politics before art.

THE EVOLUTION OF MUSIC AND DANCE

Some anthropologists hold that the influence of structural and infrastructural components upon art extends directly into the formal characteristics and aesthetic standards of different cultural styles. According to Alan Lomax (1968; Lomax and Arensberg 1977) and his associates, for example, certain broad characteristics of song, music, and dance are closely correlated with a culture's level of subsistence. Band and village peoples in general tend to have a different complex of music, song, and dance than chiefdoms and states. Dividing cultures into those that are "low" and those that are "high" on the scale of subsistence technology leads to the following correlations:

Musical Intervals. The less advanced subsistence systems employ musical scales in which notes are widely separated—that is, have intervals of one-third or more. Advanced subsistence systems employ scales that are marked by more and smaller intervals.

Repetition in Song Text. The less advanced subsistence cultures employ more repetition in their songs—fewer words over and over again.

Figure 23.13 *SOVIET REALISM*
Gavrül Gorelov, "Honored Worker of Art," won a Stalin Prize for this painting of a steel smelter brigade leader and his comrades. This is art for politic's sake.

Complexity and Type of Orchestra. Advanced subsistence is correlated with musical performances involving more performers and a greater variety of instruments. Less advanced subsistence systems use only one or two instruments.

Dance Styles. The advanced subsistence systems are correlated with dance styles in which fingers, wrists, arms, torso, legs, feet, toes—have distinctive movements to make or "parts to play." Also, the more advanced the subsistence system, the more the dance style tends to emphasize complex curving motions, as opposed to simple up and down or side-to-side steps like hopping or shuffling.

The influence of subsistence on art may be direct or indirect. Large, complex orchestration, for example, reflects the structural ability of a society to form large, coordinated groups. Dance styles, on the other hand, may simply express the characteristic movements employed in using such implements of production as digging sticks versus plows or complex machines. Some dances can be looked upon as training for work, warfare, or self-defense.

Lomax's correlations have been criticized on technical grounds relating to sampling and coding procedures (see Kaeppler 1978). Nonetheless, Lomax's attempt to measure and compare music and dance styles, and to relate them to social structure and subsistence, must be given careful consideration as a guide to future research.

THE COMPLEXITY OF PRIMITIVE ART: CAMPA RHETORIC

Anthropologists reject the ethnocentric notion that art among band and village societies is necessarily more simple or naive than art in modern industrial societies. Although, as we have just seen, many stylistic aspects of art have undergone an evolution from simple to more complex forms, other aspects may have been as complex among Stone Age hunter-gatherers as they are today. The case of Campa rhetoric illustrates this point.

Rhetoric is the art of persuasive public discourse and is closely related to the theatrical arts. As Gerald Weiss (1977b) has discovered, the preliterate Campa who live in eastern Peru near the headwaters of the Amazon River use most of the important rhetorical devices cultivated by the great philosophers and orators of ancient Greece and Rome. Their object in public discourse is not merely to inform, but to persuade and convince. "Campa narration is 'a separate time,' where a spell-binding relationship between narrator and audience is developed, with powerful rhetorical devices employed to create and enhance the quality of that relationship" (1977b:173).

Here are a few examples of these devices, as translated by Weiss from the Campa language, which belongs to the native American family of languages known as Arawak.

Rhetorical Questions. The speaker makes the point that the Campa are deficient in their worship of their sky god, the sun, by asking a question which he will answer. *Do we supplicate him, he here, he who lives in the sky, the sun? We do not know how to supplicate him.*

Iterations *(Effect by Repetition)*. The speaker imparts an emphatic, graphic, movielike quality to the point by repeating some key words. The enemy comes out of the lake: *And so they emerged in great numbers–he saw them emerge, emerge, emerge, emerge, emerge, emerge, emerge, emerge, emerge, all, all.*

Imagery and Metaphor. Death is alluded to in the phrase: *The earth will eat him.* The body is described as: *The clothing of the soul.*

Appeal to Evidence. To prove that the oil-bird was formerly human in shape: *Yes, he was formerly human—doesn't he have whiskers?*

Appeal to Authority. *They told me long ago, the elders, they who heard these words, long ago, so it was.*

Antithesis *(Effect by Contrast).* A hummingbird is about to raise the sky rope, which the other larger creatures have failed to do: *They are all big whereas I am small and chubby.*

In addition, the Campa orator uses a wide variety of gestures, exclamations, sudden calls for attention ("watch out, here it comes"); asides ("imagine it, then"; "careful that you don't believe, now"). Altogether, Weiss lists 19 formal rhetorical devices used by the Campa.

MYTH AND BINARY CONTRASTS

Anthropologists have found considerable evidence suggesting that certain kinds of formal structures recur in widely different traditions of oral and written literature, including myths and folktales. These structures are characterized by binary contrasts—that is, by two elements or themes that can be viewed as standing in diametric opposition to each other. Many examples of recurrent binary contrasts can be found in Western religion, literature, and mythology: good versus bad; up versus down; male versus female; cultural versus natural; young versus old; and so forth. According to French anthropologist Lévi-Strauss, the founder of the research strategy known as structuralism (see p. 521), the reason these binary contrasts recur so often is that the human brain is "wired" in such a way as to make binary contrasts especially appealing or "good to think." From the structuralist point of view, the main task of the anthropological study of literature, mythology, and folklore is to identify the common, unconscious binary contrasts that lie beneath the surface of human thought and to show how these binary contrasts undergo unconscious transformation-representations.

Consider the familiar tale of Cinderella: A mother has two daughters and one stepdaughter. The two daughters are older; the stepdaughter is younger; the older ones are ugly and mean while Cinderella is beautiful and kind. The older sisters are aggressive; Cinderella is passive. Through a kind fairy godmother, as opposed to her mean stepmother, Cinderella goes to the ball, dances with the prince, and loses her magical shoe. Her sisters have big feet, she has little feet. Cinderella wins the prince. The unconscious binary oppositions in the deep structure of this story might include:

passive	aggressive
younger	older
small	large
good	evil
beautiful	ugly
culture	nature
fairy godmother	stepmother

Structuralists contend that the enjoyment people derive from such tales and their durability across space and time derive mainly from the unconscious oppositions and their familiar yet surprising representations.

Structuralist analyses can be extended from the realm of myth and ritual to the entire fabric of social life. According to David Hicks, who studied the Tetum of Timor in Indonesia, Tetum culture as a whole is structured by the following "binary matrix":

human beings	ghosts
secular	sacred
secular world	sacred world
above	below
men	women
right	left
superior	inferior
wife-givers	wife-takers
aristocrats	commoners
secular authority	sacred authority
elder brother	younger brother

Any single binary contrast can symbolize any other (Hicks 1976:107); that is, in contrasting men with women, one could just as readily be contrasting elder brothers with younger brothers (among the Tetum, younger brothers must serve elder brothers just as women must serve men). The secular, above-ground, masculine world contrasts with the ghostly, sacred, below-ground, feminine world. Thus Tetum mythology recounts how the first humans emerged from vaginalike holes in the ground and how after leading a secular life on the surface of the earth, humans return to the sacred world below and to the ghostly ancestors. Tetum house architecture also participates in the same set of symbolic oppositions (Fig. 23.14). The house has two entrances; the back entrance for the women leads to the "womb" or women's part of the house, which contains the hearth and a sacred house post. The front entrance is for the men and leads to the male living quarters.

Structuralist analyses of literature, art, myths, rituals, and religion abound in anthropology. However, they are surrounded by considerable controversy, primarily because it is not clear whether the binary matrices discerned by the anthropologists really exist as unconscious realities in the minds of the people being studied. It is always possible to reduce complex and subtle symbols to less complex symbols and then finally to emerge with such flat oppositions as culture versus nature or male versus female (Harris 1979b). But the human brain may be "wired" to move away from simple oppositions as well as toward them.

SUMMARY

Creative play, formal structure, aesthetic feelings, and symbolic transformations are the essential ingredients in art. Although the capacity for art is foreshadowed in the behavior of nonhuman primates, only *Homo sapiens* is capable of art involving "transformation-representations." The distinctive human capacity for art is thus closely related to the distinctive human capacity for symbolic transformation that underlies the semantic universality of human language.

Western emic definitions of art depend on the existence of art authorities and critics who place many examples of play, structured aesthetic, and symbolic transformation into the category of nonart. The distinction between artisans, crafts and art is part of this tradition. Anthropologists regard skilled artisans and craftspersons as artists.

Art has adaptive functions in relation to creative changes in other sectors of social life. Art and technology influence each other, as in the case of instruments of music and the hunt, or in the search for new shapes, colors, textures, and materials in ceramics and textiles.

Figure 23.14 *TETUM HOUSE*
Women's entrance around back on right. Men's entrance through door, left of center.

Despite the emphasis upon creative innovation, most cultures have art traditions or styles that maintain formal continuity through time. This makes it possible to identify the styles of cultures such as the Northwest Coast, Maori, or Mochica. The continuity and integrity of such styles provide the basic context for a people's understanding of and liking for the artist's creative transformations. Establishment art in modern Western culture is unique in emphasizing structural or formal creativity as well as creative transformations. This results in the isolation of the artist. Lack of communication and discontinuity of style may be caused by factors such as the reaction to mass production, commercial art markets, a rapid rate of cultural change, and the depersonalized milieu of urban industrial life.

Art and religion are closely related. This can be seen in the Upper Paleolithic cave paintings, songs of the vision quest, preparation of shrunken heads, singing and chanting in shamanistic performances, Tapirapé shamanistic myths, Ndembu circumcision, storytelling, singing and dancing, Arunta *churingas*, and many other aspects of individual, shamanistic, communal, and ecclesiastical cults. Art and religion satisfy many similar psychological needs, and it is often difficult to tell them apart.

Art and politics are also closely related. This is clear in state-sponsored ecclesiastical art, much of which functions to keep people in awe of their rulers. It is only in recent times, with the rise of decentralized capitalist states, that art has enjoyed any significant degree of freedom from direct political control. Even today, however, many artists in both capitalist and socialist societies regard art as an important medium of political expression, both conservative and revolutionary.

To the extent that bands, villages, chiefdoms, and states represent evolutionary levels, and to the extent that art is functionally related to technology, economy, politics, religion, and other aspects of the universal cultural pattern, it is clear that there has been an evolution of the content of art. There is evidence that styles of song, music, and dance—including musical intervals, repetition in song texts, complexity and type of orchestra, body part involvement, and amount of curvilinear motion—have also undergone evolutionary changes. This finding, however, remains highly controversial. The example of Campa rhetoric shows that extreme caution must be exercised in judging the complexity and sophistication of preliterate art styles.

A currently popular mode of anthropological analysis—structuralism—attempts to interpret the surface content of myths, rituals, and other expressive performances in terms of a series of unconscious universal binary oppositions. Common binary oppositions can be found in the Cinderella myth and in Tetum cosmology, ritual, and house architecture. This too, however, remains a controversial approach.

24 PERSONALITY AND SEX

In this chapter we examine the ways in which culture influences personality and mental illness. We examine the central concepts of Freudian theories of personality, and then go on to more recent theories that attempt to account for the variations and changes in male and female personality types. We examine evidence for a pervasive male-supremacist complex, and relate this complex to warfare. We survey mental illnesses in cross-cultural perspective and discuss varieties of human sexual experience.

CULTURE AND PERSONALITY

Culture refers to the patterned ways in which the members of a population think, feel, and behave. Personality also refers to patterned ways of thinking, feeling, and behaving, but the focus is on the individual. *Personality*, as defined by Victor Barnouw (1973:10), "is a more or less enduring organization of forces within the individual associated with a complex of fairly consistent attitudes, values, and modes of perception which account, in part, for the individual's consistency of behavior." More simply, "personality is the tendency to behave in certain ways regardless of the specific setting" (Whiting and Whiting 1978:57).

The concepts employed in describing the thinking, feeling, and behavior of personality types are different from those employed in describing infrastructure, structure, and superstructure. In describing personalities, psychologists use concepts such as aggressive, passive, anxious, obsessive, hysterical, manic, depressed, introverted, extroverted, paranoid, authoritarian, schizoid, masculine, feminine, infantile, repressed, dependent, and so forth. Here is a part of a more extensive list of terms appropriate for the study of personality that appeared in a study of culture and personality in a Mexican village (Fromm and Maccoby 1970:79).

practical	anxious
economical	orderly
steadfast, tenacious	methodical
composed under stress	loyal
careful	unimaginative
reserved	stingy
patient	stubborn
cautious	indolent
imperturbable	inert
suspicious	pedantic
cold	obsessive
lethargic	possessive

If these concepts are employed to describe an entire population, the result will not add up to a description of modes of production and reproduction, domestic and political economy, systems of war and peace, or magico-religious rites and institutions. Rather they will add up to a description of that population's personality type.

CHILDHOOD TRAINING AND PERSONALITY

Our personalities are shaped by the interaction between our genetically determined predispositions and the totality of our experiences as infants and children. While everyone's experiences are unique in some respects (just as no two people except identical twins have the same genome), parents who share the same cultural tradition tend to provide similar experiences for their children during the process of enculturation. For example, parents in a particular culture tend to follow similar *childhood training practices* involving the feeding, cleaning, and handling of infants and children. These childhood training practices vary widely from one society to another. In many cultures, for example, infants are constrained by swaddling bandages or cradle boards that immobilize their limbs. Elsewhere, freedom of movement is encouraged. Similarly, nursing may be on demand at the first cry of hunger or at regular intervals at the convenience of the mother. Nursing at the mother's breast may last for a few months or several years, or may not take place at all. Supplementary foods may be taken in the first few weeks; they may be stuffed into the baby's mouth, prechewed by the mother, played with by the baby, or omitted entirely.

Weaning may take place abruptly, as where the mother's nipples are painted with bitter substances; and it may or may not be associated with the birth of another child. In some cultures infants are kept next to their mother's skin and carried wherever the mother goes (Fig. 24.1); elsewhere, they may be left behind in the care of relatives. In some cultures infants are fondled, hugged, kissed, and fussed over by large groups of adoring children and adults. In others they are kept relatively isolated and touched infrequently.

Toilet training may begin as early as 6 weeks or as late as 24 months. The mode of training may involve many different techniques, some based on intense forms of punishment, shame, and ridicule, and others involving suggestion, emulation, and no punishment.

(a)

(b)

Figure 24.1 *CARE OF CHILDREN* Cultures vary greatly in the amount of body contact between mother and infant. *(a)* Swazi mother and child. *(b)* Arunta mother and child; mother has all-purpose carrying dish on head and digging stick in hand.

Treatment of infant sexuality also varies widely. In many cultures mothers or fathers stroke their babies' genitals to soothe them and stop them from crying; elsewhere, even the baby is prevented from touching its own genitals and masturbation is severely punished.

Another series of variables relevant to personality formation consists of later childhood and adolescent experiences: numbers of siblings; their relationships and mutual responsibilities (Fig. 24.2); patterns of play; opportunities to observe adult intercourse; opportunities to engage in homosexual or heterosexual experimentation; incest restrictions; and type of threat and punishment used against culturally prohibited sexual practices (Weisner and Gilmore 1977).

Figure 24.2 *JAVANESE GIRL AND BROTHER*
One way to free mother for work in the fields is to turn over the care of infants to 7-year-old sister.

Figure 24.3 depicts one theory of how these childhood training practices may be related to personality and to other aspects of culture. The basic variables influencing child-rearing patterns are influenced by the nature of the culture's domestic, social, political, and economic institutions. These in turn are influenced by the ecosystem. Child-rearing practices are also constrained by the necessity of satisfying certain biologically determined universal needs, drives, and capacities that all human infants share (e.g., oral, anal, and genital urges). The interaction between the child-rearing practices and these biological needs, drives, and capacities molds personality; personality, in turn, expresses itself in *secondary* institutions; that is, roughly what we have been calling "superstructure" in this book.

MALE INITIATION AND CHILDHOOD TRAINING

John Whiting (1969) and his associates have developed an interesting theory which relates childhood training experiences to the formation of adult personality. Whiting has shown that statistical correlations exist between (1) protein scarcities, (2) nursing of children for 1 year or more, (3) prohibition on sex relations between husband and wife for 1 year or more after the birth of their child, (4) polygyny, (5) domestic sleeping arrangements in which mother and child sleep together and father sleeps elsewhere, (6) child training by women, (7) patrilocality, and (8) severe male initiation rites.

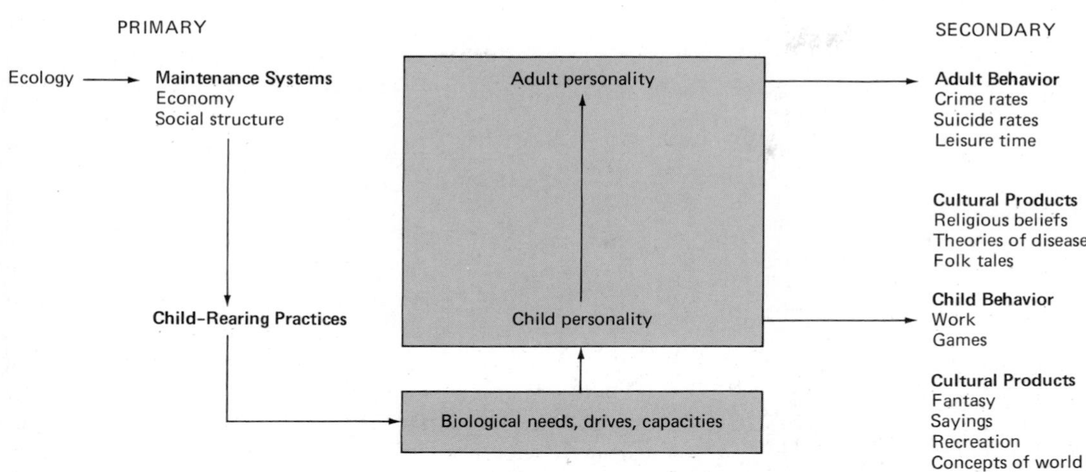

Figure 24.3 *THE RELATIONSHIP OF BASIC PERSONALITY TO ECOLOGY, CHILD-REARING PRACTICES, AND SECONDARY AND PROJECTIVE INSTITUTIONS*
After LeVine 1973, p. 57.

Following our model, the following chain develops: Low protein availability and the risk of Kwashiorkor [a protein deficiency disease] were correlated with an extended postpartum sex taboo to allow the mother time to nurse the infant through the critical stage before becoming pregnant again. The postpartum sex taboo was significantly correlated with the institution of polygyny, providing alternate sexual outlets for the male. Polygyny, in turn, is associated with mother-child households, child training by women, resultant cross-sex identity, and where patrilocality is also present, with initiation rites to resolve the conflict and properly inculcate male identity (Harrington and Whiting 1972:491).

"Cross-sex identity" refers to the psychodynamic process by which boys who are reared exclusively by their mothers and older women identify themselves with their mothers and other women. Where patrilocality is present, reasons Whiting, functional consistency demands that adult males must make a strong identification with their fathers and other males. Hence there is a conflict between what the male must do and think as an adult and what he is trained to do and think as an infant. Severe male initiation ceremonies involving circumcision or other forms of mutilation, prolonged seclusion, beatings, and trials of courage and stamina are thus required to resolve this conflict by breaking the prepubescent identity. The functional-causal links in Whiting's model are diagramed in Figure 24.4.

PATTERNS AND THEMES

Many other proposals have been made concerning how to treat the relationship between personality and culture. One popular option acknowledges the fact that culture and personality are two different ways of looking at the propensity to think, feel, and behave characteristic of a given population and uses psychological terms to characterize both personality and the cultural system. For example, Ruth Benedict in her famous book *Patterns of Culture* (1934) characterized the institution of the Kwakiutl potlatch (see Ch. 12) as a "megalomaniacal" performance—behavior dominated by fantasies of wealth and power. She saw potlatch as part of a *Dionysian* pattern that was characteris-

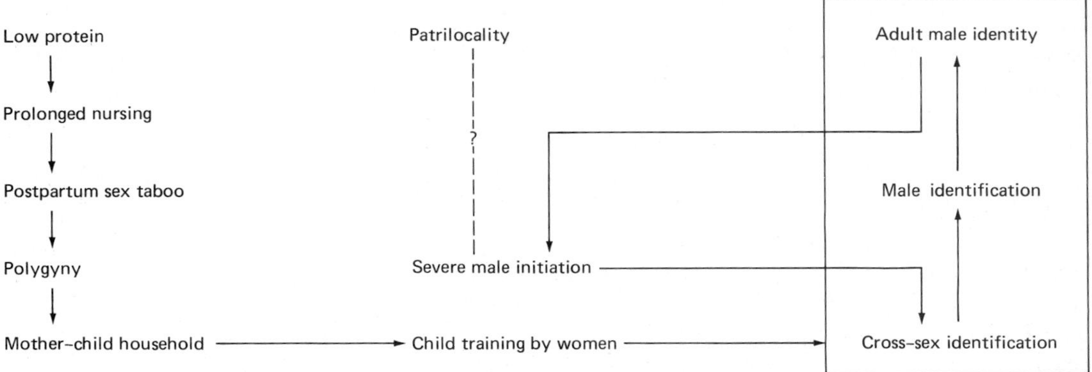

Figure 24.4 *PSYCHODYNAMIC MODEL OF RELATIONSHIP BETWEEN LOW-PROTEIN DIET AND SEVERE MALE INITIATION*

tic of all the institutions of Kwakiutl culture. By Dionysian she meant the desire to achieve emotional excess, as in drunkenness or frenzy. Other cultures, such as that of the Pueblo Indians, she saw as *Apollonian*—given to moderation and the "middle of the road" in all things. Benedict's *patterns* were psychological elements reputedly found throughout a culture, "comparable to the chromosomes found in most of the cells of a body" (Wallace 1970:149). Most anthropologists have rejected such attempts to use one or two psychological terms to describe whole cultures. Even the most simple hunter-gatherer cultures have too many different kinds of personalities to be summed up in such a manner.

Rather than attempt to sum up whole cultures under one or two psychological concepts, some anthropologists point to dominant themes or values which express the essential or main thought and feeling of a particular culture. The "image of limited good" is one such theme (p. 370). Themes and values are readily translatable into personality traits. For example, the image of limited good reputedly produces personalities that are jealous, suspicious, secretive, and fearful. The culture of poverty also has its psychological components—improvidence, lack of future-time orientation, sexual promiscuity. An important theme in Hindu India is the "sacredness of life," and an important theme in the United States is "keeping up with the Joneses." The problem with attempts to portray cultures in terms of a few dominant values and attitudes is that contradictory values and attitudes can usually be identified in the same cultures and even in the same individuals. Thus, although Hindu farmers believe in the sacredness of life (Opler 1968), they also believe in the necessity of having more bullocks than cows (see p. 124); and although many people in the United States believe in trying to keep up with the Joneses, there are others who believe that conspicuous consumption is foolish and sinful.

BASIC PERSONALITY AND NATIONAL CHARACTER

A somewhat different approach to culture and personality postulates that every culture produces a basic or deep personality structure that can be found in virtually every individual member of the culture. When the populations involved are organized into a state, the basic personality is often called *national character*. The notion of basic personality structure has always enjoyed considerable popularity among travelers to foreign lands as well as among scholars. One often hears it said that the English are "reserved," the Brazilians "carefree," the French "sexy," the Italians "uninhibited," the Japanese "orderly," the Americans "outgoing," and so forth. Gerardus Mercator, the father of mapmaking, wrote the following descriptions of European basic personalities in the sixteenth century (see if you can guess Mercator's nationality):

Franks: Simple, blockish, furious.
Bavarians: Sumptuous, gluttons, brazen-faced.
Swedes: Light, babblers, boasters.
Saxons: Dissemblers, double-hearted, opinionative.
Spaniards: Disdainful, cautious, greedy.
Belgians: Good horsemen, tender, docile, delicate.

Modern scholarly versions of basic personality structure make use of more sophisticated psychological concepts, most of which owe something to the influence of Sigmund Freud and psychoanalysis.

The concept of basic personality type must not be permitted to obscure the fact that there is a great range of personalities in every society and that the more populous, complex, and stratified the society, the greater the variability. In every society many individuals have personalities that deviate widely from the *statistical mode* (most frequent type), and the range of individual personalities produces wide overlaps among different cultures. For example, it would certainly be correct to characterize the basic type of Plains native American male personality as an aggressive, independent, and fearless person. Yet it is known from the institution called *berdache* (Fig. 24.5), that there were always some young men who found themselves temperamentally unsuited to the male role. Donning female dress and dedicating themselves to female domestic and sexual specialties, these men combined both male and female attributes and were accepted as a third sex (Callender and Kochems 1983).

Figure 24.5 *BERDACHE*
Finds-Them-And-Kills-Them, last of the Crow male homosexual transvestites.

Very little is actually known about the amount of personality variance in different societies. It is certain, however, that complex state-level populations consisting of millions of people contain an enormous variety of personality types (Fig. 24.6). Japan, for example, appears superficially to possess a homogeneous national character which leads individuals to subordinate themselves to group consensus and to refrain from challenging authority. This is a misleading stereotype, since many Japanese are highly individualistic and outspoken in their opposition to traditional norms (Sugimoto and Mouer 1983). The more complex the criteria used to define the basic personality, the more likely that the modal type of personality will be found in relatively few individuals. Anthony Wallace (1952), using 21 dimensions to define basic personality among the Iroquois, found that the modal type was shared by only 37 percent of the total sample.

OEDIPUS AND PERSONALITY

According to Sigmund Freud, a traumatic, universal, and unavoidable conflict takes place during the years preceding puberty. This is called the *Oedipus conflict,* and it is

Figure 24.6 *PERSONALITY IN A COMPLEX SOCIETY*
As this demonstration against a visit by President Reagan indicates, all Japanese can scarcely be described as having deferential and conformist personalities.

caused by biologically determined sexual strivings and jealousies within the nuclear family. The early sexual feelings of a young boy are directed first toward his mother. But he soon discovers that mother is the sexual object of his father, and he finds himself in competition with his father for sexual mastery of the same woman. The father, while providing protection, also provides stern discipline (Fig. 24.7). He suppresses his son's attempt to express sexual love for his mother. The son is frustrated and fantasizes that he is strong enough to kill his father. This seething hostility and jealousy arouse fear and guilt in the young boy: fear, because the father in fact or in fancy threatens to cut off his penis and testicles; and guilt, because the father is not only hated but also loved. To resolve this conflict successfully, the young boy must redirect his sexuality toward females other then his mother and learn how to overcome his fear and how to express his hostility in constructive ways.

For the young girl, Freud envisioned a parallel but fundamentally different trauma. A girl's sexuality is also initially directed toward her mother, but at the phallic stage the little girl makes a fateful discovery: She lacks a penis. She blames her mother for this and redirects her sexual desires away from her mother and toward her father.

Why this takes place depends upon the girl's reaction of disappointment when she discovers that a boy possesses a protruding sex organ, the penis, while she has only a cavity. Several important consequences follow from this traumatic discovery. In the first place she holds her mother responsible for her castrated conditon. . . .In the second place, she transfers her love to her father because he has the valued organ which she aspires to share with him. However, her love for

Figure 24.7 *FREUD'S MILIEU* A turn-of-the-century middle-class father with his two sons. Stern but protective.

> the father and for other men as well is mixed with a feeling of envy because they possess something she lacks. Penis envy is the female counterpart of castration anxiety in the boy (Hall and Lindzey 1967:18).

Girls are supposed to suffer the lifelong trauma of penis envy as a result of their discovery that they are anatomically "incomplete." In this fashion, Freud sought to ground the psychological supremacy of males in the unalterable facts of anatomy—hence the Freudian aphorism: "Anatomy is destiny." Freud thought that not having a penis "debases" women and dooms them to a passive and subordinate role—the role of the "second sex." Freud believed the best hope a woman has of overcoming her penis envy is to accept a passive, secondary role in life, develop her charm and sexual attractiveness, marry, and have male babies.

> Her happiness is great if later on this wish for a baby finds fulfillment in reality, and quite especially so if the baby is a little boy who brings the longed-for penis with him. (Freud, in Millet 1970:185).

Needless to say, this theory remains highly controversial.

Is the Oedipus Complex Universal?

Starting with Bronislaw Malinowski's (1927) research on the avunculocal Trobriand family (see Ch. 14), anthropologists have criticized the concept of the Oedipus complex on the grounds that it imposes on the rest of the world a view of personality development appropriate to nineteenth-century middle-class Vienna, where Freud practiced and developed his theories. According to Malinowski, Trobriand males did not develop the same kind of complex because it was their mother's brother and not their father who exercised authority over them. Thus, Trobriand males grew up without the hate-love feelings toward their father which Freud postulated as being universal. Melford Spiro (1982) has attempted to rescue the Freudian position by separating the hate-love engendered by sexual jealousy from the hate-love engendered by authority. The Trobriand male lives with his father and mother until he is an adolescent. While his father is an easy-going and nonauthoritarian figure, there is still plenty of opportunity for father and son to develop feelings of sexual rivalry over the mother and wife. Spiro concludes, therefore, that Malinowski did not prove that the Trobrianders were without any basis for developing the Oedipus complex. It remains true, however, that the intensity and importance of the Oedipus complex must vary in relationship to the amount and quality of the control which fathers exercise over their sons, and such control varies in turn with the nature of the family one grows up in.

CULTURE AND MENTAL ILLNESS

Anthropologists do not agree on the role which cultural differences play in the incidence and nature of mental illness. Recent medical research has shown that there are probably important genetic and chemical-neurological bases for such classic mental disorders as schizophrenia and manic-depressive psychosis. This accords with the evidence that the rates of those diseases among groups as diverse as Swedes, Eskimos, the Yoruba of West Africa, and modern Canadians do not show marked differences (Murphy 1976). However, there is no doubt that, while broad symptoms of the same mental diseases can be found cross-culturally, there is considerable variation in the specific symptoms found in different cultures. For example, a comparison of schizophrenic patients of Irish and Italian descent in a New York hospital revealed that substantially different sets of symptoms were associated with each group. The Irish patients tended to be obsessed with sexual guilt and to be much more withdrawn and quiet than the Italian patients, while the Italian patients were sexually aggressive and far more prone to violent fits and tantrums (Opler 1959). Just as Crow Indians have a particular visionary experience based on their cultural expectations (see p. 426), so too the specific content of psychotic hallucinations varies from culture to culture.

Evidence for more powerful effects of culture on mental illness can be found in *culture-specific psychoses*—disorders that have a distinctive set of symptoms limited to only one or a few cultures. One of the best-known of these culture-specific psychoses is called Arctic hysteria, or *pibloktoq* (Fig. 24.8). Unlike classic psychoses, pibloktoq strikes suddenly. Its victims leap up, tear off their clothes, move their limbs convulsively, and roll about naked in the snow and ice. These outbursts can be compared to a severe case of "cabin fever." Cooped up in their small, crowded dwellings for long periods during which they are unable to vent their feelings of hostility, pibloktoq victims may become hysterical as a means of dealing with their pent-up frustrations. The causes of this disorder, however, are far from certain. A second explanation is that pibloktoq results from a low level of calcium in the bloodstream. Arctic diets can be poor in calcium. In addition, the long, sunless winters inhibit the synthesis of vitamin D in the skin (see p. 109)—and vitamin D is important for the uptake of calcium into the bloodstream. Convulsions are a symptom of acute calcium deficiency (Wallace 1961; Foulks 1972). A third explanation is that pibloktoq is a form of epilepsy to which certain Arctic populations are genetically predisposed. These three explanations are not necessarily mutually exclusive. Pibloktoq, like many other mental disorders, is probably a consequence of the interaction between cultural, biochemical, and genetic variables.

Windigo "Psychosis"

Among the hunter-gatherer northern Ojibwa and Cree of the Canadian subarctic forest, there is a widespread belief that humans

(a)

(b)

Figure 24.8 *ARCTIC HYSTERIA*
The victim is an Eskimo woman from Greenland.

can become possessed by the spirit of Windigo, a cannibal monster whose heart is made out of ice. This belief has given rise to the hypothesis that the Cree and Ojibwa are subject to a culture-specific malady called *Windigo psychosis*. Those who are possessed by Windigo are said to experience an overwhelming desire to kill and eat their campmates. Living in a harsh environment, the Cree and Ojibwa often found themselves snowbound and close to starvation in their isolated winter camps. The likelihood of someone becoming a Windigo is said to have been greatest under such conditions. Various reports verify the fact that famished campmates did sometimes eat the bodies of their deceased companions in order to keep themselves alive. (Similar accounts of "crisis cannibalism" have been reported from many parts of the world, most recently from a soccer team whose plane crashed in the Andes Mountains.) Once having experienced human flesh, human Windigos are said to crave more. They lose their taste for ordinary food, their hearts feel like a lump of ice, and the people around them no longer look like people but like deer, or moose, or other game animals. Unless they are killed first, they will kill and devour their companions.

As Lou Marano (1982) has shown, there are many authenticated cases of the killing of people said to be Windigos by their alarmed campmates. Recurrently, Windigo killers cite evidence which justifies their homicides: the victims looked at them strangely, tossed about and mumbled in their sleep, had saliva dripping from their mouths, or tried to attack and bite their companions. In one instance, the alleged Windigo even seemed to hover off the ground and had to be pulled down by his attackers. Recurrently, the alleged Windigos themselves are said to have asked that they be killed lest they eat their campmates one by one. What is lacking in all of these accounts, however, is any hard data showing that the alleged Windigos thought and acted in the manner described by their executioners. Without such data, the existence of a genuine Windigo psychosis remains in doubt and a much simpler explanation can be offered for the belief in Windigo possession. Under conditions of extreme hunger and stress, the northern Ojibwa and Cree accused certain troublesome campmates of being Windigos as a justification for getting rid of them, thereby increasing the chances of survival for the rest of the camp. Thus, the typical executed Windigo was a sickly individual delirious with a high fever, or someone who was too ill to walk, or a senile old man or woman, or a stranger from another ethnic group. In Marano's words, the Windigo beliefs were not evidence of a psychosis but of a system of "triage homicide" (i.e., letting some die in order that others might live) in which the fear of being eaten was used to overcome the fear of breaking the taboo on killing a campmate:

> Upon close scrutiny the Windigo psychosis discloses itself not as a culturally isolated anthropophagic (i.e., cannibal) obsession, but instead as a rather predictable—though culturally conditioned—variant of triage homicide and witch hunting typical of societies under stress. In this process, as in all witch hunts, the victims of the aggression are socially redefined as the aggressors. Here the specific form of the redefinition was determined by the constant threat of starvation, a situation in which cannibalism has proved to be a tempting recourse for persons of all cultures throughout history. By attributing society's most salient fear to the scapegoat, the group was able to project its modal anxiety onto the individual, thus generating a rationale for homicide with which everyone could identify (Marano 1982:385).

CULTURAL DEFINITIONS OF MALE AND FEMALE

Within any given society, the most obvious and pervasive example of personality differences is the difference between men and women. In recent years, an intense debate has developed concerning the extent to which certain recurrent personality traits associated, respectively, with males and females express human nature or the effects of cultural conditioning.

As discussed above, followers of Sigmund Freud hold that the anatomical characteristics and reproductive roles of males and females predestine men and women to have fundamentally different personalities: men to be more "masculine" (active, aggressive, and violent) and women to be more "feminine" (passive, meek, and peaceful).

Regardless of whether one accepts some form of Oedipus complex as being universal, ethnographic research indicates that Freud's Viennese definition of ideal male and female temperaments is not universal. Margaret Mead's (1950) study of three New Guinea tribes—the Arapesh, Mundugumor, and Tchambuli—is the classic anthropological work on the spectrum of cultural definitions of ideal masculine and feminine personalities. Mead discovered that among the Arapesh both men and women are expected to behave in a mild, sympathetic, and cooperative manner, reminiscent of what we expect from an ideal mother. Among the Mundugumor, men and women are expected to be equally fierce and aggressive, and both sexes satisfied Mead's criteria for being masculine. Among the Tchambuli, the women shave their heads, are prone to hearty laughter, show comradely solidarity, and are aggressively efficient as food providers. Tchambuli men, on the other hand, are preoccupied with art, spend a great deal of time on their hairdos, and are always gossiping about the opposite sex. Although Mead's interpretations have been challenged as too subjective, there is no doubt that marked contrasts in sex roles do exist in different cultures. In few parts of the world outside nineteenth-century Vienna can one find the precise configuration that Freud believed to be a universal ideal. For example, Mervyn Meggitt (1964) has proposed a classification of New Guinea highland cultures into two groups on the basis of the extent to which they act like "prudes" or "lechers."

Among the Mae Enga, who are Meggitt's archetypal "prudes," men and women sleep apart. A man never enters the sleeping room at the rear of his wife's hut, and a woman never enters the men's house. Contact with menstrual blood can cause sickness and death for a Mae Enga man. Mae Enga men believe that intercourse is debilitating, and after intercourse they undergo purification by sitting in a smoky hut to protect themselves. Mae Enga bachelors swear sexual abstinence until they are married and feel uneasy and anxious if sex is discussed, especially if women are present. In contrast, the Kuma men, who are Meggitt's "lechers," share sleeping quarters, have no fear of female pollution, do not practice purification or initiation rites, and gain prestige through boasting of their conquests. Kuma girls attend courting parties at which they select sexual partners from among married and unmarried males. Intercourse is discussed openly by both sexes.

Lorraine Sexton (1973) has suggested that these differences may be associated with the high population pressure being experienced by the Mae Enga and the relatively low population density of the Kuma, extreme prudery being a mechanism that cuts back on the frequency of intercourse and thus limits fertility.

A MALE-SUPREMACIST COMPLEX?

Despite these deviations from the narrow definitions of masculine and feminine in Western society, there remains considerable evidence that males tend in the overwhelming majority of societies to be more aggressive and violent than females (Fig. 24.9). Moreover, although the Oedipus complex as Freud envisioned it is not universal, sexually charged hostility between older-generation males and their sons or nephews does occur very widely (see Barnouw 1973; Foster 1972; A. Parsons 1967; Roheim 1950).

(a)

Figure 24.9 *AGGRESSIVE MALE GAMES*
There is evidence of a close correlation between warfare and aggressive male sports: Afghan game *(a)* requires daring feats of horsemanship; the sporting life in England—rugby *(b)*; boxing, United States *(c)*; mock combat in Indonesia *(d)*; the gentle art of football, United States *(e)*.

(b)

(c)

(d)

A great variety of evidence suggests that the relatively more aggressive masculine male personality is associated with a pervasive complex that accords males a more dominant role than females in many spheres of social life. The clearest manifestation of this complex is to be found in the sphere of political economy. From our previous discussion (Ch. 15) of the evolution of political organization, it is clear that males have always preempted the major centers of public power and control. Headmen rather than headwomen dominate both egalitarian and stratified forms of trade and redistribution. The Semai and Mehinacu headmen; the Solomon Island *mumis*, and the New Guinea big men; the Nuer leopard skin chief; the Kwakiutl, Trobriand, and Tikopian chiefs; the Bunyoro Mukama; the Inca, the pharaohs, and the emperors of China and Japan all show the same male preeminence. If queens reign in Europe or Africa, it is always as temporary holders of power that belongs to the males of the lineage. Nothing more dramatically exposes the political subordination of women than the fact that among the members of the United Nations, only two effective heads of state—Margaret Thatcher and Vigdis Finnbogadottir (Iceland)—are women. Of course, this body of evidence does not justify the conclusion that women are powerless or that they never exert significant political authority. Moreover, it is clear that extremes of male dominance are incompatible with the bilateral organi-

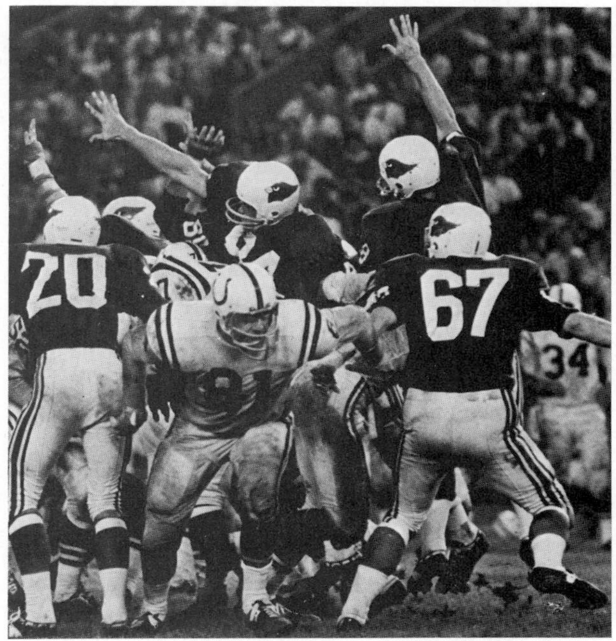

(e)

zation of egalitarian hunter-gatherer bands (Leacock 1978, 1981).

It was formerly believed that political control by women, or *matriarchy* (the opposite of patriarchy or political control by men), occurred as a regular stage in the evolution of social organization. Today virtually all anthropologists concur in rejecting the existence of any authentically matriarchal society. One exception is Ruby Rohrlich-Leavitt (1977:57), who contends that in Minoan Crete "women participated at least equally with men in political decision making, while in religion and social life they were supreme." Rohrlich-Leavitt's contention, however, is based on inferences from archaeological data that can be given contradictory interpretations. There is no doubt that Minoan Crete was matrilineal and that women enjoyed a relatively high status. However, the basis of Crete's economy was maritime trade and it was men, not women, who dominated this activity. Rohrlich-Leavitt contends that the Cretan matriarchy was made possible by the absence of warfare and a male military complex. However, it seems likely that military activities were focused on naval encounters that have left little archaeologically retrievable evidence. There is no reason, therefore, not to accept the following generalization of Michelle Rosaldo and Louise Lamphere:

> Whereas some anthropologists argue that there are, or have been truly egalitarian societies . . . and all agree that there are societies in which women have achieved considerable recognition and power, none has observed a society in which women have publicly recognized power and authority surpassing that of men (1974:3).

The idea that matriarchies once existed often arises from a confusion between matrilineality and matriarchy. Matrilineality does not mean that women reverse the male domination of politics and become dominant, as implied in the concept of matriarchy. At most, matrilineality brings about a greater degree of political equality between the sexes; it does not lead to female dominance. This can be seen in the case of the matrilineal Iroquois. Among the Iroquois, senior women had the power to raise and depose the male elders who were elected to the highest ruling body, called the council. Through a male representative on the council they could influence its decisions and exercise power over the conduct of war and the establishment of treaties. Eligibility for office passed through the female line, and it was the duty of women to nominate the men who served on the council. But women themselves could not serve on the council, and the incumbent males had a veto over the women's nomination. Judith Brown (1975:240–241) concludes that the Iroquois nation "was not a matriarchy as claimed by some."

SEXUAL POLITICS

Males in many cultures believe they are spiritually superior to females and that females are dangerous and polluting, weak and untrustworthy. One must dismiss the notion that any subjugated group really accepts the reason the subjugators give for keeping them down (see pp. 330ff). But if men do, in fact, enjoy power advantage over women with respect to access to strategic resources, then these stereotypes, whether or not shared by women, will in all likelihood be associated with deprivations and disadvantages.

This point has been stressed by Shirley Lindenbaum with respect to two strongly male-biased societies in which she has done fieldwork. In Bangladesh, Lindenbaum notes the existence of a pervasive symbolism of female pollution.

> Men are associated with the right, preferred side of things, women with the left. Village practitioners state that a basic physiological difference between the sexes makes it necessary to register a man's pulse in his right wrist, a woman's in her left, and they invariably examine patients in this way. Most villagers wear amulets to avert illness caused by evil spirits; men tie the amulet to the right upper arm, women to the left. Similarly, palmists and spiritualists read the right hands of men and the left hands of women. In village dramas, where both male and female parts are played by male actors, the audience may identify men gesturing with the right arm, women with the left. During religious celebrations there are separate entrances at such public places as the tombs of Muslim saints or Hindu images, the right avenue being reserved for men and the left for women. In popular belief, girls are said to commence walking by placing the left foot forward first, men the right.
>
> In some instances, this right-left association indicates more than the social recognition of physiological difference, carrying additional connotations of prestige, honour and authority. Women who wish to behave respectfully to their husbands say they should, ideally, remain to the left side while eating, sitting and lying in bed. The same mark of respect should be shown also to all social superiors: to the rich, and in present times to those who are well educated.
>
> Thus, the right-left dichotomy denotes not only male-female but also authority-submission. It also has connotations of good-bad and purity-pollution. Muslims consider the right side to be the side of good augury, believing that angels dwell on the right shoulder to record good deeds in preparation for the Day of Judgment, while on the left side, devils record misdeeds. The left side is also associated with the concept of pollution. Islam decrees that the left hand be reserved for cleansing the anus after defecation. It must never, therefore, be used for conveying food to the mouth, or for rinsing the mouth with water before the proscribed daily prayers (1977:142).

Lindenbaum found similar notions of female pollution and inferiority among the Foré of highland New Guinea. Here a woman is confined to special seclusion huts during pregnancy and childbirth:

> Her seclusion there is a sign of the half-wild condition brought on by the natural functions of her own body. Other women bring the food, for if she visited her gardens during this period of isolation she would blight all domesticated crops. Nor should she send food to her husband: ingesting food she had touched would make him feel weak, catch a cold, age prematurely (Lindenbaum 1979:129).

If a Foré woman gives birth to a deformed or stillborn child, the woman is held solely responsible. Her husband and the men of the hamlet denounce her, accuse her of trying to obstruct male authority, and kill one of her pigs. Among the Foré as among many other New Guinea cultures, men appropriate the best sources of animal protein for themselves. The men argue that women's sources of protein—frogs, small game, and insects—would make men sick. These prejudices can have lethal effects. Throughout New Guinea they are associated with much higher death rates for young girls than for young boys (Buchbinder n.d.). The same lethal results are evident in Bangladesh:

> The male child receives preferential nutrition. With his father he eats first, and if there is a choice, luxury foods or scarce foods are given to him rather than to his female siblings. The result is a Bengalese population with a preponderance of males, and a demographic picture in which the mortality rate for females under 5 years of age is in some years 50% higher than that for males (Lindenbaum 1977:143).

RELIGION AND SEXUAL POLITICS

Women are often excluded from tapping the principal sources of religious power. Even where individualistic rituals prevail, women tend to have less access to the supernatural than men (Fig. 24.10), Women rarely participate in the vision quests that give males the confidence to be aggressive and to kill with impunity. Women are seldom permitted to take the hallucinogenic substances that give males direct knowledge of the reality that lies behind worldly appearances.

One of the most widespread of all religious complexes has as its explicit aim the retention of a male monopoly on knowledge of the myths and rituals of human origins and of the nature of supernatural beings. This complex involves secret male initiation rites; male residence in a separate men's house (Fig. 24.11) from which women and children are excluded; masked male dancers who impersonate the gods and other spiritual beings; the bull roarer, which is said to be the voice of the gods and which is whirled about in the bush or under cover of darkness to frighten the women and uninitiated boys (see p. 436); storage of the masks, bull roarer, and other sacred paraphernalia in the men's house; threat of death or actual execution of any woman who admits to knowing the secrets of the cult; and threat of death or execution of any man who reveals the secrets to women or uninitiated boys.

Ecclesiastical types of religions are also characterized by a pervasive functional in-

Figure 24.10 *FEMALE SHAMAN*
Piegan "medicine woman." Not all shamans are men.

Figure 24.11 *INTERIOR OF MEN'S HOUSE, NEW GUINEA*
The men use the masks to terrify the women and children.

terconnection between male-dominated rituals and myths on the one hand, and male political-religious supremacy on the other. The established high priests of Rome, Greece, Mesopotamia, Egypt, ancient Israel, and the entire Muslim and Hindu world were men. Highranking priestesses with autonomous control over their own temples, as in Minoan Crete, are the exception, even when the ecclesiastical cults include female deities. Today males continue to dominate the ecclesiastical organization of all the major world religions. All three major religions of Western civilization—Christianity, Judaism, and Islam—stress the priority of the male principle in the formation of the world. They identify the creator god as "He," and to the extent that they recognize female deities, as in Catholicism, assign them a secondary role in myth and ritual. They all hold that men were created first, and women second, out of a piece of a man.

SEX ROLES AND ETHNOGRAPHY

It is important to guard against using advanced state-level stratified forms of political hierarchy as the model for all sexual politics. We cannot go from the proposition that "women are subordinate as regards political authority in most societies" to "women are subordinate in all respects in all societies." As Eleanor Leacock (1978:247) points out, the very notion of "equality" and "inequality" may represent an ethnocentric misunderstanding of the kind of sex roles that exist in many societies. Leacock (1978:225) does not dispute the fact that when "unequal control over resources and subjugation by class and by sex developed," it was women who in general became subjugated to men (recognizing, of course, that the degree of subjugation varied depending on local ecological, economic, and political conditions). But in the absence of classes and the state, Leacock argues that sex roles were merely different, not unequal. There is certainly much evidence to indicate that power of any sort, whether of men over men or men over women, was trivial or nonexistent in many (but not all) band and village societies, for reasons discussed in Chapter 15. And there is much evidence, supplied principally by women ethnographers (Kaberry 1970; Sacks 1971; Sanday 1981), that the power of women has been substantially underestimated or misconstrued by male anthropologists who until recently were the main sources of cross-cultural data on sex roles.

TROBRIANDS REVISITED

Even one of the greatest ethnographers, Bronislaw Malinowski, could fall short of providing a balanced view of sex roles in his classic study of the Trobriand Islanders. As discussed in Chapter 15, at harvest time in the Trobriands brothers give their sisters' husbands gifts of yams. These yams provide much of the material basis for the political power of the Trobriand chiefs. Malinowski viewed the harvest gift as a kind of annual tribute from the wife's family to her husband, and therefore as a means of enhancing and consolidating male power. Annette Weiner has shown, however, that the harvest yams are given in the name of the wife and are actually as much a means of bolstering up the value of being a woman as a means of conferring power on men. Malinowski overlooked the fact that the gift of yams had to be reciprocated, and that the counter-gift had to go not to a man's wife's brother but to a man's wife. In return for the yams received in his wife's name, the Trobriand husband had to provide her with a distinct form of wealth consisting of women's skirts and bundles of pandanus and banana leaves used for making skirts. Much of a husband's economic activity is devoted to trading pigs and other valuables in order to supply his wife with large quantities of women's wealth. The skirts and bundles of leaves are publicly displayed and given away at huge funeral ceremonies known as *sagali* (which Malinowski knew about but did not see fit to describe in detail). Weiner (1977:118) states that the *sagali* is one of the most important public events in Trobriand life. "Nothing is so dramatic as women standing at a *sagali* surrounded by thousands of bundles. Nor can anything be more impressive than watching the deportment of women as they attend to the distribution. When women walk to the center (of the plaza) to throw down their wealth, they carry themselves with a pride as characteristic as that of any Melanesian bigman."

Failure of a husband to equip his wife with sufficient women's wealth to make a good showing at the *sagali* adversely affects his own prospects for becoming a big man. His brothers-in-law may reduce or eliminate their yam harvest gift if their sister cannot display and give away large quantities of bundles and skirts to relatives of the deceased. In Weiner's account not only are men more dependent on women for their power than in Malinowski's account, but also women themselves emerge as having far more influence in their own right. She concludes that all too often anthropologists "have allowed 'politics by men' to structure our thinking about other societies . . . leading us to believe erroneously that if women are not dominant in the political sphere of interaction, their power, at best, remains peripheral" (Weiner 1977:228).

Machismo Revisited

Male-supremacist ideals in Latin America are known as *machismo*. Throughout Latin America men are expected to be *macho;* that is, brave, sexually aggressive, virile, and dominant over women. At home, they dole out money to their wives, eat first, expect instant obedience from their children, especially from their daughters, go and come as they please, and make decisions which the entire family must follow without discussion. They "wear the pants," or at least they think they do. But as May Diaz has shown in her study of Tonalá, a small town near Guadalajara, Mexico, there are significant discrepancies between *machismo* as a masculine ideal and *machismo* as it is actually practiced in the bosom of the family. While women overtly seem to acquiesce to being bossed about by their fathers, husbands, and older brothers, they possess certain strategies for overcoming male control and for getting their own way. One such strategy is to play a *macho* male off against another *macho* male. The case of Lupita, a young unmarried Tonalá woman, illustrates how this works. Lupita's married brother caught her in the act of talking to a young man through the front window of her house. The brother demanded to know who the young man was but Lupita refused to tell him, fearing that her brother would go to their father and convince him to put an end to Lupita's flirtation. Lupita decided to manipulate the rules of *machismo* in her own favor. While helping her mother prepare the evening meal, Lupita complained that the brother's wife was a nag and had made him butt into Lupita's affairs. Lupita knew this would elicit a sympathetic response from her mother (more sympathetic than if she had complained about her brother directly). She knew that her mother was antagonistic toward her daughter-in-law who had gained much influence over Lupita's brother and had come between mother and son. That night, as soon as the father sat down for dinner, Lupita's mother began to scold him for letting his son take over his authority and for not wearing the pants in the family. This convinced the father not to listen to what his son wanted to tell him about Lupita and he left the house as soon as he finished eating without forbidding Lupita to continue with her plans to gain a suitor. So Lupita and her mother achieved their ends, despite their lack of power, by appealing to the very rule that supposedly deprived them of power—a father should be boss in his own house (Diaz 1966:85 – 87).

The distribution of power between the sexes is seldom simply a matter of women being completely at the mercy of men (or vice versa). As the Trobriand and Tonalá studies show, male anthropologists in the past may not have grasped the more subtle aspects of sexual hierarchies. Yet we must not fall into the trap of minimizing the real power differences embodied in many sexual hierarchies by placing too great an emphasis on the ability of subordinates to manipulate the system in their favor. It is well-known that slaves can sometimes outwit masters, that privates can frustrate generals, and that children can get parents to wait on them like servants. The ability to buffer the effects of systemic inequality is not the same as systemic equality.

WARFARE AND THE MALE-SUPREMACIST COMPLEX

One theory—still controversial—is that the widespread practice of warfare accounts for the male-supremacist complex in preindustrial societies, including the ideal of a masculine male personality and the ideal of a feminine female personality. Warfare is linked to male supremacy because in preindustrial combat with hand-held weapons, victory belongs to the group that can put the largest number of the fiercest and brawniest warriors into combat. Men on the average have a physical advantage over women with respect to the force they can exert with a club, the distance they can throw a spear, shoot an arrow, throw a stone, or the speed with which they can run short distances (see Table 24.1 and Fig. 24.12). This means the group that can put the largest number of male warriors into combat will have the best chance of victory under preindustrial modes of warfare. How is this to be achieved? In band, village, and chiefdom societies, ecological constraints drastically limit the growth of population. It is not only enemy warriors that threaten survival, but also overpopulation. The problem, therefore, is twofold: to maximize the number of male warriors and at the same time minimize the pressure of population on resources. The solution to this twofold problem is to rear boys preferentially over girls, as indicated in the correlation between warfare, high male sex ratios in the junior age bracket, female infanticide, preference for male children, higher rates of junior female mortality from neglect and nutritional deprivation (see p. 223).

There remains the question of how men are to be trained to be fierce and aggressive so they will risk their lives in combat. Since the preference for rearing males over females means there will be a shortage of women as marriage partners, one way to ensure that men will be aggressive in combat is to make sex and marriage contingent on being a fierce warrior. Logically, one might suppose that the solution to the problem of a shortage of women would be to have several men share a wife. But as we have seen, polyandry is extremely rare. Indeed, just the opposite occurs: in prestate societies practicing warfare there is a strong tendency for men to take several wives—that is, to be polygynous. Thus, instead of sharing women, men compete for them, and the shortage of women is made even more se-

Table 24.1 WORLD RECORDS (1982)

Event	Men (min:sec)	Women (min:sec)
100-meter dash	0:09.95	0:10.88
1 mile	3:48.80	4:21.68
400-meter hurdle	0:47.13	0:48.60*
	(ft) (in)	(ft) (in)
High jump	7 8¾	6 7

*Women's hurdles are set lower than men's.

SOURCE: Guiness Book of World Records, 1982.

vere by the fact that some men have two or three wives. This leads to much jealousy, adultery, and sexually charged antagonism between men and women, as well as hostility between men and men, especially between juniors with no wives and seniors with several (Divale and Harris 1976, 1978a, 1978b; Divale et al. 1978; Howe 1978; Lancaster and Lancaster 1978; Norton 1978).

Note that this theory relates the intensity of the preindustrial male-supremacist complex to the intensity of warfare and of reproductive pressures. It predicts that wherever the intensity of warfare and reproductive pressure are low, the male-supremacist complex will be weak or virtually absent. This prediction conforms to the widely held view that many hunter-gatherer band societies had both low levels of warfare and considerable sexual equality, and that both warfare and sexual inequality increased with the development of agriculture and the state. Moreover, it also accounts for the reported occurrences of strong male-supremacist complexes in warlike hunter-gatherer band societies—as, for example, in Australia. Not all band societies confronted similar ecological conditions and similar degrees of reproductive pressure (Leacock 1978).

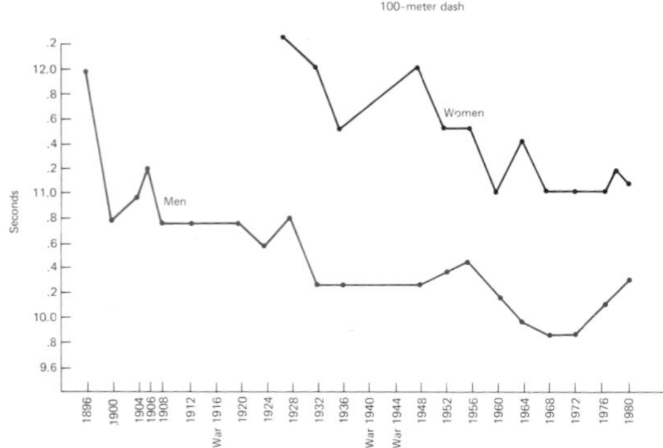

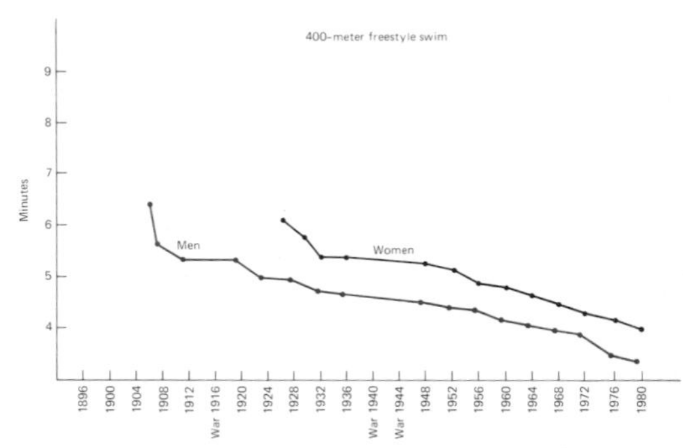

Figure 24.12 *CAN THE GAP BE CLOSED?*
Comparison of male and female Olympic records. It is possible that women may eventually surpass men in certain athletic performances, such as swimming, but not those most closely related to success in preindustrial warfare, such as running.

MASCULINITY, WAR, AND THE OEDIPUS COMPLEX

The above theory reverses the causal arrows in Freudian explanations of warfare. Freud regarded the aggressivity and sexual jealousy of males to be instinctual. He saw both war and the Oedipus complex as products of this aggressive instinct. There is much evidence, however, to indicate that the aggressive and sexually jealous male personality is itself caused by warfare, whereas warfare itself is caused by ecological, demographic, and political-economic stresses. Similarly, the Oedipus complex can be seen not as the cause of warfare, but as the consequence of having to train males to risk their lives in combat. Wherever the objective of child-rearing institutions is to produce aggressive, manipulative, fearless, virile, and dominant males, some form of sexually charged hostility between the junior and senior males is inevitable. But this does not mean the Oedipus complex is an inevitable expression of human nature. Rather, it is a predictable outcome of training males to be combative and "masculine" (see Fig. 24.10).

VARIETIES OF SEXUAL EXPERIENCE

Anatomy does not destine males and females to continue to display the personality characteristics of the past in the future. It is true that men are taller, heavier, and stronger than women; that men have higher levels of testosterone (the male sex hormone); that women menstruate, become pregnant, and lactate. Nonetheless, modern anthropology stands opposed to the view that anatomy is destiny. Males are not born with an innate tendency to be hunters or warriors or to be sexually and politically dominant over women. Nor are women born with an innate tendency to care for infants and children and to be sexually and politically subordinate. Rather, it has been the case that under a broad but finite set of cultural and natural conditions, certain sex-linked specialties have been selected for in many cultures. As demographic, technological, economic, and ecological conditions that underlie these sex-linked roles change, new cultural definitions of sex-linked roles will emerge.

Anthropological research lends strong support to the view that the particular definitions of masculinity and femininity found in many contemporary societies may be unnecessarily restrictive and unrealistically demanding. The prevalent fear of sexual deviance; the male's preoccupation with sexual potency; and the female's obsession with motherhood, sexual competence, and sexual attractiveness cannot be accounted for or justified by purely biological factors. Alternative standards of masculinity and femininity more responsive to individual differences are perfectly compatible with human nature (Hite 1976; Murphy 1976). Very little of a reliable nature is actually known about human sexuality in relation to culture. Anthropologists are certain, however, that knowledge about sexuality gained from the study of people living in one culture can never be taken as representative of human sexual behavior in general (Gregersen 1982). All aspects of sexual relationships from infantile experiences through courtship and marriage exhibit an immense amount of cultural variation. Many different arrangements of Meggitt's "lechery" and "prudery" occur. For example, among the Mangaians of Polynesia, according to Donald Marshall (1971), boys and girls never hold hands and husbands and wives never embrace in public. Brothers and sisters must never be seen together. Mothers and daughters and fathers and sons do not discuss sexual matters with one another. And yet both sexes engage in intercourse well before puberty. After puberty, both sexes enjoy an intense premarital sex life. Girls receive varied nightly suitors in the parents' house, and boys compete with their rivals to see how many orgasms they can achieve. Mangaian girls are not interested in romantic protestations, extensive petting, or foreplay. Sex is not a reward for masculine affection; rather, affection is the reward for sexual fulfillment:

> Sexual intimacy is not achieved by first demonstrating personal affection; the reverse is true. The Mangaian . . . girl takes an immediate demonstration of sexual virility and masculinity as the first test of her partner's desire for her and as the reflection of her own desirability. . . .Personal affection may or may not result from acts of sexual intimacy, but the latter are requisite to the former—exactly the reverse of the ideals of western society (Marshall 1971:118).

According to a consensus reached by Marshall's informants, males sought to reach orgasm at least once every night, and women expected each episode to last at least 15 minutes. They agreed on the data presented in Table 24.2 as indicative of typical male sexual activity.

A very different attitude toward sexual activity appears to be characteristic of Hindu India. There is a widespread belief among Hindu men that semen is a source of strength and that it should not be squandered:

> Everyone knew that semen was not easily found; it takes forty days and forty drops of blood to make one drop of semen. . . .Everyone was agreed . . . that the semen is ultimately stored in a reservoir in the head, whose capacity is twenty tolas (6.8 ounces). . . .Celibacy was the first requirement of true fitness, because every sexual orgasm meant the loss of a quantity of semen, laboriously formed (Carstairs 1967; quoted in Nag 1972:235).

Contrary to popular stereotypes concerning Hindu eroticism (Fig. 24.13), there is evidence that coital frequency among Hindus is considerably less than among U.S. whites in comparable age groups. Moni Nag gives a summary (Table 24.3) of average weekly coital frequency for Hindu and white U.S. women. It is also clear, again contrary to popular impressions, that India's high level of fertility and population growth is not the result of sexual overindulgence caused by "not having anything else to do for entertainment at night."

HOMOSEXUALITY

Attitudes toward homosexuality range from horror to chauvinistic enthusiasm. Knowledge of male homosexuality is more extensive than knowledge of female homosexuality. Several cultures studied by anthropologists incorporate male homosexuality into their system for developing masculine male personalities. For example, the *berdache*, or feminized male of the Crow

Figure 24.13 *HINDU EROTIC ART*
Erotic themes are common in the sacred art of India. Shown: Lord Shiva and Parvati.

Table 24.2 MANGAIAN SEXUALITY

Approximate age	Average Number of Orgasms per Night	Average Number of Nights per Week
18	3	7
28	2	5–6
38	1	3–4
48	1	2–3

SOURCE: D. Marshall 1971:123.

Table 24.3 AMERICAN AND HINDU COITAL FREQUENCY

Age group	White U.S. women average weekly	Hindu women average weekly
10–14	—	0.4
15–19	3.7	1.5
20–24	3.0	1.9
25–29	2.6	1.8
30–34	2.3	1.1
35–39	2.0	0.7
40–44	1.7	0.2
Over 44	1.3	0.3

SOURCE: Adapted from Nag 1972:235.

discussed earlier, performed sexual favors for great warriors without diminishing the latter's masculine status. On the contrary, to be served by a *berdache* was a proof of manliness. Similarly, among the Azande of the Sudan, renowned for their prowess in warfare, the unmarried warrior age grade, which lived apart from women for several years, had homosexual relations with the boys of the age grade of warrior apprentices. After their experiences with "boy-wives," the warriors graduated to the next age status, got married, and had many children (Evans-Pritchard 1970).

Male homosexuality in New Guinea is highly institutionalized and closely associated with male-supremacist attitudes and fear of pollution and witchcraft by women. These, in turn, are closely related to reproductive and ecological stress. Among the Etoro studied by Raymond Kelly (1976) men believe that semen is the substance that gives them life. Like the men of Hindu India, they believe that each man has only a limited supply of semen. When the supply is exhausted, a man dies. While coitus with one's wife is necessary to prevent the population from becoming too small, husbands stay away from wives most of the time. Indeed, sex is taboo between husband and wife for over 200 days per year. The Etoro males regard wives who want to break this taboo as witches. To complicate matters, the supply of semen is not something that a man is born with. Semen can be acquired only from another male. Etoro boys get their supply by having oral intercourse with older men. But it is forbidden for young boys to have intercourse with each other and, like the oversexed wife, the oversexed adolescent boy is regarded as a witch and condemned for robbing his age-mates of their semen supply. Such wayward youths can be identified by the fact that they grow faster than ordinary boys. Although the Etoro have carried male homosexuality to a point that is unusual among cultures studied by anthropologists, they serve as a warning against confusing one's own culturally determined expressions of sexuality with human nature.

SEX ROLES IN INDUSTRIAL SOCIETY

Under industrial conditions, most of the male-dominated roles in agriculture, warfare, industry, and government cannot be said to need the extra musclepower associated with the male physique. Although menstruation, pregnancy, and lactation involve disadvantages in a few situations requiring rapid mobility or continuous effort under stress, modern governments and corporations are already adjusted to high levels of absenteeism and frequent change of personnel. With the long-range trend toward decreased fertility under industrial conditions, women are pregnant, on the average, less than 3 percent of their lives.

It is sometimes argued that menstruation interferes with the capacity of women to make rational decisions under stress, and hence that the exclusion of women from positions of industrial, governmental, or military leadership continues to be based upon a realistic adjustment to biological givens. However, the association between menstruation and irritability, depression, and physical pain is not necessarily a biological given. There is wide variation in the psychological states associated with menstruation among women in different cultures. An alternative hypothesis is that the folklore about menstrual disabilities is itself at least in part a product of male supremacy rather than one of its causes.

Menstruation cannot be considered a barrier to sexual parity in positions of leadership and control. The top leadership of the U.S. military-industrial-educational establishment and of the equivalent groups in the Soviet Union and other contemporary great powers consists of men who are chronologically well past their physical prime. Many of these leaders suffer from high blood pressure, diseases of the teeth and gums, poor digestion, failing eyesight, hearing losses, backaches, fallen arches, and other clinical syndromes associated with advancing age. Like menstruation, these disorders also frequently produce psychological stress. Healthy, premenopausal women certainly enjoy a biological edge over the typical male "elder statesman." As for older, postmenopausal women, they tend to be healthier than men and to live longer.

SEX ROLES FOR THE FUTURE

One of the most remarkable trends of the twentieth century has been the rapid redefinition of sex roles and the restructuring of family life in the industrial nations. Everyone is aware of a profound change in attitude toward sexual experimentation and novel living arrangements. Couples are living together more often without being married; both men and women are getting married later; when they get married husband and wife are continuing to work; married couples are having fewer children, and they are getting divorced more often. One-child households, no-child households, single-parent households, and homosexual households are all on the increase (see Westoff 1978; Harris 1980).

What accounts for these changes? Wanda Minge-Kalman (1978a and b) suggests that many of these changes can be understood as a consequence of the rising costs and diminishing benefits of child labor. With industrialization, the cost of rearing children, especially after the introduction of child labor laws and compulsory education statutes, rose rapidly. The skills required for earning a living took longer to acquire. Hence parents had to wait longer before they could receive any economic benefits from their children. At the same time, the whole pattern of how people earned their living changed. Work ceased to be something done by family members on the family farm or in the family shop. Rather, people earned wages as individuals in factories and offices. What the family did together was to consume; its only product was children. The return flow of benefits from rearing children came to hinge more and more on their willingness to help out in the medical and financial crises that beset older people. But longer life spans and spiraling medical costs make it increasingly unrealistic for parents to expect such help from their children. The industrial nations have increasingly been obliged to substitute old age and medical insurance and old age homes for the preindustrial system in which children cared for their aged parents.

Attempts to measure the actual cost of rearing a child to middle-class status in the United States and Canada are beset by methodological difficulties. But it is clear that the costs are rising fast. Family income required to feed, clothe, house, medicate, and educate a middle-class child from birth to 18 years of age is estimated to amount to $80,000. But this does not take into consideration the income the middle-class mother would have earned had she not stayed at home to take care of her child. This could easily amount to another $150,000. Small wonder, therefore, that in many industrial nations the fertility rate is now well below the 2.1 children per woman needed for replacement. With continuing inflation, high unemployment, and the need for two wage earners per family to maintain middle-class standards, one can predict that the fertility rate will drop still further and that it will continue to drop until the economic value of motherhood is recognized and paid for. For as Minge-Kalman concludes, the entire industrial labor force is now being produced by underpaid workers in that "cottage industry" we call the family. As long as this situation continues, more and more men and women will probably decide to have only one child or none, and more and more individuals will probably find that the traditional forms of family sexual and emotional togetherness are prohibitively expensive.

SUMMARY

Culture and personality are closely related concepts concerned with the patterning of thoughts, feelings, and behavior. Personality is primarily a characteristic of individuals; culture is primarily a characteristic of groups. Yet it is possible to speak of the personality of a group—of a basic, modal, or typical personality. The two approaches, however, use different technical vocabularies to describe the patterning of thought, feelings, and behavior.

Anthropologists who study personality generally accept the Freudian premise that personality is molded by childhood experiences. This has led to an interest in how adults interact with and relate to infants and young children, especially in such matters as toilet training, nursing, weaning, and sexual discipline. In some theories these experiences are seen as determining the nature of "secondary" institutions such as art and religion, or as John Whiting has shown, the practice of severe male puberty rituals.

Other approaches to culture and personality attempt to characterize whole cultures in terms of central themes, patterns, basic personality, or national character. Care is necessary in order to avoid overgeneralizing the applicability of such concepts. A wide range of personality types is found in any large population.

The relationship between culture and mental disease remains problematical. Classic disorders such as schizophrenia and manic-depressive psychosis are somewhat modified by cultural influences, yet they occur in many different societies and probably are the result of interactions among cultural, biochemical, and genetic variables. Culture-specific psychoses such as pibloktoq indicate that cultural factors may powerfully influence the state of mental health, but as the case of Windigo psychosis shows, caution is needed in evaluating allegations concerning the existence of such psychoses.

Pervasive personality differences are associated with being male and female. Freudians emphasize the role of instincts and anatomy in the formation of the active, aggressive "masculine" personality and a passive, subordinate "feminine" personality. These differences reflect typical male versus female expressions of what Freud called the Oedipus complex. Freud's notions of typical male and female personalities have been challenged by anthropological data as being too ethnocentric. Nineteenth-century Viennese sex stereotypes cannot represent the ideal male or female personality in other cultures.

Nonetheless, a great variety of evidence suggests that in most societies males do have more aggressive and dominating personalities than females and that there is a residual core of truth in Freud's notions of antagonism between adjacent generations of males. The evidence in question consists first of the general preeminence of males in headship, redistribution, chieftainship, and monarchical and imperial political institutions on the one hand, and the absence of matriarchies on the other. Second, the pervasive male belief in the female as a focus of pollution and witchcraft reflects real power differences, regardless of whether females concur. Such beliefs, as in Bangladesh or among the Foré, are part of a system for depriving women of access to strategic resources (for example, animal fats and protein) and do not enable women to achieve autonomy or a balance of power. Third, there is pervasive male control over the offices, rituals, and symbols of religion at all levels, from the shamanistic to the ecclesiastical.

Anthropologists, however, have recently been sensitized to the possibility of exaggerating or misconstruing the extent and nature of male dominance. As illustrated in the elaborate female-run Trobriand funeral distributions, even the best of male ethnographers may overlook data relevant to women's status. And, as illustrated by Tonalá domestic life, even in stronly *macho* societies, women may get their own way by manipulating the "rules of the game."

In prestate societies the male-supremacist complex can be explained by the pervasive need to rear maximum numbers of fierce, combat-ready males in overpopulated habitats. The theory predicts that the intensity of the male-supremacist complex will vary directly with the intensity of warfare and reproductive stress. It also may explain why the Oedipus complex occurs, reversing Freud's causal arrows by viewing war as the cause rather than the effect of aggression and sexual jealousy. This shows that anatomy is not destiny. The role of cultural factors in male initiation, patrilocality, and polygyny, as discussed by John Whiting, also suggests that anatomy is not destiny. It is culture that determines how the anatomical differences between males and females are to be used in the definition of masculinity and femininity.

Anthropological studies lend support to the view that contemporary definitions of masculinity and femininity may be unnecessarily restrictive. Cross-cultural variations in sexual standards and sexual behavior prevent any single culture from serving as the model for what is natural in the realm of sex. Mangaian heterosexual standards contrast with those of Hindu India, which contrast with those of contemporary industrial societies. Homosexuality also defies neat stereotyping, as can be seen in the examples of the Crow, Azande, and Etoro.

Sex roles in industrial society cannot be attributed to anatomical and physiological differences. As the technology of production has changed, so has the definition of ideal masculine and feminine roles. Industrialization has increased the costs of rearing children while lowering the benefits. It has therefore fundamentally altered marriage and domestic life. The continuation of these trends will further modify the ideal personalities of the man and woman of the future.

25 HISTORY OF THEORIES OF CULTURE

In this chapter we recount the history of the attempts that have been made to explain cultural differences and similarities. The main research strategies employed by contemporary anthropologists are described. Special attention is devoted to raciological and biological interpretations of culture. The probabilistic nature of the determinism that operates in human history is viewed from the perspective of its implications for human will and consciousness.

The impulse lying behind the development of cultural anthropology is probably as old as our species. Members of different human groups have always been curious about the customs and traditions of strangers. The fact that people who live in different societies build different kinds of shelters, wear different kinds of clothing, practice different kinds of marriages, worship different spirits and gods, and speak different languages has always been a source of puzzlement. The most ancient and still most common approach to these differences is to assume that one's own beliefs and practices are normal expressions of the true or right way of life, as justified by the teachings of one's ancestors and the commandments or instructions of supernatural beings. Most cultures have origin myths that set forth the sequence of events leading to the beginning of the world and of humanity and to the adoption of the group's way of life. The failure of other groups to share the same way of life can then be attributed to their failure to be true, real, or normal human beings.

THE ENLIGHTENMENT

As Europe entered the age of exploration and mercantile expansion, interest in describing and explaining cultural diversity increased. The discovery and exploration of a whole "New World"—the Americas—opened the eyes of philosophers, statesmen, theologians, and scientists to astonishing contrasts in the human condition.

Toward the middle of the eighteenth century, during the period known as the Enlightenment, the first systematic attempts to offer scientific theories of cultural differences began to emerge. The common theme of these theories was the idea of progress. It was held by scholars such as Adam Smith, Adam Ferguson, Jean Turgot, and Denis Diderot that cultures were different not because they expressed innate differences in human capacities or preferences, but because they expressed different levels of rational knowledge and achievement. It was believed that humankind, including Europe's ancestors, had at one time lived in an "uncivilized" condition, lacking a knowledge of farming and animal husbandry, laws and governments. Gradually, however, guided by the ever-expanding role of reason in human affairs, humankind was supposed to have progressed from a "state of nature" to a state of enlightened civilization. Cultural differences were thus largely attributed to the different degrees of intellectual and moral progress achieved by different peoples.

NINETEENTH-CENTURY EVOLUTIONISM

The idea of cultural progress was the forerunner of the concept of cultural evolution that dominated theories of culture during the nineteenth century. Cultures were usually seen as moving through various stages of development, ending up with something resembling Euramerican life-styles. Auguste Comte, for example, postulated a progression from theological to metaphysical to positivistic (scientific) modes of thought. Friederick Hegel saw a movement from a time when only one man was free (the Asiatic tyrant) to a time when some were free (Greek city-states) to a time when all would be free (European constitutional monarchies). Others wrote of an evolution from status (such as slave, noble, or commoner) to contract (employee and employer, buyer and seller); from small communities of people who knew each other face to face to large, impersonal societies; from slave to military to industrial societies; from animism to polytheism to monotheism; from magic to science; from female-dominated horticultural societies to male-dominated agricultural societies, and from many other hypothetical earlier and simpler stages to later and more complex ones.

One of the most influential schemes was that proposed by the American anthropologist Lewis Henry Morgan in his book *Ancient Society.* Morgan divided the evolution of culture into three main stages: savagery, barbarism, and civilization. These stages had figured in evolutionary schemes as early as the sixteenth century, but Morgan subdivided them and filled them out in greater detail and with greater reference to ethnographic evidence than anyone else. (Morgan himself carried out a lifelong study of the Iroquois who lived near his home town of Rochester, New York.) Morgan held that in "lower savagery" subsistence had been gained exclusively by gathering wild foods, that people mated promiscuously, and that the basic unit of society was the small nomadic "horde" which owned its resources communally. By "upper savagery," the bow and arrow had been invented, brother-sister marriage was prohibited, and descent was reckoned primarily through women. With the invention of pottery and the beginning of farming came the transition to barbarism. In lower barbarism, incest prohibitions were extended to include all descendants in the female line, and clan and village became the basic social units.

The development of metallurgy marked the upper phase of barbarism; descent shifted from the female to the male line, men married several women at one time (polygyny), and private property appeared. The invention of writing, the development of civil government, and the emergence of the monogamous family marked the beginning of "civilization."

Few of Morgan's ideas about the sequences of cultural institutions have survived modern empirical tests. For example, there is no evidence for a uniform stage of promiscuity or of matrilineal descent, nor for the association between monogamy and civilization. Virtually all modern anthropologists reject Morgan's evolutionary stages. Yet Morgan's influence can be detected in evolutionary strategies which see bands, villages, chiefdoms, and states as recurrent sequences of sociopolitical organizations.

SOCIAL DARWINISM AND RACISM

In addition to the greater complexity and detail of the nineteenth-century evolutionary schemes, there was one fundamental difference between them and the eighteenth-century schemes of universal progress. Almost all the nineteenth-century schemes (with the conspicuous exception of Marxism) postulated that cultures evolved in conjunction with the evolution of human biological types and races. Not only were the cultures of modern-day Europe and America seen as the pinnacle of cultural progress, but the white race (especially its male half) was seen as the pinnacle of biological progress.

This fusion of biological evolutionism with cultural evolutionism is often but incorrectly attributed to the influence of Charles Darwin. In fact, however, the development of biological interpretations of cultural evolution preceded the appearance of Darwin's *Origin of Species*, and Darwin was himself greatly influenced by social philosophers such as Thomas Malthus and Herbert Spencer. Malthus's notion that population growth led to an inevitable "struggle for existence" had been elaborated by Spencer into the idea of the "survival of the fittest" before Darwin published his theories of biological evolution.

The success of Darwin's theory of the survival of the fittest (he called it "natural selection") greatly enhanced the popularity of the view that cultural evolution was dependent on biological evolution. After the publication of Darwin's *Origin of Species*, there appeared a movement known as Social Darwinism based on the belief that cultural and biological progress were dependent on the free play of competitive forces in the struggle of individual against individual, nation against nation, and race against race. The most influential Social Darwinist was Herbert Spencer, who went so far as to advocate the end of all attempts to provide charity and relief for the unemployed and impoverished classes and the so-called backward races on the grounds that such assistance interfered with the operation of the so-called law of the survival of the fittest and merely prolonged the agony and deepened the misery of those who were "unfit." Spencer used Social Darwinism to justify the capitalist free enterprise system, and his influence continues to be felt among advocates of unrestrained capitalism as well as among advocates of white supremacy.

In the nineteenth century almost all educated Westerners believed that Asians, Africans, and native Americans could achieve industrial civilization only slowly and imperfectly. Nineteenth-century scientists insisted that they had scientific proof whites were intellectually superior and that an unbridgeable biological gulf separated them from the rest of humanity (Haller 1971). They conceded the possibility of an occasional native American, Asian, or African "genius." But they insisted that the average hereditary capabilities of the races were drastically different. These raciological theories were based on the fact that in the nineteenth century Europeans had fought, tricked, and traded their way to control over almost the entire human species. The apparent inability of Asians, Africans, and native Americans to resist the encroachment of European armies, businessmen, missionaries, and administrators was interpreted as living proof that Europeans were biologically superior.

The racial explanation of European political domination was a convenient excuse for colonialism and for the exploitation and enslavement of people unable to defend themselves against technologically advanced European armaments. Today few informed scientists would wish to attribute the temporary technological superiority of Europe and North America to genetic factors. Europe has not always had the most advanced technology. At various stages in the evolution of culture, non-Europeans in Asia or Africa have temporarily held the lead. Moreover, with the breakup of the great colonial empires, it would be extremely foolhardy for the advanced industrial nations to imagine that their genetic heritage will protect them from the rising political and economic power of the Third World.

Today the emergence of Japan as the economic match of the United States discourages anyone from believing the achievement of advanced technology can be attributed to genes that are more common in one race than in another. The problem with racial interpretations of cultural evolution is that they cannot account for the ups and downs of different regions and races except by adding or subtracting hypothetical genes for this or hypothetical genes for that.

To take another example, in the nineteenth century the British believed the Irish were an inferior "race." To account for the economic success of the Irish in the New World, a racist would have to assume that the genes had suddenly changed or that there was something special about the genes of those who emigrated. Such explanations are scientifically undesirable because they depend on the appearance and disappearance of genes for economic success that no one has ever identified. Cultural explanations of the ups and downs of different human populations are scientifically preferable to racial explanations because they depend on factors such as rainfall, soil conditions, and population density, which are far more concrete and visible than hypothetical genes for technological ingenuity and economic success. The explanation for the rise of Japan as a great industrial power would become *unnecessarily* complicated, and hence scientifically undesirable, if in addition to cultural and ecological factors one were to posit the sudden appearance of Japanese genes for videorecorders and Toyotas.

MARXIST EVOLUTIONISM

While the writings and thoughts of Karl Marx were diametrically opposed to Social Darwinism, Marxism was also heavily influenced by the prevailing nineteenth-century notions of cultural evolution and progress. Marx saw cultures passing through the stages of primitive communism, slave society, feudalism, capitalism, and communism. Also, like many of his contemporaries, Marx stressed the importance of the role of struggle in achieving cultural evolution and progress. All history, according to Marx, was the outcome of the struggle between social classes for control over the means of production. The proletarian class, brought into existence by capitalism, was destined to abolish private property and bring about the final stage of history: communism. Upon reading Morgan's *Ancient Society,* Marx and his associate Frederick Engels thought they had found a confirmation of their idea that during the first stage of cultural evolution there was no private property and that the successive stages of cultural progress had been brought about by changes in the "mode of production"—as, for example, in the coincidence of the development of agriculture and the transition between savagery and barbarism in Morgan's scheme. Morgan's *Ancient Society* provided the basis for Engels' *The Origin of the Family, Private Property and the State* which, until the middle of the twentieth century, served as a cornerstone of Marxist anthropology.

THE REACTION TO NINETEENTH-CENTURY EVOLUTIONISM

Early in the twentieth century, anthropologists took the lead in challenging the evolutionary schemes and doctrines of both the Social Darwinists and the Marxist Communists. In the United States, the dominant theoretical position was developed by Franz Boas and his students and is known as *historical particularism.* According to Boas, nineteenth-century attempts to discover the laws of cultural evolution and to schematize the stages of cultural progress were founded on insufficient empirical evidence. Boas argued that each culture has its own long and unique history. To understand or explain a particular culture, the best one can do is to reconstruct the unique path it had followed. This emphasis upon the uniqueness of each culture amounted to a denial of the prospects for a generalizing science of culture. Another important feature of historical particularism is the notion of *cultural relativism,* which holds that there are no higher or lower forms of culture. Terms like "savagery," "barbarism," and "civilization" merely express the ethnocentrism of people who think that their way of life is more normal than other people's ways of life.

To counter the speculative "armchair" theories and ethnocentrism of the evolutionists, Boas and his students also stressed the importance of carrying out ethnographic fieldwork among non-Western peoples. As the ethnographic reports and monographs produced by the historical particularists multiplied, it became clear that the evolutionists had indeed misrepresented or overlooked the complexities of so-called primitive cultures and that they had grossly underestimated the intelligence and ingenuity of the non-Caucasoid, non-European people of the world.

Boas's most important achievement was his demonstration that race, language, and culture were independent aspects of the human condition. Since both similar and dissimilar cultures and languages would be found among people of the same race, there was no basis for the Social Darwinist notion that racial and cultural evolution were part of a single process. Boas, however, did not hold that cultural evolution and biological evolution were completely independent of each other. He stressed the importance of combining the study of physical anthropology with archaeology, linguistics, and cultural anthropology.

DIFFUSIONISM

Another early twentieth-century reaction to nineteenth-century evolutionism is known as *diffusionism.* According to its advocates, the principal source of cultural differences and similarities is not the inventiveness of the human mind, but the tendency of humans to imitate one another. Diffusionists see cultures as a patchwork of elements derived from a haphazard series of borrowings among near and distant peoples. In the critical case of the origin of American Indian civilizations, for example, diffusionists argued that the technology and architecture of the Inca of Peru and the Aztecs of Mexico were diffused from Egypt or from Southeast Asia, rather than invented independently (see p. 121 for a critique of diffusionism).

BRITISH FUNCTIONALISM AND STRUCTURAL FUNCTIONALISM

In Great Britain, the dominant early twentieth-century research strategies are known as *functionalism* and *structural-functionalism.* According to the functionalists, the main task of cultural anthropology is to describe the recurrent *functions* (i.e., useful contributions) of customs and institutions, rather than to explain the origins of cultural differences and similarities. According to one of the leading functionalists, Bronislaw Malinowski (see p. 503), the attempt to discover the origins of cultural elements was doomed to be speculative and unscientific because of the absence of written records. Once we have understood the function of an institution, argued Malinowski, then we have understood all we will ever understand about its orgins. The origin of food utensils, for example, lies in the service they render in conveying food to the mouth. Thus, for Malinowski, the question of why the Chinese use chopsticks and Europeans and Americans use forks was both unanswerable and uninteresting.

A. R. Radcliffe-Brown was the principal advocate of structural functionalism. According to Radcliffe-Brown, the main task of cultural anthropology was even narrower than that proposed by Malinowski. Whereas Malinowski emphasized the contribution of cultural elements to the biological and psychological welfare of individuals, Radcliffe-Brown and the structural-functionalists emphasized the contribution of the biological and psychological welfare of individuals to the maintenance of the social system. For the structural-functionalists, the function of maintaining the system took precedence over all others. But like Malinowski, the structural-functionalists labeled all attempts to find origins as speculative history.

Thus, the functionalists and structural-functionalists evaded the question of the general, recurrent causes of cultural differences, while emphasizing the general, recurrent functional reasons for similarities. This set the functionalists and structural-functionalists apart from the diffusionists as much as from the nineteenth-century evolutionists. Nor were the functionalists and structural-functionalists sympathetic to Boas's historical particularism. But like Boas and his students, the British functionalists and structural-functionalists stressed the importance of carrying out fieldwork, insisting that only after 2 years or more of being immersed in the language, thoughts, and events of another culture could anthropologists provide valid and reliable ethnographic descriptions.

CULTURE AND PERSONALITY

In turning away from the nineteenth-century notions of causality and evolution, many anthropologists, influenced by the writings of Sigmund Freud, attempted to interpret cultures in psychological terms. The writings of Freud and the anti-evolutionism of Boas set the stage for the development of the approach known as *culture and personality*. Two of Boas's most famous students, Ruth Benedict and Margaret Mead, pioneered in the development of culture and personality theories (see pp. 489 and 497). Such theories in general may be described as psychological forms of functionalism that relate cultural beliefs and practices to individual personality and individual personality to cultural beliefs and practices. As we saw in Chapter 24, many advocates of the culture and personality approach stress the importance of early childhood experiences such as toilet training, breast feeding, and sex training in the formation of a basic or modal type of adult personality or national character. Some culture and personality theories attempt to explain cultural differences and similarities as a consequence of basic or modal personality. In general, however, culture and personality advocates do not deal with the problem of why the beliefs and practices that mold particular personality types or national characters occur in some cultures but not in others.

THE NEW EVOLUTIONISM

After World War II, increasing numbers of anthropologists became dissatisfied with the anti-evolutionism and lack of generalizations and causal explanations characteristic of historical particularism, diffusionism, functionalism, structural-functionalism, and the culture and personality approach. Under the influence of Leslie White, a broad effort was launched to reexamine the works of the nineteenth-century evolutionists such as Lewis Henry Morgan, to correct their ethnographic errors, and to identify their positive contribution to the development of a science of culture. White pioneered in postulating that the overall direction of cultural evolution was largely determined by the quantities of energy that could be captured and put to work per capita per year.

At the same time (about 1940 to 1950), Julian Steward laid the basis for the development of the approach known as *cultural ecology,* which stressed the role of the interaction of natural conditions such as soils, rainfall, and temperature with cultural factors such as technology and economy as causing both cultural differences and similarities.

The return to broad evolutionary points of view in the second half of the twentieth century among American cultural anthropologists was stimulated by archaeological evidence that diffusion could not account for the remarkable similarities between the development of states and empires in the New and Old Worlds. The step-by-step process by which native American peoples in the Andean and Mesoamerican regions independently developed their own elaborate civilizations is now fairly well known, thanks to modern archaeological research (see Ch. 10).

Julian Steward was especially impressed with the parallels in the evolution of the ancient civilizations of Peru, Mexico, Egypt, Mesopotamia, and China, and called for a renewed effort on the part of anthropologists to examine and explain these remarkable uniformities. Yet Steward was careful to distinguish his scheme of cultural evolution from the more extreme versions of nineteenth-century evolutionism. According to Steward, the problem with the latter was that they postulated a single or "unilinear" set of stages for all cultures, whereas there are actually many or "multilinear" paths of development depending on initial environmental, technological, and other conditions.

DIALECTICAL MATERIALISM

Both White and Steward were influenced by Marx and Engels' emphasis upon changes in the material aspects of modes of production as the mainspring of cultural evolution. However, neither accepted the full set of Marxist propositions embodied in the point of view known as *dialectical materialism,* which gained considerable popularity among Western anthropologists for the first time in the 1960s and 1970s. Dialectical materialists hold that history has a determined direction—namely, that of the emergence of communism and of classless society. The sources of this movement are the internal contradictions of sociocultural systems and the revolutionary class warfare of the proletariat. To understand the causes of sociocultural differences and similarities, social scientists must not only study these contradictions, but they must take part in the "dialectical" resolutions that lead to progress toward communism. The most important contradiction in all societies is that between the means of production (roughly, the technology) and the relations of production (who owns the means of production). In the words of Karl Marx: "The mode of production in material life determines the general character of the social, political, and spiritual processes of life. It is not the consciousness of men that determines their existence, but on the contrary, their social existence determines their consciousness" [1970 (1859):21].

CULTURAL MATERIALISM

Further elaboration of the theoretical perspectives of Marx, White, and Steward has led to the appearance of the point of view known as *cultural materialism* (see p. 7). This is a research strategy which holds that the primary task of anthropology is to give causal explanations for the differences and similarities in thought and behavior found among human groups. Like dialectical materialists, cultural materialists hold that this task can best be carried out by studying the material constraints to which human existence is subjected. These constraints arise from the need to produce food, shelter, tools, and machines, and to reproduce human populations within limits set by biology and the environment. These are called *material* constraints or conditions in order to distinguish them from constraints or conditions imposed by ideas and other mental or spiritual aspects of human life such as values, religion, and art. For cultural materialists, the most likely causes of variation in the mental or spiritual aspects of human life are the variations in the material constraints affecting the way people cope with problems of satisfying basic needs in a particular habitat.

Cultural materialists differ from dialectical materialists mainly in their rejection of the notion that anthropology must become part of a political movement aimed at destroying capitalism and at furthering the interests of the proletariat. Cultural materialists allow for a diversity of political motivation among anthropologists united by a common commitment to the development of a science of culture. In addition, cultural materialists reject the notion that all important cultural changes result from the playing out of dialectical contraditions, holding that much of cultural evolution has resulted from the gradual accumulation of useful traits through a process of trial and error and the optimization of benefits versus costs in the fulfillment of genetically determined needs and drives.

STRUCTURALISM

Not all post-World War II approaches to cultural theory are aimed at explaining the origin of cultural differences and similarities. In France, under the leadership of Claude Lévi-Strauss, the point of view known as *structuralism* has been widely accepted. Structuralism is concerned only with the psychological uniformities that underly apparent differences in thought and behavior. According to Lévi-Strauss, these uniformities arise from the structure of the human brain and of unconscious thought processes (see p. 481). The most important structural feature of the human mind is the tendency to dichotomize, or to think in terms of binary oppositions (culture-nature) and then to attempt to mediate this opposition by a third concept, which may serve as the basis for yet another opposition. This idea owes much to the dialectical ingredient in Marxism, although structuralism pays no heed to the priority of material conditions which is the essence of dialectical materialism. Unlike Marxism, from the structuralist point of view, the more cultures change, the more they remain the same, since they are all merely variations on the theme of recurrent oppositions and their resolutions. Structuralism, therefore, is concerned with explaining the similarities among cultures, but not with explaining the differences. See pages 481–482 for an example of a structuralist analysis.

PARTICULARIZING APPROACHES

Mention must also be made of the fact that many anthropologists continue to reject all general causal viewpoints, holding that the chief aim of ethnography ought to be the study of the emics of different cultures—their world views, symbols, values, religions, philosophies, and systems of meanings—purely for their own sake, as a form of humanistic enlightenment.

RACIAL DETERMINISM: IQ

Although racial determinism has been rejected by most anthropologists, it still holds sway in other disciplines and continues to have a large popular following. More space will be devoted to this approach, because if race significantly determines culture, many of the basic concepts of anthropology such as enculturation, cultural relativism, and culture itself would have to be modified or abandoned.

During the twentieth century, the dispute between the racial determinists and the cultural determinists focused increasingly on the measurement of intelligence. Intelligence was at first regarded as a completely fixed essence or trait that could not be affected by life experience and culture. Karl Pearson, one of the most influential figures in the application of statistical measures to biological variation, wrote in 1924:

> The mind of man is for the most part a congenital product, and the factors which determine it are racial and familial; we are not dealing with a mutable characteristic of being moulded by the doctor, the teacher, the parent or the home environment (Pearson quoted in Hirsch 1970:92).

The era of large-scale intelligence testing began when the United States entered World War I. To determine their military assignments, thousands of draftees were given so-called alpha and beta tests. After the war, psychologists arranged the results according to race, found the expected correlations between blacks and lower scores, and concluded that the innate intellectual inferiority of the blacks had been proved scientifically (Yerkes 1921).

The army tests were scored by grades lettered A to E. The percentage of distribution for 93,073 whites and 18,891 blacks on, above, and below the middle grade of C was as follows:

	Below C	C	Above C
Whites	24	64	12
Blacks	79	20	1

These results were seized upon to justify the maintenance of inferior social status for blacks in and out of the army. Subsequent analysis, however, showed that the scores were useless as measurements of the genetic factors governing intelligence (Bagley 1924). They were useless because the tests had not distinguished between the assumed hereditary effects and the equally plausible effects of cultural and other nongenetic factors. The strength of these nongenetic factors became apparent when the scores of blacks from five northern states were compared with the scores of blacks from four southern states:

	Below C	C	Above C
Northern blacks	46	51	3
Southern blacks	86	14	0

The most plausible explanation for the superiority in the performance of northern over southern blacks is that the northerners had been exposed to cultural and other environmental conditions favorable to achieving higher test scores. Among such conditions would be the quality and amount of schooling, experience with test situations, diet, and conditions of life in home and neighborhood. Further attempts to interpret the test results in terms of possible nongenetic effects showed that the differences between the races disappeared when the comparison was restricted to literate New York blacks and literate Alabama whites:

	Below C	C	Above C
New York blacks	72	28	0
Alabama whites	80	20	0

Some of the scientific racists insisted that the difference between New York and southern blacks could be explained genetically. They proposed that it was the more intelligent blacks who had migrated to the North. To counter this suggestion, Otto Klineberg (1935, 1944), an anthropologically trained social psychologist, studied the relationship between the length of time that southern black migrants had lived in the North and their IQs. Klineberg found that the scores of 12-year-old southern-born black girls improved proportionately to the number of years that had elapsed since they had left the South:

Years in New York City	Average IQ
1–2	72
3–4	76
5–6	84
7–9	92
Born in New York	92

As Klineberg's data indicated, the change in residence brought the IQs of southern black girls up to the level of northern blacks in 7 to 9 years. For the first time, it was now freely admitted by all concerned that IQ scores could be influenced by life experience. Obviously the gap between black and white IQ scores could be narrowed—but could it ever be closed? The IQs of southern migrants merely rose to the limit of the average black northerner's score, but the score remained some 10 points below the average of the northern white IQ. This difference between the northern black and northern white IQ persists to the present moment. If black and white IQs are compared on a national basis, the difference is still greater, amounting to about 15 points (McGurk 1975; Shuey 1966).

The still numerous and influential racial determinists in the field of psychology and genetics no longer propose that the entire 15-point difference between blacks and whites is due to innate, hereditary factors. It is now generally recognized that environmental influences are capable of raising or lowering a group's average. But by how much?

In the late 1960s, psychologists Arthur C. Jensen (1969), R.J. Herrnstein (1973), and H.J. Eysenck (1973) contended that there was proof that only about 3 points of the differences in IQ could be attributed to the environment. This held not only for IQ differences between blacks and whites, but for IQ differences between upper- and lower-class children of the same race. Intelligence, they claimed, had a "heritability" rating of 80 percent; that is, 80 percent of the *variance* (statistical dispersal around the mean) was due to hereditary and 20 percent was due to environment. This contention has not yet been proved.

How is the heritability figure of 80 percent arrived at? To measure "heritability," one must be able to observe the development of samples of individuals who have similar genotypes (see p. 13) but who are reared in dissimilar environments. This is easily done in the case of plants and laboratory animals, but it is difficult and immoral to do in the case of human beings. The closest one can get to the controlled conditions suitable for calculating heritability in humans is to see what happens when monozygotic twins (twins born of the same ovum and same sperm) are given to foster parents and reared apart in different families. Since monozygotic twins have the same heredity, any differences in IQ scores theoretically should be due to environmental factors. It is difficult to find and test a large sample of monozygotic twins who were for one reason or another reared apart in different families, so the IQs of dizygotic twins (same ovum, different sperm) and siblings reared apart have also been studied. It has generally been recognized that the IQs of the monozygotes are more similar than those of the dizygotes reared apart, who in turn have IQs that are more similar than siblings reared apart, whose scores in turn show more similarity than those of unrelated individuals. Thus the heritability value of 80 percent is based on the progressively similar IQ scores of the individuals who are progressively closer relatives.

The use of this method involves the assumption that the amount of difference in the home environment of twins and siblings is as great as the amount of difference in the home environment of unrelated children. This assumption has been called into question, however. Adoption agencies make a considerable effort to place siblings in foster homes that match the ethnic and socioeconomic characteristics of the parents, and they also attempt to place siblings in similar situations. The motivation and feasibility for such matching is probably greatest with identical twins and least with siblings in different age groups. Moreover, the difference between monozygotic twins and dizygotic twins is readily explicable by the fact that monozygotes are always the same sex, while one-half of the time dizygotes are a boy and a girl. Hence all existing estimates of the heritability of intelligence merit extreme skepticism (Kamin 1974; Osborne 1978; Lochlin and Nichols 1976).

Many of the conclusions of Jensen, Eysenck, Herrnstein, and other IQ hereditarians have also recently been thrown into doubt because of their reliance on the work of Sir Cyril Burt. This English psychologist was considered the world's leading authority on the distribution of IQs within families and classes. His studies showing the close resemblance of the IQs of twins and of the IQs of fathers and children within different classes were based on larger samples than anyone else's and held to be irrefutable evidence in favor of the hereditarian position. It is now clear that Burt not only fudged his numbers—changing results to suit his hereditarian convictions—but invented the data and signed the names of fictitious collaborators to his most revered publications (Dorfman 1978, 1979; Hechinger 1979; Hirsch 1981; Kamin 1974; Gillie 1980).

Even if one could have confidence in the claim that the heritability of intelligence is 80 percent, such a finding would have little significance for educational policy. At best, heritability is a valid predictor of intelligence only under a given set of environmental conditions. Heritability says nothing about what IQ scores or other heritable traits will be like under a different set of environmental conditions. And heritability does not define the limits of change. Even if IQ heritability is as high as the hereditarians claim, unknowably large changes in IQ scores could still be produced by altering the environment of low-IQ children. For "whatever the heritability of IQ (or, it should be added, for any characteristic), large phenotypic changes may be produced by creating appropriate, radically different environments never before encountered by [the] genotype" (Scarr-Salapatek 1971a: 1224). This can best be seen by brief reference to the relationship between heritability and changed environment in the classic case of human stature. Identical twins tend to be very similar in height; so there is a high index of heritability for stature—90 percent. But this high value of heritability for stature has not prevented an increase in the average height of twins (and of everyone else) in the past few generations as a result of improved nutrition (J. Tanner 1968). As Lee J. Cronback (1969:342) has pointed out, although the term "heritability" is standard in genetics, it "is mischievous in public discussion, for it suggests to the unwary that it describes the limit to which environmental change *can be* influential." In the words of behavior geneticist Jerry Hirsch (1970:101): "High or low heritability tells us absolutely nothing about how a given individual might have developed under conditions different from those in which he actually did develop." More recently, Hirsch (1981:36) has condemned the preoccupation with measuring racial intelligence differences as scientifically "impossible (and thus worthless)."

The greater the amount of cultural difference between populations, the more trivial and futile the heritability measurements. Thus, the highest recorded IQ gains in controlled studies are reported from populations with the greatest cultural contrasts. In Israel, for example, Jewish immigrants from Arab countries show a 20-point gain in 1 year (Bereiter and Engelmann 1966:55–56).

When psychologists first began to recognize that the Stanford-Binet IQ test was "culture-bound," they attempted to develop substitutes that would be "culture-free" or "culture-fair" (Cattell 1940). It is a contradiction in terms, however, to suppose that any enculturated human being can be approached in such a way as to overcome or cancel out the effects of enculturation (Lynn 1978). In the words of Paul Bohannan:

> There is no possibility of any "intelligence" test *not* being culturally biased. The content of an intelligence test must have something to do with the ideas or with the muscle habits or with habitual modes of perception and action of the people who take the test. All these things are culturally mediated or influenced in human beings. . . .This is not a dictum or a definition—it is a recognition of the way in which cultural experience permeates everything human beings perceive and do (1973:115).

SOCIOBIOLOGY

Sociobiology is a research strategy that attempts to explain some sociocultural differences and similarities in terms of natural selection. It is based on a refinement of natural selection known as the principle of *inclusive fitness*. This principle states that natural selection favors traits which spread an individual's genes not only by increasing the number of an individual's offspring, but by increasing the number of offspring of close relatives such as brothers and sisters, who carry many of the same genes. What controls biological evolution, therefore, is whether a trait increases the inclusive total of an individual's genes in succeeding generations and not merely the number of one's own progeny.

Inclusive fitness has been used to account for certain infrahuman social traits that traditional versions of natural selection found mysterious. For example, it accounts for the evolution of sterile castes among social insects such as bees and ants. By not having progeny of its own and by feeding and caring for its fertile brothers and sisters, it can be shown that each sterile individual's inclusive fitness is increased. Other "altruistic" traits of social species can also be explained in this manner (Barash 1977; Wilson 1975).

Sociobiologists are in effect committed to the principle that human beings work as hard and efficiently as they can in order to have as many children, nephews, nieces, grandchildren, and other descendants as they can. This principle may apply to nonhuman primates, but it appears to be overridden in the human case, at least after cultural takeoff (see p. 61) has occurred. It is very difficult to see how cultural practices aimed at curbing reproductive success (e.g., infanticide, abortion, polyandry, and contraception) conform to the principle in question. Sociobiologists attempt to overcome this objection by arguing that the slowing down of population growth in the long run actually maximizes reproductive success (Fernandez 1981). There is no evidence, however, that by letting their fertility rate drop below 2.1 children per mother, modern industrial societies will enable individuals to achieve maximum inclusive fitness as compared with the people of Nigeria or India. There is a more plausible and testable view of restrictions on reproduction among industrial societies. According to this view, by limiting the effort and resources devoted to reproduction, individuals achieve a greater degree of satisfaction of the biopsychological drives that define human nature (see ch. 3). Such satisfaction is achieved at the expense of inclusive fitness.

Although sociobiology is a strategy that emphasizes the basic importance of genetic factors as determinants of human social life, its advocates do not necessarily accept the theories of scientists who believe that races and classes differ in intellectual capacity and in other important behavioral traits because they have different genotypes. Most sociobiologists, in fact, stress the unity of the human *biogram*—the basic genetic heritage that defines human nature. They have shown little interest in studying the possibility that each race has its own biogram. One must be careful, therefore, not to lump sociobiologists indiscriminately with scientific raciologists and political racists.

Sociobiologists do not deny that the bulk of human social responses is socially learned and therefore not directly under genetic control. Sociobiologist E. O. Wilson (1977: 133) writes: "The evidence is strong that almost but probably not quite all differences among cultures are based on learning and socialization rather than on genes." Sociobiologist Richard Alexander (1976:6) also states: "I hypothesize that the vast bulk of cultural variations among peoples alive today will eventually be shown to have virtually nothing to do with their genetic differences." Few, if any, sociobiologists are interested in linking variations in human social behavior to the variable frequencies with which genes occur in different human populations.

It must be granted that the sociobiologists' interest in identifying the constants of human nature can lead to an understanding of the outer "envelope," to use a metaphor proposed by E. O. Wilson (Harris and Wilson 1978), within which cultural evolution has thus far been constrained. Virtually all anthropologists agree that there is a human nature which corresponds to the genetic heritage of *Homo sapiens* (one-fifth of this book is devoted to propositions about human nature). But most anthropologists differ from sociobiologists in attributing few cultural practices, such as warfare or male supremacy, directly to the expression of human nature. Moreover, it is clear that human nature can only account for the universals of culture, not for the enormous range of variations at any particular moment in history.

As we have seen, a scant 12,000 years ago, virtually all of humankind lived in band-organized societies. The transitions to village, chiefdoms, states, and empires occurred in less than 400 generations. It has only taken another 10 generations to bring various forms of industrialism, capitalism, socialism, and other novel forms of state societies into existence. And yet we know that all of these changes have taken place within the same subspecies—*Homo sapiens sapiens*.

To suppose that there are genes for traits such as matrilineality, patrilineality, and cognatic descent groups; nuclear and polygamous families; kinship terminologies; reciprocity; redistribution; feudalism; capitalism; and all the other cultural variations discussed in this book is further contradicted by established facts concerning the processes of enculturation and diffusion. We know that adopted children who are brought up in cultures different from their parents' cultures acquire the culture of their foster parents. And we know that traits which originate in one culture can spread around the world to all cultures far too fast for any genetic change to have taken place. Infants reared apart from their parents always acquire the cultures of the people among whom they are reared. Children of English-speaking American whites reared by Chinese parents grow up speaking perfect Chinese. They handle their chopsticks with precision and have no urge to eat at McDonald's. Children of Chinese reared in white American households speak the standard English dialect of their foster parents, are inept at using chopsticks, and do not yearn for bird's nest soup or Peking duck. Moreover, a variety of populations have repeatedly demonstrated the ability to acquire every conceivable aspect of the world cultural inventory. Native Americans brought up in Brazil incorporate complex African rhythms into their religious performances; American blacks who attend the schools that emphasize Western classical knowledge become stars in classical European opera. Jews brought up in Germany prefer German cooking; Jews brought up in Yemen prefer Middle Eastern dishes. Under the influence of fundamentalist Christian missionaries, the sexually uninhibited people of Polynesia began to dress their women in long skirts and to follow rules of strict premarital chastity. Native Australians reared in Sydney show no inclination to hunt kangaroo or mutilate their genitals; they do not experience uncontrollable urges to sing about witchetty-grubs and the Emu ancestors (see p. 431–433). The Mohawk Indians of New York State specialized in construction trades and helped to erect the steel frames of skyscrapers. Walking across narrow beams 80 stories above street level, they were not troubled by an urge to build wigwams rather than office buildings.

The evidence of enculturation and diffusion on every continent and among every major race and microbreeding population proves that the overwhelming part of the response repertory of any human population can be acquired by any other human population through learning processes and without the slightest exchange or mutation of genes.

When our species achieved semantic universality and crossed the threshold of cultural takeoff, it completed a transition to a level of existence as momentous as the creation of matter out of energy, or of life out of matter. *Homo sapiens* is not just another animal to be studied like ants or beavers; we are the only animal on earth (and for at least a dozen light years around in the heavens as well) whose primary mode of evolving new ways of coping with the problems of survival and reproduction depends overwhelmingly on cultural selection rather than natural selection. Culture is encoded not in the genes, but in the brain. Therefore, the great preponderance of cultural differences and similarities cannot be explained by the principle of inclusive fitness.

DETERMINISM, SCIENCE, AND THE INDIVIDUAL

This book has presented a number of deterministic explanations of sociocultural differences and similarities. Although tentative and approximate, these explanations nonetheless confront the concerned student and citizen with a major dilemma. If individual behavior is largely a predictable outcome of cultural conditioning, what significance does anthropology attribute to the strivings of individuals to change their personalities or to modify their cultures? Are we all robots fated to act out our particular predestined personal and cultural configuration? Is our sense of free will merely an illusion? Can we hold ourselves and each other responsible for the personal and cultural life-style that we have been brought up to value as our own?

A determinist view of cultural evolution can lead either to fanaticism or fatalism. *Fanaticism* is the belief that history is on one's side and that there is no legitimate or rational alternative course of action. *Fatalism* is the belief that an outcome, whether desirable or undesirable, will occur regardless of individual striving. Neither of these attitudes is justified by the facts and theories described in this book. The research strategy behind this book rejects both fanaticism and fatalism on the grounds that the determinism governing cultural phenomena is a matter of probability rather than of certainty.

PROBABILISTIC CAUSALITY

As we have seen, correlations based on causal cultural processes are never fulfilled in 100 percent of the cases. Indeed, most of the generalizations discussed in this book have weak levels of predictability compared with what a chemist or a physicist would be willing to accept (although anthropology's "batting average" would be quite respectable among meteorologists and geologists).* Poor predictability may arise from several different sources: errors may be made in data collection and processing; the statement of the initial conditions may be inadequate; the conditions may be undergoing evolutionary change; the generalization itself may be poorly constructed; or finally, human will and consciousness may have produced an unpredictable result.

Regardless of the source of the uncertainties in human affairs, the fact remains that no one can be absolutely confident that a particular set of conditions and causes will always produce a particular culture or personality type. If you are a fatalist and believe that you cannot alter your personality or your culture, and if you act or do not act accordingly, you simply render the most probable outcome more probable. On the other hand, if you believe that you can change the outcome and act accordingly, you may increase the probability of changing the outcome, but you can never render it a certainty.

Thus, recognition of the probabilistic nature of scientific prediction effectively solves the classical problem of how to account for free will in a universe that exhibits unifor-

*Many readers will be familiar with the fact that even in physics no claim for 100 percent predictability is made. In the realm of microparticles, Heisenberg's uncertainty principle reigns. One practical consequence of Heisenberg's principle is the inability to predict the order in which the atoms in a radioactive substance will undergo decay. Probability rather than certainty also reigns in macrophysics. For example, it has never been shown that gravitational force is constant for all regions of space or for all phases of cosmic evolution. Thus, the rule that "one exception falsifies the law" is no more applicable to physics than it is to anthropology. True, the predictability normally associated with physics is much higher than that associated with anthropology. But that is because physics eliminates all poorly controlled conditions and variables; that is, it avoids the study of actual historic events and of evolutionary novelties.

mitarian regularities. The findings of anthropology are opposed to the view that the individual is helpless before the implacable march of history and that resignation and despair are appropriate responses for those who are discontented with present-day social conditions. The future is never so completely predictable as to render all alternatives irrelevant or superfluous. The probabilistic nature of cultural evolution, therefore, imposes nothing so certainly upon the individual as the necessity of making choices. Each decision to accept, resist, or change the current order alters the probability that a particular evolutionary outcome will occur.

This book does not, however, support the view that by mere force of will inspired individuals can change an entire cultural system in any direction they choose. Convergent and parallel developments far outnumber divergent developments in cultural evolution. History repeats itself in countless acts of individual obedience to cultural rule and pattern, and individual wills seldom prevail in matters requiring radical alterations of deeply conditioned beliefs and practices.

If anthropology has any suggestion to those seeking to participate in the creation of novel varieties of personal and cultural life, it is that to change the world one should first try to understand it. The importance of this advice varies directly with the odds against the desired personal or cultural innovation. When the odds are drastically against a hoped-for outcome, avoidable ignorance of the causal factors at work is a moral fault, especially if others are called upon to risk their lives and sacrifice their well-being. In this sense disciplined knowledge of culture, people, and nature is a moral obligation and an essential condition for achieving full human consciousness.

SUMMARY

Systematic attempts to develop scientific theories of culture were initiated during the eighteenth century. Early theories of culture focused on the phenomenon of "progress," which was seen as being linked to the ongoing perfection of rational thought among "progressive" peoples. In the nineteenth century, Herbert Spencer, Charles Darwin, and other social Darwinists, joined the concept of progress with the concept of evolution. It was believed that the principle of the "survival of the fittest," which was equated with "natural selection," accounted for the alleged superiority of "civilized" Europeans over "savages and barbarians." Many different schemes of cultural evolution were proposed by the nineteenth-century evolutionists. Most of these schemes involved some degree of racial determinism. As in the case of Lewis Henry Morgan, few of these schemes with their unilinear stages have survived the test of modern empirical research. Yet social Darwinism and racial determinism are still popular viewpoints, especially among advocates of racial and sexual supremacy and of unrestrained varieties of free-enterprise capitalism. With European and American technological leadership threatened by the industrialization of non-Caucasoid peoples, however, racial determinist theories of history are increasingly difficult to believe.

Marxism was in several respects a typical nineteenth-century evolutionary strategy concerned with unilinear stages of progress from primitive communes to communism, based on the struggle for survival between antagonistic classes.

In reaction to nineteenth-century evolutionism, Franz Boas and his students urged that more attention be paid to the actual history and condition of particular societies through more field research. In advocating cultural relativism, Boas and his students urged that pejorative ethnocentric concepts such as "savagery" and "barbarism" be eliminated from scientific writings. The Boasians also insisted that race, language, and culture could vary independently of each other and that therefore social Darwinist and racial determinist schemes of cultural evolution were fundamentally erroneous.

Diffusionist, functionalist, structural-functionalist, and culture-and-personality strategies were four alternatives that arose in the early twentieth century in reaction to nineteenth-century evolutionism. Diffusionism stressed the single origin of traits and their spread through migrations and contact. Functionalism and structural-functionalism abandoned the attempt to reconstruct evolutionary stages; the latter emphasized how culture contributed to the maintenance of social systems; the former emphasized how culture contributed to the satisfaction of biopsychological needs. Culture-and-personality was another form of functionalism, stressing the fit among personality, child-rearing practices, and cultural institutions.

After World War II, there was a renewal of interest in making broad evolutionary generalizations. Energy and other material and ecological aspects of the interaction between culture and nature were emphasized as the key to understanding the multilinear pathways of cultural evolution. Cultural materialism (with its insistence upon distinguishing between emic and etic and mental and behavioral aspects of culture, and with its emphasis upon infrastructure) as an expression of the culture–nature interface is a derivative of these revived evolutionary strategies. These new evolutionary strategies also derive much of their interest in material conditions from Marxism.

Cultural materialism, however, explicitly rejects the dialectical ingredient in Marxism and the dialectic materialist commitments to viewing the world from the political vantage point of the proletariat class. Structuralism, with its emphasis upon dialectical contradictions, also shows the influence of Marxism. But in other respects, structuralism is fundamentally opposed to dialectical materialism since it ignores the determining influence of material conditions upon the evolution of cultures.

Biological explanations of cultural differences and similarities continue to be offered. Even racial-determinist strategies continue to flourish. But modern-day raciological studies focus increasingly on intelligence testing as means of measuring racial differences. At first it was believed that intelligence tests were measuring an innate characteristic that could not be changed by environmental factors. The results of the army alpha and beta tests, however, and of Klineberg's northern immigrant study suggested that if environmental conditions were controlled, much of the difference between black and white scores could be eliminated.

The main source of disagreement between the hereditarians and environmentalists now concerns what portion of the 15-point gap in the IQs of blacks and whites is genetically determined. The hereditarians claim that the heritability of intelligence is about 80 percent; that is, only 20 percent of the variance in IQ scores can be attributed to environmental factors. This estimate is based on studies of twins, siblings, and other relatives who have been reared apart. However, the home environments have been improperly or inadequately controlled as possible sources of the highly similar scores found among close relatives. Burt's classic studies of the heritability of intelligence in twins are now known to have been fraudulent.

Heritability is not a measure of the limits

to which a trait can be changed under the influence of radically new environments. This can be seen by the fact that IQs can be shifted upwards by as much as 35 points by special programs.

The greater the amount of cultural differences between populations, the more meaningless the concept of heritability. It is a contradiction in terms to try to devise culture-free measures of the heritability of intelligence. No human being is culture-free.

Sociobiology is a biological research strategy that stands somewhat apart from scientific raciology. It is concerned with the effects of human nature on culture and it seeks to explain cultural similarities and differences in relationship to the principle of inclusive fitness. This principle stresses the measurement of reproductive success of closely related individuals as the key to natural selection in social species.

While the principle of inclusive fitness may apply to nonhuman primates and to other nonhuman social species, it is contradicted and overridden in the human case by the phenomenon of cultural takeoff. Thus, sociobiologists cannot explain the momentous changes which have occurred since 10,000 B.P. involving the transition from hunter-gatherer bands to states and empires independently of genetic changes in *Homo sapiens sapiens*. Nor can they explain population-limiting cultural practices which raise individual standards of well-being at the expense of maximizations of reproductive success.

The existence of some form of probabilistic determinism in human social life cannot be denied. Because of the probabilistic nature of that determinism, no one is obliged to be fatalistic. It is false, however, to believe that human will can create any kind of change under any circumstances. The understanding of the probabilities associated with alternative choices depends on systematic knowledge of the subjects covered in this book. To study the relationships among culture, people, and nature, therefore, can be said to be a moral obligation of concerned citizens who want to change the world for the better, rather than make it worse.

GLOSSARY

adaptation The process by which organisms, or cultural elements, undergo change in form or function in response to threats to their existence and replication.
adaptive capacity Previously established ability of a minority to compete for upward mobility in a given sociocultural context.
affinal A relationship based on marriage.
affixes Bound **morphemes** that occur at the initial position in a word.
age grades In some societies, formally institutionalized segmentation of the population, by sex and chronological age, with **rites of passage** announcing the transition from one status to the next.
agriculture The cultivation of domesticated crops.
alleles Variants of **genes** that occupy the same location on corresponding **chromosomes.**
allophone A variant of a **phoneme;** all the contrastive sounds with the class of sounds designated by a particular phoneme.
ambilineal descent The reckoning of descent through a combination of male and female ancestors establishing a descent relationship with a particular ancestor; resembles **bilateral descent** but maintains a narrow rather than a broadening span of kin on each ascending generation.
ambilocality Residence of a couple after marriage alternatively with either the husband's or wife's kin.
animatism The attribution of humanlike consciousness and powers to inanimate objects, natural phenomena, plants, and animals.
animism Belief in personalized yet disembodied beings, such as souls, ghosts, spirits, and gods. Compare **animatism.**
anthropological linguistics The study of the great variety of languages spoken by human beings.
archaeology The scientific study of the remains of cultures of past ages.
artifacts Material objects made by human hands, and having specifiable uses and functions.
ascribed status The attributes of an individual's position in **society** that are involuntary and often inevitable, based on sex or descent.
ascription See **ascribed status.**
assemblage In the archaeological sense, a patterned set of artifacts used by an occupational group that represents the sum of its social activities.
assimilation Disappearance of a group—usually a **minority**—through the loss of biological and/or cultural distinctiveness.
avunculocality Residence of a couple after marriage with or near the groom's mother's brother.
band, local A small, loosely organized group of hunter-gatherer families, occupying a specifiable territory and tending toward self-sufficiency.
basic personality Certain culturally defined traits expected to characterize generally members of a societal group.
berdache A male transvestite who assumes a sanctioned female role among the native American peoples of the Great Plains.
Bergmann's Rule Warm-blooded species tend to develop larger, heavier bodies in the colder limits of their range.
biface tools Modules worked by percussion on both surfaces to yield well-formed cutting and scraping edges.
bilateral descent Rule by which ego traces descent equally through both parents and through both sexes in all ascending and descending generations and collateral lines.
biogram The basic genetically determined propensities for behavior characteristics of a species.
bipedalism Two-leggedness.
blade tools Long, thin flakes with relatively parallel edges, struck from a core.
blood feud Vengeful confrontation between opposing groups of kin, set off by real or alleged homicide or other crimes, and involving continuing alternative retaliation in kind.
blood groups The several types of blood cells classified according to their ability to provoke an immunological reaction when combined with each other.
brachiation Locomotion, usually through trees, by swinging by the forelimbs held overhead. Gibbons are especially noted for this.
breeding population A segment of a population, usually delimited on geographical or cultural

lines, characterized by a high level of interbreeding in which one or more distinctive genes occurs with particular frequency. See also **gene pool.**

bride-price Goods or valuables transferred by the groom's kin to recompense the bride's relatives for her absence.

cargo cult A **revitalization movement** native to Melanesia based on the expectation of the imminent return of ancestors in ships, planes, and trains bringing treasures of European-manufactured goods.

carrying capacity The population of a species that a particular area or **ecosystem** can support without suffering irreversible deterioration.

caste Widely applied as a term to a self-enclosed **class** or **minority;** a stratified, endogamous descent group.

charisma The personal magnetism of extraordinary individuals.

choppers Stone core **biface** implements with broad, crude cutting edges at one end.

chromosomes Threadlike structures within the cell nucleus, containing **DNA,** that transmit information that determines heredity.

circulating connubia A system of marriages in which several groups exchange spouses in one direction in a circle or in directions that alternate in each generation.

circumcision The ritual removal of the foreskin of a man's penis.

clans Kin groups whose members assume—but need not demonstrate—descent from a common ancestor.

class, social One of the stratified groupings within a society, characterized by specific attitudes and behavior and by differential access to power and to basic resources. Less endogamous and more open than **castes** or **minorities.**

clines The gradual changes in traits and gene frequencies displayed by the populations of a species as the distance between them increases.

clitoridectomy The ritual removal of a portion of a woman's clitoris.

cognatic lineage A group whose members trace their descent genealogically from a common ancestor through the application of ambilineal descent.

collaterals Persons who are **consanguineal** kin, sharing a common ancestor, but in different lines of descent, such as cousins.

communal rites Ceremonies, largely religious, carried out by the social group—usually by nonprofessional specialists and celebrants.

complementary opposition The process by which groups unite into more and more inclusive units as they are confronted with more and more inclusive coalitions of antagonistic groups.

consanguineal A relationship between persons based on descent, in contrast with the **affinal** relationship of marriage.

core tools Stone implements made by shaping a large lump or core, such as the hand ax; the tool consists of the core rather than of the pieces detached from it as in the case of *flake tools.*

corvée A forced labor draft imposed by a government for public road and building construction, often in lieu of taxes.

couvade Customary restrictions on the activities of a man often associated with his wife's lying-in and birth of their child.

cranium The part of the skull that encloses the brain.

cross cousins Persons of either sex whose parents are siblings of the opposite sex; offspring of a father's sister and mother's brother. Compare **parallel cousins.**

cultural anthropology The analysis and description of cultures of past and present ages.

cultural materialism The research strategy that attempts to explain the differences and similarities in thought and behavior found among human groups by studying the material constraints to which humans are subjected. These material constraints include the need to produce food, shelter, tools, and machines, and to reproduce human populations within limits set by biology and the environment.

cultural relativism The principle that all cultural systems are inherently equal in value and that the traits characteristic of each need to be assessed and explained within the context of the system in which they occur.

culture The learned patterns of behavior and thought characteristic of a societal group.

culture area A geographical region characterized by a certain complex of trait elements, occurring as shared by several cultural groups, due to common ecological adaptation and/or history.

deep structure The form of an utterance that is not directly observable but that accounts for the intelligibility of its **surface structure.**

dental formula A coding of the numbers of incisor, canine, premolar, and molar teeth, in sequence, in one quadrant of the lower and upper jaws. Used as a trait in anthropoid classification.

descent reckoning The rule for ascertaining an individual's kinship affiliation from among the range of actual or presumed connections provided by birth to a particular culturally defined father and/or mother.
determinism The assumption that in cultural phenomena, as in physiochemical and biological spheres, similar causes under similar conditions give rise to similar effects.
diffusion The process by which cultural traits, ways, complexes, and institutions are transferred from one cultural group to another.
dimorphism, sexual The occurrence of differentiation as in color, structure, size, and other traits between male and female members of the same species.
displacement The ability to communicate about items or events with which the communicators are not in direct contact.
divination Arrival at an expectation or judgment of future events through the interpretation of omens construed as evidence.
DNA (deoxyribonucleic acid) The long-stranded molecules that are the principal component of **chromosomes.** Varied arrangements of DNA determine the **genetic code** and the **genotype.**
domesticate A domesticated plant or animal.
double descent Customary reckoning of affiliation of an individual in unilineal **kin groups** of both parents.
dowry Compensation given at marriage to a husband or his group by his wife's group; in some instances, it is the wife who controls the compensation, in which case the transfer of wealth resembles a predeath form of inheritance for the bride.
duality of patterning The use of a limited set of code units in different combinations and sequences to generate different messages.
ecology The study of the total system of relationships among all the organisms and environmental conditions characteristic of a given area or region.
economy The management of the production, distribution, and consumption of the natural resources, labor and other forms of wealth available to a cultural system.
ecosystem The community of plants and animals—including humans—within a habitat, and their relations to one another.
egalitarian A type of societal group at the cultural level lacking formalized differentiation in access to, and power over, basic resources among its members.
ego The person of reference at the center of kin terminological systems.
emics Descriptions or judgments concerning behavior, customs, beliefs, values, and so on, held by members of a societal group as culturally appropriate and valid. See also **etics.**
enculturation The process by which individuals—usually as children—acquire behavioral patterns and other aspects of their culture from others, through observation, instruction, and reinforcement.
endogamy The principle that requires ego to take a spouse from a group or status of which ego is a member.
epicanthic folds Flaps over the eyes, giving them a slanted look.
ethnocentrism The tendency to view the traits, ways, ideas, and values observed in other cultural groups as invariably inferior and less natural or logical than those of one's own group.
ethnocide The deliberate extinction of one culture by another.
ethnography The systematic description of contemporary cultures.
etics The techniques and results of making generalizations about cultural events, behavior patterns, artifacts, thought, and ideology that aim to be verifiable objectively and valid cross-culturally. See also **emics.**
evolution, general The observation that in cultural systems as well as in living organisms there has been a directional emergence of progressively more complex levels of organization, integration, adaptation, and efficiency.
exogamy The rule that forbids an individual from taking a spouse from within a prescribed local, kin, status, or other group with which they are both affiliated.
extended family A domiciliary aggregate of the members of two or more **nuclear families,** comprised of siblings and their spouses and children, and often including their parents and married children.
family, linguistic A group of related languages historically derived from a common antecedent language.
family, societal A domiciliary and/or kin grouping, variously constituted of married and related persons and their offspring, residing together for economic and reproductive purposes. See also **nuclear family; extended family.**
family, taxonomic A category employed in the

phylogenetic classification of plants and animals, just above the level of genus.

feudal system A type of historical socioeconomic organization involving a network of obligations, in which the **peasants** are structured inferiors to their lord and are bound to provide certain payments and services in exchange for apparent privileges.

fossils Remains or traces of plants or animals preserved—usually by mineralization—from the geological past.

functions The systemic needs served by artifacts, patterns of behavior, and ideas; the ways in which cultural traits contribute toward maintenance, efficiency, and adaptation of the cultural system.

gene flow The movement of genetic material from one **gene pool** to another as a consequence of interbreeding.

gene pool The sum and range of variety of genes present within a given **breeding population.**

genes The basic chemical units of heredity, found at particular loci on the chromosomes.

genetic code The arrangement of chemical components in the **DNA** molecules and on **chromosomes,** carrying information concerning the inheritance of traits.

genitors The etic male source of the sperm responsible for the birth of a particular child.

genocide The deliberate extinction of one population by another.

genotype The total gene complement received by an individual organism from its parents; as distinguished from the external appearance manifest in the **phenotype.**

geographic race A **breeding population,** usually of considerable spatial extent, that can be expressed in terms of the frequencies of specifiable, characterizing genetic traits.

ghost dance A **revitalization movement** that appeared on the North American Plains during the nineteenth century, awaiting the departure of the whites and the restoration of Indian traditional ways.

glottochronology The reckoning of the time at which two languages diverged from an examination of the extent to which their basic vocabularies are the same.

groom price Compensation given to a man's **matrilineal group** when he resides with his wife's matrilineal group. Very rare.

headman In an **egalitarian** group, the titular head who may lead those who will follow, but is usually unable to impose sanctions to enforce his decisions or requests, or deprive others of equal access to basic resources.

heritability In biology, the extent to which the manifestation of a particular trait can be attributed to transmission by genetic inheritance under a specific set of environmental conditions.

hominids (Hominidae) The taxonomic family, including all living and extinct types and races of humans and protohumans. See also **hominoids.**

hominoids (Hominoidea) The taxonomic superfamily of the anthropoids, including all extinct and contemporary varieties of apes and humans, and excluding the monkeys and prosimians. See also **hominids.**

iconographic symbols Symbols that bear a direct resemblance to the items they symbolize.

ideology Cognitive and emotional aspects of the emic superstructure.

incest Socially prohibited mating and/or marriage, as within certain specified limits of real or putative **kinship.**

independent assortment The process by which hereditary information on one chromosome is passed along independently of the information on all other **chromosomes.**

industrialization An advanced stage of techno-economic development observed particularly in modern states and colonizing powers, characterized by centralized control of tools, labor input, the techniques and organization of production, the marketing of goods and cash wages.

irrigation civilization An advanced type of preindustrial society associated with the control of extensive man-made facilities for crop irrigation and land drainage. Usually characterized by highly centralized political institutions.

kindred A **bilateral kin group** in which ego traces relationships in ever-widening collateral and lineal descent and ascent through both ego's maternal and paternal kin and ego's sons and daughters.

kin group A social aggregate of individuals related by either **consanguineal** ties of descent or **affinal** ties of marriage.

kin selection An exclusion of the principle of **natural selection** that takes into consideration the reproductive success not only of individuals but of their close biological kin in explaining the frequency of **genes** and **alleles.**

kinship The network of culturally recognized interpersonal relations through which individuals are related to one another by ties of descent or marriage.

kinship terminology The system of terms by which members of a **kin group** customarily address or refer to one another, denoting their relationship.

kitchen middens Seacoast mounds formed by the debris of centuries of Mesolithic shellfish eating.

levirate Custom favoring the remarriage of a widow with her deceased husband's brother.

Liebig's Law Points out that in biological evolution the processes of adaptation and selection respond to the given minimal potentialities of the environment.

lineage A **kin group** whose members can actually trace their relationship through specific, known genealogical links along the recognized line of descent, as either **matrilineal** or **patrilineal.**

magic The practice of certain rituals that are presumed to coerce desired practical effects in the material world, or in persons.

majority The superordinate group in a hierarchy of racial, cultural, or religious minorities. The majority is usually, but not necessarily, not only politically and economically dominant but more numerous as well.

mana A term for the impersonal pervasive power expected in certain objects and roles. See also **animatism.**

marriage A socially sanctioned form of heterosexual mating and coresidence establishing duties and obligations with respect to sex and reproduction; variant forms are homosexual matings and childless marriages.

matriarchy The political and economic dominance of men by women; no cases have been confirmed.

matrifocal family A domiciliary group comprised of one or more adult women, and their offspring, within which husbands-fathers are not permanent residents.

matrilineal groups Persons whose descent reckoning is through females exclusively.

matrilocality Residence of a couple after marriage in or near the wife's mother's domicile.

messianic movement A movement offering **revitalization** or salvation through following the spiritual or activist leadership of a prophetic individual or messiah; often against vested authority.

microliths Small, trapezoidal-shaped flakes of flinty stone; usually set in rows in wooden or bone hafts.

midden See **kitchen middens.**

minority Subordinate endogamous descent groups based on racial, cultural, or religious criteria found in all state societies.

modal personality The type of basic **personality** perceived to be characteristic of a cultural system, or of one of its strata or subgroups.

monogamy Marriage between one man and one woman at a time.

morpheme The smallest sequence of sounds to which a definite meaning is attached.

mutation Innovative change in hereditary material, transmitted to the offspring.

natural selection The process by which differential reproductive success changes the frequency of genes in populations. One of the major forces of **evolution.**

neolocality Residence of a couple after marriage apart from the parental domicile of either spouse.

nuclear family The basic social grouping comprised of married male and female parents and their offspring.

Oedipus conflict Sexually charged hostility, usually repressed, between parents and children of the same sex.

parallel cousins Persons whose parents are siblings of the same sex; the sons and daughters of two sisters or of two brothers.

parallel cultural evolution Represented by instances in which significant aspects, patternings, or institutions in two or more cultural systems undergo similar adaptations and transformations; presumably in response to the operations of similar causal and dynamic factors.

pastoral nomads Peoples who raise domesticated animals and do not depend upon hunting, gathering, or the planting of their own crops for a significant portion of their diet.

patrilineal groups Persons whose descent reckoning is through males exclusively.

patrilocality Residence of a couple after marriage in or near the husband's father's domicile.

peasants Food-producing farm workers who form the lower economic stratum in preindustrial and underdeveloped societies, subject to exploitative obligations in the form of rent, taxes, tribute, forced labor service (**corvée**), and the like.

personality The structuring of the inherent constitutional, emotional, and intellectual factors that determine how a person feels, thinks, and behaves in relation to the patterning of a particular cultural context.

phenotype The characteristics of an individual organism that are the external, apparent manifestations of its hereditary genetic composition, resulting from the interaction of its genotype with its environment. See also **genotype.**

phoneme A single vocal sound (**phone**), or the several variants of such a sound (**allophones**), which a listener recognizes as having a certain linguistic function.

phones The emic units of sound that contrast with each other and that are the building blocks of phonemes.

phonetic laws Statements about the shifts in the sound values of certain vowel and consonant **phonemes** that have occurred regularly in time within languages and reveal past historic relations between languages.

phyletic gradualism The theory of speciation (held by Darwin) that populations evolve gradually, by the slow accumulation of adaptive changes, so that eventually they become unable to interbreed with other populations. Compare **punctuated equilibrium.**

physical anthropology The study of the animal origins and biologically determined nature of humankind and of physical variations among human populations.

placenta Nutrient-and-waste-exchanging structure that enhances fetal development within the mother's body.

pluralism Where a national or regional population is composed of several social, cultural, or religious minorities concerned with maintaining their separate identities.

political economy Treating the role of political authority and power in production, distribution, and consumption of goods and services.

polyandry Marriage of one woman with two or more males simultaneously.

polygamy Marriage involving more than one spouse of either sex.

polygyny Marriage of one male with two or more women simultaneously.

polymorphism Genetic traits for which there are two or more **alleles** at the same chromosome locus.

punctuated equilibrium A theory of speciation holding that evolutionary changes are triggered by species-forming "events" representing disturbances in the equilibrium between a population and its environment and that such changes may occur within a relatively short span of time—for example, several centuries. Compare **phyletic gradualism.**

race Large populations characterized by a bundle of distinctive gene frequencies and associated with continents or extensive regions.

raciology The scientific study of the relationship between race and culture.

racism The attitude that the genetic composition of various **races** determines the principal cultural differences manifested by different groups of people.

reciprocity The principle of exchanging goods and/or valuables without overt reckoning of economic worth or overt reckoning that a balance need be reached, to establish or reinforce ties between persons.

redistribution A system of exchange in which the labor products of several different individuals are brought to a central place, sorted by type, counted, and then given away to establish producers and nonproducers alike.

rent A payment in kind or in money for the opportunity to live or work on the owner's land.

reproduction The process by which an organism makes a copy of itself and of its plans or heredity instructions.

revitalization movement Reaction by a minority group to coercion and disruption, often under **messianic** leadership, aiming to reclaim lost status, identity, and well-being.

rites of passage Communally celebrated rituals that mark the transition of an individual from one institutionalized **status** to another.

rites of solidarity Rites that confirm the unity of a group.

roles Patterns of behavior associated with specific statuses.

semantic universality Potentiality of all human languages for generating utterances capable of conveying information relevant to all aspects of experience and thought, without limits as to time or place.

shaman A part-time practitioner of magicoreligious rites of **divination** and curing, skilled in sleight of hand and the techniques of trance and possession.

sister exchange A form of marriage in which two males marry each other's sister (or sisters).

society A group within which all aspects of the **universal pattern** occur with a high density of interaction among its members and that has a geographical locus.

sodality A group based on nonkinship principles such as a club or a professional association.
sororate Custom by which a deceased wife is replaced by a sister.
status Position or standing, socially recognized, ascribed to be achieved by an individual or group. Compare **role.**
subculture A culture associated with a **minority, majority, class, caste,** or other group within a larger sociocultural system.
suitor service **Bride-price** rendered in the form of labor.
surface structure The directly observed form of an utterance.
taboo A culturally determined prohibition on an activity, plant, animal, person, or place.
taxons The groups of organisms designated by the taxonomic labels of biology.
tool An object, not part of the user's body, that the user holds or carries during or just prior to use and that is used to alter the form or location of a second object with which it was previously unconnected.
totems Plants, animals, phenomena, or objects symbolically associated with particular descent groups as identifying insignia.
unilineal descent The reckoning of descent either exclusively through males or exclusively through females.
universal pattern A set of categories comprehensive enough to afford logical and classificatory organization for the range of artifacts, traits, ways, and institutions to be observed in any or all cultural systems.
uxorilocal residence When the husband lives in the wife's home.
virilocal residence When the wife lives in the husband's home.
warfare Formalized armed combat by teams of people who represent rival territories or political communities.
zygote A fertilized egg; the first cells of a new individual.

BIBLIOGRAPHY

In the citation system used in this text, the names in parentheses identify the authors of the publications mentioned, or of publications which support the descriptions or interpretations of matters being discussed. The years following the names are the years of publication, and should be used to identify specific sources when more than one publication of the author is included. Letters following a date (e.g. 1982a) distinguish different publications of one author for the same year. "Cf." (compare) is used to refer to points of view opposed to those given in the text. Specific page numbers are provided only for direct quotes or controversial points.

Abrams, Leon
1983 "Cross Cultural Survey of Preferences for Animal Protein and Animal Fat." Paper read at the Wenner Gren Symposium 94. Cedar Key, Florida.

Abruzzi, William
1982 "Ecological Theory and Ethnic Differentiation Among Human Populations." *Current Anthropology* 23:13–35.

Acheson, James M.
1972 "Limited Good or Limited Goods: Response to Economic Opportunity in a Tarascan Pueblo." *American Anthropologist* 74:1152–1169.
1974 "Reply to George Foster." *American Anthropologist* 76:57–62.

Adams, M., and J. V. Neil
1967 "The Children of Incest." *Pediatrics* 40:55–62.

Adams, Richard N.
1968 "An Inquiry into the Nature of the Family." In *Selected Studies in Marriage and the Family,* R. F. Winch and L. W. Goodman, eds., pp. 45–57. New York: Holt, Rinehart and Winston.
1970 *Crucifixion by Power.* Austin: University of Texas Press.

Adams, Richard, W. Brown, and T. P. Culbert
1981 "Radar Mapping, Archaeology and Ancient Maya Land Use." *Science* 213:1457–1463.

Adams, Robert McC.
1966 *The Evolution of Urban Society: Early Mesopotamia and Prehispanic Mexico.* Chicago: Aldine.
1972 "Patterns of Urbanization in Early Southern Mesopotamia." In *Man, Settlement, and Urbanism,* P. J. Ucko, R. Tringham, and G. W. Dimbleby, eds., pp. 735–749. Cambridge, Mass.: Schenkman.

Adovasio, J. M., and R. Carlisle
1984 "An American Hunter's Camp for 20,000 Years." *Scientific American* vol. 250, no. 5:130–136.

Aigner, S.
1976 "Chinese Pleistocene Cultural and Hominid Remains." 9th Congress, USIPP; *Nice. Colloq.* 7:65–90.

Alexander, Richard
1974 "Evolution of Social Behavior." *Annual Review of Ecological Systems* 5:325–383.
1976 "Evolution: Human Behavior and Determinism." *PSA* 2:3–21.
1977 "Natural Selection and the Analysis of Human Sociology." In *The Changing Scenes in the Natural Sciences, 1776–1976,* C. E. Goulden, ed., pp. 283–337. Academy of Natural Science. Special Publication 12.

Alland, Alexander, Jr.
1970 *Adaptation in Cultural Evolution: An Approach to Medical Anthropology.* New York: Columbia University Press.
1977 *The Artistic Animal: An Inquiry into the Biological Roots of Art.* Garden City, N.Y.: Doubleday (Anchor Books).

Amin, Samir
1976 *Unequal Development: An Essay on the Social Formations of Peripheral Capitalism,* trans. Brian Pearce. New York: Monthly Review Press.

Ammerman, A. J., and L. L. Cavalli-Sforza
1973 "A Population Model for the Diffusion of Early Farming in Europe." In *The Explanation of Culture Change,* C. Renfrew, ed., pp. 343–357. Pittsburgh: University of Pittsburgh Press.

Angel, Lawrence
1975 "Paleoecology, Paledemography and

Health." In *Population, Ecology and Social Evolution*, Steven Polgar, ed., pp. 167–190. The Hague: Mouton.

Ardrey, Robert
1961 *African Genesis: A Personal Investigation into the Animal Origins and Nature of Man.* New York: Atheneum.

Ariel, Irving (ed.)
1981 *Malignant Melanoma.* New York: Appleton-Century Crofts.

Armelagos, George, and A. McArdle
1975 "Population, Disease, and Evolution." *American Antiquity* 40:1–10.

Armstrong, Louise
1978 *Kiss Daddy Goodnight.* New York: Hawthorne.

Aron, Raymond
1966 "Social Class, Political Class, Ruling Class." In *Class, Status, and Power: Social Stratification in Comparative Perspective,* R. Bendix and S. M. Lipset, eds., pp. 201–210. New York: Free Press.

Bada, Jeffrey F., R. A. Schroeder, and G. F. Carter
1974 "New Evidence for the Antiquity of Man in North America." *Science* 184:791–793.

Bagley, William C.
1924 "The Army Tests and the Pro-Nordic Propaganda." *Educational Review* 67:179–187.

Bairoch, Paul
1975 *The Economic Development of the Third World Since 1900,* trans. Cynthia Postan. Berkeley: University of California Press.

Baker, Paul
1958 "Racial Differences in Heat Tolerance." *American Journal of Physical Anthropology* 16:287–305.

Bakos, L., and A. L. MacMillan
1973 "Malignant Melanoma in East Anglia, England: An Eleven Year Survey by Type and Site." *British Journal of Dermatology* 88(6):551–556.

Baksh, Michael
1982 "The Impact of Increased Fish and Game Scarcity on Machiguenga Subsistence Behavior." Paper read at the Annual Meeting of the American Anthropological Association, Washington, D.C.

Bao, Ruo Wang (Jean Pasqualini), and Rudolph Chelminski
1973 *Prisoner of Mao.* New York: Coward-McCann & Geoghegan.

Barash, David
1977 *Sociobiology and Behavior.* New York: Elsevier.

Barber, Bernard
1968 "Social Mobility in Hindu India." In *Social Mobility in the Caste System,* J. Silverberg, ed., pp. 18–35. The Hague: Mouton.

Barnard, Alan
1983 "Contemporary Hunter-Gatherers: Current Theoretical Issues in Ecology and Social Organization." *Annual Review of Anthropology* 12:193–214.

Barnes, J. A.
1960 "Marriage and Residential Continuity." *American Anthropologist* 62:850–866.

Barnouw, Victor
1973 *Culture and Personality.* Homewood, Ill.: Dorsey Press.

Barrau, Jacques
1967 *"De l'homme cueilleur à l'homme cultivateur: L'exemple océanien." Cahiers d' Histoire Mondiale* 10:275–292.

Bayard, Donn T.
1968 "Excavations at Non Nok Tha, Northeastern Thailand: An Interim Report." *Asian Perspective* 13:109–143.

Beadle, George
1981 "The Ancestor of Corn." *Scientific American* 242(1):96–103.

Beattie, John
1960 *Bunyoro: An African Kingdom.* New York: Holt, Rinehart and Winston.

Beaumont, Peter, and J. C. Vogel
1972 "On a New Radiocarbon Chronology for Africa South of the Equator." *African Studies* 31:155–182.

Beck, Benjamin
1975 "Primate Tool Behavior." In *Socioecology and Psychology of Primates,* R. H. Tuttle, ed., pp. 413–447. The Hague: Mouton.

Belmonte, Thomas
1979 *The Broken Fountain.* New York: Columbia University Press.

Bender, Donald R.
1967 "A Refinement of the Concept of Household: Families, Co-residence and Domestic Functions." *American Anthropologist* 69:493–503.

Bendix, Reinhard, and S. M. Lipset (eds.)
1966 *Class, Status, and Power: Social Stratification in Comparative Perspective.* New York: Free Press.

Benedict, Ruth
1934 *Patterns of Culture.* Boston: Houghton Mifflin.
1938 "Religion." In *General Anthropology,* F. Boas, ed., pp. 627–665. New York: Columbia University Press.
Bereiter, Carl, and S. Engelmann
1966 *Teaching Disadvantaged Children in Preschool.* Englewood Cliffs, N.J.: Prentice-Hall.
Berreman, Gerald D.
1966 "Caste in Cross-cultural Perspective." In *Japan's Invisible Race: Caste in Culture and Personality,* G. de Vos and H. Wagatsuma, eds., pp. 275–324. Berkeley: University of California Press.
1975 "Bazar Behavior: Social Identity and Social Interaction in Urban India." In *Ethnic Identity: Cultural Continuity and Change,* L. Romanucci-Ross and G. de Vos, eds., pp. 71–105. Palo Alto, Calif.: Mayfield.
Berreman, Gerald (ed.)
1981 *Social Inequality.* New York: Academic.
Bettleheim, Charles
1978 "The Great Leap Backward." *Monthly Review* 30(3):37–130.
Bigelow, Robert
1975 "The Role of Competition and Cooperation in Human Evolution." In *War: Its Causes and Correlates,* M. Nettleship, R. D. Givens, and A. Nettleship, eds., pp. 235–261. The Hague: Mouton.
Binford, Lewis
1972 *An Archaeological Perspective.* New York: Seminar Press.
1982 "Comments on Randall White's Rethinking the Middle/Upper Paleolithic Transition." *Current Anthropology* 23:177–182.
1983 *In Pursuit of the Past.* New York: Thames and Hudson.
Binswanger, Hans
1977 "The Economics of Tractors in the Indian Subcontinent." Hyderabad: ICRISAT.
Birch, Herbert
1968 "Boldness and Judgement in Behavior Genetics." In *Science and the Concept of Race,* M. Mead et al., eds., pp. 49–58. New York: Columbia University Press.
Birdsell, Joseph B.
1968 "Some Predictions for the Pleistocene Based on Equilibrium Systems Among Recent Hunter-Gatherers." In *Man the Hunter,* R. Lee and I. DeVore, eds., pp. 229–249. Chicago: Aldine.
1981 Human Evolution: An Introduction to the New Physical Anthropology. Boston: Houghton, Mifflin.
Bischoff, J. L., R. Merriam, W. Childers, and R. Protsch
1976 "Antiquity of Man in America Indicated by Radiometric Dates on the Yuha Burial Site." *Nature* 261:129–130.
Bischoff, J. L., et al.
1979 "Reply to Payen et al., II." *American Antiquity* 44:599.
Bixler, Ray
1981 "Incest Avoidance as a Function of Environment and Heredity." *Current Anthropology* 22:639–654.
1982 "Comment on the Incidence and Purpose of Royal Sibling Incest." *American Ethnologist* 9:580–582.
Black, Francis
1975 "Infectious Disease in Primitive Societies." *Science* 187:515–518.
Blake, Judith
1961 *Family Structure in Jamaica: The Social Context of Reproduction.* New York: Free Press.
Blau, Peter, and O. D. Duncan
1967 *The American Occupational Structure.* New York: Wiley.
Bloch, Marc
1961 *Feudal Society.* Chicago: University of Chicago Press.
1964 "Feudalism as a Type of Society." In *Sociology and History: Theory and Research,* W. J. Cahnman and A. Boskoff, eds., pp. 163–170. New York: Free Press.
Blum, Harold
1964 "Does Sunlight Cause Skin Cancer?" *University Magazine* 21:10–13.
Boas, Franz
1948 *Race, Language and Culture.* New York: Macmillan.
Boaz, Neal
1983 "Implications of the Redating of the Hadar Australopithecus." *American Journal of Physical Anthropology* 60:174 (abstract).
Bodley, John H.
1975 *Victims of Progress.* Menlo Park, Calif.: Cummings.
1981 "Inequality: An Energetics Approach." In *Social Inequality,* Gerald Berreman, ed., pp. 183–197. New York: Academic Press.

Bodmer, W., and L. L. Cavalli-Sforza
1970 "Intelligence and Race." *Scientific American* 223(4):19–29.
Bohannon, Paul
1973 "Rethinking Culture: A Project for Current Anthropologists." *Current Anthropology* 14:357–372.
Bökönyi, Sandor, R. J. Braidwood, and C. A. Reed
1973 "Earliest Animal Domestication Dated?" *Science* 182:1161.
Bordes, Francois
1968 *The Old Stone Age.* New York: McGraw-Hill.
Bose, Nirmal
1975 *The Structure of Hindu Society.* New Delhi: Orient Longman.
Boserup, Ester
1965 *The Condition of Agricultural Growth: The Economics of Agrarian Change Under Population Pressure.* Chicago: Aldine.
1981 *Population and Technological Change: A Study of Long-term Trends.* Chicago: University of Chicago Press.
Bottomore, T. B.
1966 *Classes in Modern Society.* New York: Random House (Vintage Books).
Bowles, S., and H. Gintis
1976 *Schooling in Capitalist America.* New York: Basic.
Boulding, Kenneth
1973 *The Economy of Love and Fear.* Belmont, Calif.: Wadsworth.
Braidwood, Robert J., and G. R. Willey (eds.)
1962 *Courses Toward Urban Life: Archaeological Considerations of Some Cultural Alternates.* Chicago: Aldine.
Brain, C. K.
1978 "Some Aspects of the South African Australopithecine Sites and Their Bone Accumulations." In *Early Hominids of Africa,* C. Jolly, ed., pp. 131–164. New York: St. Martin's Press.
1981 *The Hunters or the Hunted? An Introduction to African Cave Taphonomy.* Chicago: University of Chicago Press.
Brandon, S. F. G.
1968a *Jesus and the Zealots: A Study of the Political Factor in Primitive Christianity.* New York: Scribner.
1968b *The Trial of Jesus of Nazareth.* London: B. T. Batsford.
Bricker, Harvey
1976 "Upper Paleolithic Archaeology." *Annual Review of Anthropology* 5:133–148.
Bronson, Bennet
1972 "Farm Labor and the Evolution of Food Production." In *Population Growth: Anthropological Implications,* B. Spooner, ed., pp. 190–218. Cambridge, Mass.: M.I.T. Press.
Browman, David
1976 "Demographic Correlations of the Wari Conquest of Junin." *American Antiquity* 41:465–477.
Brown, Judith K.
1970 "A Note on the Division of Labor by Sex." *American Anthropologist* 72:1073–1078.
1975 "Iroquois Women: An Ethnohistoric Note." In *Toward an Anthropology of Women,* Rayna Reiter, ed., pp. 235–251. New York: Monthly Review Press.
Brown, Lester
1978 *The Global Economic Prospect: New Sources of Economic Stress.* Washington, D.C.: Worldwatch Institute. Worldwatch Paper 20.
Brown, Roger, and A. Gilman
1960 "The Pronouns of Power and Solidarity." In *Style in Language,* T. Sebeok, ed., pp. 253–276. Cambridge, Mass.: M.I.T. Press.
Brown, Roy E., and J. D. Wray
1974 "The Starving Roots of Population Growth." *Natural History* 83(1):46–53.
Brunton, Ron
1975 "Why do the Trobriands Have Chiefs?" *Man* 10(4):545–550.
Bryan, Alan, et al.
1978 "An El Jobo Mastodon Kill at Taima-Taima, Venezuela." *Science* 200:1275–1277.
Buchbinder, Georgeda
n.d. *Nutrition and Population Dynamics: A Case Study from Papua, New Guinea.* Unpublished manuscript.
Buettner-Janusch, John
1973 *Physical Anthropology: A Perspective.* New York: Wiley.
Burton, Michael, Lilyan Brudner, and Douglas White
1977 "A Model of the Sexual Division of Labor." *American Ethnologist* 4(2):227–251.
Butzer, Karl
1971 *Environment and Archaeology: An Ecological Approach to Prehistory.* Chicago: Aldine.

Caldwell, J. C.
1981 "The Mechanism of Demographic Change in Historical Perspective." Population Studies 35:5–27.
Callender, Charles and L. Kochems
1983 "The North American Berdache." *Current Anthropology* 24:443–470.
Carasco, Pedro
1978 *"Le economía del México prehispánico."* In *Economía política e ideologia en el México prehispánico*, Pedro Carasco and Johanna Broda, eds., pp. 15–76. Mexico City: Editorial Nueva Imagen.
Carlisle, Ronald, and M. Siegel
1974 "Some Problems in the Interpretation of Neanderthal Speech Capabilities: A Reply to Lieberman." *American Anthropologist* 76:319–322.
Carlstein, Tony
1981 *Time, Resources, Society and Ecology*. London: George Allen and Unwin.
Carneiro, Robert
1970 "A Theory of the Origin of the State." *Science* 169:733–738.
1978 "Political Expansion as an Expression of the Principle of Competitive Exclusion." In *Origins of the State*, Ronald Cohen and E. Service, eds., pp. 205–223. Philadelphia: ISHI.
Carneiro, Robert, and Daisy F. Hilse
1966 "On Determining the Probable Rate of Population Growth During the Neolithic." *American Anthropologist* 68:177–181.
Carpenter, Clarence
1940 "A Field Study in Siam of the Behavior and Social Relations of the Gibbons, Hylobateslar." *Comparative Psychological Monographs* 16:1–212.
Carroll, Lucy
1977 " 'Sanskritization,' 'Westernization,' and 'Social Mobility': A Reappraisal of the Relevance of Anthropological Concepts to the Social Historian of Modern India." *Journal of Anthropological Research* 33(4):355–371.
Carstairs, G. M.
1967 *The Twice-born*. Bloomington: Indiana University Press.
Cartmill, Matt
1974 "Rethinking Primate Origins." *Science* 184:436–443.
Casteel, Richard
1979 "The Relationship Between Population Size and Carrying Capacity in a Sample of North American Hunter-Gatherers." In *Prehistoric Cultural Adaptations in Western North America*, D. Browman, W. Irving, and W. Powers, eds. The Hague: Mouton.
Casteneda, Carlos
1969 *The Teachings of Don Juan*. New York: Ballantine Books.
Cattell, R. B.
1940 "A Culture-free Intelligence Test." *Journal of Educational Psychology*, 31:161–179.
Cavalli-Sforza, L. L.
1972 "Origin and Differentiation of Human Races." *Proceedings of the Royal Anthropological Institute for 1972*, pp. 15–26.
Cavalli-Sforza, L. L., and W. F. Bodmer
1965 *The Genetics of Human Populations*. San Francisco: Freeman.
Chagnon, Napoleon
1974 *Studying the Yanomamö*. New York: Holt, Rinehart and Winston.
1983 *Yanomamö: The Fierce People*, 3d ed. New York: Holt, Rinehart and Winston.
Chagnon, Napoleon, and Raymond Haynes
1979 "Protein Deficiency and Tribal Warfare in Amazonia: New Data." *Science* 203:910–913.
Chang, K. C.
1973 "Radiocarbon Dates from China: Some Initial Interpretations." *Current Anthropology* 14:525–528.
1976 *Early Chinese Civilization: Anthropological Perspectives*. Cambridge, Mass.: Harvard University Press.
1977a "Chinese Paleoanthropology." *Annual Review of Anthropology* 6:137–159.
1977b *The Archaeology of Ancient China*, 3d ed. New Haven: Yale University Press.
1980 *Shang Civilization*. New Haven: Yale University Press.
Charlton, Thomas
1978 "Teotihuacán, Tepeapulco, and Obsidian Exploitation." *Science* 200:1227–1236.
Charteris, J., J. C. Wall, and J. Nottrodt
1982 "Pliocene Hominid Gait: New Interpretations Based on the Available Footprint Data from Laetoli." *American Journal of Physical Anthropology* 58:133–144.
Chesnov, Ia. V.
1973 "Domestication of Rice and the Origin of Peoples Inhabiting East and Southeast Asia." Paper read at the International Congress of Anthropological and Ethnological Sciences, Chicago.

Chilcote, Ronald (ed.)
1972 *Protest and Resistance in Angola and Brazil.* Berkeley: University of California Press.

Childe, V. Gordon
1952 *New Light on the Most Ancient East.* London: Kegan Paul.

Childers, W., and H. Minshall
1980 "Evidence of Early Man Exposed at Yuha Pinto Wash." *American Antiquity* 45:297–308.

Chomsky, Noam
1973 "The General Properties of Language." In *Explorations in Anthropology: Readings in Culture, Man, and Nature,* Morton Fried, ed., pp. 115–123. New York: Crowell.
1975 *Reflections on Language.* New York: Pantheon.

Christenson, Andrew
1982 "Maximizing Clarity in Economic Terminology." *American Antiquity* 47:419–426.

Chu'u Tung-Tsu
1964 "Chinese Class Structure and Its Ideology." In *Sociology and History: Theory and Research,* W. J. Cahnman and A. Boskoff, eds., pp. 218–235. New York: Free Press.

Clark, Grahame
1967 *The Stone Age Hunters.* New York: McGraw-Hill.

Clark, Guy
1981 "On Preagricultural Adaptations." *Current Anthropology* 22:444–445.

Clark, J. Desmond
1972 "Mobility and Settlement Patterns in Sub-Saharan Africa: A Comparison of Late Prehistoric Hunter-Gatherers and Early Agricultural Occupation Units." In *Man, Settlement, and Urbanism,* P. J. Ucko, R. Tringham, and G. W. Dimbleby, eds., pp. 127–148. Cambridge, Mass.: Schenkman.
1975 "A Comparison of Late Acheulian Industries of Africa and the Middle East." In *After the Australopithecines: Stratigraphy, Ecology, and Culture Change in the Middle Pleistocene,* K. Butzer and G. Isaac, eds., pp. 605–659. The Hague: Mouton.

Clarke, David (ed.)
1972 *Models in Archaeology.* New York: Harper & Row.

Clarke, R. J., F. C. Howell, and C. K. Brain
1970 "More Evidence of an Advanced Hominid at Swartzkrans." *Nature* 225:1219–1222.

Clarke, William
1976 "Maintenance of Agriculture and Human Habitats Within the Tropical Forest Ecosystem." *Human Ecology* 4(3):247–259.

Cleaver, Harry
1975 "Will the Green Revolution Turn Red?" In *The Trojan Horse: A Radical Look at Foreign Aid,* Steve Weisman, ed., pp. 171–200. New York: Monthly Review Press.

Cloud, Wallace
1973 "After the Green Revolution." *The Sciences* 13(8):6–12.

Clutton-Brock, Juliet
1969 "The Origins of the Dog." In *Science in Archaeology,* D. Brothwell and E. Higgs, eds., pp. 303–309. London: Thames and Hudson.

Cockburn, T. A.
1971 "Infectious Diseases in Ancient Populations." *Current Anthropology* 12:45–62.

Coe, Michael
1966 *The Maya.* New York: Praeger.
1968 *America's First Civilization: Discovering the Olmec.* New York: American Heritage.
1977 *Mexico,* 2d ed. New York: Praeger.

Coe, Michael, and K. V. Flannery
1966 "Microenvironments and Mesoamerican Prehistory." In *Ancient Mesoamerica: Selected Readings,* J. A. Graham, ed., pp. 46–50. Palo Alto, Calif.: Peek Publications.

Cohen, Mark N.
1975 "Population Pressure and the Origins of Agriculture." In *Population, Ecology and Social Evolution,* Steven Polgar, ed., pp. 79–121. The Hague: Mouton.
1977 *The Food Crisis in Prehistory.* New Haven: Yale University Press.

Cohen, Mark, and G. Armelagos, eds.
1984 "Paleopathology and the Origin of Agriculture." New York: Academic Press.

Cohen, Myron
1976 *House United, House Divided.* New York: Columbia University Press.

Cohen, Ronald
1978a "State Origins: A Reappraisal." In *The Early State,* H. Claessen and P. Skalnik, eds. The Hague: Mouton.
1978b "Ethnicity." *Annual Review of Anthropology* 7:379–403.

Cohen, Ronald, and Elman Service (eds.)
1978 *Origins of the State: The Anthropology of*

Political Evolution. Philadelphia: Institute for the Study of Human Issues.

Cohen, Yehudi
1978 "The Disappearance of the Incest Taboo." *Human Nature* 1(7):72–78.

Cohn, Bernard
1955 "Changing Status of a Depressed Caste." In *Village India: Studies in the Little Community,* M. Mariott, ed., American Anthropological Memoirs 83:55–77.

Cohn, Norman
1962 *The Pursuit of the Millenium.* New York: Harper & Row (Torchbooks).

Cole, M., J. Gray, J. Glick, and D. Sharp
1971 *The Cultural Context of Learning and Thinking.* New York: Basic Books.

Collier, George, Renato Rosaldo, and John Wirth (eds.)
1982 *The Inca and Aztec States, 1400–1800: Anthropology and History.* New York: Academic.

Condominas, Georges
1972 "From the Rice Field to the Miir." *Social Science Information* 11:41–62.
1978 *We Have Eaten The Forest: The Story of a Montagnard Village in the Central Highlands of Vietnam.* New York: Hill and Wang.

Conkey, Margaret
1981 "A Century of Paleolithic Art." *Archaeology* 34:20–28.

Connor, Walter
1979 *Hierarchy and Change in Eastern Europe and the U.S.S.R.* New York: Columbia University Press.

Conroy, Glenn, Clifford Jolly, Douglas Cramer, and Jon Kalb
1978 "Newly Discovered Fossil Hominid Skull from the Afar Depression, Ethiopia." *Nature* 276:67–70.

Constable, George
1973 *The Neanderthals.* New York: Time-Life.

Cook, D., J. Buikstra, J. DeRousseau, and C. Johanson
1983 "Vertebral Pathology in the Afar Australopithecines." *American Journal of Physical Anthropology* 60:83–102.

Cook, J., C. B. Stringer, A. P. Current, H. P. Schwartz, and A. G. Wintle
1982 "A Review of the Chronology of the European Middle Pleistocene Hominid Record." *Yearbook of Physical Anthropology* 25:19–65.

Cook, Sherburne F.
1972 *Prehistoric Demography.* Reading, Mass.: Addison-Wesley.

Coon, Carleton
1962 *The Origin of Races.* New York: Knopf.
1965 *The Living Races of Man.* New York: Knopf.

Cooter, William
1978 Ecological Dimensions of Medieval Agrarian Systems." *Agricultural History* 52:458–477.

Cowgill, G. L.
1964 "The End of Classic Maya Culture: A Review of Recent Evidence." *Southwestern Journal of Anthropology* 20:145–159.

Craig, Daniel
1979 "Immortality Through Kinship: The Vertical Transmission of Substance and Symbolic Estate." *American Anthropologist* 81:94–96.

Cronback, Lee J.
1969 "Heredity, Environment, and Educational Policy." *Harvard Educational Review* 39:338–339.

Culbert, T. P.
1973 *The Classic Maya Collapse.* Santa Fe and Albuquerque: University of New Mexico Press.

Curvin, Robert, and Bruce Porter
1978 "The Myth of Blackout Looters . . ." *New York Times,* July 13, p. 21.

Dahl, Gudron
1979 *Suffering Grass: Subsistence and Society of Waso Borana.* Stockholm: Department of Anthropology, University of Stockholm.

Dahl, Robert
1961 *Who Governs? Democracy and Power in the American City.* New Haven: Yale University Press.

Dalton, George
1965 "Primitive Money." *American Anthropologist* 67:44–65.
1969 "Theoretical Issues in Economic Anthropology." *Current Anthropology* 10:63–102.
1972 "Peasantries in Anthropology and History." *Current Anthropology* 13:385–416.
1974 "How Exactly Are Peasants Exploited?" *American Anthropologist* 76:553–561.

Daniel, Glynn
1980 "Megalithic Monuments." *Scientific American* 243:78–91.

Davis, Kingsley
1967 "Population Policy: Will Current Programs Succeed?" *Science* 158:730–739.
Davis, Shelton
1977 *Victims of the Miracle: Development and the Indians of Brazil.* New York: Cambridge University Press.
Dawes, Robyn
1972 "I.Q.: Methodological and Other Issues." *Science* 178:229–230.
Day, M., M. Leakey, and C. Magori
1980 "A New Hominid Skull (L.H. 18) from the Ngaloba Beds, Laetoli, Northern Tanzania." *Nature* 284:55–56.
Deacon, H. J.
1975 "Demography, Subsistence, and Culture During the Acheulian in Southern Africa." In *After the Australopithecines: Stratigraphy, Ecology, and Culture Change in the Middle Pleistocene,* K. Butzer and G. Isaac, eds., pp. 543–569. The Hague: Mouton.
De Laguna, Frederica
1968 "Presidential Address: 1967." *American Anthropologist* 70:469–476.
Deloria, Vine
1969 *Custer Died for Your Sins.* London: Collier-Macmillan.
De Lumley, Henry, and M. A. De Lumley
1974 "Pre-Neanderthal Human Remains from Arago Cave in Southeastern France." *Yearbook of Physical Anthropology* 17:162–168.
Demarest, William
1977 "Incest Avoidance Among Human and Non-Human Primates." In *Primate Bio-Social Development: Biological, Social and Ecological Determinants,* S. Chevalier-Skolinikoff and F. Poirer, eds., pp. 323–342. New York: Garland.
De Mott, Benjamin
1980 "The Pro-Incest Lobby." *Psychology Today* (March):11–16.
Dent, C. E., et al.
1973 "Effect of Chapattis and Ultra-Violet Radiation on Nutritional Rickets in an Indian Immigrant." *Lancet* 1:1282–1284.
Dentan, Robert
1968 *The Semai: A Non-Violent People of Malaya.* New York: Holt, Rinehart and Winston.
Despres, Leo
1975 "Ethnicity and Resource Competition in Guyanese Society." In *Ethnicity and Resource Competition in Plural Societies,* L. Despres, ed., pp. 87–117. The Hague: Mouton.
Devereaux, George
1967 "A Typological Study of Abortion in 350 Primitive, Ancient, and Pre-Industrial Societies." In *Abortion in America,* H. Rosen, ed., pp. 95–152. Boston: Beacon Press.
Dickeman, Mildred
1979 "Female Infanticide and the Reproductive Strategies of Stratified Human Societies: A Preliminary Model." In *Evolutionary Biology and Human Social Behavior: An Anthropological Perspective,* Napoleon Chagnon and William Irons, eds., pp. 321–367. North Scituate, Mass.: Duxbury.
Dickson, D. Bruce
1981 "Further Simulations of Ancient Agriculture at Tikal, Guatemala." *American Antiquity* 46:922–928.
Diener, Paul, and E. Robkin
1978 "Ecology, Evolution, and the Search for Cultural Origins: The Question of the Islamic Pig Prohibition." *Current Anthropology* 19:493–540.
Dillingham, Beth, and B. Isaac
1975 "Defining Marriage Cross-culturally." In *Being Female: Reproduction, Power and Change,* D. Raphael, ed., pp. 55–63. The Hague: Mouton.
Divale, William
1972 "Systematic Population Control in the Middle and Upper Paleolithic: Inferences Based on Contemporary Hunters and Gatherers." *World Archaeology* 4:221–243.
1974 "Migration, External Warfare, and Matrilocal Residence." *Behavior Science Research* 9:75–133.
Divale, William, and Marvin Harris
1976 "Population, Warfare and the Male Supremacist Complex." *American Anthropologist* 78:521–538.
1978a "Reply to Lancaster and Lancaster." *American Anthropologist* 80:117–118.
1978b "The Male Supremacist Complex: Discovery of a Cultural Invention." *American Anthropologist* 80:668–671.
Divale, William, M. Harris, and D. Williams
1978 "On the Misuse of Statistics: A Reply to Hirschfeld et al." *American Anthropologist* 80:379–386.
Djilas, Milovan
1957 *The New Class: An Analysis of the Communist System.* New York: Praeger.

Dobyns, Henry
1966 "Estimating Aboriginal American Population: An Appraisal of Technique with a New Hemisphere Estimate." *Current Anthropology* 7:395–449.
Dolberg, Frands
1982 *Livestock Strategies in India*. PhD dissertation, Institute of Political Science, University of Aarhus, Denmark.
Dole, Gertrude
1966 "Anarchy Without Chaos: Alternatives to Political Authority Among the Kui-Kuru." In *Political Anthropology*, M. J. Swartz, V. W. Turner, and A. Tuden, eds., pp. 73–88. Chicago: Aldine.
Domhoff, G. William
1970 *The Higher Circles: The Governing Class in America*. New York: Random House.
1980 *Power Structure Research*. London: Sage.
Dorfman, D. D.
1978 "The Cyril Burt Question: New Findings." *Science* 201:1177–1186.
1979 "Letter on 'Burt's Tables.' " *Science* 204:246–255.
Douglas, Jack
1970 *Understanding Everyday Life: Toward the Reconstruction of Sociological Knowledge*. Chicago: Aldine.
Dreher, Melanie C.
1982 *Working Men and Ganja: Marihuana Use in Rural Jamaica*. Philadelphia: ISHI Publications.
Driver, Harold
1966 "Geographical versus Psycho-Functional Explanations of Kin Avoidances." *Current Anthropology* 7:131–182.
Dumond, Don
1975 "The Limitation of Human Population: A Natural History." *Science* 187:713–721.
Dumont, Louis
1970 *Homo Hierarchicus: The Caste System and Its Implications*, trans. Mark Sainsbury. Chicago: University of Chicago Press.
Efron, Edith
1972 *The News Twisters*. New York: Manor Books.
Eisenstadt, S. N., ed.
1968 *The Protestant Ethic and Modernization: A Comparative View*. New York: Basic Books.
Eldredge, Niles, and S. Gould
1972 "Punctuated Equilibria: An Alternative to Phyletic Gradualism." In *Models in Paleobiology*, J. M. Schopf, ed., pp. 82–115. San Francisco: Freeman, Cooper and Co.
Eldredge, Niles, and Ian Tattersall
1982 *The Myths of Human Evolution*. New York: Columbia University Press.
Eliade, M.
1958 *Birth and Rebirth: The Religious Meaning of Initiation in Human Culture*. New York: Harper & Row.
Ellis, David
1979 "The Advent of Food Production in West Africa." In *West African Cultural Dynamics: Archaeological and Historical Perspectives*, B. K. Swartz, ed. The Hague: Mouton.
Ellul, Jacques
1965 *Propaganda: The Formation of Men's Attitudes*, trans. K. Kellen and J. Lerner. New York: Knopf.
Elvin, Mark
1974 *The Pattern of the Chinese Past*. Stanford, Calif.: Stanford University Press.
Ember, Carol
1983 "The Relative Decline in Women's Contribution to Agriculture with Intensification." *American Anthropologist* 85:285–304.
Ember, Carol, M. Ember, and B. Pasternak
1974 "On the Development of Unilineal Descent." *Journal of Anthropological Research* 30:69–94.
Ember, Melvin
1982 "Statistical Evidence for An Ecological Explanation of Warfare." *American Anthropologist* 84:645–649.
Ember, Melvin, and Carol R. Ember
1971 "The Conditions Favoring Matrilocal versus Patrilocal Residence." *American Anthropologist* 73:571–594.
Epstein, T. Scarlett
1968 *Capitalism, Primitive and Modern: Some Aspects of Tolai Economic Growth*. East Lansing: Michigan State University Press.
Evans-Pritchard, E. E.
1940 *The Nuer, A Description of the Modes of Livelihood and Political Institutions of a Nilotic People*. Oxford: Clarendon Press.
1970 "Sexual Inversion Among the Azande." *American Anthropologist* 72:1428–1433.
Eysenck, H. J.
1973 *The Inequality of Man*. London: Temple Smith.
Fagan, Brian
1983 *People of the Earth: An Introduction to*

World Prehistory, 4th ed. Boston: Little, Brown.

Fainsod, Merle
1967 *How Russia Is Ruled.* Cambridge, Mass.: Harvard University Press.

Fallers, L.
1977 "Equality and Inequality in Human Societies." In *Horizons of Anthropology*, 2d ed., S. Tax and L. Freeman, eds., pp. 257–268. Chicago: Aldine.

Fei Hsaio-t'ung and Chang chih-I
1947 *Earthbound China: A Study of Rural Economy in Yunnan.* Chicago: University of Chicago Press.

Feifar, Oldrich
1976 "Recent Research at Prezletice." *Current Anthropology* 17:343–344.

Feldmersen, Robert A.
1966 "Toward the Classless Society?" In *Class, Status, and Power: Social Stratification in Comparative Perspective*, R. Bendix and S. M. Lipset, eds., pp. 527–533. New York: Free Press.

Fellers, Joan, and G. Fellers
1976 "Tool Use in a Social Insect and Its Implications for Competitive Interactions." *Science* 192:70–72.

Ferguson, Brian
1979 "War and Redistribution on the Northwest Coast." Paper read at the meetings of the American Ethnological Association, Vancouver, B.C.

Fernandez, Renate
1981 "Comments on Tibetan Polyandry: A Test of Sociobiological Theory." *American Anthropologist* 83:896–897.

Finkelhor, D.
1979 *Sexually Victimized Children.* New York: Free Press.

Firth, Raymond
1957 *We, The Tikopia: A Sociological Study of Kinship in Primitive Polynesia.* Boston: Beacon Press.

Fittkau, E. J., and H. Klinge
1973 "On Biomass and Trophic Structure of the Central Amazon Rain Forest Ecosystem." *Biotropica* 5:1–14.

Flannery, Kent
1972 "The Origin of the Village as a Settlement Type in Mesoamerica and the Near East: A Comparative Study." In *Man, Settlement, and Urbanism*, P. J. Ucko, R. Tringham, and G. W. Dimbleby, eds., pp. 23–53. Cambridge, Mass.: Schenkman.
1973 "The Origins of Agriculture." *Annual Review of Anthropology* 2:270–310.

Flannery, Kent (ed.)
1982 *Maya Subsistence: Studies in Memory of Dennis E. Puleston.* New York: Academic Press.

Fleming, Stuart
1977 *Dating in Archaeology: A Guide to Scientific Techniques.* New York: St. Martin's Press.

Fortes, Meyer
1969 *Kinship and the Social Order: The Legacy of Lewis Henry Morgan.* Chicago: Aldine.

Fortune, Reo
1965 *Manus Religion.* Lincoln: University of Nebraska Press.

Foster, George M.
1967 *Tzintzuntzán: Mexican Peasants in a Changing World.* Boston: Little, Brown.
1972 "The Anatomy of Envy: A Study in Symbolic Behavior." *Current Anthropology* 13:165–202.
1974 "Limited Good or Limited Goods: Observations on Acheson." *American Anthropologist* 76:53–57.

Foulkes, Edward
1972 *The Arctic Hysteria.* Washington, D.C.: The American Anthropological Association.

Franke, Richard W.
1973 *The Green Revolution in a Javanese Village.* Ph.D. dissertation, Harvard University.
1974 "Miracle Seeds and Shattered Dreams." *Natural History* 83(1):10ff.

Frazer, James
1911–1915 *The Golden Bough*, 3d ed. London: Macmillan.

Fried, Morton H.
1967 *The Evolution of Political Society: An Essay in Political Anthropology.* New York: Random House.
1968 "The Need to End the Pseudoscientific Investigation of Race." In *Science and the Concept of Race*, M. Mead et al., eds., pp. 122–131. New York: Columbia University Press.
1972 *The Study of Anthropology.* New York: Crowell.
1975 *The Notion of Tribe.* Menlo Park, Calif.: Cummings.

1978 "The State, the Chicken, and the Egg; or What Came First?" In *Origins of the State*, Ronald Cohen and Elman Service, eds., pp. 35–47. Philadelphia: Institute for the Study of Human Issues.

Friere, Paulo
1973 *Pedagogy of the Oppressed*. New York: Seabury Press.

Frisch, Rose
1978 "Reply to Trussel." *Science* 200:1509–1513.

Frisch, Rose, and Janet MacArthur
1974 "Menstrual Cycles: Fatness as a Determinant of Minimum Weight for Height Necessary for Their Maintenance or Onset." *Science* 185:949–951.

Fromm, Erich, and M. Maccoby
1970 *A Mexican Village: A Sociopsychoanalytic Study*. Englewood Cliffs, N.J.: Prentice-Hall.

Furstenberg, Frank, Theodore Hershberg, and John Medell
1975 "The Origin of the Female-Headed Black Family: The Impact of the Urban Experience." *Journal of Interdisciplinary History* 6(2):211–233.

Galbraith, John
1958 *The Affluent Society*. New York: Houghton Mifflin.
1967 *The New Industrial State*. New York: Houghton Mifflin.

Galdikas-Brindamour, B.
1975 "Orangutans, Indonesia's 'People of the Forest.' " *National Geographic* 184:444–473.

Galdikas, B. M. F., and G. Teleki
1981 "Variations in Subsistence Activities of Female and Male Pongids: New Perspectives on the Origins of Hominid Labor Division." *Current Anthropology* 22:241–256.

Gandhi, Mohandas K.
1954 *How to Serve the Cow: Ahmedabad*. Navajivan Publishing House.

Gardner, B. T., and R. A. Gardner
1971 "Two-Way Communication with a Chimpanzee." In *Behavior of Non-Human Primates*, A. Schrier and F. Stollnitz, eds., vol. 4, pp. 117–184. New York: Academic.

Gardner, R. A., and B. T. Gardner
1975 "Early Signs of Language in Child and Chimpanzee." *Science* 187:752–753.

Gearing, Fred, and B. A. Tindale
1973 "Anthropological Studies of the Educational Process." *Annual Review of Anthropology* 2:95–105.

Geertz, Clifford
1963 *Agricultural Involution: The Process of Ecological Change in Indonesia*. Berkeley: University of California Press for The Association of Asian Studies.

Gilder, George
1981 *Wealth and Poverty*. New York: Basic Books.

Gillie, O.
1980 "Burt: The Scandal and the Cover Up." Supplement to the Bulletin of the British Psychological Association 33:9–16.

Givens, R. D.
1975 "Aggression in Nonhuman Primates: Implications for Understanding Human Behavior." In *War: Its Causes and Correlates*, M. Nettleship, R. D. Givens, and A. Nettleship, eds., pp. 263–280. The Hague: Mouton.

Glassow, Michael
1978 "The Concept of Carrying Capacity in the Study of Cultural Process." In *Advances in Archaeological Theory and Method*. Michael Schiffer, ed., pp. 31–48. New York: Academic.

Gluckman, Max
1955 *Custom and Conflict in Africa*. Oxford: Blackwell.

Godfrey, L., and J. Cole
1979 "Biological Analogy, Diffusionism, and Archaeology." *American Anthropologist* 81:37–45.

Gold, Sonia
1973 "Alternative National Goals and Women's Employment." *Science* 179:565–660.

Goldstein, Melvyn
1978 "Pahari and Tibetan Polyandry Revisited." *Ethnology* 17:325–337.

González, Nancy L.
1970 "Towards a Definition of Matrilocality." In *Afro-American Anthropology: Contemporary Perspectives*, N. E. Whitten and J. F. Szwed, eds., pp. 231–243. New York: Free Press.

Good, Kenneth
1982 "Limiting Factors in Amazonian Ecology." Paper read at the Annual Meeting of the American Anthropological Association, Washington, D.C.

Goodenough, Florence L.
1926 *Measurement of Intelligence by Drawings*. Chicago: World Book.

Goodenough, Ward H.
1970 *Description and Comparison in Cultural Anthropology.* Chicago: Aldine.
Goody, Jack
1976 *Production and Reproduction.* New York: Cambridge University Press.
Gorenstein, Shirley (ed.)
1974 *Prehispanic America.* New York: St. Martin's Press.
Gorman, Chester F.
1969 "Hoabinhian: A Pebble-Tool Complex with Early Plant Associations in Southeast Asia." *Science* 163:671–673.
1978 "*A priori* Models and Thai Prehistory: A Reconsideration of the Beginnings of Agriculture in Southeastern Asia." In *Origins of Agriculture,* C. Reed, ed., pp. 321–355. The Hague: Mouton.
Gough, E. Kathleen
1959 "Criterion of Caste Ranking in South India." *Man In India* 39:115–126.
1968 "The Nayars and the Definition of Marriage." In *Marriage, Family, and Residence,* P. Bohannan and J. Middleton, eds., pp. 49–71. Garden City, N.Y.: Natural History Press.
1978 "The Green Revolution in South India and North Vietnam." *Monthly Review* 29(8):10–21.
Gould, Harold
1971 "Caste and Class: A Comparative View." *Module* 11:1–24. Reading, Mass.: Addison-Wesley.
Gould, Richard, D. Koster, and A. Sontz
1971 "The Lithic Assemblage of the Western Desert Aborigines of Australia." *American Antiquity* 36:149–169.
Gramby, Richard
1977 "Deerskins and Hunting Territories: Competition for a Scarce Resource of the Northeastern Woodlands." *American Antiquity* 42:601–605.
Graves, Theodore
1974 "Urban Indian Personality and the Culture of Poverty." *American Ethnologist* 1:65–86.
Greenberg, Joseph
1968 *Anthropological Linguistics, An Introduction.* New York: Random House.
Gregerson, Edgar
1982 *Sexual Practices: The Story of Human Sexuality.* London: Mitchell Beazley.
Gregor, Thomas A.
1969 *Social Relations in a Small Society: A Study of the Mehinacu Indians of Central Brazil.* Ph.D. dissertation, Columbia University Press.
Gross, Daniel
1970 *Sisal and Social Structure in Northeastern Brazil.* Ph.D. dissertation, Columbia University.
1975 "Protein Capture and Cultural Development in the Amazon Basin." *American Anthropologist* 77:526–549.
1982 "Proteinas y Cultura en la Amazonia." Amazonia Peruana 3:127–144.
Gross, Daniel, and B. Underwood
1969 "Technological Change and Caloric Costs on Northeastern Brazilian Sisal Plantations." Paper read at the Annual Meeting of the American Association for the Advancement of Science, Boston.
Haas, Jonathan
1982 *The Evolution of the Prehistoric State.* New York: Columbia University Press.
Hadley, Arthur
1978 *The Empty Polling Booth.* Englewood Cliffs, N.J.: Prentice-Hall.
Hall, Calvin, and G. Lindzey
1967 "Freud's Psychoanalytic Theory of Personality." In *Personalities and Cultures: Readings in Psychological Anthropology,* Robert Hunt, ed., pp. 3–29. Garden City, N.Y.: Natural History Press.
Haller, John S.
1971 *Outcastes from Evolution.* Urbana: University of Illinois Press.
Hallpike, C. R.
1977 *Bloodshed and Vengeance in the Papuan Mountains.* London: Oxford University Press.
Hamblin, Dora Jane
1973 *The First Cities.* New York: Time-Life.
Hamblin, R. L., and B. L. Pitcher
1980 "The Classic Maya Collapse: Testing the Class Conflict Model." *American Antiquity* 45:246–267.
Hames, Raymond
1983 "The Settlement Pattern of a Yanomamo Population Bloc: A Behavioral Ecological Interpretation." In *Adaptive Responses of Native Amazonians,* R. Hames and W. Vickers, eds., pp. 393–427. New York: Academic.
Hamilton, W. J., and C. D. Busse
1978 "Primate Carnivory and Its Significance to Human Diets." *BioScience* 28:761–766.

Hammond, Norman
1982 *Ancient Maya Civilization.* New Brunswick, N.J.: Rutgers University Press.
Hammond, Norman (ed.)
1978 *Social Process in Maya Prehistory.* New York: Academic.
Hammond, Norman, et al.
1979 "The Earliest Lowland Maya: Definition of the Swasey Phase." *American Antiquity* 44:92–109.
Hammond, Norman, and Charles Miksicek
1981 "Ecology and Economy of a Formative Maya Site at Cuello, Belize." *Journal of Field Archaeology* 8:259–269.
Handwerker, W. P.
1983 "The First Demographic Transition: An Analysis of Subsistence Choices and Reproductive Consequences." *American Anthropologist* 85:5–27.
Hanks, Lucien
1972 *Rice and Man: Agricultural Ecology in Southeast Asia.* Chicago: Aldine.
Hanley, Susan, and Kozo Yamamura
1977 *Economic and Demographic Change in Preindustrial Japan, 1600–1868.* Princeton: Princeton University Press.
Harding, Robert
1975 "Meat Eating and Hunting in Baboons." In *Socioecology and Psychology of Primates.* R. H. Tuttle, ed., pp. 245–257. The Hague: Mouton.
Harlan, Jack
1978 "Origins of Cereal Agriculture in the Old World." In *Origins of Agriculture,* C. Reed, ed., pp. 357–383. The Hague: Mouton.
Harlow, Harry, M. Dodsworth, and A. Arling
1966 "Maternal Behavior of Rhesus Monkeys Deprived of Mothering and Peer Association in Infancy." *Proceedings of the American Philosophical Society* 110:58–66.
Harner, Michael J.
1970 "Population Pressure and the Social Evolution of Agriculturalists." *Southwestern Journal of Anthropology* 26:67–86.
1972a "The Role of Hallucinogenic Plants in European Witchcraft." In *Hallucinogens and Shamanism,* Michael Harner, ed., pp. 127–150. New York: Oxford University Press.
1972b *The Jivaro: People of the Sacred Waterfalls.* Garden City, N.Y.: Natural History Press.
1977 "The Ecological Basis for Aztec Sacrifice." *American Ethnologist* 4:117–135.
1978 "Reply to Ortiz de Montellano." Paper read at the New York Academy of Sciences, November 17, 1978.
Harrell, Barbara
1981 "Lactation and Menstruation in Cultural Perspective." *American Anthropologist* 83:796–823.
Harrington, Charles, and J. Whiting
1972 "Socialization Process and Personality." In *Psychological Anthropology,* Francis Hsu, ed., pp. 469–507. Cambridge, Mass.: Schenkman.
Harris, David
1976 "Traditional Systems of Plant Food Production and the Origins of Agriculture in West Africa." In *Origins of African Plant Domestication,* J. Harlan, J. de Wet, and A. Stemler, eds., pp. 311–356. The Hague: Mouton.
Harris, Marvin
1958 *Portugal's African "Wards": A First Hand Report on Labour and Education in Mozambique.* New York: American Committee on Africa.
1968 *The Rise of Anthropological Theory.* New York: Crowell.
1970 "Referential Ambiguity in the Calculus of Brazilian Racial Identity." *Southwestern Journal of Anthropology* 26:1–14.
1972 "Portugal's Contribution to the Underdevelopment of Africa and Brazil." In *Protest and Resistance in Angola and Brazil,* Ronald Chilcote, ed., pp. 209–223. Berkeley: University of California Press.
1974a *Patterns of Race in the Americas.* New York: Norton.
1974b *Cows, Pigs, Wars, and Witches: The Riddle of Culture.* New York: Random House.
1977 *Cannibals and Kings: The Origins of Cultures.* New York: Random House.
1979a "Reply to Sahlins." *New York Review of Books,* June 28, pp. 52–53.
1979b "Reply to Simoons." *Current Anthropology* 20:479–482.
1979c *Cultural Materialism: The Struggle for a Science of Culture.* New York: Random House.
1981 *America Now: The Anthropology of a Changing Culture.* New York: Simon & Schuster.
1984 "Animal Capture and Yanomamo Warfare: Retrospect and New Evidence." *Journal of Anthropological Research* 40:183–201.

Harris, Marvin, and E. O. Wilson
1978 "The Envelope and the Twig." *The Sciences* 18(8):10–15, 27.
Harrison, Gail
1975 "Primary Adult Lactase Deficiency: A Problem in Anthropological Genetics." *American Anthropologist* 77:812–835.
Harrison, Peter
1982 "Subsistence and Society in Eastern Yucatan." In *Maya Subsistence: Studies in Memory of Dennis E. Puleston.* Kent Flannery, ed. pp. 119–128. New York: Academic Press.
Harrison, Peter, and B. L. Turner (eds.)
1978 *Pre-Hispanic Maya Agriculture.* Albuquerque: University of New Mexico Press.
Harrison, R. J., and W. Montagna
1969 *Man.* Englewood Cliffs, N.J.: Prentice-Hall.
Harrison, T.
1976 "The Upper Paleolithic in Malaysia (Malaya and Borneo) and Adjacent Areas." 14th Congress, VISST. *Nice. Colloq.* 18:12–27.
Hart, C. W. M., and A. R. Pilling
1960 *The Tiwi of North Australia.* New York: Holt, Rinehart and Winston.
Hasegawa, Toshikazu, et al.
1983 "New Evidence of Scavenging Behavior in Wild Chimpanzees." *Current Anthropology* 24:231–232.
Hassan, Ferki
1973 "On Mechanisms of Population Growth During the Neolithic." *Current Anthropology* 14:535–540.
1978 "Demographic Archaeology." In *Advances in Archaeological Method and Theory,* Michael Schiffer, ed., pp. 49–103. New York: Academic.
1981 *Demographic Archaeology.* New York: Academic.
Haswell, M. R.
1953 *Economics of Agriculture in a Savannah Village: Report on Three Years Study in Genieri Village.* London: Colonial Research Studies, No. 8, H.M.S.O.
Haugen, Einar
1977 "Linguistic Relativity: Myths and Methods." In *Language and Thought: Anthropological Issues,* W. C. McCormack and S. A. Wurm, eds., pp. 11–28. The Hague: Mouton.
Haviland, William
1970 "Tikal, Guatemala and Mesoamerican Urbanism." *World Archaeology* 2:186–198.
Hayden, Brian
1981 "Subsistence and Ecological Adaptations of Modern Hunter/Gatherers." In *Omnivorous Primates: Gathering and Hunting in Human Evolution,* Geza Teleki and S. O. Harding, eds., pp. 344–421. New York: Columbia University Press.
Haynes, Vance
1973 "The Calico Site: Artifacts or Geofacts?" *Science* 181:305.
Hazard, Thomas
1960 "On the Nature of the Numaym and Its Counterparts Elsewhere on the Northwest Coast." Paper read at the Annual Meeting of the American Association for the Advancement of Science, Denver.
Heber, Rick F.
1969 *Rehabilitation of Families at Risk for Mental Retardation.* Milwaukee: University of Wisconsin Rehabilitation Center.
Hechinger, Fred
1979 "Further Proof that I.Q. Data Were Fraudulent." *New York Times,* January 30, p. C4.
Heider, Karl G.
1969 "Visiting Trading Institutions." *American Anthropologist* 71:462–471.
1972 *The Dani of West Iran.* Reading, Mass.: Addison-Wesley.
Heilbroner, Robert L.
1966 *The Limits of American Capitalism.* New York: Harper & Row.
Heizer, Robert F.
1960 "Agriculture and the Theocratic State in Lowland Southeastern Mexico." *American Antiquity* 26:215–222.
Hellburn, Suzanne, et al.
1976 *Economics in Society: Third World Economics.* Reading, Mass.: Addison-Wesley.
Helm, June
1980 "Female Infanticide, European Diseases, and Population Levels Among the Mackenzie Dene." *American Ethnologist* 7:259–284.
Henderson, John
1981 *The World of the Ancient Maya.* Ithaca: Cornell University Press.
Henry, Jules
1963 *Culture Against Man.* New York: Random House.

Herbers, John
1978 "Black-White Split Persists a Decade After Warning." *New York Times*, February 26, pp. 1ff.
Herre, Wolf, and M. Röhrs
1978 "Zoological Considerations in the Origin of Farming and Domestication." In *Origins of Agriculture*, C. Reed, ed., pp. 245–279. The Hague: Mouton.
Herrnstein, R. J.
1973 *I.Q. in the Meritocracy*. Boston: Little, Brown.
Hersh, Burton
1978 *The Mellon Family: A Fortune in History*. New York: Morrow.
Herskovits, Melville J.
1938 *Dahomey, An Ancient West African Kingdom*. New York: J. J. Augustin.
Hertzler, Joyce O.
1965 *A Sociology of Language*. New York: Random House.
Hewitt de Alcantara, Cynthia
1976 *Modernizing Mexican Agriculture*. Geneva: United Nations Research Institute for Social Development.
Heyerdahl, Thor
1950 *Kon Tiki—Across the Pacific by Raft*. Chicago: Rand McNally.
Hicks, David
1976 *Tetum Ghosts and Kin*. Palo Alto, Calif.: Mayfield.
Hiernaux, Jean
1969 *Egalité ou inegalité des races?* Paris: Hachette.
Higgs, E. S., and M. R. Jarman
1972 "The Origins of Animal and Plant Husbandry." In *Papers in Economic Prehistory*, E. S. Higgs, ed., pp. 3–13. Cambridge, England: Cambridge University Press.
Hill, Jane
1978 "Apes and Language." *Annual Review of Anthropology* 7:89–112.
Hirsch, Jerry
1970 "Behavior-Genetic Analysis and Its Biosocial Consequences." *Seminars in Psychiatry* 2:89–105.
1981 "To Unfrock the Charlatans." *Sage Race Relations Abstracts* 6:1–67.
Hirschfeld, Lawrence, J. Howe, and B. Levin
1978 "Warfare, Infanticide and Statistical Inference: A Comment on Divale and Harris." *American Anthropologist* 80:110–115.
Hite, S.
1976 *The Hite Report: A Nationwide Study of Female Sexuality*. New York: Macmillan.
Ho, Ping-C
1975 *The Cradle of the East: An Inquiry into the Indigenous Origins of Techniques and Ideas of Neolithic and Early Historic China, 5,000–1,000 B.C.* Chicago: University of Chicago Press.
1978 "The Indigenous Origins of Chinese Agriculture." In *Origins of Agriculture*, C. Reed, ed., pp. 413–484. Chicago: Aldine.
Hobsbawm, E. J.
1965 *Primitive Rebels*. New York: Norton.
Hockett, Charles, and R. Ascher
1964 "The Human Revolution." *Current Anthropology* 5:135–147.
Hoffer, Carol
1975 "Bundu: Political Implications of Female Solidarity in a Secret Society." In *Being Female: Reproduction, Power, and Change*, Dana Raphael, ed., pp. 155–164. The Hague: Mouton.
Hogbin, H. Ian
1964 *A Guadalcanal Society: The Kaoka Speakers*. New York: Holt, Rinehart and Winston.
Holloway, Ralph L.
1973 "New Endocranial Values for the East African Early Hominids." *Nature* 243:97–99.
Hopkins, D. M. (ed.)
1967 *The Bering Land Bridge*. Stanford: Stanford University Press.
Hopkins, Keith
1980 "Brother-Sister Marriage in Ancient Egypt." *Comparative Studies in Society and History* 22:303–354.
Hoselitz, Bert
1977 "Selected Publications of Bert F. Hoselitz." In *Essays on Economic Development and Cultural Change in Honor of Bert F. Hoselitz*, Manning Nash, ed., pp. 449–460. Chicago: University of Chicago Press.
Howe, James
1978 "Ninety-two Mythical Populations: A Reply to Divale et al." *American Anthropologist* 80:671–673.
Howell, F. C., and Y. Coppens
1976 "An Overview of Hominidae from the Omo Succession, Ethiopia." In *Human Origins: Louis Leakey and the East African*

Evidence, G. D. Isaac and E. R. McCown, eds. Menlo Park, Calif.: Benjamin.

Howell, Nancy
1976a "The Population of the Dobe Area !Kung." In *Kalahari Hunter-Gatherers,* Richard Lee and Irven DeVore, eds., pp. 137–151. Cambridge, Mass.: Harvard University Press.
1976b "Toward a Uniformitarian Theory of Human Paleodemography." In *The Demographic Evolution of Human Populations,* R. H. Ward and K. M. Weiss, eds., pp. 25–40. New York: Academic.

Howells, William W.
1973 *Evolution of the Genus Homo.* Reading, Mass.: Addison-Wesley.
1975 "Neanderthal Man: Facts and Figures." In *Paleoanthropology: Morphology and Paleoecology,* R. H. Tuttle, ed., pp. 389–407. The Hague: Mouton.

Huffman, Sandra, A. K. M. Chowdhury, and W. H. Mosley
1978 "Postpartum Amenorrhea: How Is It Affected by Maternal Nutritional Status?" *Science* 200:1155–1157.
1979 "Reply to Frisch." *Science* 203:922–923.

Hulse, Frederick
1973 *Human Species: An Introduction to Physical Anthropology,* 2d ed. New York: Random House.

Hunn, Eugene
1982 "Did the Aztec Lack Potential Animal Domesticates?" *American Ethnologist* 9:578–579.

Hunt, J. M.
1969 "Has Compensatory Education Failed? Has It Been Attempted?" *Harvard Educational Review* 39:278–300.

Hutterer, Karl
1976 "An Evolutionary Approach to the Southeast Asian Cultural Sequence." *Current Anthropology* 17:221–242.

Hymes, Dell
1971 "Introduction." In *The Origin and Diversification of Language,* M. Swadesh, J. F. Sherzer, eds. Chicago: Aldine.

Ianni, F. A. J., and E. Story (eds.)
1973 *Cultural Relevance and Educational Issues: A Reader in Anthropology and Education.* Boston: Little, Brown.

ICRISAT
n.d. *This is Icrisat.* Hyderabad: ICRISAT.

Inkeles, Alex
1966 "Social Stratification and Mobility in the Soviet Union." In *Class, Status, and Power: Social Stratification in Comparative Perspective,* R. Bendix and S. M. Lipset, eds., pp. 516–526. New York: Free Press.

Irons, William
1979 "Natural Selection, Adaptation, and Human Social Behavior." In *Evolutionary Biology and Human Social Behavior,* N. Chagnon and W. Irons, eds, pp. 4–39. North Scituate, Mass.: Duxbury Press.

Irving, W., and C. Harrington
1973 "Upper Pleistocene Radiocarbon-Dated Artifacts from the Northern Yukon." *Science* 179:335–340.

Isaac, Glynn
1971 "The Diet of Early Man: Aspects of Archaeological Evidence from Lower and Middle Pleistocene Sites in Africa." *World Archaeology* 2:278–298.
1978 "The Food Sharing Behavior of Protohuman Hominids." *Scientific American* 238(4):90–108.

Isaac, G. and D. Crader
1981 "To What Extent Were Early Hominids Carnivorous? An Archaeological Perspective." In *Omnivorous Primates: Gathering and Hunting in Human Evolution.* R. Harding and G. Teleki, eds. pp. 37–103. New York: Columbia University Press.

Isbell, W., and K. Schreiber
1978 "Was Huari a State?" *American Antiquity* 43:372–389.

Itani, Jun'ichiro
1961 "The Society of Japanese Monkeys." *Japan Quarterly* 8:421–430.

Itani, J., and A. Nishimura
1973 "The Study of Infra-Human Culture in Japan." In *Precultural Primate Behavior,* E. W. Menzell, ed., pp. 26–50. Basel: S. Karjer.

Jacob, T.
1975 "Morphology and Paleoecology of Early Man in Java." In *Paleoanthropology: Morphology and Paleoecology,* R. H. Tuttle, ed., pp. 311–326. Chicago: Aldine.

Jacobs, Norman
1958 *The Origin of Modern Capitalism and East Asia.* Hong Kong: Hong Kong University Press.

Jacobson, Jerome
1979 "Recent Developments in South Asian

Prehistory and Protohistory." *Annual Review of Anthropology* 8:467–502.

Janzen, Daniel
1973 "Tropical Agroecosystems." *Science* 182:1212–1219.

Jelinek, Arthur
1977 "The Lower Paleolithic: Current Evidence and Interpretation." *Annual Review of Anthropology* 6:11–32.

Jelinek, Jan
1969 "Neanderthal Man and *Homo sapiens* in Central and Eastern Europe." *Current Anthropology* 10:475–503.

Jenkins, Farish
1972 "Chimpanzee Bipedalism: Cineradiographic Analysis and Implications for the Evolution of Gait." *Science* 178:877–879.

Jennings, Jesse
1974 *Prehistory of North America*, 2d ed. New York: McGraw-Hill.
1983 *Ancient South America*. San Francisco: W. Freeman.

Jensen, Arthur
1969 "How Much Can We Boost I.Q. and Scholastic Achievement?" *Harvard Educational Review* 29:1–123.

Jensen, Neal
1978 "Limits to Growth in World Food Production." *Science* 201:317–320.

Jochim, Michael
1981 *Strategies for Survival: Cultural Behavior in an Ecological Context*. New York: Academic.

Johanson, Donald, and Maitland Edey
1981 *Lucy: The Beginnings of Humankind*. New York: Warner.

Johanson, Donald, and T. D. White
1979 "A Systematic Assessment of Early African Hominids." *Science* 203:321–330.

Johnson, Allen W.
1975 "Time Allocation in a Machiguenga Community." *Ethnology* 14:301–310.
1978 *Quantification in Cultural Anthropology*. Stanford: Stanford University Press.

Jolly, Clifford
1970 "The Seed-Eaters: A New Model of Hominid Differentiation Based on Baboon Analogy." *Man* 5:5–36.

Jones, Peter
1979 "Effects of Raw Materials on Biface Manufacture." *Science* 204:835–836.
1980 "Experimental Butchery with Modern Stone Tools and Its Relevance for Paleolithic Archaeology." *World Archaeology* 12:153–165.

Jorgenson, Joseph
1971 "On Ethics and Anthropology." *Current Anthropology* 12(3):321–334.

Joseph, Suad
1978 "Muslim-Christian Conflicts in Lebanon: A Perspective on the Evolution of Sectarianism." In *Muslim-Christian Conflicts: Economic, Political, and Social Origins*, S. Joseph and B. Pillsbury, eds., pp. 63–98. Boulder, Colo.: Westview Press.

Josephus, Flavius
1970 *The Jewish War*, trans. G. A. Williamson. Baltimore: Penguin.

Jungers, William
1978 "On Canine Reduction in Early Hominids." *Current Anthropology* 19(1):155–156.

Kaberry, Phyllis
1970 (1939) *Aboriginal Woman, Sacred and Profane*. London: Routledge.

Kaeppler, Adrienne
1978 "Dance in Anthropological Perspective." *Annual Review of Anthropology* 7:31–49.

Kaffman, M.
1977 "Sexual Standards and Behavior of the Kibbutz Adolescent." *American Journal of Orthopsychiatry* 47:207–217.

Kamin, L. J.
1974 *The Science and Politics of I.Q.* New York: Halstead Press.

Kang, Elizabeth
1979 "Exogamy and Peace Relations of Social Units: A Cross-Cultural Test." *Ethnology* 18:85–99.

Kaplan, L., T. Lynch, and C. Smith
1973 "Early Cultivated Beans (*Phaseolus vulgaris*) from an Intermontane Peruvian Valley." *Science* 179:76–77.

Karnes, M. B.
1968 "A Research Program to Determine the Effects of Various Pre-School Programs." Paper presented to the American Educational Research Association, Chicago.

Katz, Jerold
1971 *The Underlying Reality of Language and Its Philosophical Import*. New York: Harper & Row (Torchbooks).

Kay, Paul, and W. Kempton
1984 "What Is the Sapir-Whorf Hypothesis?" *American Anthropologist* 86:65–79.

Kehoe, Alice
1968 "The Ghost Dance Religion in Sasketchewan, Canada." *Plains Anthropologist* 13:296–304.

Kelly, Raymond
1976 "Witchcraft and Sexual Relations." In *Man and Woman in the New Guinea Highlands*, P. Brown and G. Buchbinder, eds., pp. 36–53. Washington, D.C.: Special Publication No. 8, American Anthropological Association.

Kelso, A. J.
1974 *Physical Anthropology*, 2d ed. Philadelphia: Lippincott.

Kendall, A. C.
1972 "Rickets in the Tropics and Subtropics." *Central African Journal of Medicine* 18:47–49.

Kephart, M. J.
n.d. "Economic Anthropology and the Problem of European Hexenwahn." Unpublished manuscript.

Kertzer, David
1978 "Theoretical Developments in the Study of Age Group Systems." *American Ethnologist* 5(2):368–374.

Key, Wilson
1976 *Media Sexploitation*. New York: Signet.

Kitahara-Frisch, J.
1980 "Apes and the Making of Stone Tools." *Current Anthropology* 21:359.

Klass, Morton
1979 *Caste: The Emergence of the South Asian Social System*. Philadelphia: ISHI.

Klein, Richard
1973 "Geological Antiquity of Rhodesian Man." *Nature* 244:311–312.

Klineberg, Otto
1935 *Negro Intelligence and Selective Migration*. New York: Columbia University Press.
1944 *Characteristics of the American Negro*. New York: Harper & Row.

Knight, Rolf
1974 "Grey Owl's Return: Cultural ecology and Canadian Indigenous Peoples." *Reviews in Anthropology* 1:349–359.

Koch, K. F.
1974 *War and Peace in Jalemo: The Management of Conflict in Highland New Guinea*. Cambridge, Mass.: Harvard University Press.

Kopper, John, and M. Grishman
1978 "Ice Age Idols." *The Sciences*, September, pp. 4–5.

Kortlant, A.
1967 "Experimentation with Chimpanzees in the Wild." In *Progress in Primatology*, D. Starck, R. Schneider, and H. Kuhn, eds., pp. 185–194. Stuttgart: Gustav Fischer.

Koskoff, David
1978 *The Mellons: The Chronicle of America's Richest Family*. New York: Crowell.

Kozol, Jonathan
1967 *Death at an Early Age: The Destruction of the Hearts and Minds of Negro Children in the Boston Public Schools*. Boston: Houghton Mifflin.

Krantz, G.
1980 "Sapienization and Speech." *Current Anthropology* 21:773–779.

Kroeber, Alfred L.
1948 *Anthropology*. New York: Harcourt Brace.

Krzyzaniak, Lech
1981 "Origin and Early Development of Food-Producing Cultures in Northeastern Africa." *Current Anthropology* 22:693–694.

Kuhn, Thomas
1970 *The Structure of Scientific Revolutions*, 2d ed. Chicago: University of Chicago Press.

Kurtén, Bjorn
1972 *The Ice Age*. New York: Putnam.

La Barre, Weston
1938 *The Peyote Cult*. Yale University Publications in Anthropology, No. 19. New Haven: Yale University Press.

Labov, William
1972a *Language in the Inner City*. Philadelphia: University of Pennsylvania Press.
1972b *Sociolinguistic Patterns*. Philadelphia: University of Pennsylvania Press.

Ladd, Everett, Jr.
1978 *Where Have All the Voters Gone?* New York: Norton.

Laitman, J., and R. Heimbuch
1982 "The Basicranium of Plio-Pleistocene Hominids as an Indicator of Their Upper Respiratory Systems." *American Journal of Physical Anthropology* 59:323–343.

Laitman, J., R. Heimbuch, and E. Crelin
1979 "The Basicranium of Fossil Hominids as an Indicator of Their Upper Respiratory Systems." *American Journal of Physical Anthropology* 51:15–34.

Lakatos, I.
1970 "Falsification and the Methodology of Scientific Research Programmes." In *Criticism and the Growth of Knowledge*, I. Lakatos and

A. Musgrave, eds., pp. 91–195. Cambridge, Mass.: Harvard University Press.

Lakoff, R.
1973 "Language and Woman's Place." *Language in Society* 2:45–79.

Lancaster, Chet, and J. B. Lancaster
1978 "On the Male Supremacist Complex: A Reply to Divale and Harris." *American Anthropologist* 80:115–117.

Langdon, Steve
1979 "Comparative Tlingit and Haida Adaptation to the West Coast of the Prince of Wales Archipelago." *Ethnology* 18:101–119.

Lanning, Edward P.
1974 "Western South America." In *Prehispanic America*, S. Gorenstein, ed., pp. 65–86. New York: St. Martin's Press.

Lanternari, Vittorio
1963 *The Religion of the Oppressed.* New York: Knopf.

Laritchev, V. E.
1976 "Discovery of Hand Axes in China and the Problem of Local Cultures of Lower Paleolithic of East Asia." 9th Congress, I.S.P.P. *Nice. Colloq.* (7):154–178.

Lattimore, Owen
1962 *Inner Asian Frontiers of China.* Boston: Beacon Press.

Laudan, Larry
1977 *Progress and Its Problems: Towards a Theory of Scientific Growth.* Berkeley: University of California Press.

Lawrence, Peter
1964 *Road Belong Cargo: A Study of the Cargo Movement in the Southern Madang District, New Guinea.* Manchester: University of Manchester.

Layzer, David
1974 "Heritability Analyses of I.Q. Scores: Science or Numerology?" *Science* 183:1259–1266.

Leach, Edmund R.
1968 "Polyandry, Inheritance, and the Definition of Marriage, with Particular Reference to Sinhalese Customary Law." In *Marriage, Family, and Residence*, P. Bohannan and J. Middleton, eds., pp. 73–83. Garden City, N.Y.: Natural History Press.

Leacock, Eleanor
1972 "Introduction" to F. Engels' *Origin of the Family, Private Property and the State*, pp. 7–67. New York: International Publishers.
1973 "The Montagnais-Naskapi Band." In *Cultural Ecology: Readings on the Canadian Indians and Eskimos*, B. Cox, ed., pp. 81–100. Toronto: McClelland and Stewart.
1975 "Class, Commodity, and the Status of Women." In *Women Cross-Culturally: Change and Challenge*, R. Leavitt, eds., pp. 601–616. The Hague: Mouton.
1978 "Women's Status in Egalitarian Society: Implication for Social Evolution." *Current Anthropology* 19:247–275.
1981 *Myths of Male Dominance.* New York: Monthly Review Press.

Leakey, Louis, and V. M. Goodall
1969 *Unveiling Man's Origins.* Cambridge, Mass.: Schenkman.

Leakey, Mary
1975 "Cultural Patterns in the Olduvai Sequence." In *After the Australopithecines: Stratigraphy, Ecology, and Culture Change in the Middle Pleistocene*, K. Butzer and G. Isaac, eds., pp. 477–493. The Hague: Mouton.
1979 "Footprints Frozen in Time." *National Geographic* 155:446–457.

Leakey, Mary, et al.
1976 "Fossil Hominids from the Laetoli Beds." *Nature* 262:460–466.

Leakey, Richard, and R. Lewin
1978 *People of the Lake.* Garden City, N.Y.: Anchor Books.

Leakey, Richard, and Alan Walker
1980 "On the Status of *Australopithecus afarensis*." *Science* 207:1103.

Lee, Richard B.
1968 "What Do Hunters Do for a Living, or How to Make Out on Scarce Resources." In *Man the Hunter*, R. B. Lee and I. DeVore, eds., pp. 30–43. Chicago: Aldine.
1969 "!Kung Bushman Subsistence: An Input-Output Analysis." In *Environment and Cultural Behavior: Ecological Studies in Cultural Anthropology*, A. P. Vayda, ed., pp. 47–79. Garden City, N.Y.: Natural History Press.
1972a "The !Kung Bushmen of Botswana." In *Hunters and Gatherers Today*, M. G. Bichiere, ed., pp. 327–367. New York: Holt, Rinehart and Winston.
1972b "Population Growth and the Beginning of Sedentary Life Among the !Kung Bushmen." In *Population Growth: Anthropological Implications*, Brian Spooner, ed., pp. 329–342. Cambridge, Mass.: M.I.T. Press.

1973 "Mongongo: The Ethnography of a Major Wild Food Resource." *Ecology of Food and Nutrition* 2:307–321.
1976 "!Kung Spatial Organization." In *Kalahari Hunter-Gatherers*, Richard Lee and Irven DeVore, eds., pp. 73–97. Cambridge, Mass.: Harvard University Press.
1979 *The !Kung San: Men, Women and Work in a Foraging Society*. New York: Cambridge University Press.

Leeds, Anthony
1970 "The Concept of the Culture of Poverty: Conceptual, Logical, and Empirical Problems, with Perspectives from Brazil and Peru." In *The Culture of Poverty: A Critique*, E. Leacock, ed., pp. 226–284. New York: Simon & Schuster.

Lees, Susan, and D. Bates
1974 "The Origins of Specialized Nomadic Pastoralism: A Systemic Model." *American Antiquity* 39:187–193.

Lenin, V. I.
1965 (1917) *The State and Revolution*. Peking: Foreign Languages Press.

Leonard, Karen I.
1978 *Social History of an Indian Caste*. Berkeley: University of California Press.

Leroi-Gourhan, Andre
1968 "The Evolution of Paleolithic Art." *Scientific American* 218(2):58–70.

Lesser, Alexander
1968 "War and the State." In *War: The Anthropology of Armed Conflict and Aggression*, M. Fried, M. Harris, and R. Murphy, eds., pp. 92–96. Garden City, N.Y.: Natural History Press.

LeVine, Robert
1973 *Culture, Behavior, and Personality*. Chicago: Aldine.

Lévi-Strauss, Claude
1963a *Totemism*. Boston: Beacon Press.
1963b *Tristes Tropiques*. New York: Atheneum.

Lewin, Roger
1983 "Were Lucy's Feet Made for Walking?" *Science* 220:700–702.

Lewis, Oscar
1961 *The Children of Sanchez: Autobiography of a Mexican Family*. New York: Random House.
1964 *Pedro Martinez: A Mexican Peasant and His Family*. New York: Random House.
1966 *La Vida: A Puerto Rican Family in the Culture of Poverty—San Juan and New York*. New York: Random House.

Lichtheim, George
1961 *Marxism: An Historical and Critical Study*. New York: Praeger.

Lieberman, Philip
1978 "More Talk on Neanderthal Speech." *Current Anthropology* 19(2):407.

Lieberman, Philip, and E. S. Crelin
1974 "Speech in Neanderthal Man: A Reply to Carlisle and Siegel." *American Anthropologist* 76:323–325.

Lieberman, Philip, E. S. Crelin, and D. H. Klatt
1972 "Phonetic Ability and Related Anatomy of the Newborn, the Adult Human, Neanderthal Man, and the Chimpanzee." *American Anthropologist* 74:287–307.

Liebow, Elliot
1967 *Tally's Corner: A Study of Negro Street Corner Men*. Boston: Little, Brown.

Lindenbaum, Shirley
1977 "The Last Course: Nutrition and Anthropology in Asia." In *Nutrition and Anthropology in Action*, Thomas Fitzgerald, ed., pp. 141–155. Atlantic Highlands, N.J.: Humanities Press.
1979 *Kuru Society*. Palo Alto, Calif.: Mayfield.
1983 "Loaves and Fishes in Bangladesh." Paper read at Wenner-Gren Symposium 94, Cedar Key, Florida.

Linton, Ralph
1959 "The Natural History of the Family." In *The Family: Its Function and Destiny*, R. Anshen, ed., pp. 30–52. New York: Harper & Row.

Littlefield, Alice, L. Lieberman, and L. Reynolds
1982 "Redefining Race: The Potential Demise of a Concept in Physical Anthropology." *Current Anthropology* 23:641–655.

Livingstone, Frank B.
1968 "The Effects of Warfare on the Biology of the Human Species." In *War: The Anthropology of Armed Conflict and Aggression*, M. Fried, M. Harris, and R. Murphy, eds., pp. 3–15. Garden City, N.Y.: Doubleday.
1969 "Genetics, Ecology, and the Origins of Incest and Exogamy." *Current Anthropology* 10:45–62.
1981 "Comments on Bixler 1981." *Current Anthropology* 22:645–656.
1982 "Comment on Littlefield, Lieberman, and Reynolds." *Current Anthropology* 23:651.

Lizot, Jaques
1977 "Population, Resources and Warfare Among the Yanomamo." *Man* 12:497–517.
1979 "On Food Taboos and Amazon Cultural Ecology." *Current Anthropology* 20:150–151.
Lochlin, J. C., and R. C. Nichols
1976 *Heredity, Environment and Personality.* Austin: University of Texas Press.
Lomax, Alan (ed.)
1968 *Folksong Style and Culture.* Washington, D.C.: American Association for the Advancement of Science, Publication 88.
Lomax, Alan, and Conrad Arensberg
1977 "A Worldwide Evolutionary Classification of Cultures by Subsistence Systems." *Current Anthropology* 18:659–708.
London, Miriam, and Ivan London
1979 "China's Victimized Youth." *New York Times,* February 10, p. 19.
Lorenz, Konrad Z.
1966 *On Aggression.* New York: Harcourt Brace Jovanovich.
Lovejoy, C. Owen
1974 "The Gait of the Australopithecines." *Yearbook of Physical Anthropology* 17:147–161.
Lovejoy, C. O., K. G. Heiple, and A. Burstein
1973 "The Gait of *Australopithecus.*" *American Journal of Physical Anthropology* 38:757–780.
Lovins, Amory
1976 "Energy Strategy: The Road Not Taken." *Foreign Affairs* 55:65–96.
Lowie, Robert
1920 *Primitive Society.* New York: Boni and Liveright.
1948 (1924) *Primitive Religion.* New York: Liveright.
Lumsden, Charles, and Edward Wilson
1983 *Promethean Fire: Reflections on the Origin of Mind.* Cambridge, Mass.: Harvard University Press.
Lundberg, Ferdinand
1968 *The Rich and the Super Rich.* New York: Lyle Stuart.
Lynch, Thomas
1983 "The Paleo-Indians." In *Ancient South Americans,* Jessie Jennings, ed., pp. 87–137. San Francisco: Freeman.
Lynn, Richard
1978 "Ethnic and Racial Differences in Intelligence: International Comparison." In *Human Variation: The Biopsychology of Age, Race, and Sex,* R. T. Osborne, C. Noble, and N. Weyl, eds., pp. 261–286. New York: Academic.
Macdougall, J. D.
1976 "Fission-Track Dating." *Scientific American* 235(6):114–122.
MacLeish, Kenneth
1972 "The Tasadays: The Stone Age Cavemen of Mindanao." *National Geographic* 142:219–248.
MacNeish, Richard
n.d. "The Transition to Statehood (As Seen from the Mouth of a Cave)." Unpublished paper.
1972 "The Evolution of Community Patterns in the Tehuacan Valley of Mexico, and Speculation About the Cultural Processes." In *Man, Settlement, and Urbanism,* P. J. Ucko, R. Tringham, and G. W. Dimbleby, eds., pp. 67–93. Cambridge, Mass.: Schenkman.
1978 *The Science of Archaeology?* Belmont, Calif.: Duxbury Press.
Magubane, B.
1975 "The Native Reserves (Bantustans) and the Role of the Migrant Labor System in the Political Economy of South Africa." In *Migration and Development: Implications for Ethnic Identity and Political Conflict,* H. I. Safa and B. Du Toit, eds., pp. 225–267. The Hague: Mouton.
Mair, Lucy
1969 *Witchcraft.* New York: McGraw-Hill.
Malefijt, Annemarie
1968 *Religion and Culture: An Introduction to the Anthropology of Religion.* New York: Macmillan.
Malinowski, Bronislaw
1920 "War and Weapons Among the Natives of the Trobriand Islands." *Man* 20:10–12.
1922 *Argonauts of the Western Pacific.* New York: Dutton.
1927 *Sex and Repression in Savage Society.* London: Routledge & Kegan Paul.
1935 *Coral Gardens and Their Magic* (2 vols.). London: Allen and Unwin.
Malkenson, Frederich, and J. Keane
1983 "Radiobiology of the Skin." In *Biochemistry and Physiology of the Skin,* Lowell Goldsmith, ed., pp. 769–814. New York: Oxford.
Mamdani, Mahmood
1973 *The Myth of Population Control: Family, Caste, and Class in an Indian Village.* New York: Monthly Review Press.
Mangelsdorf, Paul
1974 *Corn: Its Origin, Evolution, and*

Improvement. Cambridge, Mass.: Harvard University Press.

Mann, Alan, and E. Trinkaus
1974 "Neanderthal and Neanderthal-like Fossils from the Upper Pleistocene." *Yearbook of Physical Anthropology* 17:169–193.

Marano, Lou
1982 "Windigo Psychosis: The Anatomy of an Emic-Etic Confusion." *Current Anthropology* 23:385–412.

Marcus, Joyce
1983 "Lowland Maya Archaeology at the Crossroads." *American Antiquity* 48:454–488.

Marett, R. R.
1914 *The Threshold of Religion*. London: Methuen.

Marshack, Alexander
1972a "Upper Paleolithic Notation and Symbol." *Science* 178:817–828.
1972b *The Roots of Civilization*. New York: McGraw-Hill.
1976 "Some Implications of the Paleolithic Symbolic Evidence for the Origin of Language." *Current Anthropology* 17:274–282.

Marshall, Donald
1971 "Sexual Behavior on Mangaia." In *Human Sexual Behavior*, D. Marshall and R. Suggs, eds., pp. 103–162. Englewood Cliffs, N.J.: Prentice-Hall.

Marshall, Mac
1978 *Weekend Warriors: An Interpretation of Drunkenness in Micronesia*. Palo Alto, Calif.: Mayfield.

Martinez, Augustin
1979 "9,700 Years of Maritime Subsistence on the Pacific." *American Antiquity* 44:309–320.

Marx, Karl
1970 (1859) *A Contribution to the Critique of Political Economy*. New York: International Publishers.
1973 *On Society and Social Change*, Neil Smelser, ed. Chicago: University of Chicago Press.

Marx, Karl, and F. Engels
1948 (1848) *The Communist Manifesto*. New York: International.

Mason, Carol
1964 "Natchez Class Structure." *Ethnohistory* 11:120–133.

Mason, J. Alden
1957 *The Ancient Civilizations of Peru*. Harmondsworth, England: Penguin.

Matheny, Ray
1976 "Maya Lowland Hydraulic Systems." *Science* 193:639–646.

Matheny, Ray, and D. Gurr
1983 "Variations in Prehistoric Agricultural Systems of the New World." *Annual Review of Anthropology* 12:79–103.

Maw, B., R. Ciochon, and D. Savage
1979 "Late Eocene of Burma Yields Earliest Anthropoid Primate, *Pondaungia cotteri*." *Nature* 282:65–67.

McAskie, M., and A. M. Clarke
1976 "Parent-Offspring Resemblances in Intelligence; Theories and Evidence." *British Journal of Psychology* 67:243–273.

McCall, R. B., M. I. Applebaum, and P. S. Hogarty
1973 *Development Changes in Mental Performance*. Monographs, vol. 38, no. 3, Society for Research in Child Development.

McDonald, David
1977 "Food Taboos: A Primitive Environmental Protection Agency (South America)." *Anthropus* 72:734–748.

McEwen, Gordon, and D. B. Dickson
1978 "Was Huari a State?" *American Antiquity* 43:372–389.

McGrew, W. C.
1977 "Socialization and Object Manipulation of Wild Chimpanzees." In *Primate Bio-Social Development*, Susan Chevalier-Skolinkoff and Frank Poirier, eds., pp. 261–288. New York: Garland.

McGrew, W. C., and C. E. G. Tutin
1973 "Chimpanzee Tool Use in Dental Grooming." *Nature* 241:477–478.

McGrew, W. C., C. Tutin, and P. Baldwin
1979 "New Data on Meat Eating by Wild Chimpanzees." *Current Anthropology* 20:238–239.

McGurk, F. C. J.
1975 "Race Differences Twenty Years Later." *Homo* 26:219–239.

McHenry, Henry
1974 "How Large Were the Australopithecines?" *American Journal of Physical Anthropology* 40:329–340.
1982 "The Pattern of Hominid Evolution: Studies on Bipedalism, Mastication, and Encephalization." *Annual Review of Anthropology* 11:151–173.

McIntosh, Susan, and Roderick McIntosh
1981 "West Africa Prehistory." *American Scientist* 69:602–613.

1983 "Current Directions in West African Prehistory." *Annual Review of Anthropology* 12:215–258.

McNamara, Robert
1984 "Time Bomb or Myth: The Population Problem." *Foreign Affairs* 62:1107–1131.

Meacham, William
1977 "Continuity and Local Evolution in the Neolithic of South China." *Current Anthropology* 18:419–440.

Mead, Margaret
1949 *Male and Female.* New York: Morrow.
1950 *Sex and Temperament in Three Primitive Societies.* New York: Mentor.
1970 *Culture and Commitment.* Garden City, N.Y.: Natural History Press.

Meggitt, Mervyn
1964 "Male-Female Relationships in the Highlands of Australian New Guinea." *American Anthropologist* 66:204–224.
1977 *Blood is Their Argument: Warfare Among Mae Enga Tribesmen of New Guinea Highlands.* Palo Alto, Calif.: Mayfield.

Meintel, Deirdre
1978 *Cape Verde Americans: Their Cultural and Historical Background.* Unpublished Ph.D. dissertation, Brown University.

Mellaart, James
1967 *Çatal Hüyük: A Neolithic Town in Anatolia.* New York: McGraw-Hill.
1975 *The Earliest Civilizations in the Near East.* London: Thames and Hudson.

Mencher, Joan
1974a "Conflicts and Contradictions in the Green Revolution: The Case of Tamil Nadu." *Economic and Political Weekly* 9:309–323.
1974b "The Caste System Upside Down: Or, the Not So Mysterious East." *Current Anthropology* 15:469–478.
1978 *Agricultural and Social Structure in Tamil Nadu.* New Delhi: Allied Publishers.
1980 "On Being an Untouchable in India: A Materialist Perspective." In *Beyond the Myths of Culture: Essay in Cultural Materialism.* Eric Ross, ed., pp. 261–294. New York: Academic Press.

Menozzi, P., A. Piazza, and L. Cavalli-Sforza
1978 "Synthetic Maps of Human Gene Frequencies in Europeans." *Science* 201:786–792.

Miller, Barbara
1983 *The Endangered Sex: Neglect of Female Children in Rural North India.* Ithaca: Cornell University Press.

Miller, Frank
1977 "Knowledge and Power: Anthropology, Policy Research, and the Green Revolution." *American Ethnologist* 4(1):190–198.

Millet, Kate
1970 *Sexual Politics.* Garden City, N.Y.: Doubleday.

Millon, René
1970 "Teotihuacán: Completion of the Map of the Giant Ancient City in the Valley of Mexico." *Science* 170:1077–1082.
1973 *The Teotihuacán Man.* Austin: University of Texas Press.

Milton, Katherine
1984 "Primate Diets and Gut Morphology: Implications for Early Human Evolution." Revised paper read at the Wenner Gren Symposium at Cedar Key, Florida.

Minaguchi, H., and J. Meites
1967 "Effects of Norethynodrel-Mestranol Combination (Enovid) on Hypothalamic and Pituitary Hormones in Rats." *Endocrinology* 81(4):826–834.

Minge-Kalman, Wanda
1974 "Private Property and Social Behavior in the Monogamous Stage of the History of the Family." Mimeographed.
1977 *Family Production and Reproduction in Industrial Society: A Field Study of Changes During the Peasant to Worker Transition in Europe.* Ph.D. dissertation, Columbia University.
1978a "Household Economy During the Peasant-to-Worker Transition in the Swiss Alps." *Ethnology* 17(2):183–196.
1978b "The Institutionalization of the European Family: The Institutionalization of 'Childhood' as a Market for Family Labor." *Comparative Studies in Society and History* 20:454–468.

Minturn, Leigh, and John T. Hitchcock
1963 "The Rajputs of Khalapur, India." In *Six Cultures, Studies of Child Rearing*, B. B. Whiting, ed., pp. 203–361. New York: Wiley.

Mitchell, William
1973 "The Hydraulic Hypothesis: A Re-appraisal." *Current Anthropology* 14:532–535.

Miyadi, D.
1967 "Differences in Social Behavior Among Japanese Macaque Troops." In *Progress in Primatology*, D. Starck, R. Schneider, and H. Kuhn, eds. Stuttgart: Gustav Fischer.

Molnar, Stephen
1983 *Human Variation: Races, Types, and*

Ethnic Groups, 2d ed. Engelwood Cliffs, N.J.: Prentice-Hall.

Mondlane, Eduardo
1969 *The Struggle for Mozambique*. Baltimore: Penguin.

Montagu, Ashley M. F.
1974 *Man's Most Dangerous Myth: The Fallacy of Race*, 5th ed. New York: Oxford University Press.

Montague, S. P., and R. Morais
1976 "Football Games and Rock Concerts: The Ritual Enactment." In *The American Dimension: Cultural Myths and Social Realities*, W. Arens and S. P. Montague, eds., pp. 33–52. Port Washington, N.Y.: Alfred.

Montgomery, Edward, and A. Johnson
1976 "Machiguenga Energy Expenditure." *Ecology of Food and Nutrition* 6:97–105.

Mooney, James
1965 (1896) *The Ghost Dance Religion*. Chicago: University of Chicago Press.

Morlan, Richard
1978 "Early Man in North Yukon Territory: Perspectives as of 1977." In *Early Man In America From a Circum-Pacific Perspective*, Alan Bryan, ed., pp. 78–95. Edmonton: University of Alberta.

Morren, George
1973 "Woman the Hunter." Paper presented to the Annual Meeting of the American Anthropological Association, New Orleans.
1977 "From Hunting to Herding: Pigs and the Control of Energy in Montane New Guinea." In *Subsistence and Survival: Rural Ecology in the Pacific*, T. P. Bayless-Smith and Richard G. Teacham, eds., pp. 273–315. New York: Academic.

Morris, C.
1976 "Master Design of the Inca." *Natural History* 85(10):58–67.

Mosely, Michael
1975 *The Maritime Foundations of Andean Civilization*. Menlo Park, Calif.: Cummings.
1983 "Central Andean Civilization." In *Ancient South America*, Jessie Jennings, ed., pp. 179–239. San Francisco: Freeman.

Moskos, Charles
1969 "Why Men Fight." *Transaction* 7:13–23.

Moskowitz, Breyne
1978 "The Acquisition of Language." *Scientific American* 239(5):92–108.

Moynihan, Daniel P.
1965 *The Negro Family, the Case for National Action*. Washington, D.C.: U.S. Dept. of Labor.

Mullings, Leith
1978 "Ethnicity and Stratification in the Urban United States." *Annals of the N.Y. Academy of Science* 318:10–22.

Mundinger, Paul
1980 "Animal Cultures and a General Theory of Cultural Evolution." *Ethology and Sociobiology* 1:183–223.

Munson, P. J.
1976 "Archaeological Data on the Origins of Cultivation in the Southwestern Sahara and Their Implications for West Africa." In *The Origin of African Plant Domestication*, J. D. Harlan et al., eds., pp. 187–209. The Hague: Mouton.

Munzel, Mark
1973 *The Aché Indians: Genocide in Paraguay*. International Work Group for Indigenous Affairs (IWGIA), 11.

Murdock, George P.
1949 *Social Structure*. New York: Macmillan.
1967 *Ethnographic Atlas*. Pittsburgh: University of Pittsburgh Press.

Murdock, George P., C. S. Ford, A. E. Hudson, et al.
1961 *Outline of Cultural Materials*. New Haven: Human Relations Area Files.

Murphy, Robert
1956 "Matrilocality and Patrilineality in Mundurucu Society." *American Anthropologist* 58:414–434.
1976 "Man's Culture and Women's Nature." *Annals of the New York Academy of Sciences* 293:15–24.

Murray, Gerald
1980 "Population Pressure, Land Tenure, and Voodoo: The Economics of Haitian Peasant Ritual." In *Beyond the Myths of Culture: Essays in Cultural Materialism*, Eric Ross, ed., pp. 295–321. New York: Academic.

Murray, Jacqueline
1970 *The First European Agriculture*. Chicago: Aldine.

Myrdal, Gunnar
1957 *Rich Lands and Poor: The Road to World Prosperity*. New York: Harper & Row.

Nadel, S. F.
1952 "Witchcraft in Four African Societies." *American Anthropologist* 54(1):18–29.

Nader, Laura
1972 "Up the Anthropologist—Perspectives

Gained from Studying Up." In *Reinventing Anthropology,* Dell Hymes, ed., pp. 284–311. New York: Random House.
1980 *No Access to Law.* New York: Academic.
Nag, Moni
1972 "Sex, Culture, and Human Fertility: India and the United States." *Current Anthropology* 13:231–238.
Nag, Moni, B. White, and R. Peet
1978 "An Anthropological Approach to the Study of the Value of Children in Java and Nepal." *Current Anthropology* 19:293–306.
Napier, John
1970 *The Roots of Mankind.* Washington, D.C.: Smithsonian Institution.
Naroll, Raul
1973 "Introduction" to *Main Currents in Anthropology,* R. Naroll and F. Naroll, eds., pp. 1–23. Englewood Cliffs, N.J.: Prentice-Hall.
Nash, Jil
1974 *Matriliny and Modernization: The Nagovisi of South Bougainville.* New Guinea Research Bulletin.
National Research Council
1974 *Agricultural Production Efficiency.* Washington, D.C.: National Academy of Sciences.
Needham, Joseph
1970 *Clerks and Craftsmen in China and the West.* Cambridge, England: Cambridge University Press.
Needham, Joseph, and W. Ling
1959 *Science and Civilization in China,* vol. 3. Cambridge, England: Cambridge University Press.
Neville, Gwen
1979 "Community Form and Ceremonial Life in Three Regions of Scotland." *American Ethnologist* 6:93–109.
Newcomer, Peter
1977 "Toward a Scientific Treatment of Exploitation: A Critique of Dalton." *American Anthropologist* 79:115–119.
Newman, Philip L.
1965 *Knowing the Gururumba.* New York: Holt, Rinehart and Winston.
Newmeyer, Frederick
1978 "Prescriptive Grammar: A Reappraisal." In *Approaches to Language: Anthropological Issues,* W. C. McCormack and S. A. Wurm, eds., pp. 581–593. The Hague: Mouton.
Nichols, Deborah
1982 "A Middle Formative Irrigation System Near Santa Clara Coatitlán in the Basin of Mexico." *American Antiquity* 47:133–144.
Nishida, T.
1973 "The Ant-Gathering Behavior by the Use of Tools Among Wild Chimpanzees of the Mahali Mountains." *Journal of Human Evolution* 2:357–370.
Norman, Collin
1978 *Soft Technologies, Hard Choices.* Washington, D.C.: Worldwatch Institute; Worldwatch Paper.
Norton, Helen
1978 "The Male Supremacist Complex: Discovery or Invention?" *American Anthropologist* 80:665–667.
Nurge, Ethel
1975 "Spontaneous and Induced Abortion in Human and Non-Human Primates." In *Being Female: Reproduction, Power and Change,* D. Raphael, ed., pp. 25–35. The Hague: Mouton.
Obrien, Eileen
1981 "The Projectile Capabilities of an Acheulian Hand-axe from Olorgesailie." *Current Anthropology* 22:76–79.
Odend'hal, Stuart
1972 "Energetics of Indian Cattle in Their Environment." *Journal of Human Ecology* 1:3–22.
Odum, Howard
1970 *Environment, Power, and Society.* New York: Wiley.
Ohel, Milla
1977 "On the Clactonian: Redefined, Reexamined, and Reinterpreted." *Current Anthropology* 18:329–333.
O'Laughlin, B.
1975 "Marxist Approaches In Anthropology." *Annual Review of Anthropology* 4:341–370.
Oliver, Douglas
1955 *A Solomon Island Society: Kinship and Leadership Among the Sivai of Bougainville.* Cambridge, Mass.: Harvard University Press.
Olson, Gerald
1978 "Effects of Activities of the Ancient Maya Upon Some of the Soils in Central America." Paper read at the Meetings of the Society for American Archaeology, Tuscon, Arizona.
Opler, Morris
1959 "Cultural Differences in Mental Disorders: An Italian and Irish Contrast in the

Schizophrenias—U.S.A." In *Culture and Mental Health,* Morris Opler, ed., pp. 425–442. New York: Atherton.

1968 "The Themal Approach in Cultural Anthropology and Its Application to North Indian Data." *Southwestern Journal of Anthropology* 24:215–227.

Orans, Martin

1968 "Maximizing in Jajmaniland: A Model of Caste Relations." *American Anthropologist* 70:875–897.

Ortiz de Montellano, B. R.

1978 "Aztec Cannibalism: An Ecological Necessity?" *Science* 200:611–617.

1983 "Counting Skulls: Comment on the Aztec Cannibalism Theory of Harner-Harris." *American Anthropologist* 85:403–406.

Osborne, R. T.

1978 "Race and Sex Differences in Heritability of Mental Test Performance: A Study of Negroid and Caucasoid Twins." In *Human Variation: The Biopsychology of Age, Race, and Sex,* R. T. Osborne, C. Noble, and N. Weyl, eds., pp. 137–169. New York: Academic.

Ottenheimer, Martin

1984 "Some Problems and Prospects in Residence and Marriage." *American Anthropologist* 86:351–358.

Otterbein, Keith

1973 "The Anthropology of War." In *The Handbook of Social and Cultural Anthropology,* J. Honigman, ed., pp. 923–958. Chicago: Rand McNally.

Paddock, William, and E. Paddock

1973 *We Don't Know How: An Independent Audit of What They Call Success in Foreign Assistance.* Ames, Iowa: Iowa State University Press.

Paige, David, and Theodore Bayless (eds.)

1978 *Lactose Digestion: Clinical and Nutritional Implications.* Baltimore: Johns Hopkins Press.

Paolisso, Michael, and Ross Sackett

1982 "Hunting Productivity Among the Yukpa Indians of Venezuela." Paper read at the Annual Meeting of the American Anthropologist Association. Washington, D.C.

Parker, Seymour, and R. Kleiner

1970 "The Culture of Poverty: An Adjustive Dimension." *American Anthropologist* 72:516–527.

Parsons, Anne

1967 "Is the Oedipus Complex Universal?" In *Personalities and Cultures: Readings in Psychological Anthropology,* Robert Hunt, ed., pp. 352–399. Garden City, N.Y.: Natural History Press.

Parsons, Jeffry

1976 "The Role of Chinampa Agriculture in the Food Supply of Aztec Tenochtitlán." In *Cultural Change and Continuity: Essays in Honor of James Bennett Griffin,* C. Cleland, ed., pp. 233–257. New York: Academic.

Parsons, Talcott

1970 "Equality and Inequality in Modern Society, or Social Stratification Revisited." In *Social Stratification: Research and Theory for the 1970's,* Edward Laumann, ed., pp. 13–72. New York: Bobbs-Merrill.

Pasternak, Burton, Carol Ember, and Melvin Ember

1976 "On the Conditions Favoring Extended Family Households." *Journal of Anthropological Research* 32(2):109–123.

Pastore, José, and A. Haller

1977 "The Socioeconomic Status of the Brazilian Labor Force." *Luso-Brazilian Review* 14:1–28.

Patterson, Frances

1981 *The Education of Koko.* New York: Holt, Rinehart and Winston.

Patterson, Orlando

1977 *Ethnic Chauvinism: The Reactionary Impulse.* New York: Stein and Day.

Peckman, Joseph, and B. Okner

1974 *Who Bears the Tax Burden?* Washington, D.C.: Brookings Institution.

Pellet, Peter

1983 "Problems and Pitfalls in the Assessment of Human Nutritional Status." Paper read at the Wenner Gren Symposium 94, Cedar Key, Florida.

Pelto, Perttie, and Gretl Pelto

1973 "Ethnography: The Fieldwork Enterprise." In *Handbook of Social and Cultural Anthropology,* J. Honigman, ed., pp. 241–248. Chicago: Rand McNally.

1976 *The Human Adventure: An Introduction to Anthropology.* New York: Macmillan.

Perlo, Victor

1976 *Economics of Racism U.S.A.: Roots of Black Inequality.* New York: International Press.

Philips, Susan

1980 "Sex Differences and Language." *Annual Review of Anthropology* 9:523–544.

Pickersgill, B., and C. B. Heiser

1975 "Origins and Distributions of Plants in the

New World Tropics." In *The Origins of Agriculture,* C. A. Reed, ed., pp. 803–835. The Hague: Mouton.

Pickford, M.
1982 "New Higher Primate Fossils from the Middle Miocene Deposits at Majiwa and Kaloma, Western Kenya." *American Journal of Physical Anthropology* 58:1–19.

Piddocke, Stuart
1965 "The Potlatch System of the Southern Kwakiutl: A New Perspective." *Southwestern Journal of Anthropology* 21:244–264.

Piggott, Stuart
1965 *Ancient Europe.* Chicago: Aldine.

Pilbeam, David
1978 "Rearranging Our Family Tree." *Human Nature* 6:38–45.
1982 "New Hominoid Skull Material from the Miocene of Pakistan." *Nature* 295:232–234.

Pilbeam, David, and J. R. Vaišnys
1975 "Hypothesis Testing in Paleoanthropology." In *Paleoanthropology: Morphology and Paleoecology,* R. H. Tuttle, ed., pp. 3–14. The Hague: Mouton.

Pimentel, David, L. E. Hurd, A. C. Bellotti, et al.
1973 "Food Production and Energy Crisis." *Science* 182:443–449.

Pimentel, David, et al.
1975 "Energy and Land Constraints in Food Protein Production." *Science* 190:754–761.

Piven, Frances, and R. Cloward
1971 *Regulating the Poor: The Functions of Public Welfare.* New York: Random House (Vintage Books).

Plog, Fred T.
1974 *The Study of Prehistoric Change.* New York: Academic.

Podolefsky, Aaron
1984 "Contemporary Warfare in the New Guinea Highlands." *Ethnology* 23:73–87.

Poirier, Frank
1982 *An Introduction to Physical Anthropology and the Archaeological Record.* Minneapolis: Burgess.

Polgar, Steven
1972 "Population History and Population Policies from an Anthropological Perspective." *Current Anthropology* 13:203–215.
1975 "Population, Evolution, and Theoretical Paradigms." In *Population, Ecology, and Social Evolution,* Steven Polgar, ed., pp. 1–25. The Hague: Mouton.

Pospisil, Leopold
1963 *The Kapauku Papuans of West New Guinea.* New York: Holt, Rinehart and Winston.
1968 "Law and Order." In *Introduction to Cultural Anthropology,* J. Clifton, ed., pp. 200–224. Boston: Houghton Mifflin.

Premack, David
1971 "On the Assessment of Language Competence in the Chimpanzee." In *The Behavior of Nonhuman Primates,* A. M. Schrier and F. Stollnitz, eds., vol. 4, pp. 185–228. New York: Academic.
1976 *Intelligence in Ape and Man.* Hillsdale, N.J.: Erlbaum.
1983 "The Codes of Man and Beast." *The Behavioral and Brain Sciences* 6:125–167.

Price, Barbara
1977 "Shifts of Production and Organization: A Cluster-Interaction Model." *Current Anthropology* 18:209–233.
1979 "Turning States' Evidence: Problems in the Theory of State Formation." In *New Directions in Political Economy: An Approach from Anthropology,* M. B. Leons and F. Rothstein, eds., pp. 269–306. Westport, Conn.: Greenwood Press.

Price, Douglas T.
1983 "The European Mesolithic." *American Antiquity* 48:761–778.

Pronko, N. H.
1969 *Panorama of Psychology.* Belmont, Calif.: Brooks/Cole.

Protsch, Reiner, and Rainer Berger
1973 "Earliest Radiocarbon Dates for Domesticated Animals." *Science* 179:235–239.

Puleston, Dennis
1974 "Intersite Areas in the Vicinity of Tikal and Uaxactun." In *Mesoamerican Archaeology:* New Approaches, Norman Hammond, ed., pp. 303–311. Austin: University of Texas Press.

Puleston, D. E., and O. S. Puleston
1971 *"An Ecological Approach to the Origin of Maya Civilization."* Archaeology 24:330–337.

Quilter, J., and T. Stocker
1983 "Subsistence Economies and the Origin of Andean Complex Societies." *American Anthropologist* 85:545–562.

Radcliffe-Brown, A. R.
1952 *Structure and Function in Primitive Society: Essays and Addresses.* London: Cohen and West.

Raj, K. N.
1977 "Poverty, Politics and Development." *Economic and Political Weekly* (Bombay), February 1977:185–204.
Rambaugh, D. M.
1977 *Language Learning by a Chimpanzee: The Lana Project.* New York: Academic.
Ramirez, F., and J. Meyer
1980 "Comparative Education: The Social Construction of the Modern World System." *Annual Review of Sociology* 6:369–399.
Rappaport, Roy
1968 *Pigs for the Ancestors: Ritual in the Ecology of a New Guinea People.* New Haven: Yale University Press.
1971a "Ritual, Sanctity, and Cybernetics." *American Anthropologist* 73:59–76.
1971b "The Sacred in Human Evolution." In *Explorations in Anthropology,* Morton Fried, ed., pp. 403–420. New York: Crowell.
1983 *Pigs for the Ancestors: Ritual in the Ecology of a New Guinea People,* 2d ed. New Haven: Yale University Press.
Rasmussen, Knud
1929 *The Intellectual Culture of the Iglulik Eskimos.* Report of the 5th Thule Expedition, 1921–1924, vol. 7, no. 1., trans. W. Worster. Copenhagen: Glydendal.
Raymond, J. Scott
1981 "The Maritime Foundations of Andean Civilization: A Reconsideration of the Evidence." *American Antiquity* 46:806–821.
Reagan, Michael, et al.
1978 "Flake Tools Stratified Below Paleo-Indian Artifacts." *Science* 200:1272–1275.
Rein, Martin, and Lee Rainwater
1977 "How Large Is the Welfare Class?" *Change* September-October, pp. 20–23.
Reite, Martin, and Nancy Caine (eds.)
1983 *Child Abuse: The Nonhuman Primate Data.* New York: Alan R. Liss.
Renfrew, Collin
1973 *Before Civilization: The Radiocarbon Revolution and Prehistoric Europe.* New York: Knopf.
Ribeiro, Darcy
1971 *The Americas and Civilization.* New York: Dutton.
Richards, Paul
1973 "The Tropical Rain Forest." *Scientific American* 229:58–68.
Riegelhaupt, J. F., and S. Forman
1970 "Bodo Was Never Brazilian: Economic Integration and Rural Development Among a Contemporary Peasantry." *Journal of Economic History* 30:100–116.
Rightmire, G. P.
1978 "Florisbad and Human Population Succession in Southern Africa." *American Journal of Physical Anthropology* 48:475–486.
1979 "Cranial Remains of *Homo erectus* from Beds II and IV, Olduvai Gorge, Tanzania." *American Journal of Physical Anthropology* 51:99–116.
1983 "The Lake Ndutu Cranium and Early *Homo sapiens* in Africa." *American Journal of Physical Anthropology* 61:245–254.
Riner, Reed
1981 "The Supranational Network of Boards of Directors." *Current Anthropology* 22:167–172.
Riscutia, Cantemir
1975 "A Study of the Majokerto Infant Calvarium." In *Paleoanthropology: Morphology and Paleoecology,* Russell Tuttle, ed., pp. 373–375. The Hague: Mouton.
Roach, Jack L., L. Gross, and O. R. Gursslin (eds.)
1969 *Social Stratification in the United States.* Englewood Cliffs, N.J.: Prentice-Hall.
Roberts, Paul
1964 *English Syntax.* New York: Harcourt Brace Jovanovich.
Roberts, Ron, and D. Brintnall
1982 *Reinventing Inequality.* Boston: Schenkman.
Robinson, John T.
1973 *Early Hominid Posture and Locomotion.* Chicago: University of Chicago Press.
Rohdes, M. L.
1978 "Aquatic Weeds in Man-Made Lakes: Disease Vectors." In *Environmental Effects of Large Dams,* pp. 93–95. New York: American Society of Civil Engineers.
Roheim, Geza
1950 *Psychoanalysis and Anthropology.* New York: International University Press.
Rohner, Ronald
1969 *The Ethnography of Franz Boas.* Chicago: University of Chicago Press.
Rohrlich-Leavitt, Ruby
1977 "Women in Transition: Crete and Sumer." In *Becoming Visible: Women in European History.* Renate Bridenthal and C. Koonz, eds., pp. 38–59. Boston: Houghton Mifflin.
Roper, Marilyn K.
1969 "A Survey of the Evidence for Intrahuman

Killing in the Pleistocene." *Current Anthropology* 10:427–459.
1975 "Evidence of Warfare in the Near East from 10,000 to 4,300 B.C." In *War: Its Causes and Correlates*, W. Nettleship, R. D. Givens, and A. Nettleship, eds., pp. 299–340. The Hague: Mouton.

Rosaldo, Michelle, and Louise Lamphere (eds.)
1974 *Women, Culture, and Society.* Stanford: Stanford University Press.

Rosenthal, Bernice
1975 "The Role and Status of Women in the Soviet Union: 1917 to the Present." In *Women Cross-Culturally: Change and Challenge*, R. Leavitt, ed., pp. 429–455. The Hague: Mouton.

Ross, Eric
1978 "Food Taboos, Diet, and Hunting Strategy: The Adaptation to Animals in Amazon Cultural Ecology." *Current Anthropology* 19:1–36.
1979 "Reply to Lizot." *Current Anthropology* 20:151–155.

Rothberg, Abraham
1972 *The Heirs of Stalin: Dissidence and the Soviet Regime*, 1953–1970. Ithaca, N.Y.: Cornell University Press.

Rukang, Wu
1982 "Paleoanthropology in China, 1949–1979." *Current Anthropology* 23:473–477.

Ruyle, Eugene E.
1973 "Slavery, Surplus, and Stratification on the Northwest Coast: The Ethnoenergetics of an Incipient Stratification System." *Current Anthropology* 14:603–631.
1975 "Mode of Production and Mode of Exploitation: The Mechanical and the Dialectical." *Dialectical Anthropology* 1:7–23.

Saban, Roger
1977 "The Place of Rabat Man (Kebibat, Morocco) in Human Evolution." *Current Anthropology* 18:518–524.

Sacks, Karen B.
1971 *Economic Bases of Sexual Equality: A Comparative Study of Four African Societies.* Ph.D. dissertation, University of Michigan.

Safa, Helen I.
1967 *An Analysis of Upward Mobility in Lower Income Families: A Comparison of Family and Community Life Among American Negro and Puerto Rican Poor.* Syracuse, N.Y.: Youth Development Center.
1968 "The Case for Negro Separatism: The Crisis of Identity in the Black Community." *Urban Affairs Quarterly* 4:45–63.

Sahlins, Marshall
1961 "The Segmentary Lineage: An Organization of Predatory Expansion." *American Anthropologist* 63:322–345.
1972 *Stone Age Economics.* Chicago: Aldine.
1978 "Culture as Protein and Profit." *The New York Review of Books*, November 23, pp. 45–53.

Salzman, Philip
1978 "Does Complementary Opposition Exist?" *American Anthropologist* 80:53–70.

Salzman, Philip (ed.)
1971 "Comparative Studies of Nomadism and Pastoralism." *Anthropological Quarterly.* 44(3):104–210.

Samulsson, Kurt
1964 *Religion and Economic Action: A Critique of Max Weber.* New York: Harper & Row (Torchbooks).

Sanday, Peggy
1973 "Toward a Theory of the Status of Women." *American Anthropologist* 75:1682–1700.
1981 *Female Power and Male Dominance: On the Origins of Sexual Inequality.* New York: Cambridge University Press.

Sanders, William T.
1972 "Population, Agricultural History, and Societal Evolution in Mesoamerica." In *Population Growth: Anthropological Implications*, B. Spooner, ed., pp. 101–153. Cambridge, Mass.: M.I.T. Press.

Sanders, William T., and B. Price
1968 *Mesoamerica: The Evolution of a Civilization.* New York: Random House.

Sanders, William T., R. Santley, and J. Parsons
1979 *The Basin of Mexico: Ecological Processes in the Evolution of a Civilization.* New York: Academic.

Sanjek, Roger
1972 *Ghanian Networks: An Analysis of Interethnic Relations in Urban Situations.* Ph.D. dissertation, Columbia University.
1977 "Cognitive Maps of the Ethnic Domain In Urban Ghana: Reflections on Variability and Change." *American Ethnologist* 4:603–622.

Sapir, Edward
1921 *Language.* New York: Harcourt Brace Jovanovich.

Saraydar, S., and I. Shimada
1971 "A Quantitative Comparison of Efficiency

Between a Stone Axe and a Steel Axe." *American Antiquity* 36:216–217.

Sarich, Vincent

1974 "Just How Old Is the Hominid Line?" *Yearbook of Physical Anthropology* 17:98–112.

Sartono, S.

1975 "Implications Arising from *Pithecanthropus* VIII." In *Paleoanthropology: Morphology and Paleoecology*, R. H. Tuttle, ed., pp. 327–360. The Hague: Mouton.

Scarborough, Vernon

1983 "A Preclassic Maya Water System." *American Antiquity* 48:720–744.

Scarr-Salapatek, S.

1971a "Unknowns in the I.Q. Equation." *Science* 174:1223–1228.

1971b "Race, Social Class, and I.Q." *Science* 174:1285–1295.

Schaller, George B., and G. Lowther

1969 "The Relevance of Carnivore Behavior to the Study of Early Hominids." *Southwestern Journal of Anthropology* 25:307–341.

Scheffler, Harold

1973 "Kinship, Descent, and Alliance." In *Handbook of Social and Cultural Anthropology*, J. Honigman, ed., pp. 747–793. Chicago: Rand McNally.

Schermerhorn, R. A.

1970 *Comparative Ethnic Relations*. New York: Random House.

Schiff, Michel, et al.

1978 "Intellectual Status of Working Class Children Adopted Early into Upper-Middle-Class Families." *Science* 200:1503–1504.

Schiffer, Michael (ed.)

1978 *Advances in Archaeological Method and Theory*. New York: Academic.

Schlegel, Alice

1972 *Male Dominance and Female Autonomy*. New Haven, Conn.: Human Relations Area Files.

Schlegel, Alice, and H. Barry

1979 "Adolescent Initiation Ceremonies: A Cross-Cultural Code." *Ethnology* 18:199–210.

Schneider, Harold

1977 "Prehistoric Transpacific Contact and the Theory of Culture Change." *American Anthropologist* 79:9–25.

Schurmann, H. Franz, and O. Schell (eds.)

1967 *The China Reader*. New York: Random House

Schwartz, Jeffrey, I. Tattersal, and N. Eldredge

1978 "Phylogeny and Classification of the Primates Revisited." *Yearbook of Physical Anthropology* 21:95–133.

Scrimshaw, Nevin

1977 "Through A Glass Darkly: Discerning the Practical Implications of Human Dietary Protein-Energy Interrelationships." *Nutrition Reviews* 35:321–337.

Scrimshaw, Susan

1978 "Infant Mortality and Behavior in the Control of Family Size." Paper read at the Meeting of the American Association for the Advancement of Science, Washington, D.C.

1981 "Infant Mortality and Behavior in the Regulation of Family Size." In *Fertility Decline in the Less Developed Countries*, Nick Eberstadt, ed., pp. 295–318. New York: Praeger.

1983 "Infanticide as Deliberate Fertility Regulation." In *Determinants of Fertility in Developing Nations: Supply and Demand for Children*. R. Bulatao and R. Lee, eds., New York: Academic.

Sengal, Randal

1973 "On Mechanism of Population Growth During the Neolithic." *Current Anthropology* 14:540–542.

Service, Elman R.

1975 *Origins of the State and Civilization: The Processes of Cultural Evolution*. New York: Norton.

1978 "Classical and Modern Theories of the Origin of Government." In *Origins of the State: The Anthropology of Political Evolution*, R. Cohen and E. Service, eds., pp. 21–34. Philadelphia: ISHI.

Sexton, Lorraine

1973 "Sexual Interaction and Population Pressure in Highland New Guinea." Paper read at the Annual Meeting of the American Anthropological Association, New Orleans.

Shabecoff, Philip

1977 "Why Blacks Still Don't Have Jobs." *New York Times*, September 11, 1977, sec. 4, p. 4.

Sharff, Jagna

1981 "Free Enterprise and the Ghetto Family." *Psychology Today*, March.

Shaw, T.

1976 "Early Crops in Africa: A Review of the Evidence." In *The Origins of African Plant Domestication*, J. R. Harlan et al., eds., pp. 107–153. The Hague: Mouton.

Sheets, John, and James A. Gavan

1977 "Dental Reduction from *Homo erectus* to Neanderthal." *Current Anthropology* 18:587–589.

Shepher, J.
1971 "Mate Selection Among Second Generation Kibbutz Adolescents and Adults." *Archives of Sexual Behavior* 1:293–307.
Sherratt, Andrew
1982 "Mobile Resources: Settlement and Exchange in Early Agricultural Europe." In *Ranking Resource, and Exchange: Aspects of the Archaeology of Early European Society.* C. Renfrew and S. Shennan eds., pp. 13–26. Cambridge: University of Cambridge Press.
Shipler, David
1977 "In Russia, the Revolutionary Dream Has Run Its Course." *New York Times*, November 6, sec. 4, p. 5.
Short, R. V.
1984 "Breast Feeding." *Scientific American* 250(4):35–41.
Shuey, Audrey M.
1966 *The Testing of Negro Intelligence.* New York: Social Science Press.
Sigmon, B. A., and J. S. Cybulski (eds.)
1981 *Homo erectus: Papers in Honor of Davidson Black.* Toronto: University of Toronto Press.
Sillitoe, P.
1977 "Land Shortage and War in New Guinea." *Ethnology* 16:71–81.
Silverstein, Michael
1972 "Linguistic Theory: Syntax, Semantics, Pragmatics." *Annual Review of Anthropology* 3:349–382.
Simons, Elwyn L.
1968 "A Source for Dental Comparison of *Ramapithecus* with *Australopithecus* and *Homo.*" *South African Journal of Science* 64:92–112.
Simons, Elwyn L., and P. Ettel
1970 "Gigantopithecus." *Scientific American* 222(1):77–85.
Simoons, Frederick
1979 "Questions in the Sacred Cow Controversy." *Current Anthropology* 20:467–493.
1982 "Geography and Genetics as Factors in the Psychobiology of Human Food Selection." In *The Psychobiology of Human Food Selection*, L. M. Barker, ed., pp. 205–224. Westport, Conn.: AVI.
Simpson, George, and J. M. Singer
1962 *Racial and Cultural Minorities*, 2d ed. New York: Harper & Row.
Smith, C. T.
1970 "Depopulation of the Central Andes in the 16th Century." *Current Anthropology* 11:453–460.
Smith, David
1974 *Who Rules the Universities? An Essay in Class Analysis.* New York: Monthly Review Press.
Smith, Fred
1982 "Upper Pleistocene Hominid Evolution in South-Central Europe: A Review of Evidence and Analysis of Trends." *Current Anthropology* 23:667–703.
Smith, James D.
1973 *The Concentration of Personal Wealth in America.* Washington, D.C.: The Urban Institute.
Smith, J., S. Franklin, and D. Wion
1973 *The Distribution of Financial Assets.* Washington, D.C.: The Urban Institute.
Smith, M. G.
1966 "A Survey of West Indian Family Studies." In *Man, Settlement, and Urbanism: West Indian Perspectives*, L. Comitas and D. Lowenthal, eds., pp. 365–408. Garden City, N.Y.: Anchor Books.
1968 "Secondary Marriage Among Kadera and Kagoro." In *Marriage, Family, and Residence*, P. Bohannan and J. Middleton, eds., pp. 109–130. Garden City, N.Y.: Natural History Press.
Smith, Philip
1972 "Land Use, Settlement Patterns, and Subsistence Agriculture." In *Man, Settlement, and Urbanism*, P. J. Ucko, R. Tringham, and G. W. Dimbleby, eds., pp. 409–425. Cambridge, Mass.: Schenkman.
Smith, Raymond T.
1973 "The Matrifocal Family." In *The Character of Kinship*, Jack Goody, ed., pp. 121–144. London: Cambridge University Press.
Smith, Thomas C.
1955 *Political Change and Industrial Development in Japan: Government Enterprise, 1868–1880.* Stanford: Stanford University Press.
Smith, Waldemar
1977 *The Fiesta System and Economic Change.* New York: Columbia University Press.
Solecki, Ralph
1971 *Shanidar: The First Flower People.* New York: Knopf.
Solecki, Rose
1964 "Azwi Chemi Shanidar, a Post-Pleistocene Site in Northern Iraq." In *Report of the VIth International Quaternary*, pp. 405–412. Warsaw, 1961.

Solheim, William

1970 "Relics from Two Diggings Indicate the Thais Were the First Agrarians." *New York Times*, January 12.

Solzhenitsyn, Alexander

1974 *Gulag Archipelago.* New York: Harper & Row.

Sorenson, Richard

1972 "Socio-Ecological Change Among the Fore of New Guinea." *Current Anthropology* 13:349–383.

Sorenson, Richard, and P. E. Kenmore

1974 "Proto-Agricultural Movement in the Eastern Highlands of New Guinea." *Current Anthropology* 15:67–72.

Soustelle, Jacques

1970 *Daily Life of the Aztecs.* Stanford: Stanford University Press.

Southworth, Franklin

1974 "Linguistic Masks for Power: Some Relationships Between Semantic and Social Change." *Journal of Anthropological Linguistics* 16:177–191.

1969 " 'Standard' Language and Social Structure." Paper read at the Annual Meeting of the American Anthropological Association, New Orleans.

Souza, Herbert, C. Afonso, and J. Jungueira

1976 *Introduction to Latin American Politics.* Toronto: Brazilian Studies.

Speck, Frank

1915 "The Family Hunting Band as the Basis of the Algonkian Social Organization." *American Anthropologist* 17:289–305.

Spencer, Baldwin, and F. J. Gillen

1968 *The Native Tribes of Central Australia.* New York: Dover.

Spencer, P.

1965 *The Samburu: A Study of Gerontocracy in a Nomadic Tribe.* Berkeley: University of California Press.

Spengler, Joseph

1974 *Population Change, Modernization, and Welfare.* Englewood Cliffs, N.J.: Prentice-Hall.

Spicer, Edward

1954 *Potam: A Yaqui Village in Sonora.* Memoir 77, American Anthropological Association.

Spiro, Melford

1954 "Is the Family Universal?" *American Anthropologist* 56:839–846.

1982 *Oedipus in the Trobriands.* Chicago: University of Chicago Press.

Srinivas, M. N.

1955 "The Social System of a Mysore Village." In *Village India: Studies in the Little Community,* M. Marriot, ed., pp. 1–35. Memoir 83, American Anthropological Association.

Stack, Carol

1974 *All Our Kin: Strategies for Survival in a Black Community.* New York: Harper & Row.

Stahl, Ann

1984 "Hominid Dietary Selection Before Fire." *Current Anthropology* 25:151–168.

Stavenhagen, Rudolfo

1975 *Social Classes in Agrarian Societies.* Garden City, N.Y.: Anchor Books.

Stein, Howard, and R. F. Hill

1977 *The Ethnic Imperative: Examining the New White Ethnic Movement.* University Park, Pa.: Pennsylvania State University Press.

Steinhart, John, and Carol Steinhart

1974 "Energy Use in the U.S. Food System." *Science* 184:307–317.

Stern, Curt

1973 *Principles of Human Genetics,* 3d ed. San Francisco: Freeman.

Stern, Jack, and Randall Susman

1983 "The Locomotor Anatomy of *Australopithecus afarensis.*" *American Journal of Physical Anthropology* 60:279–318.

Steward, Julian H.

1955 *Theory of Culture Change: The Methodology of Multilinear Evolution.* Urbana: University of Illinois Press.

Stewart, Omer C.

1948 *Ute Peyotyism.* University of Colorado Studies, Series in Anthropology, no. 1. Boulder: University of Colorado Press.

1968 "Lorenz Margolin on the Ute." In *Man and Aggression.* M. F. Ashley Montagu, ed., pp. 103–110. New York: Oxford University Press.

Stiles, Daniel

1979 "Early Acheulian and Developed Oldowan." *Current Anthropology* 20:126–129.

Stoltman, James

1978 "Temporal Models in Prehistory: An Example from Eastern North America." *Current Anthropology* 19:703–746.

Straus, Lawrence

1982 "Comments on White's Middle/Upper Paleolithic Transition." *Current Anthropology* 23:185–186.

Street, John

1969 "An Evaluation of the Concept of Carrying Capacity." *Professional Geographer* 21(2):104–107.

Sturtevant, Edgar H.
1964 *An Introduction to Linguistic Science.* New Haven: Yale University Press.

Subrahmanyam, K. V., and J. Ryan
1975 "Livestock as a Source of Power in Indian Agriculture: A Brief Review." Hyderabad: ICRISAT Occasional Paper 12.

Sugimoto, Y. and R. Mover
1983 *Japanese Society: A Study in Social Reconstruction.* London: Kegan Paul.

Sugiyama, Yukimaru
1969 "Social Behavior of Chimpanzees in the Budongo Forest, Uganda." *Primates* 10:197–225.

Sussman, Robert
1972 "Child Transport, Family Size, and Increase in Population During the Neolithic." *Current Anthropology* 13:258–259.

Suttles, Wayne
1960 "Affinal Ties, Subsistence, and Prestige Among the Coast Salish." *American Anthropologist* 62:296–305.

Suzuki, Akira
1975 "The Origin of Hominid Hunting: A Primatological Perspective." In *Socioecology and Psychology of Primates,* R. H. Tuttle, ed., pp. 259–278. The Hague: Mouton.

Suzuki, H., and F. Takai (eds.)
1970 *The Amud Man and His Cave Site.* Tokyo: University of Tokyo Press.

Swanson, Guy E.
1960 *The Birth of the Gods: The Origin of Primitive Beliefs.* Ann Arbor: University of Michigan Press.

Sweezy, Paul
1978 "Is There a Ruling Class in the USSR? *Monthly Review* 30(5):1–17.

Tanner, J. M.
1968 "Earlier Maturation in Man." *Scientific American* 218(1):21–27.

Tanner, Nancy
1974 "Matrifocality in Indonesia and Africa and Among Black Americans." In *Woman, Culture and Society,* M. Rosaldo and L. Lamphere, eds., pp. 129–156. Stanford: Stanford University Press.
1983 "Hunters, Gatherers, and Sex Roles in Space and Time." *American Anthropologist* 85:335–341.

Tápia, Andres de
1971 *"Relación Hecha por El Señor Andrés de Tápia Sobre la Conquista de México."* In *Colección de Documentos para la Historia de México,* vol. 2, J. G. Icazbalceta, ed., pp. 554–594. Nendeln/Liechtenstein: Kaus reprint.

Taylor, R. E., et al.
1983 "Middle Holocene Age of the Sunnyvale Human Skeleton." *Science* 220:1271–1273.

Tefft, Stanton
1975 "Warfare Regulation: A Cross-Cultural Test of Hypotheses." In *War: Its Causes and Correlates,* M. Nettleship, R. D. Givens, and A. Nettleship, eds., pp. 693–712. The Hague: Mouton.

Teleki, Geza
1973 "The Omnivorous Chimpanzee." *Scientific American,* 288(1):32–42.
1981 "The Omnivorous Diet and Eclectic Feeding Habits of Chimpanzees in Gombe National Park, Tanzania." In *Omnivorous Primates: Gathering and Hunting in Human Evolution,* G. Teleki and S. O. Harding, eds., pp. 303–343. New York: Columbia University Press.

Terrace, Herbert
1979 "Is Problem Solving Language?" *Journal of the Experimental Analysis of Behavior* 31:161–175.
1981 *Nim: A Chimpanzee Who Learned Sign Language.* New York: Washington Square Press.

Thomas, David H.
1974 *Predicting the Past.* New York: Holt, Rinehart and Winston.
1979 *Archaeology.* New York: Holt, Rinehart and Winston.

Thorndike, R. L.
1968 "Intelligence and Intelligence Testing." *International Encyclopedia of the Social Sciences* 7:421–429.

Thrupp, Sylvia (ed.)
1962 *Millennial Dreams in Action.* The Hague: Mouton.

Tiger, Lionell
1970 *Men in Groups.* New York: Random House (Vintage Books).

Todd, I. A.
1978 *Çatal Hüyük in Perspective.* Menlo Park, Calif.: Cummings.

Trevathan, Wenda
1982 "Comment on Littlefield, Lieberman, and Reynolds 1982." *Current Anthropology* 23:657–662.

Trigger, Bruce
1978 "Iroquois Matriliny." *Pennsylvania Archaeologist* 48:55–65.

Turner, B. L.
1974 "Prehistoric Intensive Agriculture in the Mayan Lowlands." *Science* 185:118–124.

Turner, B. L., and Peter Harrison
1981 "Prehistoric Raised Field Agriculture in the Maya Lowlands." *Science* 213:399–405.

Turner, Victor W.
1967 *The Forest of Symbols: Aspects of Ndembu Ritual.* Ithaca, N.Y.: Cornell University Press.

Tuttle, Russell H.
1969 "Knuckle-Walking and the Problem of Human Origins." *Science* 166:953–961.

Tylor, Edward B.
1871 *Primitive Culture.* London: J. Murray.

Tyson, J. E., and A. Perez
1978 "The Maintenance of Infecundity in Post-Partum Women." In *Nutrition and Human Reproduction,* W. H. Moseley, ed., pp. 11–27. New York: Plenum.

Uberoi, J. P. Singh
1962 *Politics of the Kula Ring: An Analysis of the Findings of Bronislaw Malinowski.* Manchester, England: Manchester University Press.

Ucko, Peter J., and A. Rosenfeld
1967 *Paleolithic Cave Art.* London: Weidenfeld and Nicolson.

Ulman, Garry
1979 *The Science of Society.* The Hague: Mouton.

United Nations
1974a *Study of the Problems of Raw Materials and Development: Evolution of Basic Commodity Prices Since 1950* (A/9544).
1974b *Problems of Raw Materials and Development.* Note by the Secretary-General of UNCTAD (UNCTAD/OSG/52).

U.S. Agency for International Development
1971 *Rice in the Philippines.* Country Crop Papers. Washington, D.C.: East Asia Technical Advisory Office.

U.S. Economic Council
1974 *Economic Report to the President, Transmitted to Congress.* Washington, D.C.: U.S. Government Printing Office.

U.S. Senate Committee on Governmental Affairs
1978 *Voting Rights in Major Corporations.* 95th Congress, 1st Session. Washington, D.C.: U.S. Government Printing Office.

Vaidyanathan, A.
1978 "Aspects of India's Bovine Economy: Some Preliminary Results." *Indian Journal of Agricultural Economics* 33:1–29.

Vaidyanathan, A., N. Nair, and M. Harris
1982 "Bovine Sex and Age Ratios in India." *Current Anthropology* 23:365–383.

Vaillant, George C.
1966 (1941) *The Aztecs of Mexico.* Baltimore: Penguin.

Valentine, Charles
1970 *Culture and Poverty: Critique and Counterproposals.* Chicago: University of Chicago Press.

van den Berghe, Pierre
1972 "Sex Differentiation and Infant Care: A Rejoinder to Sharlotte Neely Williams." *American Anthropologist* 74:770–771.

van den Berghe, Pierre, and Gene Mesker
1980 "Royal Incest and Inclusive Fitness." *American Ethnologist* 7:300–317.

van Lawick-Goodall, Jane
1965 "Chimpanzees on the Gombe Stream Reserve." In *Primate Behavior: I.* DeVore, ed., pp. 425–473. New York: Holt, Rinehart and Winston.
1968 "Tool-Using Bird: The Egyptian Vulture." *National Geographic* 133:630–641.
1972 "Expressive Movements and Communication in Chimpanzees." In *Primate Patterns,* P. Dolhinow, ed., pp. 25–84. New York: Holt, Rinehart and Winston.
1972 *In the Shadow of Man.* Boston: Houghton Mifflin.
1979 "Life and Death at Gambe." *National Geographic* 155(5):592–620.

Vayda, Andrew P.
1971 "Phases of the Process of War and Peace Among the Marings of New Guinea." *Oceania* 42:1–24.

Verdon, Michel
1982 "Where Have All Their Lineages Gone? Cattle and Descent Among the Nuer." *American Anthropologist* 84:566–579.

Vicek, Emanuel
1978 "A New Discovery of *Homo erectus* in Central Europe." *Journal of Human Evolution* 7:239–251.

Vickers, William
1980 "An Analysis of Amazonian Hunting Yields as a Function of Settlement Age." In *Working Papers on South American Indians,* no. 2., Spring, Raymond H. Hames, ed., pp. 7–30.

Vishnu-Mittre
1975 "The Archaeobotanical and Palynological Evidences for the Early Origin of Agriculture in South and Southeast Asia." In *Gastronomy, the Anthropology of Food and Food Habits,*

M. Arnott, ed., pp. 13–21. The Hague: Mouton.

Vogt, Evon Z.
1969 *Zinacantan.* Cambridge, Mass.: Harvard University Press.

Vogt, Evon Z., and F. Cancian
1970 "Social Integration and the Classic Maya: Some Problems in Haviland's Argument." *American Antiquity* 35:101–102.

Von Koenigswald, G. H. R.
1975 "Early Man in Java: Catalogue and Problems." In *Paleoanthropology: Morphology and Paleoecology,* R. H. Tuttle, ed., pp. 303–309. The Hague: Mouton.

Von Koenigswald, G. H. R., and P. Tobias
1964 "A Comparison Between the Olduvai Hominids and Those of Java and Some Implications for Hominid Phylogeny." *Nature* 204:515–518.

Wade, Nicholas
1973 "The World Food Situation: Pessimism Comes Back into Vogue." *Science* 181:634–638.

Wadel, Cato
1973 *Now, Whose Fault is That?: The Struggle for Self-Esteem in the Face of Chronic Unemployment.* Institute of Social and Economic Research. Memorial University of Newfoundland.

Wagley, Charles
1943 "Tapirapé Shamanism." *Boletim Do Museu Nacional* (Rio De Janiero) *Antropología* 3:1–94.
1977 *Welcome of Tears: The Tapirapé Indians of Central Brazil.* New York: Columbia University Press.

Wagley, Charles, and M. Harris
1958 *Minorities in the New World.* New York: Columbia University Press.

Walker, Alan
1981 "Diet and Teeth." *Philosophical Transaction of the Royal Society.* London. B292:57–64.
1983 Paper read at the Annual Meeting of the American Association of Physical Anthropologists.

Walker, Alan, and Richard Leakey
1978 "The Hominids of East Turkana." *Scientific American* 239(2):54–66.

Walker, Deward
1972 *The Emergent Native Americans.* Boston: Little, Brown.

Wallace, Anthony F. C.
1952 *The Modal Personality Structure of the Tuscarora Indians, as Revealed by the Rorschach Test.* Bulletin 150, Bureau of American Ethnology. Washington, D.C.: U.S. Government Printing Office.
1961 "Mental Health, Biology, and Culture." In *Psychological Anthropology,* F. Hsu, ed., pp. 255–295. Homewood, Ill.: Dorsey.
1966 *Religion: An Anthropological View.* New York: Random House.
1970 *Culture and Personality,* 2d ed. New York: Random House.

Wallace, Wilson
1943 *Messiahs: Their Role in Civilization.* Washington, D.C.: American Council on Public Affairs.

Wallerstein, Emmanuel
1974 *The Modern World System.* New York: Academic.

Walsh, John
1983 *Mexican Agriculture: Crisis Within Crisis.* Science 219:825–826.

Walter, R. C., and Aronson, J. L.
1982 "Revisions of K/Ar Ages for the Hadar Hominid Site, Ethiopia." *Nature* 296:122–127.

Warner, W. Lloyd (ed.)
1963 *Yankee City.* New Haven: Yale University Press.

Warner, W. Lloyd, M. Meeker, and K. Eells
1949 *Social Class in America: A Manual for the Social Status.* Chicago: Chicago Research Association.

Wasserstrom, Robert
1977 "Land and Labor in Central Chiapas." *Development and Change* 8:441–463.

Watson, James
1977 "Pigs, Fodder, and the Jones Effect in Postipomean New Guinea." *Ethnology* 16:57–70.

Wax, Murray, S. Diamond, and F. O. Gearing
1971 *Anthropological Perspectives on Education.* New York: Basic Books.

Weaver, Muriel Porter
1972 *The Aztec, Maya, and Their Predecessors.* New York: Seminar Press.

Weisman, Steven
1978 "City Constructs Statistical Profile in Looting Cases." *New York Times,* August 14, p. 1.

Weisner, Thomas, and Ronald Gilmore
1977 "My Brother's Keeper: Child and Sibling Caretaking." *Current Anthropology* 18:169–190.

Weiss, Gerald
1977a "The Problem of Development in the Non-Western World." *American Anthropologist* 79:887–893.
1977b "Rhetoric in Campa Narrative." *Journal of Latin American Lore* 3, pp. 169–182.
Wendorf, F., and R. Schild
1981 "The Earliest Food Procedures." *Archaeology* 34:30–36.
Wendorf, F., R. Schild, and S. Rushdi
1970 "Egyptian Prehistory: Some New Concepts." *Science* 169:1161–1171.
Wendorf, Fred, et al.
1984 "New Radio Carbon Dates of the Cereals from Wadi Kubaynya." *Science* 225:645–646.
Wenke, Robert
1980 *Patterns in Prehistory*. New York: Oxford.
Werner, Dennis
1982 "Why do the Mekranoti Trek?" In *Adaptive Responses of Native Amazonians*, Raymond Hames and William Vickers, eds., pp. 225–238. New York: Academic.
West, James
1945 *Plainville, U.S.A.* New York: Columbia University Press.
Westoff, Charles
1978 "Marriage and Fertility in the Developed Countries." *Scientific American* 239(6):51–57.
White, Benjamin
1973 "Demand for Labor and Population Growth in Colonial Java." *Human Ecology* 1:217–236.
1975 "The Economic Importance of Children in a Javanese Village." In *Population and Social Organization*, Moni Nag, ed., pp. 127–146. The Hague: Mouton.
1982 "Child Labour and Population Growth in Rural Asia." *Development and Change* 13:587–610.
1983 *"Agricultural Involution" and Its Critics: Twenty Years After Clifford Geertz*. The Hague: Institute of Social Studies.
White, Douglas, et al.
1977 "Entailment Theory and Method: A Cross-Cultural Analysis of the Sexual Division of Labor." *Behavior Science Research* 12:1–24.
White, Randall
1982 "Rethinking the Middle/Upper Paleolithic Transition." *Current Anthropology* 23:169–192.
Whiting, John M.
1969 "Effects of Climate on Certain Cultural Practices." In *Environment and Cultural Behavior: Ecological Studies in Cultural Anthropology*, A. P. Vayda, ed., pp. 416–455. Garden City, N.Y.: Natural History Press.
Whiting, John, and Beatrice Whiting
1978 "A Strategy for Psychocultural Research." In *The Making of Psychological Anthropology*, George Spindler, ed., pp. 41–61. Berkeley: University of California Press.
Whorf, Benjamin
1956 *Language, Thought, and Reality*. New York: Wiley.
Wilkinson, J. C.
1977 *Water and Tribal Settlement in Southeast Asia: A Study of the Aflai of Oman*. Oxford: Claredon.
Willey, Gordon
1977 "The Rise of Maya Civilization: A Summary View." In *The Origins of Maya Civilization*, Richard E. Adams, ed., pp. 383–423. Albuquerque: University of New Mexico Press.
Willey, G. R., and D. B. Shimkin
1971 "Why Did the Pre-Columbian Maya Civilization Collapse?" *Science* 173:656–658.
Williams, Nancy, and Eugene Hunn (eds.)
1982 *Resource Managers: North American and Australian Hunter-Gatherers*. Boulder: Westview.
Williams, Sharlotte N.
1971 "The Limitations of Male/Female Activity Distinction Among Primates." *American Anthropologist* 73:805–806.
1973 *"The Argument Against the Physiological Determination* of Female Roles." *American Anthropologist* 75:1725–1728.
Wilmsen, Edwin
1979 "Diet and Fertility Among Kalahari Bushmen." African Studies Center, Boston University. Working paper 14.
Wilson, E. O.
1975 *Sociobiology: The New Synthesis*. Cambridge, Mass.: Harvard University Press.
1977 "Biology and the Social Sciences." *Daedalus* 106(4):127–140.
1978 *Human Nature*. Cambridge, Mass.: Harvard University Press.
Wilson, Monica
1963 *Good Company: A Study of Nyakyusa Age-Villages*. Boston: Little, Brown.
Witowski, Stanley, and Cecil A. Brown
1978 "Lexical Universals." *Annual Review of Anthropology* 7:427–451.

Wittfogel, Karl A.
1957 *Oriental Despotism: A Comparative Study of Total Power*. New Haven: Yale University Press.
1960 "A Stronger Oriental Despotism." *China Quarterly* January-March, pp. 32ff.
1979 Introduction to the 2d English edition of *Oriental Despotism*. New York: Vintage.
Wolf, Arthur P.
1968 "Adopt a Daughter-in-Law, Marry a Sister: A Chinese Solution to the Problem of the Incest Taboo." *American Anthropologist* 70:864–874.
1974 "Marriage and Adoption in Northern Taiwan." In *Social Organization and the Applications of Anthropology: Essays in Honor of Lauristan Sharp*, Robert Smith, ed., pp. 128–160. Ithaca, N.Y.: Cornell University Press.
Wolf, A. P., and C. S. Huang
1980 *Marriage and Adoption in China, 1845–1945*. Stanford: Stanford University Press.
Wolf, Eric R.
1959 *Sons of the Shaking Earth*. Chicago: University of Chicago Press.
1966 *Peasants*. Englewood Cliffs, N.J.: Prentice-Hall.
1969 *Peasant Wars of the Twentieth Century*. New York: Harper & Row.
1982 *Europe and the People Without History*. Berkeley: University of California Press.
Wolf, Eric (ed.)
1976 *The Valley of Mexico: Studies in Pre-Hispanic Ecology and Society*. Albuquerque: University of New Mexico Press.
Wolf, Eric R., and Sidney Mintz
1957 "Haciendas and Plantations in Middle America and the Antilles." *Social and Economic Studies* 6:380–412. Kingston, Jamaica: University College of the West Indies.
Wolpoff, Milford H.
1975 "Sexual Dimorphism in the Australopithecines." In *Paleoanthropology: Morphology and Paleoecology*, R. Tuttle, ed., pp. 245–289. The Hague: Mouton.
1982 "Ramapithecus and Hominid Origins." *Current Anthropology* 23:501–522.
Wolpoff, M., et al.
1976 "Some Aspects of the Evolution of Early Hominid Sexual Dimorphism." *Current Anthropology* 17:579–606.
Wood, Corinne
1975 "New Evidence for the Late Introduction of Malaria into the New World." *Current Anthropology* 16:93–104.
World Bank
1978 *World Development Report*. Washington, D.C.: World Bank.
Worsley, Peter
1968 *The Trumpet Shall Sound: A Study of "Cargo" Cults in Melanesia*. New York: Schocken.
Wright, Henry
1977 "Recent Research on the Origin of the State." *Annual Review of Anthropology* 6:379–397.
Yellen, John
1976 "Settlement Patterns of the !Kung." In *Kalahari Hunter-Gatherers*, Richard Lee and Irven DeVore, eds., pp. 47–72. Cambridge, Mass.: Harvard University Press.
Yellen, John, and R. Lee
1976 "The Dobe/Du/de Environment." In *Kalahari Hunter-Gatherers*, Richard Lee and Irven DeVore, eds., pp. 27–46. Cambridge, Mass.: Harvard University Press.
Yen, Douglas
1977 "Hoabhinian Horticulture: The Evidence and Questions from Northern Thailand." In *From Sunda to Sahel*, J. Allen, J. Golson, and Rhys Jones, eds., pp. 567–600. New York: Academic.
Yerkes, Robert
1921 *Psychological Examining in the United States Army*. National Academy of Science Memoirs No. 15. Washington, D.C.: National Academy of Science.
Yessner, David
1981 "Reply to G. Clark; 'On Preagricultural Adaptations.' " *Current Anthropology* 22:445–446.
Yi, Seonbok, and G. A. Clark
1983 "Observations on the Lower Paleolithic of Northeast Asia." *Current Anthropology* 24:181–202.
Young, L. M.
1982 "The Shang of Ancient China." *Current Anthropology* 23:311–314.
Zihlman, Adrienne, and J. Lowenstein
1979 "False Start of the Human Parade." *Natural History* 88(7):86–91.
Zohary, Daniel, and M. Hopf
1973 "Domestication of Pulses on the Old World." *Science* 182:887–894.

CREDITS

Chapter-opening photos:

Chapter 1 Walker, Anthro-Photo.
Chapter 2 Rotker, Taurus/Science Photo Library.
Chapter 3 © Ambler, NAS, Photo Researchers.
Chapter 4 Baron Hugo Van Lawick, © National Geographic Society.
Chapter 5 DeVore/Anthro-Photo.
Chapter 6 Courtesy of United Nations.
Chapter 7 Robert Ginn.
Chapter 8 Courtesy of the Library Services Department, American Museum of Natural History.
Chapter 9 Ralph S. Solecki.
Chapter 10 Menzel, Stock, Boston.
Chapter 11 China Pictures, Eastfoto.
Chapter 12 United Nations.
Chapter 13 Rosenthal, Stock, Boston.
Chapter 14 The Bettman Archive.
Chapter 15 Kenneth R. Good.
Chapter 16 From a photo by the late Dr. A. T. Schofield in *The Uganda Journal*, courtesy Dr. J. Beattie.
Chapter 17 UPI/Bettmann Archive.
Chapter 18 Tracy B. Ehlers.
Chapter 19 United Nations.
Chapter 20 Terrace, Anthro-Photo.
Chapter 21 Courtesy of the Library Services Department, American Museum of Natural History.
Chapter 22 © Muller, 1982, Woodfin Camp.
Chapter 23 UPI/Bettmann Archive.
Chapter 24 Vandermark, Stock, Boston.
Chapter 25 © Frerck, Woodfin Camp.

Figures:

1.1 *(a)* AP/Wide World Photos; *(b)* Ralph Skinner; *(c)* Walker, Anthro-Photo; *(d)* DeVore, Anthro-Photo.

2.2 Rotker, Taurus Photos, Inc.

3.1 *(a)* Arthur W. Ambler/National Audubon Society/Photo Researchers; *(b)* Australian Information Service.
3.2 © Zoological Society of San Diego.
3.3 Gordon S. Smith/National Audubon Society/Photo Researchers.
3.5 *(a)* Arthur W. Ambler/National Audubon Society/Photo Researchers; *(b)* James Welgos/National Audubon Society/Photo Researchers.
3.6 L. M. Chace/National Audubon Society/Photo Researchers.
3.7 *(a)* Arthur W. Ambler/National Audubon Society/Photo Researchers; *(b)* © Ambler, NAS, Photo Researchers; *(c)* © Kinne, 1977, Photo Researchers.
3.9 *(a)* © Ambler, NAS, Photo Researchers; *(b)* Arthur W. Ambler/National Audubon Society/Photo Researchers.
3.10 DeVore/Anthro-Photo.
3.11 Claude Schoepf.
3.12 Claude Schoepf.
3.20 Ron Garrison/© Zoological Society of San Diego.
3.21 Mark Boulton/National Audubon Society/Photo Researchers.

4.2 E. L. Simons.
4.4 Eric Delson.
4.5 E. L. Simons.
4.6 Eric Delson.
4.7 Courtesy of the Library Services Department, American Museum of Natural History.
4.8 Courtesy of the Library Services Department, American Museum of Natural History.
4.9 Cleveland Museum of Natural History.
4.10 UPI/Bettmann Archive.
4.11 Ward, Anthro-Photo.
4.12 Photo by Alun R. Hughes, by permission of Professor Phillip V. Tobias.
4.13 *(a)* Photo of cast of australopithecine skull courtesy of Wenner-Gren Foundation and with permission of C. K. Brain, Transvaal Museum; *(b)* National Museums of Kenya.
4.14 Tim White.
4.15 Donald Johanson.
4.16 Cannon, Anthro-Photo.
4.17 Cooper, Anthro-Photo.
4.18 National Museums of Kenya.
4.19 Cannon, Anthro-Photo.
4.20 H. V. Merrick.
4.21 Baron Hugo Van Lawick, © National Geographic Society.
4.22 Baron Hugo Van Lawick, © National Geographic Society.
4.23 Masao Kawai.
4.24 *(a)* Masao Kawai; *(b)* Mitsuo Iwamoto.
4.25 Nicolson, Anthro-Photo.

5.2 Photo of cast courtesy of the Wenner-Gren Foundation for Anthropological Research, Inc., and with permission of the owner, G. H. R. von Koenigswald.

5.3 Photo of cast courtesy of the Wenner-Gren Foundation for Anthropological Research, Inc., and with permission of the owner, G. H. R. von Koenigswald.
5.4 Photo of cast courtesy of the Wenner-Gren Foundation for Anthropological Research, Inc., and with permission of the owner, G. H. R. von Koenigswald.
5.6 From "The Hominids of 'East Turkana' " by Alan Walker and Richard Leakey, *Scientific American,* August 1978. © 1978, *Scientific American,* Inc., All rights reserved.
5.7 DeVore/Anthro-Photo.
5.12 Clark Howell.
5.13 UPI/Bettmann Archive.
5.14 By courtesy of the British Museum (Natural History).
5.16 Staatliches Museum für Naturkunde, Stuttgart.
5.17 By courtesy of the British Museum (Natural History).
5.18 Photo of cast courtesy of the Wenner-Gren Foundation for Anthropological Research, Inc., and with permission of owner, G. H. R. von Koenigswald.
5.19 W. W. Howells 1973.
5.21 Musée de l'homme.
5.22 Ralph S. Solecki.
5.23 By courtesy of the British Museum (Natural History).
5.24 Photo of cast courtesy of the Wenner-Gren Foundation for Anthropological Research, Inc., and with permission of owner, Peabody Museum.

6.1 Gatha, DeWys.
6.3 Consulate General of Denmark—no. 5; Consulate General of Finland—no. 10; others courtesy of United Nations.
6.4 National Institute of Health.
6.6 Photo by Jacob A. Riis, the Jacob A. Riis Collection, Museum of the City of New York.
6.7 Lester Bergman and Assoc.

7.1 FAO.
7.2 *(a)* UPI/Bettmann Archive. *(b)* Eugene Gordon; *(c)* UPI/Bettmann Archive. *(d)* Museum of the American Indian, Heye Foundation, N.Y.
7.3 *(a)* Johnson, DeWys; *(b)* Jacques Henri Lartique: *Beach at Villerville,* 1908. Photo Researchers.
7.4 Robert Ginn.
7.5 *(a)* DeVore, Anthro-Photo; *(b)* Cartier-Bresson, Magnum; *(c)* UPI/Bettmann Archive.
7.6 *(a)* Albertson, Stock, Boston; *(b)* Zimbel, Monkmeyer; *(c)* Hamlin, Stock, Boston.

8.1 Courtesy of the Library Services Department, American Museum of Natural History.
8.2 Lee Boltin.
8.6 Lee Boltin.
8.7 After H. Martin.
8.8 Alexander Marshack.
8.9 Lee Boltin.
8.12 Musee de l'Homme, courtesy of Alexander Marshack.
8.13 Neg. no. 298390, courtesy of the Library Services Department, American Museum of Natural History.
8.14 Courtesy of the Library Services Department, American Museum of Natural History
8.15 *(a)* © Alexander Marshack, 1972; *(b)* © Alexander Marshack.
8.16 Courtesy of the Library Services Department, American Museum of Natural History.

9.1 Ralph S. Solecki.
9.2 Ralph S. Solecki.
9.3 Ralph S. Solecki.
9.5 Robert Braidwood and Oriental Institute, University of Chicago.
9.6 AP/Wide World Photos.
9.7 *(a)* Ralph S. Solecki; *(b)* AP/Wide World Photos.
9.8 Guler, Magnum.
9.9 AP/Wide World Photos.
9.10 Rogers, Monkmeyer.
9.11 AP/Wide World Photos.
9.12 *(a)* Historical Museum, Beijing; *(b)* Institute of Archaeology, Beijing.
9.13 Jen and Des Bartlett, Bruce Coleman, Inc.

10.1 Dr. J. M. Adovasio, Dept. of Anthropology, University of Pittsburgh.
10.3 Courtesy of the Library Services Department, American Museum of Natural History.
10.4 AP/Wide World Photos.
10.5 Gordon Ekholm and American Museum of Natural History.
10.6 Norman Hammond.
10.7 Courtesy of the Library Services Department, American Museum of Natural History.
10.8 Menzel, Stock, Boston.
10.9 AP/Wide World Photos.
10.10 © George W. Gardner.
10.11 Greene, Frederic Lewis.
10.12 Brain, Anthro-Photo.
10.13 UPI/Bettmann Archive.
10.14 Courtesy of the Library Services Department, American Museum of Natural History.
10.15 Sergio Larrain, Magnum.
10.16 Courtesy of the Library Services Department, American Museum of Natural History.
10.17 *(a)* © Walter R. Aguiar; *(b)* © George W. Gardner.

11.1 Robert Carneiro and American Museum of Natural History.

11.2 Harold C. Conklin, Yale University.
11.4 Richard B. Lee/Anthro-Photo.
11.5 Roy Rappaport.
11.6 Cherry Lowman.
11.7 CPS/Eastfoto.
11.8 George Rodger, Magnum.
11.9 Chester, DeWys.
11.10 *(a)* AP/Wide World Photos; *(b)* UPI/Bettmann Archive.
11.11 Allen and Orna Johnson.
11.12 Konner, Anthro-Photo.

12.1 Richard B. Lee/Anthro-Photo.
12.2 United Nations.
12.3 Leopold Pospisil.
12.4 AP/Wide World Photos.
12.5 Courtesy of the Library Services Department, American Museum of Natural History.
12.6 Courtesy of the Library Services Department, American Museum of Natural History.
12.7 Courtesy of the Library Services Department, American Museum of Natural History.
12.8 UPI/Bettmann Archive.
12.9 Courtesy of the Library Services Department, American Museum of Natural History.

13.1 Japan Information Center.
13.2 *(a)* United Nations; *(b)* Museum of the American Indian, Heye Foundation, N.Y.
13.3 Schuler, Anthro-Photo.
13.4 The Bettman Archive.
13.5 Myron L. Cohen.
13.6 Leopold Pospisil.
13.7 Hopker, Woodfin Camp © 1978.
13.8 Goldberg, Stock, Boston.
13.9 The Granger Collection, N.Y.

15.1 Napoleon Chagnon/Anthro-Photo.
15.2 Courtesy of Royal Danish Ministry of Foreign Affairs.
15.3 Thomas Gregor.
15.4 Pitt Rivers Museum, Oxford.
15.5 Australian Information Service.
15.6 Kenneth R. Good.
15.7 Kenneth R. Good.

16.1 © Eugene Gordon, 1984.
16.2 The Granger Collection, N.Y.
16.3 © Eugene Gordon, 1984.
16.4 From a photo by the late Dr. A. T. Schofield, in *The Uganda Journal,* courtesy Dr. J. Beattie.
16.5 Neg. no. 336689, courtesy of the Library Services Department, American Museum of Natural History.
16.6 UPI/Bettmann Archive.
16.7 Henle, Monkmeyer.
16.8 *(a)* AP/Wide World Photos; *(b)* Franck, Woodfin Camp.
16.9 UPI/Bettman Archive.

17.1 Charles Gatewood.
17.2 Tass, Sovfoto.
17.3 Sovfoto/Eastfoto.
17.4 China Photo Service.
17.5 © Walter R. Aguiar.
17.6 United Nations.
17.7 *(a)* UPI/Bettmann Archive; *(b)* AP/Wide World Photos; *(c)* AP/Wide World Photos.
17.8 Kroll, Taurus Photos, Inc.
17.9 Vanderwall, DeWys.
17.10 UPI/Bettmann Archive.
17.11 United Nations.
17.12 Israeli Information Service.
17.13 United Nations.
17.14 UPI/Bettmann Archive.
17.15 Myron L. Cohen.

18.1 Eugene Gordon.
18.2 United Nations.
18.3 Richard W. Franke.
18.4 UPI/Bettmann Archive.
18.5 Redenius, Monkmeyer.
18.6 United Nations.
18.7 Daniel Gross.
18.8 Tracy B. Ehlers.

19.1 Herwig, Stock, Boston.
19.2 Kalvar, Magnum.
19.3 © Berry, Magnum.
19.4 Running, Stock, Boston.
19.5 St. Louis Post-Dispatch.
19.6 Meyers, NYT Pictures.
19.7 Carol Stack.
19.8 Hispanic Study Project/J. W. Sharff, Director. Photo by Jennifer Benepe.
19.9 Thomas Belmonte.

20.2 R. S. Fouts.
20.3 Yerkes Regional Primate Research Center of Emory University.
20.4 © Dr. Ronald H. Cohn, The Gorilla Foundation.
20.5 Terrace, Anthro-Photo.
20.6 AP/Wide World Photos.

21.1 Courtesy of the Library Services Department, American Museum of Natural History.
21.2 UPI/Bettmann Archive.
21.3 DeVore, Anthro-Photo.
21.4 *(a)* Eugene Gordon; *(b)* United Nations.
21.5 Museum of the American Indian, Heye Foundation, N.Y.
21.6 Charles Wagley.
21.7 The Granger Collection, N.Y.
21.8 Courtesy of the Library Services Department, American Museum of Natural History.
21.9 Neg. no. 298398, courtesy of the Library Services Department, American Museum of Natural History.

21.10 *(a)* Courtesy of the Library Services Department, American Museum of Natural History; *(b)* Eugene Gordon; *(c)* Museum of the American Indian, Heye Foundation, N.Y. *(d)* Courtesy of the Library Services Department, American Museum of Natural History.
21.11 From Victor Turner: *The Forest of Symbols: Aspects of Ndembu Ritual.* Copyright © 1967 by Cornell University. Used by permission of the publisher, Cornell University Press.
21.12 Neg. no. 324767, courtesy of the Library Services Department, American Museum of Natural History.
21.13 From Victor Turner: *The Forest of Symbols: Aspects of Ndembu Ritual.* Copyright © 1967 by Cornell University. Used by permission of the publisher, Cornell University Press.
21.14 Charles Gatewood.
21.15 Mexican National Tourist Council.
21.16 Courtesy of the Library Services Department, American Museum of Natural History.

22.1 Sergio Larrain, Magnum.
22.2 Courtesy of the Library Sevices Department, American Museum of Natural History.
22.3 © Peter Menzel.
22.4 Nevada Historical Society.
22.5 *(a)* Museum of the American Indian, Heye Foundation, N.Y. *(b)* Wide World Photos.
22.6 Painting by Ernest Spybuck, Museum of the American Indian, Heye Foundation, N.Y.
22.7 © Muller, 1982, Woodfin Camp.
22.8 UPI/Bettmann Archive.
22.9 UPI/Bettmann Archive.
22.10 © Burnett, 1979/Contact, Woodfin Camp.
22.11 Baldwin, DeWys.
22.12 *(a)* Moni Nag; *(b)* UPI/Bettmann Archive.
22.13 Paul L. Bourguignon.

23.1 AP/Wide World Photos.
23.2 Museum of the American Indian, Heye Foundation, N.Y.
23.4 Courtesy of the Library Services Department, American Museum of Natural History.
23.5 Courtesy of the Library Services Department, American Museum of Natural History.
23.6 Courtesy of the Library Services Department, American Museum of Natural History.
23.7 Oppenheim, Meret. *Object* (1936). Fur-covered cup, saucer, and spoon; cup, 4⅜″ diameter; saucer, 9⅜″ diameter; spoon, 8″ long; overall height 2⅞″. Collection, The Museum of Modern Arts, New York. Purchase.
23.8 de Havenon Collection.
23.9 Eugene Gordon.
23.10 UPI/Bettmann Archive.
23.11 Photograph by Egyptian Expedition, The Metropolitan Museum of Art.
23.12 French Government Tourist Office.
23.13 Sovfoto/Eastfoto.
23.14 Maxine Hicks.

24.1 Courtesy of the Library Services Department, American Museum of Natural History.
24.2 United Nations.
24.5 Museum of the American Indian, Heye Foundation, N.Y.
24.6 AP/Wide World Photos.
24.7 The Bettmann Archive, Inc.
24.8 Courtesy of the Library Services Department, American Museum of Natural History.
24.9 *(a)* and *(c)* Eugene Gordon; *(b)* © George W. Gardner; *(d)* and *(e)* UPI/Bettmann Archive.
24.10 Museum of the American Indian, Heye Foundation, N.Y.
24.11 Courtesy of the Library Services Department, American Museum of Natural History.
24.13 Sharma, DPI.

INDEX

Abejas phase, 181
Abortion methods, 223
ABO system (blood groups), 100–103
Aché Indians (Paraguay), genocide of, 327
Acheson, James, on development, 371
Acheulian tool industry, 76–79, 82, 131–134, 143
Achievement
descent and, 273
drive for, 383–385
Achuara, food taboos of, 459
Adaptive capacity, 348
Adaptive radiations, defined, 42
Adena phase, 192
Adolescent sexuality, 260–261, 488, 509
Adoption
enculturation and, 527
of twins, 524
Adornment
Middle Paleolithic, 134–135
Upper Paleolithic, 142–143
vaygu'a of Kula trade as, 233–234
Adultery, incest as, 267
Aegyptopithecus, 44
Aelopithecus, 44
Aesthetic, art and, 468
Afar (Ethiopia), fossil finds, 75, 85
Affinity, defined, 272
Africa
archaic *Homo sapiens* in, 85–86
Homo erectus in, 75, 76–78, 85
Homo sapiens sapiens in, 89
Mesolithic age in, 148
Middle/Upper Paleolithic transition in, 143
Neolithic age in, 158–160, 171
racial characteristics and, 95–96, 106, 111
skin cancer in, 107–109
African Genesis (Ardrey), 65
Age set
defined, 252
sex, class and, 331
sodalities based on, 299–300
Agglutinative stage, grammar, 404
Agriculture. *See also* Food production; Green Revolution
Chinampas, 189–190, 206
input-output ratio in, 213–214, 216–217
irrigation. *See* Irrigation agriculture
leisure in, 160–161, 211
mixed farming in, 205–206
Neolithic origins of, 155–157. *See also* Domestication, animal; Domestication, plant
New World origins of, 178–180, 191–194
rainfall, 186, 205, 365
raised-field, 182, 205
reasons for growth of, 160–161
slash-and-burn method. *See* Slash-and-burn method
types of, 205–206, 209
Aid to Families with Dependent Children (AFDC), 385–389
Ajalpan phase, 181
Ajuereado phase, 180
Alcohol, personal values and, 384–385
Alexander, Richard, 526
Alienation, art and, 474–475
Alland, Alexander, on art, 468, 470
Alleles. *See also* Genes
defined, 13, 100
dominant and recessive, 14–15
fitness of, 16–17
Allomorphs, 398, 399
Allophones, 398
Alorese (Indonesia), concept of descent of, 273
Altruistic sterility, 17, 525
Alveolar ridge, 397
Alveolar stops, 397
Ambilineal descent, 279–280
cognatic lineage in, 277
defined, 274
Ambilocality, 279–280
America, discovery of, 174–175
Ameslan (American Sign Language), 400–401, 402–403
Amitalocality, 283–284
Anasazi culture, 191–192
Ancient Society (Morgan), 515, 517
Animalia (kingdom), 20
Animatism, 418
Animism, 416–417
Jívaro, 417–418, 427
Anthropoidea (suborder), 26–38
Anthropological linguistics, defined, 2–6

Anthropology
application of, 6–7
biological, 6
cultural, 2, 114
defined, 2
fields of study within, 2–6
general, 6
physical, 6. *See also* Races
social, 114
theories of, 7–8
Anting, by chimpanzees, 60, 61–64
Antithesis, 481
Apes
characteristics of, 28
common ancestry of, with *Homo sapiens,* 30
dental formula of, 26
language and, 400–403
tools of, 38–39, 59–61, 64
Appollonian patterns, 490
Arago (France), fossil finds, 76
Arapesh (New Guinea), sex roles of, 497
Arbitrariness, language, 395–396
Arboreal life, 23, 25–26, 28
Archaeology
defined, 2
periods in, 131
Archaic traditions, 177–178
Archetypes, racial frequencies versus, 94–96
Architecture. *See also* Monuments; Pyramids
Inca, 319
Mayan, 182, 183, 187
Neolithic Middle Eastern, 164
Arctic hysteria, 495
Ardrey, Robert, 65
Argonauts of the Western Pacific (Malinowski), 233–234
Ariel, Irving, 109
Art
as cultural category, 468–470
cultural patterning and, 472–475
defined, 468
evolution of structures of, 479–480
invention and, 470–472
Neolithic, 163
politics and, 477–479
religion and, 475–477
Upper Paleolithic, 137, 138–143
Articulatory features, 397
Artisans, 470
Artists
artisans versus, 470
political control of, 477–478
Arunta (Australia)
art and, 475
totemic ritual of, 431–433
Ascription, 344
descent and, 273
Ashanti (West Africa)
concept of descent of, 273
domestic life of, 252
Asia
archaic *Homo sapiens* in, 86
Homo erectus in, 72–75
Homo sapiens sapiens in, 89
Mesolithic age in, 148
Middle/Upper Paleolithic transition in, 143
Neolithic age in, 167–171
origin of first Americans in, 175
racial characteristics and, 95
Aspirated bilabial unvoiced stop, 398
Aspiration (phonetic), 398
Assemblages, defined, 177
Assimilation, pluralism versus, 347–349
Atlanthropus, 75
Aurignacian tool industry, 137
Australia, skin cancer in, 107
Australopithecines, 49, 51–52
Australopithecus afarensis, 47–49, 51, 74
Australopithecus africanus, 49, 51, 52, 54, 75
Australopithecus boisei, 54
Australopithecus robustus, 49, 51, 52, 54, 55, 57
bipedalism of, 51–52, 74
discovery of earliest, 46–51
extinction of, 55–56
later forms of, 52–54
as omnivores, 68–69
tool use by, 57–58, 61
Authority, 481
Avunculocality
causes of, 283–284
matrilineality and, 280–281, 283–284, 312–313
Ayatollah Khomeini, 457
Azande (Sudan), sexuality among, 509
Aztec empire, 189, 198–199
cannibalism of, 190, 441, 446–448
ceremonial centers of, 439–441
ecclesiastical cult of, 438–441, 446–448

Baksh, Michael, 306–307
Band and village societies, 180, 205. *See also* Hunting-and-gathering societies
art of, 479–481
blood feuds in, 298–299
enculturation in, 252

end of, 325–327
headmanship in, 296–298, 310–312, 499–500
incest in, 264–265, 266–267
landownership in, 246–247
language of, 404–405
law enforcement in, 290–300
matrilocality and, 281–283
New World, 180–181
primitive capitalism in, 245–246
primitive communism in, 290–292
reciprocal exhange in, 229, 230, 231, 235–236, 238–239
redistributive exchange among, 236–238, 239–240
sodalities in, 299–300
song duels in, 292–294
trade among, 231–234
warfare among, 300, 301, 302, 303–307, 311–312
witchcraft accusations in, 294–296
Bangladesh
Green Revolution in, 363–365
sexual politics in, 501
Barber, Bernard, 352
Bar Kochva, 456
Barnouw, Victor, on personality, 486
Barotse (Zambia), extended families of, 257
Barter, 241
Bathonga (Mozambique)
bride-price among, 262
extended families of, 255–256
Beans, domestication of, 192–193
Beattie, John, 316–317
Behavioral aspects of culture, 122–123
Belmonte, Thomas, on culture of poverty, 389–391
Benedict, Ruth, 236–237, 239, 421, 489–490, 519
Berdache, 491, 508–509
Beringia Bridge, 175
Bering Straits migration, 175
Biface tools, 76–79
Bigmanship, 310–312. *See also* Headmanship
Bilabial stops, 397–398
Bilateral descent
causes of, 279
defined, 273
Eskimo, 284–285
Hawaiian, 285–286
kindred groups in, 276–277
Bilocality, 279
Bilzingsleben (Germany), fossil finds, 76
Binary contrasts, 481–482
Biogram, 526
Biological anthropology, defined, 6
Bipedalism, 28, 31, 32, 58, 130
of *Australopithecus*, 51–52, 74
early homonid diet and, 69
Blacks
African, as slaves, 179
dialects of, 407
futility of work and poverty of, 380–382
intelligence tests and, 522–525
matrifocal families of, 385–389
physical characteristics of, 95–96, 106, 111
skin color of, 107–109, 110–111
Blade tools, 131
Upper Paleolithic, 135–139, 143
Blood feuds, 298–299
Blood groups, race and, 100–101
Blood proteins (immunological distance), 30, 46
Boas, Franz, 239, 404, 517–518, 519
Bohannon, Paul, on intelligence tests, 525
Borlaug, Norman, 361
Boserup, Ester, 209
Bound morphemes, 398–399
Bovicide, 124–125
Braceros (migrant laborers), 370–371
Brachiation, 28, 31
Brains
hominid evolution and, 130
Primate, 22, 25
Brazil
legitimacy of children in, 260
sisal production in, 372
Breast feeding, 487
population control through, 160, 221, 223, 224
Breeding populations, 114
Bride-price, 241, 243–244, 261–262
defined, 258
Bride-service, 262
Broad spectrum food production
Mesolithic, 147–148
Neolithic. *See* Neolithic age
New World, 177–181, 192
Brown, Judith, 500
Brown, Lester, 365
Buddhism, as universalistic religion, 445–446
Bull roarer, 435
Bunyoro (Uganda), chiefdoms of, 316–318
Burial. *See* Funerary rituals
Burt, Cyril, 524

Cacao, domestication, 179
Calcium
Arctic hysteria and, 495

Calcium (*Continued*)
lactase deficiency and, 105, 110
vitamin D and, 109–110
Calendars, 408
Aztec, 440
cave paintings and, 140
Mayan, 196–197
Campa, rhetoric of, 480–481
Cancer, skin, 107–111
Cannibalism
Aztec, 190, 441, 446–448
Windigo psychosis and, 495–496
Capital, defined, 244
Capitalism, 244–245
art and, 478–479
in Guatemala, 372–375
in Japan, 360–361
peasant classes in, 336–337
primitive, 245–246
Carbon fourteen dating, 48
Cargo cults, 453–454
Carpenter, C. R., 394
Carrying capacity, 208–209, 224
Caste. *See also* Class
in India, 349–353
reproduction and, 258
Castration, 221
Çatal Hüyük (Turkey), Neolithic development of, 161–163
Cattle
as bride-price, 241, 243–244, 262
domestication of, in the Middle East, 161–163, 164
domestication of, in Northeast Africa, 159
emics and etics of, in India, 124–125
Indian taboos against eating, 459–462
Cave painting, 139–140
Ceboidea (superfamily), 26
Cercopithecoidea (superfamily), 26
Ceremonial centers
Aztec, 439–441
Maya, 182, 183–184, 186–189
Chang Chih-I, 213
Châtelperronian tool industry, 136–137, 143
Cherokee, chiefdoms of, 313
Cheyenne, military associations of, 300
Chiefdoms
Cherokee, 313
headmanship versus, 296, 312–314
Inca, 318–320
limitations of, 314–315
Olmec, 181–182
South American, 193–194, 318–320
transition to states from, 315–317
Trobriand Islander, 312–313, 314
Child abuse, in Primates, 24
Childhood training practices, 487–489
Children
age hierarchies and, 331
economic position and number of, 369–370
growth of agricultural society and, 160–161
increased costs of, 510–511
legitimacy of, 258, 259–261
reciprocal exchange and, 231
training of, and personality, 486–488
welfare and, 385–389
Chimpanzee
art and, 468
blood proteins of, 30
hands of, 32
language and, 400–401
pelvic girdle of, 32
sexual receptivity, 38
suspensory feeding of, 28
tool use by, 59–64
walking of, 28
Chimu empire, 194
China
archaic *Homo sapiens* in, 86
extended families in, 256–257
Homo erectus in, 74–75, 78, 79
irrigation agriculture in, 213–214
Neolithic age in, 167–169
peasant class in, 335–336
phonemic system of, 398
revolution in, 345
Chinampas agriculture, 189–190, 206
China Peking man, 74
Chomsky, Noam
on language of apes, 403
on linguistic behavior, 399–400
Chon-Gok-Ni (Korea), fossil finds, 78
Chopper-chopping tool tradition, 78
Chordata (phylum), 20–21, 42
Christianity, 416
male supremacy in, 503
revitalization of, 454–458
as universalistic religion, 445–446
Chromosomes
defined, 10
in evolution process, 11–14
genes, DNA and, 10–11
Churinga, art, 431, 475
Circulating connubia, 268
Circumcision rites, 433–437, 489
Circumscribed habitats, 315–316

Ciston, defined, 11
Cities
  epidemics and, 224
  Mayan, 182, 183–184, 186–189
  poverty in. *See* Poverty
  rise of, in China, 169
  rise of, in the Middle East, 164–166
Clacton (Essex, England), fossil finds, 79
Clans, cognatic, 277, 279–280
Class
  assimilation versus pluralism in, 347–349
  communism and, 335–336, 337–338
  defined, 330
  development of, in states, 316
  economic exploitation and, 333
  emics, etics, and consciousness of, 331–333
  ethnicity and, 345–347, 405–407
  incest and, 264, 267
  intelligence and, 524
  language and, 405–407, 409
  life-style and, 341–344
  minority and majority groups versus, 345–347
  mobility and, 344–345
  in the Neolithic state, 164–166, 169
  in Olmec society, 181–182
  peasant. *See* Peasant class
  physical coercion and, 324–325
  poverty and. *See* Poverty
  power and, 330–331, 338–341, 344–345
  religion and, 444–445
  ruling, 337–344
  sex, age and, 331
  in the Soviet Union, 337–338
  thought control and, 323–324
  in the United States, 338–341
  values and, 378–379
Cleopatra, 264
Climate, racial characteristics and, 106–111
Clines, 96–100
Clitoridectomy, 221, 437
Clocks, 408
Clovis tool assemblages, 177, 178
Codes of conduct, 122–123
Coffee, 358–359
Cognatic descent
  ambilineal, 274, 277, 279–280
  bilateral, 273, 276–277, 279, 284–286
  causes of, 279–280
  defined, 273
  in hunting-and-gathering societies, 280–281, 285
Cognatic lineage
  defined, 277
  determinants of, 279–280
Colonialism
  in Japan, 357, 358, 360–361
  in Java, 357–360, 361, 369–370
  race as basis of, 516
  revitalization movements and, 448–458
  underdevelopment and, 356–357
Color, language for, 405
Communal cults
  art and, 475
  described, 422–423, 430
  Haitian voodoo and, 462–463
  rites of passage of, 433–437
  rites of solidarity of, 430–433
Communal societies
  "primitive communism" in, 290–292
  reciprocal exchange in. *See* Reciprocal exchange
  redistributive exchange in. *See* Redistributive exchange
Communism, 244–245
  art and, 479
  capitalism versus, 244–245
  class and, 335–336, 337–338
  indoctrination in, 323
  primitive, in band and village societies, 290–292
  state versus, 325
Complementary distribution, sound, 398
Composite tools, Upper Paleolithic, 135–136, 138–139
Comte, Auguste, 515
Consanguine, defined, 273
Consciousness, 412
Consensual marriage, 260
Contraception
  breast feeding as form of, 160, 221, 223, 224
  population control through, 221, 367–369
  techniques for, 221
Copper, 204–205
Corporation(s)
  in colonial Java, 358–360
  control of United States, 340–341
  extended family as, 255–257, 261–263, 268
Cortes, Hernando, 189, 198–199, 446
Corvée (forced labor)
  colonialism and, 356
  and Mayan monuments, 185
  as taxation, 247
Cotton, domestication of, 179
Cousins
  cross, 266, 275, 286
  double, 277

Cousins (*Continued*)
parallel, 266, 286
Coxcatlan phase, 181
Craig, Daniel, 272
Cranium
Australopithecine, 53
display of, in cannibalism, 446
Hominoidea, 33–34, 73
Homo erectus, 72–76
Homo sapiens, 34, 84–91
Homo sapiens sapiens, 87–91
Vertebrata, 21
Cree, Windigo psychosis of, 495–496
Crime. *See also* Homicide
matrifocal families and, 388–389
stealing, 292, 293–294, 381
Cronback, Lee J., 525
Cross cousins, 266, 286
defined, 275
Crossing over (chromosome), 12
Cross-sex identity, 489
Crow
berdache and, 491, 508–509
hallucinatory experiences of, 426
kin terminological system of, 287
military associations of, 300
sex roles among, 508–509
Cultural anthropology
defined, 2
social anthropology versus, 114
Cultural ecology, 520
defined, 204
of exchange, 238–239
Cultural evolution
cultural materialism in, 521
dialectical materialism in, 520
diffusionism in, 119–122, 518
Enlightenment views on, 514
functionalism and structural-functionalism in, 518–519
genetic evolution and, 130, 166
historical particularism in, 517–518
Marxism in, 517
new evolutionism in, 519–520
nineteenth-century views of, 514–515, 517–518
population pressure and, 224–225
Social Darwinism and racism in, 515–517
sociobiology and, 525–527
structuralism in, 481–482, 521
Cultural materialism, 521
defined, 7
Cultural patterning, art and, 472–475
Cultural relativism, 117, 518
Cultural selection
cattle and, 124–125
infanticide in. *See* Infanticide
Culture
alternative research strategies for, 125–127
art as form of, 468–470
consciousness and, 412
cultural relativism and, 117, 518
defined, 114
diffusion of, 119–122, 179–180
emic and etic aspects of, 123–125, 126, 331–333
enculturation and. *See* Enculturation
evolution of. *See* Cultural evolution
gender identity and, 497
Hominidae, 38–39, 61–69
Homo erectus, 76–84
impact of language on, 407–409
intelligence and. *See* Intelligence
mental and behavioral aspects of, 122–123
mental illness and, 494–496
personality and, 486, 489–490, 519
of poverty, 378–379, 389–390
universal pattern of, 125, 126
Culture Against Man (Henry), 323–324
Culture-specific psychoses, 495–496
Cures by shamans, 427, 428

Dalton, George, 244, 334
Dance
evolution of, 479–480
Ghost, 450–452
Sun, 431
Dani (New Guinea), warfare among, 302
Dart, Raymond, 52, 54, 57
Dar Tichitt (Mauritania), domestication in, 171
Darwin, Charles, 17–18, 516
Davis, Kingsley, on family planning, 368
Deep structure, language, 399–400
Deferred gratification, 380–385
Deforestation, in slash-and-burn method, 211–212
De Laguna, Frederica, on scope of anthropology, 7
Dental formula
of *Aegyptopithecus*, 44
australopithecine, 52–53
of carnivores, 68
Hominoidea, 26, 35–38
Pongidae, 35
Dentan, Robert
on reciprocal exchange, 235–236

on Semai leadership, 296
Descent, 272–273
ambilineal, 274, 277, 279–280
bilateral, 273, 276–277, 279, 284–286
defined, 272
postmarital residence practices and, 278–279
rules of, 273–276
unilineal. *See* Unilineal descent
Despotism, 324–325
Despres, Leo, 348
Determinism, individual change and, 527–528
Development, 158. *See also* Green Revolution
in Brazil, 372
colonialism and, 356–361
in Guatemala, 372–375
image of limited good and, 370–371, 374, 378, 490
oxen versus tractors in, 366–367
population and, 367–370
Dialectical materialism, 520
Dialects, 405–407
black, 407
linguistic change and, 410–412
Diaz, May, 504–505
Diet. *See also* Feeding
bipedalism and early hominid, 69
Mesolithic, 146–148, 153–154
Paleolithic, 146
in preagricultural versus agricultural societies, 160, 161
Diffusionism, 119–122, 179–180, 518
Dionysian pattern, 489–490
Disease
damming of rivers and, 206
population control through, 223–224
spread of, in the New World, 325
Displacement, language, 395
Divale, William, 300, 303–304
Divination, 294
Dizygotic twins, 524
DNA (deoxyribonucleic acid), 10
Dobuans, Kula trade by, 233–234, 313
Dog
domestication of, 146–147
in domestication of other animals, 158
Dole, Gertrude, 294–295
Domestication, animal, 164
cattle, 124–125, 159, 161–163, 164, 459–462
in China, 168–169
described, 152
dogs, 146–147, 158
in Europe, 166–167
loss of plant food energy and, 214–215
in the Middle East, 153, 157–158, 161
Neolithic age, 152, 157–158, 159, 161–163, 164, 166–169
New World, 178, 190–191, 193
in Northeast Africa, 159
pigs, 169, 213
Domestication, plant, 155–157
in Africa, 171
in China, 168–169
in Europe, 166–167
irrigation and. *See* Irrigation agriculture
in the Middle East, 153–157
New World, 178–181, 192–194
in Northeast Africa, 158–159
process of, 152
in Southeast Asia, 169–171
Domestic economies, 125
Domestic life
alternatives to nuclear family in, 251–252
avoidance of incest in, 263–268, 458
extended family in. *See* Extended family
functions of, 250
legitimacy of children and, 258, 259–261
male/female bonding and, 38, 69
marriage and. *See* Marriage
nuclear family in. *See* Nuclear family
one-parent groups in, 257–258
polyandry in, 254, 257, 273, 505
polygamy in, 252–255
polygyny in, 253–256, 282, 505
Dominant genes, 14–15
Double cousins, defined, 277
Double descent, 275
Dowry, defined, 262
Drift, genetic, 15
Drinking, personal values and, 384–385
Drugs
alcohol as, 384–385
hallucinogenic, in religious rites, 425, 426–428
in native American revitalizations, 452–453
tobacco as, 122, 179, 428
Dryopithecinae, 44, 45
Duality of patterning, language, 396
Duckbill *(Ornithorhynchus)*, 21
Durkheim, Emile, 419–420, 458

Ecclesiastical cults
art and, 475–476
Aztec, 438–441, 446–448
described, 423, 437–438
imperial religion of, 445–446
political economy and, 444–445

Ecclesiastical cults (*Continued*)
sexual politics of, 502–503
shamans and, 429–430
Ecology
cultural, 204, 238–239, 520
defined, 204
ecosystems and, 204
food taboos and, 458–462
of hunting-and-gathering societies, 210–211
Economic exploitation, 333
Economy
defined, 228
exchange, 228. *See also* Price-market exchange; Reciprocal exchange; Redistributive exchange
political, 444–445, 499–501. *See also* Capitalism; Communism; Socialism
Ecosystems, 204
Education. *See* Enculturation
Ego
in ambilineal descent, 274
defined, 274*n*
in unilineal descent, 274–275
Egypt
Fayum fossil find, 44
inbreeding in, 264
Elitism, linguistic, 409–410
El Riego phase, 180–181
Emics
defined, 124
etics, cattle sex ratios and, 124–125
etics, class consciousness and, 331–333
universal pattern and, 125, 126
Enculturation
adoption and, 527
art and, 472–475
defined, 115
intelligence tests and, 522–525
language in, 395–396, 405–407
limitations of, 117–119
nuclear family and, 251
personality and, 486–489
social heredity in, 61–65
in village and band societies, 252
Endogamy, 263–268
among closed classes, 344–345
in Indian castes, 349–353
minority group, 347–349
Energy production. *See also* Food production
carrying capacity in, 208–209, 224
cattle and, 460–462
evolution of, 204–205
law of diminishing returns in, 208–209, 365–366
Engels, Frederick, 517
England
enculturation in, 252
feudal system of, 317–318
Neolithic age in, 166, 167
Enlightenment, 514
Environment
carrying capacity of, 208–209, 224
changes in, and Paleolithic society, 143–146
cultural diffusion and, 120–121
influence of, on food production, 206–208
intelligence and, 522–525
law of diminishing returns and, 208–209, 365–366
New World animal extinctions and, 178
Epicanthic folds, 95, 100, 105–106
defined, 96
Eskimo
climate adaptation by, 106
concept of descent of, 273
food production by, 205
kin terminological system of, 284–285
religious cults of, 423–424
song duels of, 293–294
vitamin D, calcium and, 110
Ethnicity. *See also* Majority groups; Minority groups
language, class and, 405–407
Ethnocentrism, defined, 115–117
Ethnocide, defined, 325
Ethnographic Atlas (Murdock), 285–286
Ethnography
defined, 2
sex roles and, 503–505
Etics
defined, 124
emics, cattle sex ratios and, 124–125
emics, class consciousness and, 331–333
universal pattern and, 125, 126
Etoro (New Guinea), sexuality among, 509
Europe
archaic *Homo sapiens* in, 84–85
Homo erectus in, 75–76, 78–79, 82
Homo sapiens sapiens in, 87–89
Mesolithic age in, 146–148
Middle/Upper Paleolithic transition in, 136–138, 143
Neandertals in, 87–89, 90–91
Neolithic age in, 166–167
racial characteristics and, 95, 96, 106
skin cancer in, 107
Eutheria (infraclass), 21–22
Evidence, 481
Evolution

of art forms, 479–480
chromosomes and, 11–14
cultural. *See* Cultural evolution
of energy production methods, 204–205
of food production methods, 209
gene-culture, 130, 166
genetic forces of, 15–17, 130, 166
of Primates, 42–46
sociocultural, 122, 199
Evolutionism
Marxist, 517
new forms of, 519–520
nineteenth-century, 514–515, 517–518
Exchange
defined, 228
market. *See* Price-market exchange
reciprocal. *See* Reciprocal exchange
redistributive. *See* Redistributive exchange
Exogamy, 263–268
class and, 344–345
warfare and, 267
Expansion, technological, 209
Exploitation, economic, 333
Extended family, 255–257, 268
incest and, 263–264, 266
marriage in, 255–258, 261–263
matrilocal, 252, 257–258
Eyes
epicanthic folds and, 95, 96, 100, 105–106
in Primates, 23, 25–26
Eysenck, H. J., 523–524

Facial expression
Hominoidea, 34–35
Primate, 26
Family
extended. *See* Extended family
nuclear. *See* Nuclear family
Family planning, 221, 367–368
Fanaticism, 528
Fatalism, 528
Fathers. *See also* Men
cultural versus genetic, 258, 260–261, 272
Oedipus conflict and, 492–494, 507
Fauresmith (South Africa), tool finds, 143
Fayum fossil find, 44
Feeding. *See also* Diet
alternatives to nuclear family for, 252
Hominid diet and, 68–69
Hominoidea jaws and teeth and, 35–38
redistributive exchange and, 235, 239, 310–313, 315
sharing of food in, 69
social heredity and, 61–65
suspensory, of Pongidae, 28, 31
Feet, of Primates, 22–23, 25–26
Fei Hsiao-t'ung, 213
Female husband, 258
Ferguson, Brian, 240
Fergusson, Adam, 412
Fertility rates, 220–221
cost of raising children and, 511
decline in, 370, 511
inclusive fitness and, 526
Feudalism, 317–318
in Japan, 360
in Java, 358–360
peasant class in, 334–335
religious revitalization and, 456–457
Feuds
blood, 298–299
song duels and, 292–294
witchcraft and, 294–296
Fire, 82, 204
Firth, Raymond, on kinship in chiefdoms, 315
Fishing
Kwakiutl potlatches and, 236–238, 239–240, 489–490
law of diminishing returns in, 366
Mesolithic age, 147–148
New World, 192, 193
ocean, 209
Fission track dating, 48
Fitness, genetic, 16–17
Flake tools, 131–133
Levalloisian, 133–134, 135
New World Paleolithic, 175–177
Upper Paleolithic, 135–139, 143
Flannery, Kent, 155
Folsom tool assemblages, 177, 178
Food production. *See also* Agriculture
broad spectrum, 147–148, 177–181, 192. *See also* Neolithic age
carrying capacity in, 208–209, 224
expansion of, 209, 224
fishing in. *See* Fishing
in hunter-gatherer societies. *See* Hunting-and-gathering societies
industrial, 216–217
influence of environment on, 206–208
intensification of, 209, 224
land ownership and, 247
law of diminishing returns in, 208–209, 365–366
methods of, 205–206, 209
pastoral nomadism in, 214–216
population pressure and, 367–370

Food production (*Continued*)
  slash-and-burn method of. *See* Slash-and-burn method
  taboos and, 458–462
Foré (New Guinea), sexual politics of, 501
Forelimbs
  of Hominoidea, 32
  of Primates, 23, 25–26, 28
Forests, 146–147
Form, art and, 468
Fossil fuels, 204, 205
  agribusiness and, 365–366
  in industrial food energy systems, 216–217
Fossils
  dating of, 48, 76
  defined, 42
  geological time periods and, 42
Foster, George, 378
  on image of limited good, 370–371
Founder effect, 15
France
  Homo erectus tool use in, 78–79, 82
  Upper Paleolithic cave art in, 139–140
Francis Xavier, 358, 360
Franke, Richard, 362
Frazer, James, 421
Freeloading, 229–231
Free morphemes, 398
Frequencies, racial, 96
  archetypes versus, 94–96
Freud, Sigmund, 491, 492–494, 497, 519
Frumm, John, 453–454
Functionalism, 518–519
Functions, defined, 518
Funerary rituals
  art and, 475
  Neandertal, 135
  Trobriand Islander, 504
  in voodoo, 463
Fur (Sudan), domestic life, 252
Fur trade, Kwakiutl, 240

Galbraith, John Kenneth, 339
Gandhi, Mohandas, 462
Gene-culture coevolution, 130, 166
Gene flow, 15–16, 94
  clines and, 96–100
General anthropology, 6
Generality, language, 404–405
Generation gap, 117
Genes
  blood group, race and, 100–101
  chromosomes, DNA and, 10–11
  clines and, 96–100
  defined, 11
  dominant and recessive, 14–15
  evolution and, 15–17, 130, 166
  gene flow and, 15–16, 94, 96–100
  incest and, 264–265, 267–268
  inheritance of, 11–14
  intelligence and, 522–525
  language development and, 395–396
  mental illness and, 494–496
  polymorphisms and, 101–111
  Social Darwinism and, 515–517
Genetrix, cultural mothers versus, 272
Genitor
  cultural father versus, 272
  defined, 258
  premarital sex and, 260–261
Genocide
  defined, 325
  of minority groups, 348
  New World, 325–327
Genotype, defined, 13–14
Geology, time periods of, 42
Geomagnetic dating, 48
Ghost Dance, 450–452
Gibbon
  blood proteins of, 30
  as brachiator, 28
  hands of, 32
  language of, 394–395
Gigantopithecus, 45
Gilder, George, 379
Gill pouches, 20
Glaciers, 146, 171, 175
Glottochronology, 412
Gluckman, Max, 257
Goats, domestication of, 157–158
Goiter, 103–105
Golden Bough (Frazer), 421
Goldenweiser, Alexander, 419
Gombe National Park (Tanzania), 59–60, 64, 67, 68
Gorilla
  blood proteins of, 30
  cranium of, 34, 53
  face of, 35
  hands of, 32
  language and, 401–403
  neck of, 33
  suspensory feeding of, 28
  vertebral column of, 33
  walking of, 28
Gorman, Chester, 171

Gough, Kathleen, 352
  on marriage, 258–259
Government, defined, 315
Grain domestication. *See* Domestication, plant
Grammar
  construction of morphemes and, 399
  deep structure and, 400
  equivalences of, 404
  syntax of, 399
Grasslands, end of, 146
Graves, Theodore, 383–385
Gravettian tool industry, 137
Greece, Neolithic age in, 166
Greenberg, Joseph, 394
Green Revolution, 361–362
  in Bangladesh, 363–365
  limits to technification and industrial growth in, 365–366
  in Mexico, 362–363
Gregory, Thomas, on Mehinacu Indian leadership, 297–298
Groom-price, 263
Gross, David, 372
Guardian spirits, 425
Guatemala, capitalism in, 372–375
Guinea pig, domestication of, 191
Gururumba (New Guinea), supernatural forces of, 419

Hadar (Ethiopia), fossil finds, 46–47, 49–51, 52, 54, 55, 58, 131
Hair form
  climate and, 106
  clinal patterns of, 96–100
  racial category and, 95–96
  radiation exposure and, 106, 107
Haiti, voodoo in, 462–464
Hallucination
  in individualistic cults, 425–426
  by shamans. *See* Shamanistic cults
  witchcraft accusations and, 430
Hand ax, 76–79
  Lower Paleolithic, 131–132
  Middle Paleolithic, 133
Hands
  of Hominoidea, 32
  prehensile, of Primates, 22–23, 25–26
Harding, Robert, 67
Harlan, J. D., 154–155
Harner, Michael, 280, 431, 441, 446–448
Harrison, William Henry, 449
Hart, C. W., 301
Hawaiians, kin terminological system of, 285–286
Hazardous wastes, 208
Headmanship, 296–298
  bigmanship in, 310–312
  chiefdoms versus, 296, 312–314
  Kapauku Papuan, 246
  male supremacy and, 499–500
Head tax, 356, 454
Health care, population growth and, 369
Heat stroke, 111
Hegel, Frederick, 515
Heider, Karl G., 302
Henry, Jules, 323–324
Herrnstein, R. J., 523–524
Heterozygosity
  defined, 13
  in dominant and recessive genes, 14–15
  superiority in, 15
Hewitt de Aloantara, Cynthia, 363
Hicks, David, 482
Hinduism
  caste hierarchy of, 349–353
  sacred cow in, 459–462
  sexuality and, 508
  as universalistic religion, 445–446
Hirsch, Jerry, 525
Historical particularism, 517–518
Hogbin, H. Ian, 311
Hohokam culture, 191
Homicide. *See also* Cannibalism
  blood feuds and, 298–299
  in urban ghettos, 389
  wife stealing and, 294
  witchcraft and, 294
Hominidae (family), 30
  archaic *Homo sapiens* in, 84–86
  Australopithecines in. *See* Australopithecines
  bipedalism of, 51–52, 58, 69, 130
  culture and evolution of, 38–39, 61–65, 130
  evolution from Hominoidea to, 42–46
  Homo erectus in, 72–84, 130, 132
  Homo habilis in. *See Homo habilis*
  Homo sapiens in. *See Homo sapiens*
  Homo sapiens sapiens in. *See Homo sapiens sapiens*
  hunting by Plio-Pleistocene, 65–69
  language and culture of, 38–39
  meat eating by, 68–69
  physical characteristics of, 30–38
  Plio-Pleistocene, 46–51, 56–58, 65–69
  sexuality of, 38
  tools and Plio-Pleistocene, 56–58

Hominoidea (superfamily), 26, 73
  characteristics of, 28
  evolution of, to Hominidae, 42–46
  physical characteristics of, 30–38
Homo erectus
  in Africa, 75, 76–78, 85
  characteristics of, 72
  in China, 74–75, 78, 79
  cultures of, 76–84
  in Europe, 75–76, 78–79, 82
  evolution of, to *Homo sapiens,* 84–85
  fire and, 82, 204
  hunting by, 79, 82–84
  in Java, 72–74
  tools of, 76–79, 132, 82
Homo habilis, 54–56
  evolution of, to *Homo erectus,* 72, 75
  hunting by, 58, 69
  mixed economy of, 58, 69
  tools of, 57–58
Homologous chromosomes, defined, 11
Homo sapiens, 2
  African archaic, 85–86
  Asian archaic, 86
  bipedalism of, 28
  common ancestry of, with apes, 30
  cranium of, 34, 84–91
  cultural versus biological evolution and, 130–131
  European archaic, 84–85
  evolution of, to *Homo sapiens sapiens,* 89–91, 142
  incest avoidance among, 268
  jaw of, 35
  Neandertal, 87–89, 90
  population density of, 220, 221
  tools of, 132
Homo sapiens neanderthalensis, 87–89, 90–91, 134, 143
Homo sapiens sapiens
  in Europe, 87–89
  evolution of *Homo sapiens* to, 89–91, 142
  in the Middle East, 89
  tools of, 132, 143
  transition of, to Upper Paleolithic culture, 143
Homosexuality, 491, 508–509
  contraception and, 221
  marriage and, 259
Homozygosity
  defined, 12–13
  in dominant and recessive genes, 14–15
  incest and, 264–265, 267
Hopewell phase, 192
Hopi, time sense of, 408
Horses, New World conquest and, 190, 195
Howell, Nancy, 223
Human ecology, defined, 204
Human sacrifice, Aztec, 190, 441, 446–448
Hunting
  agricultural development and, 158
  cave paintings of, 139–140
  by chimpanzees, 60–61, 65–68
  hair form and, 107
  Homo erectus, 79, 82–84
  Homo habilis, 58, 69
  Mesolithic age, 146–148
  by Plio-Pleistocene Hominidae, 65–69
  skin color and, 111
  Upper Paleolithic, 138–140, 143, 146
Hunting-and-gathering societies, 205. *See also* Band and village societies; Paleolithic age
  cognatic descent in, 280–281, 285
  contemporary, 82–84
  food energy system of, 210–211
  Homo erectus, 83–84
  male-supremacist complex in, 505–507
  New World, 174–178, 180, 191–192
  population control and, 160–161, 171, 221–224
  selective harvesting by, 155–156
  sex roles of, 58, 67–69
  South American, 192–193
  transition from, 153–154, 160–161, 169, 171
  warfare among, 300–303
Hutterites (Canada), reproduction of, 220–221
Hylobatidae (family), 28, 30

Iconographic symbols, 396
Ideographic strategies, defined, 125
Image of limited good, 370–371, 374
  in culture of poverty, 378
  personality formation and, 490
Imagery, 481
Immunological distance, 30, 46
Imperial religion, 445–446
Inbreeding, 264–265
Inca empire, 121, 192–193, 194, 318–320
  land ownership in, 247
  state system of, 318–320
Incest, 263–268, 458
Inclusive fitness, 525–527
Independent assortment (chromosome), 12
India
  bovicide in, 124–125
  caste system of, 349–353
  food production in, 217

irrigation in, 206
Neolithic age in, 167
oxen versus tractors in, 366–367
sacred cow of, 459–462
Individualistic cults
art and, 475
described, 422
Eskimo, 423–424
patterning of beliefs and rituals in, 425–426
Indo-European family of languages, 407, 411
Industrial Revolution, 205
Industry
food production through, 216–217
influence of environment on, 206–208
limits to technification and growth of, 365–366
myth of increased leisure and, 218–220
sex roles and, 509–510
Infanticide, 223
as cultural selection method, 106, 110
female versus male, 304
population control through, 160, 368–369
among Primates, 24
Infants
betrothal of, 260
enculturation of, 487
mortality of, 223, 368, 369
of Primates, 24–25
sexuality of, 488
Infibulation, 221
Inflective stage, grammar, 404
Infrastructure
defined, 125
in the universal pattern, 125, 126
Input-output ratio, agricultural, 213–214, 216–217
Intelligence
in Hominoidea, 28
language and, 39
natural selection and, 130
in Primates, 25
racial determinism and, 522–525
Intensification, technological, 209, 224
Intichiuma, totemic rituals of, 431–433
Invention, art and, 470–472
Iran, 457
Iron, 205
Iroquois
kin terminological system of, 286
matrilineality of, 500
matrilocality of, 282
Irrigation agriculture, 205
environmental factors in, 206
Green Revolution and, 361–362
Hohokam, 191
Mayan, 186
Neolithic, 164, 165–166
New World, 181, 194
relative productivity of, 213–214
soil fertility and, 206
Islam
in Indonesia, 358
male supremacy in, 503
as universalistic religion, 445–446
Isolating stage, grammar, 404
Italy, Neolithic age in, 166
Iterations, 480

Jacobson, Jerome, 148
Japan
colonialism in, 357, 358, 360–361
economic power of, 517
national character of, 492
population growth of, 369
Jarmo (Iraq), domestication in, 158
Jatis (Hindu subcastes), 350–352
Java
colonialism in, 357–360, 361, 369–370
Green Revolution in, 362
Homo erectus in, 72–74
Homo sapiens in, 86
population growth of, 369–370
Jaws, Hominoidea, 34–38
Jelinek, Arthur, on the Lower Paleolithic age, 132
Jensen, Arthur C., 523–524
Jericho (Jordan)
domestication in, 158
walled town of, 161, 300
Jesus, 455, 456
Jívaro (Ecuador)
animism of, 417–418, 427
art and, 475
Johanson, Donald, 47, 49, 51, 52
Johnson, Allen, 219
Johnson, Lyndon, 454
John the Baptist, 455
Jolly, Clifford, 36
Jones, Jim, 457
Jones, Peter, 132
Josephus, Flavius, 455
Judaism
adaptive capacity and, 348
food taboos in, 458–459
male supremacy in, 503
revitalization and, 454–456

Kader (Nigeria), premarital sex and, 260–261
Kaingang (Brazil), inbreeding of, 265
Kanakuk (prophet), 449–450
Kaoka (Solomon Islands), bigmanship among, 311
Kapauku (New Guinea)
capitalism of, 245–246
leadership among, 298
silent trade by, 232
Karma, 349, 351–352
Kayastks caste (India), 352
Kelly, Raymond, 509
Kibbutz marriages, 263, 264
Kindreds, defined, 276
Kingdoms
Bunyoro (Uganda), 316–318
English feudal, 317–318
Kinship
avunculocality in, 280–281, 283–284, 312–313
blood feuds and, 298–299
in chiefdoms, 315
defined, 272
descent in. *See* Descent
landownership groups and, 245–246
matrilocality in, 280, 281–283
patrilocality in, 280, 281
public opinion and, in band and village societies, 292–296
reciprocal exchange and, 229–230, 231
redistributive exchange and, 235
terminologies in, 284, 286, 287
Kin terminological system
Crow, 287
Eskimo, 284–285
Hawaiian, 285–286
Iroquois, 286
Kitchen middens, 147, 148
Klineberg, Otto, 523
Knuckle walking, 28
Kroeber, Alfred, on language changes, 412
Kuikuru (Brazil), witchcraft of, 294–295
Kula trade, 30, 233–234
Kuma (New Guinea), sex roles of, 497
!Kung San
food energy system of, 210–211
infant mortality of, 223
population growth of, 220
reciprocal exchange among, 229, 236, 238
warfare of, 302
Kwakiutl
cognatic lineages of, 279–280
marriage and, 259
potlatches of, 236–238, 239–240, 489–490

Labor, industrialization and, 366
Labov, William, on black speech, 407
Lactase deficiency, 105, 110
Laetoli, fossil finds, 46–47, 51, 54, 55, 85
Lake Turkana (Kenya), fossil finds, 54, 55, 58, 75
Landownership, 245–247
communal, 290–292
peasant, 336–337
voodoo and, 463
Language. *See also* Speech
acquisition of, 403–404
apes and, 400–403
arbitrariness of, 395–396
Campa rhetoric and, 480–481
change and, 410–412
class, ethnicity and, 405–407, 409
consciousness and, 412
deep structure theory of, 399–400
duality of patterning of, 396
elitism and sexism in, 409–410
enculturation and, 395–396, 405–407
generality and specificity of, 404–405
grammar and, 399, 404
Hominidae, 38–39
in the Lower Paleolithic age, 132
morphemes in, 398–399
phonemic systems of, 396–398
semantic universality of, 394–395
sign, 400–401, 402–403
thought, causality and, 407–409
Law enforcement
in band and village societies, 290–300
physical coercion and, 324–325
in states, 324–325
thought control in. *See* Thought control
Law of diminishing returns, 208–209, 224, 365–366
Leach, Edmund, on functions of marriage, 261
Leacock, Eleanor, 503
Leadership
chiefdoms as. *See* Chiefdoms
headmanship as. *See* Headmanship
menstruation as barrier to, 510
Leakey, Louis, 55, 57–58
Leakey, Mary, 51, 55
Leakey, Richard, 49–51, 55, 58
Lee, Richard S., 210, 223, 229, 236, 296
Legitimacy of children, 258, 259–262

Leibig's law of the minimum, 208
Leisure
 in agricultural versus preagricultural societies, 160–161, 211
 in industrial versus preindustrial societies, 218–220
Leonard, Karen, 352
Levallois technique, tool production, 133–134, 135
Levirate, 268
Lévi-Strauss, Claude, 296, 430–431, 481, 521
Lewis, Oscar, 378
Lieberman, Philip, 90–91
Liebow, Elliot, 380–382
Lifestyle, class and, 341–344
Lindenbaum, Shirley, on sexual politics, 500–501
Linton, Ralph, 250
Literature, binary contrasts and, 481–482
Livingstone, Frank, 264–265
Llama, domestication of, 191
Lomax, Allan, on evolution of art, 479–480
Lowie, Robert, 419, 426
Luther, Martin, 456

Maba, Guangdong (China), fossil finds, 86
Macaque, social learning by, 64
McHenry, Henry, 54
Machiguenga (Peru)
 leisure time of, 219–220
 protein needs of, 307
Machismo
 black culture, 389
 Latin American, 504–505
MacNeish, Richard S., 180–181, 193
Mae Enga (New Guinea), sex roles of, 497
Magdalenian tool industry, 138–139
Magic
 freeloading and, 230
 religion and, 421–422, 476–477
Maize
 domestication of, 152, 179–180, 181, 193
 spread of cultivation of, 192
Majority groups, class versus, 345–347
Malaita (Solomon Islands), silent trade by, 232
Malaria, sickle cell anemia and, 103, 105
Male-supremacist complex
 of Latin American *machismo*, 504–505
 Oedipus conflict in, 492–494, 507
 prevalence of, 498–500
 sexuality and, 507–509
 sexual politics and, 500–503
 Trobriand Islander, 503–504
 warfare and, 505–507
Malignant melanoma, 107–111
Malik, Bos (prophet), 454
Malinowski, Bronislaw, 230, 233–234, 259, 312, 314, 494, 503–504, 518–519
Malthus, Thomas, 17, 516
Mammalia (class), 21–22
Mana (animatist power), 418
Manahem (prophet), 455–456
Mangaians (Polynesia), sexuality of, 507–508
Manioc, 179
Maori, sculpture of, 472–473
Marano, Lou, on Windigo psychosis, 496
Marett, Robert R., 418, 419
Market exchange. *See* Price-market exchange
Marriage
 arranged, 260–261
 avoidance of incest and, 263–268, 458
 bride-price and, 241, 243–244, 258, 261–262
 defined, 258, 259
 descent and. *See* Descent
 extended family and, 255–258, 261–263
 functions of, 261
 Indian castes and, 352
 legitimacy of children and, 258, 259–261
 monogamous, 254, 256–257
 nature of, 258–259
 polygamous, 253–256
 preferential, 268
 residence practices after, 278–284
 wife stealing and, 293–294
Marshack, Alexander, 134, 142
Marshall, Donald, 507–508
Marsupials, 21–22
Marx, Karl, 325, 333, 457–458, 517, 520
Marxism
 dialectical materialism of, 520
 evolutionism of, 517
 sociobiology and, 131
Masai (East Africa), enculturation of, 252
Mass production, art and, 475
Materialism
 cultural, 521
 dialectical, 520
Matriarchy, 500
Matriclan, defined, 278
Matrifocal families, 257–258, 385–389
Matrilineality
 avunculocality and, 280–281, 283–284, 312–313

Matrilineality (*Continued*)
  defined, 274
  kin groups in, 277–278
  matriarchy versus, 500
Matrilocality
  causes of, 281–283
  extended family and, 252, 257–258
  matrilineality and, 280, 281–283
Matrisib, defined, 278
Maya
  agriculture of, 182, 184–189
  ceremonial centers of, 182, 183–184, 186–189
  decline of, 186–189
  economic development of, 373–375
  technology of, 196–197
Mbuti (Ituri Forest), silent trade by, 231
Mead, Margaret, 497, 519
  on generation gap, 117
Meadowcraft (Pennsylvania), fossil finds, 174–175
Meat eating, 68–69
Media, thought control and, 321
Mediums, 426
Megalithic monuments, 167
Meganthropus, 74
Meggitt, Mervyn, 497
Mehinacu Indians (Brazil), leadership among, 297–298
Melanin, 107–111
Mellon, Thomas, 340
Mellon family, 340, 342
Men. *See also* Male-supremacist complex
  bonding of, with women, 38, 69
  castration and, 221
  circumcision rituals and, 433–437, 489
  culturally defined traits of, 497
  as fathers. *See* Fathers
  groom-price and, 263
  homosexuality of, 221, 259, 491, 508–509
  in hunting-and-gathering societies, 58, 67–69, 210–211
  initiation and childhood training of, 488–489
  in matrifocal families, 257–258, 385–389
  procreative role of, 273
  war-related deaths of, 302–304
Mencher, Joan, 351
Mendel, Gregor, 14
Men's houses, 252, 497, 502
Menstruation
  as handicap to women, 509–510
  sexual receptivity and, 38
Mental aspects of culture, 122–123
Mental illness
  culture and, 494–495
  Windigo psychosis and, 495–496
Mercator, Gerardus, on basic personalities, 491
Mesoamerica
  development of highland societies in, 180–181, 186–190
  development of lowland societies in, 181–186
Mesolithic age, 131, 146–147, 153
  in Africa, 148
  broad spectrum food production in, 147–148
  New World, 177–178
Mesopotamia, state formation in, 165–166
Messianic movements. *See* Revitalization, religious
Metallurgy
  energy production and, 204–205
  New World techniques in, 196
Metaphors, 481
Metatheria (infraclass), 21–22
Mexico
  Green Revolution in, 362–363
  population growth of, 369
  wheat experiment in, 361, 362–363
Middle East
  Homo sapiens sapiens in, 89
  Neandertals in, 89
  Neolithic age in, 152–158, 161–166
Military. *See also* Law enforcement
  Native American associations as, 300
  revitalization movements and, 449–458
Milk. *See also* Breast feeding
  Arctic hysteria and, 495
  lactase deficiency and, 105, 110
  vitamin D and, 109–110
Millenarian movements. *See* Revitalization, religious
Millet, domestication of, 168–169
Milling stones, 177
Milton, Katherine, 68–69
Minge-Kalman, Wanda, 510–511
Minoan Crete, matriarchy of, 500
Minority groups
  assimilation versus pluralism of, 347–349
  class versus, 345–347
  poverty of. *See* Poverty
Mississippian phase, 192
Mixed economy, sex roles and, 58, 67–69
Mixed farming, 205–206
Mobility, class, 344–345
Mochica (Peru), art of, 473–474
Mode, statistical, 491
Mode of production, 125
Mode of reproduction, 125

Money
  characteristics of, 243
  class and. *See* Class
  in price-market exchange, 241
Monkeys
  dental formula of, 26
  New World ceboidean, 174
  tools of, 59–61, 64
Monogamy, 254, 256–257
Monozygotic twins, 523–525
Montmaurin (France), fossil finds, 76
Monuments. *See also* Pyramids
  megalithic, 167
  Olmec, 181–182
  stelae, 181, 183
  thought control through use of, 321
Morgan, Lewis Henry, 284, 515, 517, 520
Morocco
  Homo erectus fossil finds in, 75
  Homo sapiens in, 85
Morphemes
  defined, 398–399
  in grammar development, 404
Morphs, defined, 398
Moseley, Michael, on South American fishing, 193
Mother-in-law, extended family, 256–257
Mothers. *See also* Women
  abortion and, 223
  cultural versus genetic, 272
  in extended families, 255–258
  legitimacy of children of, 258, 259–261
  in matrifocal households, 257–258
  Oedipus conflict and, 492–494
  in Primates, 24–25
Mt. Carmel, Israel, Natufians in, 154
Mousterian tool industry, 133–135, 143
Moynihan, Daniel P., 385
Mumi (big man), 310–312
Mundugumor (New Guinea), sex roles of, 497
Mundurucu (Amazon), matrilocality of, 282
Müntzer, Thomas, 456
Münzel, Mark, 327
Murdock, George Peter, 250, 254, 281, 285, 286
Murngin (Australia)
  battle-related deaths of, 302
  concept of descent of, 273
Murray, Gerald, 463–464
Music
  early weapons and, 472
  evolution of structures of, 479–480
Mutations, genetic, 16
Myth, 481–482
Nag, Moni, 508
Nambikwara Indians (Brazil), leadership among, 296–297
Natchez, class system of, 345
National character, personality and, 490–492
Native Americans. *See also* New World
  genocide of, 325–327
  military associations of, 300
  religious revitalization of, 449–453
  sexual identity and, 491
Nativistic movements. *See* Revitalization, religious
Natufians, 148
  dwellings of, 154
  seed collecting by, 160
Natural selection
  development of concept of, 516–517
  incest and, 264
  inclusive fitness and, 525–527
  intelligence and, 130
  polymorphism and, 101, 103, 105, 110
  process of, 16–17
  survival and, 17–18
  tool use and, 58
Navajo
  personal values and economic success of, 383–385
  prayer of, 421
Nayar (Kerala)
  avunculocality of, 283
  extended families of, 252, 257–258
Ndembu (Zambia)
  art and, 475
  circumcision ritual of, 433–437
Neandertal
  in Europe, 87–89, 90–91
  funerary rituals of, 135
  Middle Eastern, 89
Neck, in Hominoidea, 33
Neolithic age, 131, 152
  in Africa, 158–160, 171
  art in, 163
  causes of, 160–161
  in China, 167–169
  domestication of animals in, 152, 157–158, 159, 161–163, 164, 166–169
  in East Asia, 167–169
  energy production in, 204
  in the Middle East, 152–158, 161–166
  New World, 178–180, 191–194
  origins of agriculture in, 155–157, 169–171
  "revolution" in, 161–163
  rise of the state in, 164–166, 169

Neolithic age (*Continued*)
in Southeast Asia, 169–171
spread of, 166–167
warfare in, 300, 301
Neolocality, 279
Newman, Philip, on supernatural forces, 419
New World
animal domestication in, 178, 190–191, 193
archaic traditions in, 177–178
Aztecs in. *See* Aztec empire
discovery of America, 174–175
end of band and village societies in, 325–327
feudal peasant class in, 334–335
Mayas in. *See* Maya
Mesoamerica, 180–191
native American revitalization in, 449–453
Neolithic age in, 178–180, 191–194
North America, 174–175, 191–192
Paleolithic age in, 175–177
South America, 192–194
technology in, 194–199
Niah Cave (Borneo), fossil finds, 89
Nomothetic strategies, defined, 125
Non Nok Tha (Thailand), domestication in, 171
Norman, Collin, 366
Norms, 122–123
North America, 174–175, 191–192
Northwest Coast, art of, 472
Nose shape, 106
Notochord, 20–21
Nuchal crest, 33–34
Nuchal plane, 33–34
Nuclear energy, 205
Nuclear family
alternatives to, 251–252
in band and village societies, 291–292
bilateral descent and, 279
functions of, 250–251
incest and, 263–268, 458
polygamy and, 252–255
Nuer (Sudan), blood feuds among, 298–299
Number system, Mayan, 197
Nyakyusa (Tanzania), enculturation and, 252

Occipital condyles, 33
Odend'hal, Stuart, 461–462
Odum, Howard, on agricultural production, 217
Oedipus conflict, 492–494
masculinity, war and, 507
Oldowan tool industry, 76–78, 131–132, 135
Olduvai Gorge (Tanzania), 55, 57–58, 68
Homo erectus in, 75, 76–78
tool industry in, 76–78, 131–132, 135
Oliver, Douglas, 310–312
Olmec empire, 181–182
Omnivores, 38
Hominidae as, 60–61, 65–69
Omo (Ethiopia), fossil finds, 85
One-parent groups, 257–258
Orangutan
blood proteins of, 30
hands of, 32
suspensory feeding of, 28
walking of, 28
Orchestra, 480
Origin of Species (Darwin), 516
Origin of the Family, Private Property and the State (Engels), 517
Orthognathism, 35
Osteomalacia, 109–110
Oxen
cattle versus, in India, 460–462
in China, 169
tractors versus, in India, 366–367

Paintings
Neolithic wall, 163
Paleolithic cave, 139–140
Pakistan, Neolithic age in, 167
Paleo-Indian traditions, 177
Paleolithic age, 131, 153
art and technology in, 470–472
end of, 143–148
Homo sapiens population growth in, 220, 221–224
infanticide and child neglect in, 223
Lower, 131–132
Middle, 131, 133–135, 143
New World, 175–177
Upper, 131, 135–143, 146, 160, 161, 175–177
warfare in, 300
Pan-p'o (China), Neolithic agriculture in, 168–169
Paolisso, Michael, 307
Parallel cousins, 266, 286
defined, 275
Parsons, Jeffry, on *Chinampa* agriculture, 189
Pastoral nomadism, 214–216
Patriclan, defined, 278
Patrilineality
defined, 274
kin groups in, 277–278
patrilocality and, 280, 281
Patrilocality
causes of, 281
patrilineality and, 280, 281

Patrisib, defined, 278
Patronymic, defined, 276
Patterns of Culture (Benedict), 236–237, 239, 489–490
Patterson, Francine, 402–403
Paundaungia, 44
Pearson, Karl, 522
Peasant class, 333–337
  agromanagerial state, 335–336
  capitalist, 336–337
  colonialism and, 356–361, 369–370
  feudal, 334–335
  image of limited good and, 370–371
  revitalization movements and, 456
Peking man, 74
Pelto, Gretel, 300
Pelto, Perttie, 300
Pelvic girdle, in Hominoidea, 32–33
Penis envy, 493–494
Penny capitalism, 336–337
People's Temple, 457
Perigordian tool industry, 136–137
Personality
  childhood training and, 486–488
  culture and, 486, 489–490, 519
  defined, 486
  male versus female traits in, 497
  national character and, 490–492
  Oedipus conflict and, 492–494
  poverty and, 383–385
Perturbations, defined, 225
Peten (Yucatan), abandonment of, 185–186
Pets, Mesolithic age, 158
Peyote rituals, 452–453
Phenotype, defined, 14
Phenylthiocarbamide (PTC), 103–105
Phonemes
  defined, 396
  systems of, 396–398
Phones, defined, 396–397
Phonetic sounds, 397
Phyletic gradualism, 17–18
Physical anthropology
  defined, 6
  race in. *See* Races
Pibloktoq (psychosis), 495
Piddocke, Stuart, 239
Pig
  domestication of, 169, 213
  Jewish taboo against eating, 458–459
Pilling, Arnold, 301
Pimentel, David, 365
Pithecanthropus erectus, 72–74
Placenta, 21–22
Play, art and, 468, 470
Pleistocene megafauna, 146
Plows
  in China, 169
  invention of, 164
  New World, 195–196
Pluralism, assimilation versus, 347–349
Point of diminishing returns, 208–209, 224, 365–366
Polanyi, Karl, 229
Polgar, Steven, 370
Political economy, 125
  capitalist. *See* Capitalism
  Communist. *See* Communism
  religion and, 444–445
  sexual politics and, 499–501
  Socialist. *See* Socialist
Politics
  art and, 477–479
  exchange systems and, 241. *See also* Exchange
  revitalization movements and, 448–449
  sexual, 500–503
Pollution, 208
Polyandry, 254, 505
  matrifocal households and, 257
  reproduction and, 273
Polygamy, 252–256
Polygyny, 253–255, 505
  extended family and, 255–256
  matrilocality and, 282
Polyhedrals, 131
Polymorphisms
  defined, 101
  explanation of, 101–105
  racial antiquity and, 105–106
  skin color and, 107–111
Pondaung Hills (Burma), fossil find, 44
Pongidae (family), 28, 30, 31, 35
Pontiac, 449
Popé (prophet), 449
Population
  breeding, 114
  carrying capacity and, 208–209, 224
  contraception and regulation of, 221, 367–369
  cultural checks on growth of, 220–221
  defined, 94
  disease and regulation of, 223–224
  early methods of controlling, 160, 221–224
  economic development and, 367–370
  hunter-gatherer societies and, 160–161, 171, 221–224
  law of diminishing returns and, 208–209

Population (*Continued*)
  Neolithic age and growth of, 160–161
  postconception methods of regulating, 160, 221–223, 224
  potlatches and shifts in, 239–240
  pressure on, and cultural evolution, 224–225
  race as, 94
  warfare in regulation of, 302–304
Pospisil, Leopold, 245–246
Possession, defined, 426
Potassium-argon dating, 48
Potato, domestication, 179
Potlatches, 236–238, 239–240, 489–490
Pottery, 204
Poverty, 118–119
  culture of, 378–379, 389–390
  deferred gratification, futility of work and, 380–382
  matrifocal families and, 385–388
  personality attributes and, 383–385
  responsibility for, 382–383
  welfare and, 388–389
Power
  animatistic, 418
  of chiefs, 314–315
  class and, 330–331, 338–341, 344–345
  defined, 330
Preferential marriages, 268
Pregnancy
  abortion methods and, 223
  Primate, 24
  role of parents in, 272–273
  sexual politics and, 501
Premack, David, 401
Price-market exchange, 232, 244–246
  buying and selling in, 241
  capitalism and, 244–246. *See also* Capitalism
  culture of, 38–39
  incest avoidance and, 267
  landownership and, 246–247
  language systems of, 38–39
  money in, 241–244
Primates (order)
  arboreal life of, 23, 25–26, 28
  categories leading to, 20–22
  characteristics of, 22–25
  evolution of, 42–46
  language systems of, 394–395, 396, 400–403
  sexuality of, 38
  social heredity of, 61–65
  suborder Anthropoidea of, 26–38
  suborder Prosimii of, 26
  tool use by, 59–61, 64
Primitive communism, 290–292
Primitive Culture (Tylor), 416
Probabilistic causality, 528–529
Productivity of language, 394–395, 405
Profane realm, 419–420
Prognathism, 34
Propliopithecus, 44
Prosimii (suborder), 26
Protein
  animal versus plant, 212–213
  cannibalism and need for, 446–448, 495–496
  resistance to disease and, 224
  sexual politics and access to, 501
  taboos against types of, 458–462
  warfare and, among Yanomamo, 304–307
Protestant reformation, 456
Proto-Indo-European languages, 411
Prototheria (subclass), 21
Proto-West Germanic language, 410–411
Psychosis, cultural differences in, 494–496
Public opinion. *See* Thought control
Pueblo
  cultural patterns of, 490
  revitalization of, 449
Pueblo Bonito, 191
Punctuated equilibrium, 18
Punnett square, 14
Pyramid of the Sun (Maya), 187
Pyramids
  Aztec, 439–440
  at Cholula, Mexico, 189
  Mayan, 183, 187–188
  Olmec, 181

Races
  ages of, 105–106
  blood groups and, 100–101
  clines in, 96–100
  defined, 94
  frequencies versus archetypes in, 94–96
  polymorphisms and, 101–111
  as populations, 94
  skin color and, 95–96, 107–111
  Social Darwinism and, 515–517
Rachis seeds, 156–157, 180
Racial determinism, 522–525
Racism, 515–517
  intelligence tests and, 522–523
Radcliffe-Brown, R., 519
Rainfall agriculture, 205
  Green Revolution and, 365
  Mayan, 186
Rainwater, Lee, 389

Raised-field method, 205
  Mayan, 182
Rajputs (India), extended families of, 257
Ramapithecinae, 44–46
Ramapithecus, 45–46
Rappaport, Roy, 211, 212
Raymond, J. S., 193–194
Recessive genes, 14–15
Reciprocal exchange
  cultural ecology of, 238–239
  described, 229
  freeloading and, 229–231
  incest avoidance and, 266–267
  Kula trade as, 233–234, 313
  money and, 241
  redistribution versus, 235–238
  trade and, 231–234
Redistributive exchange
  cultural ecology of, 238–239
  described, 235
  egalitarian, 235–236, 240, 245
  money and, 241
  potlatches in, 236–238, 239–240, 489–490
  reciprocal exchange versus, 235–238
  stratified, 235, 240–241
Red Power movement, 453
Reduction division (chromosome), 12
Rein, Martin, 389
Relativism, cultural, 117, 518
Religion
  animatism in, 418
  animism in, 416–418
  art and, 475–477
  cannibalism in, 190, 441, 446–448
  communal cults in. *See* Communal cults
  defined, 416
  ecclesiastical cults in. *See* Ecclesiastical cults
  Hindu caste system and, 349–353
  imperial, 445–446
  individualistic cults in, 422, 423–426, 475
  levels of organization of, 422–423
  magic and, 421–422, 476–477
  natural and supernatural forces in, 418–419
  political economy and, 444–445
  revitalization of, 448–458
  sacred and profane in, 419–420
  sexual politics and, 502–503
  shamanistic cults in. *See* Shamanistic cults
  taboo, ecology and, 458–463
  thought control through use of, 320–321
Rent, defined, 247
Reproduction. *See also* Genes; Sexuality
  altruistic sterility and, 17, 525
  blood type and, 101–103
  descent in. *See* Descent
  inbreeding in, 264–265
  inclusive fitness and, 525–526
  mode of, 125
  among Primates, 24, 25
  purpose of, 10
  rate of. *See* Fertility rates
  roles of parents in, 272–273
Reproductive isolation, 17
Research strategies
  defined, 7, 125
  idiographic, 125
  nomothetic, 127
Revitalization, religious
  Christianity and, 454–458
  Native American, 449–453
  process of, 448–449
Revolution
  in China, 345
  Green. *See* Green Revolution
Rhetoric, defined, 480
Rhetorical questions, 480
Rhinarium, Prosimii, 26
Rhodesian man, 85
Rice
  domestication of, 170–171
  "miracle," 361
Rickets, 109–110
Rites of passage, 433–434, 489
  circumcision, 433–437
Rites of solidarity, 430–433
Ritual objects
  cave paintings as, 139–140
  Middle Paleolithic, 135
  totemic, 240, 430–433, 475
  Upper Paleolithic, 137
Rohrlich-Leavitt, Ruby, 500
Romance languages, 409, 410–411
Roman empire, 318
  religious revitalizations and, 454–456
Ross, Eric, 306, 459
Rossel Islanders (New Guinea), money of, 244
Rules
  cultural, 114
  descent, 273–276
  linguistic, 396–400, 404
Ruling class
  Soviet Union, 337–338
  United States, 338–341

Sabbats, 429
Sackett, Ross, 307

Sacred realm, 419–420. *See also* Religion
taboo and, 459–462
Safa, Helen Icken, 378
Sagali (funeral ceremonies), 504
Saldanha man, 85
Sanjek, Roger, 349
Sapir, Edward, 404
Sarich, Vincent, 30, 46
Scavenging, end of, 143
Schizophrenia, 494–495
Science, magic versus, 421
Scotland, clans in, 277
Scrimshaw, Susan, 223
Sculpture, cultural patterning and, 472–474
Sedentary villages. *See* Band and village societies; Villages
Selection
cultural. *See* Cultural selection
natural. *See* Natural selection
Selective harvesting, 155–156
Semai (Malaya)
leadership among, 296
reciprocal exchange of, 235–236
Semantic universality, 394–395
Semen
Etoro attitude toward, 509
Hindu attitude toward, 508
role of, in reproduction, 273
Serfs, 334–335
Sex (gender)
age, class and, 331
alleles and, 13–14
cultural definitions of, 497
in language, 409–410
Sexism, linguistic, 409–410
Sex ratios
of cattle in India, 124–125
Homo erectus, 82–84
infanticide and, 223, 304
sexual politics and, 501
war-related deaths and, 303–304
Sex roles. *See also* Male-supremacist complex
cross-sex identity and, 489, 491, 508–509
cultural definition of, 497
ethnography and, 503–505
future, 510–511
Homo erectus, 82–84
hunting and gathering as, 58, 67–69
in industrial society, 509–510
in Latin American *machismo*, 504–505
mixed economy and, 58, 67–69
nuclear family and, 251
patrilocality and, 281
sexuality and, 497, 507–508
Trobriand Islander, 503–504
warfare and, 505–507
Sexton, Lorraine, 497
Sexual dimorphism
Australopithecine, 49, 51–52
decrease in, and sapienization, 90
defined, 49
Sexuality
adolescent, 260–261, 488, 509
contraception and. *See* Contraception
Hominidae, 38
homosexuality in. *See* Homosexuality
incest in, 263–268, 485
infant, 488
male aggression and, 505–507
marriage and, 253–254, 255–259, 261
nuclear family and, 250
Oedipal conflict and, 492–494
premarital, 260–261
sex roles and, 497, 507–508
varieties of experience in, 507–508
Sexual politics
prevalence of, 500–501
religion and, 502–503
sex roles, ethnography and, 503
Shaanxi (China), fossil finds, 86
Shamanistic cults, 294–296
art and, 475
described, 422, 426
individualistic visions versus, 426–427
Tapirapé, 427–428
witchcraft, witchhunts and, 429–430
Shang (China), Neolithic development of, 169
Shanidar Cave (Iraq)
burial ritual, 135
fossil finds, 89
Sharff, Jagna, 388–389
Sharing behavior, 69
Shawnee, revitalization of, 449
Sheep, domestication of, 157–158
Shell money, 244, 245–246
Shriver site (Missouri), tools, 176, 177
Siamang
blood proteins of, 30
as brachiator, 28
Sickle-cell anemia, 103, 105
Sign language, ape use of, 400–401, 402–403
Silent trade, 231–232
Sinanthropus pekinensis, 74
Siona-Sicoya (Ecuador), protein needs of, 307
Sioux, revitalization of, 450–452
Sisal, 372–373

Sister exchange, 261
Site stratification, 315
Sitting Bull, 452
Siuai (Solomon Islands), bigmanship among, 310–312
Skhūl cave (Israel)
  burial ritual, 135
  fossil finds, 89
Skin color
  clinal patterns of, 96–100
  racial category and, 95–96, 107–111
Slash-and-burn method, 166, 205, 211–213
  environmental factors in, 206
  food energy system and, 211–213
  leisure time and, 211, 219–220
  Mayan, 182, 186
Slavery, New World, 179
Sleeping arrangements
  alternatives to nuclear family and, 252
  polygamy and, 254
  sex roles and, 497
Smith, M. G., 260
Smith, Waldemar, 373–375
Smohalla (prophet), 450
Snails, 206
Social anthropology, 114
Social behavior
  hunting and, 58, 67–69
  Primate, 24–25
Social Darwinism, 515–517
Social heredity, 61–65
Socialism, 244–245
  capitalism versus, 244–245
  class and, 335–336
  indoctrination in, 323
Society, defined, 114
Sociobiology, 131, 525–527
Sociocultural systems
  defined, 115
  evolution of, 122, 199
Sodalities, 299–300
Soil depletion
  Mayan, 186, 188–189
  prevention of, 205–206
Solidarity, rituals of, 430–433
Solo man, 86
Solutrean tool industry, 137–138
Song
  duels with, 292–296
  hallucinatory experiences and, 426
Sorcery, freeloading and, 230
Sororate, 268
South America
  chiefdoms of, 193–194, 318–320
  Neolithic age in, 192–194
Southworth, Frank, 410
Soviet Union, ruling class in, 337–338. *See also* Communism
Spain
  New World conquest by, 189, 198–199, 334–335, 446
  Upper Paleolithic cave art in, 139–140
Speciation, 17–18
Specificity, language, 404–405
Speech. *See also* Language
  Campa rhetoric and, 480–481
  Homo sapiens cranium and, 90–91
  in learning of languages, 403–404
  physical mechanisms for, 396–398
Spencer, Herbert, 516
Spiny anteater *(Echidna)*, 21
Spirit Cave (Thailand), plant domestication and, 169–170
Spiro, Melford, 494
Stack, Carol, 387–388
Star Carr (England), fossil find, 146–147
States
  control of thought and, 320–324
  defined, 315
  development of South American, 194
  end of band and village societies and, 325–327
  energy production and, 204
  feudalism versus, 317–318
  Inca, 318–320
  law enforcement in, 324–325
  Mayan, 182–190
  Mississippian, 192
  national character of, 490–492
  Olmec, 181–182
  pastoral societies and, 216
  peasant class in, 335–337
  religion in. *See* Ecclesiastical cults
  rise of, in the Neolithic age, 164–166, 169
  transition from chiefdoms to, 315–317
Statistical mode, 491
Stature, racial category and, 95–96
Stealing
  in band and village societies, 292, 293–294
  wage levels and, 381
Steel, 205
Stelae
  defined, 181
  Mayan, 183
  Olmec, 181
Sterility, altruistic, 17, 525

Steward, Julian, 520
Stonehenge, 167
Stratified redistribution, 235, 240–241
Striking platform, tool, 133
Structural-functionalism, 518–519
Structuralism, 521
  literature and, 481–482
Structure
  defined, 125
  in the universal pattern, 125, 126
Subcultures
  class, 342–343
  defined, 114–115
Subincision, 437
Sublineages, 245–246
Sugar
  domestication of, 179
  in Java, 359–360
  slave trade and, 179
Suitor-service, 262
Sunburn, 107–109
Sun Dance, 431
Supernatural forces, 418–419
Superstructure
  defined, 125
  in the universal pattern, 125, 126
Supraorbital torus, 35
Surface structure, language, 399–400
Surplus, agricultural, 213
Suspensory feeding, 28, 31
Suttles, Wayne, 239
Swartkrans (South Africa), fossil finds, 75
Syntax, grammar, 399–400

Taboo, 458–459
  sacred cow and, 459–462
Taima-taima (Venezuela), tools, 176
Tally's Corner (Liebow), 380–382
Tamil (India), concept of descent of, 273
Tapirapé
  art and, 475
  shamanism among, 427–428
Taro, 169, 170–171
Taste, phenylthiocarbamide (PTC), 103–105
Tata (Hungary), fossil find, 135
Taung fossil find, 52, 54, 57
Tax, Sol, 336
Taxes
  forced labor as form of, 185, 247, 356
  head, 356, 454
  rents compared to, 247
Taxons, 20
  racial, 94–96, 105–106
Tchambuli (New Guinea), sex roles of, 497
Technology
  art and, 470–472
  of energy production, 204–205
  intensification of, 209, 224
  interaction of, with environment, 206–208, 209
  in Japan, 360–361
  leisure time and increase of, 218–220
  limits on growth of, 365–366
  Neolithic, 164, 169
  New World, 194–199
  oxen versus, 366–367
Tecumseh, 449
Teeth. *See* Dental formula
Tehuacán (Mexico)
  domestication of maize and, 100
  village in, 181
Tell Abu Hureya (Syria), domestication in, 157
Tell Mureybat (Syria), village life in, 154
Tenochititlán (Mexico), 189–196, 198–199, 441, 446
Tenskwatawa (prophet), 449
Teosinte, 180
Teotihuacán (Mexico), Mayas in, 186–188
Termiting, by chimpanzees, 60, 61–64
Ternifine (Algeria), fossil finds, 75
Tetrapoda (superclass), 21, 42
Tetum (Timor), binary matrix of, 482
Thatcher, Margaret, 499
Theria (subclass), 21
Thought control
  in band and village societies, 292–296
  language in, 407–409
  limitations of, 325
  modern contexts of, 321–324
  in preindustrial states, 320–321
Thyroid gland, 103–105
Tikal (Yucatan), Mayan center, 184, 186
Tikopia (Solomon Islands), chiefdoms of, 314–315
Time
  calendars and. *See* Calendars
  clocks and, 408
  orientation to, and economic success, 383–385
  sense of, in language, 408
Tin, 204–205
Tiwi (Australia), warfare among, 301–302
Tobacco
  in shaman curing rituals, 428
  slavery and, 179
  smoking of, 122
Toilet training, 487